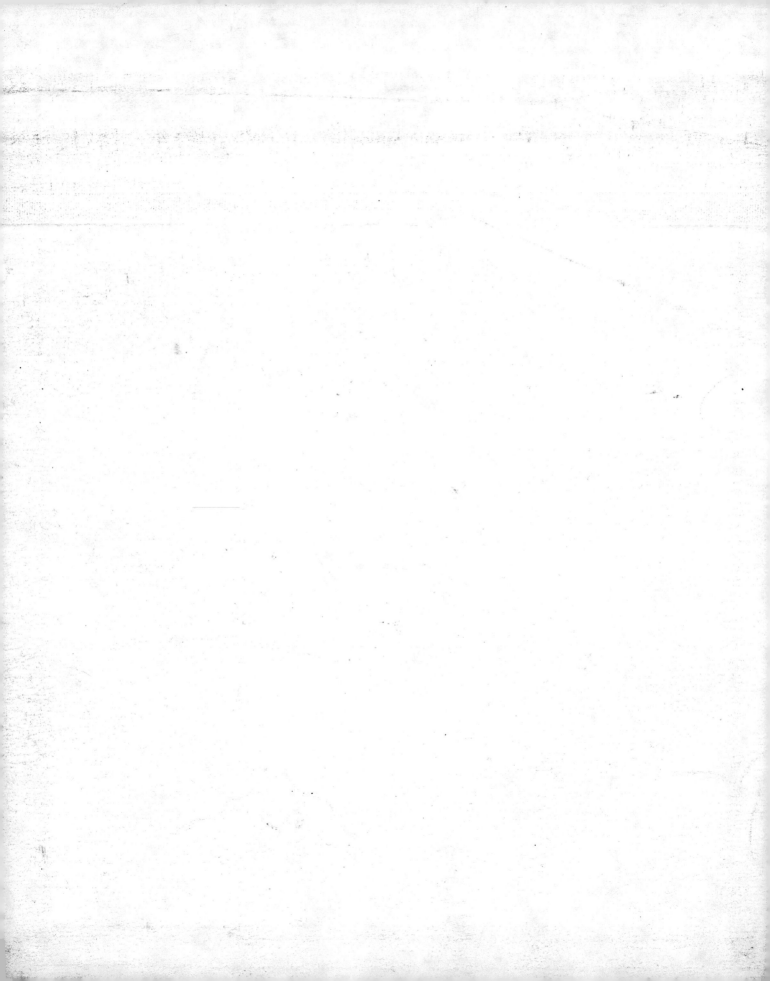

Gregg College

Complete Course

Keyboarding & Document Processing

For Microcomputers

7th Edition

(formerly Gregg College Typing)

Scot Ober, Ph.D.
Professor, Department of Business Education
and Office Administration
Ball State University
Muncie, Indiana

Robert P. Poland, Ph.D.
Professor Emeritus, Business and Distributive Education
Michigan State University
East Lansing, Michigan

Robert N. Hanson, Ed.D.
Professor Emeritus, Department of Office Systems
and Business Education
Northern Michigan University
Marquette, Michigan

Albert D. Rossetti, Ed.D.
Dean, School of Business Administration
Montclair State College
Montclair, New Jersey

Jack E. Johnson, Ph.D.
Professor, Department of Administrative Systems
and Business Education, School of Business
West Georgia College
Carrollton, Georgia

GLENCOE

Macmillan/McGraw-Hill

New York, New York Columbus, Ohio Mission Hills, California Peoria, Illinois

REVIEWERS:

Ms. Beverly Bell
Bryant & Stratton Business Institute
Amherst, New York

Ms. Anita Landenberger
Brookhaven College
Dallas, Texas

Ms. Debbie Hinkle
Forsyth Technical Community College
Hickory, North Carolina

Ms. Rose Mary Pressly
Pellissippi State Technical Community College
Knoxville, Tennessee

Ms. Patricia King
Blackhawk Technical College
Janesville, Wisconsin

Mrs. Arlene Rice
Los Angeles City College
Los Angeles, California

Mrs. Marilyn Satterwhite
Danville Area Community College
Danville, Illinois

Library of Congress Cataloging-in-Publication Data

Gregg college keyboarding and document processing for microcomputers,
complete course/Scot Ober . . . [et al.].—7th ed.
p. cm.—(Gregg college typing, series six)
"Formerly Gregg college typing."
Includes index.
ISBN 0-02-801737-4
1. Electronic data processing—Keyboarding. I. Ober, Scot, Date.
II. Title: Gregg college typing. III. Series.
QA76.9.K48G75 1993
652.5′536—dc20 93-25886
CIP

Gregg College Keyboarding and Document Processing for Microcomputers, Complete Course, 7th edition

Imprint 1995

Send all inquiries to:

Glencoe/McGraw-Hill
936 Eastwind Drive
Westerville, OH 43081

ISBN 0-02-801737-4

Printed in the United States of America.

3 4 5 6 7 8 9 10 11 12 13 14 15 RRDW/MC 03 02 01 00 99 98 97 96 95

Contents

PART 1

PART 2

PRODUCTION ASSIGNMENTS

PART 

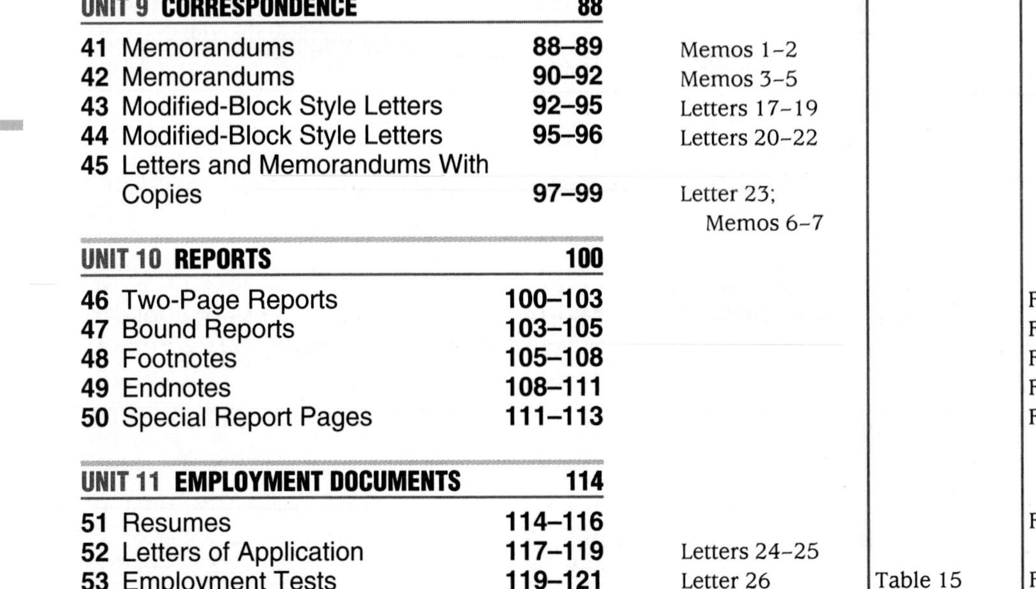

PART 4

PART 5

PART

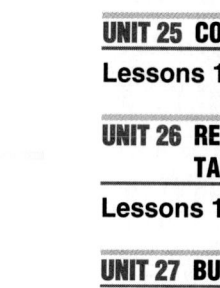

PART 9

INDEX

Preface

Gregg College Keyboarding and Document Processing, Seventh Edition, is a multicomponent instructional program designed to give the student and the instructor a high degree of flexibility and a high degree of success in meeting their respective goals. To facilitate the choice and use of materials, the core components of this teaching-learning program are available in either a kit format or a book format. *The Keyboarding, Third Edition,* text is also available for the development of touch keyboarding skills for use in shorter computer keyboarding classes.

THE KIT FORMAT

Gregg College Keyboarding and Document Processing, Seventh Edition, provides a complete kit of materials for each of the three courses in the keyboarding curriculum generally offered by colleges. Each kit, which is briefly described below, contains a softcover textbook with an easel back, optional computer courseware, and supplementary instructional materials.

The text in each kit contains 60 lessons, with each lesson requiring approximately 45–50 minutes of class time.

Kit 1: Basic. This kit provides the text and courseware for Lessons 1–60. In addition, an 8-page supplemental forms unit is included which contains instructions for completing such items as ruled forms and envelopes. Since this kit is designed for the beginning student, its major objectives are to develop touch control of the keyboard and proper keyboarding techniques; build basic speed and accuracy skill; and provide practice in applying those basic skills to the formatting of letters, reports, tables, memos, and other kinds of personal, personal-business, and business communication.

Kit 2: Intermediate. This kit includes the textbook and courseware for Lessons 61–120. This second course continues the development of basic keyboarding skills and emphasizes the formatting of various kinds of business correspondence, reports, tabulations, and electronic forms from unarranged and rough-draft sources.

Kit 3: Advanced. This kit containing the text and computer courseware, which covers Lessons 121–180, is designed for the third course. After a brief review of basic document processing techniques and an integrated office project in Part 7, students are introduced to various tasks involving desktop publishing in Part 8. In Part 9, students are placed in three different office situations that emphasize such modern office skills as editing, decision making, abstracting information, setting priorities, maintaining a smooth work flow, following directions, and working under pressure and with interruptions.

Format Guides. A pad of self-check keys is available for each of the three kits to enable students to check the correct format of all documents processed.

THE BOOK FORMAT

For the convenience of those who wish to obtain the core instructional materials in separate volumes, the *Gregg College Keyboarding and Document Processing, Seventh Edition,* program offers the following textbooks and self-check keys. In each instance, the content of these components is identical with that of the corresponding part or parts in the kit format.

Textbooks. *Gregg College Keyboarding and Document Processing, Intensive,* contains Lessons 1–120. The content and objectives of this two-semester hardcover text exactly match the content and objectives of the softcover textbooks in the *Basic* and *Intermediate* kits.

Gregg College Keyboarding and Document Processing, Complete Course, contains Lessons 1–180. Thus it combines into one hardcover volume all the lessons contained in the three softcover textbooks included in the three kits.

Format Guides. These self-check keys of formatted documents are also available for use with the *Intensive* and *Complete* hardcover texts.

SUPPORTING MATERIALS

The *Gregg College Keyboarding and Document Processing, Seventh Edition,* program includes the following additional components.

Instructor's Materials. The special materials provided for the instructor can be used with either the *Gregg College Keyboarding and Document Processing, Seventh Edition,* kits or the hardcover textbooks. These materials include special Instructor's Editions containing annotated student pages and solution keys for all of the formatting exercises in each of the three courses. Also available is a separate Instructor's Manual which contains teaching and grading suggestions.

Computer Courseware. The complete computer courseware program (IBM only) is available as a complete package or in sections: Lessons 1–180 (Complete), Lessons 1–120 (Intensive), Lessons 1–60 (Basic), Lessons 61–120 (Intermediate), and Lessons 121–180 (Advanced). Also available is *Keyboarding* (Lessons 1–20) in both IBM and Macintosh versions.

The computer courseware directs students through all activities in the lessons and scores most of the activities including timed writings and formatted documents.

ACKNOWLEDGEMENTS

We wish to express our appreciation to all the instructors and students who have used the previous editions and who have contributed much to this Seventh Edition.

The Authors

Reference Section

MICROCOMPUTER SYSTEM

CORRESPONDENCE

REPORTS

EMPLOYMENT DOCUMENTS

TABLES AND FORMS

MISCELLANEOUS

LANGUAGE ARTS

MAJOR PARTS OF A MICROCOMPUTER SYSTEM

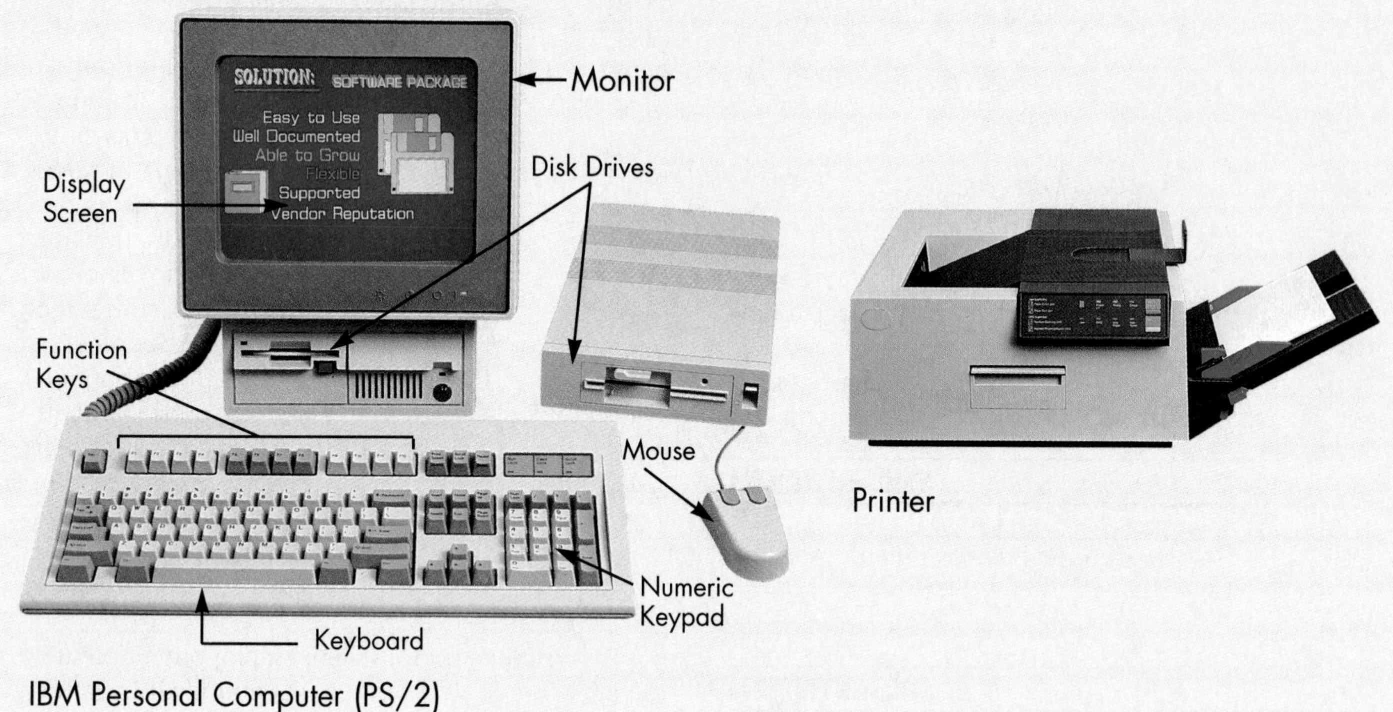

IBM Personal Computer (PS/2)

THE COMPUTER KEYBOARD

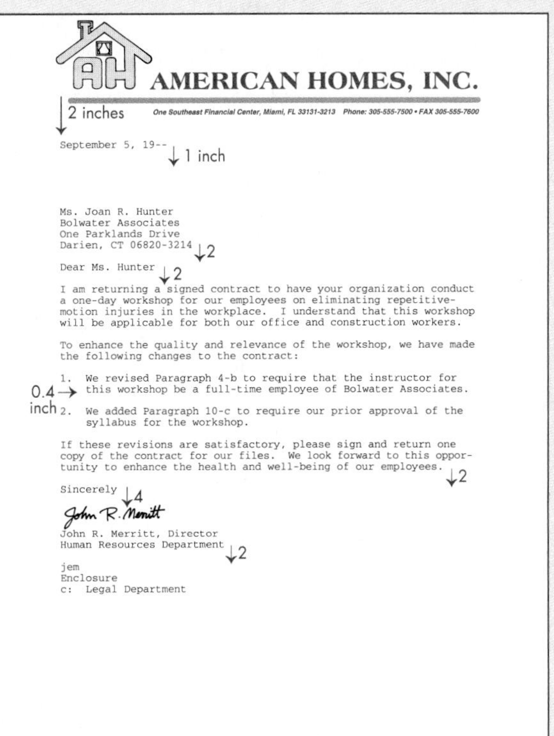

AMERICAN HOMES, INC.
One Southeast Financial Center, Miami, FL 33131-3213 Phone: 305-555-7500 • FAX 305-555-7600

September 5, 19--

Ms. Joan R. Hunter
Bolwater Associates
One Parklands Drive
Darien, CT 06820-3214

Dear Ms. Hunter

I am returning a signed contract to have your organization conduct a one-day workshop for our employees on eliminating repetitive-motion injuries in the workplace. I understand that this workshop will be applicable for both our office and construction workers.

To enhance the quality and relevance of the workshop, we have made the following changes to the contract:

1. We revised Paragraph 4-b to require that the instructor for this workshop be a full-time employee of Bolwater Associates.
2. We added Paragraph 10-c to require our prior approval of the syllabus for the workshop.

If these revisions are satisfactory, please sign and return one copy of the contract for our files. We look forward to this opportunity to enhance the health and well-being of our employees.

Sincerely

John R. Merritt

John R. Merritt, Director
Human Resources Department

jem
Enclosure
c: Legal Department

BUSINESS LETTER IN BLOCK STYLE
(open punctuation)

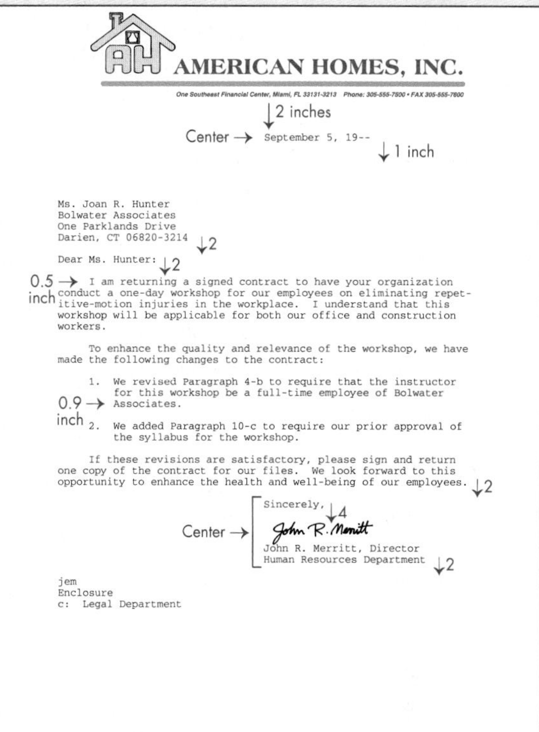

AMERICAN HOMES, INC.
One Southeast Financial Center, Miami, FL 33131-3213 Phone: 305-555-7500 • FAX 305-555-7600

September 5, 19--

Ms. Joan R. Hunter
Bolwater Associates
One Parklands Drive
Darien, CT 06820-3214

Dear Ms. Hunter:

I am returning a signed contract to have your organization conduct a one-day workshop for our employees on eliminating repetitive-motion injuries in the workplace. I understand that this workshop will be applicable for both our office and construction workers.

To enhance the quality and relevance of the workshop, we have made the following changes to the contract:

1. We revised Paragraph 4-b to require that the instructor for this workshop be a full-time employee of Bolwater Associates.
2. We added Paragraph 10-c to require our prior approval of the syllabus for the workshop.

If these revisions are satisfactory, please sign and return one copy of the contract for our files. We look forward to this opportunity to enhance the health and well-being of our employees.

Sincerely,

John R. Merritt

John R. Merritt, Director
Human Resources Department

jem
Enclosure
c: Legal Department

BUSINESS LETTER IN MODIFIED-BLOCK STYLE
(standard punctuation; indented paragraphs)

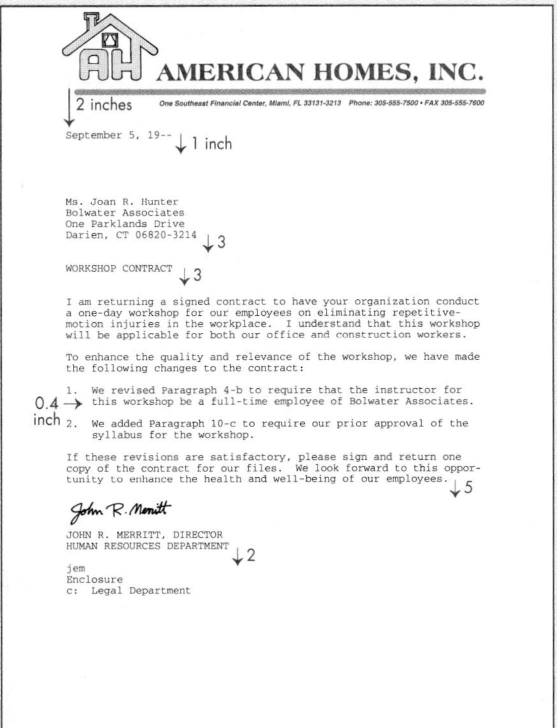

AMERICAN HOMES, INC.
One Southeast Financial Center, Miami, FL 33131-3213 Phone: 305-555-7500 • FAX 305-555-7600

September 5, 19--

Ms. Joan R. Hunter
Bolwater Associates
One Parklands Drive
Darien, CT 06820-3214

WORKSHOP CONTRACT

I am returning a signed contract to have your organization conduct a one-day workshop for our employees on eliminating repetitive-motion injuries in the workplace. I understand that this workshop will be applicable for both our office and construction workers.

To enhance the quality and relevance of the workshop, we have made the following changes to the contract:

1. We revised Paragraph 4-b to require that the instructor for this workshop be a full-time employee of Bolwater Associates.
2. We added Paragraph 10-c to require our prior approval of the syllabus for the workshop.

If these revisions are satisfactory, please sign and return one copy of the contract for our files. We look forward to this opportunity to enhance the health and well-being of our employees.

John R. Merritt

JOHN R. MERRITT, DIRECTOR
HUMAN RESOURCES DEPARTMENT

jem
Enclosure
c: Legal Department

BUSINESS LETTER IN SIMPLIFIED STYLE

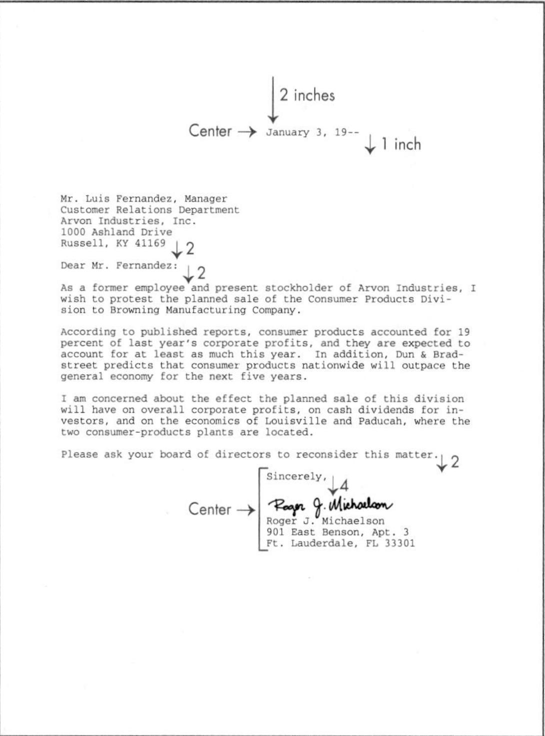

January 3, 19--

Mr. Luis Fernandez, Manager
Customer Relations Department
Arvon Industries, Inc.
1000 Ashland Drive
Russell, KY 41169

Dear Mr. Fernandez:

As a former employee and present stockholder of Arvon Industries, I wish to protest the planned sale of the Consumer Products Division to Browning Manufacturing Company.

According to published reports, consumer products accounted for 19 percent of last year's corporate profits, and they are expected to account for at least as much this year. In addition, Dun & Bradstreet predicts that consumer products nationwide will outpace the general economy for the next five years.

I am concerned about the effect the planned sale of this division will have on overall corporate profits, on cash dividends for investors, and on the economics of Louisville and Paducah, where the two consumer-products plants are located.

Please ask your board of directors to reconsider this matter.

Sincerely,

Roger J. Michaelson

Roger J. Michaelson
901 East Benson, Apt. 3
Ft. Lauderdale, FL 33301

PERSONAL-BUSINESS LETTER
(modified-block style; standard punctuation)

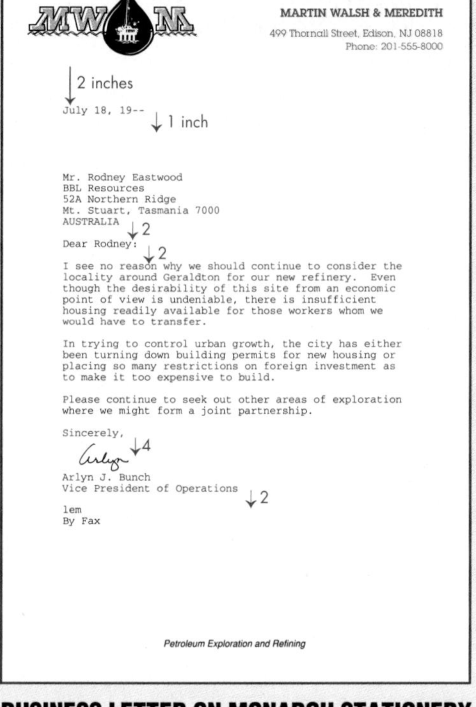

MARTIN WALSH & MEREDITH
499 Thornall Street, Edison, NJ 08818
Phone: 201-555-8000

↓ 2 inches

July 18, 19--

↓ 1 inch

Mr. Rodney Eastwood
BBL Resources
52A Northern Ridge
Mt. Stuart, Tasmania 7000
AUSTRALIA

↓ 2

Dear Rodney:

↓ 2

I see no reason why we should continue to consider the locality around Geraldton for our new refinery. Even though the desirability of this site from an economic point of view is undeniable, there is insufficient housing readily available for those workers whom we would have to transfer.

In trying to control urban growth, the city has either been turning down building permits for new housing or placing so many restrictions on foreign investment as to make it too expensive to build.

Please continue to seek out other areas of exploration where we might form a joint partnership.

Sincerely,

↓ 4

Arlyn J. Bunch
Vice President of Operations

↓ 2

lem
By Fax

Petroleum Exploration and Refining

BUSINESS LETTER ON MONARCH STATIONERY
(1-inch side margins; $7^1/_4$" × $10^1/_2$")

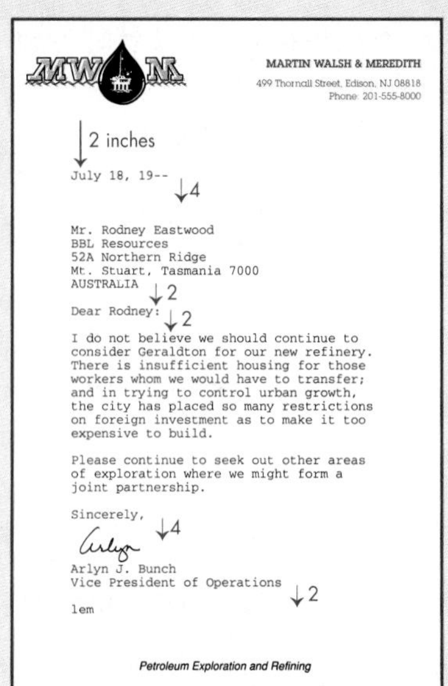

MARTIN WALSH & MEREDITH
499 Thornall Street, Edison, NJ 08818
Phone: 201-555-8000

↓ 2 inches

July 18, 19--

↓ 4

Mr. Rodney Eastwood
BBL Resources
52A Northern Ridge
Mt. Stuart, Tasmania 7000
AUSTRALIA

↓ 2

Dear Rodney:

↓ 2

I do not believe we should continue to consider Geraldton for our new refinery. There is insufficient housing for those workers whom we would have to transfer; and in trying to control urban growth, the city has placed so many restrictions on foreign investment as to make it too expensive to build.

Please continue to seek out other areas of exploration where we might form a joint partnership.

Sincerely,

↓ 4

Arlyn J. Bunch
Vice President of Operations

↓ 2

lem

Petroleum Exploration and Refining

BUSINESS LETTER ON BARONIAL STATIONERY
(0.75-inch side margins; $5^1/_2$" × $8^1/_2$")

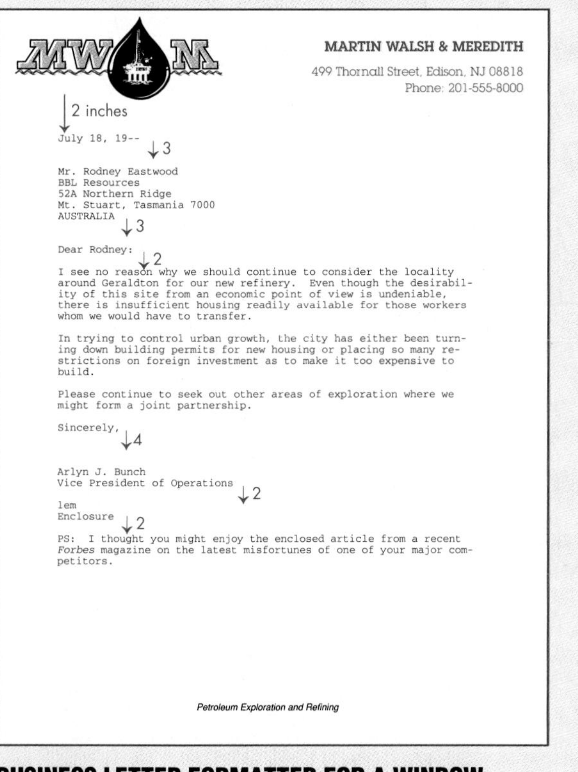

MARTIN WALSH & MEREDITH
499 Thornall Street, Edison, NJ 08818
Phone: 201-555-8000

↓ 2 inches

July 18, 19--

↓ 3

Mr. Rodney Eastwood
BBL Resources
52A Northern Ridge
Mt. Stuart, Tasmania 7000
AUSTRALIA

↓ 3

Dear Rodney:

↓ 2

I see no reason why we should continue to consider the locality around Geraldton for our new refinery. Even though the desirability of this site from an economic point of view is undeniable, there is insufficient housing readily available for those workers whom we would have to transfer.

In trying to control urban growth, the city has either been turning down building permits for new housing or placing so many restrictions on foreign investment as to make it too expensive to build.

Please continue to seek out other areas of exploration where we might form a joint partnership.

Sincerely,

↓ 4

Arlyn J. Bunch
Vice President of Operations

↓ 2

lem
Enclosure

↓ 2

PS: I thought you might enjoy the enclosed article from a recent *Forbes* magazine on the latest misfortunes of one of your major competitors.

Petroleum Exploration and Refining

BUSINESS LETTER FORMATTED FOR A WINDOW ENVELOPE

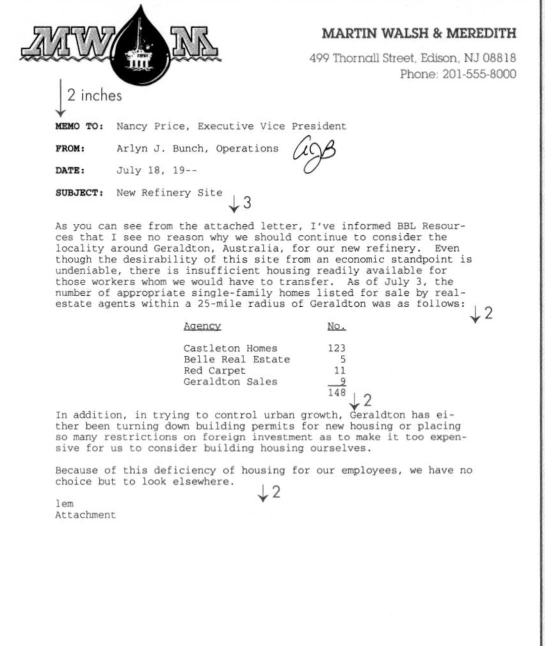

MARTIN WALSH & MEREDITH
499 Thornall Street, Edison, NJ 08818
Phone: 201-555-8000

↓ 2 inches

MEMO TO: Nancy Price, Executive Vice President
FROM: Arlyn J. Bunch, Operations
DATE: July 18, 19--
SUBJECT: New Refinery Site

↓ 3

As you can see from the attached letter, I've informed BBL Resources that I see no reason why we should continue to consider the locality around Geraldton, Australia, for our new refinery. Even though the desirability of this site from an economic standpoint is undeniable, there is insufficient housing readily available for those workers whom we would have to transfer. As of July 3, the number of appropriate single-family homes listed for sale by real-estate agents within a 25-mile radius of Geraldton was as follows:

↓ 2

Agency	No.
Castleton Homes	123
Belle Real Estate	5
Red Carpet	11
Geraldton Sales	9
	148

↓ 2

In addition, in trying to control urban growth, Geraldton has either been turning down building permits for new housing or placing so many restrictions on foreign investment as to make it too expensive for us to consider building housing ourselves.

Because of this deficiency of housing for our employees, we have no choice but to look elsewhere.

↓ 2

lem
Attachment

Petroleum Exploration and Refining

MEMORANDUM

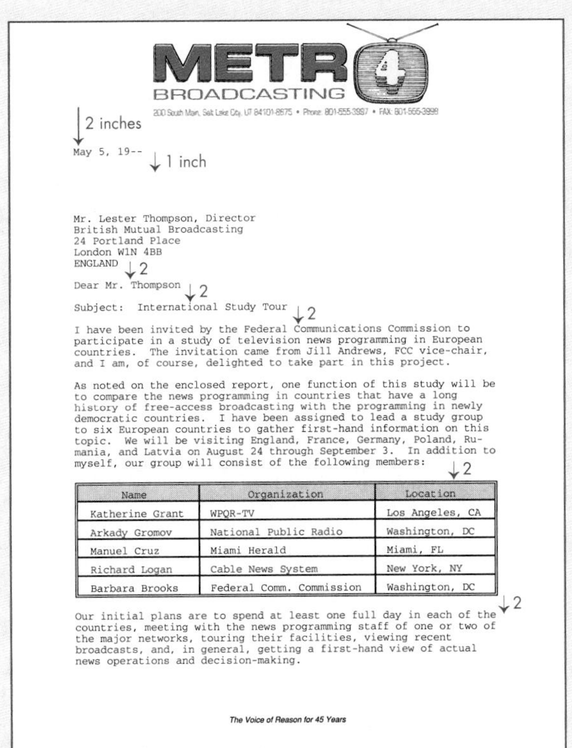

METRO 4 BROADCASTING

200 South Main, Salt Lake City, UT 84101-8675 • Phone: 801-555-3997 • FAX: 801-555-3998

↓ 2 inches

May 5, 19-- ↓ 1 inch

Mr. Lester Thompson, Director
British Mutual Broadcasting
24 Portland Place
London W1N 4BB
ENGLAND ↓ 2

Dear Mr. Thompson ↓ 2

Subject: International Study Tour ↓ 2

I have been invited by the Federal Communications Commission to participate in a study of television news programming in European countries. The invitation came from Jill Andrews, FCC vice-chair, and I am, of course, delighted to take part in this project.

As noted on the enclosed report, one function of this study will be to compare the news programming in countries that have a long history of free-access broadcasting with the programming in newly democratic countries. I have been assigned to lead a study group to six European countries to gather first-hand information on this topic. We will be visiting England, France, Germany, Poland, Rumania, and Latvia on August 24 through September 3. In addition to myself, our group will consist of the following members: ↓ 2

Name	Organization	Location
Katherine Grant	WPQR-TV	Los Angeles, CA
Arkady Gromov	National Public Radio	Washington, DC
Manuel Cruz	Miami Herald	Miami, FL
Richard Logan	Cable News System	New York, NY
Barbara Brooks	Federal Comm. Commission	Washington, DC

↓ 2

Our initial plans are to spend at least one full day in each of the countries, meeting with the news programming staff of one or two of the major networks, touring their facilities, viewing recent broadcasts, and, in general, getting a first-hand view of actual news operations and decision-making.

The Voice of Reason for 45 Years

↓ 1 inch

Mr. Lester Thompson
Page 2
May 5, 19-- ↓ 2

Our tentative itinerary calls for us to arrive at Heathrow Airport at 7:10 p.m. on Tuesday evening, August 27. Would it be possible for us to do the following: ↓ 2

1. Meet with various members of your staff on August 28. We would be available from 8:30 a.m. until 1:30 p.m.

0.4 inch →

2. Receive a copy of your programming log for the week of August 26-30 and especially a minute-by-minute listing of the programming segments for your national news reporting. ↓ 2

I would appreciate your contacting Barbara Brooks, our liaison at the Federal Communications Commission (1919 M Street, NW, Washington, DC 20554; phone: 202-555-3894), to let us know whether we may study your operations on August 28.

So that we can finalize our plans and make the necessary arrangements, may we please hear from you by May 15. If your decision is positive, I will work directly with you in coordinating the details of our visit. ↓ 2

Sincerely ↓ 2

METRO BROADCASTING ↓ 4

Denise J. Watterson

Denise J. Watterson
General Manager ↓ 2

urs
Enclosure: FCC Report
By International Express Mail
c: Barbara Brooks ↓ 2

PS: The Federal Communication Commission will reimburse your organization for any expenses associated with our visit, including phone calls, duplicating, and the like.

SPECIAL CORRESPONDENCE FEATURES

FOREIGN ADDRESS. Key the name of a foreign country in all capital letters on a line by itself.

SUBJECT LINE. If used, key a subject line in upper- and lowercase letters below the salutation, with 1 blank line above and below; the terms *Re:* or *In re:* may also be used.

TABLE. Leave 1 blank line above and below a table without a title (regardless of whether the table has column headings) and 3 blank lines above and below a table with a title.

MULTI-PAGE LETTERS. Key the first page on letterhead stationery and the second page on matching plain stationery. On the second page, key the addressee's name, page number, and date beginning 1 inch from the top, blocked at the left margin. Leave 1 blank line between the page-2 heading and the first line of the body.

ENUMERATION. Key the number followed by a period at the point where paragraphs begin (the left margin for blocked paragraphs or indented 0.5 inch for indented paragraphs). Leave 2 spaces after the number and period and indent turnover lines 0.4 inch. Single-space the items within an enumeration and double-space between items.

COMPANY NAME IN CLOSING LINES. If included, key the company name in all capital letters below the complimentary closing, with 1 blank line above and 3 blank lines below it.

REFERENCE INITIALS. Key only the keyboarder's initials (not the signer's) in lowercase letters a double space below the writer's name and/or title. (Optional: You may also include the computer filename; for example: *urs/SMITH.LET*).

ENCLOSURE NOTATION. Key an enclosure notation a single space below the reference initials if an item is enclosed with a letter. Use the term "Attachment" if an item is attached to a memo instead of enclosed in an envelope. Examples: *3 Enclosures, Enclosure: Contract, Attachment.*

DELIVERY NOTATION. Key a delivery notation a single space below the enclosure notation. Examples: *By Certified Mail, By Fax, By Federal Express.*

COPY NOTATION. Key a copy notation *(c:)* a single space below the delivery notation if someone other than the addressee is to receive a copy of the message.

POSTSCRIPT NOTATION. Key a postscript notation as the last item, preceded by 1 blank line. Indent the first line of the postscript if the paragraphs in the body are indented.

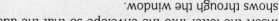

FORMATTING ENVELOPES

A standard large (No. 10) envelope is $9^1/_2$ by $4^1/_8$ inches. A standard small (No. $6^3/_4$) envelope is $6^1/_2$ by $3^5/_8$ inches. Although either address format shown below is acceptable, the format shown for the large envelope (all capital letters and no punctuation) is recommended by the U.S. Postal Service for mail that will be sorted by an electronic scanning device.

Window envelopes are often used in a word processing environment because of the difficulty of aligning envelopes correctly in some printers. A window envelope requires no formatting, since the letter is formatted and folded so that the inside address is visible through the window.

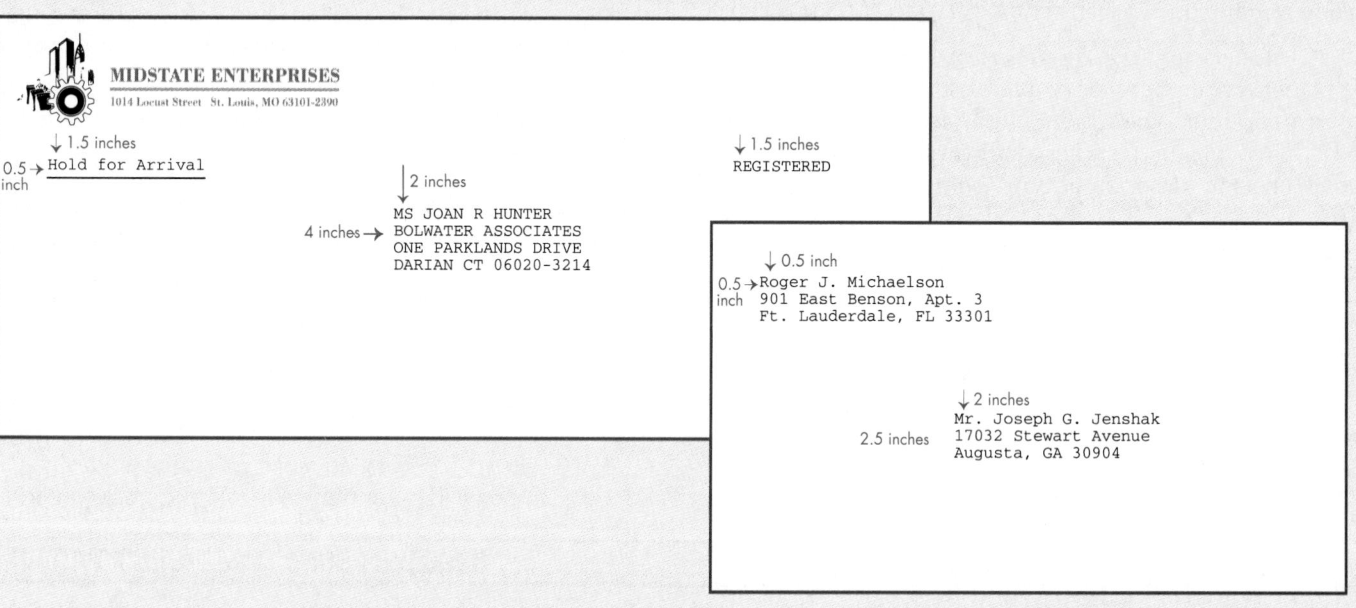

FOLDING LETTERS

To Fold a Letter for a Large Envelope:

1. Place the letter *face up* and fold up the bottom third.
2. Fold the top third down to 0.5 inch from the bottom edge.
3. Insert the last crease into the envelope first, with the flap facing up.

To Fold a Letter for a Small Envelope:

1. Place the letter *face up* and fold up the bottom half to 0.5 inch from the top.
2. Fold the right third over to the left.
3. Fold the left third over to 0.5 inch from the right edge.
4. Insert the last crease into the envelope first, with the flap facing up.

To Fold a Letter for a Window Envelope:

1. Place the letter *face down* with the letterhead at the top and fold the bottom third of the letter up.
2. Fold the top third down so that the address shows.
3. Insert the letter into the envelope so that the address shows through the window.

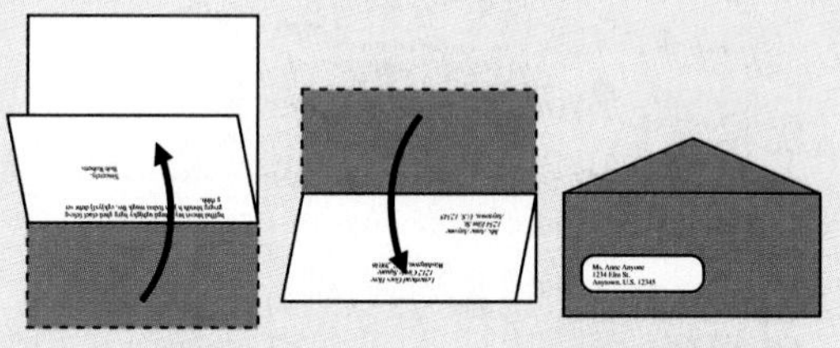

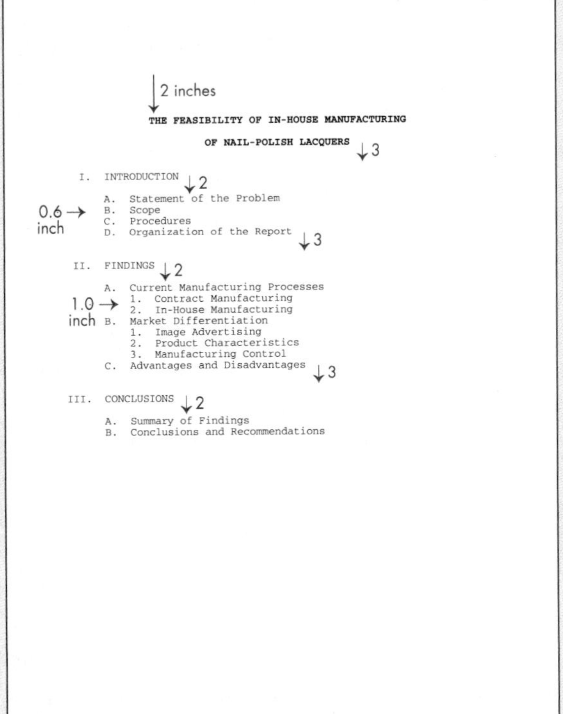

2 inches

THE FEASIBILITY OF IN-HOUSE MANUFACTURING

OF NAIL-POLISH LACQUERS ↓3

I. INTRODUCTION ↓2

0.6 inch →
A. Statement of the Problem
B. Scope
C. Procedures
D. Organization of the Report ↓3

II. FINDINGS ↓2

A. Current Manufacturing Processes
1.0 inch →
1. Contract Manufacturing
2. In-House Manufacturing
B. Market Differentiation
1. Image Advertising
2. Product Characteristics
3. Manufacturing Control
C. Advantages and Disadvantages ↓3

III. CONCLUSIONS ↓2

A. Summary of Findings
B. Conclusions and Recommendations

OUTLINE

(Equal top and bottom margins)

CONSOLIDATION OF THE PARTS WAREHOUSES AT ↓2

SIOUX CITY AND CEDAR FALLS ↓2

Maintaining Profitability in a Declining Market ↓15

Prepared by ↓2

Catherine Rogers-Busch
Chief Product Engineer
Helene Ponds and Associates ↓15

December 3, 19--

(Equal top and bottom margins)

TITLE PAGE

2 inches

CONTENTS ↓3

I. DEVELOPMENT ALTERNATIVES . . . . 1 ↓2

0.6 inch →
A. Young Family 2
B. Growing Family 2
C. Empty Nest 3
D. Custom Home . . . . 3 ↓3

II. FINANCIAL ANALYSES . . . . 4 ↓2

A. Land-Development Costs 4
B. Structural Costs 5
C. Selling Prices . . . . 7 ↓3

III. RISK ANALYSIS . . . . 8 ↓2

A. Supply 8
B. Demand . . . . 10 ↓3

IV. SUMMARY, CONCLUSIONS, AND RECOMMENDATIONS . . . . 14 ↓3

APPENDIX ↓2

A. Questionnaire 17
B. Lot Plan 19
C. Cash-Flow Tables . . . . 20 ↓3

REFERENCES 24

TABLE OF CONTENTS

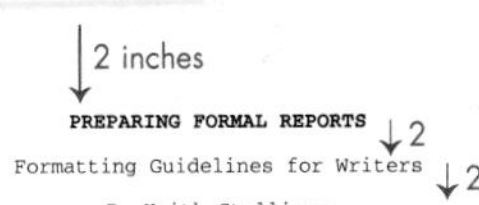

PREPARING FORMAL REPORTS ↓2

Formatting Guidelines for Writers ↓2

By Keith Stallings ↓3

Formatting formal reports is not a difficult task if you just take the time to study the technical aspects involved. This report discusses report headings, page numbers, margins, reference citations, and the bibliography.

Headings

The major heading in a report is the title. It should be centered in all capital letters 2 inches from the top. A subtitle or byline, if used, is keyed in initial capital letters a double space below the title. The body of the report begins on the third line below the title or byline.

Side Headings. A side heading (such as "Page Numbering" shown below) is keyed at the left margin in initial capital letters and in bold, with double-spacing before and after it.

Paragraph Headings. A paragraph heading is indented and keyed in initial capital letters and in bold a double space below the preceding paragraph. The paragraph heading is followed by a period and two spaces, with the text beginning on the same line.

Page Numbering

The first page of the body of a report is counted as page 1 but is not numbered. All other pages are numbered flush right at the top margin, with the first line of the text beginning a double

UNBOUND REPORT (first page)

↓ 1 inch

2 ↓ 2

a real-estate agent from Central Michigan/Tucker Realty, provided a copy of selected reports that are available only to real estate agents.[1] The relevant statistics for the Mt. Rainey school district for those homes selling for $60,000 or more during the past year are shown in Table 2. ↓ 4

TABLE 2. MT. RAINEY HOME SALES FOR $60,000 OR MORE

Jan-Dec 19--

Selling Price	No. of Homes	Days Listed	Average Sq. Ft.
$60,000-$79,999	55	145	1,571
$80,000-$99,999	29	81	1,917
$100,000-$119,999	7	105	2,094
$120,000-$149,999	8	85	2,291
$150,000 or more	6	109	2,659

↓ 4

The data reflected in Table 2 are based on used homes, so comparisons to newly constructed homes are not always appropriate. According to one source, the typical residential community offers fewer new homes than resales, new homes sell faster, and they average about 20 percent larger than resales.[2] ↓ 2

Young Family ↓ 2

The young family submarket is moving from rental or otherwise limited accommodations into their first new home. The mobile-home ↓ 1

↓ 2

[1]Jacqueline Miller, *Residential Real Estate: Central Michigan Edition*, Michigan Real Estate Association, Lansing, Michigan, 1994, pp. 216-224. ↓ 2

[2]Benjamin J. Ashley, "New Sales Versus Resales: Apples to Oranges?" *Real Estate Quarterly*, September 1993, p.143.

UNBOUND REPORT WITH FOOTNOTES (second page)

↓ 1 inch

13

↓ 2 inches

BIBLIOGRAPHY ↓ 3

0.5 inch →

Ashley, Benjamin J., "New Sales Versus Resales: Apples to Oranges?" *Real Estate Quarterly*, September 1993, pp. 143-149. ↓ 2

Barrett, R. J., "Planning Your First Home," *The Long Island Herald*, September 13, 1992, pp. A3, A16. ↓ 2

Bullard, Mary Helen, *The Bullard Real Estate Report*, Bullard Consulting Group, Nyack, New York, 1994. ↓ 2

Heydenburg, Peter, and Rhonda Silver, "Restrictive Covenants and the Law," *Journal of Real Estate Law*, Vol. 24, No. 3, Fall 1991, pp. 81-87. ↓ 2

Miller, Jacqueline. *Residential Real Estate: Central Michigan Edition*, Michigan Real Estate Association, Lansing, Michigan, 1994.

BIBLIOGRAPHY FOR UNBOUND REPORT

↓ 1 inch

3 ↓ 2

1.5 inches → product was eliminated as an option for this submarket because of the numerous developments of this type that already exist or are under construction in the area.[1]

Modular homes, which have been partially constructed before being brought to the building site, were likewise rejected because: ↓ 2

> 0.5 inch → Contrary to popular belief, modular homes are generally not less expensive than conventionally constructed homes. Their advantage, instead, is the speed with which they can be constructed. Their major disadvantage relates to the restrictions often placed on them by municipal zoning ordinances.[2] ← 0.5 inch ↓ 2

Since the River Road development is not subject to time pressures, conventional construction methods were evaluated as the most appropriate for this submarket.

Most of the homes sold in Mt. Rainey contain at least three bedrooms, but in the lowest price bracket most contain less than 1,600 square feet, as shown below. ↓ 2

Selling Price	No. of Homes	Days Listed	Average Sq. Ft.
$60,000-$79,999	55	145	1,571
$80,000-$99,999	29	81	1,917
$100,000-$119,999	7	105	2,094
$120,000-$149,999	8	85	2,291
$150,000 or more	6	109	2,659

↓ 2

Because several planning experts have noted the importance of overall outside dimensions for first-time home buyers,[3] the home plan selected for this submarket is only 37 feet wide, allowing it to be placed on a 67-foot-wide lot, with ample setback from the lot lines both from a zoning standpoint and from an aesthetic point of view.

BOUND REPORT WITH ENDNOTES (third page)

↓ 1 inch

13

↓ 2 inches

NOTES ↓ 3

0.5 inch → 1. Jacqueline Miller, *Residential Real Estate: Central Michigan Edition*, Michigan Real Estate Association, Lansing, Michigan, 1994, pp. 216-224. ↓ 2

1.5 inches → 2. Benjamin J. Ashley, "New Sales Versus Resales: Apples to Oranges?" *Real Estate Quarterly*, September 1993, p. 143.

3. Mary Helen Bullard, *The Bullard Real Estate Report*, Bullard Consulting Group, Nyack, New York, 1994, p.3.

4. Peter Heydenburg and Rhonda Silver, "Restrictive Covenants and the Law," *Journal of Real Estate Law*, Vol. 24, No. 3, Fall 1991, pp. 85-87.

5. Bullard, p. 13.

6. R. J. Barrett, "Planning Your First Home," *The Long Island Herald*, September 13, 1992, pp. A3, A16.

7. Heydenburg and Silver, p. 82.

ENDNOTES FOR BOUND REPORT

3

product was eliminated as an option for this submarket because, as Bullard (1994) has noted, numerous developments of this type already exist or are under construction in the area.

Modular homes, which have been partially constructed before being brought to the building site, were likewise rejected for the following reasons (Modlin, 1994, p. 232):

1. Contrary to popular belief, modular homes are generally not less expensive than conventionally constructed homes.

2. Zoning regulations and restrictive covenants often forbid the construction of modular homes, especially in upscale areas.

The big advantage of modular homes is the speed with which they can be constructed. However, since the River Road development is not subject to time pressures, conventional construction methods were evaluated as the most appropriate for this submarket.

Home Requirements. Based on current mortgage criteria in the Mount Rainey area, a buyer in this submarket cannot afford more than $70,000 for a home. Since family size is still small (fewer than four family members), a 1,250-square-foot model with one full bath on each level was selected for planning purposes.

Lot Requirements. Because several planning experts have noted the importance of overall outside dimensions for first-time home buyers (see, for example, Barrett, 1992; Heydenburg and Silver, 1994), the home plan selected for this submarket is only 37 feet wide, which allows it to be located on a 67-foot-wide lot with ample setback from the lot lines.

UNBOUND REPORT WITH AUTHOR/DATE CITATIONS

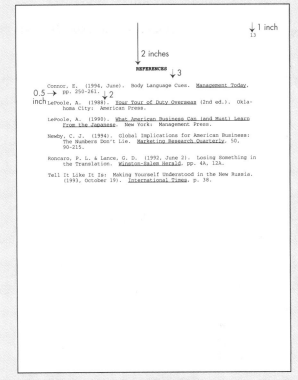

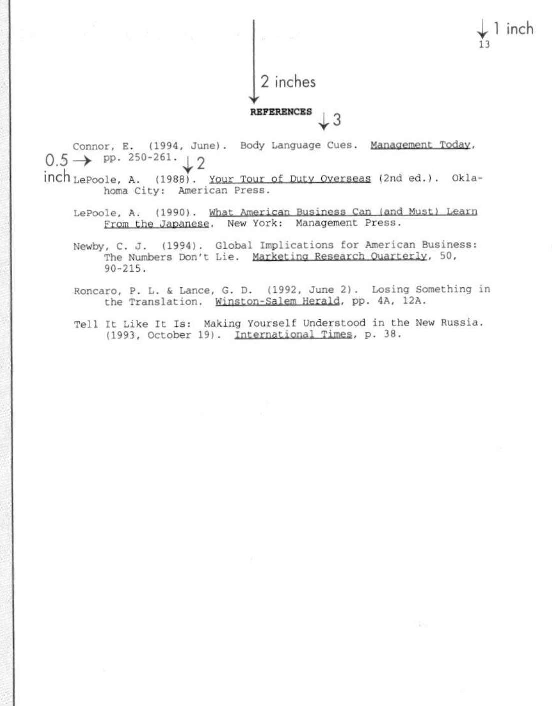

13

REFERENCES

Connor, E. (1994, June). Body Language Cues. Management Today, pp. 250-261.

LePoole, A. (1988). Your Tour of Duty Overseas (2nd ed.). Oklahoma City: American Press.

LePoole, A. (1990). What American Business Can (and Must) Learn From the Japanese. New York: Management Press.

Newby, C. J. (1994). Global Implications for American Business: The Numbers Don't Lie. Marketing Research Quarterly, 50, 90-215.

Roncaro, P. L. & Lance, G. D. (1992, June 2). Losing Something in the Translation. Winston-Salem Herald, pp. 4A, 12A.

Tell It Like It Is: Making Yourself Understood in the New Russia. (1993, October 19). International Times, p. 38.

REFERENCES PAGE IN APA FORMAT

Jenson 1

Sherlon Jenson

Professor Zhao

Comm 201

8 October 19--

Communication Skills Needed in International Business

International business plays an increasingly important role in the U.S. economy, and U.S. companies recognize that to be competitive nationally, they must be competitive internationally. Reflecting this trend, direct investment by U.S. private enterprises in foreign countries increased from $309 billion in 1987 to $415 billion in 1991, an increase of 34 percent in four years (Connor 253). Today, more than 3,000 U.S. corporations have over 25,000 subsidiaries and affiliates in 125 foreign countries, and more than 25,000 American firms are engaged in international marketing (Newby 193, 205).

International business is highly dependent on communication. According to Arnold LePoole, chief executive officer of Armstrand Industries, an international supplier of automotive parts:

> If a company cannot communicate with its foreign subsidiaries, customers, suppliers, and governments, it cannot achieve success. And the sad fact is that most American managers are ill-equipped to communicate with their international counterparts. (143-144).

Because competent business communication skills are one of the most important components for success in international business affairs, a survey was designed to explore the importance of, level of competence in, and methods of developing four types of

REPORT IN MLA FORMAT

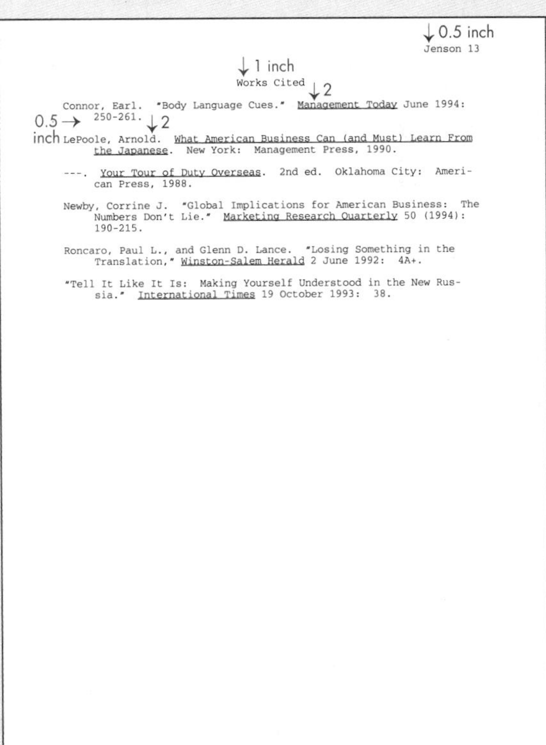

Jenson 13

Works Cited

Connor, Earl. "Body Language Cues." Management Today June 1994: 250-261.

LePoole, Arnold. What American Business Can (and Must) Learn From the Japanese. New York: Management Press, 1990.

---. Your Tour of Duty Overseas. 2nd ed. Oklahoma City: American Press, 1988.

Newby, Corrine J. "Global Implications for American Business: The Numbers Don't Lie." Marketing Research Quarterly 50 (1994): 190-215.

Roncaro, Paul L., and Glenn D. Lance. "Losing Something in the Translation," Winston-Salem Herald 2 June 1992: 4A+.

"Tell It Like It Is: Making Yourself Understood in the New Russia." International Times 19 October 1993: 38.

WORKS-CITED PAGE IN MLA FORMAT

2 inches

BUCK HARDWARE EXECUTIVE COMMITTEE ↓2

Meeting Agenda ↓2

June 7, 19--, 3 p.m. ↓3

1. Call to order ↓2
2. Approval of minutes of May 5 meeting
3. Progress report on building addition and parking lot (Norman Hedges)
4. Unfinished business: (0.4 inch →)
   a. May 15 draft of Five-Year Plan
   b. Review of National Hardware Association annual convention
5. New business:
   a. Employee grievance filed by Ellen Burrows (John Lennon)
   b. New expense-report forms (Anne Richards)
   c. Home office visit by Jay Nelson
6. Announcements
7. Program: "The One-Second Manager" (30-minute videotape)
8. Adjournment

MEETING AGENDA

2 inches

RESOURCE COMMITTEE ↓2

Minutes of the Meeting ↓2

March 13, 19-- ↓3

ATTENDANCE (1.5 inches →) The Resource Committee met on March 13, 19--, at the Airport Sheraton in Portland, Oregon, in conjunction with the western regional meeting. Members present were Michael Davis, Cynthia Giovanni, Don Madsen, and Edna Pintar. Michael Davis, chairperson, called the meeting to order at 2:30 p.m. ↓3

OLD BUSINESS The members of the committee reviewed the sales brochure on electronic copyboards. They agreed to purchase an electronic copyboard for the conference room. Cynthia Giovanni will secure quotations from at least two suppliers.

NEW BUSINESS The committee reviewed a request from the Purchasing Department for three new electronic typewriters. After extensive discussion regarding the appropriate uses of electronic typewriters versus microcomputers, the committee approved the request.

A request from the Marketing Department for a new photocopier was sent back to the department for more justification.

ADJOURNMENT The meeting was adjourned at 4:45 p.m. The next meeting has been scheduled for May 4 in the headquarters conference room. Members are asked to bring with them copies of the latest resource planning document. ↓2

Center → Respectfully submitted, ↓4

D. S. Madsen, Secretary

MINUTES OF MEETING

2 inches

PORTLAND SALES MEETING ↓2

Itinerary for Arlene Gilsdorf ↓2

March 12-15, 19-- ↓3

Thursday, March 12 ↓2

Detroit/Minneapolis . . . . Northwest 83
(0.4 inch →) Leave 5:10 p.m.; arrive 5:55 p.m.
Seat 8D; nonstop ↓2

Minneapolis/Portland . . . . Northwest 2363
Leave 6:30 p.m.; arrive 8:06 p.m.
Seat 15C; nonstop; dinner ↓3

Sunday, March 15

Portland/Minneapolis. . . . . Northwest 360
Leave 7:30 a.m.; arrive 12:26 p.m.
Seat 15H; one stop; breakfast

Minneapolis/Detroit . . . . Northwest 748
Leave 1 p.m.; arrive 3:32 p.m.
Seat 10D; nonstop; snack ↓3

NOTES ↓2

1. Jack Weatherford, assistant western regional manager, will meet your flight on Thursday and return you to the airport on Sunday.
2. All seat assignments are aisle seats; smoking is not allowed on any of the flights.
3. A single-room reservation (Reservation 36812-0), guaranteed for late arrival, has been made at the Airport Sheraton for March 12-14.
4. Important phone numbers:
   Jack Weatherford . . . . .503-555-8029, Ext. 87
   Airport Sheraton 503-555-4032
   Northwest Reservations 800-555-1289

ITINERARY

2 inches

POWER OF ATTORNEY ↓3

(1.0 inch →) KNOW ALL MEN BY THESE PRESENTS that I, ANTHONY LEE FERNANDEZ, of the City of Tulia, County of Swisher, State of Texas, do hereby appoint my son, Robert Fernandez, of this City, County, and State as my attorney-in-fact to act in my name, place, and stead as my agent in the management of my real estate transactions, chattel and goods transactions, banking and securities transactions, and business operating transactions.

I give and grant unto my said attorney full power and authority to do and perform all and every act and thing whatsoever requisite and necessary to be done in the said management as fully, to all intents and purposes, as I might or could do if personally present, with full power of revocation, hereby ratifying and confirming all that my said attorney shall lawfully do or shall cause to be done in my behalf by virtue hereof:

IN WITNESS WHEREOF, I have hereunto set my hand and seal this thirteenth day of April, 1994. ↓3

Center → ______________________ (L.S.) ↓2

SIGNED and affirmed in the presence of: ↓3

______________________ ↓3

____

Page 1 of 1

↑ 1 inch

LEGAL DOCUMENT

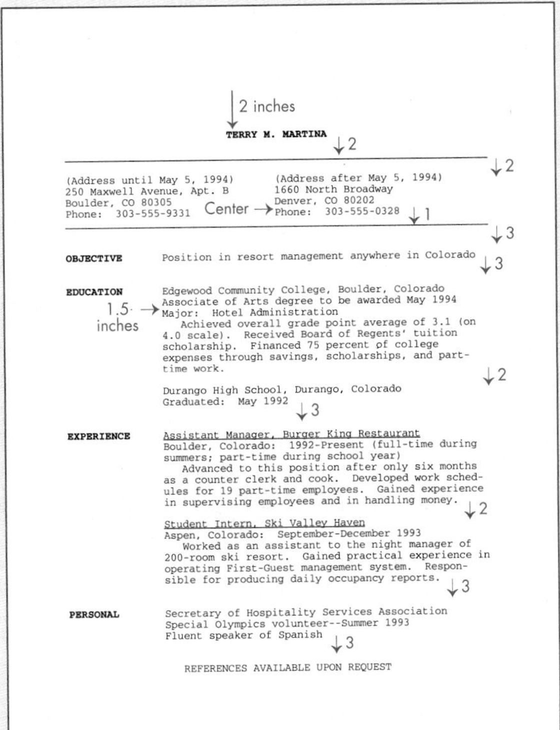

TERRY M. MARTINA

(Address until May 5, 1994)
250 Maxwell Avenue, Apt. B
Boulder, CO 80305
Phone: 303-555-9331

(Address after May 5, 1994)
1660 North Broadway
Denver, CO 80202
Phone: 303-555-0328

OBJECTIVE Position in resort management anywhere in Colorado

EDUCATION Edgewood Community College, Boulder, Colorado
Associate of Arts degree to be awarded May 1994
Major: Hotel Administration
Achieved overall grade point average of 3.1 (on 4.0 scale). Received Board of Regents' tuition scholarship. Financed 75 percent of college expenses through savings, scholarships, and part-time work.

Durango High School, Durango, Colorado
Graduated: May 1992

EXPERIENCE Assistant Manager, Burger King Restaurant
Boulder, Colorado: 1992-Present (full-time during summers; part-time during school year)
Advanced to this position after only six months as a counter clerk and cook. Developed work schedules for 19 part-time employees. Gained experience in supervising employees and in handling money.

Student Intern, Ski Valley Haven
Aspen, Colorado: September-December 1993
Worked as an assistant to the night manager of 200-room ski resort. Gained practical experience in operating First-Guest management system. Responsible for producing daily occupancy reports.

PERSONAL Secretary of Hospitality Services Association
Special Olympics volunteer--Summer 1993
Fluent speaker of Spanish

REFERENCES AVAILABLE UPON REQUEST

RESUME

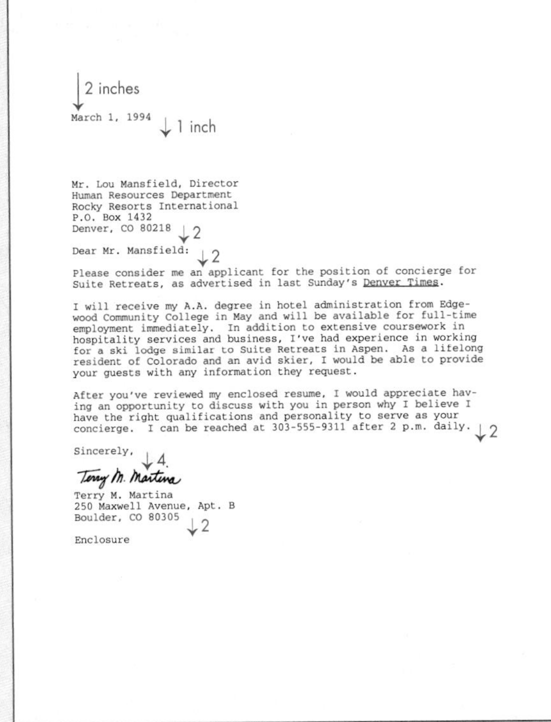

March 1, 1994

Mr. Lou Mansfield, Director
Human Resources Department
Rocky Resorts International
P.O. Box 1432
Denver, CO 80218

Dear Mr. Mansfield:

Please consider me an applicant for the position of concierge for Suite Retreats, as advertised in last Sunday's Denver Times.

I will receive my A.A. degree in hotel administration from Edgewood Community College in May and will be available for full-time employment immediately. In addition to extensive coursework in hospitality services and business, I've had experience in working for a ski lodge similar to Suite Retreats in Aspen. As a lifelong resident of Colorado and an avid skier, I would be able to provide your guests with any information they request.

After you've reviewed my enclosed resume, I would appreciate having an opportunity to discuss with you in person why I believe I have the right qualifications and personality to serve as your concierge. I can be reached at 303-555-9311 after 2 p.m. daily.

Sincerely,

Terry M. Martina

Terry M. Martina
250 Maxwell Avenue, Apt. B
Boulder, CO 80305

Enclosure

LETTER OF APPLICATION

PLACING INFORMATION ON PRINTED LINES

Because of the difficulty of aligning copy on a printed line with a computer and printer, lined forms such as job-application forms are most efficiently completed on a typewriter.

When keying on a lined form, use the typewriter's variable spacer to adjust the paper so that the line is in the position that a row of underlines would occupy. (On many machines, this is accomplished by pressing in the left platen knob.)

Do not leave any requested information blank; use "N/A" (not applicable) if necessary. Because of space limitations, it may be necessary to abbreviate some words.

Because first impressions are important, ensure that all your employment documents are in correct format, are neat in appearance, and are free from errors.

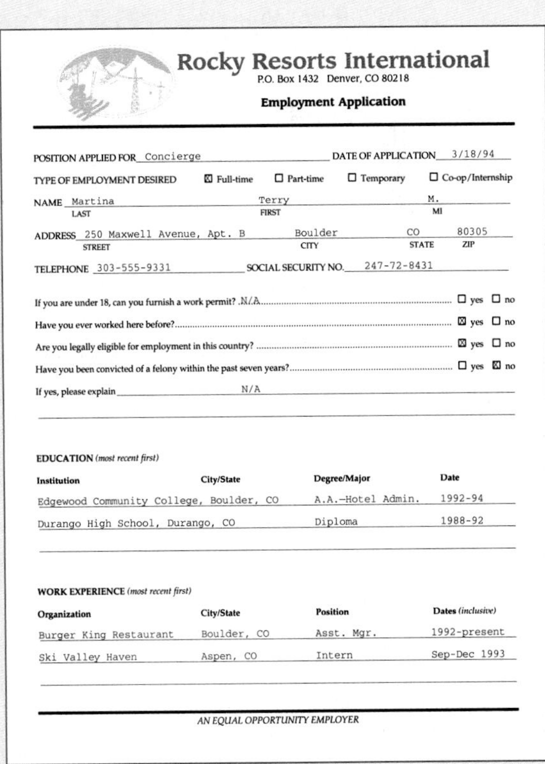

Rocky Resorts International
P.O. Box 1432 Denver, CO 80218
Employment Application

POSITION APPLIED FOR Concierge DATE OF APPLICATION 3/18/94

TYPE OF EMPLOYMENT DESIRED ☒ Full-time ☐ Part-time ☐ Temporary ☐ Co-op/Internship

NAME Martina (LAST) Terry (FIRST) M. (MI)

ADDRESS 250 Maxwell Avenue, Apt. B (STREET) Boulder (CITY) CO (STATE) 80305 (ZIP)

TELEPHONE 303-555-9331 SOCIAL SECURITY NO. 247-72-8431

If you are under 18, can you furnish a work permit? N/A ☐ yes ☐ no
Have you ever worked here before? ☒ yes ☐ no
Are you legally eligible for employment in this country? ☒ yes ☐ no
Have you been convicted of a felony within the past seven years? ☐ yes ☒ no
If yes, please explain N/A

EDUCATION (most recent first)

Institution	City/State	Degree/Major	Date
Edgewood Community College	Boulder, CO	A.A.–Hotel Admin.	1992-94
Durango High School	Durango, CO	Diploma	1988-92

WORK EXPERIENCE (most recent first)

Organization	City/State	Position	Dates (inclusive)
Burger King Restaurant	Boulder, CO	Asst. Mgr.	1992-present
Ski Valley Haven	Aspen, CO	Intern	Sep-Dec 1993

AN EQUAL OPPORTUNITY EMPLOYER

JOB-APPLICATION FORM (first page)

ARCHER-DANIELS PHARMACEUTICALS
FRINGE-BENEFIT ANALYSIS ↓2

January 1, 19-- ↓3

Component	Total Costs	Gain ↓2
Paid Time Off	$ 5,080	7%
Retirement	3,105	5%
Taxes	2,750	3%
Medical Plan	2,495	107%
Miscellaneous	2,650	14%
TOTALS	$16,080	16%

OPEN TABLE (with blocked column headings)

Table 14 ↓2

COMPOUND INTEREST ↓1

Year	Rate of 9%[a] ↓1		
	Beginning Amount	Interest	Ending Amount ↓1
1	$50.00	$ 4.50	$54.50
2	54.50	4.91	59.41
3	59.41	5.35	64.76
4	64.76	5.83	70.59
5	70.59	6.35	76.94 ↓1
TOTAL	......	$26.94	...... ↓1

[a]Accrued annually.

BOXED TABLE (with centered column headings)

FORMATTING BUSINESS FORMS

Most business forms can be formatted most efficiently on a typewriter. Whether formatted on a typewriter or computer, follow these guidelines:

- Align number columns at the right, centered visually within each ruled area.
- Align word columns (or combination word and number columns) at the left, 2 or 3 spaces after the vertical rule.
- Set the left margin for the first column and set left or decimal tabs for each additional column.
- Do not key a dollar sign for amount columns.
- Indent turnover lines 2 or 3 spaces.

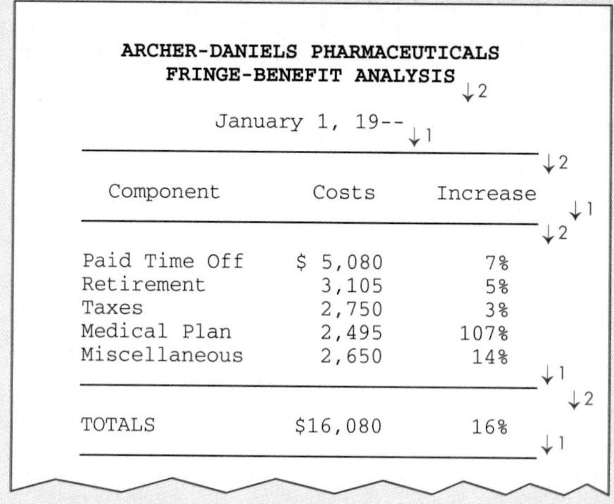

ARCHER-DANIELS PHARMACEUTICALS
FRINGE-BENEFIT ANALYSIS ↓2

January 1, 19-- ↓1

Component	Costs	Increase
Paid Time Off	$ 5,080	7%
Retirement	3,105	5%
Taxes	2,750	3%
Medical Plan	2,495	107%
Miscellaneous	2,650	14%
TOTALS	$16,080	16%

RULED TABLE (with centered column headings)

CHIEF EXECUTIVE ALMA MATERS

As of January 1992

Company	Chief Executive	Education: Undergraduate	Education: Graduate
Apple	John Sculley	Brown	Princeton
Compaq	Joseph R. Canion	Houston	Houston
IBM	John F. Akers	Yale	
Unisys	James A. Unruh	Jamestown	Denver
Zenith	Jerry Pearlman	Princeton	Harvard

BOXED TABLE (prepared in WordPerfect)

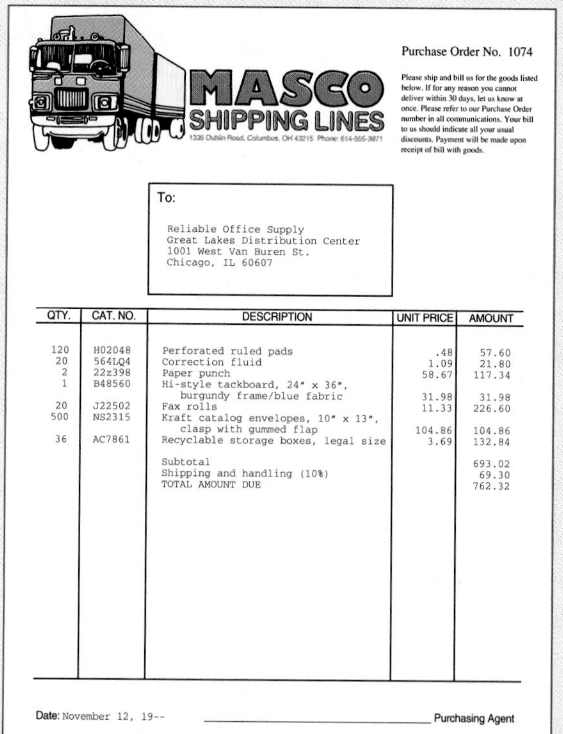

Purchase Order No. 1074

Please ship and bill us for the goods listed below. If for any reason you cannot deliver within 30 days, let us know at once. Please refer to our Purchase Order number in all communications. Your bill to us should indicate all your usual discounts. Payment will be made upon receipt of bill with goods.

To:

Reliable Office Supply
Great Lakes Distribution Center
1001 West Van Buren St.
Chicago, IL 60607

QTY.	CAT. NO.	DESCRIPTION	UNIT PRICE	AMOUNT
120	H02048	Perforated ruled pads	.48	57.60
20	564LQ4	Correction fluid	1.09	21.80
2	22z398	Paper punch	58.67	117.34
1	B48560	Hi-style tackboard, 24" x 36", burgundy frame/blue fabric	31.98	31.98
20	J22502	Fax rolls	11.33	226.60
500	NS2315	Kraft catalog envelopes, 10" x 13", clasp with gummed flap	104.86	104.86
36	AC7861	Recyclable storage boxes, legal size	3.69	132.84
		Subtotal		693.02
		Shipping and handling (10%)		69.30
		TOTAL AMOUNT DUE		762.32

Date: November 12, 19-- _______________ Purchasing Agent

BUSINESS FORM

WORD-DIVISION RULES

1. Do not divide words pronounced as one syllable *(thoughts, planned)*, contractions *(shouldn't, haven't)*, or abbreviations *(UNICEF, assoc.)*.
2. Divide words only between syllables. Whenever you are unsure of where a syllable ends, consult a dictionary.
3. Leave at least three characters (the last will be a hyphen) on the upper line, and carry at least three characters (the last may be a punctuation mark) to the next line. Thus *de- lay* and *af- ter*, but not *a- maze* or *trick- y*.
4. Divide compound words either at the hyphen *(self-confidence)* or where the two words join to make a solid compound. Thus *master- piece*, not *mas- terpiece*.

PROOFREADERS' MARKS

Proofreaders' Mark	Draft	Final Copy
SS Single-space	SS [first line / second line	first line second line
ds Double-space	ds [first line second line	first line / second line
V or ∧ Insert punctuation	if he's not,	if he's not,
new/~~old~~ Change word	and ~~if~~ when you	and when you
Delete and close up	co-operation	cooperation
/ Use lowercase letter	our President	our president
○ Spell out	the only ①	the only one
⊐ Move right	Please send	Please send
⊏ Move left	May I	May I
⌢ Omit space	data base	database
∽ Transpose	they all see	they see all
∧ Insert	she may ∧ go (not)	she may not go
≡ Capitalize	Maple street	Maple Street
Delete	a ~~final~~ draft copy	a draft copy
Move as shown	no copy machine	no machine
¶ Paragraph	¶ Most of the	Most of the
# Insert space	allready to	all ready to
⊙ Make a period	one way ⊙	one way.
··· Don't delete	a ~~true~~ story	a true story

PUNCTUATION AND SPACING POINTERS

AMPERSAND. One space before and after.

CLOSING QUOTATION MARK. *(a)* Keyed *after* a period or comma and *before* a colon or semicolon. *Always. (b)* Keyed *after* a question mark or exclamation point if the quoted material is a question or an exclamation; otherwise, it is keyed *before* the question mark or exclamation point.

COLON. Two spaces after.

COMMA. One space after.

EQUALS SIGN. One space before and after.

EXCLAMATION POINT. Two spaces after.

PERIOD. *(a)* Two spaces after a period at the end of a sentence; *(b)* one space after the period following someone's initials or the abbreviation of a single word (e.g., *Mrs. Jones*); *(c)* no space after each internal period in an abbreviation (e.g., *a.m.*).

QUESTION MARK. Two spaces after.

SEMICOLON. One space after.

TABLE COLUMNS. Six spaces between.

UNDERLINE. *(a)* To key a magazine or book title, underline the entire title, including internal spaces and punctuation. *(b)* To stress individual words, underline them separately; do not underline the punctuation or the spaces between the words.

ZIP CODE. One space before.

COMMAS

1. Use a comma to separate two independent clauses in a compound sentence when they are joined by *and, but, or,* or *nor.*

   I want to attend, but Dee has tickets to the game.

   Ellen left her job in May, and she and her sister went to Paris.

   But: Ellen left her job and went to Paris with her sister.

2. Use commas to separate three or more items in a series when the last item is preceded by *and, or,* or *nor.*

   Patsy, Kris, or Bill will be elected.

   They saved their work, exited the program, and turned their computers off.

3. When a dependent clause *precedes* the independent clause, separate the clauses with a comma.

   Before we can make a decision, we need the facts.

4. Use commas to set off a nonessential expression (a word, phrase, or clause that may be omitted without changing the basic meaning of the sentence). When an expression is essential to the completeness of a sentence, do not set it off with commas.

   Our present projections, you must admit, are inadequate.

   But: You must admit the projections are inadequate.

   It was mailed on Tuesday, the day your order was received.

   But: It was mailed the day your order was received.

5. Use commas to set off the year when it follows the month and day.

   The reunion will be held on May 2, 1995, in Chicago.

   But: The reunion will be held on May 2 in Chicago.

   But: In March 1988 the firm was incorporated.

6. When two adjectives modify the same noun, use a comma to separate the adjectives if they are not joined by *and.* (Note: If the first adjective modifies the combined idea of the second adjective plus the noun, do not separate the adjectives with a comma.)

   Rue is an intelligent, understanding counselor.

   But: Rue is an intelligent and understanding counselor.

7. Use commas to set off a transitional expression (such as *therefore*) or an independent comment (such as *of course*).

   Thomas told her, however, that the new printers would arrive today.

   In the first place, the members have not yet reached an agreement.

8. Use commas to set off an expression in apposition (that is, a word, phrase, or clause, that identifies or explains other terms).

   The projectionist, Kelsey Auland, will show the film tonight.

OTHER PUNCTUATION MARKS

1. Use a semicolon to separate two independent clauses that are not joined by *and, but,* or *nor*.

   Leslie worked on Labor Day; Jean did not.

   But: Leslie worked on Labor Day but Jean did not.

2. If either of the independent clauses in a compound sentence contains a comma, separate the clauses with a semicolon rather than a comma.

3. Use a semicolon to separate items in a series if any of the items already contain commas.

   Staff meetings were held on Thursday, May 7; Monday, June 7; and Friday, June 12.

4. Hyphenate a compound adjective (two or more words that function as a unit to describe a noun) that comes *before* a noun. Exception: If the first word is an adverb ending in *ly,* do not hyphenate such adjectives.

   The determination of production goals for each of the plants is a high-level decision.

   But: Decisions about production goals are made at a high level.

5. Underline titles of complete published works, and use the quotation marks around titles that represent only a part of a complete published work.

   The chapter entitled "IRAs and Personal Financial Planning" will be discussed tomorrow.

   The sales director reported that excellent results had been obtained from advertisements in the Chicago Tribune.

6. Use a period to end a sentence that is a polite request, suggestion, or command if you expect the reader to respond by acting rather than by giving a yes-or-no answer.

   Will you please send the report by overnight express.

   May I have a copy of your report before you leave.

7. To make a singular noun possessive, add the apostrophe before the *s.*

   a customer's request   the company's profits

8. To make a possessive from a singular noun that ends in an *s* sound, be guided by the way the word is pronounced. If a new syllable is formed by making the noun possessive, add an apostrophe and an s (my *boss's* office, the *witness's* testimony). If the addition of an extra syllable to a singular noun would make a word that is hard to pronounce, add only an apostrophe (*Mr. Phillips'* career, *Mrs. Hodges'* friend).

9. To make a plural noun not ending in s possessive, place the apostrophe before the s.

   the women's offices   the children's school

10. To make a possessive from a plural noun ending in *s,* place the apostrophe after the *s.*

    the secretaries' computers   the Halls' reception

11. Do not use an apostrophe with possessive pronouns.

    The new house is ours. The team won its first three debates.

    But: It's time for their mid-semester exams.

CAPITALIZATION

1. Capitalize the first word of all sentences and the first word of expressions used as a sentence.
   How may I help you?
   Enough said about that!
2. Capitalize every proper noun. A proper noun is the official name of a particular person, place, or thing.
   Ohio State University   Memorial Day
3. Capitalize common organization terms such as *advertising department* and *finance committee* when they are the actual names of units within the writer's own organization and are modified by the word *the*.
   The Board of Trustees of our college meets on Thursday.
   The advertising department of A & G will reorganize.
4. Capitalize adjectives derived from proper nouns.
   America (n.)   American (adj.)
5. Capitalize the names of places such as *streets, buildings, parks, monuments, rivers, oceans,* and *mountains.* Do not capitalize short forms used in place of the full name.
   Northland Mall   Front Street
   Pacific Ocean   Washington Monument
6. Capitalize *north, south, east, west,* and derivative words when they designate definite regions or are an integral part of a proper name.
   She lives in the Southwest.
   Go north for two blocks, then head west.
   He is a southern gentleman.
7. Capitalize the names of the days of the week, months, holidays, and religious days.
   Veterans Day   Tuesday, October 8
8. Do not capitalize the names of the seasons.
   We will publish the book in the fall.
   During the spring, my allergies bother me.
9. Capitalize the names of specific course titles. Do not, however, capitalize the names of subjects or areas of study (except for any proper nouns or adjectives in such names).
   I'm enrolled in American History 201.
   She's studying modern art.
10. Capitalize a noun followed by a number or letter that indicates sequence. Exceptions: Do not capitalize the nouns *line, note, page, paragraph, size.*
    The Section 2 class was assigned Chapter 5.
    Many read only pages 15–27.

NUMBERS

1. Spell out numbers 1 though 10, and use figures for numbers above 10. Exception: If two or more *related* numbers both below and above 10 are used in the same sentence, use figures for all numbers.
   She invited seven managers to the meeting.
   There were 20 people at the seminar.
2. To express even millions or billions, use the following style: 35 million; 7 billion.
   20 million (**not** 20,000,000)
   $45 billion (**not** 45,000,000,000)
3. When two numbers come together in a sentence and one is part of a compound adjective, spell out the first number unless the second number would make a much shorter word.
   three 9-room suites   175 six-page reports
4. When expressing numbers in words, hyphenate all compound numbers between 21 and 99 (or *21st* and *99th*), whether they stand alone or are part of a number over 100.
   They sent forty-six invitations.
5. Spell out (and hyphenate) fractions that stand alone, and use figures for mixed numbers.
   four-fifths of the market $7\frac{3}{8}$ yards
6. To form the plural of figures, add *s* (without the apostrophe).
   the 1990s
7. Spell out a number at the beginning of a sentence.
   Seven students missed the class.
8. Use commas to separate thousands, millions, and billions.
   $12,752,099   10,000   199,999
9. Use figures for house numbers.
   They live at 10 Eastland Drive.
10. Do not use a decimal with even amounts of money.
    $550 (**Not:** $550.00)
11. Use the word *cents* for amounts under $1.
    75 cents (**Not:** $.75 or 75¢)
12. Use *st, d,* or *th* only if the day precedes the month.
    Start the work on the 3rd of June.
    But: Start work on June 1.

13. Use figures to express time with *o'clock* or with *a.m.* and *p.m.* (The abbreviations *a.m.* and *p.m.* should be keyed in small letters without spaces.)
    9 o'clock (**Not:** nine o'clock)
    I left at 8:30 a.m. and returned at 5 p.m.

14. Express percentages in figures and spell out the word *percent.* Note: The percent sign (%) may be used in tables.
    7 percent 15.6 percent

15. When ages are used as significant statistics, express them in figures. Otherwise, spell them out.
    You may drive at the age of 16.
    My father is seventy-five years old.

ABBREVIATIONS

1. In lowercase abbreviations made up of single initials, use a period after each initial but no space after each internal period.
   p.m. i.e. f.o.b.

2. Always abbreviate *Mr., Mrs., Ms.,* and *Dr.*, when they are used with personal names. In general, spell out all other titles used with personal names.
   Ms. Joan Brandt Dr. James Rich

3. Always abbreviate *Jr., Sr.,* and *Esq.* when they follow personal names.
   Mr. Harold A. Smith, Jr. George Barr, Esq.

4. Spell out compass points used as ordinary nouns and adjectives or when included in street names. Exception: Abbreviate compass points without periods when they are used *following* a street name.
   He bought a lot on the southeast corner.
   18 Front Street, NW
   12 North Adams Street

5. In nontechnical writing, spell out units of measure.
   a 5-quart bottle 12 yards of material
   3½ by 5 inches a 110-acre development

6. Abbreviate units of measure when they occur frequently, as in technical or scientific works, on forms, and in tables. Do not use periods.
   14 oz 6 qts 5 ft 10 in 55 mph

GRAMMAR

1. A verb must agree with its subject in number and person.
   They are looking for the dog.
   He is looking for them.

2. The following pronouns are always singular and take singular verbs: *each, either, neither, much,* and pronouns ending in *body, thing,* and *one.*
   Neither of the assistants is busy.
   Everybody has to participate.

3. When establishing agreement between subject and verb, disregard intervening phrases and clauses.
   The doctor, not the interns, is working there.
   Only one of the students finished the test.

4. Verbs in the subjunctive mood (those that talk of conditions which are improbable, doubtful, or contrary to fact) require the plural form.
   I wish I were on that harbor cruise.
   If I were she, I would use a different format.

5. Use a singular pronoun with a singular antecedent (the word for which the pronoun stands) and a plural pronoun with a plural antecedent.
   Neither Karla nor Marie must change her coat.
   Neither Mr. Brown nor his aides finished their work.

6. Use nominative pronouns (*I, he, she, we, they,* and so on) as subjects of a sentence or clause.
   The programmer and he are reviewing that.
   It is she who likes this software program.

7. Use objective pronouns (*me, him, her, us, them,* and so on) as objects in a sentence or clause.
   The folders are for Susan and him.
   She went out with him and me.

8. Use comparative adjectives and adverbs (*er, more,* and *less*) in referring to two persons, places, or things; use superlative adjectives and adverbs (*est, most,* and *least*) in referring to more than two.
   He is the quicker of the two ball players.
   He is the quickest of the two ball players.
   This computer is faster than the other.
   This computer is the fastest of all.

Orientation Lesson

WordPerfect 6 users: See the Orientation Lesson, pages OL-1–OL-9 in the Student Guide.

This orientation lesson provides an overview of the basic WordPerfect commands you will need to use in the first several lessons. Study these commands; then return to this lesson for review as you progress through the first several lessons.

A. OPENING WORDPERFECT

DOS prompt > WP

Example:
C:*WP*

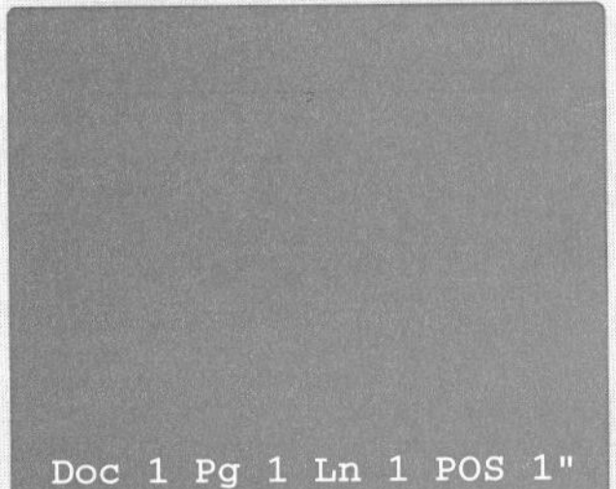

Follow the directions for your computer system for turning on your computer and beginning WordPerfect (usually you would key "WP" at the DOS prompt).

WordPerfect opens with a blank screen. The *cursor* (a blinking underline at the top left of the screen) indicates your current position. The *status line* at the bottom right of the screen shows the cursor position. When you begin, the status line will show that the cursor is positioned in Document 1, Page 1, Line 1″ (vertical position in inches from the top of the page), and Position 1″ (horizontal position in inches from the left edge of the page).

To enter text, you begin keying. Text will be inserted at the cursor position. When the cursor reaches the end of a line, it will automatically move to the beginning of the next line. This feature, called *word wrap,* means you press Enter only to begin a new line or a new paragraph.

B. ENTERING COMMANDS

Display menu bar: Alt-=
Remove menu bar: Esc or Alt-=

Exit (execute a command): F7

Cancel: F1

Help: F3

WordPerfect features may be selected by pressing a function key—either alone or in combination with the Alt (Alternate), Ctrl (Control), or Shift keys.

WordPerfect 5.1 also offers pull-down menus. To turn on pull-down menus, hold down the Alt key while pressing the equal (=) key. To select a function from the pull-down menu, either key the highlighted letter of the function you want or use the arrow keys or a mouse to highlight the selection.

Although using pull-down menus may be helpful for the new or occasional user, using function keys requires fewer keystrokes. For this reason, the WordPerfect commands in this text are given only for function keys.

With the use of function keys or pull-down menus, many commands require you to press F7 to exit (or execute) a command. To cancel a command, you would press F1.

If you need help, press F3 once to display the help screen and twice to display a keyboard template showing the keystrokes for the most common commands.

C. MOVING AROUND WITHIN A DOCUMENT

In the commands that follow, a hyphen joins keys that must be held down together; a comma separates keys that are pressed one after the other. For example, the command "Sh-F7, 1" means to *(a)* hold down the shift key, and while still holding it down, *(b)* press the F7 key; *(c)* release the shift and F7 keys; and *(d)* key *1.*

To move the cursor around within a document, you can use either the arrow (cursor movement) keys or a mouse to reposition the cursor. The arrow keys are located at the bottom right of most keyboards. When used alone or with other function keys, they enable you to quickly move to any position within your document. Use the commands shown at the right to move the cursor to the positions indicated.

Word left	Ctrl- ←
Word right	Ctrl- →
Beginning of line	Home, ←
End of line	Home, → (*or* End)
Top of screen	Home, ↑
Bottom of screen	Home, ↓
Previous page	PgUp
Next page	PgDn
Beginning of document	Home, Home, ↑
End of document	Home, Home, ↓

D. CORRECTING ERRORS

To insert new text into your document, position the cursor where you want to add the text and begin keying. Text to the right of the cursor will move to the right to make room for the new text. Use the commands shown at the right to delete unwanted text.

Character at cursor	Delete
Character to the left of cursor	Backspace
Word at cursor	Ctrl-Backspace
From cursor to end of line	Ctrl-End
Undelete (restore deleted text)	F1, 1

E. PRINTING A DOCUMENT

Print:
Document: Sh-F7, 1
Page: Sh-F7, 2

Once a printer has been selected during the installation of WordPerfect, the print feature enables you to print all or part of a document on screen or a document that has previously been saved. To print an entire document that is on screen, press Sh-F7 (Print) and enter "1" (Full Document). To print a single page, position the cursor on the page you want to print, then press Sh-F7 (Print) and "2" (Page). To print multiple pages of a single document, press Sh-F7 and enter "5." Next, enter the page numbers of those pages that you want to print (for example, 3–6).

F. SAVING A DOCUMENT

Save:
First time: F10, *file name,* Enter
Thereafter: F10, Enter, *Y*

To avoid accidental loss of data, you should save your work frequently. To save a document periodically while you are working on it, press F10 (Save). The first time you save a document, you must give it a file name, such as "MEMO-3." The file name can be up to 8 characters with no spaces. Once you have named the file, pressing F10 will give you a choice of replacing the earlier version of the document with the new version (the usual choice) or saving the new version under a different name.

G. EXITING A DOCUMENT AND WORDPERFECT

WP

Exit: F7

To exit a document you are working on, press F7 (Exit). You will be asked if you want to save your work. Enter "Y" if you wish to do so. If you are saving the document for the first time, you will be asked to give the document a name. If the document has already been named, you will be asked if you want to replace it with the new version. Then you will be asked if you want to exit WordPerfect. Enter "Y" to exit the program and return to a DOS prompt or "N" to clear the screen and start a new document. If you choose to exit WordPerfect, do not remove your disk from the drive until you see a DOS prompt on the screen.

WP

File name known:
Sh-F10, *file name,* Enter
File name unknown (List Files):
F5, Enter, *highlight file name,* 1

H. RETRIEVING A FILE

To work on a previously saved file (document), first start WordPerfect as usual. Then to retrieve the file, press Sh-F10 (Retrieve), enter the name of the file you want, and press Enter. If you cannot remember the name of the file, press F5 (List Files) and Enter. Use the arrow keys to highlight the name of the file you want to retrieve, then enter "1."

Delete file:
F5, *highlight file name, 2, Y*

I. DELETING A FILE

When you are sure you no longer need a file that has been saved on disk, you should delete it. Keep in mind that once you delete a file, you can never retrieve it. To delete a file, press F5 (List) to list the file names, then use the arrow keys to highlight the file you want to delete. Enter "2" (Delete) and "Y" (Yes).

WP

12-point monospaced font
10-point monospaced font

```
LINE SPACING
single 1.5 double triple
single
       1.5
single     double
single 1.5        triple
```

J. LEARNING ABOUT FONTS AND LINE SPACING

Fonts (different styles and sizes of type) are available through your printer or through WordPerfect. Dot-matrix printers usually have fonts of 10 cpi (characters per inch) and 12 cpi. Laser printers and some of the more sophisticated dot-matrix printers also have fonts available in different point sizes (measured by the height of the letters), different typefaces (style of characters), and proportional spacing.

The jobs in this text have been planned for using 10 cpi, a monospaced font where each character of space in a line takes the same amount of space. This is the default for most dot-matrix printers.

The default line spacing for WordPerfect is 1 (single spacing) which leaves no blank lines between keyed lines. Line spacing can be changed to any number, including fractions. Line spacing of 1.5 leaves a half line between keyed lines; 2 leaves 1 blank line; 3 leaves 2 blank lines, and so on.

K. LEARNING ABOUT MARGINS

Margins are the white (empty) space around all sides of a printed document. The default top, bottom, and side margins for a standard sheet of paper (8 1/2″ × 11″) are 1 inch. No matter what size font you use, the margins will not change.

When you begin a new document in WordPerfect, the status line indicates that your cursor is on Ln 1″ (top margin) and Pos 1″ (left margin). Even though no margins show on the screen, the printed page will have 1-inch margins.

In order for your printer to print with the appropriate margins, you must insert the paper correctly into the printer. Learn how to operate the printer you will be using so that your documents will print with the correct margins.

When a key or the space bar is tapped, the cursor advances 1 space. The default font (that is, the preset style of the printed characters for most printers is a monospaced font, where each character occupies the same amount of space.

Font sizes are measured in points; 1 point = 1/72 of an inch. The most common font size for business documents is either 10 points or 12 points, measured vertically. A 10-point monospaced font prints 12 characters per inch, corresponding to elite type on a typewriter. A 12-point monospaced font prints 10 characters per inch, corresponding to pica type.

Although fonts and font sizes can be changed, a 12-point monospaced font (pica-size) is the default setting for most printers and is the font used for all jobs in this text. A 12-point font prints 6 lines per inch (72 points per inch ÷ 12). The default setting is single-spacing, which contains no blank space between printed lines.

Margins are the white (empty) space around each side of your document. Most word processing software programs have default margins of 1 inch, meaning that a full printed page will have 1 inch of blank space at the top, bottom, left, and right.

When you open a new document in WordPerfect, the status line indicates that your cursor is on Ln 1" (top margin) and Pos 1" (left margin). Even though no margins show on the computer screen, the printed page will have 1-inch margins.

In order for your printer to print with the appropriate margins, you must insert the paper correctly into the printer. Learn how to operate the printer you will be using in class so

L. PRACTICING BASIC WORDPERFECT COMMANDS

1. To begin WordPerfect, you will need to be in the WordPerfect directory. At the DOS prompt (C:>), key CD\WP51. At the WordPerfect prompt (C:\WP51>), key WP to start the program (or use the correct procedure for your system).

2. Files created in WordPerfect are called data files. Data files can be saved on a disk in a drive other than the default drive (the drive letter showing when you turn on your computer). To save a file, you must enter the path (drive where it is to be saved) and the name of the document.

3. To move the cursor around in a document, use the cursor movement commands shown in Section C, page OL-2.

4. If you were working on the document shown in Illustration 1, when you retrieved the document, your cursor would be positioned under the "T" in "To," with Ln 1" Pos 1" showing on the status line at the bottom right of the screen.

5. If you press tab, the first line of the paragraph will be indented 0.5 inch (the default tab).

Note in Illustration 2 that when the tab key is pressed, the last words on the first line moved (wrapped around) to the second line.

6. To delete a word and the space after it, position the cursor any place within that word and press Ctrl-Backspace. Note that when a word is deleted (such as *automatically* in the fourth line), the space around the word is closed up.

7. To save a document on a separate data disk, press F10. When asked for the document name, key the complete path name for the file (for example, A:\PRACTICE).

8. To print a document, press Sh-F7, 1.

9. To exit a document and return to a new document screen, press F7. If you have not saved the file before now, or if you have made any changes to the file, answer *yes* to save; then enter the path name.

10. To exit a document and WordPerfect, press F7. Answer *yes* or *no* to save the document, and answer *yes* to exit WordPerfect.

11. When you see the DOS prompt and that the disk drive light is off, you may safely remove your data disk.

ILLUSTRATION 1

```
To enter text, simply begin keying.  The text will be inserted at
the current cursor location.  Errors can be corrected easily by
simply backspacing and keying the correct letter.  When the
cursor reaches the end of a line, it will automatically move to
the next line.  This feature, called word wrap, means you do not
have to press Enter unless you wish to begin a new paragraph or a
new drill line.  Many other features of WordPerfect make creating
business documents fast and simple.
```

ILLUSTRATION 2

```
     To enter text, simply begin keying.  The text will be
inserted at the current cursor location.  Errors can be corrected
easily by simply backspacing and keying the correct letter.  When
the cursor reaches the end of a line, it will move to the next
line.
     This feature, called word wrap, means you do not have to
press Enter unless you wish to begin a new paragraph or a new
drill line.  Many other features of WordPerfect make creating
business documents fast and simple.
```

M. STARTING A LESSON

Margins: 1 inch
Spacing: single
Drills: 2 times

Goals:
To key 39 wam/5'/5e; to format a letter of application.

If you use the software correlated with this program, the software will direct you in completing each part of the lesson. If you are not using the software, follow the directions given with each lesson.

Each lesson heading includes instructions that tell you what software settings to use to format your document. Unless told otherwise, use 1-inch side margins and single spacing (usually the default settings). For example, the instructions in the left margin tell you to use 1-inch margins, single spacing, and to key each drill line 2 times. The goals for this lesson are to key 39 wam (words a minute) on a 5-minute timed writing with no more than 5 errors and to format a letter of application.

N. BUILDING STRAIGHT-COPY SKILL

Speed	Accuracy
aw awaken awhile	aw awaken awhile
aw awaken awhile	se severe seized
se severe seized	rd ordeal burden
se severe seized	aw awaken awhile
rd ordeal burden	se severe seized
rd ordeal burden	rd ordeal burden

Warmups. Beginning with Lesson 15, each lesson or unit starts with a 3-line warmup paragraph. All alphabet and number keys are included, as well as several common symbols. Key the Warmup twice or take three 1-minute timed writings on the paragraph.

Back-of-Book Drills. In addition to the specially constructed drills contained within the lessons, you will frequently be asked to turn to a specific drill in the back of the book for individualized practice on the passage most appropriate for your skill level. Always start at the point where you left off the previous time.

Pretest/Practice/Posttest Routines. When practicing P/P/P drills, your practice routine depends on whether you reached your accuracy goal on the Pretest. If you did, emphasize speed by keying each *individual* drill the specified number of times. If you did not reach your speed goal, emphasize accuracy by keying each *group* of lines (as though it were a paragraph) the specified number of times. These two practice routines are illustrated in the left margin.

O. MEASURING STRAIGHT-COPY SKILL

```
   20                    21
20      Ethical people sh
           24
21 they say and what they
           28
22 are in the best intere
                   32
23 should always try to a
     35          36
24 in an ethical manner.
```

All timed writings in the text are the exact length needed to reach the speed goal that is set for each lesson or unit. Thus, if you finish the timed writing, you know you have reached your speed goal.

All timed writings in the same course (that is, in the Basic, Intermediate, and Advanced courses) are of equivalent difficulty as measured by syllabic intensity (the average number of syllables per word). Thus, you can be sure that any change in your speed is due to a change in your skill rather than a change in the difficulty level of the timed writing.

If you use the software correlated with this program, your timed writings will be automatically scored for you. Your speed on a timed writing is the number of words you keyed divided by the number of minutes you keyed. Round off a fraction to the nearest whole number.

All timed writings in this book contain small numbers, called speed markers, above the copy. When you take a 5-minute timed writing, the highest number that you pass is your *wam* (words-a-minute) speed.

In addition to the timed writings in the lessons and units, the back of the book contains eight additional timed writings that may be used at any time for additional skill measurement.

P. BUILDING FORMATTING SKILL

↓ 2 inches

→4 inches Mr. Edward Whitman
Smith & Whitman Inc.
1047 Fifth Avenue
New York, NY 10028

Leave 1 space between state and ZIP Code

Marginal notes and arrows are sometimes used to remind you of margins, spacing, and so on. These aids are gradually reduced as you gain experience in formatting each kind of job.

Some jobs have special explanations which are positioned as close to the point of use as possible. Always look for and read any marginal notes before you begin to key.

Horizontal arrows (→) indicate the point at which to begin keying. For example, → 4 inches means to begin keying 4 inches from the left edge of the page (the status line should indicate Pos 4"). Down arrows (↓) indicate how far down the page a line should be keyed. For example, ↓2 inches means to begin keying 2 inches from the top edge of the page (the status line should indicate Ln 2"). Likewise, ↓4 means to press Enter 4 times before keying the next line.

Q. KEYBOARDING TECHNIQUE

Assuming the correct position at the computer enables you to key with greater speed and accuracy and less fatigue. When keying for long periods of time, rest your eyes periodically by looking away from the screen, shifting your position, or moving about.

To the extent possible, adjust your work station as follows:

Chair. Adjust the chair height so that your upper and lower legs form a 90 degree angle and your lower back is supported by the back of the chair.

Keyboard. Center your body opposite the J key, leaning forward slightly. Keep your forearms horizontal and raise your hands slightly when keying so that your wrists do not touch the keyboard or desk.

Screen. Position the monitor so that the top of the screen is just below eye level, about 18 to 26 inches away.

Text. Position your textbook (or other copy) on either side of the monitor as close to the monitor vertically and horizontally as possible to minimize head and eye movements and to avoid neck strain.

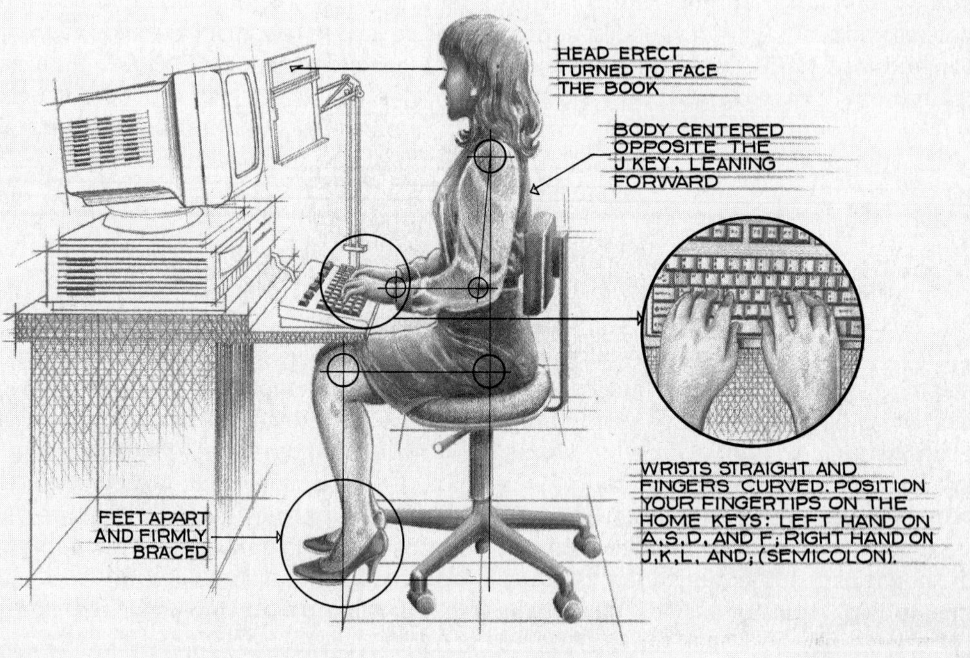
HEAD ERECT TURNED TO FACE THE BOOK
BODY CENTERED OPPOSITE THE J KEY, LEANING FORWARD
WRISTS STRAIGHT AND FINGERS CURVED. POSITION YOUR FINGERTIPS ON THE HOME KEYS: LEFT HAND ON A,S,D, AND F; RIGHT HAND ON J,K,L, AND; (SEMICOLON).
FEET APART AND FIRMLY BRACED

PART 1

THE ALPHABET, NUMBER, AND SYMBOL KEYS

OBJECTIVES

KEYBOARDING

To operate the letter, number, and symbol keys by touch.

To make all machine adjustments needed: set margins (if default margins are not used), tabs, and line spacing.

To key 28 words a minute on a 2-minute timed writing with no more than 5 errors.

LANGUAGE ARTS

To divide words correctly.

To proofread documents and correct errors.

To use quotation marks correctly.

TECHNICAL

To answer correctly at least 90 percent of the questions on an objective test.

WORD PROCESSING

To use the following WordPerfect commands: Tab Set, Hyphenation, Underlining, Reveal Codes, and Blocking Text.

TEST 9-D
TABLE 74
BOXED TABLE WITH BRACED HEADINGS

BI-LEVEL CRT WORK DESK
Prices by Choice of Two Widths

Stock Item	Top Size		Price Each	
	Depth (in inches)	Width (in inches)	1-2	2+
WED-312	30	48	$299	$284
WED-313	30	48	299	284
WED-314	30	60	399	319
WED-315	30	60	399	319

TEST 9-E
FORM 32
INVOICE

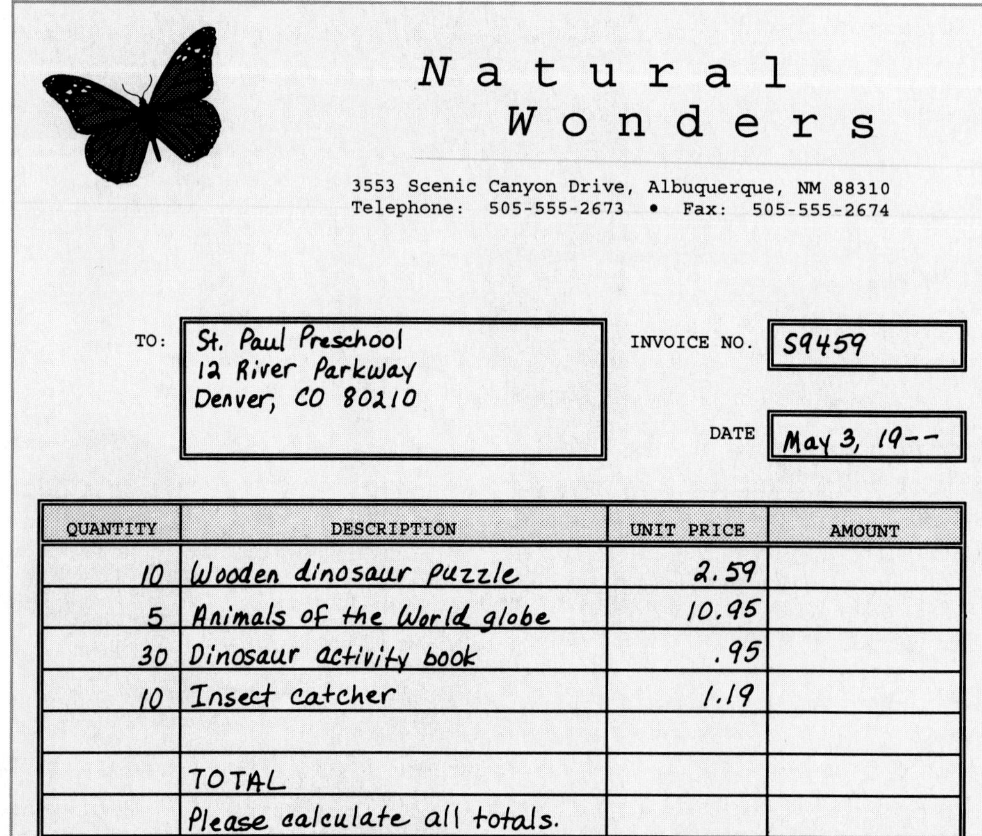

Natural Wonders

3553 Scenic Canyon Drive, Albuquerque, NM 88310
Telephone: 505-555-2673 • Fax: 505-555-2674

TO: St. Paul Preschool
12 River Parkway
Denver, CO 80210

INVOICE NO. 59459

DATE May 3, 19--

QUANTITY	DESCRIPTION	UNIT PRICE	AMOUNT
10	Wooden dinosaur puzzle	2.59	
5	Animals of the World globe	10.95	
30	Dinosaur activity book	.95	
10	Insect catcher	1.19	
	TOTAL		
	Please calculate all totals.		

Home Keys

Margins: 1 inch • Spacing: Single • Drills: 2 times

Goals:
To control the home keys (A S D F J K L ;), the enter key, and the space bar.

A. THE HOME KEYS

The A S D F J K L ; keys are known as the home keys. Place your fingers on the home keys as follows. **Left hand:** first finger on F; second finger on D; third finger on S; fourth finger on A. **Right hand:** first finger on J; second finger on K; third finger on L; and fourth finger on ;. Keep your fingers curved.

B. THE *SPACE BAR*

The space bar is used to space between words and after marks of punctuation.

With fingers held motionless on the home keys, poise your right thumb about 1/4 inch above the space bar. Tap the space bar in the center, and bounce your thumb off.

Space once (*tap the space bar once*) . . . twice (*tap the space bar twice*) . . . once . . . once . . . twice . . . once . . . twice . . . once . . . twice . . . twice

NEW KEYS

C. THE *ENTER* KEY

Tap the enter key twice to leave a blank line between drills.

Reach to the enter key with the fourth finger of your right hand. Keep your J finger at home. Lightly tap the enter key returning the cursor to the beginning of a new line.

Practice using the enter key until you can do so with confidence and without looking at your hands.

Space once . . . twice . . . once . . . twice . . . Enter! Home! (*return fingers to home-key position*) . . . Repeat.

D. THE F AND J KEYS

Use first fingers on F and J keys. Tap the space bar with your right thumb.

```
1 fff fff jjj jjj fff jjj ff jj ff jj f j
2 fff fff jjj jjj fff jjj ff jj ff jj f j
```

TEST 9-C
REPORT 118
EMPLOYMENT CONTRACT

EMPLOYMENT CONTRACT

ds This agreement, made and concluded this *(current)* day of *(current)*, 19-- between Westfield Department Store located at 3704 Peach Street, Hattiesburg, MS 39402, party of the first part, and Delphine Ann Silver, 8406 Whisperin g Pines Drive, Hattiesburg, Mississippi 39402, party of the second part.

Article 1. Services. The party of the ~~first~~ second part, DelphineAnn Silver, covenants and agrees to and with the party of the first part , Westfield department store, to furnish ~~his~~ her services to the said party of the first part as Assistant Office Systems Manager for a period of six (6) months, beginning on March 1, 19--, and ending on August 31, 19--. The said party of the second part covennants and agrees to perform office systems services delegated to her by the Office Systems Manager.

Article 2. Wages. The party of the first part, Westfield department store, covenants and agrees to pay the said party of the second part, for the same the sum of two thousand eight hundred dollars ($2,800) per ~~week~~ month, on a biweekly basis beginning March 22, 19--. ¶ In Witness Whereof, the parties to the employment contract have here unto set their hands the day and year first above written.

SS Delphine Ann Silver	Jarvis L. Winters
	Westfield Department Store
SS Witness to Signature	Witness to Signature

LEFT HAND
Forefinger F
Second Finger D
Third Finger S
Fourth Finger A

RIGHT HAND
J Forefinger
K Second Finger
L Third Finger
; Fourth Finger
Space Bar Thumb

Leave 1 blank line (strike the enter key twice) between drills.

Use second fingers on D and K. A and Sem fingers remain in home position.

E. THE D AND K KEYS

3 ddd ddd kkk kkk ddd kkk dd kk dd kk d k
4 ddd ddd kkk kkk ddd kkk dd kk dd kk d k

Use third fingers on S and L. A and Sem fingers remain on home keys.

F. THE S AND L KEYS

5 sss sss lll lll sss lll ss ll ss ll s l
6 sss sss lll lll sss lll ss ll ss ll s l

Use fourth fingers on A and Sem. F and J fingers remain on home keys.

G. THE A AND ; KEYS

7 aaa aaa ;;; ;;; aaa ;;; aa ;; aa ;; a ;
8 aaa aaa ;;; ;;; aaa ;;; aa ;; aa ;; a ;

SKILLBUILDING

H. Key lines 9–15 twice, leaving a blank line after each pair. Note the word patterns.

Space once after a semicolon.

H. WORD BUILDING

9 aaa ddd ddd add aaa lll lll all add all
10 aaa sss kkk ask ddd aaa ddd dad ask dad
11 lll aaa ddd lad fff aaa ddd fad lad fad
12 aaa ddd ;;; ad; aaa sss ;;; ad; as; ad;
13 f fa fad fads; a as ask asks; d da dad;
14 l la las lass; f fa fal fall; s sa sad;
15 a ad add adds; l la lad lads; a ad ads;

I. Key lines 16–17 twice, leaving a blank line after each pair. Note the phrase patterns.

I. PHRASES

16 dad ask; ask a lad; dad ask a lad; as a
17 a fall; a lass; ask a lass; a lad asks;

J. Take three 1-minute timed writings. Try to complete the line each time.

J. 1-MINUTE TIMED WRITING

18 ask a sad lad; a fall fad; add a salad;

TEST 9-B
LETTER 123
MODIFIED-BLOCK STYLE
WITH STANDARD
PUNCTUATION

(Current Date)

Mr. Nathan Avani
1330 Melbourne Avenue
Oklahoma City, OK 73102

Dear Mr. Avani:

Subject: Dividend Reinvestment Program

Thank you for your letter concerning Oklahoma Bank's Dividend Reinvestment Program. The program provides stockholders the opportunity to purchase stocks through their stock dividends. A report of their accumulated dividends is distributed to stock-holders each month in the following areas:

1. Amount of funds carried forward from the previous quarter.
2. Cash dividends for the quarter as well as the total number of shares held by the stockholder and the total dividend in relation to the number of shares held.
3. Market price for Oklahoma Bank's stock on the day of pur-chase and number of stocks purchased under the program.
4. Amount of funds remaining to be carried to the next quarter.

If you have further questions about our Dividend Reinvestment Program or our services, please call Darla Rodbaugh or Ann Hammer at 405-555-8361.

Sincerely yours,

Charles T. Longworth
Stockholder Relations Department

New Keys

Margins: 1 inch • Spacing: Single • Drills: 2 times

Goal:
To control the H, E, O, and R keys.

Fingers are named for home keys. (Example: second finger of the left hand is the D finger.)

A. WARMUP

1 fff jjj ddd kkk sss lll aaa ;;; fff jjj
2 a salad; a lad; alas a fad; ask a lass;

NEW KEYS

B. THE H KEY

Use the J finger.

Space once after a semicolon.

3 jjj jhj jhj hjh jjj jhj jhj hjh jjj jhj
4 has has hah hah had had aha aha ash ash
5 hash half sash lash dash hall shad shah
6 as dad had; a lass has half; add a dash

C. THE E KEY

Use the D finger.

Keep your eyes on the copy as you key.

7 ddd ded ded ede ddd ded ded ede ddd ded
8 lea led see he; she eke fed sea lee fee
9 keel fake head feed seal ease lead held
10 she held a lease; he fed a seal; a keel

D. THE O KEY

Use the L finger.

Keep fingers curved.

11 lll lol lol olo lll lol lol olo lll lol
12 doe off foe hod oh; oak odd ode old sod
13 shoe look kook joke odes does solo oleo
14 he held a hook; a lass solos; old foes;

E. THE R KEY

Use the F finger.

Keep A finger at home.

15 fff frf frf rfr fff frf frf rfr fff frf
16 red ark ore err rah era rod oar her are
17 oars soar dear fare read role rare door
18 he read a rare reader; a dark red door;

Progress Test on Part 9

TEST 9-A
5-MINUTE TIMED WRITING

Spacing: Double

Many employers provide an opportunity for employees to 12
enhance their education in various ways. Some workers are 24
able to attend courses held during and after work hours in 36
their place of work. Such courses often provide the latest 48
information about new systems and related procedures for 59
completing tasks. These courses help employees to advance 71
on the job as well as help their companies to become more 82
competitive. Many times the instructors are those workers 94
who enrolled in such courses earlier and are being rewarded 106
for doing so. 109

Some companies reimburse employees for some or all of 121
their tuition expenses if they have enrolled in recognized 132
educational programs. Employees often enroll in college 144
programs to obtain degrees which will help them find more 155
rewarding jobs in their firms. If changing technology has 167
affected their work or the competitive edge of the firm, 179
improving the workers' efficiency is well worth the time 190
and money invested in the workers. In some instances, a 201
worker will move on to a different firm as a result of the 213
additional education. This can be expected. 222

Many firms also provide workers with the time and the 234
money for them to attend workshops or conferences conducted 246
by known experts in the field. These short-term programs 257
will often cover ways to improve management and employee 269
relations and handle other common problems. Many of these 281
programs are held away from the firm so that nothing will 292
distract employees from these programs. 300

| 1 | 2 | 3 | 4 | 5 | 6 | 7 | 8 | 9 | 10 | 11 | 12

SKILLBUILDING

F. WORD FAMILIES

Do not pause at the vertical lines that mark off the word families.

19 hale sale kale dale | sold fold hold old;
20 seed heed deed feed | sash dash lash ash;
21 rake sake fake lake | rear sear dear ear;

G. 1-MINUTE TIMED WRITING

G. Take three 1-minute timed writings. Try to complete both lines each time. Use word wrap.

22 he asked for a rare old deed; she had a
23 door ajar;

New Keys

Margins: 1 inch • Spacing: Single • Drills: 2 times

Goal:
To control the M, T, I, and C keys.

A. WARMUP

1 aa ;; ss ll dd kk ff jj hh ee oo rr aa;
2 he held a sale for her as she had asked

NEW KEYS

B. THE M KEY

Use the J finger.

3 jjj jmj jmj mjm jjj jmj jmj mjm jjj jmj
4 mad mom me; am jam; ram dam ham ma; mar
5 same lame room fame make roam loam arms
6 she made more room for some of her ham;

C. THE T KEY

Use the F finger.

7 fff ftf ftf tft fff ftf ftf tft fff ftf
8 hot jot rat eat tam mat lot sat art tar
9 mate tool fate mart date late told take
10 he told her to set a later date to eat;

REPORT 117
NEWSLETTER

WordPerfect 6 users: See Student Guide, p. 118.

Create this first page of a newsletter, using the guidelines provided here and in the illustration. Be sure to note the changes indicated. Use View Document frequently to check the placement of graphic items and text; then adjust as necessary.

1. Set the left margin to 0.75″; right, top, and bottom margins, to 0.6″.
2. Select full justification.
3. Use a 2-space paragraph indention.
4. Create Figure Box 2, then define and turn on the columns.

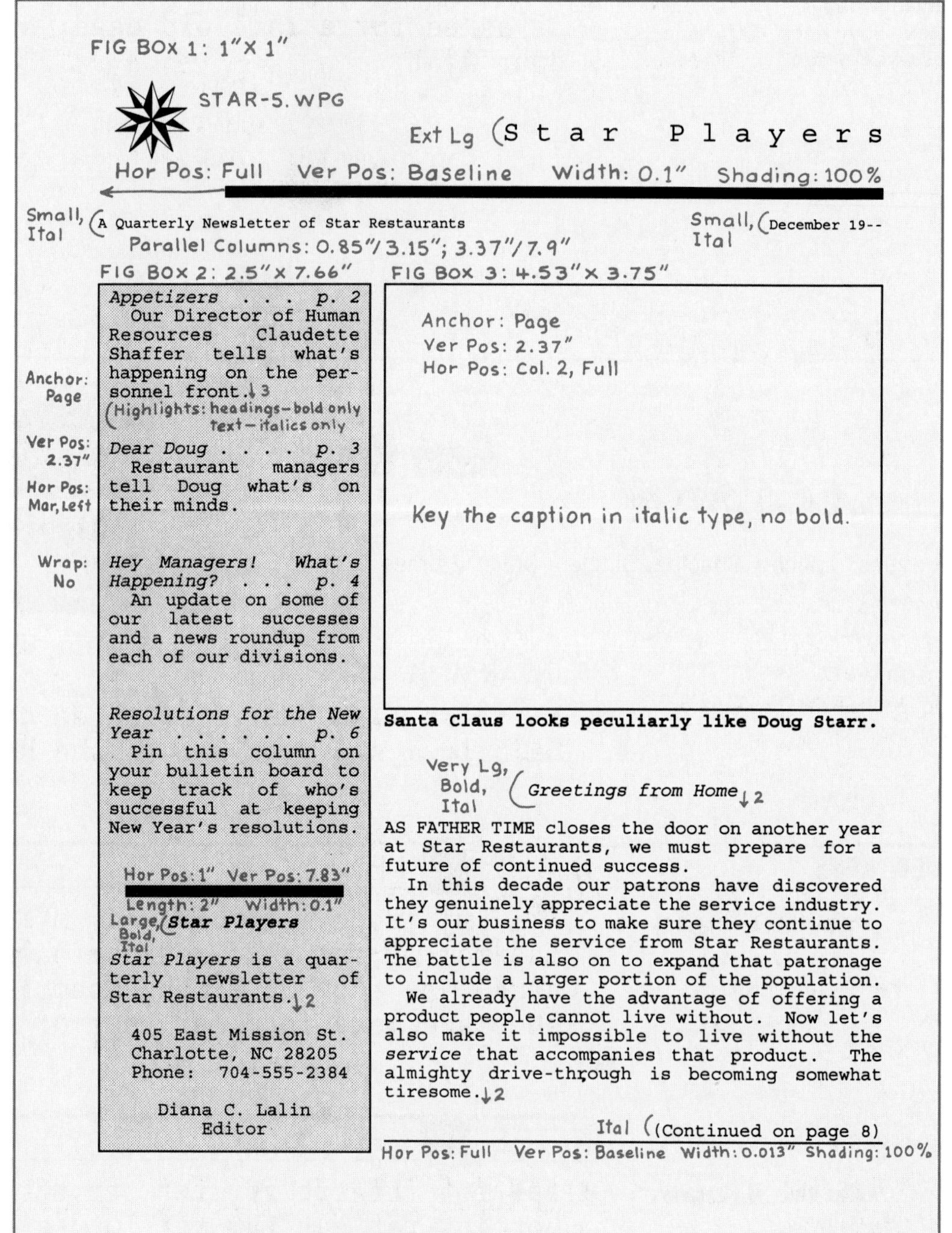

FIG BOX 1: 1″ X 1″

STAR-5.WPG

Ext Lg (S t a r   P l a y e r s

Hor Pos: Full   Ver Pos: Baseline   Width: 0.1″   Shading: 100%

Small, Ital (A Quarterly Newsletter of Star Restaurants

Small, Ital (December 19--

Parallel Columns: 0.85″/3.15″; 3.37″/7.9″

FIG BOX 2: 2.5″ X 7.66″

Anchor: Page
Ver Pos: 2.37″
Hor Pos: Mar, Left
Wrap: No

Appetizers . . . p. 2
  Our Director of Human Resources Claudette Shaffer tells what's happening on the personnel front.↓3
(Highlights: headings—bold only
text—italics only

Dear Doug . . . . p. 3
  Restaurant managers tell Doug what's on their minds.

Hey Managers! What's Happening? . . . p. 4
  An update on some of our latest successes and a news roundup from each of our divisions.

Resolutions for the New Year . . . . . . p. 6
  Pin this column on your bulletin board to keep track of who's successful at keeping New Year's resolutions.

Hor Pos: 1″ Ver Pos: 7.83″
Length: 2″ Width: 0.1″

Large, Bold, Ital (***Star Players***

Star Players is a quarterly newsletter of Star Restaurants.↓2

405 East Mission St.
Charlotte, NC 28205
Phone: 704-555-2384

Diana C. Lalin
Editor

FIG BOX 3: 4.53″ X 3.75″

Anchor: Page
Ver Pos: 2.37″
Hor Pos: Col. 2, Full

Key the caption in italic type, no bold.

Santa Claus looks peculiarly like Doug Starr.

Very Lg, Bold, Ital (*Greetings from Home*↓2

AS FATHER TIME closes the door on another year at Star Restaurants, we must prepare for a future of continued success.
  In this decade our patrons have discovered they genuinely appreciate the service industry. It's our business to make sure they continue to appreciate the service from Star Restaurants. The battle is also on to expand that patronage to include a larger portion of the population.
  We already have the advantage of offering a product people cannot live without. Now let's also make it impossible to live without the *service* that accompanies that product. The almighty drive-through is becoming somewhat tiresome.↓2

Ital ((Continued on page 8)

Hor Pos: Full   Ver Pos: Baseline   Width: 0.013″   Shading: 100%

NOTE: Do not be concerned if you make errors in these early lessons. Making errors is expected at this stage of your learning.

If you forget where a key is located, look at the keyboard chart, not at your fingers.

D. THE I KEY

Use the K finger.

11 kkk kik kik iki kkk kik kik iki kkk kik
12 air fir dim sir him rim kit sit did lid
13 iris tide site item fire idea tile tire
14 this time he left his tie at the store;

E. THE C KEY

Use the D finger.

15 ddd dcd dcd cdc ddd dcd dcd cdc ddd dcd
16 cot sac cod act car coo cat arc ice ace
17 rich tack chat face aces itch coat deck
18 he liked to race cars at the old track;

SKILLBUILDING

Sit in the correct position as you key these drills. Refer to the illustration on page OL-6.

F. WORD FAMILIES

19 sail tail rail fail | mace face lace ace;
20 dots tots jots lots | mire tire fire ire;
21 jade fade made ade; | seed deed feed heed
22 hale tale sale dale | cads lads fads ads;

G. SHORT PHRASES

23 as so | do as | if it | she is | he did | she had
24 so as | as if | it is | did it | it had | has met
25 to it | do it | if he | for it | as she | let her
26 he is | as do | of it | far as | of her | had his

H. 1-MINUTE TIMED WRITING

H. Take three 1-minute timed writings. Try to complete both lines each time. Use word wrap. Press Enter only at the end of line 28.

27 their old store had lots of deck chairs
28 for his leased home;

FORM 30
PURCHASE ORDER

WordPerfect 5.1
Create é: Ctrl-V,'e

WordPerfect 6
Create é: Ctrl-W,'e

Retrieve the purchase order form (Form 29), immediately save it under another file name, and format the following purchase order.

Leslie Morris Co. **Purchase Order**
One Dupont Circle
Washington, DC 20036
Telephone: 202-555-2460

December 27, 19--

TO: Taylor Leather Shop
Attention: John Reigle
530 North Capitol Street, NW
Washington, DC 20001

Order No. M-2074

QTY.	CAT. NO.	DESCRIPTION	UNIT PRICE	AMOUNT
4	14A91	Attaché cases	81.95	327.80
8	14A75	Three-piece luggage sets	133.49	1,067.92
12	23J073	European-style weekend cases	48.50	582.00
2	82806	Nylon garment bags	45.25	90.50
		TOTAL		2,068.22

________________________ Purchasing Agent

FORM 31
PURCHASE ORDER

Use the purchase order form created on page 443.

Change the Qty. column to left justify for this form because the column contains both figures and words.

Use Purchase Order No. M-2075, dated December 31, 19—, to order the following items from Consolidated Bank Forms, 143 Meridian North, Indianapolis, IN 46204:

8 bx (Catalog No. 513) of EFT authorization forms @ 9.35 = 74.80
3 rm (No. 204) of FDIC transmittal forms @ 6.75 = 20.25
1,000 (No. 3529) ABA 2-part compliance forms @ 1.35 = 1,350.00
12 bx (No. 8933) of MICR cash-receipts forms, "LMC" imprint (see attached), @ 13.75 = 165.00
750 (No. H-2805) Universal cash statements @ .60 = 450.00
TOTAL = 2,060.05

New Keys

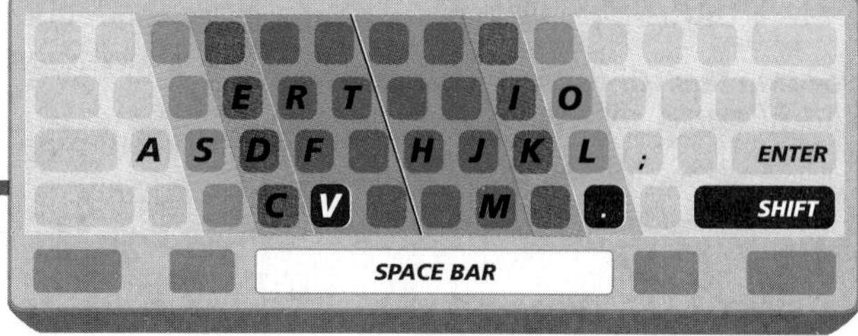

Margins: 1 inch • Spacing: Single • Drills: 2 times

Goals:
To control the right shift, V, and period keys; to count errors.

A. WARMUP

1 the farmer hired her to feed the mares;
2 the first callers came to see the iris;

NEW KEYS

B. THE RIGHT SHIFT KEY

To capitalize letters on the left half of the keyboard:
1. With the J finger at home, press and hold down the right shift key with the Sem finger.
2. Strike the letter key.
3. Release the shift key and return fingers to home position.

3 ;;; ;A; ;A; ;;; ;S; ;S; ;;; ;D; ;D; ;;;
4 Art Alf Sal Tom Sam Dee Ted Rae Sam Ada
5 Chet Edie Elsa Carl Amos Todd Sara Dick
6 Sara Edie Carter married Carl Sam Amos;

C. THE V KEY

Use the F finger.

7 fff fvf fvf vfv fff fvf fvf vfv fff fvf
8 Val eve Eva via vim vis Viv vet Ava vie
9 live have Vida ever vast Vera move vote
10 Victor Vida moved to Vassar to see Val;

D. THE . KEY

Use the L finger.

Space once after a period following an abbreviation; none after a period within an abbreviation; twice after a period ending a sentence.

11 lll l.l l.l .l. lll l.l l.l .l. lll l.l
12 sr. sr. dr. dr. ea. ea. Dr. Dr. Sr. Sr.
13 misc. D.C. jr. A.D. loc. cit. i.e. a.m.
14 Eva left. David came. Elsa came home.

SKILLBUILDING

E. PHRASES

15 as some | let him | are so | has had | ask them
16 to move | see her | for it | had the | did some
17 do have | her old | did he | jot the | had this
18 so ever | let her | she is | see him | for them

FORM 29
PURCHASE ORDER

WordPerfect 6 users: See Student Guide, p. 117.

Create the purchase order shown below, using these guidelines. Your form should match the illustration as closely as possible.

1. Use side margins of 0.5″; center the page vertically.
2. Key the first line in Extra-Large, bold type. Key the next three lines in Large, bold type.
3. Return to normal font. Create a 5-column, 14-row table, with Position of Table: Left.
4. Join Cells A1-A3 and D1-D3.
5. Block Cells B1-C1, extend the highlight to Cells B3-C3, then join the cells.
6. Delete unnecessary lines from Row 4.
7. Justify cells and columns as necessary; adjust lines as appropriate.
8. Key table text and the signature line in Fine type.
9. Decrease the width of Columns A and B by 5 spaces each; Columns D and E, 3 spaces each. Increase the width of Column C by 16 spaces.

Leslie Morris Co. **Purchase Order**
One Dupont Circle
Washington, DC 20036
Telephone: 202-555-2460 **(Current Date)**

TO:

Order No.

QTY.	CAT. NO.	DESCRIPTION	UNIT PRICE	AMOUNT

______________________________ Purchasing Agent

F. COUNTING ERRORS

Count an error when:

1. Any stroke is incorrect.
2. Any punctuation after a word is incorrect or omitted. Count the word before the punctuation.
3. The spacing after a word or after its punctuation is incorrect. Count the word as incorrect.
4. A letter or word is omitted.
5. A letter or word is repeated.
6. A direction about spacing, indenting, and so on, is violated.
7. Words are transposed.

Note: Only one error is counted for each word, no matter how many errors it may contain.

Compare the copy with lines 19–21 below.

```
Ada mailwd a letter; Dee mailed a card.
Ada mailed a letter. Dee mailed a card.
Dell soldsome of the food to a market.
Dell sold some the food to to a market.
 Alma asked for Dick three more tickets.
Alma asked Dick for three more tockits.
```

G. After keying each line 2 times, count your errors.

G. SENTENCES

```
19 Ada mailed a letter; Dee mailed a card.
20 Dell sold some of the food to a market.
21 Alma asked Dick for three more tickets.
```

H. Take three 1-minute timed writings. Try to complete both lines each time.

H. 1-MINUTE TIMED WRITING

```
22 Vic asked them to tell the major to see
23 Carla at the local firm.
```

Review

Margins: 1 inch • Spacing: Single • Drills: 2 times

Goals:
To reinforce new-key reaches; to compute speed.

A. WARMUP

```
1 Val called Dale to ask for a ride home.
2 Edie took three old jars to her mother.
```

TABLE 71
OPEN TABLE

Center horizontally and vertically. Use single spacing.

FOREIGN EXCHANGE RATES
Currency Units per Dollar

Country	Currency	U.S. Value
Australia	Dollar	0.78
Canada	Dollar	1.17
China	Yuan	4.79
France	Franc	5.45
Germany	Deutsche mark	1.62
Italy	Lira	1,198.27
Japan	Yen	145.00
Mexico	Peso	3.01
Spain	Peseta	101.96
United Kingdom	Pound	1.78

TABLE 72
RULED TABLE

Using the Table feature, create a table with 5 columns; then leave the third column blank.

Center horizontally and vertically.

AMERICAN TRADE
(As a Percentage of Total)

Exports			Imports	
Canada	22		Japan	20
Japan	12		Canada	19
Mexico	7		Mexico	6
United Kingdom	6		Germany	5
Germany	5		Taiwan	5
South Korea	4		South Korea	4
Other countries	44		Other countries	41

TABLE 73
BOXED TABLE

Center horizontally and vertically.

CHIEF EXECUTIVE ALMA MATERS

As of January 1992

Company	Chief Executive	Education	
		Undergraduate	Graduate
Apple	John Sculley	Brown	Princeton
Compaq	Joseph R. Canion	Houston	Houston
IBM	John F. Akers	Yale	
Unisys	James A. Unruh	Jamestown	Denver
Zenith	Jerry Pearlman	Princeton	Harvard

B. WORD FAMILIES

3 lace face mace race | fame tame lame same
4 mail tail sail rail | fold cold mold told
5 mate late date fate | feed seed deed heed

C. PHRASES

6 or there | did he | for the | some mail | is he
7 is after | has it | ask the | come home | if it
8 he liked | she is | did she | late date | he is
9 it faces | had he | her hat | same mail | as if

D. If you are using the software that comes with this course, your speed will be computed automatically.

D. COMPUTING SPEED

Compare with line 12.

```
Carl asked him to deed the farm to Ted.
Carl asked him to deed the farm to Ted.
Carl asked
| 1 | 2 | 3 | 4 | 5 | 6 | 7 | 8
```

Compare with lines 13–15.

```
Della asked David to take her to school
for a short time.  She had to meet Fred
or Sarah at the school office at three.
Della asked David to
| 1 | 2 | 3 | 4 | 5 | 6 | 7 | 8
```

Keyboarding speed is measured in words a minute (wam). To compute wam, count every 5 strokes, including spaces, as 1 "word." Horizontal word scales (see E) divide lines into 5-stroke words. In paragraph copy, words are cumulatively totaled at the end of each line (see F).

In Example 1, speed is 18 wam (8 + 8 + 2). In Example 2, speed is 28 wam (24 + 4). For timed writings other than a minute, divide the number of words keyed by the number of minutes in the timed writing. For example, if you key 28 words in 2 minutes, your speed is 14 wam (28 ÷ 2); in 1 minute, 28 wam (28 ÷ 1); or in 1/2 minute, 56 wam (28 ÷ 1/2).

E. Take a 1-minute timed writing on each line. Compute your speed and count errors.

E. SENTENCES

10 Vickie loved the fame she had achieved.
11 Art dashed to take the jet to his home.
12 Carl asked him to deed the farm to Ted.

| 1 | 2 | 3 | 4 | 5 | 6 | 7 | 8 = 5-stroke words

F. Take two 1-minute timed writings on the paragraph. Press Enter only at the end of the paragraph. Compute your speed and count errors.

F. PARAGRAPH

CUMULATIVE WORDS

13 Della asked David to take her to school 8
14 for a short time. She had to meet Fred 16
15 or Sarah at the school office at three. 24

| 1 | 2 | 3 | 4 | 5 | 6 | 7 | 8

G. Take three 1-minute timed writings. Compute your speed and count errors.

G. 1-MINUTE TIMED WRITING

16 Cass said she asked Al Rice to meet her 8
17 at five to look for a jacket. 14

| 1 | 2 | 3 | 4 | 5 | 6 | 7 | 8

REPORT 116
TWO-PAGE UNBOUND REPORT WITH FOOTNOTES

Remember to use italics for titles shown here underlined.

WELCOME TO CAPITAL COMMUNICATION COMPANY

Richard Edmunds, Director, Human Resources Department

Capital Communication Company operates the fourth largest network in the United States (CXC) with 222 affiliates. In addition, CCC owns 8 television stations (including WMIX in Salt Lake City), 3 radio stations, and 4 newspapers.

History

CCC was started in 1926 by a subsidiary of Heartland Publications as a public service network. It began with three radio stations which sold commercial air time. The company gradually added both radio and television stations until in 1956, when it went public, it was made up of 157 affiliate stations. A 1987 merger with Pacific Media Company added four newspapers to the growing list of communications media.[1]

Broadcasting. In addition to its network shows, CCC also produces cable programming and owns part of a cable service. It's nightly news show, *World News Direct,* finished second in the Nielsen ratings last year. CCC's three radio stations are all in major markets and two of them three (Phoenix and Miami) are market leaders in terms of listenership.[2]

Newspapers. CCC's largest newspaper, the San Antonio Tribune, won a Pulitzer Prize for feature writing, bring to seven the total number of Pulitzers won by the company's four newspapers. The Albuquerque Star is the home syndicate for the award-winning and popular political cartoonist Peter J. Benson.

Earnings

With sales of $4.9 billion for the most recent period and net income of $486 million,[3] CCC continues to lead the buy list of most stockbrokers. With its recent move into the videotext market, CCC appears well-posed to take advantage of new technology to provide even greater service in the future.

---

[1]Jane O'Malley, The History of Television, Western Publishing Co., Los Angeles, 1994, pp. 132-34.

[2]Anne Waggoner, "CCC News Shoots to the Top," Media Weekly, March 18, 1994, p. A3.

[3]W. J. Stewart, "Network Earnings Down," Financial News, February 3, 1994, p. 16.

New Keys

Margins: 1 inch • Spacing: Single • Drills: 2 times

Goals:
To control the N, W, comma, and G keys; to key 15 wam/1′/3e.

"15 wam/1′/3e" means to key at the rate of 15 words a minute for 1 minute with no more than 3 errors.

A. WARMUP

1 A major firm sold office items at cost.
2 Viola had her office clerks assist her.

NEW KEYS

B. THE N KEY

Use the J finger.

Keep other fingers at home as you reach to N.

3 jjj jnj jnj njn jjj jnj jnj njn jjj jnj
4 man fan ran sin den kin tin tan and not
5 sane rain even cent find seen then none
6 Dan and Al can enter the main entrance.

C. THE W KEY

Use the S finger.

7 sss sws sws wsw sss sws sws wsw sss sws
8 now two tow how wow row who law few saw
9 want will when wine warm wait saws wave
10 Walt Shaw will want to walk with Wanda.

D. THE , KEY

Use the K finger.

Space once after a comma.

11 kkk k,k k,k ,k, kkk k,k k,k ,k, kkk k,k
12 or, of, to, oh, it, no, if, is, so, do,
13 too, if it is, as soon as, if so, what,
14 Dale, Annie, Sadie, and Edith left too.

E. THE G KEY

Use the F finger.

Keep wrists low, but not resting on keyboard.

15 fff fgf fgf gfg fff fgf fgf gfg fff fgf
16 log rag egg age nag tag sag get leg got
17 sage grow rage wing grew gown wage gain
18 Gail greeted the Garden Town Gardeners.

MEMO 46
(Continued)

You are already scheduled to produce six documentaries next year. When each one is completed, would you please edit a five-minute version of the documentary to be used on the newscast. The format and content of the condensed version will naturally be left up to you. We will plan to air each segment as a teaser on the night of your full documentary.

MEMO 47

Create a memorandum form for Station KMIX (200 South Main, Salt Lake City, UT 84101-8675, Phone: 801-555-3997, FAX: 801-555-3998). Use the heading lines *MEMO TO:, FROM:, DATE:* (use Date Insert), and *SUBJECT:*.

After preparing the form, revise Memo 46 and key the memo on the new memorandum form.

LETTER 122
PERSONAL-BUSINESS LETTER
MODIFIED-BLOCK STYLE
STANDARD PUNCTUATION

Format the following personal-business letter from Denise J. Watterson (301 Goodyear, Apt. 6-B, Salt Lake City, UT 84115) to Professor Richard D. Hartley (see Letter 119). Date the letter May 30, 19—.

Dear Professor Hartley:

When I invited my old economics professor to present his views on the problems of growth in the Salt Lake City area, I had no idea the editorial would create such a controversy. The station was swamped with requests for equal time.

I serve as vice president of the Salt Lake City Civic Club, a volunteer organization. We would like to cordially invite you, Professor Hartley, to present an expanded version of your comments at our July 15 meeting. We meet at The Tamarack Manor from noon to 2 p.m. and would like you to speak from 1 to 1:45 p.m.

Although we cannot offer you an honorarium, we would be pleased to provide you with lunch and to give you a forum to present your views to the approximately 75 people who will attend. Please call me at 555-2834 weekdays after 6 p.m. or anytime during the weekend to let me know if you can accept our offer.

Sincerely,

SKILLBUILDING

F. TECHNIQUE PRACTICE: SPACE BAR

19 Al is here. Ed is fine. Cal can meet.
20 Do it. See them. Rae did. Del is it.
21 Dora is home. Fred went. Cal is here.
22 Take the tram. Ed is in. Art is home.
23 Walt is there. Edith lost it. She is.

G. Take two 1-minute timed writings. Compute your speed and count errors.

G. 1-MINUTE TIMED WRITING

	WORDS
24 Ted joined the firm one month ago. Ted	8
25 will see Valerie for a review too.	15
| 1 | 2 | 3 | 4 | 5 | 6 | 7 | 8	

LESSON 7

New Keys

Margins: 1 inch • Spacing: Single • Drills: 2 times

Goals:
To control the left shift, U, B, and colon keys; to key 16 wam/1'/3e.

A. WARMUP

1 Evie jogged more than a mile with Walt.
2 Will Shea joined the Georgia Five team.

NEW KEYS

To capitalize letters on the right half of the keyboard:
1. With the F finger at home, press and hold down the left shift key with the A finger.
2. Strike the letter key.
3. Release the shift key and return fingers to home position.

B. THE LEFT SHIFT KEY

3 aaa Jaa Jaa aaa Kaa Kaa aaa Laa Laa aaa
4 Lee Joe Kim Ira Hal Ned Kit Mel Ken Jed
5 John Hans Mark Nita Iris Kate Hank Lian
6 Kate Mace went with Ned Hall to Kenton.

Use the J finger.

Keep other fingers at home as you reach to U.

C. THE U KEY

7 jjj juj juj uju jjj juj juj uju jjj juj
8 dug cue rut run due jug sue lug sun urn
9 just hulk nuns dunk sulk hums must junk
10 Hugh Unger urged that Hugo must unload.

LETTER 120
(continued)

Our initial plans are to spend at least one full day in each of the countries, meeting with the news programming staff of one or two of the major networks, touring their facilities, viewing recent broadcasts, and, in general, getting a firsthand view of actual news operations and decision making.

Our tentative itinerary calls for us to arrive at Heathrow Airport at 7:10 p.m. on Tuesday evening, August 27. Would it be possible for us to meet with various members of your staff all day on August 28? We would be available from 8:30 a.m. until 6:30 p.m. and would leave the exact events up to you and your staff.

I would appreciate your contacting Barbara Brooks, our liaison at the Federal Communications Commission (1919 M Street, NW, Washington, DC 20554; phone: 202-555-3894), to let us know whether we may study your operations on August 28.

So that we can finalize our plans and make the necessary arrangements, may we please hear from you by May 20. If your decision is positive, I will work directly with you in coordinating the details of our visit.

Sincerely / Denise J. Watterson / General Manager / *Notations?*

LETTER 121
MODIFIED-BLOCK STYLE
STANDARD PUNCTUATION
INDENTED PARAGRAPHS

Although different formats are illustrated in Letters 120–121, in a real office situation, all letters would be prepared in the same format.

May 29, 19— / Ms. Laura W. Alspach / 1800 East Hollywood Avenue / Salt Lake City, UT 84108 / Dear Ms. Alspach:

Our station is delighted to provide you with an opportunity to reply to Professor Richard Hartley's commentary "The Economic Fallacy of Growth for Salt Lake Country," which aired on May 15. A transcript of his commentary is enclosed.

Professor Hartley's comments generated much interest throughout our viewing area. In fact, we received more than 100 letters and 10 requests for equal time to reply. We ultimately selected you to present the opposing view because your letter touched on most of the relevant points of this topic.

Please use the enclosed guidelines when drafting your comments. We will tape your commentary on June 4 and will broadcast it sometime during the week of June 7.

Sincerely, / KMIX BROADCASTING COMPANY / Denise J. Watterson / General Manager / *Notations?*

MEMO 46

Send a memo from Denise J. Watterson today (May 30) to Alice Cameron, Special Projects Director, on the topic of the expanded newscast:

As you know, we intend to expand our newscast to a full hour this fall. While your department is not directly involved with the news, I thought you may be able to provide some support services for the news department.

(Continued on next page)

D. THE B KEY

Use the F finger.

11 fff fbf fbf bfb fff fbf fbf bfb fff fbf
12 big orb cab bun bow bid bit bin bag job
13 bush back bask bulb bent bunt blew bend
14 Bob backed Bill in a bid for a big job.

E. THE : KEY

The colon is the shift of the semicolon key.

Use the Sem finger.

Space once after a period following an abbreviation; twice after a colon.

15 ;:; ;:; ;:; :;: ;:; ;:; ;:; :;: ;:; ;:;
16 Mr. Uhl: Mrs. Low: Dr. Roe: Ms. See:
17 Dear Mrs. Mills: Dear John: Dear Lee:
18 Date: To: From: Subject: as listed:

SKILLBUILDING

F. KEYBOARD PRACTICE

Top row

19 We were told to take our truck to Hugo.
20 There were two tired men waiting there.
21 Write to their hometown to inform them.

Home row

22 Jake asked his dad for small red flags.
23 Sara added a dash of salt to the salad.
24 Dale said she had a fall sale in Elson.

Bottom row

25 He can come at five for nine old canes.
26 Burton came to vote with vim and vigor.
27 Bob had nerve to come via a Boston bus.

G. 1-MINUTE TIMED WRITING

G. Take two 1-minute timed writings. Compute your speed and count errors.

Goal: 16 wam/1′/3e

WORDS

28 Dear Jack: Fred would like to take Ben 8
29 and us to a home game at five tomorrow. 16

| 1 | 2 | 3 | 4 | 5 | 6 | 7 | 8

DOCUMENT PROCESSING

LETTER 119
BLOCK STYLE
STANDARD PUNCTUATION

May 5, 19— / Professor Richard D. Hartley / Department of Economics / Baldwin College / Orem, UT 84057-5234 / Dear Professor Hartley: / Subject: Guidelines for Preparing Commentary

The following guidelines will help you to make your commentary on our 6 p.m. *Newswatch* show as explicit and informative as possible. Please consult these guidelines as you prepare your remarks.

1. You will be allowed three minutes for your comments. Please stay within these time constraints, and confine your remarks to the issues involved, avoiding statements that cannot be proved.
2. Do not go overboard in advocating a particular point of view. A balanced presentation that discusses all sides of an issue will get the best results.
3. Please submit your comments at least two days in advance of taping. This will allow our editorial and legal departments time to review your remarks.

By following these guidelines, you will be able to give our viewers informed, perceptive insights into matters of current interest to the community.

Sincerely, / Denise J. Watterson / General Manager / urs

LETTER 120
TWO-PAGE,
BLOCK STYLE
OPEN PUNCTUATION

May 5, 19— / Mr. Lester Thompson, Director / British Mutual Broadcasting / 24 Portland Place / London W1N 4BB / ENGLAND / Dear Mr. Thompson

I have been invited by the Federal Communications Commission to participate in a study of television news programming in European countries. The invitation came from Jill Andrews, FCC vice-chair; and I am, of course, delighted to take part in this project.

One function of this study will be to compare the news programming in countries that have a long history of free-access broadcasting with the programming in newly democratic countries. I have been assigned to lead a study group to six European countries to gather firsthand information on this topic. We will be visiting England, France, Germany, Poland, Romania, and Latvia from August 24 through September 3. In addition to me, our group will consist of the following members:

Katherine Grant	Station Manager WPQR-TV	Boston, Mass.
Arkady Gromov	News Director National Public Radio	Washington, D.C.
Manuel Cruz	Executive Editor *Miami Herald*	Miami, Fla.
Richard Logan	Operations Manager Cable News System	New York, N.Y.
Barbara Brooks	FCC Staff Assistant	Washington, D.C.

(Continued on next page)

New Keys

Margins: 1 inch • Spacing: Single • Drills: 2 times

Goals:
To control the P, Q, slash, and X keys; to key 17 wam/1'/3e.

A. WARMUP

1 Jack asked Morgan if Charlie came home.
2 Keith went to lunch with Vic and Baker.

NEW KEYS

B. THE P KEY

Use the Sem finger.

3 ;;; ;p; ;p; p;p ;;; ;p; ;p; p;p ;;; ;p;
4 pan sap rap pad pen sip lip dip pat rip
5 page pale stop trip pace peep palm park
6 Pat Page kept him in step with Pauline.

C. THE Q KEY

Use the A finger.

7 aaa aqa aqa qaq aaa aqa aqa qaq aaa aqa
8 quip aqua quick quiet equip quack quite
9 quell quark quotas quarts quills quests
10 The quiet quints quilted an aqua quilt.

D. THE / KEY

Use the Sem finger.

Do not space before or after a slash.

11 ;;; ;/; ;/; /;/ ;;; ;/; ;/; /;/ ;;; ;/;
12 his/her him/her he/she either/or ad/add
13 do/due/dew hale/hail fir/fur heard/herd
14 Ask him/her if he/she and/or Al can go.

E. THE X KEY

Use the S finger.

15 sss sxs sxs xsx sss sxs sxs xsx sss sxs
16 vex box tax nix mix wax lux lax hex fox
17 axle next taxi flux text flax flex apex
18 Max coaxed six men to fix a sixth taxi.

O. Take three 30-second timed writings on each line. Remember to use the caps lock key when keying in all-capital letters.

O. TECHNIQUE PRACTICE: CAPS LOCK KEY

Their supervisors should read the book HOW TO MANAGE TODAY.
If the CAPS LOCK is used, Hamilton will look like HAMILTON.
We must ship that GRAY-BROWN order by the end of NEXT week.
The CLASSIFIED section of the DAILY ADVANCE had many pages.

| 1 | 2 | 3 | 4 | 5 | 6 | 7 | 8 | 9 | 10 | 11 | 12

P. Spacing: Double
Take two 5-minute timed writings. Compute your speed and count errors.

Goal: 60 wam/5′/5e

P. 5-MINUTE TIMED WRITING

There is only one total escape from the crazy demands 12
of our day-to-day lives: Sleep. Every evening we take a 23
lengthy break, giving ourselves a well-deserved rest. In 35
many respects, sleep is even more essential to our mental 47
health than to our physical well-being. We can relax our 58
tired muscles by having a massage or sitting down for a 69
minute, but this does very little to recharge our mental 81
batteries. By the end of every day, we have amassed quite 93
a confusion of new ideas, concerns, and experiences that we 105
need about eight hours of sleep to get this new material 116
filed away in our memory banks. 122

Our brains are busy not just filing but also sorting 134
through the various contradictions and conflicts that have 146
arisen during the day. This is what dreaming is all about. 158
What we remember afterwards as our dream is merely the tip 170
of the nocturnal iceberg. Modern studies of sleepers have 181
revealed that we are actively dreaming in repeated bouts 193
every night, regardless of whether we have dream memories 204
when we awaken or whether we feel we have spent a dreamless 216
night of totally empty sleep. 222

Dreaming does not, as was once believed, occur in a 234
rapid flash. Experts believe we all dream several times a 246
night, with every incident lasting approximately twenty 257
minutes. While in this state, the body is withdrawn from 268
consciousness but at that same time seems ready for action. 280
Dreaming is the way we keep our brains in working order, 292
ready to undertake tomorrow's dilemmas. 300

| 1 | 2 | 3 | 4 | 5 | 6 | 7 | 8 | 9 | 10 | 11 | 12

SKILLBUILDING

F. PHRASES

19 and it is | she can do | will he come | he is
20 she said so | who left them | can she drive
21 after all | he voted | just wait to | ask her
22 some needed it | for the firm | did he seem

G. TECHNIQUE PRACTICE: SHIFT KEY

23 Ada, Idaho; Sitka, Alaska; Eaton, Ohio;
24 Mr. and Mrs. Lee; Miss Sabin; Mr. Neal;
25 Mr. Don King; Ms. Sue Bell; Ames, Iowa;
26 Dr. Jo Smith; Mr. Ault; Mrs. Dean Bell;

H. Take two 1-minute timed writings. Compute your speed and count errors.

Goal: 17 wam/1′/3e

H. 1-MINUTE TIMED WRITING

27 George planned that Lu should have five 8
28 boxed lunches. Quint was to pack seven 16
29 mugs. 17

| 1 | 2 | 3 | 4 | 5 | 6 | 7 | 8

New Keys

Margins: 1 inch • Spacing: Single • Drills: 2 times

Goals:
To control the hyphen, Z, Y, and ? keys; to key 18 wam/1′/3e.

A. WARMUP

1 I have quit the marketing job in Idaho.
2 Alice packed two boxes of silver disks.

NEW KEYS

B. THE - KEY

Use the Sem finger.

Do not space before or after a hyphen.

Keep the J finger in home position.

3 ;;; ;p; ;-; ;-; -;- ;;; ;-; -;- ;;; ;-;
4 one-sixth one-fifth one-third self-made
5 tie-in ha-ha show-off has-been ice-cold
6 Mr. Ward-Hughes is a well-to-do patron.

J. Take three 12-second timed writings on each line. The scale gives wam for a 12-second timed writing.

J. 12-SECOND SPRINTS

43 The Paradise Island Beach Club in Nassau is opening in May.
44 Sarah Rocconi of Peoria will wed John Price of Rock Island.
45 The Elk City Police Athletic League team went to Pocatello.
46 Ms. Diane Aimone lives at 11 Wayne Street, Lancaster, Ohio.

| | | | 5 | | | | 10 | | | | 15 | | | | 20 | | | | 25 | | | | 30 | | | | 35 | | | | 40 | | | | 45 | | | | 50 | | | | 55 | | | | 60

K. Key each sentence twice. Keep your eyes on the copy so that you do not lose your place as you key the longer words.

K. TECHNIQUE PRACTICE: CONCENTRATION

47 The delicatessen served delightful petite cream delicacies.
48 A presumptuous professional aided in restoring the library.
49 The philanthropist from Massachusetts was a septuagenarian.
50 A subcommittee chided a young sergeant for insubordination.

L. These sentences are made up of very short words, requiring frequent use of the space bar. Key each sentence twice. Do not pause before or after striking the space bar.

L. TECHNIQUE PRACTICE: SPACE BAR

51 We can do it if you or he can go on a jet to see a big dog.
52 If she is so bad, why did she win the bet a day or two ago?
53 Her dog dug up an old bag and a jar of jam at the oak tree.
54 I can buy a new bat for my son so that he can use it today.

M. PROGRESSIVE PRACTICE: NUMBERS

Turn to the Progressive Practice: Numbers routine at the back of the book. Take five 30-second timed writings, starting at the point where you left off the last time.

N. Take a 1-minute timed writing on the first paragraph to establish your base speed. Then take four 1-minute timed writings on the remaining paragraphs. As soon as you equal or exceed your base speed on one paragraph, advance to the next one.

N. SUSTAINED PRACTICE: SYLLABIC INTENSITY

55 If you want to do well in any new job, you should know 12
56 and follow one important guideline: find out how your boss 24
57 prefers to be dealt with, and learn how to do it. Pursuing 36
58 this one rule will serve you well by helping you get ahead. 48

59 There are numerous ways you can put this strategy into 12
60 effect in your job. The first is to discover how your boss 24
61 enjoys being contacted. Does he or she prefer face-to-face 36
62 chats or a discussion of all the issues over the telephone? 48

63 Another consideration is the timing of your petitions. 12
64 Is it appropriate? An observant worker recognizes when the 24
65 boss is most receptive to new ideas. It can also be useful 36
66 for you to notice when your boss is most likely to be busy. 48

67 Finally, remember to always be professional. Managers 12
68 select the degree of formality or informality they are most 24
69 comfortable having in their office. To avoid embarrassment 36
70 for one or both of you, keep your private problems at home. 48

| 1 | 2 | 3 | 4 | 5 | 6 | 7 | 8 | 9 | 10 | 11 | 12

Elbow Control. Keep your elbows in close, hanging loosely by your sides. Do not let elbows swing out. Keep your shoulders relaxed, fingers curved, and wrists level.

C. THE Z KEY

Use the A finger.

Keep the F finger at home as you reach to Z.

7 aaa aza aza zaz aaa aza aza zaz aaa aza
8 zoo zap zig zip fez daze buzz jazz fizz
9 zing gaze zoom zone zinc quiz zest doze
10 The size of the prized pizza amazed us.

D. THE Y KEY

Use the J finger.

11 jjj jyj jyj yjy jjj jyj jyj yjy jjj jyj
12 ray say way may you joy yam yet yes eye
13 yarn year yawn yard holy fray eyed duty
14 Lucy, Nancy, and Peggy may try to stay.

E. THE ? KEY

The question mark is the shift of the slash.

Use the Sem finger.

Space twice after a question mark at the end of a sentence.

15 ;;; ;/? ;/? ?;? ;;; ;/? ;/? ?;? ;;; ;?;
16 Can Ken go? If not him, who? Can Joe?
17 Is that you? Can it be? Who will see?
18 Did he ask? Can they go? Why not her?

SKILLBUILDING

F. TECHNIQUE PRACTICE: HYPHEN

Hyphens are used:
1. To show that a word is divided (line 19).
2. To make a dash (two hyphens with no space before or after, see lines 20 and 23).
3. To join words in a compound (lines 21, 22, and 24).

19 Can Larry go to the next tennis tourna-
20 ment? I am positive he--like you--will
21 find it a first-class sports event. If
22 he can go, I will get first-rate seats.
23 Zane--like Ellen--liked to write texts.
24 Tony took Liza to a drive-in for lunch.

G. PHRASES

25 and the | for the | car is able | can they go
26 did they fly | ask her | for him | they still
27 of what | with us | ought to be | can he send
28 has been able | they need it | he will call

SKILLBUILDING

D. PACED PRACTICE

Turn to the Paced Practice routine at the back of the book. Take three 2-minute timed writings, starting at the point where you left off the last time.

PRETEST. Take a 1-minute timed writing; compute your speed and count errors.

E. PRETEST: DISCRIMINATION PRACTICE

Wisdom and genius are two important traits sought from 12
leaders and managers. Of course, the need for productivity 24
and loyalty is also very strong. Many businesses and firms 36
place quite a premium on finding leaders with these traits. 48

| 1 | 2 | 3 | 4 | 5 | 6 | 7 | 8 | 9 | 10 | 11 | 12

PRACTICE.
Speed Emphasis: If you made no errors on the Pretest, key each line twice.
Accuracy Emphasis: If you made 1 or more errors on the Pretest, key each group of lines (as though it were a paragraph) twice.

F. PRACTICE: LEFT HAND

rtr barter assert carton straw trace artist fort truck trip
asa basket asking ascent safer essay biased sand sadly safe
sds inside wisdom sadden dense desks beside kids cases dose
rer secure reason adhere purer after reflex redo alert doer

G. PRACTICE: RIGHT HAND

mnm manage solemn alumni named denim unmade main enemy mean
pop poorer oppose pompon roped pound option open point pool
olo locale oiling oblige along blown boldly loot loyal solo
iui united induce genius quite using medium suit quiet unit

POSTTEST. Repeat the Pretest (E) and compare performance.

H. POSTTEST: DISCRIMINATION PRACTICE

I. Take a 1-minute timed writing on the first paragraph to establish your base speed. Then take four 1-minute timed writings on the remaining paragraphs. As soon as you equal or exceed your base speed on one paragraph, advance to the next one.

I. SUSTAINED PRACTICE: NUMBERS

There are many people in our society who are hoping to 12
help others. This help can come in many different ways. A 24
person may provide some assistance via a local organization 36
or through the personnel office at the place of employment. 48

The employees of Bentley Financial Service were having 12
a blood drive for five of their coworkers. Tentative plans 24
were set to recruit 75 donors for May 19 starting at 8 a.m. 36
All the donors would be given a certificate of recognition. 48

Each unit was assigned a goal for the number of donors 12
to recruit. Personnel had 14; Customer Service, 7; Records 24
Management, 8; Purchasing, 19; Accounting, 21; and Mail, 6. 36
The company will be extremely pleased to get its 75 donors. 48

As May 19 approached, there were 17 donors assigned to 12
give blood from 8 to 9 a.m.; 23 were assigned from 9 to 10; 24
and 24 were assigned for 10 to 11 a.m.--a sum of 64 donors. 36
The leader of this drive will try to get a few more donors. 48

| 1 | 2 | 3 | 4 | 5 | 6 | 7 | 8 | 9 | 10 | 11 | 12

H. Space once after a semicolon and comma, twice after a period and question mark at the end of a sentence, twice after a colon.

H. PUNCTUATION PRACTICE

```
29 John sings; Paul writes.  Is she there?
30 Can Morgan drive?  I will drive; hurry.
31 Pat, Janice, and May left.  I will fly.
```

I. Take two 1-minute timed writings. Compute your speed and count errors.

Goal: 18 wam/1′/3e

I. 1-MINUTE TIMED WRITING

```
32 Zelig judged six keying contests that a      8
33 local firm held in Piqua.  Vic Bass was     16
34 a winner.                                   18
   | 1 | 2 | 3 | 4 | 5 | 6 | 7 | 8
```

Review

Margins: 1 inch • Spacing: Single • Drills: 2 times

Goals:
To strengthen controls; to format paragraph copy; to key 19 wam/1′/3e.

A. WARMUP

```
1 Gwen Dunne expects too much from a job.
2 Keith had a very quiet, lazy afternoon.
```

FORMATTING

The word counts in this book credit you with 1 word (5 strokes) for each paragraph indention in a timed writing. Press the tab key after the timing starts.

B. PARAGRAPH INDENT

When paragraphs are double spaced, the first line of each paragraph should be indented 0.5 inches or 5 spaces (the default setting). Use the tab key to indent. Reach to the tab key with the A finger.

When paragraphs are single spaced, leave 1 blank line between them. The first line may be either indented 0.5 inches or blocked at the left margin. (See illustrations below.)

```
     I would like to visit you

next month.  What plans do you

have during June?

     We could go to Avon for a

trip down the river.  We had a

good time last year.
```

Double-spaced, indented.

```
     I would like to visit you
next month.  What plans do you
have during June?

     We could go to Avon for a
trip down the river.  We had a
good time last year.

     Can you let me know how a
trip like this sounds?  A raft
is a lot of fun, as you know.
```

Single-spaced, indented.

```
I would like to visit you next
month.  What plans do you have
during June?

We could go to Avon for a trip
down the river.  We had a good
time last year.

Can you let me know how a trip
like this sounds?  A raft is a
lot of fun, as you know.
```

Single-spaced, blocked.

LESSONS 176-180

Margins: 1 inch • Spacing: Single • Drills: 2 times • Format Guide: 155–161

Goals for Unit 36

Begin each day with approximately 15 minutes of skill-building, selecting activities from pages 434–437. In the remaining class time, complete as many production jobs from pages 438–445 as you can.

1. To improve accuracy and speed on alphabet and number keys.
2. To key 60 wam for 5 minutes with no more than 5 errors.
3. To improve proofreading skills when reviewing formatted work.
4. To use desktop publishing features in formatting a variety of documents.
5. To format a variety of letters—block-style, modified-block style, and personal-business.
6. To format memorandums.
7. To format open, ruled, and boxed tables.
8. To format a variety of reports and forms—unbound with footnotes, two-column newsletter, and purchase orders.

A. WARMUP

```
1      Jack analyzed the supply.  On the basis of findings, a   12
2 purchase request for 7 items @ $140, 13 items @ $56, and 20   24
3 items @ $89 was completed.  Jack expected a quick delivery.   36
  | 1 | 2 | 3 | 4 | 5 | 6 | 7 | 8 | 9 | 10 | 11 | 12
```

LANGUAGE ARTS

B. APOSTROPHES

Study the rules at the right. Then key lines 4–7, making necessary changes.

Rule: To make a possessive from a plural noun ending in *s*, place the apostrophe after the *s*.

Investors' protests were voiced at the annual meeting.

Rule: Do not use an apostrophe with possessive pronouns.

The design department will prepare its own calendar.

```
4 The universities presidents presented a joint statement.
5 The four secretaries' positions were properly upgraded.
6 Their new products will be marketed along with our's.
7 The plant was designed to recycle it's own waste products.
```

C. PROOFREADING

C. Compare this paragraph with the third paragraph of the 5-minute timed writing on page 437. Key a list of the words that contain errors, correcting the errors as you key.

```
8       Dreaming does not, as was once beleived, occur in a
9  rapid flash.  Experts believe we all dream sevarel times a
10 night, with every incident lasting aproximately twenty
11 minets.  While in this state, the body is withdrawn from
12 conciousness but at that same time seems ready for action.
13 Dreaming is the way we keep hour brains in work order,
14 ready to undertake tomorrow's dilemas.
```

REVEAL CODES
Alt-F3 or F11

WordPerfect 6 users: See Student Guide, page 1.

C. WORDPERFECT: REVEAL CODES

When you issue a command, WordPerfect sometimes inserts a hidden code into the document. For example, pressing Enter at the end of a line inserts a hard return code [Hrt]. Use Reveal Codes (Alt-F3 or F11) to view these codes. Reveal Codes splits the screen. The top portion shows text as you keyed it. The bottom portion shows the same text with the codes. To delete a code, position the cursor to the right of the code and press Backspace or position the cursor on the code and press Delete.

To return to the normal screen, press Alt-F3 or F11 again.

LINE SPACING
Sh-F8, 1, 6, *No.*, F7, F7

WordPerfect 6 users: See Student Guide, page 2.

D. WORDPERFECT: LINE SPACING

Line Spacing sets the amount of space between keyed lines. Single spacing (1) leaves no blank lines; double spacing (2) leaves 1 blank line; triple spacing (3) leaves 2 blank lines, and so forth.

To change line spacing at any point in a document, position the cursor where you wish the new spacing to begin. Enter the appropriate commands (Sh-F8, 1, 6). The default setting is "1" for single spacing. Key "2" for double spacing and so on. All text after the line-spacing code will reflect the new spacing. Line spacing can be changed as often as you wish within a document.

SKILLBUILDING

E. Spacing: double; tab: default. Take a 1-minute timed writing on each paragraph, or key lines 3–8 once. Compute your speed and count errors. Use the tab key to indent the first line of each paragraph.

E. SHORT PARAGRAPHS

```
     You can now use your keying skills      8
to do many jobs.  Quite a few will have     16
to be printed.                              19
     It will amaze you to find how easy      8
and exact keying is used to rough out a     16
good thought.                               19
| 1 | 2 | 3 | 4 | 5 | 6 | 7 | 8
```

F. Spacing: double; tab: default. Key each sentence on a separate line. Tab to indent each line.

Technique hint: Keep your eyes on the copy as you make the reach to the tab key.

F. TECHNIQUE PRACTICE: ENTER AND TAB KEYS

```
Edna asked Quincy to order some stamps.
Joseph left for New York at noon today.
Mary was amazed to find Robert at home.
When is Mary or Lucy to be interviewed?
Oscar ordered some pizza for the class.
The manager was explicit in directions.
Kyle was on time for the short meeting.
Who left their worksheets on the table?
```

REPORT 114
COMPOSITION: HUMAN RELATIONS

A man rushes into the office area. He insists that he has a serious problem and needs to see a doctor immediately. Both doctors have a full schedule. Briefly describe how you would handle this situation.

REPORT 115
COVER PAGE FOR BROCHURE

Please revise this cover page of our new living will brochure. Double-space the title lines for a better visual appearance.

The graphic image is CNTRCT-2.WPG.

Q U E S T I O N S
A N D   A N S W E R S . . .
About Living Wills

The LIVING WILL, a health-care declaration, is a legal document ~~which~~ that competent adults may write concerning their preferences and instructions for care and treatment that are to be applied when they are in a terminal condition and are no longer able to participate in treatment decisions.

Accidents and diseases cause the deaths of many young people; living wills are not only for older persons. No matter what the age, a declaration can help to avoid guilt feelings, family disagreements, and any doubts about treatment when one is in a terminal condition.

In writing their declarations, some persons name a proxy to carry out their wishes. A living will for a competent person goes into effect only when ~~one~~ that person has a terminal condition and cannot make decisions.

This brochure was prepared by Surgical Associates for the purpose of answering questions about ~~the~~ preparat~~ion~~ing ~~of~~ a health-care declaration (a living will) and appointing a proxy. A list of factors to be considered and an appropriate form are included in this brochure.

Produced by Surgical Associates, 19--

Reset the line spacing to 1.

G. Key each line twice.

Keep fingers curved and wrists low but not resting on the keyboard as you practice these lines.

G. ALPHABET REVIEW

17 Alma Adams asked Alda to fly to Alaska.
18 Both Bill and Barbara liked basketball.
19 Can Cass accept a classic car in Clare?
20 David did dine in the diner in Drayton.
21 Earl says Elmer edited the entire text.
22 Four fables focused on the five friars.
23 Gina gave a bag of green grapes to Gil.
24 Hal hoped Seth had helped haughty Hugh.
25 Irene liked to pickle pickles in brine.
26 Jody Judd joined a junior jogging team.
27 Keith kept a kayak for a trip to Koyuk.
28 Lance played a razzle-dazzle ball game.
29 Martha made more money on many markups.
30 Nan knew ten men in a main dining room.
31 Opal Olah opened four boxes of oranges.
32 Pat paid to park the plane on the ramp.
33 Quincy quickly quit his quarterly quiz.
34 Robin read rare books in their library.
35 Sal signed, sealed, and sent the lease.
36 Todd caught trout in the little stream.
37 Uncle Marty urged Julie to go to Utica.
38 Viva Vista vetoed the five voice votes.
39 Walt waited while Wilma went to Weston.
40 Xu mixed extra extract exactly as told.
41 Yes, your young sister played a cymbal.
42 Zesty zebras zigzagged in the Ohio zoo.

H. Take two 1-minute timed writings. Compute your speed and count errors.

Goal: 19 wam/1′/3e

H. 1-MINUTE TIMED WRITING

43 Zoe expected a quiet morning to do 8
44 her work. Joy was to bring five of the 16
45 ruled tablets. 19

| 1 | 2 | 3 | 4 | 5 | 6 | 7 | 8

LETTER 118

Use August 8 as the date for this letter for Dr. Michaels, and provide an appropriate subject line. The letter is to go to Mrs. Rebecca F. Pedrin, 1230 Mount Vernon Drive, Normal, IL 61761.

The postoperative report from the audiologist indicates that there is still a 50 percent hearing loss in your right ear. You may wish to consider the use of a hearing aid. A copy of an article entitled "Hearing Aid Update" is enclosed for your review.

I do recall that you were not pleased with the hearing aid you had about four or five years ago. However, the new technology has significantly improved the quality of these instruments.

I would like both you and your husband to read the article and discuss the contents.

PS: Please call me in a week to let me know your reaction.

FORM 28
PATIENT DATA FORM

WordPerfect 5.1
Compose small boxes: Ctrl-V, 4,38.

WordPerfect 6
Compose small boxes: Ctrl-W, 4,48

Create the following patient data form to be given to patients on their first visit to our offices. Double-space the form and save it for future use.

PATIENT DATA FORM

(Preliminary Report)

NAME____ ☐ Male ☐ Female
(first) (middle initial) (last)
HEIGHT___________________ WEIGHT___________________ AGE________
SOC. SEC. NO._______________ MEDICAID NO.______________________
BIRTHDATE__________________ OCCUPATION________________________
CURRENT PAYMENT SOURCE(S)______________________________________
RESPONSIBILITY/LEGAL GUARDIAN____________________________________
LIVING WILL ☐ YES ☐ NO ORGAN DONATION ☐ YES ☐ NO
HEARING ☐ GOOD ☐ POOR ☐ HEARING AID
VISION ☐ GOOD ☐ POOR ☐ CORRECTIVE LENSES
Toilet use and personal hygiene________________________________
Bowel and bladder control______________________________________
Present health problems_______________________________________
____
Present medications____
____
Previous health problems/surgery________________________________
____

LESSON 11 Number Keys

Margins: 1 inch • Tab: 0.5 inch • Spacing: Single •
Drills: 2 times

Goals:
To control the 4, 7, 3, and 8 keys; to key 19 wam/2'/5e.

Key the paragraph twice from now on.

A. WARMUP

    Robert Vaughn wrote a good article in one of 10
our new magazines. He quotes Paul Jones, William 20
Paley, and Xenia May. Read it--you will like it. 30
| 1 | 2 | 3 | 4 | 5 | 6 | 7 | 8 | 9 | 10

NEW KEYS

B. THE 4 KEY

Use the F finger.

Do not space after a colon used with figures to express time.

fr4f fr4f f44f f44f f4f4 f4f4 4 44 444 4,444 4:44
44 fins 44 fish 44 feet 44 figs 44 fans 44 flakes
The 44 boys had 44 tickets for the games at 4:44.
Fred Lyons had read 44 articles and 44 magazines.

C. THE 7 KEY

Use the J finger.

ju7j ju7j j77j j77j j7j7 j7j7 7 77 777 7,777 7:77
77 jigs 77 jobs 77 jugs 77 jets 77 jars 77 jewels
The 77 men bought Items 77 and 777 for their job.
Joe had 47 books and 77 tablets for a 7:47 class.

D. THE 3 KEY

Use the D finger.

de3d de3d d33d d33d d3d3 d3d3 3 33 333 3,333 3:33
33 doze 33 died 33 dine 33 days 33 dogs 33 drains
The 33 vans moved 73 cases in less than 33 hours.
If Charles adds 43, 44, and 347, he will get 434.

E. THE 8 KEY

Use the K finger.

ki8k ki8k k88k k88k k8k8 k8k8 8 88 888 8,888 8:88
88 inks 88 inns 88 keys 88 kits 88 kids 88 knives
Bus 38 left at 3:38 and arrived here at 8:37 p.m.
Kenny called Joe at 8:38 at 883-7878 or 484-3878.

SKILLBUILDING

F. NUMBER PRACTICE: 4, 7, 3, AND 8

The 47 tickets were for the April 3 show at 8:48.
Mary was to read pages 33, 47, 84, and 87 to him.
Kate planted 43 tulips, 38 mums, and 87 petunias.
Only 387 of the 473 coeds could register at 4:38.

REPORT 113
CONSULTATION REPORT

Please prepare a consultation report form for Dr. Sia. Center *BLOOMINGTON GENERAL HOSPITAL, 2013 MAIN STREET SOUTH, BLOOMINGTON, IL 61704* in bold, 1 inch from the top of a page. Then add the following headings in bold at the left just as you would position them for a memorandum. *PATIENT:, ROOM:, CONSULTANT:, DATE:*. The patient's name is J. Kurt Filezetti, he's in Room 358, and I examined him on a consulting basis on August 7.

Mr. Filezetti has been observed for several years for progressive end-stage obstructive chronic pulmonary disease. He fell and broke his hip last night and was admitted through the emergency room.

1. Blood gases last night showed a partially compensated severe respiratory acidosis. This morning his pH was a little better, at 7.29. He was quite dyspneic last night and still so this morning but somewhat better.
2. On examination he was found to be in mild respiratory distress at rest, using accessory muscles with a rate of about 26-28. Lungs revealed marked, decreased breath sounds; they were otherwise clear. Cardiac examination was normal. Chest films showed no acute infiltrates.
3. My recommendation to DR. Melvin Haugen, the attending physician, is to pin Mr. Filezetti's hip if possible under spinal anesthesia this Fri. with IV steroids pre-operatively and continue bronchodilators. There is a fairly high risk, including respiratory failure. He should be intubated after the surgery.

Mr. Filzetti has designated his son Jason Filezetti as his proxy. If necessary, any decisions about ventilator support withdrawal should be made at a later date.

would

TABLE 70
BOXED TABLE

Please format this egg-comparison table in boxed form. Center the table vertically on a printed page for my review.

EGG AND EGG SUBSTITUTE COMPARISONS

Product	Calories	Protein (Grams)	Fat (Grams)	Cholesterol (Milligrams)
1 large egg	79	6	6	213
1 large egg white	16	3	0	0
Conda Foods, Better 4U (1/4 cup)	60	5	2	0
Healthfoods, Egg Sub (1/4 cup)	35	5	0	0

G. Take a 1-minute timed writing on the first paragraph to establish your base speed. Then take successive 1-minute timed writings on the other paragraphs. As soon as you equal or exceed your base speed on one paragraph, advance to the next one.

G. SUSTAINED PRACTICE: NUMBERS

In the past 34 months, we constructed stores 10
in 38 states. We hope to build 47 stores in some 20
of the 48 states in which we are currently found. 30

Of the 37 stores built, many will have 73 to 10
84 employees. In 33 stores, most of the managers 20
supervise 34 to 48 employees in all of the units. 30

In Ohio, 38 stores serve 43 counties. In 37 10
stores, we have over 483 varieties of products to 20
sell. All 38 stores sell the Bates 877 products. 30

The top 447 stores meet the needs of 874,374 10
people in 38 cities in 34 states. Our 43 leading 20
stores are found in 33 major cities in Louisiana. 30

| 1 | 2 | 3 | 4 | 5 | 6 | 7 | 8 | 9 | 10

H. Keep other fingers at home as you reach to the shift keys.

H. TECHNIQUE PRACTICE: SHIFT KEY

Joe Sal Ann Yuk Sue Pat Jae Tab Fay Vera Rosa Tao
Dick Fern Juan Mike Andre Fidel Pedro Chong Alice
Karen Ojars Marta Scott Carlos Maria Julie Caesar
Al Ken Bob Ray Joan Marge Mary Ted Bill Jerry Mel

I. Keep other fingers and elbow still as you reach to the hyphen.

I. PUNCTUATION PRACTICE

Jan Brooks-Smith was a go-between for the author.
The off-the-record comment led to a free-for-all.
Louis was a jack-of-all-trades as a clerk-typist.
Ask Barbara--who is in Central Data--to find out.
Joanne is too old-fashioned to be that outspoken.

J. PROGRESSIVE PRACTICE: ALPHABET

Turn to the Progressive Practice: Alphabet routine at the back of the book. Take six 30-second timed writings. Follow the directions at the top of the page for beginning the activity.

K. Spacing: Double
Take two 2-minute timed writings. Compute your speed and count errors.

Goal: 19 wam/2'/5e

K. 2-MINUTE TIMED WRITING

If you are seeking a job, do you possess the 10
expected skills? Quite often just a list of them 20
will let you size up those which you already have 30
or may be acquired in your new position. 38

| 1 | 2 | 3 | 4 | 5 | 6 | 7 | 8 | 9 | 10

LETTER 116 Please use August 6, 19—, as the date for this letter that Dr. Sia has handwritten to Ms. Gladys R. Laechelt, 1717 Bolivia Street, Peoria, IL 61607.

Your consideration of a move from your home to a nursing home is a major decision for you. You are wise to seek the counsel of your family members and health professionals.

You should be aware that there is a Federal Bill of Rights for residents at care facilities. A copy may be obtained from the Illinois Department of Health.

If competent, the Illinois resident has the right to choose a personal attending physician and participate in planning for medical care and treatment. Examples of other rights discussed in the document are those that relate to privacy, visitation, quality of life, grievance procedures, and transfer and discharge.

You will also find that the laws of the state of Illinois are designed to ensure that your rights to a dignified existence are respected.

Please let me know if I can be of further help as you do your planning.

LETTER 117 Retrieve the letter to Ms. Laechelt, and revise it as needed for mailing to Mr. Adolph Knaus at Room 280, Bloomington General Hospital, 2013 Main Street South, Bloomington, IL 61704. Change the reference in the first sentence to appropriately reflect his transfer from the hospital to a nursing home. Also, delete the second sentence of the first paragraph. As Mr. Knaus is contemplating a move to a nursing home in Minnesota, replace *Illinois* with *Minnesota* throughout the body of the letter.

REPORT 112
APPOINTMENT SCHEDULE

Sally Taylor (a new patient, aged 27) telephoned, requesting a diagnostic appointment with Dr. Sia on August 27 at 2 p.m. Retrieve the schedule for that day, and make the appropriate entries.

LESSON 12

Review

Margins: 1 inch • Tab: 0.5 inch • Spacing: Single • Drills: 2 times

Goal:
To key 20 wam/2'/5e.

A. WARMUP

Alex said 37 men quit unexpectedly. The men worked in 48 firms. At least 34 have found a job in 33 firms. Amazingly, the men like their jobs.

SKILLBUILDING

B. Take a 1-minute timed writing on the first paragraph to establish your base speed. Then take successive 1-minute timed writings on the other paragraphs. As soon as you equal or exceed your base speed on one paragraph, advance to the next one.

B. SUSTAINED PRACTICE: SYLLABIC INTENSITY

There is no question that we have entered an age of information. Many new processes and smart equipment can now provide more data in less time.

The entire telecommunications industry has a very bright future. With the use of the computer and the phone, much stored data is now available.

The ease with which financial records can be updated and revised is truly phenomenal. Visit a nearby financial institution for a demonstration.

Inventory control has become simpler with an emphasis on technology. Optical scanning devices can help businesses with their inventory records.

C. ALPHABET PRACTICE

Packing jam for the dozen boxes was quite lively.
Fay quickly jumped over the two dozen huge boxes.
We vexed Jack by quietly helping a dozen farmers.
The quick lynx from the zoo just waved a big paw.
Lazy brown dogs do not jump over the quick foxes.

D. NUMBER PRACTICE

Mary was to read pages 37, 48, 74, and 83 to Zoe.
He invited 43 boys and 48 girls to the 7:34 show.
The 8:37 bus did not come to our stop until 8:44.
Purchase Order 43 listed Items 34, 77, 83, and 8.
Flight 374 will be departing Gate 37 at 8:48 p.m.

REPORT 110
COMPOSITION: HUMAN RELATIONS

A patient approaches your desk and says, "My neighbor, Janice Berg, was in here last week. Is it true that she has cancer and has to have a mastectomy?" Briefly describe how you would handle this situation.

REPORT 111
COMPOSITION: ABSTRACT OF A REPORT

Our patients often have to be reminded about our office hours and payment policies. In addition, I'm not sure that they really know what information we need when they call for an appointment. I'd like you to compose, from the information in the *Procedures Manual,* a one-page information sheet explaining these three things. Use *Surgical Associates* as the title, and use three questions as side headings. Double-space the copy on one page. We'll duplicate the information sheet and distribute it to new patients as well as others who request this information.

MEMO 45

You have edited the following draft memorandum, which Drs. Sia and Michaels had prepared. Format a copy that can be duplicated for distribution.

ds **MEMO TO:** All Staff Members
FROM: R. L. Sia, M.D.
Ann M. Michaels, M.D.

ds **DATE:** August 6, 19--
SUBJECT: Adult Abuse and Neglect

All of us have to become more aware of the possibilities for abuse and neglect of our adult patients. Legislation has been passed that is designed to protect anyone 18 years and older regardless of place of residence from any intentional and nontherapeutic infliction of pain or injury that produces mental or emotional distress. ¶ Even actions that are not intended must be avoided. ~~As an~~ For example, some health practitioners do not provide proper guidance for the self-administration of insulin shots. All of our diabetic patients ~~must~~ should be familiar with the following easy-to-remember rotation schedule:

DAY	Site for injection
Mon.	Right Leg
Tuseday	Left Leg
Wednesday	Right Arm
Thursday	Right Buttock
Friday	Left Arm
Saturday	Left Buttock
Sunday	Optional

All of us have the ~~obligation~~ responsibility to report in ~~good~~ faith any act of patient abuse or neglect that we observe. The law prohibits facilities or other persons from retaliation against those who ~~who~~ make good-faith reports.

E. Key each sentence on a separate line.

E. TECHNIQUE PRACTICE: ENTER KEY

26 Can he go? If so, what? I am lost. Joe is ill.
27 Did he key the memo? Tina is going. Susan lost.
28 Max will drive. Xenia is in Ohio. He is taller.
29 Nate is fine; Ty is not. Who won? Where is Nan?
30 No, he cannot go. Is he here? Where is Roberta?

F. Space without pausing.

F. TECHNIQUE PRACTICE: SPACE BAR

31 a b c d e f g h i j k l m n o p q r s t u v w x y
32 to an is of we no it in as go by me be or but for
33 Do you go to Ada or Ida for work every day or so?
34 I am sure he can go with you if he has some time.
35 He is to be at the car by the time you get there.

G. Spacing: Double
Take two 2-minute timed writings. Compute your speed and count errors.

Goal: 20 wam/2′/5e

G. 2-MINUTE TIMED WRITING

36 Skills in expressing our thoughts are needed 10
37 more than ever. One who can write and speak well 20
38 quite often does well on the job. You really can 30
39 learn these amazing skills if you will take time. 40

| 1 | 2 | 3 | 4 | 5 | 6 | 7 | 8 | 9 | 10

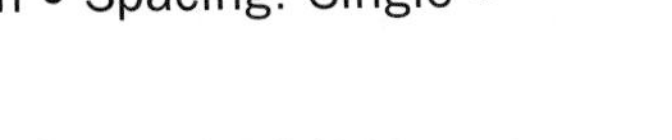

LESSON 13 Number Keys

Margins: 1 inch • Tab: 0.5 inch • Spacing: Single • Drills: 2 times

Goals:
To control the 2, 9, 1, and 0 keys; to key 21 wam/2′/5e.

A. WARMUP

1 Quincy Loven took the 3:34 jet to Chicago to 10
2 attend an 8:37 meeting tomorrow. He expects Fran 20
3 Ladda will have a short buzz session before 7:34. 30

| 1 | 2 | 3 | 4 | 5 | 6 | 7 | 8 | 9 | 10

NEW KEYS

Use the S finger.

B. THE 2 KEY

4 sw2s sw2s s22s s22s s2s2 s2s2 2 22 222 2,222 2:22
5 22 subs 22 suns 22 seas 22 sons 22 sets 22 sports
6 The 22 seats sold at 2:22 to 22 coeds in Room 22.
7 He added Items 22, 23, 24, 27, and 28 on Order 2.

MEMO 44 Create a macro for each of the following frequently used paragraphs. Use a name you can easily remember and add a complete description. For example, you may want to name the first macro *denopt* with *dental and optical coverage* as the description.

You indicated on your employment form that you would like to have both supplemental dental and optical coverage under your health insurance coverage. Please provide the necessary information on the attached form.

You indicated on your employment form that you do not wish to have supplemental dental and optical insurance, as you have this coverage under your spouse's health plan. Please provide the necessary waiver information on the attached form.

You indicated on your employment form that you would like to have supplemental dental coverage under your health insurance coverage. Please provide the necessary information on the attached form.

You indicated on your employment form that you would like to have supplemental optical coverage under your health insurance coverage. Please provide the necessary information on the attached form.

A new employee, Kate Petersen, has just begun working at Surgical Associates; she wishes to have both supplemental dental and optical coverage. Please prepare this memorandum to be sent to her, inserting the appropriate paragraph as the second paragraph of the memorandum.

MEMO TO:

FROM: R.L. Sia, M.D.
Ann M. Michaels, M.D.

DATE: August 5, 19--

SUBJECT: Supplemental Dental and Optical Insurance Coverage

We welcome you to Surgical Associates. We are confident that you are the type of person who will provide the kind of care that our patients need.

Insert appropriate paragraph.

Both of us want you to know that we wish everyone at Surgical Associates to have a positive feeling about our work environment. If at any time you have a concern, please let either of us know so that remedial action can be taken.

C. THE 9 KEY

Use the L finger.

lo91 lo91 1991 1991 1919 1919 9 99 999 9,999 9:99
99 lads 99 lights 99 labs 99 legs 99 lips 99 logs
Their 99 cans of No. 99 were sold to 99 managers.
He had 29 pens, 39 pads, 93 pencils, and 9 clips.

D. THE 1 KEY

Use the A finger.

aq1a aq1a a11a a11a a1a1 a1a1 1 11 111 1,111 1:11
11 adds 11 arts 11 aims 11 axes 11 aces 11 arenas
Sam left here at 1:11; Sue at 11:11; Don at 9:11.
Eric moved from 1992 Main Street to 1994 in 1991.

E. THE 0 KEY

Use the Sem finger.

;p0; ;p0; ;00; ;00; ;0;0 ;0;0 0 00 000 0,000 0:00
10 pads 10 pegs 10 pits 10 pins 10 pens 100 parks
You will get 220 when you add 30, 40, 70, and 80.
The 20 men met at 2:02 with 10 agents in Room 20.

SKILLBUILDING

F. NUMBER PRACTICE

Jill bought 44 tickets for the 7:30 or 8:30 show.
When you add 44, 30, 40, 80, and 90, you get 284.
Maxine called from 829-7430 or 829-7431 for Mary.
Sally had 12 cats, 20 dogs, and 30 birds at home.

Items 37, 38, 39, and 40 were sent on October 18.
Did Flight 1478 leave from Gate 19 at 2:30 today?
Sue went from 380 29th Street to 471 27th Street.
He sold 43 tires, 28 air filters, and 139 wipers.

G. Indent and key each sentence on a separate line.

G. TECHNIQUE PRACTICE: ENTER AND TAB KEYS

Casey left. Susan asked for Tom. Where is John?
How fast do you key? Is Maxine faster? I drive.
She lived at 1991 Main Street. He sold old cars.
Do you have the software? If not you, who could?

REPORT 108
APPOINTMENT SCHEDULE

Your first task is to create the appointment schedule form. After saving the form, retrieve it and record an appointment for Bruce S. Holasek with Dr. Sia on August 27 at 3:30 p.m. Mr. Holasek is 43 years old, and this is a follow-up visit to his stomach surgery on July 9. Save the form for scheduling other August 27 appointments.

APPOINTMENT SCHEDULE

DOCTOR:

DATE:

Time	Patient	Age	Reason for Appointment
9:00	Continue times through		4:30
9:30			
10:00			
10:30			
11:00			
11:30			
12:00			
12:30			
1:00			
1:30			

REPORT 109
SURGERY REPORT

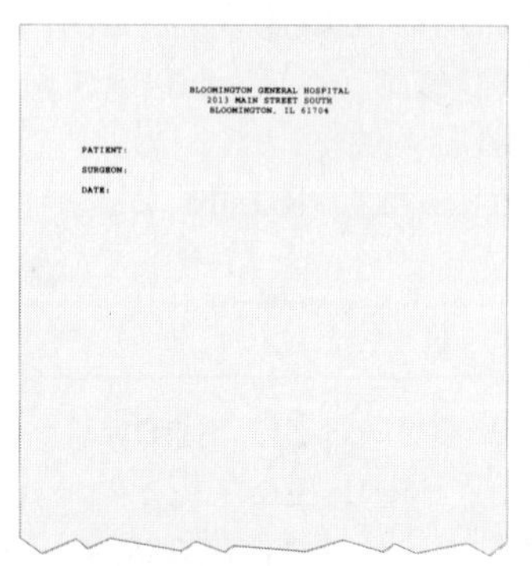
BLOOMINGTON GENERAL HOSPITAL
2013 MAIN STREET SOUTH
BLOOMINGTON, IL 61704

PATIENT:
SURGEON:
DATE:

WordPerfect 5.1
Degree symbol (°): Ctrl-V, 6,36

WordPerfect 6
Degree symbol (°): Ctrl-W, 6,36

Please prepare a surgery report form for Dr. Michaels. Center *BLOOMINGTON GENERAL HOSPITAL, 2013 MAIN STREET SOUTH, BLOOMINGTON, IL 61704* in bold, 1 inch from the top of a page. Then add the following headings in bold at the left just as you would position them for a memorandum. *PATIENT:, SURGEON:, DATE:*. The patient is Edna F. Appelwick; the surgery was performed on August 4, 19—. Complete the report as follows:

The right hip was prepped and draped in the usual sterile fashion. A standard lateral incision was made through skin and subcutaneous tissue down to the tensor fascia, which was incised along its length. The vastus lateralis was then reflected away from the lateral femoral cortex.

Under image intensification, a guidewire was placed at a 140° angle through the lateral cortex into the femoral head. A 125-mm Ambi nail with 140° four-hole sideplate was then placed over the guidewire and attached to the femur with four bone screws, each appropriately drilled, measured, and placed.

The wound was irrigated with lactated Ringer's. The vastus lateralis was closed using interrupted 0 Dexon; the tensor fascia was closed using interrupted 0 Dexon over a medium Hemovac drain. The subcutaneous tissue was closed with 3-0 Dexon, and the skin was closed with staples. A light compression dressing was applied. The patient tolerated the procedure well and left the operating room in satisfactory condition. Estimated blood loss was 250 cc.

H. Take a 1-minute timed writing on the first paragraph to establish your base speed. Then take successive 1-minute timed writings on the other paragraphs. As soon as you equal or exceed your base speed on one paragraph, advance to the next one.

H. SUSTAINED PRACTICE: NUMBERS

In the past quarter, we have added the names of 178 clients to our database. This gives us an exciting total of 249 clients in this first year.

Of the 249 clients, 92 were being handled by Charles Thompson; 84 were controlled by Charlotte Baines; and 73 were being serviced by Gail Banks.

We got 24 clients in July from 108 contacts; August brought us 20 clients from 138 contacts; a record of 34 clients was gained during September.

We were able to get 249 clients in our first year; our aim is 470, 733, and 880 clients in the next three years--or 2,332 clients in four years.

| 1 | 2 | 3 | 4 | 5 | 6 | 7 | 8 | 9 | 10

I. Spacing: double. Take two 2-minute timed writings. Compute your speed and count errors.

Goal: 21 wam/2′/5e

I. 2-MINUTE TIMED WRITING

We can expect quite a few changes in our job market in the next few years. There will be jobs that have new skills due to the many uses of the computer. The labor market will increase in its size, too.

| 1 | 2 | 3 | 4 | 5 | 6 | 7 | 8 | 9 | 10

Number Keys

Margins: 1 inch • Tab: 0.5 inch • Spacing: Single • Drills: 2 times

Goals:
To control the 5 and 6 keys; to key 22 wam/2′/5e.

A. WARMUP

Liza Quigley moved to 4397 South Main Street on July 20. She expected Frank would spend a few extra hours helping her move 18 chairs and books.

| 1 | 2 | 3 | 4 | 5 | 6 | 7 | 8 | 9 | 10

P. INTEGRATED OFFICE PROJECT

SURGICAL ASSOCIATES

Situation: Today is Monday, August 4, 19—. You are a medical office assistant for Surgical Associates, which is located in the Fairview Clinic at 2608 Empire Street East in Bloomington, IL 61704. You are working for R. L. Sia, M.D., and Ann M. Michaels, M.D.

Your work includes making, changing, and canceling appointments; preparing medical documents; composing or transcribing medical reports, letters, and memorandums; and dealing directly with patients in the reception area or by phone.

No matter how carefully the day is planned, interruptions and emergencies will alter your schedule. You will just rearrange your work and move ahead. Begin by carefully studying the first page of the *Surgical Associates Procedures Manual* before the first patients arrive at 11 a.m. The early morning hours are reserved for surgery at Bloomington General Hospital.

SURGICAL ASSOCIATES PROCEDURES MANUAL

At the present time the medical staff at Surgical Associates performs diagnoses and follow-up surgery in most general areas. However, referrals are made to other surgeons for specialized needs, such as heart and brain surgery.

The office is open from 9 a.m. to 5 p.m. Monday through Friday and from 9 a.m. to 12 noon on Saturdays. Patients are seen by appointment only; those needing emergency care are referred to Emergency Admissions at Bloomington General Hospital.

It is important to inform or remind a caller that payment is collected for clinic visits immediately upon completion of the appointment. The patient is responsible for dealing with the insurance company. When surgery is required, the patient is responsible for any balance within 30 days after partial reimbursement is received from an insurance company.

Appointments are to be made on a computer form. The name, age, and reason for the appointment are to be entered on the form for the appropriate doctor. New patients require 1-hour appointments; others are to be scheduled for 30 minutes.

The hours during which each physician is available for appointments are as follows:

Dr. Sia	Dr. Michaels
Mon.: off	Mon.: 11–12, 1–5
Tues.: 11–1, 2–5	Tues.: 11–12, 1–5
Wed.: 11–1, 2–5	Wed.: 11–12, 1–5
Thurs.: 11–1, 2–5	Thurs.: 11–12, 1–5
Fri.: 11–1, 2–5	Fri.: off
Sat.: 9–12	Sat.: 9–12

Each day your first task is to print two copies of each doctor's schedule for the day. One copy is kept on the doctors' desks, and the other copy is kept in the office so that the necessary files can be pulled. New patients are identified with an asterisk after their names.

Letters are to be formatted in block style with standard punctuation. The closing lines are as follows:

Sincerely yours,	Sincerely yours,
R. L. Sia, M.D.	Ann M. Michaels, M.D.

NEW KEYS

B. THE 5 KEY

Use the F finger.

4 fr5f fr5f f55f f55f f5f5 f5f5 5 55 555 5,555 5:55
5 55 fury 55 foes 55 fibs 55 fads 55 furs 55 favors
6 The 55 students read the 555 pages in 55 minutes.
7 She found Items 5, 10, and 29; I found 47 and 38.

C. THE 6 KEY

Use the J finger.

8 jy6j jy6j j66j j66j j6j6 j6j6 6 66 666 6,666 6:66
9 66 jots 66 jams 66 jump 66 jabs 66 join 66 jewels
10 Tom Lux left at 6:16 on Train 66 to go 600 miles.
11 There were 53,640 people in Bath; 28,179 in Hale.

SKILLBUILDING

D. NUMBER PRACTICE: 5 AND 6

12 The 65 adults went to 5566 Wooster Avenue on 6/5.
13 On 5/6 at the age of 6, Andrew weighed 55 pounds.
14 If Gail takes 10 percent of 650, she will get 65.
15 Call Jeffrey at 555-8407 or 555-5143 by 8:30 p.m.

E. NUMBER PRACTICE

NOTE: Focus on accuracy rather than speed as you practice the number drills.

16 Adding 10 and 20 and 30 and 40 and 70 totals 170.
17 On July 25, 1994, 130 girls ran in a 4-mile race.
18 Al selected Nos. 16, 17, 18, 19, and 20 to study.
19 The test took 10 hours and 8 minutes to complete.
20 Alice took 14 men and 23 women to the 128 events.

21 Did the 33 men drive 567 miles on Route 23 or 27?
22 On 10/29/94, she keyed lines 16-47 in 35 minutes.
23 In 1993 there were 2,934 people in the 239 camps.
24 The 18 shows were sold out by 8:37 on October 18.
25 On April 29-30 we will be open from 7:45 to 9:30.

F. PROGRESSIVE PRACTICE: NUMBERS

Turn to the Progressive Practice: Numbers routine at the back of the book. Take six 30-second timed writings.

Follow the directions at the top of the page for beginning the activity.

N. Take three 30-second timed writings on each line as you concentrate on infrequently used letters.

N. ALPHABET REVIEW: INFREQUENT-LETTER PRACTICE

K Kent kept the keys to the truck and took Kim's kitten home.
X Max boxed six bouts in the Texas exhibition for extra cash.
Q He requested many quality quilts to fill his quota quickly.
Z Dozens of crazy zookeepers zipped past the zebras and zebu.

O. Spacing: Double
Take two 5-minute timed writings. Compute your speed and count errors.

Goal: 60 wam/5′/5e

O. 5-MINUTE TIMED WRITING

Have you ever observed what happens when two friends meet and talk in an easy manner? They adopt similar body postures. If they are really friendly and share the same attitudes toward the subjects being discussed, the poses in which they hold their bodies are liable to become yet more alike, to the point where they virtually become carbon copies of each other. This is not a deliberate imitative process. Rather, the friends in question are indulging in an unconscious act called postural echo.

There is a good reason for this. A true friendship is usually only possible between people of roughly equal status. This likeness is demonstrated in many indirect ways, but it is reinforced in face-to-face encounters by a matching of the postures of relaxation or alertness. In this way the body sends a quiet message of acceptance to the other party. This message not only is sent without the sender realizing it but also is comprehended in that same manner.

The precision of the postural echo is quite amazing. Two friends reclining in armchairs both have their legs crossed in just the same way, and both have an arm across their lap. Even more surprising is the fact that they may synchronize their movements as they talk. When one person uncrosses the legs, the other soon follows suit, and when one leans back a little, so does the partner. If, for some reason, one does not participate, a loss of synchrony might occur. Both people will feel irritable and not know why.

G. Spacing: double. Take two 1-minute timed writings. Compute your speed and count errors.

G. HANDWRITTEN PARAGRAPH

Jobs in business require good skills in oral 10
and written communications. Confirmation of this 20
fact can be found in various magazines and books. 30

H. Spacing: double. Take two 2-minute timed writings. Compute your speed and count errors.

Goal: 22 wam/2′/5e

H. 2-MINUTE TIMED WRITING

New equipment is letting us share more and 10
more data in less time than ever. Experts tell 20
us if we link phones and computers, we could have 30
data that will quickly zoom from site to site to 40
help all jobholders. 44

| 1 | 2 | 3 | 4 | 5 | 6 | 7 | 8 | 9 | 10

LESSON 15 Review

Margins: 1 inch • Tab: 0.5 inch • Spacing: Single • Drills: 2 times

Goals:
To key 23 wam/2′/5e; to set tabs; to align text right and left; to align decimals.

A. WARMUP

Hazel Jacobson asked the attendant what time 10
Flight 948 was expected to arrive in Quincy. She 20
said probably at 2:30 or 2:35 at Gate 16A or 17B. 30

| 1 | 2 | 3 | 4 | 5 | 6 | 7 | 8 | 9 | 10

FORMATTING

B. WORDPERFECT: TAB SET

TAB SET
Sh-F8, 1, 8, *tab position,* Enter F7, F7

Clear all tabs: Ctrl-End

Set tabs in spaces rather than inches: *tab position,* U

Set multiple tabs: *tab position for first tab, comma, amount of space between tabs*

WordPerfect 6 users: See Student Guide, page 3.

WordPerfect has default tabs set every 0.5 inch (5 spaces). Pressing the tab key moves the cursor 0.5 inch to the right.

Enter the appropriate commands to access the tab ruler (Sh-F8, 1, 8). To clear the default tabs, position the cursor at the beginning of the line and press Ctrl-End; to clear an individual tab, position the cursor under the tab and press Delete.

To set a left tab (indicated by the letter "L"), enter the position number (e.g., "0.5") and press Enter. You must enter 0 (zero) and a decimal point before any number less than 1. To set a tab in terms of spaces rather than inches, enter "U" (for units) after the number (e.g., "3u" for a tab 3 spaces from the left margin).

To set tabs at regular intervals, enter the position number for the first tab, a comma, and the amount of space between tabs (e.g., "0,1.5" for tabs 1.5 inches apart beginning at the left margin).

To set a right tab (for aligning at the right), enter the position number, press Enter, then change L to R. To set a decimal or dec tab (for aligning at the decimal point), enter the position number, press Enter, then change L to D.

I. PROGRESSIVE PRACTICE: ALPHABET

Turn to the Progressive Practice: Alphabet routine at the back of the book. Take five 30-second timed writings, starting at the point where you left off the last time.

J. Take three 12-second timed writings on each line. The scale gives wam for a 12-second timed writing.

J. 12-SECOND SPRINTS

Orders #57, #92, and #115 were 15% of your total purchases.
Roberta is (1) dependable, (2) competent, and (3) pleasant.
Send checks for $15, $29, and $36 to this club's treasurer.
Eng & Chen, Lin & Wang, and Ping & Pai sent eleven members.

K. Insert the necessary capital letters as you key these sentences twice.

K. TECHNIQUE PRACTICE: CONCENTRATION

The buffalo bills and denver broncos will meet next sunday.
Ken, joe, mike, ann, sue, and liz went to orlando, florida.
The members of phi beta lambda left for st. louis on may 8.
Bill murphy moved to 15 lincoln avenue in albany, new york.

L. Clear all tabs. Then set four new tabs every 1.2 inches. Key lines 44–47, using the tab key to go across from column to column.

L. TECHNIQUE PRACTICE: TAB KEY

Thomas	Brenda	Wesley	Carolyn	Michael
Albina	Gina	Valentino	Ludevina	Dino
Venice	Munich	London	Moscow	Tokyo
Italy	Germany	England	Russia	Japan

M. Take a 1-minute timed writing on the first paragraph to establish your base speed. Then take four 1-minute timed writings on the remaining paragraphs. As soon as you equal or exceed your base speed on one paragraph, advance to the next one.

M. SUSTAINED PRACTICE: ALTERNATE-HAND WORDS

The panel members will handle the problem of the audit when it comes to them. They wish that the chair will allow them to meet with the city leaders to make a formal request for their help. Then, they also wish to sign needed forms.

Of course, the chair will want to make sure that those panel members do their job right. The goal of the audit is to assure city leaders that they have taken the right steps in managing funds. The chair of that panel should be firm.

The auditor will want to speak to the panel members on an individual basis. In addition, the auditor will want to make some calls to clients. The auditor will also hope for a complete review of all elements of receipts and expenses.

Obviously, every leader in any major organization must be concerned with how receipts and expenditures are handled by personnel. Therefore, having someone review all entries in accounting records can be an issue of utmost importance.

C. Spacing: double. Set multiple left tabs every 1.2 inches. Press tab to begin the first column.

C. TECHNIQUE PRACTICE: ALIGN WORDS LEFT

dear	business	loan	office
computer	disk	yours	sincerely
keying	budget	our	employees

D. Spacing: double. Set multiple right tabs every 1.5 inches. Clear existing tabs before setting new tabs. Change the Ls to Rs for right tabs.

D. TECHNIQUE PRACTICE: ALIGN NUMBERS RIGHT

109	780,331	10,456	1
9,456	67	273	8,780
33	1,489	410,345	105

E. Spacing: double. Decimal tabs every 1.5 inches. Clear existing tabs before setting new tabs. Change the Ls to Ds for dec tabs.

E. TECHNIQUE PRACTICE: ALIGN DECIMALS

.05	10.33	100.25	1.6
9.25	133.66	1,345.66	100.67
106.09	1.333	.025	56.89

SKILLBUILDING

PRETEST.
Take a 1-minute timed writing; compute your speed and count errors.

F. PRETEST: VERTICAL REACHES

A few of our business managers attribute the success of the bank to a judicious and scientific reserve program. The bank cannot drop its guard.

PRACTICE.
Speed Emphasis: If you made 2 or fewer errors on the Pretest, key each line twice.
Accuracy Emphasis: If you made 3 or more errors, key each group of lines (as though it were a paragraph) twice.

G. PRACTICE: UP REACHES

at atlas plate water later batch fatal match late
dr draft drift drums drawn drain drama dress drab
ju jumpy juror junky jumbo julep judge juice just
es essay press bless crest quest fresh rises less

H. PRACTICE: DOWN REACHES

ca cable cabin cadet camel cameo candy carve cash
nk trunk drink prank rinks brink drank crank sink
ba batch badge bagel baked banjo barge basis bank
sc scale scald scrub scalp scare scout scarf scan

POSTTEST.
Repeat the Pretest (F) and compare performance.

I. POSTTEST: VERTICAL REACHES

J. Spacing: double. Take two 2-minute timed writings. Compute your speed and count errors.

Goal: 23 wam/2′/5e

J. 2-MINUTE TIMED WRITING

One of the reasons for all the technology is to help us become more productive. If this does happen, we would have an amazing amount of extra time off. Quite a few of our job skills would be changed to meet new standards.

SKILLBUILDING

PRETEST. Take a 1-minute timed writing; compute your speed and count errors.

PRACTICE.
Speed Emphasis: If you made no errors on the Pretest, key each line twice.
Accuracy Emphasis: If you made 1 or more errors on the Pretest, key each group of lines (as though it were a paragraph) twice.

POSTTEST. Repeat the Pretest (D) and compare performance.

D. PRETEST: VERTICAL REACHES

8 The senior lawyer was able to tackle the case in June. 12
9 She knew she would be making herself available to the court 24
10 for a third time in a month. She said she needed to revamp 36
11 her vacation plans to guard against whatever might go awry. 48

| 1 | 2 | 3 | 4 | 5 | 6 | 7 | 8 | 9 | 10 | 11 | 12

E. PRACTICE: UP REACHES

12 aw awry away paws drawer awakes spawns brawny awards aweigh
13 se self seen sewn bosses paused senior seller seizes itself
14 ki kiln kilt kite skirts joking kinder bikini making unkind
15 rd hard lard cord hurdle overdo lizard inward boards upward

F. PRACTICE: DOWN REACHES

16 ac acid ache aces jacked facial actors tacked jackal places
17 kn knot knee knob knives kneels knight knotty knocks knives
18 ab able blab ably tables fabric babies rabbit cabana cables
19 va vase vain vail evades revamp valley avails ravage canvas

G. POSTTEST: VERTICAL REACHES

H. Take a 1-minute timed writing on the first paragraph to establish your base speed. Then take four 1-minute timed writings on the remaining paragraphs. As soon as you equal or exceed your base speed on one paragraph, advance to the next one.

H. SUSTAINED PRACTICE: ROUGH DRAFT

20 Whether you are a student struggling to keep up with a 12
21 crushing course load or an avid mystery fan reading through 24
22 the most recent best-seller, raising your reading speed may 36
23 help make your day a little easier and much less stressful. 48
24 When building your read speed, consider some of the 12
25 most common read errors. The first, vocalizing is when 24
26 you say the words out load as you read them. Try holding a 36
27 pen with your teeth or chewing gum to get your self to stop. 48
28 An other bad reading habit is pointing. When your point 12
29 to the words with your ruler or a marker, are you adding a 24
30 mechanical stop to the reading program. The solution is too 36
31 make pointing impossable by folding you hands in your lap. 48
32 The last problem read habit happens then you follow 12
33 the lines of test with your head. Like pointing, this ads 24
34 another mechanicle step to the process. To avoid it, please 36
35 your hand against the side of your head or grasp your chin. 48

| 1 | 2 | 3 | 4 | 5 | 6 | 7 | 8 | 9 | 10 | 11 | 12

LESSON 16 Symbols and Word Division

Margins: 1 inch • Tab: 0.5 inch • Spacing: Single • Drills: 2 times

Goals:
To control the #, (, and) keys; to make correct word-division decisions; to key 24 wam/2′/5e.

A. WARMUP

Fay Jacobs drove 1,568 miles last week. She
met 39 aides in Arizona and Oregon. She expected
and required a 4:20 meeting with 17 new managers.

| 1 | 2 | 3 | 4 | 5 | 6 | 7 | 8 | 9 | 10

NEW KEYS

B. THE # KEY

NUMBER (if before a figure) or POUNDS (if after a figure) is the shift of 3. Use the D finger.

Do not space between the figure and symbol.

de3d de3#d d3#d d3#d d##d d##d #3 #33 #333 #3,333
Al wants 33# of #200 and 38# of #400 by Saturday.
My favorite seats are #2, #34, #56, #65, and #66.
Please order 45# of #245 and 13# of #24 tomorrow.

C. THE (AND) KEYS

PARENTHESES are the shifts of 9 and 0. Use the L finger on (and the Sem finger on).

Do not space between the parentheses and the text within them.

lo91 lo91 lo(l lo(l l((l ;p0; ;p0; ;p); ;p); ;));
Please ask (1) Al, (2) Pat, (3) Ted, and (4) Dee.
Sue has some (1) skis, (2) sleds, and (3) skates.
Mary is (1) prompt, (2) speedy, and (3) accurate.

Our workers (Lewis, Jerry, and Ty) were rewarded.
The owner (Ms. Parks) went on Friday (August 18).
The Roxie (a cafe) had fish (salmon) on the menu.
The clerk (Ms. Fay Green) will vote yes (not no).

LANGUAGE ARTS

D. WORD DIVISION

Whenever you key material with word wrap off, you must decide where each line should end.

If it is necessary to divide a word, follow the rules given here.

1. Do not divide (*a*) words pronounced as one syllable (*thought, planned*), (*b*) contractions (*isn't, shouldn't*), or (*c*) abbreviations (*ILGWU, Inc.*).
2. Divide words only between syllables. Whenever you are unsure of where a syllable ends, consult a dictionary.
3. Leave at least three characters (the last will be a hyphen) on the upper line, and carry at least three characters (the last may be a punctuation mark) to the next line. Thus, *al-ways* and *mat-ter,* but not *a-round* or *trick-y*.
4. Divide compound words either at the hyphen (*self-control*) or where the two words join to make a solid compound. Thus *master-mind,* not *mas-termind.*

UNIT THIRTY-FIVE • INTEGRATED OFFICE PROJECT: MEDICAL

171-175 LESSONS

Margins: 1 inch • Spacing: Single • Drills: 2 times • Format Guide: 151–155

Goals for Unit 35

To improve accuracy and speed on alphabet and number keys.
To key 60 wam for 5 minutes with no more than 5 errors.
To improve proficiency in composing at the keyboard.
To use desktop publishing features in formatting a variety of documents.
To format a variety of medical documents—appointment schedules, surgery report, consultation report, and patient data form.
To make decisions and formulate responses in situations dealing with interpersonal relations.
To format a handwritten, boxed table.
To format letters and memorandums with varied features.

Begin each day with approximately 15 minutes of skillbuilding, selecting activities from pages 422–425. In the remaining class time, complete as many production jobs from pages 426–433 as you can.

A. WARMUP

1 Three travel agencies (Jepster & Vilani, Quinn & Bott, 12
2 and Zeplin & Wexter) issued the most travel tickets for the 24
3 past 12 months. They sold 785, 834, and 960 total tickets. 36

| 1 | 2 | 3 | 4 | 5 | 6 | 7 | 8 | 9 | 10 | 11 | 12

LANGUAGE ARTS

B. COMMAS

Study the rules at the right. Then key lines 4–7, making necessary changes.

Rule: Use a comma to separate two or more adjectives that both modify the same noun.

Ms. Shell is a patient, understanding counselor.

Rule: Do not use a comma to connect items in a series if they are connected by *and, or,* or *nor.*

The plates and the cups and the saucers were neatly stacked.

4 The music enchanted the attentive wide-eyed children.
5 The sponsor of the event is a compassionate generous resident.
6 Marvin or Jon or Karl completed the page design.
7 My monitor, and laser printer, and facsimile machine need to be repaired.

C. COMPOSING

Prepare a memo to Ms. Hoover (Memo 43, page 420) suggesting that the estate planning guide include a substantial section on estates that are settled without a will and how estate law can vary on this topic from state to state. Also suggest that the guide include a section on the appointment of an executor or executrix to render the provisions of the will.

E. Select the words in each line that can be divided, and key them with a hyphen to show where the division should be (Example: *con-sult*).

E. WORD DIVISION PRACTICE

dragged	weren't	today
safety	moment	USMC
grandmother	teenagers	trailing
expect	reproach	couldn't

HYPHENATION—AUTOMATIC
Sh-F8, 1, 1, Y, F7

HYPHENATION PROMPT

Position the cursor at division point, Ctrl-Hyphen

WordPerfect 6 users: See Student Guide, page 4.

F. WORDPERFECT: HYPHENATION

Use Hyphenation to maintain a more even right margin. WordPerfect will automatically divide most words correctly. If it needs help, a screen prompt will ask you to position the hyphen (use the arrow keys) at a correct division point; then press Esc. If the word should not be hyphenated, press F1.

To manually divide a word not in WordPerfect's dictionary, position the cursor at the division point and press Ctrl-Hyphen.

G. Key the paragraph with Hyphenation on.

G. HYPHENATION PRACTICE

In order for you to become a part of the emerging telecommunications field, your course of study must consist of a preponderance of courses in that field. Not keeping up with technological advances could hurt your career.

SKILLBUILDING

H. Take a 1-minute timed writing on the first paragraph to establish your base speed. Then take successive 1-minute timed writings on the other paragraphs. As soon as you equal or exceed your base speed on one paragraph, advance to the next one.

H. SUSTAINED PRACTICE: SYLLABIC INTENSITY

One should always try to keep in good shape. As the first step in keeping in good shape, avoid starting or being tempted with the smoking habit.

A second step that helps in maintaining good health for years is drinking the proper amount of water. Most doctors suggest eight glasses a day.

Making exercise a step is another method for staying in good health. Many experts suggest one spend a few minutes each day in regular exercise.

A final step of importance is maintaining an appropriate body weight. The clue to maintaining weight is developing the positive eating pattern.

I. Spacing: double. Take two 1-minute timed writings. Compute your speed and count errors.

I. HANDWRITTEN PARAGRAPHS WITH NUMBERS

The membership in our credit union is 1,850. We need 200 new members if we are to reach 2,050. There were 46 new members in May, 33 in June, and 24 in July for a total of 103. If we are to have 93 new members, it means we must get started now.

REPORT 106
EMPLOYMENT CONTRACT

EMPLOYMENT CONTRACT

ds

This agreement, made and concluded this *(current)* day of *(current), 19--* between the Oakview mall located at 14001 Muerknoll Street, Troy, MI, party of the first part, and Raymond L.Singh, 378 Glendenin Court, Farmington, MI, party of the second part.

<u>Article 1. Services.</u> The party of the ~~first~~ second part, Raymond L. Singh, covenants and agrees to and with the party of the first part, the Oakview mall, to furnish ~~his~~ services to the said party of the first part as security consultant at least two (2) days a month for six (6) months, beginning January 1, 19--, and ending June 30, 19--; and the said party of the second part covenants and agrees to conduct training sessions for ~~senior~~ managers in the area of employee theft and both for managers and all other employees in the area of customer shoplifting.

<u>Article 2. Wages.</u> The party of the first part, the Oakview mall, covennants and agrees to pay the said party of the second part, for the same, the sum of eighty dollars ($80) per hour, on a biweekly basis beginning January 23, 19--. <u>IN WITNESS WHEREOF</u>, the parties to the employment contract have hereunto set their hands the day and year first above written.

____
Raymond L. Singh

____
ss
Virginia F. Woods, Manager
Oakview mall

____
Witness To Signature

____
Witness To Signature

REPORT 107
EMPLOYMENT CONTRACT

Spread-center *DRAFT* in extra-large, bold type on Ln = 1.5".

Set Line Numbering, as explained on page 414, to begin on the first paragraph.

An employment contract between the Oakview Mall and Franklin S. Cosell must also be prepared. Retrieve the Raymond L. Singh employment contract, and revise it as follows for a first draft.

1. Replace *Raymond L. Singh* with *Franklin S. Cosell.*
2. Change the address to that of Mr. Cosell, 2147 Wendell Street, NE, Grand Rapids, Michigan.
3. Mr. Cosell will be a special consultant for the months of November and December to coordinate special holiday themes under the supervision of the Oakview Mall director of marketing, Mr. Matt Simmons.
4. Mr. Cosell will be paid $10,400 on December 31, 19—, for his services.

J. Spacing: double. Take two 2-minute timed writings. Compute your speed and count errors.

Goal: 24 wam/2′/5e

J. 2-MINUTE TIMED WRITING

```
     The personal computer has changed all of our   10
lives in just a few years.  Since we have quite a   20
variety of software programs for our use, we can    30
expect to find that a computer will let us do an    40
amazing amount of work in less time than before.    48
 | 1 | 2 | 3 | 4 | 5 | 6 | 7 | 8 | 9 | 10
```

LESSON 17 Symbols

Margins: 1 inch • Tab: 0.5 inch • Spacing: Single • Drills: 2 times

Goals:
To control the %, ′, and ″ keys; to key 25 wam/2′/5e.

A. WARMUP

```
     Jack Xua quizzed the men about 345# of grain   10
(wheat) found by 26 boys on Lot #98.  Two men had   20
paid 17 students to place the wheat in 20# units.   30
 | 1 | 2 | 3 | 4 | 5 | 6 | 7 | 8 | 9 | 10
```

NEW KEYS

B. THE % KEY

PERCENT is the shift of 5. Use the F finger.

Do not space between the number and the percent sign.

```
ft5f ft5%f f5%f f5%f f%%f f%%f 5% 55% 555% 5,555%
Robert quoted rates of 8%, 9%, 10%, 11%, and 12%.
Pat scored 82%, Jan 89%, and Ken 90% on the test.
Only 55% of the students passed 75% of the exams.
```

C. THE ' KEY

APOSTROPHE is to the right of the semicolon. Use the Sem finger.

```
;'; ''' ;'; ''' Can't we go in Sue's or Al's car?
It's Bob's job to cover Ted's work when he's out.
What's in Mike's lunch box for Stanley's dessert?
He's left for Ty's banquet which is held at Al's.
```

D. THE " KEY

QUOTATION is the shift of the apostrophe. Use the Sem finger.

Do not space between the quotation marks and the text they enclose.

```
;"; """" ;"; """" "That's a super job," said Mabel.
The theme of the meeting is "Improving Your Job."
Jill liked "Grand Hotel"; Sharon liked "Fiddler."
Allison said, "I'll take Janice and Jo to Flint."
```

LETTER 115

Indent the second paragraph from both the left and right margins.

Please prepare this letter to Mr. Owen F. Austin at 1734 Perry Street, Flint, MI 48504.

I am sorry that time constraints shortened our phone conversation yesterday. Given the circumstances as you presented them, you would be wise to consider drafting a General Durable Power of Attorney, as described below in Section 495 of the new act:

> A Power of Attorney is only effective up to the time one is disabled or incompetent. Now, with the new statute, the General Durable Power of Attorney will remain in effect until one either revokes it or passes away.

This new law will be very helpful to many elderly and infirm people.

PS: Please call me at 555-6327 so that we can continue our discussion about this matter.

MEMO 43

ds

MEMO TO: Mabel R. Meiers
FROM: Jeanne M. Hoover
DATE: (Current)
RE: Estate planning guide

As you requested, Al Jordan and I have been doing much some preliminary work on the proposed estate planning guide. In additionto surveying the partners and all junior members in the firm, we have allso reviewed much of the literature. It is our feeling at this time that the basic purpose of the guide should be to discuss the following"Tools for Estate Planning:" the last will and testament, jointly held property, lifetime giving, revocable and irrevocable living trusts, and durable powers of attorney. At this time AL and I would like your reactions to the above listing. With your suggestions, we will then be in a position to prepare a preliminary draft.

current

ds

c: Al Jordan

LANGUAGE ARTS

E. PLACEMENT OF QUOTATION MARKS

Read these rules about the placement of quotation marks. Then key lines 16–19 twice.

1. The closing quotation mark is always keyed *after* a period or comma but *before* a colon or semicolon.
2. The closing quotation mark is keyed *after* a question mark or exclamation point if the quoted material is a question or an exclamation; otherwise, the quotation mark is keyed *before* the question mark or exclamation point.

16 "Hello," I said. "My name is Al; I am new here."
17 Zack read the article "Can She Succeed Tomorrow?"
18 John said, "I'll mail the check"; but, he didn't.
19 Did he say, "We lost"? She said, "I don't know."

SKILLBUILDING

F. ALPHABET AND SYMBOL PRACTICE

20 Gaze at views of my jonquil or red phlox in back.
21 Jan quickly moved the six dozen big pink flowers.
22 Joe quietly picked six razors from the woven bag.
23 Packing jam for the dozen boxes was quite lively.

24 Mail these "Rush": #38, #89, and #99 (software).
25 Joe's note carried a rate of 6%; Ann's only 5.5%.
26 Lee read "The Computer Today." It's here Monday.
27 Ask (1) Tom, (2) Dick, and (3) Harry (Feigleson).

G. Spacing: double. Set tabs every 1.2 inches. Press tab to begin the first column.

G. TECHNIQUE PRACTICE: TAB KEY

28	perfect	agency	office	disc
29	security	company	employer	firm
30	Monday	workers	vacation	employee
31	also	wouldn't	it's	computer

H. Spacing: double. Take two 1-minute timed writings. Compute your speed and count errors.

H. HANDWRITTEN PARAGRAPHS

32 You have now completed the first sequence of 10
33 your class and have learned how to make the right 20
34 reaches to those alpha, numeric, and symbol keys. 30
35 In the next sequence, you will be taught how 40
36 to center and to develop your keyboarding skills. 50

I. Spacing: double. Take two 2-minute timed writings. Compute your speed and count errors.

Goal: 25 wam/2′/5e

I. 2-MINUTE TIMED WRITING

37 We can expect quite a few changes in our job 10
38 market in the next few decades. People will have 20
39 jobs that will require new tasks due to the many 30
40 uses of the computer. We will have a gain in the 40
41 size of the labor force which processes our data. 50

| 1 | 2 | 3 | 4 | 5 | 6 | 7 | 8 | 9 | 10

REPORT 104
DOCKET SHEET

The docket sheet, a handwritten record of time devoted and expenses incurred, is maintained by an attorney. At periodical intervals, a keyed copy is prepared. When a handwritten line is drawn below the last entry on a docket page, it indicates that the legal action on that matter has been completed.

Key the information on the ruled lines 0.5 inch after the guide words. Be sure the cursor is past the underline code.

Single-space each entry; double-space between entries.

WordPerfect 5.1
½: Ctrl-V, /2

WordPerfect 6
½: Ctrl-W, 4,17

First, please create the printed docket form shown below. After saving the form, retrieve it and then key the handwritten information on the blank form.

DOCKET (Print this on 8½ x 11" paper.)

CLIENT Alvin R. and Gayla L. Crisman

TYPE OF MATTER Purchase of Home

FEE $95 per hour plus disbursements

Date	Explanation	Hours	Disbursements
8/12/--	Meeting with Mr. and Mrs. Crisman to discuss purchase	1	
8/13/--	Meeting at Rawlins Abstract and Title Company in Pontiac	2	
8/13/--	Travel to Pontiac		$18.20
8/14/--	Meeting at Myler Realty Co.	1½	

REPORT 105
POWER OF ATTORNEY

As is true for the last will and testament and the codicil, a power of attorney should also be double-spaced.

Set a 0.5-inch bottom margin to keep all the signature lines on one page.

POWER OF ATTORNEY

KNOW ALL MEN BY THESE PRESENTS that I, EUGENE M. SCHRAM, of the City of Lapeer, County of Lapeer, State of Michigan, do hereby appoint my daughter, Pauline L. Gobert, of the City of Mount Pleasant, County of Isabella, State of Michigan, as my attorney-in-fact to act in my name, place, and stead as my agent in the management of my real estate transactions, chattel and goods transactions, banking and securities transactions, and business operating transactions, giving and granting unto my said attorney full power and authority to do and perform all and every act and thing whatsoever requisite and necessary to be done in the said management as fully, to all intents and purposes, as I might or could do if personally present, with full power of revocation, hereby ratifying and confirming all that my said attorney shall lawfully do or cause to be done by virtue hereof:

IN WITNESS WHEREOF, I have hereunto set my hand and seal this *(current)* day of *(current)*, 19—.

____

SIGNED and affirmed in the presence of:

____________________ and ____________________

LESSON 18 Symbols

Margins: 1 inch • Tab: 0.5 inch • Spacing: Single • Drills: 2 times

Goals:
To control the &, $, and _ keys; to underline; to key 26 wam/2'/5e.

A. WARMUP

```
     Of the 345 votes cast, 279 were for Jo.  She 10
won by 81%.  Jo's quick win amazed 60 of her pals 20
from home.  The "Times" exalted the huge victory. 30
 | 1 | 2 | 3 | 4 | 5 | 6 | 7 | 8 | 9 | 10
```

NEW KEYS

B. THE & KEY

AMPERSAND (sign for *and*) is the shift of 7. Use the J finger.

Space before and after the ampersand.

```
juj ju7j j7j j7&j j&&j j&&j Max & Dee & Sue & Ken
Brown & Sons shipped goods to Crum & Lee Company.
Johnson & Loo brought a case against May & Green.
Ball & Trump vs. Vens & See is being decided now.
```

C. THE $ KEY

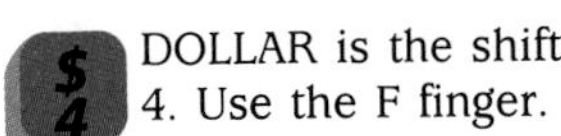

DOLLAR is the shift of 4. Use the F finger.

Do not space between the dollar sign and the number.

```
frf fr4f f4f f4$f f$$f f$$f $44 $444 $4,444 $4.44
I quoted $48, $64, and $94 for the set of chairs.
His insurance paid $150; our insurance paid $175.
First-floor seats were $25, $30, and $55 in June.
```

D. THE _ KEY

UNDERLINE is the shift of the hyphen. Use the Sem finger.

Blank lines within sentences are 5 characters long.

```
;p; ;p-; ;p-; ;p_; ;_; ;_; Use a date of _____.
My new hours are from _____ a.m. until _____ p.m.
My sales goal of $_____ is an increase of _____%.
There are _____ graduating; only _____ will stay.
```

FORMATTING

E. WORDPERFECT: BLOCK TEXT

BLOCK
Alt-F4 or F12, *highlight text*

WordPerfect 6 users: See Student Guide, page 5.

Block is used to highlight a section of text, such as a word, phrase, sentence, or paragraph. You can then perform other commands, such as underlining or deleting the block of text.

To define a block, position the cursor under the first character you wish to block and press Alt-F4 or F12. WordPerfect will display "Block On" at the bottom of your screen. Next, move the cursor to the right of the last character you wish to block. The block of text is now highlighted, and you can issue another command, such as pressing F8 to underline.

F. WORDPERFECT: UNDERLINING

WP

UNDERLINING
F8

WordPerfect 6 users: See Student Guide, page 6.

To underline text as you key it, turn on underlining by pressing F8. Then key the text and press F8 again (or the right arrow key) to turn off underlining. To underline existing text, block the text to be underlined, then press F8.

REPORT 103
CODICIL

Codicil: An appendix or supplement to a will.

WordPerfect 6 users: Do not key the dollar sign in the Value column.

FIRST CODICIL

ds

I, LAURA J. MACKLIN, declare this to be a first codicil to my Last Will and Testament dated the *(current)* day of *(current)*, 19--.

FIRST: Replace Article III with the following: "I give and bequeath the following four pieces of jewelry as follows:

Jewelry		
Item	Value	Recipient
Diamond ring	$7,400	Judith Cosgrove
String of pearls	2,600	Mavis Macklin
Wrist watch	1,800	Toni Macklin
Gold bracelet	1,300	Jill Cosgrove

ds

I give and bequeath all of my other jewelry to my beloved daughter, JUDITH MACKLIN COSGROVE."

SECOND: In all other respects I ratify and confirm my said will.

The second page of this codicil should be the same as the last page of Ms. Macklin's will, except that the document should be referred to as a First Codicil to her Last Will and Testament rather than her Last Will and Testament.

MEMO 42

Use the guide word *RE* in place of *SUBJECT*.

Please send a memo to John Carruth from me on the subject of copyright infringement, as follows:

The following citations relate to the pending Compton copyright infringement trial. While somewhat dated, the cases do have particular relevance.

1. *Universal Athletic Sales Co. v. Salkeld*, 511 F. 2d 904 (1975)
2. *Berlin v. E. C. Publications, Inc.*, 210 F. Supp. 911 (1963)
3. *International Luggage Registry v. Avery Products Corp.*, 541 F. 2d 830 (1976)

If I can provide any further help, please let me know.

SKILLBUILDING

G. Underline individual words separately; for a book title, underline the entire title, including the spaces.

G. TECHNIQUE PRACTICE: UNDERLINING

The Sindbad Voyage is an excellent story for all.
Are the words for, fore, and four used correctly?
We had an ad in The Wall Street Journal in March.
Max will not or should not attend the conference.

H. Keep your eyes on the copy so that you do not lose your place as you key these longer words.

H. CONCENTRATION PRACTICE

The provocative statement caused an insurrection.
A congregation in Connecticut intervened quickly.
A lackadaisical traveler crisscrossed continents.
All resignations were interpreted as irrevocable.

I. Spacing: double. Take two 1-minute timed writings. Compute your speed and count errors.

I. HANDWRITTEN PARAGRAPH

You will discover when you begin working in 10
industry that there are other skills you need to 20
possess beyond the basic business skills. Skills 30
in human relations are desirable for every worker. 40

J. Spacing: double. Take two 2-minute timed writings. Compute your speed and count errors.

Goal: 26 wam/2′/5e

J. 2-MINUTE TIMED WRITING

Van Clark was amazed at how quickly he could 10
key on a new computer. It took him just a little 20
time to learn the functions it can perform. He 30
expected he would surely forget how to use it his 40
first time alone, but he did not. He had learned 50
the skill. 52

| 1 | 2 | 3 | 4 | 5 | 6 | 7 | 8 | 9 | 10

LESSON 19 Symbols and Editing Text

Margins: 1 inch • Tab: 0.5 inch • Spacing: Single • Drills: 2 times

Goals:
To control the *, @, and = keys; to edit text; to key 27 wam/2′/5e.

A. WARMUP

The owner (Mr. Judd) quoted a sales price of 10
$3.86 for the items. He expects Grove & Baker to 20
buy nearly 129,457 units of these sizzling items. 30

| 1 | 2 | 3 | 4 | 5 | 6 | 7 | 8 | 9 | 10

REPORT 102
(continued)

Be sure that all the signature lines are on the same page—that of the testatrix and those of the witnesses. In order to accomplish this, it may be necessary for the next-to-last page to be just a partial page.

For the remainder of this document, Ms. Hoover has used the last page of the will that was prepared for Ms. Macklin several years ago. Make the changes as indicated.

IN WITNESS WHEREOF, I subscribe my name to this, my Last Will and Testament, consisting of three (3) [Please check] printed pages, this ~~12th~~ (current) day of ~~March~~, (current) 19~~84~~ --.

Laura J. Macklin
LAURA J. MACKLIN

On the ~~12th~~ (current) day of ~~March~~, (current) 19~~84~~ --, LAURA J. MACKLIN signed, published, and declared to us that the foregoing instrument, consisting of three (3) [Please check] printed pages, was her Last Will and Testament. Then, in her presence and in the presence of each other, we, at her request and believing her to be of sound mind, have hereunto subscribed our names as witnesses this ~~12th~~ (current) day of ~~March~~, (current) 19~~84~~ --.

After completing this page, go back to the beginning of Page 1 and insert the page numbering style. Be sure it follows the page numbering command.

Donna S. McDaniel of 8412 Layman Drive
Donna S. McDaniel
Flint, MI 48506

~~Bernard H. Huber~~ of ~~634 Devon Court~~ Rural Route 3, Box 67
~~Bernard H. Huber~~ Joyce E. Bates
~~Flint~~ Clio, MI ~~48532~~ 48420

Cynthia K. Varney of ~~905 Eighth Avenue West~~ 3810 Morton Street
~~Cynthia K. Varney~~ Trish V. Neveaux
Flint, MI ~~48504~~ 48507

NEW KEYS

B. THE * KEY

ASTERISK is the shift of 8. Use the K finger.

4 kik ki8k k8*k k8*k k**k k**k Al's book* is great.
5 Use the * to show book/table footnote references.
6 Asterisks keyed in a row (*******) make a border.
7 Harry's* article quoted Hanson* and Pyle* in May.

C. THE @ KEY

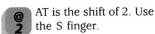

AT is the shift of 2. Use the S finger.

Space before and after @.

8 sws sw2s s2@s s2@s s@@s s@@s Buy 15 @ $5 in June.
9 Order 12 items @ $14 and another 185 items @ $16.
10 He bought 12 units @ $14.50 and 6 units @ $12.30.
11 Buy 10 shares @ $75 and another 15 shares @ $125.

D. THE = KEY

EQUAL is to the right of the hyphen. Use the Sem finger.

Space before and after =.

12 ;=; ;=; ;==; ;==; A = 40, B = 160, C = 18, D = 1.
13 If x = 4 and y = 6 and z = 8, what is the answer?
14 He learned that A = B and was able to solve that.
15 The = sign, equal, is used by our mathematicians.

SKILLBUILDING

E. TECHNIQUE PRACTICE: EDITING TEXT

E. Use the WordPerfect Block command to make the necessary changes in lines 16–19.

Key lines 16–19 as shown. Then revise each line, making these changes:

1. In line 16, change *Dr.* to *Mr.* and replace *at the Holiday Hotel* with *on "Software" for me.*
2. In line 17, change *Is Tyne* to *Tyne is* and the question mark to a period.
3. In line 18, change *house* to *lot* and *March* to *October.*
4. In line 19, underline *used computer* and change *$750* to *$875.*

16 Dr. James Garner will speak at the Holiday Hotel.
17 Is Tyne planning an address on "Software" for me?
18 A house sold, on March 4, for less than $134,000.
19 On April 6, Jill bought a used computer for $750.

F. SUSTAINED PRACTICE: NUMBERS AND SYMBOLS

F. Take a 1-minute timed writing on the first paragraph to establish your base speed. Then take successive 1-minute timed writings on the other paragraphs. As soon as you equal or exceed your base speed on one paragraph, advance to the next one.

20 Our new store enjoyed an unexpected increase 10
21 in sales. We were quite astonished and amazed by 20
22 the gain in numbers of customers served and kept. 30

23 We opened 18 new outlets in 14 cities, and a 10
24 catalog outlet in 29 counties. We were then able 20
25 to serve 150,670 possible customers in 10 states. 30

26 Our gross sales were $4,560,871 (an increase 10
27 of 9%). Knox & Sons paid $46/share and said, "It 20
28 was a great year." These figures are confirmed.* 30

| 1 | 2 | 3 | 4 | 5 | 6 | 7 | 8 | 9 | 10

REPORT 102
(continued)

A female Personal Representative, the person appointed to execute a will, is often referred to as an Executrix. A male is often referred to as an Executor.

In legal documents, important numbers are typically keyed in both figures and words.

This is a continuation of the last will and testament of Laura J. Macklin. Follow the same format that you used for the first page as you continue keying this will.

ARTICLE III

I give and bequeath all of my jewelry to my beloved daughter, JUDITH MACKLIN COSGROVE, or her surviving issue, per stirpes.

ARTICLE IV

I give and bequeath all of my remaining property, real and intangible and wheresoever situated, after payment of taxes and other payments required by Article II (including property over which I hold a power of appointment) as follows:

(A) Fifty percent (50%) to my beloved daughter, JUDITH MACKLIN COSGROVE, or her surviving issue, per stirpes;

(B) Fifty percent (50%) to my beloved son, WILLIAM L. MACKLIN, or his surviving issue, per stirpes;

(C) In the event either of my beloved children predeceases me leaving no issue surviving, I hereby give, devise, and bequeath said share of my estate to my surviving child, or her/his surviving issue, per stirpes.

ARTICLE V

I appoint JUDITH MACKLIN COSGROVE as Personal Representative of this, my Last Will and Testament. In the event my Personal Representative shall predecease me, or, for any reason, is unable or unwilling to accept the office of Personal Representative, then I appoint WILLIAM L. MACKLIN as Alternate Personal Representative. I request that no bond be required in any jurisdiction of my Personal Representative or any successors.

I hereby give my said Personal Representative all powers provided by the Michigan Revised Probate Code, as amended, and any other conferred by statute and, in addition, the full power to sell, mortgage, hypothecate, invest, reinvest, exchange, manage, and control and in any way use and deal with any and all of my estate, both real and personal, without making notice or application to any court for leave.

ARTICLE VI

I hereby direct that my eyes, or any other vital body organs which are functional at the time of my death, be removed for transplantation, if there is such a need, for the benefit of other persons.

(Continued on next page)

G. Keep your eyes on the copy while keying.

G. SYMBOL PRACTICE

```
Invoice #356 to Rice & Sons required May's reply.
My total bill was $450.65, including a tax of $7.
She (May) read How to Save Money; it costs $9.50.
Luke said, "I'll buy 1 share @ $6 and 2 @ $7.55."
```

H. Spacing: double. Take two 2-minute timed writings. Compute your speed and count errors.

Goal: 27 wam/2′/5e

H. 2-MINUTE TIMED WRITING

```
     If you have plans to be an expert on a job,    10
you must first have the skills; you must possess    20
good English skills as a second requirement; and    30
a third criterion is knowing how to proofread all   40
work.  Start to analyze your work with care and     50
find all errors.                                    54
| 1 | 2 | 3 | 4 | 5 | 6 | 7 | 8 | 9 | 10
```

Symbols

Margins: 1 inch • Tab: 0.5 inch • Spacing: Single • Drills: 2 times

Goals:
To control the ! and + keys; to improve speed and accuracy; to key 28 wam/2′/5e.

A. WARMUP

```
     Ken bought 11 prized lots @ $975.  The sizes
varied but there were 3,482* (*square feet).  Joe
was amazed that Ken expected to buy 12 more lots.
| 1 | 2 | 3 | 4 | 5 | 6 | 7 | 8 | 9 | 10
```

NEW KEYS

EXCLAMATION is the shift of 1. Use the A finger.

Space twice after an exclamation point at the end of a sentence.

PLUS is the shift of EQUAL. Use the Sem finger.

Space before and after plus.

B. THE ! KEY

```
aqa aq1a aq!a a!!a a!!a Where!  Why!  How!  When!
It's his!  Don't do that!  Stop!  No!  Exit Only!
He did say that!  Jill can't take a vacation now!
What he said was startling!  She does believe it!
```

C. THE + KEY

```
;=; ;=+; ;=+; ;++; ;++; 10 + 20 + 3 + 4 + 5 = 42.
When you add 13 + 40 + 50 + 60 + 90, you get 253.
The + sign, plus, was used in an arithmetic task.
Do you ever use the plus (+) sign in your office?
```

REPORT 102
LAST WILL AND TESTAMENT

Legal documents usually have double spacing and 10-space paragraph indentions.

Legal documents are sometimes printed on ruled stationery. A vertical double line is printed the length of the stationery on the left; a vertical single line is printed on the right. Margins are set a space or two inside the ruled lines.

Legal documents (even one page) are usually numbered at the bottom center in this format: *Page 1 of 4.* So that pages break correctly, insert the page numbering command for bottom center at the beginning of the document. Once you know how many pages are in the complete document, insert the page numbering style after the page numbering command.

Article I is the same in all wills; therefore, create a macro and save it before you begin keying the will. Then, execute the macro where indicated.

ARTICLE I

I hereby expressly revoke and cancel any and all Wills, Codicils, or other testamentary dispositions at any time heretofore made by me.

The next few pages are a rough draft of the last will and testament of Laura J. Macklin. Please key a final copy for her signature.

LAST WILL AND TESTAMENT

OF

LAURA J. MACKLIN

ds Being of sound mind and disposing memory for the purpose of making disposition upon my death of my entire estate, real, personal, and mixed, wherever situated, whether owned by

ds me me at the date of execution hereof , or acquired by me after such date, I do make hereby, publish, and declare this to be my Last Will and Testament. My present domicile is at 807 Carver St., Fenton, Michigan 48430.

Execute the ARTICLE I macro here.

ARTICLE I II

I direct my Personal Representative to pay before makeing any distributions: (1) all of the expenses of my last illness, funeral, and burial, including a grave cemetery marker in such amount as my Personal Representative may deem proper; (2)all of the expenses of administering my estate; (3) all estate, inheritance, and other taxes that may be payable by reason of my death; and (4) all of my just debts.

(Continued on next page)

D. SYMBOL PRACTICE

Al said, "Stop it at once!" He's selling 5 @ $6.
Brown & Daughters held their annual Dollar Sales.
Julie's article* was reprinted in Newsweek today.
"Can't I read Catcher in the Rye?" asked Rob Lee.

E. KEYING IN ALL CAPS

Use the A finger.

To key in all-capital letters:

1. Depress the caps lock key.
2. Key the word or words.
3. Release the caps lock by pressing the caps lock key.

E. Key each sentence on a separate line.

Remember to shift for ?, !, and :.

Is MABEL going? Attend the MINNESOTA STATE FAIR.
NO SMOKING! STOP IT! Post the sign, NO HUNTING.
Are there EXIT and ENTRANCE signs? DO NOT ENTER.
An ad read: SPEND YOUR VACATION IN NORTH DAKOTA.

F. PRETEST: ALTERNATE- AND ONE-HAND WORDS

PRETEST.
Take a 1-minute timed writing; compute your speed and count errors.

The chairman should handle their tax problem 10
downtown. If they are reversed, pressure tactics 20
might have changed the case as it was being held. 30

| 1 | 2 | 3 | 4 | 5 | 6 | 7 | 8 | 9 | 10

G. PRACTICE: ALTERNATE-HAND WORDS

PRACTICE.
Speed Emphasis: If you made 2 or fewer errors on the Pretest, key each line twice.
Accuracy Emphasis: If you made 3 or more errors, key each group of lines (as though it were a paragraph) twice.

the with girl right blame handle antique chairman
for wish town their panel formal problem downtown
sit work make tight amend profit element neighbor
pan busy they flair signs thrown signals problems

H. PRACTICE: ONE-HAND WORDS

lip fact yolk poplin yummy affect reverse pumpkin
you cast kill uphill jumpy grease wagered opinion
tea cage lump limply hilly served bravest minimum
fat tree only unhook jolly garage reserve million

I. POSTTEST: ALTERNATE- AND ONE-HAND WORDS

POSTTEST.
Repeat the Pretest (F) and compare performance.

J. 2-MINUTE TIMED WRITING

J. Spacing: double. Take two 2-minute timed writings. Compute your speed and count errors.

Goal: 28 wam/2′/5e

The purpose for all the new technology is to 10
make workers more productive. If this happens, a 20
decrease in the number of hours on the job may be 30
noticed. This could mean that workers would have 40
extra time off. This could be quite a benefit to 50
a large number of those workers. 56

| 1 | 2 | 3 | 4 | 5 | 6 | 7 | 8 | 9 | 10

FORMATTING

P. WORDPERFECT: LINE NUMBERING

 LINE NUMBERING

On: Sh-F8, 1, 5, Y, F7
Off: Sh-F8, 1, 5, N, F7

WordPerfect 6 users: See Student Guide, p. 117.

It is sometimes helpful to number the lines in a document. WordPerfect will do this automatically for you. Position the cursor where you want Line Numbering to begin, and issue the appropriate commands. The line numbers print in the left margin. You can start and stop Line Numbering anywhere in a document.

DOCUMENT PROCESSING

Q. INTEGRATED OFFICE PROJECT

CARRUTH AND MAIERS, ATTORNEYS-AT-LAW

Situation: You are a legal secretary in the office of Ms. Jeanne M. Hoover, attorney-at-law. Her employer is Carruth and Maiers, Attorneys-at-Law, at 1220 Eighth Avenue West, Flint, MI 48504.

You are responsible for all administrative duties and the preparation of correspondence and various legal documents. Ms. Hoover prefers modified-block format, standard punctuation, and the closing *Sincerely yours,* in her letters. Use the current date for all jobs. For legal documents, use 1-inch side and bottom margins. On page 1, set the top margin at 1.5″ for continuing pages. Key document titles in Extra Large font and bold on Ln = 2″.

Leave 3 blank lines before and after all signature lines. Signature and address lines should be 3 inches long, beginning at the left margin, at the center, or following a conjunction.

LETTER 114
TWO-PAGE LETTER WITH OPEN TABLE

Send this letter to mr michael d eiden . . . attorney-at-law . . . 2408 ridgecrest avenue . . . dayton . . . ohio . . . 45416 . . . dear mike . . .

it was great to see you at the convention in detroit last week . . . all of us enjoyed reminiscing about the old days in law school . . .

you may recall that i told you i had just been appointed by the court to defend a woman here in flint who has been charged with embezzling large sums of money from her previous employer . . . she was in charge of accounts receivable at a large department store . . . her previous employer . . . the plaintiff in the case . . . claims that she embezzled the following amounts . . . *(please arrange the following information in a table with two column headings, "year" and "amount")* . . .

1991 . . . $18,634 . . . 1992 . . . $39,072 . . . 1993 . . . $27,045 . . .

i recall that you mentioned you had represented a defendant in a similar case last year . . . as i prepare for this defense . . . perhaps you might help me in the following ways . . .

one . . . please send me the appropriate citations for the trial in which you participated . . .

two . . . also provide me with any other case citations that you think might be particularly helpful . . .

three . . . arrange to meet with me soon so that i can benefit from your experience as i prepare for the trial . . .

a copy of the formal complaint is enclosed for your review . . . i shall call you in about a week to arrange a time and place for our meeting . . .

i have never been involved with anything like this before . . . any help that you give me will be appreciated . . .

PART 2

SKILL DEVELOPMENT

Centering, Letters, and Reports

OBJECTIVES

KEYBOARDING

To operate the entire keyboard by touch.

To key 36 words a minute on a 3-minute timed writing with no more than 4 errors.

LANGUAGE ARTS

To improve language arts skills, including correct grammar, spelling, use of punctuation marks, capitalization, numbers, titles in business correspondence, and abbreviations.

To proofread documents and correct errors.

To develop keyboard composing skill.

WORD PROCESSING

To use the following WordPerfect commands: Horizontal Centering, Page Break, Center Page, Speller, Date Insert, View Document, Top and Bottom Margins, Left and Right Margins, Full Justification, Bold, Move, Indent, and Italics.

DOCUMENT PROCESSING

To center text horizontally and vertically.

To format business letters and personal-business letters in block style.

To format one-page unbound reports, enumerations, outlines, and bibliographies.

N. Take three 1-minute timed writings. Note that the last two digits of each number are a cumulative word count and give your wam speed.

N. NUMBER PRACTICE

1801 2902 4703 5604 6305 9106 2807 2408 2109 8610 5511 3812
4513 6714 1015 2216 9717 5618 4419 9320 4521 8122 9323 4824
1225 2026 3427 8728 7929 1530 6431 2732 8933 7434 5535 6836
8337 2138 6639 3540 7941 6842 3843 2244 3045 6046 3347 3948

O. Spacing: Double. Take two 5-minute timed writings. Compute your speed and count errors.

Goal: 59 wam/5′/5e

O. 5-MINUTE TIMED WRITING

All animals perform[1] basic actions for survival.[2] Birds 12
gather twigs to[3] make nests, while[4] squirrels hunt for nuts 24
and berries.[5] People perform very basic[6] actions too, but we[7] 36
often disregard them in[8] favor of such complex achievements[9] 47
as reading, language,[10] philosophy, and[11] math. Yet despite a 59
truly[12] amazing array of artifacts[13] that we have developed,[14] 71
devised, and built over[15] the years, we can still[16] observe 82
similar actions[17] in people from a wide range[18] of cultures. 93
There[19] are two major types of[20] actions. The first is 105
called[21] inborn actions. The idea[22] with an inborn action[23] is 116
that the brain is programmed[24] to link particular[25] reactions 128
with specific[26] stimuli. The stimulus[27] triggers a specific 139
action,[28] even though the person has[29] never experienced the[30] 151
stimulus before. The[31] classic example is the newborn[32] baby 162
who knows right[33] at birth how to take milk[34] from the bottle 174
given[35] to him or her. 178
The second[36] type is all those actions[37] we have to be 189
taught.[38] Trained actions are[39] consciously acquired through[40] 201
teaching or by self-observation[41] and practice.[42] At one end 212
of the scale[43] there are very difficult[44] physical achievements 224
such[45] as turning midair cartwheels[46] or walking on your[47] hands. 237
Only expert acrobats[48] can master these skills[49] after long 248
hours of practice.[50] At the other end[51] of the scale there 259
are very[52] simple actions such as[53] winking and shaking hands.[54] 271
Watching a child first[55] master winking provides[56] a graphic 282
reminder of how[57] difficult some apparently[58] simple actions 294
can be.[59] 295

| 1 | 2 | 3 | 4 | 5 | 6 | 7 | 8 | 9 | 10 | 11 | 12

LESSON 21 Horizontal Centering

Margins: 1 inch • Tab: 0.5 inch • Spacing: Single • Drills: 2 times • Format Guide: 1

Goals:
To improve speed and accuracy; to center material horizontally.

A. WARMUP

1 Jill gave an expert a quick breakdown of all the sizes 12
2 made. She may ask clients to call 642-3598 to get a better 24
3 understanding of the shipping charge of $10.75 on item #22. 36

| 1 | 2 | 3 | 4 | 5 | 6 | 7 | 8 | 9 | 10 | 11 | 12

LANGUAGE ARTS

B. COMPOSING

Composing at the keyboard can save you considerable time when you create first drafts of documents. When composing at the keyboard, keep the following points in mind:

1. Key at a comfortable pace as your thoughts come to you. Do not stop to correct errors.
2. Keep your eyes on the screen as you key.
3. Do not be overly concerned with correct grammar. It is more important that you get your thoughts recorded. Any errors you make can be corrected later.

B. Answer each question with a single word.

4 Do you have a computer?
5 What is your favorite sport?
6 What is your favorite color?
7 When is your favorite time of day?
8 Do you read a daily newspaper?
9 What is your favorite hobby?
10 Where would you like to spend your next vacation?
11 What is the name of the happiest person you know?

SKILLBUILDING

PRETEST.
Take a 1-minute timed writing; compute your speed and count errors.

C. PRETEST: COMMON LETTER COMBINATIONS

12 The manager tried to react with total control. He was 12
13 indeed annoyed and devoted all his efforts to being fair to 24
14 the entire staff. His daily schedule was rampant with ways 36
15 in which to confront the situation and to apply good sense. 48

| 1 | 2 | 3 | 4 | 5 | 6 | 7 | 8 | 9 | 10 | 11 | 12

PRACTICE.
Speed Emphasis: If you made 2 or fewer errors on the Pretest, key each line twice.
Accuracy Emphasis: If you made 3 or more errors, key each group of lines (as though it were a paragraph) twice.

D. PRACTICE: WORD BEGINNINGS

16 re relay react reply reuse reason record return results red
17 in index inept incur inset inning indeed insure interns ink
18 be beast berry being beeps berate belong became beavers bet
19 de dealt death decay devil detest devote derive depicts den

J. Take three 12-second timed writings on each line. The scale gives wam for a 12-second timed writing.

J. 12-SECOND SPRINTS

42 A group of 185 left on the 6:30 plane at 7:34 from Gate 29.
43 She took Route 96 for 1,804 of the 3,257 miles on her trip.
44 Please call 359-0678 for the 20 tickets on February 1 or 4.
45 Her telephone number was changed from 691-8407 to 532-4876.
46 Ed counted 278 cars, 150 trucks, 69 tractors, and 34 buses.

| | | | 5 | | | |10 | | | |15 | | | |20 | | | |25 | | | |30 | | | |35 | | | |40 | | | |45 | | | |50 | | | |55 | | | |60

K. As you key this paragraph once, change all first-person pronouns to the second person and vice versa; for example, change *I* to *you* and change *you* to *I* or *me.*

K. TECHNIQUE PRACTICE: CONCENTRATION

47 You must give me a recipe for success in your profession
48 if I intend to follow you. If I become a broker also, you
49 can help me by giving me some leads and other contacts; you
50 could also have me subcontract a few of your small accounts.

L. Take three 30-second timed writings on each line. Try not to slow down for the capital letters.

L. TECHNIQUE PRACTICE: SHIFT KEY

51 Mario, Franco, and Angela went to Rome, Naples, and Venice.
52 Mr. Tom Hart went to Toronto in May to see James G. Miller.
53 The Empire Business School in Reno opened on Monday, May 8.
54 Phyllis Mirchin will leave Hillside High School in October.
55 The White Plains Colts will play the Newburgh Lions in May.

| 1 | 2 | 3 | 4 | 5 | 6 | 7 | 8 | 9 | 10 | 11 | 12

M. Take a 1-minute timed writing on the first paragraph to establish your base speed. Then take four 1-minute timed writings on the remaining paragraphs. As soon as you equal or exceed your base speed on one paragraph, advance to the next one.

M. SUSTAINED PRACTICE: SYLLABIC INTENSITY

56 Do you want a job in one of the fastest-growing fields 12
57 in the country, where you can have a good income, work in a 24
58 nice office, and render a social service? If you said yes, 36
59 you may want to think about a career in law as a paralegal. 48

60 Most paralegals have jobs in law firms. In their work 12
61 with lawyers, they get involved in areas such as family law 24
62 and real estate law. They may perform such tasks as aiding 36
63 in the interviewing of clients and doing research on cases. 48

64 Other paralegals work in the public sector. This term 12
65 refers to a wide range of nonprofit agencies that give some 24
66 form of public service. These paralegals work as advocates 36
67 for the poor, the handicapped, the elderly, and immigrants. 48

68 The paralegal profession is ideal for someone desiring 12
69 an interesting career but lacking the time or money for law 24
70 school. It is also an excellent occupation for the student 36
71 returning to the job market who needs on-the-job education. 48

| 1 | 2 | 3 | 4 | 5 | 6 | 7 | 8 | 9 | 10 | 11 | 12

E. PRACTICE: WORD ENDINGS

```
20 ly dimly daily apply lowly barely deeply unruly finally sly
21 ed cured moved tamed tried amused billed busted creamed fed
22 nt mount blunt front stunt absent rodent splint rampant ant
23 al canal total local equal plural rental verbal logical pal
```

POSTTEST.
Repeat the Pretest (C) and compare performance.

F. POSTTEST: COMMON LETTER COMBINATIONS

G. PROGRESSIVE PRACTICE: NUMBERS

Turn to the Progressive Practice: Numbers routine at the back of the book. Take six 30-second timed writings, starting at the point where you left off the last time.

H. Take two 1-minute timed writings. The last two digits of each number provide a cumulative word count for determining wam.

H. NUMBER PRACTICE

```
24 2201 2202 2203 2204 2205 2206 2207 2208 2209 2210 2211 2212
25 8813 8814 8815 8816 8817 8818 8819 8820 8821 8822 8823 8824
26 4725 4726 4727 4728 4729 4730 4731 4732 4733 4734 4735 4736
27 9237 9238 9239 9240 9241 9242 9243 9244 9245 9246 9247 9248
```

FORMATTING

CENTER—HORIZONTAL
Sh-F6

JUSTIFICATION—CENTER
Sh-F8, 1, 3, 2, F7

WordPerfect 6 users: See Student Guide, page 7.

PAGE BREAK
Ctrl-Enter

WordPerfect 6 users: See Student Guide, page 8.

I. WORDPERFECT: HORIZONTAL CENTERING

Horizontally centered text has equal spaces to the left and the right of it.

To center a single line of text, position the cursor at the left margin, press Sh-F6, key the line, then press Enter. To center several lines of text, position the cursor at the left margin, turn on Center Justification (Sh-F8, 1, 3, 2, F7), key the lines to be centered, then turn off Center Justification (Sh-F8, 1, 3, 1, F7).

To center an existing line of text, position the cursor at the beginning of the line, press Sh-F6, then press the down arrow key. To center several lines of existing text, block the text to be centered, press Sh-F6, then answer "yes" to the screen prompt [*Just: Center*]?.

J. WORDPERFECT: PAGE BREAK

When you reach the end of a page, WordPerfect inserts a soft page break (shown by a line of dashes). Soft page breaks will shift as copy is added or deleted.

A hard page break (shown by a line of equal signs) can be inserted wherever you want a new page to begin (for example, to start a centering activity on a new page).

To insert a hard page break, position the cursor where you want the new page to start, and press Ctrl-Enter. Hard page breaks will not shift as copy is deleted.

To delete a hard page break, position the cursor at the left margin immediately below the line of equal signs, and press Backspace.

Key each practice on a new page.

Correct your errors.

WordPerfect 6 users: See Student Guide, page 9.

Practice 1. Horizontally center each line.

```
Tennessee
North Carolina
Ohio
California
Florida
Rhode Island
```

Practice 2. Horizontally center each line.

```
Nashville
Raleigh
Columbus
Sacramento
Tallahassee
Providence
```

SKILLBUILDING

D. PACED PRACTICE

Turn to the Paced Practice routine at the back of the book. Take three 2-minute timed writings, starting at the point where you left off the last time.

PRETEST. Take a 1-minute timed writing; compute your speed and count errors.

E. PRETEST: ALTERNATE- AND ONE-HAND WORDS

A few men in Cascade and Reserve are eager to join the 12
antique-car race in Ohio. It is the only authentic race in 24
the world for an antique car. It is their goal to go there 36
in July. The fare to Mantau is better than average by air. 48
The men are free to go when their usual extra work is done. 60

| 1 | 2 | 3 | 4 | 5 | 6 | 7 | 8 | 9 | 10 | 11 | 12

PRACTICE.
Speed Emphasis: If you made no errors on the Pretest, key each line twice.
Accuracy Emphasis: If you made 1 or more errors on the Pretest, key each group of lines (as though it were a paragraph) twice.

F. PRACTICE: ALTERNATE-HAND WORDS

also angle field profit problem formal signs throw and form
goal usual signs eighty element social chair blend big make
town amend world emblem visible visual their blame cut fish
firm eight lapel enrich auditor island snaps laugh aid lake

G. PRACTICE: ONE-HAND WORDS

hook craft nippy eraser average adverb draws pupil pull joy
seed draft onion afraid catered breeze hilly junky deed red
milk exact plump limply million regret fewer based moon mop
gave crave knoll extras acreage better defer award upon far

POSTTEST. Repeat the Pretest (E) and compare performance.

H. POSTTEST: ALTERNATE- AND ONE-HAND WORDS

I. Take a 1-minute timed writing on the first paragraph to establish your base speed. Then take four 1-minute timed writings on the remaining paragraphs. As soon as you equal or exceed your base speed on one paragraph, advance to the next one.

I. SUSTAINED PRACTICE: NUMBERS

Each June teenagers across the country wrap up another 12
year of school. While some students elect to lounge around 24
the house all summer, most decide to trade in their rulers, 36
notebooks, and backpacks for aprons, paintbrushes, or mops. 48

Getting, or creating, a summer job is not an easy task 12
for most teenagers. They may be inexperienced or unsure of 24
what they can do. Those who persevere, however, benefit by 36
making anywhere from $500 to $2,500 in just 10 short weeks. 48

The kinds of jobs and the wages they pay are as varied 12
as the teenagers themselves. For example, typists can make 24
$2.25 to $3.50 per page, mowing a lawn runs about $5.25 per 36
hour, and walking a pet will fetch $2.25 to $3.25 per walk. 48

Working with kids is lucrative too. Baby-sitters earn 12
$2.50 to $4.50 an hour, while running a kid's party can net 24
$25 to $40. The teen with a car can make $4.25 to $5.25 an 36
hour as a driver or plan tours for $4.50 to $5.50 per hour. 48

| 1 | 2 | 3 | 4 | 5 | 6 | 7 | 8 | 9 | 10 | 11 | 12

DOCUMENT PROCESSING

Key each centering practice on a new page.

Turn on Justification-Center.

Correct your errors.

WordPerfect 6 users: See Student Guide, page 9.

Practice 3. Horizontally center each line.

```
Phi Chi Beta
Is Sponsoring a Career Fair
Friday, April 17, 19--
Room 419
Student Center Building
```

Practice 4. Horizontally center each line.

```
COMMUNITY BLOOD DRIVE
Saturday, April 18
Sponsored by the Rotary Club
Municipal Building
Denville, New Jersey
```

Practice 5. Horizontally center each line.

```
A Report by Josephine Baker on
the INVENTORY CONTROL ANALYSIS
Completed for Harrison Supply Company
Saturday, April 18, 19--
FALL RIVER, MASSACHUSETTS
```

Vertical Centering

Margins: 1 inch • Tab: 0.5 inch • Spacing: Single • Drills: 2 times • Format Guide: 1–3

Goals:
To key 30 wam/3'/5e; to center text vertically.

A. WARMUP

```
1      Liza bought two very exquisite jackets from a downtown  12
2 shop.  The prices were $739 and $681, which included a nice  24
3 discount of 20%.  Her total savings amounted to about $145.  36
  | 1 | 2 | 3 | 4 | 5 | 6 | 7 | 8 | 9 | 10 | 11 | 12
```

LANGUAGE ARTS

B. NUMBERS

B. Study the rules at the right. Then key lines 4–7, making any necessary changes.

Rule: Spell out numbers from 1 through 10; use figures for numbers above 10.
Exception: If two or more *related* numbers both below and above 10 are used in the same sentence, use figures for all numbers.

He bought two horses. He now has 12 horses and 2 dogs.

Rule: To express even millions or billions, use the following style: 10 million (not 10,000,000) and 3.6 billion (not 3,600,000,000).

The state's population was slightly over 7 million.

```
4 Our dealers sold thirty-four cars during the weekend sale.
5 The order was for seven desks, 12 tables, and 55 chairs.
6 The county's wheat production was about 2,000,000 bushels.
7 There were 3.4 billion shares traded during the period.
```

UNIT THIRTY-FOUR • INTEGRATED OFFICE PROJECT: LEGAL

166-170 LESSONS

Margins: 1 inch • Spacing: Single • Drills: 2 times • Format Guide: 145–149

Goals for Unit 34

Begin each day with approximately 15 minutes of skill-building, selecting activities from pages 410–413. In the remaining class time, complete as many production jobs from pages 414–421 as you can.

1. To improve accuracy and speed on alphabet and number keys.
2. To key 59 wam for 5 minutes with no more than 5 errors.
3. To develop proficiency in spelling commonly misspelled words.
4. To format legal documents—last will and testament, codicil, docket sheet, power of attorney, and employment contract.
5. To format letters with many varied features.
6. To format a boxed table with a braced heading.
7. To format handwritten and rough-draft memorandums.

A. WARMUP

```
1      Jazzy requested 14 items @ $37 and 6 items @ $159.  By  12
2 taking trade discounts of 20% and 18%, the total cost would  24
3 be approximately $950.  Please verify that order carefully.  36
  | 1 | 2 | 3 | 4 | 5 | 6 | 7 | 8 | 9 | 10 | 11 | 12
```

LANGUAGE ARTS

B. CAPITAL LETTERS

Study the rules at the right. Then key lines 4–7, making necessary changes.

Rule: Capitalize the names of days of the week, months, holidays, and religious days.

He hopes to be elected on the first Tuesday in November.

Rule: Do not capitalize the names of the seasons unless they are personified.

The sales conference will be held in the early spring.

```
4 There was a parade down Main Street on the fourth of July.
5 Special evening services were held on Ash Wednesday.
6 Competition in six Winter sports will be held in Ironwood.
7 The course will be offered during the spring term.
```

C. SPELLING

C. These words are among the 500 most frequently misspelled words in business correspondence.

```
8 estimate physical directly preliminary seminar days partial
9 assure applicants special stockholders contractors delivery
10 particular appointment inventories plan ayes exists inquiry
11 bureau compressor functions quarterly net daily regulations
12 statistics guaranteed chairman requests cooperative contact
```

SKILLBUILDING

C. 12-SECOND SPRINTS

C. Take three 12-second timed writings on each line. The scale shows your wam speed for a 12-second timed writing.

8 Sixty equals only five dozen, but we promised Jackie eight.
9 Vic quickly mixed frozen strawberries into the grape juice.
10 Jeff amazed the audience by quickly giving six new reports.
11 Five big jet planes zoomed quickly by the six steel towers.

| | | | 5 | | | |10| | | |15| | | |20| | | |25| | | |30| | | |35| | | |40| | | |45| | | |50| | | |55| | | |60

D. TECHNIQUE PRACTICE: TAB KEY

D. Clear all tabs. Set new tabs every 1.0 inch. Tab to begin the first column. Key lines 12–15 using the tab key to move from column to column.

12	soggy	check	vague	awake	elite	civic
13	refer	color	error	swish	extra	sense
14	youth	month	usual	knock	puppy	peach
15	joint	ninth	level	noble	local	might

E. SUSTAINED PRACTICE: SYLLABIC INTENSITY

E. Take a 1-minute timed writing on the first paragraph to establish your base speed. Then take several 1-minute timed writings on the remaining paragraphs. As soon as you equal or exceed your base speed on one paragraph, advance to the next one.

16 One should always attempt to maintain good health. As 12
17 the first step in keeping good health, one should avoid the 24
18 habit of smoking. Volumes have been written on this topic. 36

19 A second habit that will help maintain your health for 12
20 decades is consuming an appropriate amount of water, day in 24
21 and day out; most physicians recommend eight glasses a day. 36

22 Making exercise a habit is another important trait for 12
23 staying in good health. Most experts agree that spending a 24
24 few minutes a day in regular, vigorous exercise is helpful. 36

25 A final habit of importance is maintaining appropriate 12
26 body weight. The key to maintaining weight is developing a 24
27 positive eating pattern. Calculating calorie intake helps. 36

| 1 | 2 | 3 | 4 | 5 | 6 | 7 | 8 | 9 | 10 | 11 | 12

F. 3-MINUTE TIMED WRITING

F. Spacing: Double.
Take two 3-minute timed writings. Compute your speed and count errors.

Goal: 30 wam/3′/5e

Interlinear numbers in the paragraph show wam for a 3-minute timed writing.

```
                  1                  2                  3
28      Getting a job is something that you are quite likely    12
       4                  5                  6                  7
29 thinking about as you look to your future.  It is vital for  24
       8                  9                  10                 11
30 you to learn some appropriate skills to assist you in that   35
       12                 13                 14                 15
31 venture.  Keyboarding is an extremely important skill in     47
              16                 17
32 preparing for that first job.                                53
              18                 19                 20                 21
33      Of course, you must realize that your future boss is    64
           22                 23                 24                 25
34 looking for more than skills.  He or she wants you to have   76
            26                 27                 28                 29
35 the right kind of attitude and work ethic as you begin that  88
                30
36 first job.                                                   90
```

| 1 | 2 | 3 | 4 | 5 | 6 | 7 | 8 | 9 | 10 | 11 | 12

REPORT 101
ANNOUNCEMENT

Please prepare an announcement for our February 18 seminar. Please format it just like our previous announcement, except, of course, for updating the date. Everything else is the same.

The United States Wetlands Protection Agency

announces a one-day, free seminar on

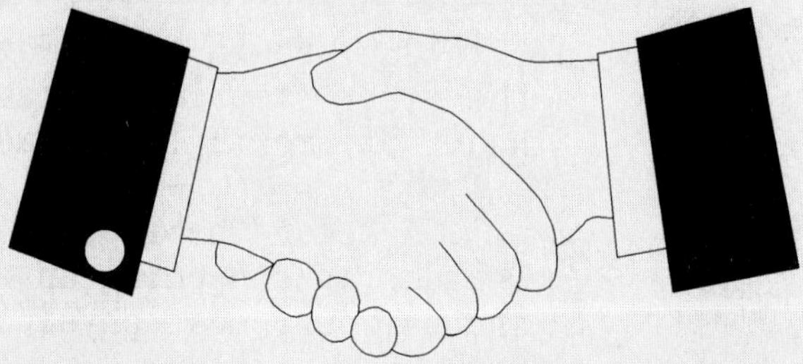

INDUSTRY/GOVERNMENT COOPERATION

November 3, 19--, 9 a.m.-3 p.m.
Hay Adams House, 800 16th Street, NW
Washington, D.C.

Learn how you can achieve your development objectives AND protect our environment.

Call 555-2090 to register.

FORMATTING

G. WORDPERFECT: VERTICAL CENTERING

CENTER PAGE
Sh-F8, 2, 1, Y, F7

WordPerfect 6 users: See Student Guide, page 9.

The concept of vertical centering is similar to horizontal centering. Text that is vertically centered has equal space above and below it. Documents should appear to be framed on all sides of the page with equal side margins and equal top and bottom margins.

To vertically center text (between the top and bottom margins) on a page, position the cursor at the top left of the page, then enter the appropriate commands (Sh-F8, 2, 1, Y, F7). Although text will not appear centered on the screen, it will be vertically centered when you print.

H. WORDPERFECT: VIEW DOCUMENT

VIEW DOCUMENT
Sh-F7, 6

WordPerfect 6 users: See Student Guide, page 11.

Using View Document, you can see what a document looks like and make any format changes before it is printed. To view a document, press Sh-F7, then enter 6. Select option 3 to see the full page. Press F7 to return to your document.

DOCUMENT PROCESSING

Spacing: Double

Practice 6. Center lines horizontally and vertically.

```
THE ELECTION RESULTS ARE:
Sharon Coleman, President
Victor Puglio, Vice President
Thomas Parciak, Treasurer
Megan Cull, Secretary
Joseph Browning, Historian
Karen Labadie, Public Relations
```

Practice 7. Center lines horizontally and vertically.

```
INTERNATIONAL ART SOCIETY
cordially invites you to attend
The Premier Showing of
ART FROM AROUND THE WORLD
Friday and Saturday, March 6–7
from 10 a.m. until 10 p.m.
CIVIC AUDITORIUM BUILDING
```

Horizontal Centering

Margins: 1 inch • Tab: 0.5 inch • Spacing: Single • Drills: 2 times • Format Guide: 3

Goals:
To improve speed and accuracy; to review vertical and horizontal centering.

A. WARMUP

```
     Invoice #1436-78 for $2,590 was billed incorrectly for   12
five (5) new quartz watches.  It was sent to Maxwell Jacobs   24
on Buckingham Boulevard in Parma, Ohio.  He was very upset.   36
| 1 | 2 | 3 | 4 | 5 | 6 | 7 | 8 | 9 | 10 | 11 | 12
```

LANGUAGE ARTS

B. PROOFREADING

B. Compare this paragraph with the Pretest (F) on the next page. Key a list of the errors, correcting the errors as you key.

```
     We were hopping to agree on the need to check the valu
of our assets.  No one should be oppossed to finding ansers
that would give us our worth.  Old records and legers will
be sorted, and we will unit in our effort to get the data.
```

REPORT 100
SCHEDULE PROPOSAL

WordPerfect 6 users: Set the column widths at 1.9″ and 4.1″.

We frequently have to prepare proposals to schedule speakers. Please format this proposal in two parallel columns with margins of 1″/2.9″ and 3.4″/7.5″.

SCHEDULE PROPOSAL FOR THE DIRECTOR

SPEECH:	"Assessing the Environmental Problems of America's Wetlands"
EVENT:	Annual Convention, Environmental Writer's Group of North America
WHEN/WHERE:	April 10, 19--, 1:30-2:30 p.m. 8:15-9:15 a.m, Gold Crest Hotel, 3601 Turtle Creek, Dallas, TX 75219 (Phone: 214-555-3601)
PARTICIPANTS:	350 environmental writers; 300 newspaper journalists (mostly from big-city newspapers), and 30 magazine journalists, and 20 book authors.
BACKGROUND:	The EWGNA has frequently given the administration negative press during this term, partly because of a preception that the President has not given the environment a high priority. Some hostile questions can be expected at the end of the speech., especially wetlands protection,
MEDIA COVERAGE:	The participants typically file stories with their home newspapers. In addition, 2 or 3 local Dallas/Fort Worth television stations would probably cover the session.
STAFF COORDINATORS:	Terry R. Hanson, your executive assistant (Extension 429), would prepare the briefing material; Janice Oliver, public information officer (Ext. 327), would draft the speech and handle meeting arrangements.
PROPOSED BY:	Janice Oliver, Public Information Office

MEMO 41

Please compose a memorandum from me to the director (memo ID M265). Tell Mr. Barzani that I'm enclosing a speaker request from Janice Oliver in PIO, and give the details. Janice needs his response by December 28.

SKILLBUILDING

C. DIAGNOSTIC PRACTICE: ALPHABET

Turn to the Diagnostic Practice: Alphabet routine at the back of this book. Take the Pretest and record your performance. Then, practice the drill lines for those reaches on which you made errors. Finally, repeat the Pretest and compare your performance.

D. Take two 1-minute timed writings. Try not to slow down for the capital letters.

D. TECHNIQUE PRACTICE: SHIFT KEY

```
     D. M. Mays from Clark, Ohio, and Dr. C. H. Miller from   12
Aurora, Utah, attended the Miss America Pageant in Atlantic   24
City, New Jersey.  They met Veronica B. Baxter from Georgia   36
and Pat D. Parr from Connecticut, who is Miss Congeniality.   48
| 1 | 2 | 3 | 4 | 5 | 6 | 7 | 8 | 9 | 10 | 11 | 12
```

E. Take two 1-minute timed writings. Focus on correct techniques and accuracy rather than speed.

E. SYMBOL PRACTICE

```
     Order #2310 was sent to Van & Blake for the following:   12
(1) 12 ribbons @ 9.75 each; (2) 8 boxes of envelopes @ 2.25   24
each; (3) 24 computer disks @ 1.75 each.  The amount of the   36
invoice came to $187.62, which included 6% for a sales tax.   48
| 1 | 2 | 3 | 4 | 5 | 6 | 7 | 8 | 9 | 10 | 11 | 12
```

PRETEST.
Take a 1-minute timed writing; compute your speed and count errors.

F. PRETEST: CLOSE REACHES

```
     We were hoping to agree on the need to check the value   12
of our assets.  No one should be opposed to finding answers   24
that would give us our worth.  Old records and ledgers will   36
be sorted, and we will unite in our effort to get the data.   48
| 1 | 2 | 3 | 4 | 5 | 6 | 7 | 8 | 9 | 10 | 11 | 12
```

PRACTICE.
Speed Emphasis: If you made 2 or fewer errors on the Pretest, key each line twice.
Accuracy Emphasis: If you made 3 or more errors, key each group of lines (as though it were a paragraph) twice.

G. PRACTICE: ADJACENT KEYS

```
as ashes cases class asset astute passes chased creased ask
op optic ropes grope snoop oppose copied proper trooper top
we weave tweed towed weigh wealth twenty fewest answers wet
rt worth alert party smart artist sorted charts turtles art
```

H. PRACTICE: CONSECUTIVE FINGERS

```
sw sweet swarm swing swift switch answer swampy swims swirl
un undue bunch stung begun united punish outrun untie funny
gr grand agree angry grade growth egress hungry group graph
ol older solid tools spool volume evolve uphold olive scold
```

POSTTEST.
Repeat the Pretest (F) and compare performance.

I. POSTTEST: CLOSE REACHES

FORMATTING

J. WORDPERFECT: BOLD

WP BOLD
F6

WordPerfect 6 users: See Student Guide, page 11.

Bold text prints darker than normal text. Use bold to highlight or display text. To bold text, press F6, key the text, then press F6 again (or the right arrow key) to turn off bold. To bold existing text, position the cursor under the first character to appear in bold, block the remaining text to appear in bold, then press F6.

TABLE 69

Mr. Barzani needs to incorporate in an upcoming report a table that was in last year's annual report. Please use WordPerfect's Table command to format this table as a boxed table. Use 0.75″ side margins, and center the table vertically and horizontally. Center and bold the column headings; then apply gray shading. Use full justification for the "Comments" column, and adjust the column widths as needed.

UNITED STATES WETLANDS POLLUTION INDICATORS

(Changes Since 1985)

Type of Pollution	**Change**	**Comments**
Suspended particulates	-22%	Essentially dust; a measure that concentrates on tiny particles thought to cause most respiratory ailments.
Sulfur dioxide	-17%	Considered to be the principal cause of acid rain.
Carbon monoxide	-25%	Similar to the familiar carbon dioxide. One measure that can help prevent carbon monoxide from forming is to add extra oxygen to gasoline.
Nitrogen dioxide	-8%	Contributes to acid rain and is one of the principal catalysts that causes ozone formation near ground level.
Ozone	-17%	Near ground level, ozone is toxic to plants and animals for reasons similar to the toxicity of carbon monoxide.
Lead	-93%	Most lead in the air comes from the burning of leaded gasoline in automobiles. Reductions in the use of leaded gasoline have resulted in substantial declines of lead in the air.

REPORT 99

From the Desk of
Terry Hanson

Mr. Barzani received a letter from a fifth-grade student asking him to explain what acid rain is.

Please go to our library and draft a 3- to 4-paragraph report on acid rain that Mr. Barzani can use to answer the student. Keep it simple -- with only a couple of footnotes.

Terry

DOCUMENT PROCESSING

Spacing: Double

Center each job vertically and horizontally on a new page.

Titles are keyed in bold, centered, and followed by a triple space. After the triple space, change to double spacing.

Remember to use the caps lock for lines keyed in all capitals.

Practice 8

ACCOUNTING CLUB INVITES YOU ↓3
Double spacing
to the 17th Annual Symposium
Wednesday, April 17, 19--
3:30-5:15 p.m.
Robin Hood Inn
SPEAKER: ALBERT ABOYOUN, C.P.A.

Practice 9

CAST IN ORDER OF APPEARANCE ↓3
Double Spacing
Sarah: Julia Primiano
Charlotte: Patricia Rocconi
Bennett: Joseph Youngquist
David: Peter Marinelli
Teresa: Paulette Dorner

Practice 10

RECEPTION REFRESHMENTS ↓3
double spacing
Cheese and crackers
Fresh vegetables with dip
Fresh fruit
Assorted pastries
Coffee, tea, soda, juices

Block Centering

Margins: 1 inch • Tab: 0.5 inch • Spacing: Single • Drills: 2 times • Format Guide: 3

Goals:
To key 30 wam/3′/5e; to block-center material.

A. WARMUP

```
     Order 14 items @ $95 and another 10 items @ $86.  When   12
you add the 7% sales tax, the total will be $2,343.30.  The   24
boxes should be sent to P. J. Quigley of Vanzant, Kentucky.   36
 | 1 | 2 | 3 | 4 | 5 | 6 | 7 | 8 | 9 | 10 | 11 | 12
```

LANGUAGE ARTS

WP

SPELLER
Ctrl-F2, 3

WordPerfect 6 users: See Student Guide, page 12.

B. WORDPERFECT: SPELLER

Proofreading and correcting errors are an essential part of document processing. The WordPerfect Speller enables you to quickly check documents for misspelled words.

To spell-check your document, press Ctrl-F2, then enter 3. The Speller compares the words in your document with words in its dictionary. When a word is not found, it is highlighted and a list of replacement words is displayed. To choose a word from the list, enter its letter.

If a highlighted word is correct, skip the word by entering 1 or 2. If the word is incorrect but no list is provided, enter 4 to edit the word. When the spell-check is complete, press any key.

Although the Speller will find misspelled words, it will not find omitted words or wrong words (such as “sing” for “sign” and “wiring” for “writing”). Therefore, you must still proofread every document carefully.

REPORT 98
TRANSPARENCY MASTERS

Do not key the numbers on the transparencies.

WordPerfect 5.1 users: Right Arrow: Ctrl-V, 6,27

WordPerfect 6 users: Right Arrow: Ctrl-W, 6,27

Mr. Barzani would like these four transparencies for his Las Vegas speech. We'll first prepare paper originals of the transparencies and then photocopy them onto transparency film.

As you can see from this sample transparency he used in another speech, Mr. Barzani likes the initials *WPA* and wide top and bottom divider lines to appear on each transparency. Using eye judgment, center the material attractively on the page, leaving wide margins all around and plenty of space between each item. Use a consistent format and right arrows for each subpoint.

W P A

REASONS FOR WETLANDS LOSS:

- Agriculture
- Commercial Development
- Residential Development
- Dumping

①

OUR DIMINISHING SWAMPS:
WHO CARES?

- Background
- Federal Efforts
- Success Stories
- Opportunities to Improve

②

BACKGROUND:

- Definition
- Diminishing Returns
- Benefits

③

FEDERAL EFFORTS:

- Clean Air Act and Amendments
- Wetlands Criteria
  - Soil Type
  - Flooding
  - Plant Growth

④

TURNING THE TIDE:

- Sawmill River Parkway
- Everglades National Park
- Arcata Wildlife Sanctuary

C. These words are among the 500 most frequently misspelled words in business correspondence.

Spell-check your lines when finished.

C. SPELLING

```
personnel information its procedures their committee system
receive employees which education services opportunity area
financial appropriate interest received production contract
important through necessary customer employee further there
property account approximately general control division our
```

SKILLBUILDING

D. Take two 1-minute timed writings. The last two digits of each number provide a cumulative word count for determining wam.

D. NUMBER PRACTICE

```
5601 3802 8203 1104 1505 2806 9207 4408 5009 6110 2811 4912
7813 4814 2915 9016 8317 5618 4419 1520 3321 8722 5623 4124
3925 2426 9627 5528 6829 1930 2831 4332 6633 7834 2135 9036
3337 5638 7439 8340 3941 2742 1043 6444 5945 1946 3447 6248
```

E. Take a 1-minute timed writing on the first paragraph to establish your base speed. Then take several 1-minute timed writings on the remaining paragraphs. As soon as you equal or exceed your base speed on one paragraph, advance to the next one.

E. SUSTAINED PRACTICE: NUMBERS

```
     In the past quarter, we have added the names of 78 new   12
clients to our list of customers.  This brings our total of   24
new clients for this entire past year to 249, a new record.   36

     Of the 249 new clients, 91 were being serviced by Pete   12
Thompson; 85 were being helped by Charlotte Anne Baine; and   24
73 of the new clients were being handled by Melanie Murphy.   36

     We got 24 clients in October from 107 contacts; during   12
November we gained 29 new clients through our 168 contacts;   24
in December we earned 35 new clients through some contacts.   36

     It was exciting to get 249 new clients this past year.   12
Next year we want 350 more; then, gains of 425 and 475 will   24
give us a total of 1,499 new clients in a four-year period.   36
| 1 | 2 | 3 | 4 | 5 | 6 | 7 | 8 | 9 | 10 | 11 | 12
```

F. Spacing: Double
Take two 3-minute timed writings. Compute your speed and count errors.

Goal: 30 wam/3′/5e

F. 3-MINUTE TIMED WRITING

```
     The first day on a new job can be quite exciting.  You   12
are looking forward to meeting the different people you may   24
be working with, as well as to finding out about the daily   36
tasks and duties you will handle.                             43
     It is very important that you approach that first day    54
in the right frame of mind.  Think carefully about the way    66
you dress.  Be friendly to all people you meet.  Show some    78
enthusiasm and zest for the tasks and duties you will have.   90
| 1 | 2 | 3 | 4 | 5 | 6 | 7 | 8 | 9 | 10 | 11 | 12
```

REPORT 97
(continued)

The Interior Department estimates that at our nation's founding, we had 250 million acres of wetlands in what is now the continental United States. Only 100 million acres now survive.

Why are we so determined to not only protect these 100 million acres but also increase them? To begin with, consider the wildlife implications. Many shorebirds and waterfowl make their homes in wetlands.

These areas also provide food and shelter for such mammals as mink, moose, and muskrats. And they provide some of the increasingly rare resting places for warblers, tanagers, and other migratory birds that spend winters in South America.

The wet areas are valuable ecologically in other ways as well. For example, they help control floods because they hold back water and provide space for rainwater to collect. They also help to purify water by slowing it down before it reaches our rivers and seas, giving time for the solids to sink and subjecting any organic pollutants to microbes in the mud.

TRANSP 3: FEDERAL EFFORTS

Because of the increasing recognition of the environmental importance of wetlands for wildlife and humankind, the Federal Clean Air Act prohibits any effort to fill in or build on a wetland or otherwise conduct business that would alter the landscape of a wetland without first obtaining a permit from the U.S. Corps of Engineers.

Our most recent legislation classifies a wetland as any area that has all three of these distinctive natural features:

WordPerfect 5.1 users:
Bullet: Ctrl-V, **

WordPerfect 6.0 users:
Bullet: Ctrl-W, 4,0

Quadruple-space before and after the bulleted list.

- Its soil is composed of mulch, peat, or other soils formed from constant soaking.
- The surface is flooded for more than 14 consecutive days during the growing season.
- More than half of all plants growing in the area are among the 7,000 species common to wetlands (such as red maples, ferns, and willows).

As I stated, anyone wishing to develop land that meets these three criteria must first secure permission from the U.S. Corps of Engineers. Failure to do so may result in heavy fines, which then are used to purchase additional wetlands to add to our wetland inventory.

TRANSP 4: TURNING THE TIDE

Working with industry, private owners, and state and local governments, we have been able to turn the tide, so to speak, so that we are no longer losing wetlands to development or agriculture. Specifically, the following three success stories each involve a different management and conservation strategy.

FORMATTING

G. WORDPERFECT: LEFT AND RIGHT MARGINS

WP

MARGINS—LEFT AND RIGHT
Sh-F8, 1, 7, *new margin settings,* F7

WordPerfect 6 users: See Student Guide, page 14.

WordPerfect's default side margins are 1 inch. To change margins, position the cursor where you want the new margins to begin, and enter the appropriate commands (Sh-F8, 1, 7, *margin settings,* F7). Margins can be changed as often as desired within a document.

CENTER
Sh-F6

H. BLOCK CENTERING

To horizontally center several lines as a group (or block) rather than individually:

1. Center (Sh-F6) and key the title in all caps; then triple-space.
2. Center and key the longest line.
3. Position the cursor under the first character of the centered line, and note its position on the status line.
4. Reset the left margin at this position.
5. Delete the longest line and the Center command.
6. Key all lines, beginning each one at the new left margin.

DOCUMENT PROCESSING

Spacing: Double
Center titles horizontally, then triple-space. Block-center the items. Center each activity vertically.

Practice 11

```
SKILLS NEEDED FOR WORK SUCCESS↓3

Communications
Interpersonal
Setting Priorities
Organization
Technical
Managing Time
Critical Thinking
```

Practice 12

BUSIEST U.S. AIRPORTS
Chicago O'Hare International
Dallas/Ft. Worth International
Los Angeles International
Atlanta International
New York (JFK) International
San Francisco International

Centering Review

Margins: 1 inch • Tab: 0.5 inch • Spacing: Single • Drills: 2 times • Format Guide: 5

Goals:
To improve speed and accuracy; to review horizontal, vertical, and block centering.

A. WARMUP

```
1      There were 567 people watching Joseph's performance as  12
2 Keith in "Always Heavy."  Zwigg's role as Baxter in "Unsung  24
3 Hero" was seen by 1,284.  There were 390 tickets requested.  36
  | 1 | 2 | 3 | 4 | 5 | 6 | 7 | 8 | 9 | 10 | 11 | 12
```

SKILLBUILDING

B. TECHNIQUE PRACTICE: CONCENTRATION

B. Key lines 4–7 inserting *you, your,* or *you're* in place of each dash.

```
4 -- quite correct when -- note that -- bill is wrong.
5 -- should balance -- checkbook with -- bank statement.
6 -- should buy -- three tickets to the show by next week.
7 -- correct in noting that -- thoughts make -- happy.
```

REPORT 97
SPEECH

Would you please prepare a draft of the first several pages of a speech that Mr. Barzani will be presenting in March. He likes his speeches double-spaced.

Please underline and capitalize each reference to a transparency, quadruple-space between paragraphs, and do not break a paragraph between two pages. Use 1.5″ side margins and standard report top margins and pagination. Here's a previous speech to use as a guide in formatting this new speech.

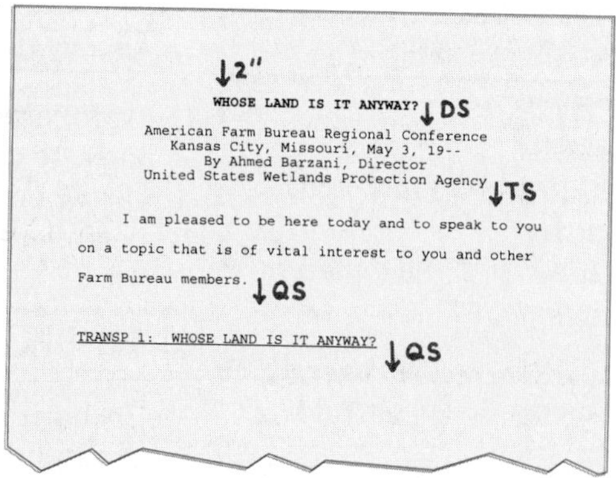
↓2″

WHOSE LAND IS IT ANYWAY? ↓DS

American Farm Bureau Regional Conference
Kansas City, Missouri, May 3, 19--
By Ahmed Barzani, Director
United States Wetlands Protection Agency ↓TS

I am pleased to be here today and to speak to you on a topic that is of vital interest to you and other Farm Bureau members. ↓QS

TRANSP 1: WHOSE LAND IS IT ANYWAY? ↓QS

OUR DIMINISHING SWAMPS: WHO CARES?

Federation of Small Businesses National Convention / Las Vegas, Nevada, March 13, 19— / By Ahmed Barzani, Director / United States Wetlands Protection Agency

Thank you, Mr. Beasley, for that nice introduction. On behalf of the 2,500 federal employees of the United States Wetlands Protection Agency, I am pleased to bring you greetings tonight and to spend a few moments talking to you on the topic "Our Diminishing Swamps: Who Cares?"

TRANSP 1: OUR DIMINISHING SWAMPS: WHO CARES?

First, I'd like to give you some background information on our wetlands—or what some of you might consider our swamps—and show why we consider them to be valuable resources. Then I'll discuss federal legislation and regulations that seek to protect these valuable resources and give a few examples of some of our early successes. Next, I'll provide an honest assessment of where we are now and the problems remaining for us to tackle in the coming years. Finally, I'll be happy to answer any questions you may have.

TRANSP 2: BACKGROUND

Wetlands are bogs, marshes, swamps, and other areas with a high proportion of water. Bogs are found primarily in the northern climates and contain large amounts of partially decayed plant life called peat. Marshes and swamps generally occur in warmer climates. Marshes are dominated by grasses, reeds, and other nonwoody plants, whereas swamps include many trees and shrubs.

It wasn't too long ago that wetlands were considered disease-harboring nuisances. These swamps were routinely filled in and built on, used as dumping grounds for car wrecks and construction debris, or drained and converted for agriculture.

(Continued on next page)

C. Use the caps lock to key a word or series of words in all caps. Reach to the caps lock with the A finger.

C. TECHNIQUE PRACTICE: CAPS LOCK

8 The new company, RINALDI SERVICES, is located in AKRON, OH.
9 MS. MARIDEL CUEVAS, 921 POTTERDAM AVENUE, won the election.
10 Did the WANT AD section of the STAR-LEDGER help her at all?
11 On the way home I saw both the YIELD and the CAUTION signs.

D. Key each sentence on a separate line.

D. TECHNIQUE PRACTICE: ENTER KEY

12 Who will be attending? How many will sing? Who is taller?
13 The file was black. The desk was brown. The rug was gray.
14 Jim ate. Jan joked. Joe danced. Vin laughed. Pat cried.
15 Jan ran two miles. Jill ran three miles. Sue did not run.

E. PROGRESSIVE PRACTICE: ALPHABET

Turn to the Progressive Practice: Alphabet routine at the back of the book. Take six 30-second timed writings, starting at the point where you left off the last time.

F. Key each line twice, striving for accuracy.

F. INFREQUENT-LETTER PRACTICE

J 16 Jill Jenkins adjusted her jogging jacket and jumped across.
K 17 Kaye Kane packed stacks of bricks in the back of the truck.
Q 18 Quentin Quamm was quite quiet but quickly requested equity.
X 19 Rex Truex got excited as he expertly fixed those six taxis.
Y 20 Bobby Yoder yearns for the day they say his story may play.
Z 21 Liza Zimmerman seized the prize of one dozen frozen pizzas.

G. Take a 1-minute timed writing on the first paragraph to establish your base speed. Then take several 1-minute timed writings on the remaining paragraphs. As soon as you equal or exceed your base speed on one paragraph, advance to the next one.

G. SUSTAINED PRACTICE: NUMBERS AND SYMBOLS

22 Our sales to Johnson & Clark showed an increase of 30% 12
23 over the same month last year. Last year we sold them $650 24
24 worth of merchandise in May; sales for this year were $845. 36

25 Shipment of items on Invoice #478 (radios, tape decks, 12
26 & stereos) was to be postponed to June 12. The delay would 24
27 mean that our cash flow for May would be reduced by $3,605. 36

28 Errors were found on some invoices. The errors (#336, 12
29 #391, and #402) resulted in a shortfall of revenue. Errors 24
30 this year have increased by 25%. We must correct this now! 36

31 The amount of $6,840 (owed by Ashe & Cull) covered all 12
32 these invoices: #242, #284, #311, & #385. Bentley & Sklar 24
33 made the last payment on the amount that was still owed us. 36

34 Two invoices had 24% discounts (#561 & #582). We gave 12
35 22% discounts on four invoices (#248, #283, #302, #347). A 24
36 total savings of $425 was realized from these six invoices. 36

| 1 | 2 | 3 | 4 | 5 | 6 | 7 | 8 | 9 | 10 | 11 | 12

MEMO 39

Please retrieve the memorandum form you created, immediately save it under another file name, and then format this rough-draft memorandum. Our office uses this format for corresponding with all governmental agencies.

Key the file reference (inserting your own initials); then use the down arrow (instead of the Enter key) to move to the subject line. After keying the inside address, move the cursor to the right of the Advance code to begin keying the body of the memo. Since this is your first day on the job, I've marked the job with various formatting guidelines.

The reference line includes the originator's initials, your initials, and a unique document ID number.

Capitalize only the first word and any proper nouns in a subject line.

The inside address is positioned so that it (and nothing else) shows through a window envelope.

Leave 3 blank lines before the closing lines.

The reference line in the heading takes the place of reference initials.

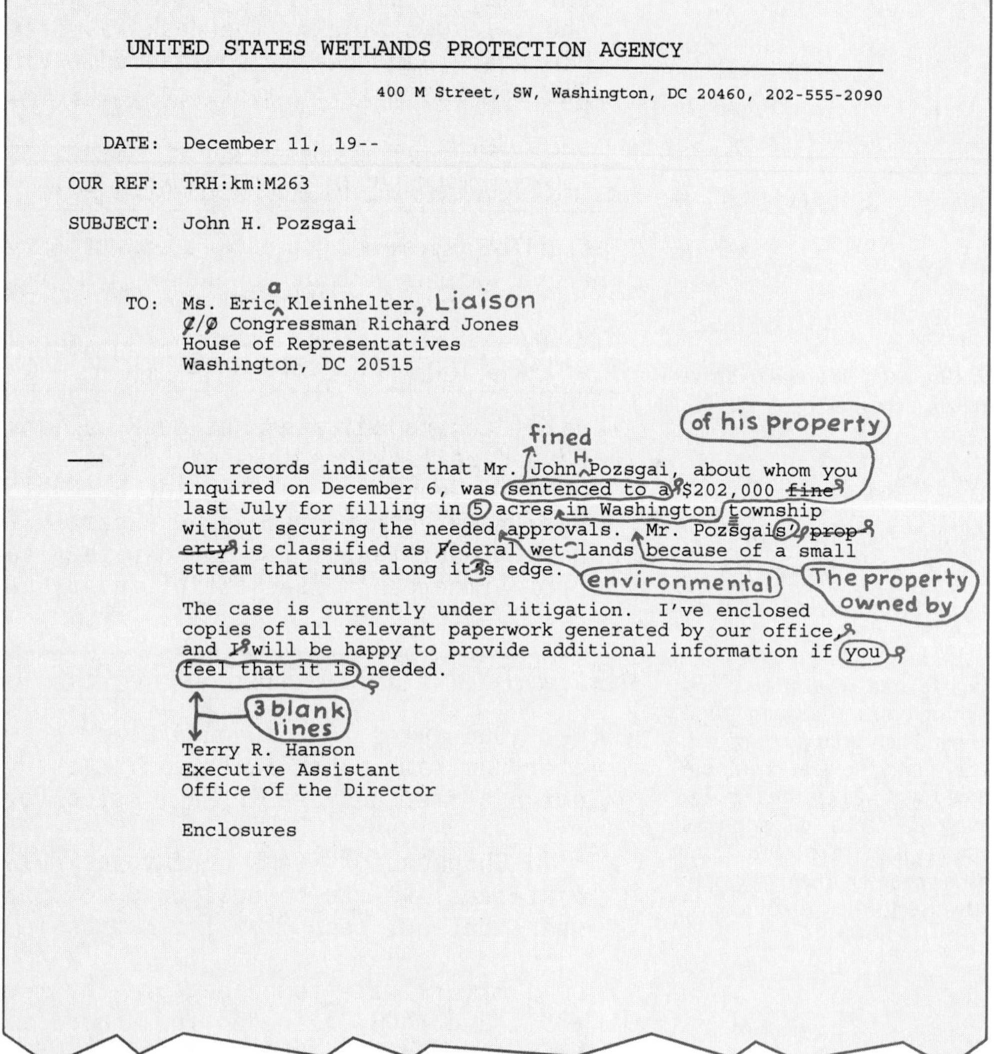

UNITED STATES WETLANDS PROTECTION AGENCY

400 M Street, SW, Washington, DC 20460, 202-555-2090

DATE: December 11, 19--

OUR REF: TRH:km:M263

SUBJECT: John H. Pozsgai

TO: Ms. Eric Kleinhelter, Liaison
c/o Congressman Richard Jones
House of Representatives
Washington, DC 20515

Our records indicate that Mr. John H. Pozsgai, about whom you inquired on December 6, was sentenced to a $202,000 fine last July for filling in 5 acres in Washington township without securing the needed approvals. Mr. Pozsgai's property is classified as Federal wet lands because of a small stream that runs along it's edge.

The case is currently under litigation. I've enclosed copies of all relevant paperwork generated by our office, and I will be happy to provide additional information if you feel that it is needed.

Terry R. Hanson
Executive Assistant
Office of the Director

Enclosures

MEMO 40

Please compose a memorandum from me to the director (you don't need to include his address) on the subject of Congressional correspondence.

Tell Mr. Barzani that I'm enclosing the letter of inquiry from Congressman Richard Jones and my reply, as well as all related backup material. Assure him that I feel this case will not generate any undue negative publicity and that he does not need to get involved personally; add that I'll keep him posted as I learn more.

DOCUMENT PROCESSING

Center each activity vertically on a new page.

Practice 13. Double-space. Center each line horizontally.

TRAINEES FOR CUSTOMER SERVICES↓3

Armando Lorenzini
Maria Rodriquez
Jane Mangiamelli
Matthew Wyble
Sharon Ostrowski
Paul Madison

Practice 14. Block-center and double-space the paragraph. Double-space after the paragraph, then block-center and key the list with single spacing.

The Smithville Community Club will be holding its annual Rummage Sale on Saturday, April 21, from 10 a.m. to 4 p.m. The sale will be on Route 206. Items for sale include:

Furniture
Toys
Household Appliances
Children's Clothing
Sporting Equipment
Garden Tools

Practice 15. Double-space. Center each line horizontally.

You are cordially invited to attend the
COMPUTER SOFTWARE DISPLAY
Sponsored by ASTD
Thursday, May 15, 19--, 4-7 p.m.
FAIRFIELD MOTOR INN
Fairfield, CT

Practice 16. Double-space. Block-center the list.

PROGRAMMING LANGUAGES
BASIC
Pascal
Fortran
COBOL
Logo
RPG

P. INTEGRATED OFFICE PROJECT

GOVERNMENT

Situation: Today is Monday, December 11, your first day as an assistant in the office of Ahmed Barzani, director of the United States Wetlands Protection Agency in Washington, D.C. Your supervisor is Terry Hanson, Mr. Barzani's executive assistant. Each government agency has its own style of formatting, which is often different from that used in industry, so pay special attention to the formatting details that are provided with each job.

FORM 27

Please prepare a memorandum form that we can use to format memorandums on plain paper. Here are the directions:

To format the letterhead:

1. Change the top margin to 0.5″, and advance the cursor to Ln = 0.6″.
2. Create a horizontal line, using all the default settings; then move the cursor to Ln = 0.5″.
3. Key the agency name in Large font; then return to normal font.
4. Press Enter 2 times, and key the address line flush right in Small font. Return to normal font. Press Enter once.
5. Format the marginal fold line by changing the left margin to 0.5″; then create a horizontal line with a horizontal position of left, a vertical position of 4″, and a length of 0.3″.

To format the memo heading:

1. Advance to Ln = 1.3″.
2. Clear all tabs, and set an absolute right tab at 1.3″ and a left tab at 1.5″.
3. Press Tab, key *DATE:*, and press Tab again. Then press Enter 2 times.
4. Press Tab, key *OUR REF:*, press Tab again, and then press Enter 2 times.
5. Press Tab, key *SUBJECT:*, press Tab again, and then press Enter 4 times.
6. Press Tab, key *TO:*, press Tab once more, and finally press Enter.
7. Change the left margin to 1.5″. Advance to Ln = 4″, and save the memorandum form.

The marginal fold line shows where to make the first fold for insertion into a window envelope. Begin the body of the memo immediately below this line (Ln = 4″).

UNITED STATES WETLANDS PROTECTION AGENCY

400 M Street, SW, Washington, DC 20460, 202-555-2090

DATE:

OUR REF:

SUBJECT:

TO:

UNIT SIX • CORRESPONDENCE

Business Letters

Margins: 1 inch • Tab: 0.5 inch • Spacing: Single • Drills: 2 times • Format Guide: 5

Goals:
To key 32 wam/3′/5e; to format business letters.

A. WARMUP

1   A 13 percent adjustment resulted in an invoice balance 12
2 of $568.49. In addition, two equal checks for $270 will be 24
3 needed as payment for six medium-sized gates for the court. 36

| 1 | 2 | 3 | 4 | 5 | 6 | 7 | 8 | 9 | 10 | 11 | 12

LANGUAGE ARTS

B. PROOFREADING

B. Compare this paragraph with the second paragraph of the letter on page 51. Key a list of the errors, correcting them as you key.

4 Please come to my office at our address, which is show in
5 the letter head above. It will be helpful if you have
6 figures relating to your volumn of copying as well as
7 information about size and color needs. After determining
8 your needs we can then visit our ajoining showroom so that
9 you can select the model that will be best for your.

SKILLBUILDING

C. TECHNIQUE PRACTICE: CONCENTRATION

C. Key line 10. Then key lines 11–13, reading the words from right to left.

10 When keying copy, always strive for complete concentration.
11 concentration. complete for strive always copy, keying When
12 errors. your on down cut may rate keying your in decrease A
13 errors. of number the reduce to rate reading your down Slow

D. 3-MINUTE TIMED WRITING

D. Spacing: Double
Take two 3-minute timed writings. Compute your speed and count errors.

Goal: 32 wam/3′/5e

14   Our legal system defines to a sizable degree what we 12
15 who work at a business can and cannot do. But it is also 23
16 true that the customs, mores, and values of our culture 34
17 play a part. The joining of these factors in the business 46
18 world can be thought of as business ethics. 55
19   Questions of ethical behaviors might be raised in this 67
20 example: A receptionist accepts gifts from a new client, 79
21 one whom she knows would like to have privileged access 90
22 to the manager. 92

| 1 | 2 | 3 | 4 | 5 | 6 | 7 | 8 | 9 | 10 | 11 | 12

N. Take three 30-second timed writings on each line as you concentrate on infrequently used letters.

N. ALPHABET REVIEW: INFREQUENT-LETTER PRACTICE

J Judge Jones justly joined Judge Jettig on a major judgment. 12
Q Quentin quietly and quickly quoted that eloquent quotation. 12
X Alex took extra time to execute the exercise on a tax exam. 12
Z Buzz was amazed at the size of the dozen zebras at the zoo. 12

| 1 | 2 | 3 | 4 | 5 | 6 | 7 | 8 | 9 | 10 | 11 | 12

O. Spacing: Double
Take two 5-minute timed writings. Compute your speed and count errors.

Goal: 58 wam/5′/5e

O. 5-MINUTE TIMED WRITING

Imagine that you have just graduated from college and 12
are starting a new job in human resources. What are the 23
major qualities you will need to perfect in order to become 35
successful in your position? While human resource experts 47
display a variety of skills, there are two competencies 58
that all must acquire: the ability to connect with their 70
clients and the knowledge to counsel them through the many 82
crises that occur on the job. 88

Connecting is the process of building relationships 99
with a wide range of customers in your business unit. When 111
connecting with an employee, there are several things to 122
keep in mind. A primary objective is determining the needs 134
and wants of that other person and working toward meeting 146
them. Remember to aim for an end result that is beneficial 158
to both parties. Another key factor is trying to establish 170
open communication. A person must feel he or she can trust 182
you in order to build a foundation for an open discussion. 194
Finally, there must be give-and-take. Both parties must be 206
given the chance to speak their minds. 214

If you wish to become a whiz in the field, you should 226
spend some time developing your counseling skills. When 237
counseling an employee, you are assisting somebody in pain 249
or in some type of crisis in his or her life. You must be 261
sure to respond empathically, stay objective, and refer 272
the employee to a more experienced professional when you 283
feel you may be in over your head. 290

| 1 | 2 | 3 | 4 | 5 | 6 | 7 | 8 | 9 | 10 | 11 | 12

E. BASIC PARTS OF A BUSINESS LETTER

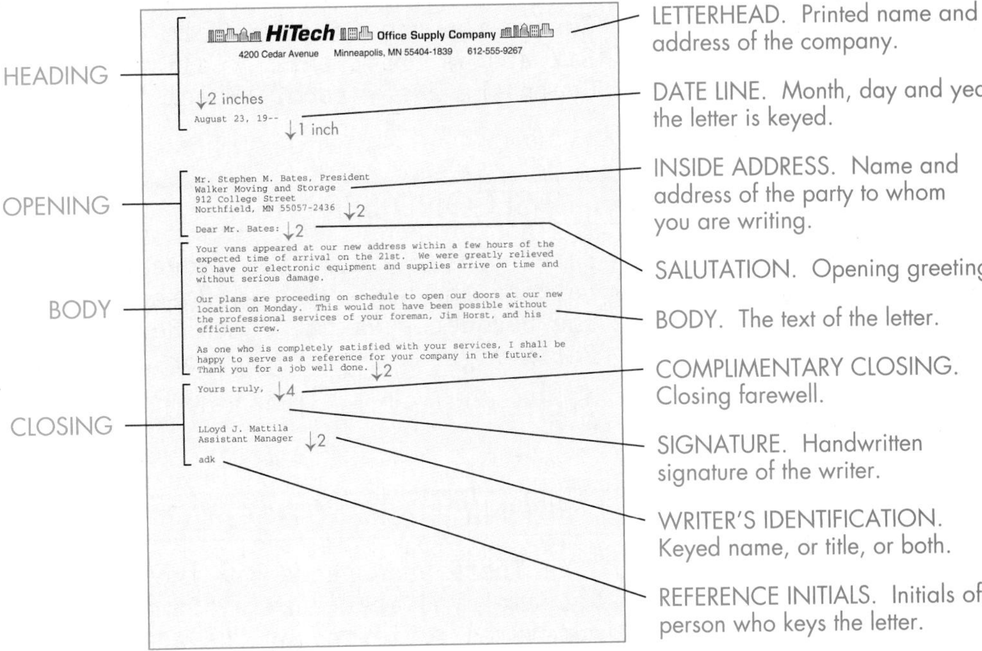

HiTech Office Supply Company
4200 Cedar Avenue Minneapolis, MN 55404-1839 612-555-9267
HEADING
↓2 inches
August 23, 19--
↓1 inch
OPENING
Mr. Stephen M. Bates, President
Walker Moving and Storage
912 College Street
Northfield, MN 55057-2436 ↓2
Dear Mr. Bates: ↓2
BODY
Your vans appeared at our new address within a few hours of the expected time of arrival on the 21st. We were greatly relieved to have our electronic equipment and supplies arrive on time and without serious damage.
Our plans are proceeding on schedule to open our doors at our new location on Monday. This would not have been possible without the professional services of your foreman, Jim Horst, and his efficient crew.
As one who is completely satisfied with your services, I shall be happy to serve as a reference for your company in the future. Thank you for a job well done. ↓2
CLOSING
Yours truly, ↓4
LLoyd J. Mattila
Assistant Manager ↓2
adk
LETTERHEAD. Printed name and address of the company.
DATE LINE. Month, day and year the letter is keyed.
INSIDE ADDRESS. Name and address of the party to whom you are writing.
SALUTATION. Opening greeting
BODY. The text of the letter.
COMPLIMENTARY CLOSING. Closing farewell.
SIGNATURE. Handwritten signature of the writer.
WRITER'S IDENTIFICATION. Keyed name, or title, or both.
REFERENCE INITIALS. Initials of person who keys the letter.

F. BUSINESS LETTERS IN BLOCK STYLE

1. Use 1-inch side margins for all letters.
2. Key all lines beginning at the left margin.
3. Key the date 2 inches from the top of the page.
4. Key the inside address 1 inch below the date.
5. Key the salutation a double space below the inside address. Double-space after the salutation.
6. Single-space the body of the letter, but double-space between paragraphs. Do not indent paragraphs.
7. Key the complimentary closing a double space below the body.
8. Key the writer's identification 4 lines below the complimentary closing.
9. Key your reference initials in lowercase letters with no periods a double space below the writer's identification.

WP

DATE INSERT
Date Text: Sh-F5, 1
Date Code: Sh-F5, 2

WordPerfect 6 users: See Student Guide, page 15.

G. WORDPERFECT: DATE INSERT

If the date on your computer is correct, use Date Insert to insert the date into your document. To insert the date as text, position the cursor where you want the date to appear and press Sh-F5. Then enter "1" to select Date Text.

If you want to insert the date and also have it change to the most current date each time you retrieve the document, enter "2" to select Date Code.

J. Key each sentence on a separate line.

J. TECHNIQUE PRACTICE: ENTER KEY

Call the nurse. Make the bed. Deliver the greeting cards.
Change the sheets. Get some water. Distribute the drinks.
Sit at the front desk. Call the doctor. Get all the food.
Go to the X-ray room. Wheel the patient. Talk to the man.

K. Take three 12-second timed writings on each line. The scale gives wam for a 12-second timed writing.

K. 12-SECOND SPRINTS

Bored junior executives request help from weekly magazines.
Seizing the wax buffers, Joseph quickly removed a big spot.
The banquet speaker, James Boxell, analyzed a few carvings.
Felix might hit your jackpot even with the bad quiz answer.

| | | | 5 | | | | 10 | | | | 15 | | | | 20 | | | | 25 | | | | 30 | | | | 35 | | | | 40 | | | | 45 | | | | 50 | | | | 55 | | | | 60

L. As you key this paragraph once, untangle the transpositions. This means that you must read ahead for understanding.

L. TECHNIQUE PRACTICE: CONCENTRATION

There been has a big increase in number the of workers who employed are today by temporary agencies. This is fact confirmed reviewing by the ads found in papers local and by checking managers with of some local personnel departments.

M. Take a 1-minute timed writing on the first paragraph to establish your base speed. Then take four 1-minute timed writings on the remaining paragraphs. As soon as you equal or exceed your base speed on one paragraph, advance to the next one.

M. SUSTAINED PRACTICE: ROUGH DRAFT

Various human responses are asymmetrical, meaning that 12
we ask more from one side of the body than the other. Each 24
time we wave, wink an eye, clap our hands, arch an eyebrow, 36
or cross our legs, we are favoring one side over the other. 48

Each such action we make demands a clear-cut desision, 12
usually unconscious and instantaneous, to start the process 24
of moving parts of the human body in two very different 36
directions. Indecision or doubt would create ineficiency. 48

All children go though a remarkably involved series of 12
stages in developping their preferred for the right or left 24
hand. As a child grows, she or he usualy favors the right 36
hand, than the left, then both equally for months at a time. 48

By the time most kids hit eight or seven years of age, 12
stability ocurrs and one hand is strongly, and permenantly, 24
domineent over the other. For some unknown reason, the vast 36
majority of people, nine out of ten, choose the right hand. 48

| 1 | 2 | 3 | 4 | 5 | 6 | 7 | 8 | 9 | 10 | 11 | 12

DOCUMENT PROCESSING

LETTER 1
BLOCK STYLE

Margins: 1 inch
Date: 2 inches

The date should begin at least 0.5 inch below the last line of the letterhead.

Standard punctuation: Colon after the salutation and comma after the complimentary closing.

Leave 1 space between the state and the ZIP Code.

Use word wrap for the paragraphs. Press Enter only at the end of each paragraph. Your lines may end differently from those shown here.

Spell-check your letter when you finish.

Key your own initials for the reference initials.

4200 Cedar Avenue Minneapolis, MN 55404-1839 612-555-9267

↓ 2 inches
August 24, 19-- ↓ 1 inch

Ms. Kathryn M. Amsbury
Home Care Nursing, P.C.
6807 Crestridge Drive
Hopkins, MN 55343-1921 ↓ 2

Dear Ms. Amsbury: ↓ 2

As you requested, I shall be happy to meet with you on August 30 at 10 a.m. to review your copy needs. I am confident that we have just the right copier for you.

Please come to my office at our new address, which is shown in the letterhead above. It will be helpful if you have some figures relating to your volume of copying as well as information about size and color needs. After determining your needs, we can then visit our adjoining showroom so that you can select the model that will be best for you.

HiTech is dedicated to providing up-to-date office services in the greater Twin Cities area. Our new, expanded facilities will help us achieve that goal. ↓ 2

Sincerely yours, ↓ 4

David G. Kramer
Customer Relations Associate ↓ 2

hsg

Business letter in block style with *(a)* all lines beginning at left margin and *(b)* standard punctuation.

SKILLBUILDING

D. PACED PRACTICE

Turn to the Paced Practice routine at the back of the book. Take three 2-minute timed writings, starting at the point where you left off the last time.

PRETEST. Take a 1-minute timed writing; compute your speed and count errors.

E. PRETEST: CLOSE REACHES

```
     Many employers often have policies that employees feel  12
do not treat everyone the same.  Employers try to avoid any  24
notion of partiality.  It is a myth to say that policies do  36
not work, for they do; policies help lift morale in offices  48
when an employee understands their usage and their results.  60
| 1 | 2 | 3 | 4 | 5 | 6 | 7 | 8 | 9 | 10 | 11 | 12
```

PRACTICE.

Speed Emphasis: If you made no errors on the Pretest, key each line twice.

Accuracy Emphasis: If you made 1 or more errors on the Pretest, key each group of lines (as though it were a paragraph) twice.

F. PRACTICE: ADJACENT KEYS

```
tr true treat straw stray strap tracer betray metric citric
po pool polar spoil epoch spoon policy podium spoken spoils
sa said sales salad essay usage salute salary sesame disarm
oi oils oiler toils hoist avoid voiced boiled poison rejoin
```

G. PRACTICE: CONSECUTIVE FINGERS

```
my army pygmy seamy foamy grimy myself mystic stormy shimmy
ft lift often after lefty nifty rafter sifted gifted deftly
ny many nymph phony loony peony canyon mutiny grainy botany
lo look locus color igloo aglow looses hollow ballot employ
```

POSTTEST. Repeat the Pretest (E) and compare performance.

H. POSTTEST: CLOSE REACHES

I. Take a 1-minute timed writing on the first paragraph to establish your base speed. Then take four 1-minute timed writings on the remaining paragraphs. As soon as you equal or exceed your base speed on one paragraph, advance to the next one.

I. SUSTAINED PRACTICE: CAPITALIZATION

```
     Almost one hundred years ago, state legislatures began  12
a practice still in existence today.  They started choosing  24
flowers and trees, fruits and vegetables, and animals great  36
and small to serve as official symbols of the fifty states.  48

     Washington was the first state to identify an official  12
symbol by designating the coast rhododendron as its flower.  24
Delaware, Maine, Montana, Nebraska, and Oklahoma soon chose  36
the trend and within a few years adopted their own flowers.  48

     Decades later, canines replaced flowers as the elected  12
symbol.  Maryland chose the Chesapeake Bay retriever as its  24
state dog, Pennsylvania named the Great Dane its own pooch,  36
and Louisiana selected the Louisiana Catahoula leopard dog.  48

     Symbols constantly change.  Currently, Connecticut has  12
the USS Nautilus as its state ship, and Colorado honors the  24
stegosaurus as its fossil.  The fiddle is now claimed to be  36
a state instrument by Oklahoma, Missouri, and South Dakota.  48
| 1 | 2 | 3 | 4 | 5 | 6 | 7 | 8 | 9 | 10 | 11 | 12
```

LETTER 2
BLOCK STYLE

Use Date Text for the date.

The slash marks in the inside address and closing lines indicate line breaks and should not be keyed.

Spell-check your letter when you finish.

(Current Date) / Ms. Judith A. Ghiardi / G & G Electrical, Inc. / 4614 12th Avenue, NW / Minneapolis, MN 55901-3281 / Dear Ms. Ghiardi:

Thank you for doing the electrical work at our new location as scheduled. A check for 80 percent of the contract amount is being sent to you by our Accounts Payable Department. The balance will be paid within 90 days if all of the work has been completed to our satisfaction.

The light intensity and quality are excellent throughout the building. However, there is one problem: Only half of the electrical outlets in the showroom have been installed.

Please arrange to have this work completed as soon as possible.

Yours truly, / Lloyd J. Mattila / Assistant Manager / *Your initials*

Business Letters

Margins: 1 inch • Tab: 0.5 inch • Spacing: Single • Drills: 2 times • Format Guide: 7

Goals:
To improve speed and accuracy; to format business letters.

A. WARMUP

```
1       Jan can't believe it!  The quick Wildcats won 29 of 34   12
2 games.  The loyal puck fans were excited and amazed as they   24
3 had scores of 6 to 1, 8 to 5, and 7 to 0 in the last games.   36
  | 1 | 2 | 3 | 4 | 5 | 6 | 7 | 8 | 9 | 10 | 11 | 12
```

SKILLBUILDING

PRETEST.
Take a 1-minute timed writing; compute your speed and count errors.

B. PRETEST: DISCRIMINATION PRACTICE

```
4       Few of you were as lucky as Bev was when she joined us   12
5 for golf.  She just dreaded the looks of the work crew when   24
6 she goofed.  But she neatly swung a club and aced the hole.   36
7 The team made her wait while they tried to match her score.   48
  | 1 | 2 | 3 | 4 | 5 | 6 | 7 | 8 | 9 | 10 | 11 | 12
```

PRACTICE.
Speed Emphasis: If you made 2 or fewer errors on the Pretest, key each line twice.
Accuracy Emphasis: If you made 3 or more errors, key each group of lines (as though it were a paragraph) twice.

C. PRACTICE: LEFT HAND

```
8  vbv verb bevy vibes bevel brave above verbal bovine behaves
9  wew west weep threw wedge weave fewer weight sewing dewdrop
10 ded deed seed bride guide dealt cried secede parted precede
11 fgf gulf gift fight fudge fugue flags flight golfer feigned
```

D. PRACTICE: RIGHT HAND

```
12 klk kiln lake knoll lanky locks liken kettle kindle knuckle
13 uyu buys your usury unity youth buoys unruly untidy younger
14 oio coin lion oiled foils foist prior oilcan iodine iodized
15 jhj jury huge enjoy three judge habit adjust slight jasmine
```

POSTTEST.
Repeat the Pretest (B) and compare performance.

E. POSTTEST: DISCRIMINATION PRACTICE

UNIT THIRTY-THREE • INTEGRATED OFFICE PROJECT: GOVERNMENT

LESSONS 161-165

Margins: 1 inch • Spacing: Single • Drills: 2 times • Format Guide: 139–145

Goals for Unit 33

1. To improve accuracy and speed on alphabet and number keys.
2. To key 58 wam for 5 minutes with no more than 5 errors.
3. To improve proofreading skills when reviewing formatted work.
4. To use desktop publishing features in formatting a variety of documents.
5. To format a variety of government documents—a speech, correspondence, transparency masters, a schedule proposal, a table, a report, and an announcement.

Begin each day with approximately 15 minutes of skillbuilding, selecting activities from pages 398–401. In the remaining class time, complete as many production jobs from pages 402–409 as you can.

A. WARMUP

```
1      Rex was quite pleased with his travel plans.  The trip   12
2 to Bozeman was on Flight #578 on January 30.  The return is   24
3 on February 12 on Flight #64.  The ticket will cost $1,090.   36
  | 1 | 2 | 3 | 4 | 5 | 6 | 7 | 8 | 9 | 10 | 11 | 12
```

LANGUAGE ARTS

B. GRAMMAR

Study the rules at the right. Then key lines 4–7, making necessary changes.

Rule: Use a singular pronoun with a singular antecedent (the word for which the pronoun stands) and a plural pronoun with a plural antecedent.

Either Susan or Valerie will bring her operations manual.

Rule: Use comparative adjectives and adverbs (*er, more,* and *less*) in referring to two persons, places, or things; use superlative adjectives and adverbs (*est, most,* and *least*) in referring to more than two.

That printer is the fastest of the three models we used.

```
4 Neither Juan nor Bob will complete their term of office.
5 Everybody must be able to do their share of the work.
6 Which of the two economists is the most conservative?
7 Ngai Chee is the most accurate of the three new employees.
```

C. PROOFREADING

C. Compare this paragraph with the third paragraph of the 5-minute timed writing on page 401. Key a list of the words that contain errors, correcting the errors as you key.

```
8      If you wish to become a whiz in the feild, you should
9  spend some time developeing your counseling skills.  When
10 counseling an employee, you are assisting some body in pain
11 or in some type of crises in his or her life.  You mast be
12 sure to respond empathically, stay objective, and refer
13 the employer to a more experienced profesional when you
14 feel you may be in over you head.
```

F. Take three 1-minute timed writings. Key these opening lines as many times as you can. Triple-space between each group.

F. TECHNIQUE PRACTICE: OPENING LINES

```
(Current Date)↓1 inch

Mr. Peter J. Phillips
Anoka Abstract & Title Co.
3104 137th Avenue, NW
Anoka, MN 55303↓2

Dear Mr. Phillips:
```

FORMATTING

G. ENCLOSURE NOTATION

To indicate that an item is enclosed with a letter, key the word *Enclosure* a single space below the reference initials.

Example: mcs
Enclosure

WP

MARGINS—TOP AND BOTTOM
Sh-F8, 2, 5, *position,* Enter, F7

WordPerfect 6 users: See Student Guide, page 16.

H. WORDPERFECT: TOP AND BOTTOM MARGINS

WordPerfect has default top and bottom margins of 1 inch. To leave a larger top margin on a single page, press Enter to space down to the correct starting line.

To change the top or bottom margin on all pages, position the cursor at the top left margin of the first page and enter the appropriate commands (Sh-F8, 2, 5, *position,* F7).

DOCUMENT PROCESSING

LETTER 3
BLOCK STYLE

Date: 2 inches

(Current Date) / Mr. Chad P. Treml / Vice President / Treml & Associates, Inc. / 12438 Lake Street East / St. Paul, MN 55117 / Dear Mr. Treml:

Miss Sue Mills has informed me that you called yesterday concerning your office needs. Three lines of modular furniture components are described in the enclosed brochure.

May I suggest an alternative to your visiting our showroom at this time. I would first like to visit the fourth-floor office areas that your firm occupies in order to discuss requirements with both you and your staff.

It is my understanding that you will be out of the office until next Thursday. I shall call on Friday of next week after you return from your trip to arrange for my visit.

Sincerely yours, / David G. Kramer / Customer Relations Associate / *(Your Initials)* / Enclosure

LETTER 4
BLOCK STYLE

Date: 2 inches

(Current Date) / Mrs. Jennifer Ann Yu / Branch Manager / Oriental Imports / 3960 Lyndale Avenue North / Minneapolis, MN 55412-6745 / Dear Mrs. Yu:

We at HiTech wish to thank you for your letter of appreciation for the recent furniture installation. We make every effort to complete projects on schedule and with full customer satisfaction.

We look forward to continuing to provide you with your office supplies. Also, if you have other furniture or equipment needs, please let us know.

Our long business relationship with you is valued very much.

Yours truly, / Lloyd J. Mattila / Assistant Manager / *(Your Initials)*

PART

9

SKILLBUILDING

Integrated Office Projects: Government, Legal, and Medical

OBJECTIVES

KEYBOARDING

To key 60 wam on a 5-minute timed writing with no more than 5 errors.

LANGUAGE ARTS

To improve language arts skills, including the correct use of punctuation marks, capitalization, numbers, abbreviations, grammar, and spelling.

To proofread and correct errors.

WORD PROCESSING

To use previously learned WordPerfect commands to format various document processing assignments.

DOCUMENT PROCESSING

To apply high-level formatting skills while completing integrated office projects in the fields of government, law, and medicine.

To format personal-business and business letters in block and modified-block style with subject lines, a company name, and a postscript.

To format tables using the Table feature.

To format a newsletter, purchase order, and advertisement using desktop publishing.

Ruttle Graphics, Inc./Maria Paraskevas

LETTER 5
BLOCK STYLE

Date: 2 inches

(Current Date) / Mr. Michael P. DeCamp / DeCamp Tax Services / 9483 Osseo Avenue South / St. Cloud, MN 56301-4732 / Dear Mr. DeCamp:

Retrieve Letter 4 and make the following changes: (1) Change the reference in the first sentence from *furniture* to *equipment,* and (2) change the first sentence of the second paragraph to read as follows: *I personally would like to discuss with you how we can provide you with office supplies in the future; I shall contact you soon.*

LESSON 28 Business Letters

Margins: 1 inch • Tab: 0.5 inch • Spacing: Single • Drills: 2 times • Format Guide: 7

Goals:
To key 32 wam/3'/5e; to format business letters.

A. WARMUP

```
1      Gravitz & Jacoby, Inc., has equipped 26 trucks with my   12
2 safety devices.  They plan to equip the remainder (15) next   24
3 week at their new warehouse located at 3970 East 48 Street.   36
  | 1 | 2 | 3 | 4 | 5 | 6 | 7 | 8 | 9 | 10 | 11 | 12
```

LANGUAGE ARTS

B. TITLES IN BUSINESS CORRESPONDENCE

Courtesy titles always precede a person's name in the inside address of a letter; for example, *Mr., Mrs., Ms.,* or *Dr.* In the closing lines, however, a man's name is not preceded by a courtesy title; a woman should include a courtesy title in either her keyed name or her signature.

A person's title may be keyed on the line with the name (preceded by a comma) or on a separate line.

INSIDE ADDRESS

Ms. Rose E. Nebel, Owner
Nebel Financial Services

Dr. Prayad Chayapruks
Executive Director
Foye Memorial Hospital

Mr. Craig R. Weiger
Manager, Dahlke Oil Co.

CLOSING LINES

Sincerely yours,

Mildred D. King

Miss Mildred D. King
Adjunct Instructor

Cordially,

(Ms.) Evelyn Marketto

Evelyn Marketto
Senior Programmer Analyst

SKILLBUILDING

C. PROGRESSIVE PRACTICE: ALPHABET

Turn to the Progressive Practice: Alphabet routine at the back of the book. Take six 30-second timed writings, starting at the point where you left off the last time.

D. 12-SECOND SPRINTS

D. Take three 12-second timed writings on each line. The scale shows your wam speed for a 12-second timed writing.

```
J 4 Judy joined a jolly group and ate jelly with Jan and Jamie.
Q 5 Queens quietly acquired quite large quails near the quarry.
Z 6 Zeke zigzagged past four dozen dozing zebras near Zanzibar.
    | | | |5| | | |10| | | |15| | | |20| | | |25| | | |30| | | |35| | | |40| | | |45| | | |50| | | |55| | | |60
```

TEST 8-D
TABLE 68
RULED TABLE

Spacing: Double

ANNUAL SPRING SALE PRICES

March 21, 19--

Item	Stock Number	Quantity	Sale Price
Guest Armchair	WFC-113	20	$164.50
Compact Kitchen	WFA-23	5	699.50
Service Cart	WES-3	31	56.50
Visible Card File	WEF-7	18	675.25
Swivel Chair	WFE-101	6	106.00
Conference Table	WFT-21	3	299.00
Oak CRT Stand	WED-102	26	71.95
Typewriter Stand	WET-1	9	46.60

TEST 8-E
MEMO 38
MEMO REPORT

Please prepare a memo report addressed to All Employees from Chun Lin Cheng, Manager. Use today's date and General Travel Policy as the subject.

The company has rewritten its travel policy for all employees. I am sure that you will see that it is more liberal in terms of employees covered. *(Now type the side heading "General Policy.")* Travel by company personnel should be in support of a specific program. Decisions regarding the use of travel funds will be made by the individual departments of the company. Travel regulations and reimbursement rates apply to company travel regardless of the source of funds. *(Paragraph)* When travel is funded by a grant or contract, the use of travel funds will be governed by whichever is most restrictive: grant, contract, or company policy. *(Now type the side heading "Eligibility.")* All individuals employed by the company or representing the company are eligible to travel. Exceptions must be approved in advance by the Accounting Department. *(Paragraph)* Copies of the new policy will be distributed as soon as they are printed. The Accounting Department is in the process of reviewing/revising the limitations and exceptions of the travel policy. Current procedures regarding domestic and foreign travel will remain in effect until all procedures have been reviewed.

E. Take three 1-minute timed writings. Key these closing lines as many times as you can. Triple-space between groups.

E. TECHNIQUE PRACTICE: CLOSING LINES

```
Sincerely yours,↓4



Ms. Adeline G. Tate-Winters
Executive Director↓2

(Your Initials)
Enclosure
```

F. Spacing: Double.
Take two 3-minute timed writings. Compute your speed and count errors.

Goal: 32 wam/3'/5e

F. 3-MINUTE TIMED WRITING

```
     We have all seen instances of misunderstandings in our   12
personal ties and in our work lives.  To a much greater       23
extent, we must be aware that such problems may arise when    35
we deal with those from foreign cultures.                     44
     The quiet manner of the people and the customs in a      55
country like Japan may be quite different from our way of     67
life.  Even when English is the language being used, lazy     78
speech patterns and slang may foul up the real message.       89
Body language also plays a part.                              96
| 1 | 2 | 3 | 4 | 5 | 6 | 7 | 8 | 9 | 10 | 11 | 12
```

DOCUMENT PROCESSING

LETTER 6
BLOCK STYLE

Date: 2 inches

When possible, use a person's name in the salutation. The correct form is the courtesy title and the last name (Dear Ms. Varney:). If no name is available, use a title (Dear Credit Manager:) or Ladies and Gentlemen:.

Some frequently used business closings are: *Sincerely, Sincerely yours, Yours truly,* and *Very truly yours.*

This letter from Marcia D. Turini / Accounting Department is to be dated August 28, 19—. Send the letter to Mr. Mark D. O'Brien / Office Manager / Wester Abstract & Title Co. / 2407 Mayo Park Drive, SE / Rochester, MN 55904 / (Supply an appropriate salutation and closing lines.)

line n

Please excuse the delay in replying to your letter of August 16. The delay was due to our company's move to our new location on August 21.

Your comments concerning Invoice 35847, dated August 11, are correct. The total amount, $279.58, should have been adjusted to reflect a 10 percent discount. We will credit your account in the amount of $27.96.

Thank you for calling this matter to our attention. We look forward to serving you even better in our new store.

TEST 8-B
LETTER 113
BLOCK STYLE WITH
OPEN PUNCTUATION

Bonnie Jean Denslow, Deputy Director, needs a letter formatted with July 11, 19—, as the date. The letter is to go to Mr. William R. Bucholz, Curator, at the Smithsonian Institution at 1000 Jefferson Drive, SW, in Washington, DC 20560. Use Re: Cabin Frame Design as a subject line, and supply an appropriate closing.

The current model of the 780 Series, manufactured by Midwest, has been designed to break into three sections in some types of crashes. In the most recent crash of a 780, all passengers survived because of the structural design of the cabin. The cabin broke before and after the wing, leaving three sections by which passengers escaped before the plane ignited.

As you requested, I am enclosing a copy of the cabin blueprint for the 780 Series. I believe this blueprint will assist you in developing your new Air Safety Exhibit.

As the exhibit is developed and you use the information from the blueprint, please remember:

1. The 780 Series has had the best safety record of all planes built in the last ten years.

2. The cabin of the 780 Series has been recognized throughout the world for its functional design.

I am pleased to provide this information for your exhibit and look forward to visiting it next month.

TEST 8-C
REPORT 96
ITINERARY

PITTSBURGH ITINERARY #
Patricia Hunter #
October 17-19, 19-- (8)

<u>Monday, October 17</u>

Philadelphia/Pittsburgh . . . . National 368
Leave 7:20 a.m.; continental breakfast
\# Seat 7C; nonstop
FRNC Meeting . . . . Pittsburgh Hilton
Exective Session, 10 P.m., Ohio Room (u; a.)
Luncheon, FNRC Officers, 12:15 p.m.
FRNC general session, 1 p.m., Ballroom B (2; A)

<u>Tuesday, October 18</u>

Pittsburgh/Philadelphi . . . . National 462 (a)
Leave 8:40 p.m.; Seat 9C; nonstop (a)

NOTES

1. Louis Cally will meet you at the airport. (e; Pittsburgh)

2. A single room reservation has been made at the Pittsburgh Hilton (No. 625934).

LETTER 7
BLOCK STYLE

Date: 2 inches

Retrieve Letter 6 and make the following changes: Send the letter to Mr. John A. Kaznowski / Director of Purchasing / Conrad Department Store / 3514 70th Street East / Minneapolis, MN 55450-8269. Mr. Kaznowski's letter was dated August 17. The problem relates to Invoice 35091, dated August 9, in the amount of $478.62. The 10 percent discount amount is $47.86. Remember to change the salutation.

LETTER 8
BLOCK STYLE

Date: 2 inches

This letter is from Lloyd J. Mattila / Assistant Manager. Use today's date, and send the letter to Ms. Erica L. Yoder, Manager / New Image Salon / 2342 Como Avenue / St. Paul, MN 55108 / (Supply an appropriate salutation and closing lines.)

First, please let me congratulate you on the rapid growth of your operation. I was pleased to learn of the success you have had by combining exercise and massage facilities with your cosmetology salon at one location.

Many new business ventures of your enterprise's size begin with a manual recordkeeping system. Your present volume, however, indicates that there is a definite need for a computerized system.

Rick Mariani, who is the director of our computer division, will be scheduling an appointment with you at your office within a few days. I am confident that the two of you will develop a plan that is just right.

Lesson 29 Personal Business Letters

Margins: 1 inch • Tab: 0.5 inch • Spacing: Single • Drills: 2 times • Format Guide: 9

Goals:
To improve speed and accuracy; to format personal-business letters.

A. WARMUP

```
     "Do you know Paul Moen?  He acquired a used 1992 Buick   12
for $13,475, which is $680 above the book value.  He enjoys   24
having an amazingly clean auto that is loaded with extras."   36
 | 1 | 2 | 3 | 4 | 5 | 6 | 7 | 8 | 9 | 10 | 11 | 12
```

Progress Test on Part 8

TEST 8-A
5-MINUTE TIMED WRITING

Spacing: Double

Business plays a major role today in the daily lives 12
of all of us, whether or not we are business employees. 23
All citizens must understand the role of business in our 34
society. It is part of all of our daily lives. Business 46
provides us with goods and services which are indispensable 58
for all citizens. We could not maintain our high standard 70
of living if we did not have business to manufacture the 81
various types of goods we buy and sell. If business did 93
not provide us with the important services of insurance and 105
banking, our life styles would certainly be quite different 117
than they are today. Business is interwoven in all aspects 129
of our society. 132

Businesses can be defined as commercial or industrial 143
enterprises. They are organizations made up of people who 155
work to provide us with the goods or services we need and 167
want. Most businesses are managed by administrative units, 179
which exert leadership to combine the resources, labor, and 191
capital needed to satisfy both our needs and our wants. A 203
corporation must justify its actions to the stockholders or 215
owners. Businesses are involved with lots of other groups, 227
too. These assorted groups include both workers and the 238
public as well as the various agencies of local, state, and 250
federal government, civic organizations, and others. It is 262
difficult to identify the different ways in which business 274
firms of all kinds and sizes can affect our daily lives. 285

| 1 | 2 | 3 | 4 | 5 | 6 | 7 | 8 | 9 | 10 | 11 | 12

LANGUAGE ARTS

B. ABBREVIATIONS

B. Study the rules at the right. Then key lines 4–7, making any necessary changes.

Rule: Always abbreviate *Mr., Mrs., Ms.,* and *Dr.* when they are used with personal names. In general, spell out all other titles used with personal names.

Ms. Mabel E. Jackson is our company's new treasurer.

Rule: Always abbreviate *Jr., Sr.,* and *Esq.* when they follow personal names. Do not use a comma before *Jr.* or *Sr.*

Lilly Ontiveros, Esq., will probably appeal the case. John Jones Jr. is here.

```
4 The surgical procedure was introduced by Doctor Eric Salo.
5 Mister and Mrs. Tom Berutti serve as our faculty sponsors.
6 Jason E. Phillips Jr. is meeting with Prof. Abrams.
7 Francis Howard Senior is a member of another committee.
```

C. COMPOSING

C. Answer each question with a single word.

8 What is your favorite pet?
9 What kind of music do you prefer listening to?
10 Have you read a novel during the past year?
11 What is one state you think has pretty scenery?
12 What is your favorite day of the week?
13 In what month is your birthday?
14 What is your favorite season of the year?
15 Have you ever had to give a speech?

D. SPELLING

D. These words are among the 500 most frequently misspelled words in business correspondence.

```
16 prior activities additional than faculty whether first with
17 subject material equipment receiving completed during basis
18 available please required decision established policy audit
19 section schedule installation insurance possible appreciate
20 benefits requirements business scheduled office immediately
```

SKILLBUILDING

E. PROGRESSIVE PRACTICE: NUMBERS

Turn to the Progressive Practice: Numbers routine at the back of the book. Take six 30-second timed writings, starting at the point where you left off the last time.

F. SYMBOL PRACTICE

F. Key lines 21–24 twice each. Then take two 1-minute timed writings on lines 25–28.

```
21 sws sw2s s2s s@s s2s@s s2@s frf fr4f f4f f$f f4f$f f4$f $44   12
22 lol lo9l l9l l(l l9l(l l9(l ded de3d d3d d#d d3d#d d3#d #33   24
23 ju7 ju7j j7j j&j j7j&j j7&j frf fr5f f5f f%f f5f%f f5%f 55%   36
24 ;p; ;p0; ;0; ;); ;0;); ;0); kik ki8k k8k k*k k8k*k k8*k ***   48

25 Dodd & Marcus collect our state's 6% sales tax ($6 for $100   12
26 in sales) at their #9 and #10 stores and then "send it on!"   24
27 Was he self-taught?  His 14 + 3 = 18 answer suggested this;   36
28 he also computed $1.80 for 1 1/2 dozen eggs @ $1 per dozen.   48
   | 1 | 2 | 3 | 4 | 5 | 6 | 7 | 8 | 9 | 10 | 11 | 12
```

REPORT 95
(Thumbnail Sketch)

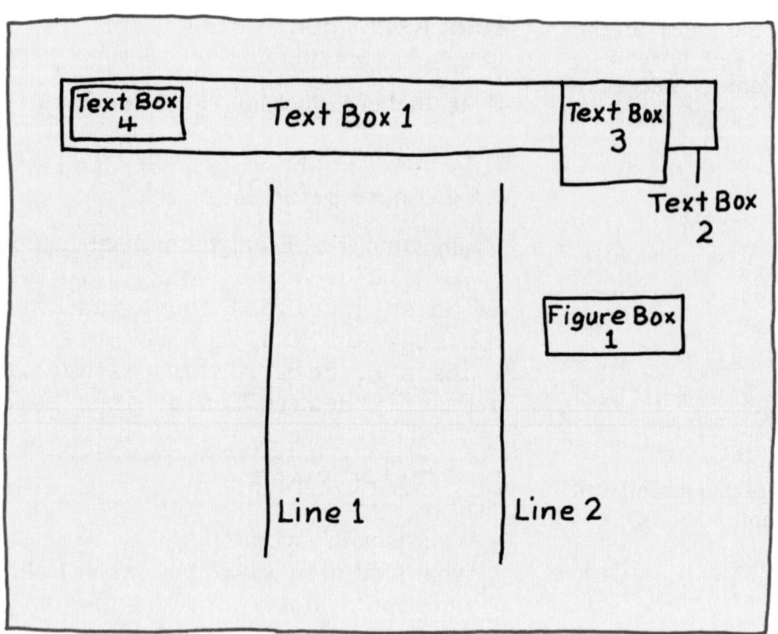

REPORT 95
(Illustrated)

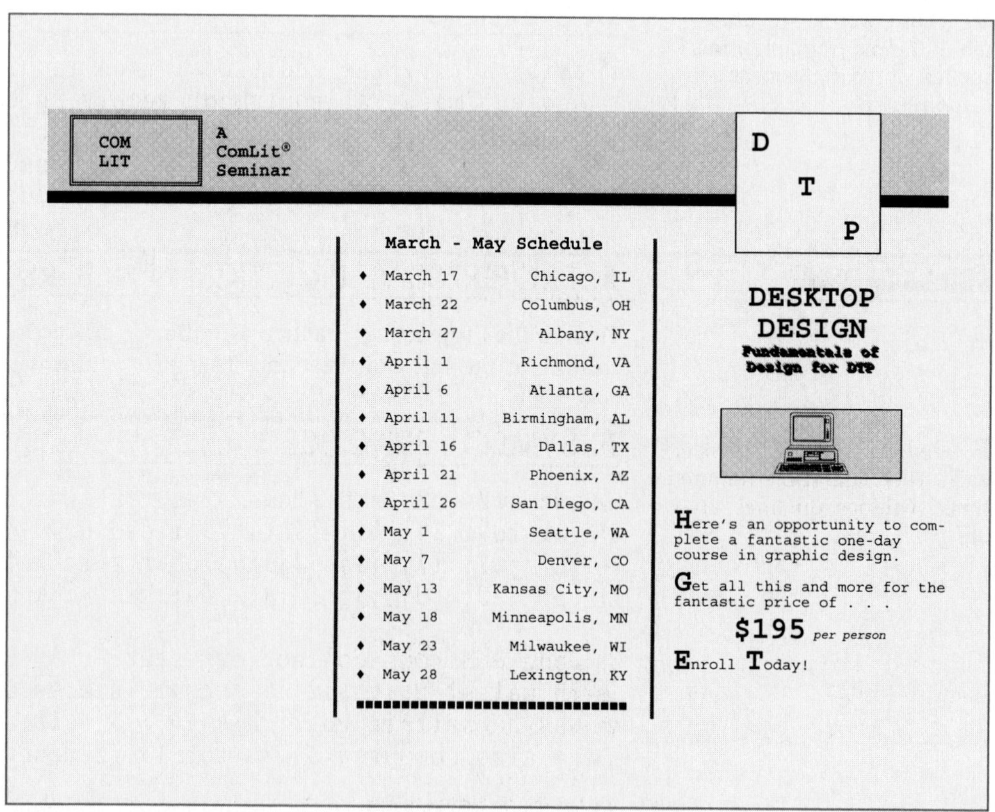

FORMATTING

G. PERSONAL-BUSINESS LETTERS

Personal-business letters are written to conduct one's personal business affairs. Personal-business letters are keyed on plain paper rather than letterhead. Therefore, the writer's return address must be included in the letter. Since the writer of the letter also prepares the letter, reference initials are not used.

In the following letter, the return address is keyed directly beneath the writer's name in the closing lines. Another acceptable format is to key the inside address before the date at the top of the page.

DOCUMENT PROCESSING

LETTER 9
PERSONAL-BUSINESS LETTER IN BLOCK STYLE

Date: 2 inches

Alternate style: Key the return address immediately above the date, starting 2 inches from the top of the page; for example,

1427 Laurel Drive
Albany, NY 12211
September 16, 19—

Reference initials are not used in letters you key for yourself.

↓ 2 inches
September 16, 19-- ↓ 1 inch

Mr. Clarence M. Hammar, Director
Family Social Services of Albany
4813 Dowling Road
Albany, NY 12205-4903

Dear Mr. Hammar:

The article in Sunday's issue of the Albany Times that told of the work of your agency impressed me very much. I was not aware of many of the community needs that your organization serves.

I am a second-year student at Franklin Business College. Although my college work and a part-time job keep me busy, I would like to spend some time each week as a volunteer with your agency.

Please let me know the steps I should take to get involved. I would particularly enjoy working with older people. However, I shall be happy to serve wherever you feel there is a need.

Sincerely, ↓ 4

(Miss) Tracy L. Ernsberger
1427 Laurel Drive
Albany, NY 12211

Personal-business letter in block style with *(a)* all lines beginning at left margin and *(b)* standard punctuation.

REPORT 95

BROCHURE, PAGE 2

Refer to the thumbnail sketch on page 393 for placement of the text and figure boxes.

Registered trademark symbol: Ctrl-V, 4,22

Diamond: Ctrl-V, 5,1

Square bullet: Ctrl-V, 4,2

WordPerfect 6 users: See Student Guide, p. 113.

Create the back page of Report 94, following these directions:

1. Change paper size to Standard—Wide and left, right, and bottom margins to 0.5″.
2. Set Text Box 1 options to no borders except an Extra Thick bottom border and 20% gray shading; then create the box:
   Anchor Type: Page
   Vertical Position: Top
   Horizontal Position: Margin, Left
   Size: 7.65″ wide × 1″ high
   Wrap Text: No
3. Key the text in Text Box 1 in Large, bold type. Tab 3 times and space twice before each line.
4. Create Text Box 2 with the same options as Text Box 1:
   Anchor Type: Page
   Vertical Position: Top
   Horizontal Position: Margin, Right
   Size: 0.75″ wide × 1″ high
   Wrap Text: No
5. Set Text Box 3 options to a single border on all sides and 0% gray shading; then create the box:
   Anchor Type: Page
   Vertical Position: Top
   Horizontal Position: 8.15″
   Size: 1.6″ wide × 1.5″ high
   Wrap Text: Yes
6. In Text Box 3, set line spacing for 1.4, and key the three letters in Extra Large, bold type. Key *D* at the margin, *T* at the center, and *P* flush right.
7. Set Text Box 4 options to a double border on all sides and 0% gray shading; then create the box:
   Anchor Type: Page
   Vertical Position: 1.1″
   Horizontal Position: 0.75″
   Size: 1.4″ wide × 0.75″ high
   Wrap Text: No
8. In Text Box 4, key the text in Large, bold type. Space once before keying each line.
9. Create the first vertical line:
   Horizontal Position: 3.75″
   Vertical Position: 2.35″
   Length of Line: 5.15″
   Width of Line: 0.04″
   Gray Shading: 80%
10. Create the second vertical line:
    Horizontal Position: 7.25″
    Vertical Position: 2.35″
    Length of Line: 5.15″
    Width of Line: 0.04″
    Gray Shading: 80%
11. Press Enter once, and advance to Ln = 2.33″.
12. Define and turn on three newspaper columns with these margins: 0.5″, 3.5″; 4.0″, 7.0″; 7.5″, 10.5″.
13. Set Figure Box 1 options to a single border on all sides and 20% gray shading; then create the box:
    Filename: PC-1.WPG
    Anchor Type: Page
    Vertical Position: 4″
    Horizontal Position: Column(s) 3, Center
    Size: 2″ wide × 0.75″ high
    Wrap Text: Yes
14. Leave Column 1 blank (insert a hard page break).
15. In Column 2, center and key *March - May Schedule* in Large, bold type. (Space once before and after the hyphen.) Then change to normal type.
16. Press Enter twice, and set line spacing to 1.83. Create the diamond, space twice, and key the dates. Key the cities flush right.
17. Set line spacing to 1, press Enter twice, and key a line of 30 square bullets. Insert a hard page break.
18. Press Enter 3 times, and center and key *DESKTOP* in Extra Large, bold type. Press Enter, and center and key *DESIGN*. Change to normal font.
19. Press Enter, add shadow, and center and key *Fundamentals of Design for DTP* in shadow, bold. Change to normal type, and press Enter 10 times.
20. Set a fixed line height of 0.167″ (the default for normal type).
21. Key *H* in Extra Large, bold type. Return to normal type, finish keying the paragraph, and press Enter twice.
22. Repeat Step 21 for the second paragraph.
23. Center and key *$195* in Extra Large, bold type and *per person* in Small, italic type; then press Enter twice.
24. Key the last two words with the first letters in Extra Large, bold type and the rest of each word in normal type.

LETTER 10
PERSONAL-BUSINESS LETTER IN BLOCK STYLE

Date: 2 inches

This personal-business letter is from Wallace G. Helfinstein, who lives at 948 Boisseau Avenue in Shreveport, LA 71103. Use today's date, and supply an appropriate salutation and closing lines. The letter is to be sent to Mr. Richard A. Alderton, Owner / The Garden Room Restaurant / 726 Bayou Drive / Shreveport, LA 71105.

Thanks to you and hundreds of other Shreveport citizens, the fall Special Olympics events were highly successful. Our planning committee is very appreciative of the ways in which you helped.

We particularly wish to thank you for the use of your conference room for our committee's meetings. And the committee members thoroughly enjoyed the refreshments that you provided. Thank you for your kindness.

The smiles on the faces of our special friends who participated in the games are the rewards we seek. As chairperson for the planning committee, however, I want to extend special thanks to you for your generous contributions.

LETTER 11
PERSONAL-BUSINESS LETTER IN BLOCK STYLE

Top margin: 2 inches

Retrieve Letter 10 and revise it as follows. Send the letter to Ms. Cynthia Spelgatti / 3526 Crofton Street / Shreveport, LA 71101. Use an appropriate salutation. Replace the second paragraph with the following: *We particularly wish to thank you for the manner in which you handled the details for the awards ceremony. You made it very clear that all participants were indeed winners. Thank you for your kindness.*

Letter Review

Margins: 1 inch • Tab: 0.5 inch • Spacing: Single • Drills: 2 times • Format Guide: 9

Goals:
To key 32 wam/3'/5e; to format business and personal-business letters.

A. WARMUP

```
     Hazel and/or Blake joined 5 others in 1980 to create a   12
quality firm.  After adding 6 or 7 people in 1993, they had   24
exactly 24 sales representatives; and it continued to grow.   36
 | 1 | 2 | 3 | 4 | 5 | 6 | 7 | 8 | 9 | 10 | 11 | 12
```

SKILLBUILDING

B. TECHNIQUE PRACTICE: CAPS LOCK

B. Use the caps lock to key a word or series of words in all caps.

```
RHONDA KORDICH was promoted on APRIL 1 to SENIOR SECRETARY.
The SOLD sign replaced the FOR SALE sign at 19 ELDER DRIVE.
The trip from LOUISVILLE to NASHVILLE was on INTERSTATE 65.
ADAMS-PAULIN, INC., is owned by Allen Adams and Hal Paulin.
The SPRING AUTO SHOW was held at LAKEVIEW ARENA on APRIL 8.
```

REPORT 94
(continued)

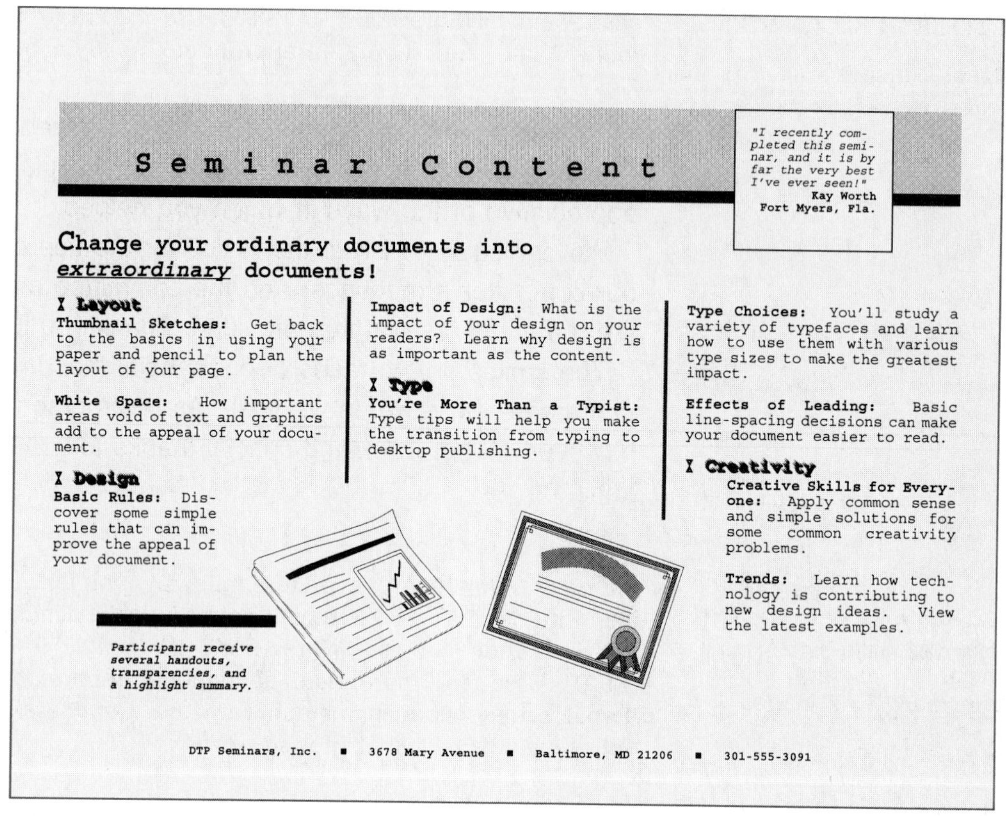

"I recently completed this seminar, and it is by far the very best I've ever seen!"
Kay Worth
Fort Myers, Fla.

Seminar Content

Change your ordinary documents into *extraordinary* documents!

Layout

Thumbnail Sketches: Get back to the basics in using your paper and pencil to plan the layout of your page.

White Space: How important areas void of text and graphics add to the appeal of your document.

Design

Basic Rules: Discover some simple rules that can improve the appeal of your document.

Impact of Design: What is the impact of your design on your readers? Learn why design is as important as the content.

Type

You're More Than a Typist: Type tips will help you make the transition from typing to desktop publishing.

Type Choices: You'll study a variety of typefaces and learn how to use them with various type sizes to make the greatest impact.

Effects of Leading: Basic line-spacing decisions can make your document easier to read.

Creativity

Creative Skills for Everyone: Apply common sense and simple solutions for some common creativity problems.

Trends: Learn how technology is contributing to new design ideas. View the latest examples.

Participants receive several handouts, transparencies, and a highlight summary.

DTP Seminars, Inc. ■ 3678 Mary Avenue ■ Baltimore, MD 21206 ■ 301-555-3091

Dual triangle: Ctrl-V, 5,32

Rotate the image 342 degrees, and scale it by pressing Page Down 3 times.

12. Add a vertical line as follows:
    Horizontal Position: 3.75″
    Vertical Position: 3.05″
    Length of Line: 2″
    Width of Line: 0.04″
    Gray Shading: 80%
13. Add a second vertical line as follows:
    Horizontal Position: 7.25″
    Vertical Position: 3.05″
    Length of Line: 2.35″
    Width of Line: 0.04″
    Gray Shading: 80%
14. On Ln = 2.33″, key the letter *C* in *Change* in Extra Large, bold type. Then switch to Very Large, bold type, and key the rest of the sentence. Press Enter twice.
15. Define and turn on three newspaper columns with the following margins: 0.5″, 3.5″; 4.0″, 7.0″; 7.5″, 10.5″. Then press Enter once, and turn on full justification.
16. Key the section headings (*Layout, Design, Type,* and *Creativity*) in Large, bold, shadowed type. First, create a dual triangle graphic, space once, and key the headings. Press Enter twice before all remaining section headings.
17. Key the remaining text in normal font, using bold for the lead-in headings (such as *Thumbnail Sketches:*).
18. After *document* at the bottom of Column 1, insert a hard page break. Begin the text in the next column on the same line as the beginning of the Column 1 text.
19. After *publishing* at the bottom of Column 2, insert a hard page break. Begin Column 3 on the same line as the beginning of the other two columns.

C. Spacing: Double. Take two 3-minute timed writings. Compute your speed and count errors.

Goal: 32 wam/3′/5e

C. 3-MINUTE TIMED WRITING

There are good reasons why a young office worker will 12
want to demonstrate that he or she uses time well. Some 23
cultures have quite different views; but in this country 35
one is expected to report to work on time, to be on time 46
for meetings, and to meet all deadlines. 54
In order to do these things, an organized plan for 65
daily action should be developed. Just as a pilot prepares 77
a flight plan, the efficient worker will start each day by 89
listing tasks in priority order. 96

| 1 | 2 | 3 | 4 | 5 | 6 | 7 | 8 | 9 | 10 | 11 | 12

FORMATTING

D. WORDPERFECT: FULL JUSTIFICATION

JUSTIFICATION—FULL: Sh-F8, 1, 3, 4, F7

WordPerfect 6 users: See Student Guide, page 17.

Full Justification is used to align text at both the left and right margins. The spaces between words are expanded or compressed as necessary to align the text.

To turn on Full Justification, position the cursor where you want Full Justification to begin and enter the appropriate commands (Sh-F8, 1, 3, 4, F7). Full Justification can be turned on or off at any point in a document.

DOCUMENT PROCESSING

LETTER 12
BLOCK STYLE

Date: 2 inches

Turn on Full Justification only for this letter. Compare the appearance of the printed letter with one using left justification.

Key this business letter for Vincent J. Robare / President. Use the current date, and send the letter to Ms. Catherine A. Cox, Manager / City-Wide Insurance Agency / 2810 Canyon View Drive East / Flagstaff, AZ 86001. Supply an appropriate salutation and complimentary closing.

Thank you for seeing me at your office last Thursday. You provided the guidance I needed in order to review our firm's present insurance coverages. I appreciate your taking time to explain to me the many new options that are available.

It seems that there are several weaknesses that must be corrected. Therefore, I would like to request that your agent, Dale Starr, meet with our senior accountant and me at my office within the next ten days. We would like to review our property, liability, and employee group health insurance policies.

There is also the likelihood that group life insurance coverage for our employees will be added within the next six months. We are in the midst of contract negotiations, and this new coverage will be a topic for discussion in the near future. Perhaps Dale can present some basic plans to us that incorporate shared premium payments by both the employer and employees.

I appreciate your seeing me on such short notice last week. As a result of our discussion, I am confident that appropriate adjustments in our coverages can be made within a short period of time. The manner in which your agency continues to satisfy our insurance needs is sincerely appreciated.

REPORT 94
BROCHURE

Square bullet: Ctrl-V, 4,2

WordPerfect 6 users: See Student Guide, p. 110.

Create all the graphic elements for the front side of the brochure shown on page 391; then add the text. Refer to the thumbnail sketch below for placement of the graphics.

1. Change paper size to Standard—Wide and left, right, and bottom margins to 0.5″.
2. Create this footer, centered in Small, bold type: *DTP Seminars, Inc.* ▪ *3678 Mary Avenue* ▪ *Baltimore, MD 21206* ▪ *301-555-3091.* Space 3 times before and after the bullets.
3. Set Text Box 1 options to no borders except an Extra Thick bottom border and 20% gray shading; then create the box:
   Anchor Type: Page
   Vertical Position: Top
   Horizontal Position: Margin, Left
   Size: 7.5″ wide × 1″ high
   Wrap Text: Yes
4. Key the text in Text Box 1 in Extra Large, bold type, leaving 1 space between letters and 3 between words on Ln = 0.333″.
5. Create Text Box 2 with the same options as Text Box 1:
   Anchor Type: Page
   Vertical Position: Top
   Horizontal Position: Margin, Right
   Size: 0.75″ wide × 1″ high
   Wrap Text: Yes
6. Set Text Box 3 options to a single border on all sides and 0% gray shading; then create the box:
   Anchor Type: Page
   Vertical Position: Top
   Horizontal Position: 8″
   Size: 1.75″ wide × 1.5″ high
   Wrap Text: Yes
7. Key the Text Box 3 quotation on Ln = 0″ in Small, italic type, left–justified. Key the name and location in Small, bold type flush right.
8. Set Text Box 4 options to no borders except an Extra Thick top border and 0% gray shading; then create the box:
   Anchor Type: Page
   Vertical Position: 6.3″
   Horizontal Position: 1″
   Size: 2″ wide × 1″ high
   Wrap Text: Yes
9. Key the Text Box 4 text in Small, bold, italic type, left–justified.
10. Set Figure Box 1 options to no borders and 0% gray shading; then create the box:
    Filename: NEWS.WPG
    Anchor Type: Page
    Vertical Position: 5.1″
    Horizontal Position: 2.5″
    Size: 2.8″ wide × 2″ high
    Wrap Text: Yes
11. Create Figure Box 2:
    Filename: CERTIF.WPG
    Anchor Type: Page
    Vertical Position: 5.1″
    Horizontal Position: 5″
    Size: 2.8″ wide × 2″ high
    Wrap Text: Yes

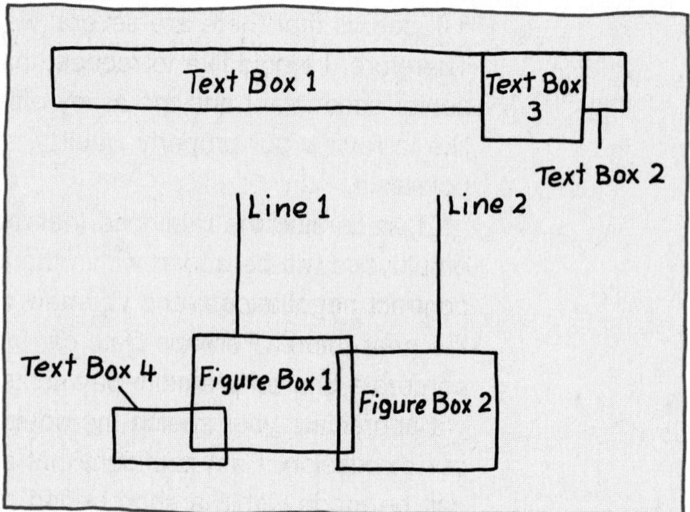

(Continued on next page)

LETTER 13
BLOCK STYLE

Date: 2 inches

Use today's date and key this letter from Lloyd J. Mattila / Assistant Manager to Ms. Erica L. Yoder, Manager / New Image Salon / 2342 Como Avenue / St. Paul, MN 55108 / (Supply an appropriate salutation and closing lines.)

Rick Mariani has told me about the progress that has been made in converting your salon's office operation to a computer system. He is confident that the Model 738 will adequately serve your needs for the foreseeable future. Incidentally, Rick was very pleased about the compliments that you have given him about the conversion process.

While the 738 has an excellent performance record, you may want to consider the purchase of a long-term maintenance contract to take effect when the warranty period expires. Our records show that approximately 80 percent of our computer sales include this coverage.

Thank you for choosing HiTech for your computer needs. We look forward to working closely with you in satisfying your software needs and in providing orientation workshops for your office employees. Our involvement extends far beyond the date of purchase.

LETTER 14
PERSONAL-BUSINESS
LETTER IN BLOCK STYLE

Date: 2 inches

This personal-business letter is from Charlene H. Washington, who lives at 2406 25th Avenue, SE, Apt. 318, in Hillsboro, OR 97123-5632. Use today's date, and supply an appropriate salutation and closing lines. The letter is to be sent to Mrs. Doris R. Hall, Manager / CDs and More / 1817 Dierdorff Road, NW / Hillsboro, OR 97124-2781.

I was in your Dierdorff Road store last evening while shopping for a birthday gift for my son. After making my purchase, I returned home, thinking that I had placed my small purse in the package with the CD.

At 10 p.m. I received a phone call from your employee, Rae Ann Marshall, informing me that my purse had been found and was safely stored in your store's safe. She was calling from her home after returning from work. I was not even aware that my purse was missing.

Ms. Marshall went out of her way to relieve me of any anxieties I might have had. You are lucky to have her working for you. I shall look forward to having her serve me again the next time I am in your store.

REPORT 93
(continued)

Telephone graphic: Ctrl-V, 5,30

6. In each box, center and key the course title in bold, underlined type. Press Enter twice; then center and key the date in bold.
7. Spread-center *COMPUTER SKILLS TRAINING* in Extra Large, bold type.
8. Press Enter 2 times; key the types of software in Very Large font at these absolute tab settings:
   Database, 1.3″
   Spreadsheet, 4.2″
   Word Processing, 7.1″
9. Move the cursor beyond the font codes; then press Enter once. Advance to Ln = 6.42″.
10. Center and key the street address in normal, bold type. Space twice.
11. In Extra Large, bold type, create a telephone graphic. Space twice.
12. In normal, bold type, key the telephone number. Space twice.
13. Create the telephone graphic as before. Space twice.
14. Key the remainder of the address in normal, bold type.
15. Press Enter twice and center and key in Very Large, bold, small caps *Call Us Today. . . .*
16. Create a horizontal line as follows:
    Horizontal Position: Center
    Vertical Position: 6″
    Length of Line: 8.25″
    Width of Line: 0.05″

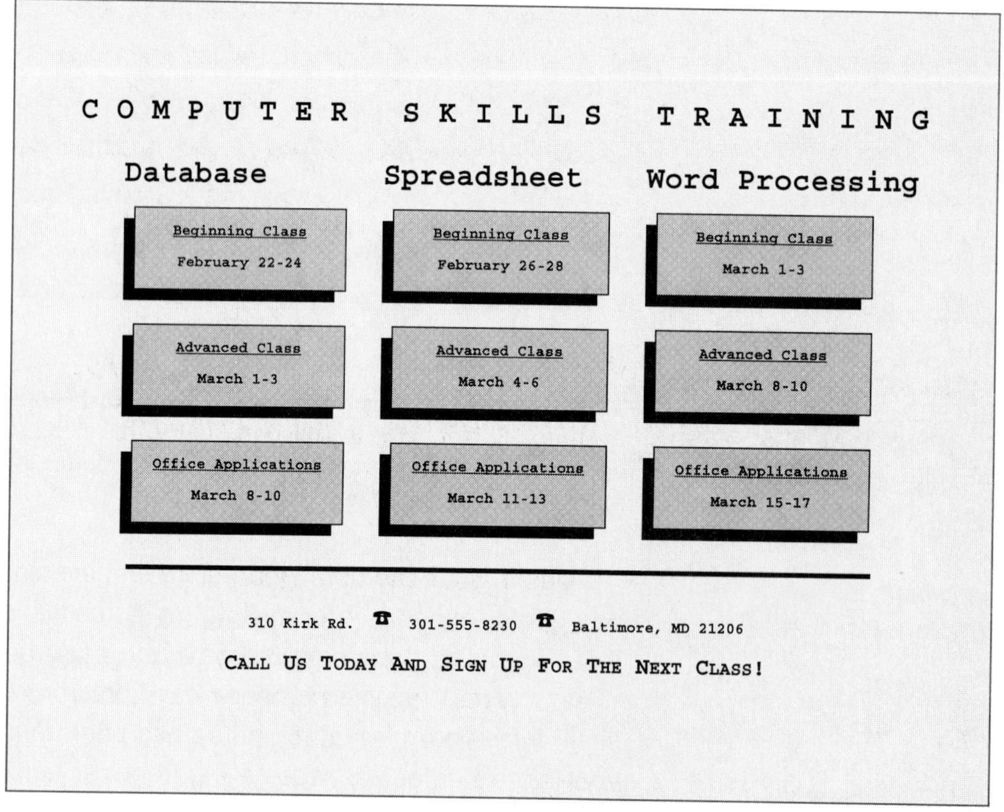

LESSON 31 One-Page Reports

Margins: 1 inch • Tab: 0.5 inch • Spacing: Single • Drills: 2 times • Format Guide: 11

Goals:
To improve speed and accuracy; to format bold text; to format a one-page report.

A. WARMUP

1   Jake volunteered quickly for the tax group. He organ- 12

2 ized 19 to 20 volunteers as well--do you believe this group 24

3 will soon "rescind" Amendments #36 and #48 on pages 7 & 25? 36

| 1 | 2 | 3 | 4 | 5 | 6 | 7 | 8 | 9 | 10 | 11 | 12

LANGUAGE ARTS

B. CAPITAL LETTERS

B. Study the rules at the right. Then key lines 4–7, making any necessary changes.

Rule: Capitalize the first word of all sentences and the first word of an expression used as a sentence.

How come? We thought there would be a lengthy delay.

Rule: Capitalize every proper noun. A proper noun is the official name of a particular person, place, or thing.

Brady Wahlstrom plans to drive his Chevrolet to Miami.

4 really? we had planned to go to the concert on the 14th.

5 both parties modified their positions on the cable issue.

6 wendy and nicholas bought the hotpoint range in flagstaff.

7 jung lee chaired one of the environmental committees.

SKILLBUILDING

PRETEST.
Take a 1-minute timed writing; compute your speed and count errors.

C. PRETEST: HORIZONTAL REACHES

8   She thinks the chief hired a loyal agent for the extra 12

9 ship. He was alarmed by hints of terrorism. The agent was 24

10 armed and received valued input daily from all his sources. 36

| 1 | 2 | 3 | 4 | 5 | 6 | 7 | 8 | 9 | 10 | 11 | 12

PRACTICE.
Speed Emphasis: If you made 2 or fewer errors on the Pretest, key each line twice.
Accuracy Emphasis: If you made 3 or more errors, key each group of lines (as though it were a paragraph) twice.

D. PRACTICE: IN REACHES

11 oy foyer loyal buoys enjoy decoy coyly royal cloy ploy toys

12 ar argue armed cared alarm cedar sugar radar area earn hear

13 pu pumps punch purse spurt input spurn purge pull spur push

14 lu lucid lunch lured bluff value blunt fluid luck lush blue

E. PRACTICE: OUT REACHES

15 ge geese genes germs agent edges dodge hinge gear ages page

16 da daily dazed dance adapt sedan adage panda dash date soda

17 hi hints hiked hired chief think ethic aphid high ship chip

18 ra radar raise raved brain moral cobra extra race brag okra

REPORT 92
BUSINESS CARD

Round bullet: Ctrl-V, 4,0

Square bullet: Ctrl-V, 4,2

WordPerfect 6 users: See Student Guide, p. 107.

Create the business card illustrated below:

1. Set the options for a text box to a single border on all sides and 0% gray shading. Then create the text box as follows:
   Anchor Type: Page
   Vertical Position: Center
   Horizontal Position: Margin, Center
   Size: 3.5″ wide × 2″ high
   Wrap Text: No
2. In Text Box 1, center and key *Diane Gilderhus* in bold type. Center and key her title in bold, italic type.
3. Press Enter twice, change to Fine type, and key the list of documents as follows. Tab once, and create a round bullet. Key the first document in Column 1; then tab twice. Create a round bullet, and key the first document in Column 2. Repeat this process for the remaining documents.
4. Press Enter once after the final document, and center a row of 32 square bullets.
5. Press Enter once, and center and key both address lines in normal, bold type.
6. Press Enter once, and center and key the telephone numbers in normal, bold type. Space once before and after the round bullet.
7. Set the options for the figure boxes to no borders and 20% gray shading. Then create the figure boxes as follows:
   Filename: PC-1.WPG
   Anchor Type: Page
   Vertical Position: 4.5″
   Horizontal Position: (1) 2.65″, (2) 5.35″
   Size: 0.5″ wide × 0.5″ high
   Wrap Text: No

Diane Gilderhus
Desktop Publishing Specialist

●Announcements	●Fliers
●Brochures	●Letterheads
●Business Cards	●Newsletters

■■■■■■■■■■■■■■■■■■■■■■■■■■■■■■■■

2500 Myrtle Avenue
Schenectady, NY 12306
518-555-1052 ● Fax 518-555-1054

REPORT 93
ADVERTISEMENT

WordPerfect 6 users: See Student Guide, p. 108.

Create the advertisement that is shown on page 389, using these directions.

1. Change paper size to Standard—Wide (11″ × 8.5″).
2. Change the left and right margins to 0.5″.
3. Set the options for the text boxes as follows: top and right borders, single; bottom and left borders, Extra Thick; gray shading, 20%.
4. Create the nine text boxes. All text boxes have the following settings:
   Anchor Type: Page
   Size: 2.5″ wide × 1″ high
   Wrap Text: No
5. Vertical and horizontal positions are as follows:
   Row 1: Vertical, 2″
   Horizontal, 1.3″, 4.2″, 7.1″
   Row 2: Vertical, 3.25″
   Horizontal, same as Row 1
   Row 3: Vertical, 4.5″
   Horizontal, same as Row 1

(Continued on next page)

POSTTEST. Repeat the Pretest (C) and compare performance.

F. POSTTEST: HORIZONTAL REACHES

G. This paragraph is made up of very short words, requiring the frequent use of the space bar. Key the paragraph twice. Do not pause before or after striking the space bar.

G. TECHNIQUE PRACTICE: SPACE BAR

19 We will all go to the race if I win the one I am going 12
20 to run today. Do you think I will be able to finish in the 24
21 front of the pack, or do you think there are lots of really 36
22 fast runners there who surely can finish ahead of me? It's 48
23 going to be a lot of fun, and I look forward to this event. 60

| 1 | 2 | 3 | 4 | 5 | 6 | 7 | 8 | 9 | 10 | 11 | 12

H. PACED PRACTICE

Turn to the Paced Practice routine at the back of the book. Take three 2-minute timed writings, following the directions at the top of the page.

FORMATTING

Titles and side headings appear in bold.

I. BASIC PARTS OF A REPORT

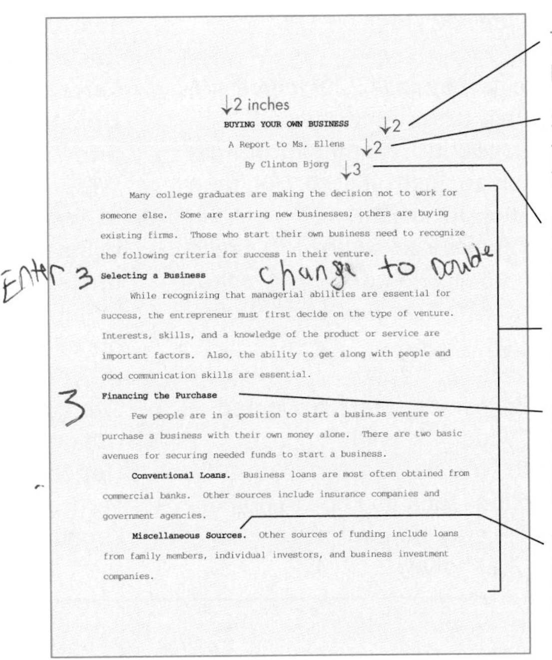
↓2 inches

BUYING YOUR OWN BUSINESS ↓2

A Report to Ms. Ellens ↓2

By Clinton Bjorg ↓3

Many college graduates are making the decision not to work for someone else. Some are starting new businesses; others are buying existing firms. Those who start their own business need to recognize the following criteria for success in their venture.

Selecting a Business

While recognizing that managerial abilities are essential for success, the entrepreneur must first decide on the type of venture. Interests, skills, and a knowledge of the product or service are important factors. Also, the ability to get along with people and good communication skills are essential.

Financing the Purchase

Few people are in a position to start a business venture or purchase a business with their own money alone. There are two basic avenues for securing needed funds to start a business.

Conventional Loans. Business loans are most often obtained from commercial banks. Other sources include insurance companies and government agencies.

Miscellaneous Sources. Other sources of funding include loans from family members, individual investors, and business investment companies.

TITLE. Subject of the report; centered in bold print; keyed in all caps.

SUBTITLE. Secondary or explanatory title; centered a double space (1 blank line) below the title, with first and principal words capitalized.

BYLINE. Name of the writer; centered a double space below the subject or, if no subtitle is used, a double space below the title.

BODY. Text of the report; separated from the heading(s) by a triple space (2 blank lines).

SIDE HEADING. Major subdivision of the report; keyed at the left margin in bold print with first and principal words capitalized; preceded and followed by a double space.

PARAGRAPH HEADING. Minor subdivision of the report; indented 0.5 inch in bold, with first and principal words capitalized; followed by a period (in bold) and 2 spaces.

J. ONE-PAGE REPORTS

Side Margins: Default (1 inch).
Top Margin: 2 inches; center the title.
Bottom Margin: Default (1 inch).
Tab Setting: Default (0.5 inch; used for indenting paragraphs).
Spacing: One blank line between the title, subtitle, and byline. Two blank lines between the title block and the body. Change to double spacing before keying the body of the report.

FORMATTING

P. WORDPERFECT: ROTATE A GRAPHIC

Rotate a graphic:

Alt-F9, 1, 2, 1, Enter, 9, 3, *enter degree,* F7, F7

Move a graphic: Alt-F9, 1, 2, 1, Enter, 9, 1, *enter left or right movement,* F7, F7

WordPerfect 6 users: See Student Guide, p. 104.

To rotate (turn) a graphic image, enter the Graphics Editor (Alt-F9, 1, 2, *Figure No.,* Enter, 9). Then use + or − to turn the image.

An alternative method is to select Rotate (3) and enter the number of degrees to rotate the image. The number of degrees you enter is always calculated from the original starting position of the image.

If you select Rotate, you will be asked if you want a mirror image. A mirror image shows the graphic in the opposite direction (for example, from left to right instead of right to left).

DOCUMENT PROCESSING

REPORT 91
BUSINESS CARD

WordPerfect 6 users: See Student Guide, p. 106.

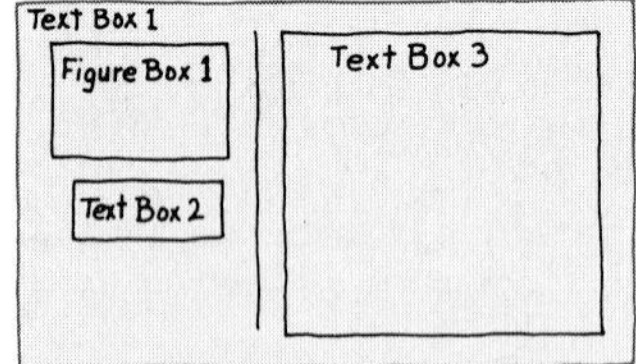

Create the business card illustrated below.

1. Set the options for a figure box to no borders and 0% gray shading. Then create Figure Box 1 as follows:
   Filename: GAVEL.WPG
   Anchor Type: Page
   Vertical Position: 4.25″
   Horizontal Position: 2.7″
   Size: 1″ wide × 2″ high
   Wrap Text: No
2. Rotate the gavel image 220 degrees (9, 3, 220); then press Enter twice.
3. Move the graphic to the left three-quarters of an inch (1, −0.75); then return to the document.
4. Set the options for a text box to a single border on all sides and 0% gray shading. Then create Text Box 1 as follows:
   Anchor Type: Page
   Vertical Position: Center
   Horizontal Position: Margin, Center
   Size: 3.5″ wide × 2″ high
   Wrap Text: No
5. Set the options for a text box to no borders and 0% gray shading. Then create Text Box 2 as follows:
   Anchor Type: Page
   Vertical Position: 5.4″
   Horizontal Position: 2.8″
   Size: 1″ wide × 0.5″ high
   Wrap Text: No
6. Center and key the letters *SLS* in Text Box 2, using Extra Large, bold type.
7. Set the options for a text box to no borders and 0% gray shading. Then create Text Box 3 as follows:
   Anchor Type: Page
   Vertical Position: Center
   Horizontal Position: 3.9″
   Size: 2.1″ wide × 2″ high
   Wrap Text: No
8. In Text Box 3, key the company name in Small, bold, italic type. Press Enter 3 times, and key *Dan Woodland* in Small, bold type; then press Enter once. Key the remaining information in Small type. Press Enter 2 times after *Manager* and after the ZIP Code.
9. Create the vertical line as follows:
   Horizontal Position: 3.9″
   Vertical Position: Center
   Length: 1.75″; Width: 0.05″

Your printed copy may look different from this, depending on your printer.

DOCUMENT PROCESSING

REPORT 1

Top margin: 2 inches
Tab: 0.5 inch
Spacing: Double

Key the title block and triple-space before changing to double spacing.

↓2 inches **THE FUTURE OF INFORMATION STORAGE**↓2

Business Technology Conference↓2

By Marianne Townsend↓3

Much of what we save as files on computers today is stored on hard disks or diskettes. The future of information storage, however, clearly rests in the technology of compact disc storage or CD-ROM as it is often labeled.↓3

Basic Features↓2

A single compact disc can store about 700 megabytes of information. With this capability, a computer user can store an entire encyclopedia or dictionary, a vast assortment of graphic images and clip art pieces, as well as a considerable number of individual software packages. A CD-ROM drive will cost between $400 and $1,200.↓3

Using CD-ROM↓2

Using a CD-ROM disc will free up space on your hard disk, and it will give you immediate access to many software packages. Thus, you can have at your disposal an entire encyclopedia or call up an image from thousands of clip art pieces stored on the disc. However, the CD-ROM drive is presently more expensive and slower than other drives, and it is impossible to erase the CD-ROM. Also, because of the vast amount of storage on just one disc, the purchase price of a prerecorded disc may be high.

Rough–Draft Reports

Margins: 1 inch • Tab: 0.5 inch • Spacing: Single • Drills: 2 times • Format Guide: 11

Goals:
To key 33 wam/3'/5e; to use proofreaders' marks; to format a report from rough-draft copy.

A. WARMUP

```
1      The quiz will cover just pages 17-28, 39-40, and 65-70  12
2 from Quinn's article called, "Back Up Your Disk."  Will any  24
3 extra pages be required for the summary that we must write?  36
  | 1 | 2 | 3 | 4 | 5 | 6 | 7 | 8 | 9 | 10 | 11 | 12
```

N. Key lines 65–68 once. Then key the four lines again. Notice that each number uses the same reaches as the word above it.

N. NUMBER PRACTICE

```
Your tree root tore up your tire.  We try to tie your rope.
6974 5433 4995 5943 70 6974 5843.  23 546 59 583 6974 4903.
Your power wire tore up your tree prior to our trip or two.
6974 09234 2843 5943 70 6974 5433 04894 59 974 5480 94 529.
```

O. Spacing: Double
Take two 5-minute timed writings. Compute your speed and count errors.

Goal: 57 wam/5′/5e

O. 5-MINUTE TIMED WRITING

When any holiday approaches, it becomes important to 12
plan all activities carefully. This is when gifts might be 24
exchanged and when special food may be prepared. To get 35
ready for these holiday periods, experts tell us that we 46
can reduce stress and enjoy the holiday more if we make 58
lists and schedules to manage our time. This will provide 69
us with time for relaxation. 75

Lists, schedules, and a definite delegation of duties 87
among family members and houseguests shape the basic plan 99
of action. When organizing a strategy, plan everything, 110
from the cooking and baking to the shopping and wrapping. 122
The most important task to remember, and the one that most 134
people forget, is to plan to relax. 141

Psychologists warn us of the dangers of cutting out 152
personal pleasures. We all need time out to recharge and 164
diffuse developing stress. Nourish yourself with walks, 175
exercise class, gardening, religious services, or a quiet 187
evening in with an old movie or a good novel. Do whatever 199
it takes to pacify your spirit. 205

When the next holiday is on the horizon, don't be a 216
person who gets all stressed out. Remember to plan all the 228
activities carefully and to enlist the help of all family 240
members in getting ready for the celebration. When this is 252
done carefully, everyone can assume some responsibility for 264
different tasks, and the end result will be a joyous time 276
that will be remembered by all family members. 285

| 1 | 2 | 3 | 4 | 5 | 6 | 7 | 8 | 9 | 10 | 11 | 12

LANGUAGE ARTS

B. SPELLING

B. These words are among the 500 most frequently misspelled words in business correspondence.

per provided international receipt commission present other
questions maintenance industrial service following position
management absence proposal corporate mortgage support well
approval recommendations facilities balance experience upon
premium currently because procedure addition paid directors

SKILLBUILDING

C. SUSTAINED PRACTICE: SYLLABIC INTENSITY

C. Take a 1-minute timed writing on the first paragraph to establish your base speed. Then take several 1-minute timed writings on the remaining paragraphs. As soon as you equal or exceed your base speed on one paragraph, advance to the next one.

When you have to give a talk and would like to impress 12
your audience, it is essential that you use graphics. Here 24
are a few suggestions to help you if you must use graphics. 36

Try to distribute your graphics evenly throughout your 12
talk. Highlight the important points as you present all of 24
your talk; be certain to spend enough time on these points. 36

Select only one graphic design for your graphics. The 12
single graphic design means that you select the layout only 24
once, thus conveying a sense of organization to your group. 36

| 1 | 2 | 3 | 4 | 5 | 6 | 7 | 8 | 9 | 10 | 11 | 12

D. 3-MINUTE TIMED WRITING

D. Spacing: Double
Take two 3-minute timed writings. Compute your speed and count errors.

Goal: 33 wam/3′/5e

Although you attend college so that you can find a job 12
upon graduation, there is a better than average chance that 24
you will not stay with that job for your entire career. If 36
you find yourself searching for a job, what is one quick 47
suggestion that you can make to help you expand your search 59
for that job? 62

An absolute must is that you organize your plan of 73
attack and focus on a final objective. Target a certain 84
company and find out before your interview as much as you 96
can about it. 99

| 1 | 2 | 3 | 4 | 5 | 6 | 7 | 8 | 9 | 10 | 11 | 12

FORMATTING

E. PROOFREADERS' MARKS

The proofreaders' marks shown on the next page are used to indicate changes or corrections to be made in a rough-draft document that is being revised for final copy. Study the chart to learn what each of the marks means.

I. Take three 12-second timed writings on each line. The scale gives wam for a 12-second timed writing.

I. 12-SECOND SPRINTS

The American Bar Association will meet in Denver, Colorado.
Sunday River in Maine holds its Ski Clinic every Wednesday.
The North Idaho Blood Drive will be in Lewiston and Moscow.
Mr. Ray Hart lives at 15 Kent Place, Apt. 4, Clinton, Iowa.

| | | | 5 | | | |10| | | |15| | | |20| | | |25| | | |30| | | |35| | | |40| | | |45| | | |50| | | |55| | | |60

J. Each of these sentences contains two words that are not used properly. Correct those words as you key each sentence twice.

J. TECHNIQUE PRACTICE: CONCENTRATION

Please except my apologies for the poor advise that I gave.
He did a through check of all cereal numbers of equipment.
She was board with the duel assignments that were disputed.
A curtesy reply to explain the access absences was needed.

K. This paragraph is made up of very short words, requiring the frequent use of the space bar. Take three 1-minute timed writings. Do not pause before or after striking the space bar.

K. TECHNIQUE PRACTICE: SPACE BAR

A man in a cab at the old pub can go up to the big bar 12
by the bay to ask the new boy for a box of cod if I ask him 24
to do so. He can fry a box of cod now, or he can put it on 36
ice for a day or two. We met an old man and his son at the 48
new inn; if they eat cod, it is up to you and me to fix it. 60

| 1 | 2 | 3 | 4 | 5 | 6 | 7 | 8 | 9 | 10 | 11 | 12

L. PROGRESSIVE PRACTICE: NUMBERS

Turn to the Progressive Practice: Numbers routine at the back of the book. Take five 30-second timed writings, starting at the point where you left off the last time.

M. Take a 1-minute timed writing on the first paragraph to establish your base speed. Then take four 1-minute timed writings on the remaining paragraphs. As soon as you equal or exceed your base speed on one paragraph, advance to the next one.

M. SUSTAINED PRACTICE: NUMBERS

Many young people soon see that their entry-level jobs 12
scarcely pay for necessities, and there is nothing left for 24
a savings plan. Difficult as it may be, however, an effort 36
should be made to begin saving at the start of your career. 48

It is easy to understand that most of us don't realize 12
the effect of starting to save at a young age. The results 24
of saving $100 a month over 20 years are really surprising. 36
Money is not everything, but senior citizens need security. 48

The dollars saved will be working for the owner. When 12
that interest rate is 5.5 percent, the savings of $100 will 24
be worth over $43,000 at the end of that time. If this sum 36
impresses you, the next illustration will just astound you. 48

Let us suppose that those savings are earning interest 12
at a rate of 15 percent for a period of 30 years. The same 24
savings will be worth $700,000. A monthly increase to $200 36
results in almost a million and a half dollars in 30 years. 48

| 1 | 2 | 3 | 4 | 5 | 6 | 7 | 8 | 9 | 10 | 11 | 12

Proofreaders' Mark	Draft	Final Copy
Omit space	data base	database
Transpose	they all see	they see all
Insert	she may go (insert: not)	she may not go
Capitalize	Maple street	Maple Street
Delete	a final draft	a draft copy
Move as shown	no copy machine	no machine
Paragraph	Most of the	Most of the

WP

MOVE (MOVE, COPY, DELETE)
Move: Ctrl-F4, *select option,* 1, *position cursor,* Enter

Copy: Ctrl-F4, *select option,* 2, *position cursor,* Enter

Delete: Ctrl-F4, *select option,* 3

WordPerfect 6 users: See Student Guide, page 18.

F. WORDPERFECT: MOVE (MOVE, COPY, DELETE)

Use Move to highlight text, and then move, copy, or delete it. Position the cursor any place within the text and press Ctrl-F4. Then select option 1 (sentence), 2 (paragraph), or 3 (page). Next, select option 1 (move), 2 (copy), or 3 (delete). If you choose to move or copy, position the cursor where you want the text to be placed and press Enter. If you choose 3 (delete), the text will be automatically deleted.

To move a partial section of text, block the text, then press Ctrl-F4. Select 1 (block), then select either move, copy, or delete. To move or copy, position the cursor where you want the copy to be placed and press Enter.

DOCUMENT PROCESSING

REPORT 2
ONE-PAGE REPORT

Top margin: 2 inches
Spacing: Double

REPORT 3

Revise Report 2 making these changes:
1. Add a byline with your name in the heading.
2. Delete the first sentence of the report.
3. Change the paragraph headings to read as follows: Time as a Cultural Difference. Space as a Cultural Difference.

INTERNATIONAL COMMUNICATIONS

Cultural Differences

The marvel of technology has changed communications in that we are seeing an emphasis increased on the inter national dimension. Because of the ease with which we can communicate with other people from a round the globe, it is becoming increasingly important that we learn about communications differences within a variety of cultures.

Cultural differences vary considerably around the world. The way we walk, smile, or use our hands can convey diferent meanings to particular cultures. A smile, for example, is used in our culture to convey friendliness; yet, it may be a sign of weakness. in another culture,

Views about time. We look at time as an element that must be planned carefully; yet others may have a much more relaxed view of time. To some, it is considered appropriate to be late because it shows that one is a busy person. **Views About space.** We prefer from two to three feet between ourselves and those with whom we communicate. People from some cultures, however, prefer to stand closer when speaking.

SKILLBUILDING

PRETEST. Take a 1-minute timed writing; compute your speed and count errors.

D. PRETEST: COMMON LETTER COMBINATIONS

The condo committee was hoping the motion would not be 12
forced upon it, realizing that viable solutions ought to be 24
developed. It was forceful in seeking a period of time for 36
tensions to cool. All concerned wanted the problem solved. 48

| 1 | 2 | 3 | 4 | 5 | 6 | 7 | 8 | 9 | 10 | 11 | 12

PRACTICE.
Speed Emphasis: If you made no errors on the Pretest, key each line twice.
Accuracy Emphasis: If you made 1 or more errors on the Pretest, key each group of lines (as though it were a paragraph) twice.

E. PRACTICE: WORD BEGINNINGS

for forum forge forced forgot formal forest foreign forerun
con conks conic consul confer convey convex contact concern
per perks peril person period perish permit percale percent
com combs comet combat comedy comics common compete complex

F. PRACTICE: WORD ENDINGS

ing tying hiking liking edging bowing hoping having nursing
ble fable pebble treble tumble viable dabble fumble fusible
ion union legion nation region motion potion option bastion
ful awful cupful fitful joyful lawful earful artful tearful

POSTTEST. Repeat the Pretest (D) and compare performance.

G. POSTTEST: COMMON LETTER COMBINATIONS

H. Take a 1-minute timed writing on the first paragraph to establish your base speed. Then take four 1-minute timed writings on the remaining paragraphs. As soon as you equal or exceed your base speed on one paragraph, advance to the next one.

H. SUSTAINED PRACTICE: ROUGH DRAFT

One of the characteristics happy marriages often share 12
is the ability of husband and wife to identify each other's 24
hidden qualities and nurture them. Improvement and growth, 36
both as individuals and as a couple, should be a major aim. 48

Marriage, as a broad comitment between two people, is 12
meant to foster the kind of mutual improvement. Helping a 24
spouse improve is a terific goal. Remember, however, that 36
a complete personality make-over is probably not realistic. 48

The easist way for spouses to better one an other are 12
to become trustworthy, to inpire confidence, to truly like 24
one another, to repsect on another, to listen carefully to 36
one another, and to out bring one anothers best quality. 48

When you thing in terms of mutul improvement, the roll 12
of friend makes sense. Friends try to better those qualities 24
that matter. Decide if whats bothering you is an little 36
anoyance you can accept or something central to your life. 48

| 1 | 2 | 3 | 4 | 5 | 6 | 7 | 8 | 9 | 10 | 11 | 12

Enumerations

Margins: 1 inch • Tab: 0.5 inch • Spacing: Single • Drills: 2 times • Format Guide: 11

Goals:
To improve speed and accuracy; to improve proofreading and composing skills; to format enumerations and outlines.

A. WARMUP

David, Jake, and Zach have quite a few baseball cards. 12
They possess 258 from the 1970s and 346 from the 1980s, and 24
in the next months they can get more from different places. 36

| 1 | 2 | 3 | 4 | 5 | 6 | 7 | 8 | 9 | 10 | 11 | 12

LANGUAGE ARTS

B. PROOFREADING

B. Key the paragraph, correcting all errors.

What is it taht makes one person more succesful than another when thier backgrounds, esperience, and education are very similar? Many studies have been conducted in an attempt to anser this particuler question, and the findings almost always reveal that the differenses in success are allmost always related to personal intiative, enthusiasm, and attitude. An individual with a postive attitude and noticable enthusiasm has great potential for success. These personnal characteristics will often play a more important role than eduction or experience when success is evalauted.

C. COMPOSING

C. Answer each question with a single word or a short phrase.

What is your favorite day of the week?
What sport do you like to watch on television?
What is the last name of your favorite female vocal artist?
How much money do you expect to pay for your next car?
What is the name of the largest state in the United States?
What is the name of the smallest state in the United States?
What is your favorite snack?
Where would you like to spend your next vacation?

SKILLBUILDING

D. PACED PRACTICE

Turn to the Paced Practice routine at the back of the book. Take four 2-minute timed writings, starting at the speed at which you left off the last time.

E. PROGRESSIVE PRACTICE: ALPHABET

Turn to the Progressive Practice: Alphabet routine at the back of the book. Take six 30-second timed writings, starting at the point where you left off the last time.

UNIT THIRTY-TWO • DESKTOP PUBLISHING: REINFORCEMENT

LESSONS 156-160

Margins: 1 inch • Spacing: Single • Drills: 2 times • Format Guide: 137–139

Goals for Unit 32

1. To improve accuracy and speed on alphabet and number keys.
2. To key 57 wam for 5 minutes with no more than 5 errors.
3. To improve proficiency in composing at the keyboard.
4. To review numerous WordPerfect features including text boxes, figure boxes, graphics, font sizes, font styles, compose characters, and other desktop publishing features.
5. To format business cards, advertisements, and brochure pages.

Begin each day with approximately 15 minutes of skillbuilding, selecting activities from pages 383–386. In the remaining class time, complete as many production jobs from pages 387–393 as you can.

A. WARMUP

```
1      Zackary was anxious to make his vacation plans.  He is   12
2 to travel to Quebec on Flight #9 for $546.  His agenda then   24
3 will take him to Japan on Flight #732 for a cost of $1,087.   36
  | 1 | 2 | 3 | 4 | 5 | 6 | 7 | 8 | 9 | 10 | 11 | 12
```

LANGUAGE ARTS

B. NUMBERS

Study the rules at the right. Then key lines 4–7, making necessary changes.

Rule: Use the word *cents* for amounts under $1.

Tonia quoted a price of 89 cents for the ballpoint pen.

Rule: Use figures to express time with *o'clock* or with *a.m.* and *p.m.* (The abbreviations *a.m.* and *p.m.* should be keyed in small letters without spaces.)

The 11 o'clock flight from Seattle arrived at 1:27 p.m.

```
4 A first-class postage stamp cost $.25 in 1990.
5 Copies can be made at the library for $.10 a page.
6 The meeting will start at three o'clock in the afternoon.
7 Lizabeth's last class for the day ends at 3:50 P.M.
```

C. COMPOSING

Compose a letter to John Burns (Letter 96, p. 302) from Beth Rutter and use the current date. Apologize to Mr. Burns for the problem he encountered with a garment purchased from J. W. Knapps, Inc. Tell him that Knapps always stands behind its merchandise and will either replace the sweater or refund his money. Also tell him that he can return the sweater to any branch of Knapps. Close the letter by telling Mr. Burns that we hope, in spite of this experience, that he will continue to shop at Knapps. Don't forget to mention (and enclose) the card that entitles Mr. Burns to a 30 percent discount on his next purchase at Knapps.

FORMATTING

WP

INDENT
Left Indent: F4
Double Indent: Sh-F4
Hanging Indent: F4, Sh-Tab

WordPerfect 6 users: See Student Guide, page 18.

F. WORDPERFECT: INDENT

Left Indent (F4) is used to indent all lines from the left margin to the first tab setting.

Double Indent (Sh-F4) is used to indent all lines from both the left and right margins the same number of spaces as the first tab setting.

Hanging Indent (F4, Sh-Tab) is used to leave the first line of a paragraph flush with the left margin and to indent all remaining lines to the first tab setting.

DOCUMENT PROCESSING

REPORT 4
ENUMERATION

Top margin: 2 inches
Tab: 0.4 inches

Turnover lines: the second and succeeding lines in an enumerated list.

G. ENUMERATIONS

Read the information in Report 4 before you key the assignments in this section. Study the format so that you get a mental picture of the layout before keying it. Use the Left Indent (F4) after keying the number and period so that turnover lines are indented.

ENUMBERATIONS

1. An enumeration may be a series of number items, Although letters may be used.) Numbers keyed at the left and followed by a period and two spaces.
2. Turn over lines are indented 4 spaces from the left margin. Use the left indent after keying the number and period to guarantee that turnover lines are indent as they are in this enumeration.
3. If numbered items take one line or less, they are singlespaced with no balnk lines between them. However, if most items have more than one line (as they do in this enumeration), they are single space with a double spaced (one blank lines) between numbered items.
4. The periods following the introductory numbers should be aligned vertically. if the enumeration runs to ten or more items, a decimal should be set to align the periods for all numbers.
5. The title of an enumberation is keyed inches from the top of the page. The title should be centered, boldfacef, and all caps. Side margins are 1 inch.

REPORT 90 (continued)

8. Press Enter and tab once; then key *KITCHEN CLOCKS* in Extra Large, bold type.
9. Return to normal font, and press Enter 3 times. Tab, and key the model number. Tab again, and key the price. Then indent, and key the description.
10. Press Enter 2 times, and create a horizontal line with a horizontal position of 1″.
11. Press Enter 3 times; then repeat Steps 9 and 10 to key the second model, price, and description.
12. Repeat Steps 7–11 to complete the catalog page. The graphic for the third figure box is TELPHONE.WPG.

16

JUST FOR THE KITCHEN SALE

. . . F O R   T H E   H O M E

All Items on This Page Will Be on Sale Until After the Holidays

---

KITCHEN CLOCKS

Model R771-0384	32.48	Case is painted in white enamel. Black hands and Roman numerals are set against a parchment-color dial with colorful floral prints. Quartz movement uses one "C" battery, not included.
Model R771-9235	37.75	Oak finish, hand-stained. Solid brass dial with Arabic numerals. Silk screen on glass front. Electric only.

KITCHEN TELEPHONES

Model 100WP-6874	65.78	One-touch redial. Ringer volume control. Tone or pulse dialing. Comes with 15-foot handset cord. Available in ivory, brown, or black.
Model 200WP-4398	129.99	Cordless model with LCD display. Digital security system protects your line. Tone sounds when out of range. Available in ivory or brown.

REPORT 5
OUTLINE

Top margin: 2 inches
Tabs: 0.4, 0.7, 1.1, 1.5 inches
Spacing: Single

The first tab in Report 5 is set as a decimal tab to align the periods following the roman numerals.

2 inches ↓ COUNTY OF DOUGLAS ↓3

I. ADMINISTRATION ↓2

A. Commissioner's Office
B. Fiscal Services
C. Planning and Evaluation ↓3

II. PLANNING AND ECONOMIC DEVELOPMENT ↓2

A. Government Center
1. Economic development and promotion policies
2. Research development and information
3. Current planning and zoning policies
B. Special Services Division
C. Technical Services Division ↓3

III. PUBLIC WORKS ↓2

A. Emergency Services
B. Garbage and Trash Disposal
C. Land Development
D. Water and Street Department

One-Page Reports

Margins: 1 inch • Tab: 0.5 inch • Spacing: Single • Drills: 2 times • Format Guide: 11–13

Goals:
To key 34 wam/3'/4e; to format reports from rough-draft copy.

A. WARMUP

1 Brazil, Mexico, and Pakistan qualified for the U.N. in 12
2 the 1940s along with 156 other countries. In the 1990s, we 24
3 saw another seven nations join. Might we see more by 2023? 36

| 1 | 2 | 3 | 4 | 5 | 6 | 7 | 8 | 9 | 10 | 11 | 12

SKILLBUILDING

B. TECHNIQUE PRACTICE: ENTER KEY

B. Key each sentence on a separate line.

4 Where is my new diskette? You placed it on my office desk.
5 Why did you miss my meeting? I was working at the exhibit.
6 When do you expect to return? We will be back on Thursday.

7 Eleven computers are missing. They must be out for repair.
8 The sessions were canceled. The speaker could not make it.
9 My telephone is now working. We all have better equipment.

10 The business trip is scheduled. Will we fly to Pittsburgh?
11 We ordered new software. On what day will it be installed?
12 You have an interview tomorrow. What time will you return?

REPORT 89
TRANSPARENCY

WordPerfect 6 users: See Student Guide, p. 103.

Create Report 89, shown below, by following these steps:

1. Select the landscape definition.
2. Create a text box with the following options:
   Border Style: Thick, top and bottom; None, left and right
   Gray Shading: 20%
   Anchor Type: Page
   Vertical Position: Top
   Horizontal Position: Margin, Center
   Size: 5″ wide × 0.95″ high
   Wrap Text: No
3. Center and key the title, *PRINTER NEEDS,* in the text box in Extra Large, bold type; then center and key the subtitle, *(LISTED BY REGION),* in Very Large, bold type and small caps.
4. Press Enter once; then advance to Ln = 3.0″.
5. Key the regions and cities in Extra Large, bold type.
6. Single-space the cities within a region; double-space between regions.
7. Tab once before keying each city; then press Alt-F6 twice (to create dot leaders and to position the copy flush right), and key the number of copies.

Depending on your printer, your report may look different than the one shown here.

PRINTER NEEDS
(LISTED BY REGION)

CENTRAL REGION
Minneapolis . . . . 18,700 copies
St. Louis . . . . 17,400 copies

EASTERN REGION
Providence . . . . 10,000 copies
Trenton . . . . 9,800 copies

WESTERN REGION
Los Angeles . . . . 32,700 copies
Seattle . . . . 16,300 copies

REPORT 90
CATALOG PAGE

WordPerfect 6 users: See Student Guide, p. 103.

To prepare the catalog page shown on page 382, follow these steps:

1. Set left and right margins of 0.5″, and change to full justification.
2. Create a figure box with these options:
   Gray Shading: 10%
   Anchor Type: Page
   Vertical Position: Top
   Horizontal Position: 1″
   Size: 2″ wide × 2″ high
   Wrap Text: No
3. Add the text to the box, using center–justification. Press Enter twice, and key *JUST FOR THE KITCHEN SALE* in Extra Large, bold type.
4. Press Enter twice; then key *16* at the left margin in Very Large, bold type. Key . . . *FOR THE HOME* flush right, with 1 space between letters and 3 spaces between words.
5. Press Enter 2 times, and key the next three lines flush right. Return to normal font, and press Enter 5 times.
6. Create a horizontal line 0.1″ wide.
7. Press Enter 3 times, and create a figure box with these options:
   Gray Shading: 0%
   Filename: CLOCK.WPG
   Anchor Type: Paragraph
   Vertical Position: 0″
   Horizontal Position: Left
   Size: 0.5″ wide × 0.5″ high

(Continued on next page)

C. DIAGNOSTIC PRACTICE: NUMBERS

Turn to the Diagnostic Practice: Numbers routine at the back of this book. Take the Pretest and record your performance. Then practice the drill lines for those reaches on which you made errors. Finally, repeat the Pretest and compare your performance.

D. 3-MINUTE TIMED WRITING

D. Spacing: Double
Take two 3-minute timed writings. Compute your speed and count errors.

Goal: 34 wam/3′/4e

What does the future of computers hold for us? Just 12
a few years ago we were amazed at the storage space of a 23
hard disk, the quickness of the dot-matrix printer, and the 35
beauty of a color screen. Now, those hardware features 46
are thought to be old technology. 53

In the future, we will be storing much of our data on 64
compact discs, our printing will most likely be produced by 76
a color laser printer, the images on our monitors will be 88
as clear as on a movie screen, and images will very likely 100
be animated. 102

| 1 | 2 | 3 | 4 | 5 | 6 | 7 | 8 | 9 | 10 | 11 | 12

DOCUMENT PROCESSING

REPORT 6
ONE-PAGE REPORT

Top margin: 2 inches
Spacing: Double

AUTO INSURANCE COVERAGE

By Andrea Parker

All of us are required to carry automobile insurance on our cars, regardless of the state in which we live. The following paragraph^s reveal coverages found in some insurance policies.

Medical Coverage Payments

This coverage will pay for ^all reasonable medical expenses incurred ~~for medical expenses~~ because of bodily injury caused by an accident. Coverage is available to the insured and ^his or her family.

Coverage for Damage to an automobile

This coverage is usually paid directly for loss to any covered automobile, minus any ~~paid~~ deductible in the policy. ¶Part of this coverage may also include insured transportation expenses incurred while the automobile is being repaired.

Certain exclusions usually apply to auto coverage. Insurance companies will ^not pay for damages if the auto was used to carry persons for a ~~nominal~~ fee. Nor they will pay for damage caused by wear and tear of the auto, freezing, or ^mechanical failure.

REPORT 88
(continued)

The vertical position for each of the bars is always different; however, when the measure is added to the length of the line, the two numbers will always equal 6.5″. Thus the base of all the bars will always be at the same horizontal position.

Length: 8″
Width: 0.013″

5. Create a vertical line for the *y* axis of the graph as follows:
   Horizontal Position: 1.5″
   Vertical Position: 3.5″
   Length: 3″
   Width: 0.013″
6. Create the vertical bars (lines) representing printer sales from 1990 to 1993 as follows.
   1990: Horizontal Position, 2.25″; Vertical Position, 4.5″; Length, 2″; Width, 1″
   1991: Horizontal Position, 4″; Vertical Position, 4.2″; Length, 2.3″; Width, 1″
   1992: Horizontal Position, 5.75″; Vertical Position, 4.75″; Length, 1.75″; Width, 1″
   1993: Horizontal Position, 7.5″; Vertical Position, 3.5″; Length, 3″; Width, 1″
7. Advance to Ln = 3.5″, and set the line spacing to 2.7.
8. Key *7* in bold, and press Enter once.
9. Key *6* in bold, press Enter once, and repeat this procedure for the remaining numbers on the vertical axis.
10. Press Enter twice after keying *1*.
11. Set absolute, center tabs at 2.75″, 4.5″, 6.25″, and 8″.
12. Tab, and key the year *1990.* Tab, and key *1991.* Repeat this procedure for the remaining numbers on the horizontal axis.

The width of each bar and the space between each bar remain constant. This is a rule that is usually followed when bar graphs are prepared.

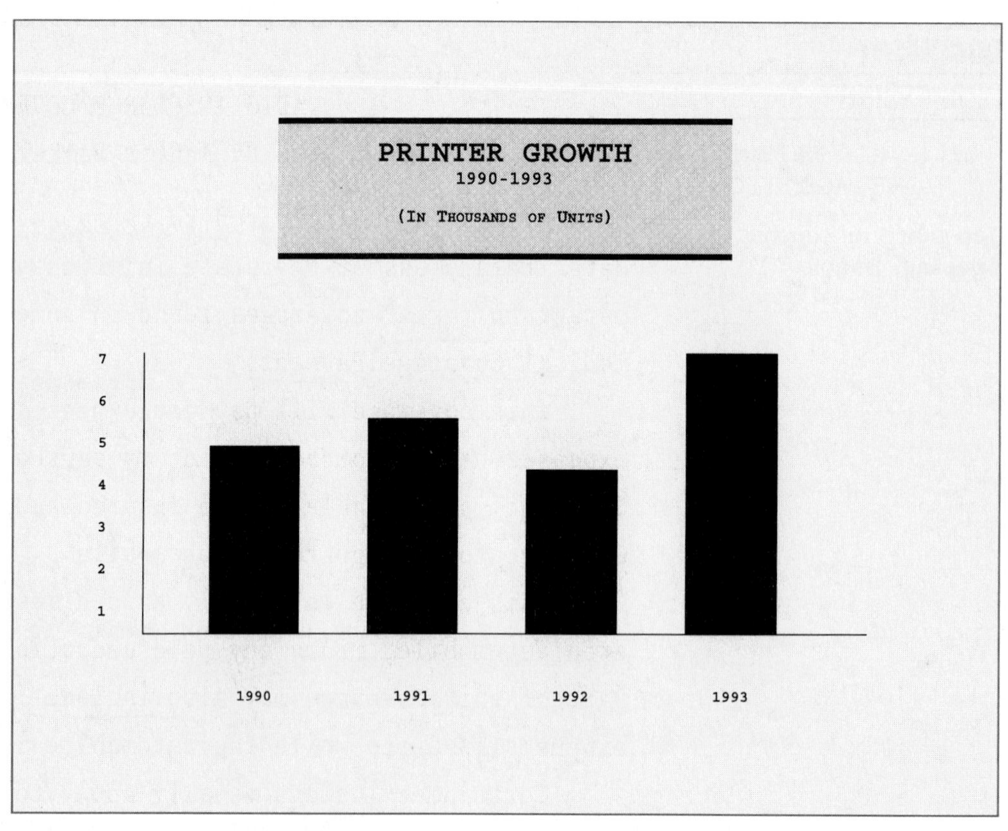

REPORT 7
ONE-PAGE REPORT

Top margin: 2 inches
Spacing: Double

MAKING A DECISION

By Candace Benedict

Making a decision is often a difficult task, but it is one that is performed on a routine basis. The steps to decision making vary, but they can be summarized in four activities that are described in the following paragraphs.

Identify the Problem

The first step in the decision-making process is to identify that you do have a problem. Unless you can focus on the problem, you may never resolve it.

List All Possible Solutions

Once the problem has been identified, you need to identify all possible solutions to the problem. "Brainstorming" is an excellent technique that is used to identify various solutions.

Analyze All Possible Solutions

In this step, you must study carefully all the solutions and narrow your list of possible choices to two or three. Study the strengths and weaknesses of each of these solutions.

Choose the Best Solution

The final step is to select the best solution from those you identified as the final two or three. This step may take several days, depending on how much input you expect from others.

S. PRESENTATION GRAPHICS

The ability to change font sizes, add graphics, and create special designs is extremely useful when you are creating transparencies to be displayed during a presentation.

Because transparencies are projected onto a screen, it is essential that the font style and size be clear and large enough to be read from a distance. It is also important, for readability, to leave plenty of white space on the page.

To create transparency masters, you can either print directly on transparency film (if you have a laser printer) or print on paper and photocopy the page onto transparency film.

DOCUMENT PROCESSING

REPORT 87
TRANSPARENCY

Right arrow: Ctrl-V, *6,27*, Enter

WordPerfect 6 users: See Student Guide, p. 101.

Follow these steps to create Report 87:

1. Create a text box with the following options:
   Border Style: None, left and right; Thick, top and bottom
   Gray Shading: 20%
   Anchor Type: Page
   Vertical Position: 1.5″
   Horizontal Position: Margin, Center
   Size: 5″ wide × 0.68″ high
2. Use Extra Large font for all type. Center and key the information in the text box in bold.
3. Press Enter once; then advance to Ln = 3.5″.
4. Key the first printer type following this sequence: tab, tab, create right arrow, tab, key printer type. Leave 1 space between letters and 3 spaces between words. Then press Enter 4 times.
5. Repeat Step 4 to key the remaining printer types.

PRINTER COMPARISONS

▸ B U B B L E   J E T

▸ D O T   M A T R I X

▸ I N K   J E T

▸ L A S E R

▸ T H E R M A L

REPORT 88
TRANSPARENCY

WordPerfect 6 users: See Student Guide, p. 101.

Follow these steps to create the bar graph shown on page 380.

1. Select the landscape definition.
2. Create a text box with the following options:
   Border Style: None, left and right; Thick, top and bottom
   Gray Shading: 20%
   Anchor Type: Page
   Vertical Position: Top
   Horizontal Position: Margin, Center
   Size: 5″ wide × 1.5″ high
3. Center and key the title, *PRINTER GROWTH,* in the text box in Extra Large, bold type. Center and key *1990–1993* in Large, bold type. Center and key the subtitle, *(IN THOUSANDS OF UNITS),* in Large, bold type and small caps.
4. Create a horizontal line for the *x* axis of the graph as follows:
   Horizontal Position: 1.5″
   Vertical Position: 6.5″

(Continued on next page)

Lesson 35: Enumerations and Bibliographies

Margins: 1 inch • Tab: 0.5 inch • Spacing: Single • Drills: 2 times • Format Guide: 13

Goals:
To improve speed and accuracy; to improve skills in formatting from rough-draft copy and word-division skills; to format a report with an enumeration and a bibliography.

A. WARMUP

```
     The quake in Brazil destroyed approximately 875 to 925   12
buildings.  We are fortunate that 12,643 buildings had been   24
reinforced just 10 months prior; they haven't been damaged.   36
 | 1 | 2 | 3 | 4 | 5 | 6 | 7 | 8 | 9 | 10 | 11 | 12
```

SKILLBUILDING

B. 12-SECOND SPRINTS

B. Take three 12-second timed writings on each line. The scale shows your wam speed for a 12-second timed writing.

```
We use the computer to prepare all of the work at our home.
All the players were ready to play their best on the court.
It will start to rain, and then our game might be canceled.
We must order all our stock by the second day of the month.
| | | | 5 | | | |10| | |15| | |20| | |25| | |30| | |35| | |40| | |45| | |50| | |55| | |60
```

C. SUSTAINED PRACTICE: ROUGH DRAFT

C. Take a 1-minute timed writing on the first paragraph to establish your base speed. Then take several 1-minute timed writings on the remaining paragraphs. As soon as you equal or exceed your base speed on one paragraph, advance to the next one.

```
     Ethics in business has always been very important.  If   12
we are honest in our work and respect the ethical standards   24
of our company, we'll be creating a positive image for all.   36
A ~~new~~ challenge to ethical standards in the work place has   12
been more apparent in the past [few] years because of the use   24
of computer[s].  How have computers challenged ethical codes?   36
     One of the most sever[e] ethical probelms has to do with   12
the use of software.  Ever[y] copy of soft ware sold car[r]ies a   24
serial  number, and it's given to the ~~user~~ [owner] of the software.   36
     Some people will take anothers software, however, and   12
copy it as ~~there~~ [their] own.  so doing violate[s] ethical code[s], and   24
people who so do are dis honest in using the soft ware.   36
 | 1 | 2 | 3 | 4 | 5 | 6 | 7 | 8 | 9 | 10 | 11 | 12
```

D. WORD DIVISION

D. Beginning at 0.5, set tabs every 1.6 inches. Tab in to key the first column. Key those words that can be divided with a hyphen to show where the word can be divided (for example, *fore-front*).

taught	address	business	counterpart
finance	weren't	expressway	alarm
monthly	USAF	thanked	self-defense
can't	knowledge	TWA	afford

FORMATTING

R. SHADOW EFFECT

WordPerfect 6 users: See Student Guide, p. 99.

A shadow effect is often used to highlight a figure or text box to attract the attention of readers. To make a shadow effect, create a box with an extra-thick border on two sides.

The illustration below (Report 86) shows the shadow effect created by using extra-thick borders on the top and left sides of text boxes.

DOCUMENT PROCESSING

REPORT 86
FLIER

WordPerfect 6 users: See Student Guide, p. 100.

Use Reveal Codes and View Document to be sure you have entered the correct codes.

Bullet: Ctrl-V, 4,0

Create this flier following these steps:

1. Create three figure boxes with these options:
   Filename: BALLOONS.WPG
   Anchor Type: Page
   Vertical Position: 1.5″ for left and right boxes; 1″ for center box
   Horizontal Position: Left, Center, and Right
   Size: 1.5″ wide × 1.5″ high
   Wrap Text: No
2. Press Enter once, and advance to Ln = 3.17″. Then spread center and key in Extra Large, bold type *SUE'S ANNUAL SALE* double-spaced.
3. Return to normal font, and press Enter 4 times.
4. Create Text Box 1 with these options:
   Border Style: Extra Thick on left and top; Single on right and bottom
   Gray Shading: 20%
   Anchor Type: Paragraph
   Vertical Position: 0″
   Horizontal Position: Left
   Size: 1.6″ wide × 0.7″ high
   Wrap Text: No
5. Center and key in the box in Extra Large, bold type *VALUE.*
6. Exit the text box, press Enter once, and advance to Ln = 5.67″.
7. Change to Extra Large type, and key the descriptions for *VALUE.* Precede each item with a *Tab-Bullet-Tab* sequence.
8. Return to normal font, then press Enter 4 times. Create Text Box 2 with these options:
   Anchor Type: Paragraph
   Vertical Position: 0″
   Horizontal Position: Left
   Size: 2.5″ wide × 0.7″ high
   Wrap Text: No
9. Center and key in the box in Extra Large, bold type *SELECTION.*
10. Exit the text box, press Enter once, advance to Ln = 7.89″, and repeat Step 7 for the descriptions.
11. Return to normal font, and press Enter 3 times.
12. Create a horizontal line, changing the width to 0.1″.
13. Press Enter 2 times. Then key *256 Elm Drive* at the left margin; *Paw Paw, MI 59079* at center; and *616-555-6823* flush right.

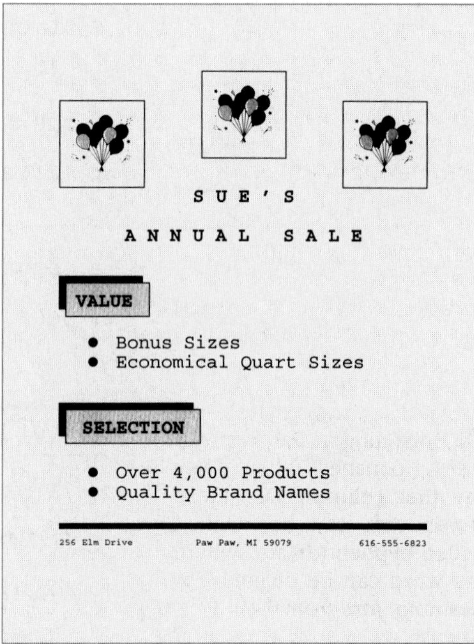

FORMATTING

E. WORDPERFECT: ITALICS

WP ITALICS
Ctrl-F8, 2, 4

WordPerfect 6 users: See Student Guide, page 20.

To italicize text, enter the appropriate commands (Ctrl-F8, 2, 4) and key the text. Next, turn off italics (Ctrl-F8, 3 or press the right arrow key). To italicize existing text, first block the text; then enter the italics commands. Be sure your printer is capable of printing italics before selecting this feature.

DOCUMENT PROCESSING

REPORT 8
REPORT WITH ENUMERATION

Tabs: 0.5 and 0.9 inch
Spacing: Double

Single-space the lines within a numbered item; double-space between numbered items.

Numbered items are indented 0.5 inch, and turnover lines are indented 0.9 inch.

Read Report 8 for the information it contains. Then carefully follow the instructions at the left, noting that a tab must be set at 0.5 inch for the numbered items.

PREPARING A BIBLIOGRAPHY

By Bonnie Sparks

A bibliography is an alphabetic listing of sources and is placed at the end of a report. Follow these instructions:

1. Use the side margins of the report (usually 1 inch).
2. Center the title in bold print, all caps, 2 inches from the top. Triple-space after the title.
3. Arrange book entries in this sequence: author, title (in italics or underlined), publisher, place of publication, and date.
4. Arrange information for journal articles in this order: author, title of article (in quotation marks), title of journal (in italics or underlined), series number, volume number, issue number, date, and page number or numbers.

REPORT 9
BIBLIOGRAPHY

Tab: 0.5 inch

Prepare Report 9 from the copy below using a 0.5-inch hanging indent to automatically indent the turnover lines. You may underline book and journal titles if your printer cannot print italics.

BIBLIOGRAPHY

Book by one author

Blanchard, Christie, *Experience a Successful Interview,* Beringson Printing, New York, 1990.

Book by two authors

Dolfeld, Kyle B., and Lisa R. Simmons, *Using an Interview to Get the Job,* Masterson Books, Aptos, California, 1989.

Article by one author

Johnston, Karen C., "What to Do After the Interview," *Journal of Communications,* Vol. XVII, No. 6, May 1980, pp. 17-20.

Article by three or more authors (*et al.* means "and others")

Lymanski, James T., et al., "The Secrets to Interviewing: Style and Organization," *HRD Journal,* Vol. LXVII, No. 5, October 1992, pp. 58-61.

Article—no author

"Preparing for the Interview," *Sales Marketing Journal,* Vol. XXVII, No. 2, August 21, 1991, pp. 103-105.

Organization as author

Secretarial Association, *The Job Interview and Your Success,* Georgia College Press, Carrollton, Georgia, 1992.

FORMATTING

Q. WORDPERFECT: SMALL CAPS

WP

SMALL CAPS
Ctrl-F8, 2, 7

WordPerfect 6 users: See Student Guide, p. 97.

Small caps are capital letters that print the same size as lowercase letters. Small caps are often used for display. When using small caps, you may also "capitalize" the first letter of a word or sentence. Depending on the fonts that are available with your printer, the "capital" letter may appear larger than the remaining small caps. To turn on small caps, press Ctrl-F8. Then key *2* and *7*. Remember to turn off small caps (right arrow or Ctrl-F8, 3) when you finish keying the display. Use View Document to see how small caps will appear when printed.

DOCUMENT PROCESSING

REPORT 85
ANNOUNCEMENT

REVIEW
Create figure box: Alt-F9, 1, 1

Create text box: Alt-F9, 3, 1

Depending on your printer, your report may look different from the one shown here.

WordPerfect 6 users: See Student Guide, p. 98.

Follow these directions to create Report 85.

1. Create Figure Box 1 with these options:
   Border Style: Single
   Gray Shading: 0%
   Filename: NEWS.WPG
   Anchor Type: Page
   Vertical Position: Top
   Horizontal Position: Margin, Center
   Size: 2.75″ wide × 1.75″ high
   Wrap Text: No
2. Press Enter once, and advance to Ln = 1.83″. In Extra Large type, key *EXTRA!!!* at the left margin and again flush right.
3. Press Enter 4 times; then center and key *READ ALL ABOUT IT!!!*
4. Return to normal font, and press Enter 2 times; then center and key *LYKKEN'S BOOKSTORE GRAND OPENING* in Very Large type.
5. Return to normal font, and press Enter 4 times.
6. Create Figure Box 2 with these options:
   Border Style: None
   Gray Shading: 0%
   Filename: CHKBOX-1.WPG
   Anchor Type: Paragraph
   Vertical Position: 0″
   Horizontal Position: Left
   Size: 1″ wide × 1″ high
   Wrap Text: Yes
7. Press Enter 3 times; then key *WHEN:* in Extra Large size, small caps.
8. Key the data for this section flush right as it appears below.
9. Press Enter 3 times, and repeat Steps 6–8 to create Figure Boxes 3 and 4 and to complete the announcement.

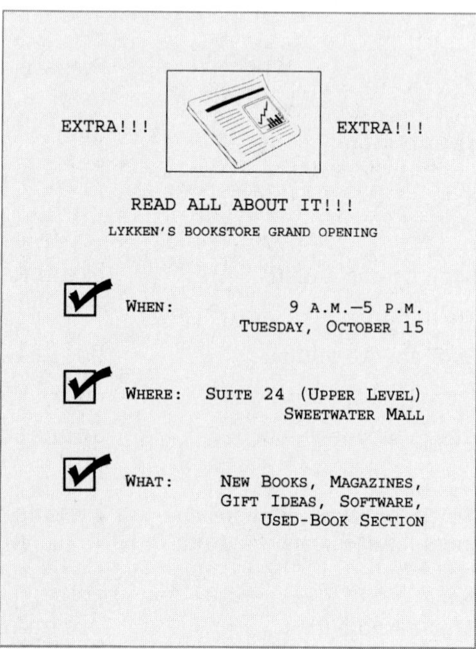

Simple Tables

Margins: 1 inch • Tab: 0.5 inch • Spacing: Single • Drills: 2 times • Format Guide: 13

Goals:
To key 35 wam/3′/4e; to format simple tables.

A. WARMUP

1 Have you read Jackie's article entitled "Civilized Ex- 12
2 ports" in yesterday's newspaper? It's on pages B34 and B67 24
3 and quotes your 1989-92 study of the Fortune 500 companies. 36

| 1 | 2 | 3 | 4 | 5 | 6 | 7 | 8 | 9 | 10 | 11 | 12

LANGUAGE ARTS

B. NUMBERS

B. Study the rules at the right. Then key lines 4–7, making any necessary changes.

Rule: Key percentages in figures, and spell out the word *percent.*
Note: The percent sign (%) may be used in tables.

An accuracy rate of 97 percent was reported for the month.

Rule: When ages are used as significant statistics, key them in figures.

He was excited because he would be able to vote at age 18.

4 The quality-control group reports a 2.7% defect rate.
5 The absentee rate was lowered by twenty-three percent.
6 Pension eligibility was reduced to the age of 62.
7 Of the executive group, only one member is age fifty-two.

SKILLBUILDING

C. TECHNIQUE PRACTICE: TABS

C. Set tabs every 1.2 inches beginning at 0.5. Tab to begin Column 1. Use the tab to move from column to column.

8	A. Allen	B. Cable	D. Drake	E. Eaton	F. Frank
9	G. Grant	H. Henry	I. Ilanu	J. Kirby	L. Lopez
10	M. Mills	N. Nolan	O. Ortiz	P. Quinn	R. Rosen
11	S. Simon	T. Tyler	U. Vidah	W. Xerox	Y. Zulch

D. 3-MINUTE TIMED WRITING

D. Spacing: double. Take two 3-minute timed writings. Compute your speed and count errors.

Goal: 35 wam/3′/4e

12 There has surely been quite an increase in emphasis on 12
13 international business in the past few years, but we should 24
14 not forget that you do not have to leave this country in 35
15 order to encounter cultures that are different from the one 47
16 with which you may be most at ease. This is true no matter 59
17 if you belong to a majority or to a minority group. Look 71
18 around the room the next time you are in a meeting. You 82
19 will be amazed at the diversity that is there. You should 94
20 learn to be comfortable with those different from you. 105

| 1 | 2 | 3 | 4 | 5 | 6 | 7 | 8 | 9 | 10 | 11 | 12

O. Take three 1-minute timed writings. Note that the last two digits of each number are a cumulative word count and give your wam.

O. NUMBER PRACTICE

6701 8202 6303 7204 8705 9606 2707 1008 7409 8510 9311 8212
7613 6714 7015 6116 1017 5618 4919 3920 2821 1622 1723 1624
9725 8626 6727 5028 4729 3930 2831 7632 6733 6534 7435 1036
8737 1938 6739 9340 8241 7742 9843 9044 5645 4046 3947 2848

P. Spacing: Double
Take two 5-minute timed writings. Compute your speed and count errors.

Goal: 56 wam/5′/5e

P. 5-MINUTE TIMED WRITING

A country innkeeper may have an idyllic life. Many 11
people often imagine leaving their demanding jobs to open 23
a country inn far from the crazy pace of the cities. They 35
dream of a spot where they can be independent, creative, 46
and peaceful, a place where they might live in financial 58
comfort and security and enjoy the quieter pleasures of 69
life. How accurate is this portrait? Owning an inn is 80
a business, and just like any other business, it is filled 92
with many and various problems and joys, heartaches and 103
challenges, and anxieties and rewards. 111

What are some qualities successful innkeepers share? 123
Although they all have a distinct personality, there are 134
a few common attributes. First and foremost, they must 145
enjoy meeting, working with, and being near lots of people. 157
They should like seeking out challenges and enjoy taking 169
risks. They should be stubborn enough to hold onto a dream 181
in the face of adversity and flexible enough to step in 192
wherever and whenever something needs to be done. 202

In addition to the right personality, a solid bank 213
account is needed to open a country inn. The exact amount 225
will vary depending on the size and scope of the inn, but 237
about one-fourth of the purchase price of the land is often 249
required for the down payment. Money will also be needed 260
for several other types of expenses, including repairs, 271
landscaping, advertisements, and furnishings. 280

| 1 | 2 | 3 | 4 | 5 | 6 | 7 | 8 | 9 | 10 | 11 | 12

FORMATTING

E. BASIC PARTS OF A TABLE

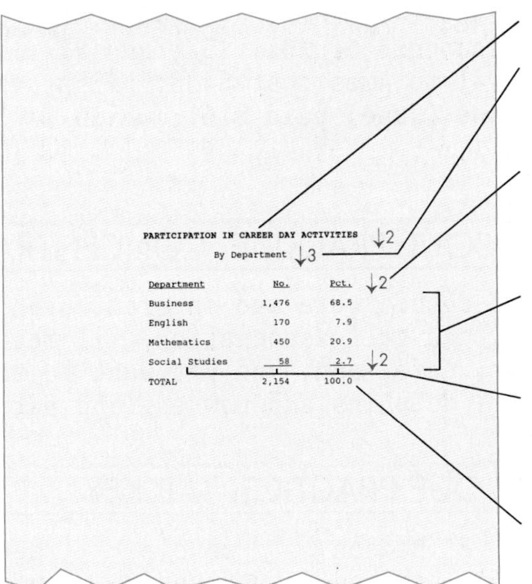

PARTICIPATION IN CAREER DAY ACTIVITIES ↓2
By Department ↓3
Department No. Pct. ↓2
Business 1,476 68.5
English 170 7.9
Mathematics 450 20.9
Social Studies 58 2.7 ↓2
TOTAL 2,154 100.0

TITLE. Center and key in all caps and in bold.

SUBTITLE (optional). Center a double space below the title, with the first and all principal words capitalized.

COLUMN HEADINGS. Align at the left for word columns and at the right for number columns; Underline, and leave 2 blank lines before and 1 after.

BODY. Center horizontally, usually with 6 spaces between columns; may be either single-spaced or double spaced.

COLUMN. Align columns of words at the left, columns of whole numbers at the right, and columns of decimal numbers on the decimal point.

TOTAL LINE. Make the underline before the total line the length of the longest number in the column. Double-space before the total line.

F. You must switch from relative tabs, which are measured from the left margin setting (the default), to absolute tabs because the position number showing on the status line is measured from the left edge of the page, not from the left margin.

WordPerfect 6 users: See Student Guide, p. 20.

F. FORMATTING A TABLE

Follow these steps to format Tables 1–3:

1. Center the table vertically using Center Page.
2. Horizontally center and key the title in all caps and bold. Double-space and center and key the subtitle in upper- and lowercase plain type followed by a triple space.
3. Horizontally center the key line—an imaginary line made up of the longest item in each column plus 6 spaces for each area between columns.
4. Use the key line to determine the tab settings: For text columns (left tabs), position the cursor under the first character in the column and note the position on the status line. For number columns (right tabs), position the cursor to the right of the last digit and note the position on the status line. For decimal columns, position the cursor under the decimal point and note the position on the status line.
5. Delete the key line and the center command.
6. Access the tab menu (Sh-F8, 1, 8), clear existing tabs (Ctrl-End), and set absolute tabs (T, 1) at the positions you noted in Step 4.
7. Change line spacing if necessary.
8. Tab to begin Column 1. Use the tab key to move from column to column.

DOCUMENT PROCESSING

TABLE 1
2-COLUMN TABLE

Spacing: Double
Set 2 left absolute tabs.

ANNUAL REPORT ASSIGNMENTS ↓2

By Priority ↓3

Letter from the CEO	Walter Behrens
The Year in Review	Anne Smithson-Elliott
Financial Picture	Auditors
Spotlight on New Products	Alan C. Wingett
A Look Ahead	Barbara J. Arno

Key Line: Spotlight on New Products123456Anne Smithson-Elliott

J. Take three 12-second timed writings on each line. The scale gives wam for a 12-second timed writing.

J. 12-SECOND SPRINTS

41 Mail these statements: (1) #897, (2) #1143, and (3) #1276.
42 Trade discounts of 20%, 15%, and 8% amounted to $143 saved.
43 Flight #41 to Ames cost $438; Flight #22 to Butte was $585.
44 On 5/1 she (Jane) paid $141, which is 24% less than I paid.

| | | | 5 | | | |10 | | | |15 | | | |20 | | | |25 | | | |30 | | | |35 | | | |40 | | | |45 | | | |50 | | | |55 | | | |60

K. Insert the necessary capital letters as you key these sentences twice.

K. TECHNIQUE PRACTICE: CONCENTRATION

45 Dave and debbie were wed in orem, utah, on sunday, july 21.
46 The american golf association will meet in kansas city, mo.
47 Jim, sue, nate, ann, and pat went to radio city music hall.
48 The miami dolphins and new england patriots meet on sunday.

L. Clear all tabs. Then set four new tabs every 1 inch. Key lines 49–52, using the tab key to go across from column to column.

L. TECHNIQUE PRACTICE: TAB KEY

49	admire	beacon	candle	desire	earful
50	shrewd	thread	unused	vision	waving
51	memory	needle	oppose	kimono	lastly
52	nickel	ordeal	plunge	agrees	runner

M. DIAGNOSTIC PRACTICE: ALPHABET

Turn to the Diagnostic Practice: Alphabet routine at the back of this book. Take the Pretest and record your performance. Then, practice the drill lines for those reaches on which you made errors. Finally, repeat the Pretest and compare your performance.

N. Take a 1-minute timed writing on the first paragraph to establish your base speed. Then take four 1-minute timed writings on the remaining paragraphs. As soon as you equal or exceed your base speed on one paragraph, advance to the next one.

N. SUSTAINED PRACTICE: ALTERNATE-HAND WORDS

53 A downturn in world fuel prices signals a lower profit 12
54 for the giant oil firms. In fact, most downtown firms will 24
55 see the usual sign of tight credit and other problems. The 36
56 city must get down to business and make plans for the fall. 48

57 The hungry turkeys ate eight bushels of corn that were 12
58 thrown to them by our neighbors next door. They also drank 24
59 the five bowls of water that were left in the yard. All in 36
60 all, the birds caused quite a bit of chaos in the barnyard. 48

61 A debate on what to do about that extra acreage in the 12
62 desert dragged on for eight hours. One problem is what the 24
63 effect may be of moving the ancient Indian ruins to a safer 36
64 place. City council has a duty to protect our environment. 48

65 Molly Babbage was dressed in a plain pink dress at the 12
66 annual meeting that was taking place at the hotel in Denver 24
67 later that last week in September. The agenda included two 36
68 very controversial topics that were generating much debate. 48

| 1 | 2 | 3 | 4 | 5 | 6 | 7 | 8 | 9 | 10 | 11 | 12

TABLE 2
3-COLUMN TABLE

Spacing: Double
Set 3 left absolute tabs.

SECTION 5: A LOOK AHEAD ↓2

Deadlines for First Drafts ↓3

New Products	Alan C. Wingett	October 15
The Economy	Chad Spencer	December 1
International Dimensions	Sherri Jordan	October 15
The Competition	Pedro Martin	November 15

TABLE 3
3-COLUMN TABLE

Spacing: Single
Set 3 left absolute tabs.

SECTION 5C: INTERNATIONAL DIMENSIONS

Agent Locations

Canada	Pearson, Ltd.	Toronto, Canada
Central America	Escadrille	Panama City, Panama
South America	Desarrollo Minero	Salvador, Brazil
Europe	Der Widermaster	Bonn, Germany
Near East	Porat Industrial	Haifa, Israel
Far East	Ito-Yokado	Osaka, Japan

LESSON 37 Tables With Number Columns

Margins: 1 inch • Tab: 0.5 inch • Spacing: Single • Drills: 2 times • Format Guide: 15

Goals:
To improve speed and accuracy; to format tables with number columns.

A. WARMUP

I'll fly Flight 1482 on 10/23/96. It departs New York 12
City at 10:57 p.m. and arrives in Caracas, Venezuela, quite 24
late the next morning. The Boeing jet is most comfortable. 36

| 1 | 2 | 3 | 4 | 5 | 6 | 7 | 8 | 9 | 10 | 11 | 12

LANGUAGE ARTS

B. COMPOSING

Answer each question with a single word or a short phrase.

What is your favorite color combination?
If you could take a "dream vacation," where would you go?
What two qualities do you look for in a friend?
What kinds of books do you like to read?
Approximately how many miles do you drive each week?
What personality traits do you admire?

SKILLBUILDING

D. PACED PRACTICE

Turn to the Paced Practice routine at the back of the book. Take three 2-minute timed writings, starting at the point where you left off the last time.

PRETEST. Take a 1-minute timed writing; compute your speed and count errors.

E. PRETEST: HORIZONTAL REACHES

Some employees were engaged in a market survey to rate 12
the data gathered from the campus. Some of the data within 24
the study eluded the employees because they were puzzled by 36
the range of ages of students and by the high dropout rate. 48

| 1 | 2 | 3 | 4 | 5 | 6 | 7 | 8 | 9 | 10 | 11 | 12

PRACTICE.
Speed Emphasis: If you made no errors on the Pretest, key each line twice.
Accuracy Emphasis: If you made 1 or more errors on the Pretest, key each group of lines (as though it were a paragraph) twice.

F. PRACTICE: IN REACHES

oy ploy toys boys voyage joyous decoys employ oyster coyote
ar arch yard fear argued market soared embark dollar artist
pu punt spun spur puzzle spunky deputy campus pushed repute
lu luck club plus luxury eluded salute unplug fluffy lugged

G. PRACTICE: OUT REACHES

ge germ ages wage genius urgent agents merged engage gentle
da data soda daze danger update payday agenda pedals daring
hi high thin chip hinder shield hiking behind hiring within
ra rate brag rare ratify traced ranged afraid ramble betray

POSTTEST. Repeat the Pretest (E) and compare performance.

H. POSTTEST: HORIZONTAL REACHES

I. Take a 1-minute timed writing on the first paragraph to establish your base speed. Then take four 1-minute timed writings on the remaining paragraphs. As soon as you equal or exceed your base speed on one paragraph, advance to the next one.

I. SUSTAINED PRACTICE: SYLLABIC INTENSITY

The art of negotiation is a key part of life each day, 12
whether you are buying a house, asking for a raise, or just 24
trying to get the kids to go to bed. Yet most people dread 36
it. They are scared of getting stuck in a battle of wills. 48

In negotiating, you never get everything you want, but 12
you often can persuade the other party to do what you would 24
like without demanding it. Keep in mind that by asking for 36
what you want amiably, you are much more likely to succeed. 48

Another suggestion for creating a win-win situation is 12
to do your homework. Many people walk up to the bargaining 24
table and reel off a long list of demands. It is vital for 36
you to do thorough research prior to starting your meeting. 48

Some folks postulate that the only way to successfully 12
negotiate is to be dishonest or devious. This is not true. 24
True negotiating is not adversarial; it is working together 36
to come up with an arrangement which is of mutual interest. 48

| 1 | 2 | 3 | 4 | 5 | 6 | 7 | 8 | 9 | 10 | 11 | 12

SKILLBUILDING

PRETEST.
Take a 1-minute timed writing; compute your speed and count errors.

C. PRETEST: COMMON LETTER COMBINATIONS

```
     At the conference last week, some person made a formal  12
motion that might be useful to us in the coming months.  It  24
should enable us to easily comply with our building permit.  36
```

| 1 | 2 | 3 | 4 | 5 | 6 | 7 | 8 | 9 | 10 | 11 | 12

PRACTICE.
Speed Emphasis: If you made 2 or fewer errors on the Pretest, key each line twice.
Accuracy Emphasis: If you made 3 or more errors, key each group of lines (as though it were a paragraph) twice.

D. PRACTICE: WORD BEGINNINGS

```
for forget formal format forces forums forked forest formed
con concur confer conned convoy consul convey convex condor
per perils period perish permit person peruse perked pertly
com combat comedy coming commit common compel comply comets
```

E. PRACTICE: WORD ENDINGS

```
ing acting aiding boring buying ruling saving hiding dating
ble bubble dabble double enable feeble fumble tumble usable
ion action vision lesion nation bunion lotion motion legion
ful armful cupful earful eyeful joyful lawful useful woeful
```

POSTTEST.
Repeat the Pretest (C) and compare performance.

F. POSTTEST: COMMON LETTER COMBINATIONS

DOCUMENT PROCESSING

TABLE 4
2-COLUMN TABLE WITH NUMBERS

Spacing: Double
Set 1 left and 1 right absolute tab.

To make the underline the width of the longest item in the column, turn on Underline and then space 3 times before keying *986*. Remember to turn off Underline.

NUMBER OF POLICIES WRITTEN

January 1-September 30

Automobile	10,076
Business liability	436
Homeowner's	4,385
Term life	1,452
Whole life	986
TOTAL	17,335

TABLE 5
3-COLUMN TABLE WITH NUMBERS

Spacing: Single
Set 1 left and 2 decimal absolute tabs.

To set a decimal tab, position the cursor under the decimal point in the key line and note its position in the status line.

Double-space before the total line.

MIDCONTINENT STATE-PRIDE AWARD WINNERS

(Annual Sales in $000)

Ohio	6,305.7	39.56%
Indiana	4,206.5	26.39%
Minnesota	2,177.4	13.66%
Iowa	1,092.7	6.86%
Michigan	945.8	5.93%
Illinois	803.6	5.04%
Wisconsin	408.2	2.56%
TOTAL	15,939.9	100.00%

UNIT THIRTY-ONE • DESKTOP PUBLISHING: PRESENTATION GRAPHICS

LESSONS 151-155

Margins: 1 inch • Spacing: Single • Drills: 2 times • Format Guide: 135

Goals for Unit 31

1. To improve accuracy and speed on alphabet and number keys.
2. To key 56 wam for 5 minutes with no more than 5 errors.
3. To develop proficiency in spelling commonly misspelled words.
4. To develop proficiency in using WordPerfect Graphics, Text Boxes, Figure Boxes, and Lines.
5. To format and key announcements, transparencies, graphs, and catalog pages.

Begin each day with approximately 15 minutes of skillbuilding, selecting activities from pages 373–376. In the remaining class time, complete as many production jobs from pages 377–382 as you can.

A. WARMUP

1 Invoice #347 from Quigley & Baxter was for $567. With 12
2 the discount of 25%, the amount came to $425.25. The order 24
3 on Invoice #219 from Jecke & Ponzi was for a total of $850. 36

| 1 | 2 | 3 | 4 | 5 | 6 | 7 | 8 | 9 | 10 | 11 | 12

LANGUAGE ARTS

B. GRAMMAR

B. Study the rules at the right. Then key lines 4–7, making necessary changes.

Rule: When establishing agreement between subject and verb, disregard intervening phrases and clauses.

The doctor, not the interns, is working there.

Rule: Verbs in the subjunctive mood (those which talk of conditions that are improbable, doubtful, or contrary to fact) require the plural form.

If I were he, I would want to charter a much larger plane.

4 The manager, not the department heads, was in control.
5 The supervisor, as well as others, were taking inventory.
6 I wish I was involved more in decision-making matters.
7 If I was she, I would have selected a different route.

C. SPELLING

C. These words are among the 500 most frequently misspelled words in business correspondence.

8 status category technology respect handicapped human number
9 secretaries exhibit company's personally essential hospital
10 agencies consistent certificate designed opinion percentage
11 receipts attorney convenience purchase specifically charges
12 submitted variety achievement processing example cost order

TABLE 6
4-COLUMN TABLE WITH NUMBERS

Spacing: double
Set 2 left and 2 decimal absolute tabs.

Leave 10 spaces between Columns 2 and 3 and 6 spaces between the other columns.

MIDCONTINENT THIRD-QUARTER SALES

As a Percentage of Sales Goal

Illinois	93.5	Minnesota	103.7
Indiana	113.7	Missouri	96.5
Iowa	100.0	Ohio	129.6
Michigan	85.6	Wisconsin	99.1

Tables With Blocked Column Headings

Margins: 1 inch • Tab: 0.5 inch • Spacing: Single • Drills: 2 times • Format Guide: 15

Goals:
To key 35 wam/3'/4e; to format tables with blocked column headings.

A. WARMUP

On our next job, we will increase our contributions to 12
a retirement plan from 18% to 20%; this should very quickly 24
bring the size of our blue-chip investments up to $375,469. 36

| 1 | 2 | 3 | 4 | 5 | 6 | 7 | 8 | 9 | 10 | 11 | 12

SKILLBUILDING

B. SUSTAINED PRACTICE: NUMBERS

B. Take a 1-minute timed writing on the first paragraph to establish your base speed. Then take several 1-minute timed writings on the remaining paragraphs. As soon as you equal or exceed your base speed on one paragraph, advance to the next one.

Michael learned through firsthand experience last week 12
that the cost of a week on the water can vary a great deal. 24
He says that a rowboat would be about right for his wallet. 36

His Uncle Al told him that when he was his age, he had 12
rented a small cabin for the huge sum of $105 for one week. 24
For $23 more, he rented a small boat and an outboard motor. 36

Then his uncle went on to say that when he rented that 12
same cabin last year, the fee had gone up to either $395 or 24
$410. The boat and motor rentals now cost from $62 to $87. 36

Aunt Kate said that she and her husband will be paying 12
either $1,946 or $2,075 for one week's sailing on a 53-foot 24
yacht. The boat has a 4-person crew and was built in 1982. 36

| 1 | 2 | 3 | 4 | 5 | 6 | 7 | 8 | 9 | 10 | 11 | 12

C. PACED PRACTICE

Turn to the Paced Practice routine at the back of the book. Take four 2-minute timed writings, starting at the speed at which you left off the last time.

FORM 25
(continued)

15. Change the left line to double in cells B2–B10, D2–D10, F2–F10, H2–H10, and J2–J10.
16. Center-justify Rows 3–6, excluding Column A.
17. Right-justify Rows 7–10, excluding Column A.
18. Change the decimal display to 0 in cells B9–K9 (in Table Edit, 2, 2, 4, 0, Enter).
19. Enter the formula B8–B7 in cell B9; then copy the formula to cells C9–K9.
20. Save the form.

W E E K L Y   A U T O   U S A G E   F O R M

For the Week of:

Auto Used	Monday		Tuesday		Wednesday		Thursday		Friday	
	Bus.	Per.	Bus.	Per.	Bus.	Per.	Bus.	Per.	Bus.	Per.
Buick, LPD-285										
Dodge, QZT-176										
Toyota, HZG-358										
Ford, VRP-823										
Beg. Odometer										
End. Odometer										
Total Miles	0	0	0	0	0	0	0	0	0	0
Misc. Expenses										

FORM 26
AUTO USAGE FORM

Be sure the cursor is positioned before the bold and Large codes before you key *March 21.*

WordPerfect 6 users:
Checkmark, Ctrl-W, 5,51

Retrieve Form 25, and save it under a new name. Then enter the following information for the week of March 21 on the form.

1. In Rows 3–6, place a check mark (Ctrl-V, 5, 23) under "Bus." or "Per." for each day an auto was used. The autos were used as follows:
   Buick: Monday, Tuesday, Thursday, and Friday for business.
   Dodge: Wednesday for business.
   Toyota: Monday, Tuesday, and Friday for personal.
   Ford: Wednesday and Thursday for personal.
2. Enter the following beginning odometer readings consecutively from Monday to Friday: 5,678; 31,094; 5,825; 31,180; 17,446; 9,340; 5,931; 9,417; 6,184; 9,637.
3. Enter the following ending odometer readings consecutively from Monday to Friday: 5,825; 31,180; 5,931; 31,223; 17,622; 9,417; 6,275; 9,485; 6,275; 9,721.
4. Calculate the total miles driven each day for each category (business and personal).
5. Enter the following miscellaneous expenses consecutively from Monday to Friday: 23.47; 12.50; 48.99; 5.00; 11.75; 6.50; 23.50; 8.00; 11.50; 13.25.

D. Spacing: double. Take two 3-minute timed writings. Compute your speed and count errors.

Goal: 35 wam/3′/4e

D. 3-MINUTE TIMED WRITING

The United States plays a major role in world trade, 12
both as a buyer and as a seller. We are now the largest 23
importer of goods in the whole world and the second largest 35
exporter. Thus it is quite important that all members of 47
an organization learn as much as they can about each of 58
the cultures with which they may be dealing. When we talk 70
about culture, we simply mean the typical traits of a group 82
of people. We need to learn how these people dress, think, 94
talk, and carry out their business and private affairs. 105

| 1 | 2 | 3 | 4 | 5 | 6 | 7 | 8 | 9 | 10 | 11 | 12

FORMATTING

E. FORMATTING BLOCKED COLUMN HEADINGS

Blocked column headings align with their columns—at the left for word columns and at the right for number columns.

If a column heading is the longest item in a column, use it as part of the key line to horizontally center the table. Triple-space before and double-space after column headings. Column headings are keyed in upper- and lowercase letters and underlined.

If a column heading is over a column with decimals, set a right tab rather than a decimal tab for the column to right align the column heading.

DOCUMENT PROCESSING

TABLE 7
3-COLUMN TABLE WITH BLOCKED COLUMN HEADINGS

Align columns that contain both words and numbers at the left.

EMPLOYEE UPDATE FILE

New Hires Since March 1

Employee Name	Soc. Sec. No.	Empl. Date
Chalupa, B. J.	246-72-8384	May 1
Dye, R. E.	382-43-8823	May 15
Grunkemeyer, R. L.	130-03-7255	August 15
Ma, P. F.	281-19-2877	July 10
Mundrake, J. A.	380-32-3476	June 9
Sanchez, E. T.	154-14-3228	August 25
Sormunen, R. A.	130-29-9931	June 18
Underwood, R. L.	222-38-0934	July 25
Zimpfer, M. A.	191-73-0221	August 10

TABLE 8
3-COLUMN TABLE WITH BLOCKED COLUMN HEADINGS

These changes require new tab settings.

Retrieve Table 7 and make the following changes:

1. Ms. Sormunen uses a hyphenated last name: Sormunen-Jones.
2. Mr. Mundrake's social security number is 308-32-3476.
3. Ms. Ma was actually hired on February 27, so her name should be deleted from the table.
4. The following name should be added to the list in alphabetic order: R. T. Allison, 379-42-3715, August 31.

FORM 23 (continued)

13. Change the gray shading option to 20%, and shade cells B12–F12 and cell G11.
14. In cell G2, enter the formula to total that row (5, 2, *B2+C2+D2+E2+F2,* Enter).
15. With the cursor still in cell G2, copy the formula to cells G3–G10 (5, 3, 2, 8, Enter). The formula will be adjusted for each row (for example, in Row 3, the formula will change to B3+C3+D3+E3+F3).
16. In cell B11, enter the formula to total the column (5, 2, *B2+B3+B4+B5+B6+B7+B8+B9+B10,* Enter).
17. With the cursor still in cell B11, copy the formula to cells C11–F11 (5, 3, 3, 4, Enter).
18. In cell G12, enter the formula to total the monthly expenses (5, 2, *B11+C11+D11+E11+F11,* Enter).
19. Save the form.

FORM 24
EXPENSE REPORT

Do not include the dollar signs on the expense report.

Position the cursor before the bold and Very Large codes before keying *May*.

Retrieve Form 23, and save it under a new name. Complete the form for the month of May, using the following information.

1. Mileage: Week 1, $75.00; Week 2, $8.75; Week 3, $24.25; Week 4, $30.00; Week 5, $20.75.
2. Tolls: Week 1, $12.00; Week 4, $1.75.
3. Parking: Week 1, $14.00; Week 2, $3.00; Week 4, $7.50; Week 5, $14.00.
4. Local Transportation: Week 3, $12.00.
5. Airfare: Week 3, $378.50; Week 5, $278.60.
6. Hotel/Motel: Week 1, $145.00; Week 3, $269.79; Week 4, $78.75; Week 5, $92.67.
7. Telephone: Week 1, $11.67; Week 2, $7.96; Week 3, $6.43; Week 4, $1.67; Week 5, $2.48.
8. Postage: Week 1, $2.90; Week 5, $10.98.
9. Meals: Week 1, $165.00; Week 2, $25.75; Week 3, $84.00; Week 4, $128.50; Week 5, $360.02.
10. Calculate all totals.

FORM 25
AUTO USAGE FORM

WordPerfect 6 users: See Student Guide, p. 96.

Create the auto usage form shown on page 372, using the information that follows:

1. Change paper size to Landscape; set 0.5″ side margins; set a fixed line height of 0.167″; change to Extra Large, bold type.
2. Center and key *WEEKLY AUTO USAGE FORM,* leaving 1 space between letters and 3 spaces between words.
3. Change to Large, bold type, and press Enter 3 times. Center and key *For the Week of:*.
4. Change to normal type, press Enter twice, and create a table with 11 columns and 10 rows. Horizontally center the table.
5. Narrow Columns B–K by 1 space each; then widen Column A by 10 spaces.
6. Join cells A1 and A2.
7. Join cells B1 and C1; D1 and E1; F1 and G1; H1 and I1; J1 and K1.
8. Set Rows 1 and 2 for center justification and bold.
9. Change the top line of cells A3–K3 to double.
10. Key *Auto Used* in cell A1. Enter the days of the week, beginning with *Monday,* in cells B1, D1, F1, H1, and J1.
11. Key *Bus.* and *Per.* in cells B2 and C2, respectively. Follow this sequence across the row.
12. Enter the following information in cells A3–A10:
    Buick, LPD-285
    Dodge, QZT-176
    Toyota, HZG-358
    Ford, VRP-823
    Beg. Odometer
    End. Odometer
    Total Miles
    Misc. Expenses
13. Change the top line of Rows 7 and 10 to double.
14. Change the left line in all Row 2 cells to double.

(Continued on next page)

TABLE 9
4-COLUMN TABLE WITH BLOCKED COLUMN HEADINGS

Spacing: Double
Tabs: 1 left and 3 right absolute tabs

WAREHOUSING DEPARTMENT

January Payroll Report

Name	Gross Pay	Deductions	Net Pay
C. S. David	2,025.00	404.75	1,620.25
P. M. Gilelsman	1,984.10	396.82	1,587.28
J. T. Peralta	1,278.32	273.66	992.66
D. J. Terrell	2,406.91	481.38	1,925.53
E.D. Wyllie	2,978.35	595.67	2382.68
Total	10,672.68	2,152.28	8,508.40

LESSON 39 Tables With Two-Line Blocked Column Headings

Margins: 1 inch • Tab: 0.5 inch • Spacing: Single • Drills: 2 times • Format Guide: 17

Goals:
To improve speed and accuracy; to format tables with two-line blocked column headings.

A. WARMUP

1 Four dozen of our taxi drivers had just quit because I 12
2 asked them to drive between 1:30 and 6:45 a.m. Their union 24
3 (Local #2798) hired Page & Lambert to overturn my decision. 36

| 1 | 2 | 3 | 4 | 5 | 6 | 7 | 8 | 9 | 10 | 11 | 12

LANGUAGE ARTS

B. SPELLING

B. These words are among the 500 most frequently misspelled words in business correspondence.

4 complete recent members enclosed determine development site
5 medical facility permanent library however purpose personal
6 electrical implementation representative discussed eligible
7 organization discuss expense minimum performance next areas
8 separate professional changes arrangements reason pay field

SKILLBUILDING

C. 12-SECOND SPRINTS

C. Take three 12-second timed writings on each line. The scale shows your wam speed for a 12-second timed writing.

9 Fritz saw many old jets at the air show held in the spring.
10 Jim kept Gil away because four dozen taxi drivers had quit.
11 They will take their rowboat when they go back to the lake.

12 They caught the last boat back to the mainland at the dock.
13 Fay's wipers quit just when Marv locked the zoo's gate box.
14 Did Mac Wiker prize the five or six big quarterly journals?

| | | | 5 | | | | 10 | | | | 15 | | | | 20 | | | | 25 | | | | 30 | | | | 35 | | | | 40 | | | | 45 | | | | 50 | | | | 55 | | | | 60

FORM 22
CALENDAR

Retrieve Form 21, and save it under a different name. Then use the information below to place entries into selected days of the month. Depending on the length of the entry, use 1, 2, or 3 lines. Horizontally center each line.

Nov. 1, DEPT. MTG. / Nov. 4, QUARTERLY REPORT DUE / Nov. 9, TOPEKA SEMINAR / Nov. 11, HOLIDAY / Nov. 15, DEPT. MTG. / Nov. 18, DISTRICT MEETING / Nov. 24, HOLIDAY / Nov. 29, DEPT. MTG. / Nov. 30, SALES RPT. DUE

FORM 23
EXPENSE REPORT

WordPerfect 6 users: See Student Guide, p. 94.

Create this monthly expense report.

1. Change paper size to wide (landscape) and side margins to 0.5″.
2. Create Figure Box 1 as follows:
   Filename: PC-1.WPG
   Anchor Type: Page
   Vertical Position: Top
   Horizontal Position: Margin, Left
   Size: 1″ wide × 1″ high
   Wrap Text: Yes
3. Create Figure Box 2 following Step 2, but change Horizontal Position to Margin, Right.
4. In Extra Large, bold type center and key *KRANDAL COMPUTER COMPANY* on Ln = 1″; then press Enter once.
5. In Very Large, bold type center and key *Monthly Expense Report.* Press Enter twice, and center and key *For the Month of:*.
6. Change to normal font, and press Enter 2 times.
7. Create a table with 7 columns and 12 rows. Horizontally center the table.
8. In Table Edit, decrease the width of Columns B–G by 3 spaces each; then increase the width of Column A by 18 spaces.
9. Center-justify and bold Row 1. Change the bottom rule to double; return to Cell A1.
10. In the document screen, increase the depth of Row 1 by 1 line (press Enter); then add these headings to Columns A–G: *Item, Week 1, Week 2, Week 3, Week 4, Week 5, Total Expenses.*
11. Add these items to cells A2–A12: *Auto Mileage @ $.25/Mile, Tolls, Parking, Local Transportation, Airfare, Hotel/Motel, Telephone, Postage, Meals, TOTAL WEEKLY EXPENSES, TOTAL MONTHLY EXPENSES.*
12. Right-justify Columns B–G, excluding the column headings (block the columns and select Cell).

Decrease the width of Columns B–G before you increase the width of Column A.

(Continued on next page)

KRANDAL COMPUTER COMPANY
Monthly Expense Report

For the Month of:

Item	Week 1	Week 2	Week 3	Week 4	Week 5	Total Expenses
Auto Mileage @ $.25/Mile						0.00
Tolls						0.00
Parking						0.00
Local Transportation						0.00
Airfare						0.00
Hotel/Motel						0.00
Telephone						0.00
Postage						0.00
Meals						0.00
TOTAL WEEKLY EXPENSES	0.00	0.00	0.00	0.00	0.00	
TOTAL MONTHLY EXPENSES						0.00

D. PROGRESSIVE PRACTICE: NUMBERS

Turn to the Progressive Practice: Numbers routine at the back of the book. Take six 30-second timed writings, starting at the point where you left off the last time.

E. TECHNIQUE PRACTICE: SHIFT KEY

E. All 26 capital letters are included in the passage. Keep your eyes on the copy, and try not to slow down for the capital letters.

```
     Z. L. Ford from Eaton, Ohio, and Dr. B. I. Quincy from   12
Venice, Utah, attended the Miss America Pageant in Atlantic   24
City, New Jersey.  They met Helen X. Wood from South Dakota   36
and Gay Y. Kane from Puerto Rico, who is Miss Congeniality.   48
| 1 | 2 | 3 | 4 | 5 | 6 | 7 | 8 | 9 | 10 | 11 | 12
```

DOCUMENT PROCESSING

TABLE 10
3-COLUMN TABLE WITH 2-LINE BLOCKED COLUMN HEADING

Leave 2 blank lines between the table title and the first line of a two-line column heading. Underline and single-space each line. The bottom lines of all column headings should align horizontally.

11 Left
17 Right

FAX PHONE DIRECTORY

3 Returns

Marketing Representative (single, 11, Double space)	Company (L 35)	Fax Phone (R 73)
Wayne, Fran	Pinnacle West	415-555-3076
Allan, May	Herman Miller	207-555-1932
Murphy, P. J.	Northern Savings	943-3211
Harp, Dolores	U.S. Markets	802-555-7453
Dawkins, Amy	Western Digital	816-555-2222
Oglesby, Peter	General States	616-555-8654
Carmichael, Robert	Quaker & Southern	481-3287
Tanton, Clay	Sears Mobil	802-555-2961
Eaton, T. Susan	Fairchild Industries	719-555-0841
Latz-Wells, Ada	Healthco	314-555-8765
Shaorenzski, Mike	Circus Pacific	943-5768
Coffin, William	Central Air	802-555-3333
Boyer, Ellen	Smithfield	816-555-3429
Kuiper, Cheryl	Union Labs	733-8655
Hebert, Marilyn	Rubbermaid	831-3288
McKenna, P. O.	Guilford Mills	605-555-3838
May, Martin	RJR Nabisco	800-555-0888
Rodriguez, Robert	Nordstrom	314-555-2907

S. WORDPERFECT: LANDSCAPE PRINTING

Change paper size: Sh-F8, 2, 7, 2, 1, 1, 2, F7, 1, F7

Select landscape: Sh-F8, 2, 7, *highlight*, 1, F7

WordPerfect 6 users: See Student Guide, p. 93.

To print landscape (the text is parallel to the long edge of the paper), edit the paper definition, change the paper size to 11″ × 8.5″, and then select landscape from the Paper Size/Type menu (Sh-F8, 2, 7, 2, 1, 1, 2, F7, 1, F7). When using a laser printer, you may also need to change font type to landscape (Sh-F8, 2, 7, 2, 1, 1, 2, 3, 2, F7, 1, F7).

Once landscape has been added to the Paper Size/Type menu, you need only to highlight landscape and select it (Sh-F8, 2, 7, *highlight*, 1, F7).

DOCUMENT PROCESSING

FORM 21
CALENDAR

Spread-center: space once between letters; space 3 times between words.

WordPerfect 6 users: See Student Guide, p. 94.

Create a monthly calendar, following these steps.

1. Change paper size to wide (landscape).
2. Set side margins of 0.5″.
3. Set a fixed line height of 0.167″.
4. Change to Extra Large, bold type, and spread-center *NOVEMBER 1995* on Ln = 1″. Press Enter 3 times.
5. Change to Very Large, bold type; then key *Krandal Computer Company* at the left margin and *Information Systems Department* flush right. Press Enter 4 times.
6. Change to Large type, and create a table with 7 columns and 5 rows. Center the table horizontally.
7. In the document screen, press Enter 4 times in cell A1. Repeat this procedure for the remaining rows.
8. In Table Edit, delete the top and left lines from cells A1 and B1.
9. Delete the bottom lines from cells E5, F5, and G5; the left lines from cells F5 and G5; and the right line from cell G5.
10. On the first line of cell C1, key *1* for the first day of the month. Enter the remaining days for the rest of the month.
11. Shade the cells for November 11 and 24 to indicate holidays (Alt-F7, 3, 8, 1).
12. Save the calendar.

N O V E M B E R   1 9 9 5

Krandal Computer Company — **Information Systems Department**

		1	2	3	4	5
6	7	8	9	10	11	12
13	14	15	16	17	18	19
20	21	22	23	24	25	26
27	28	29	30			

TABLE 11
3-COLUMN TABLE WITH 2-LINE BLOCKED COLUMN HEADING

Revise Table 10 as follows:

1. Delete the names of and information for Dolores Harp and Marilyn Hebert.
2. Double-space the body of the table.
3. Add the following name and information at the end of the table: Steven L. Pierce, Allied Fertilizer, 919-555-4022.
4. Change Clay Tanton's telephone number to 617-555-4370.
5. Change Martin May's company and telephone number as follows: Neiman Industries, 601-555-8990.

TABLE 12
4-COLUMN TABLE WITH 2-LINE BLOCKED COLUMN HEADING

Spacing: Double

ROI stands for *Return on Investment.*

STOCK PORTFOLIO ANALYSIS

For Year Ended June 30

Company	Percent of Total	Major Product	ROI %
Mellon Bank	29.3	Retail banking	23.1
Occidental Oil	21.7	Agribusiness	5.4
Stanley Works	15.6	Home improvement	8.6
Norfolk Southern	12.6	Rail shipments	12.5
Armstrong World	11.7	Floor coverings	7.4
Tyson Foods	9.1	Poultry products	9.5
TOTAL	100.0		66.5

Formatting Review

Margins: 1 inch • Tab: 0.5 inch • Spacing: Single • Drills: 2 times • Format Guide: 17–19

Goals:
To key 36 wam/3'/4e; to format a table, a report, and a letter.

A. WARMUP

Just five or six of my quarterly journals cost as much 12
as $45 a year; most cost me between $16 and $30. A sizable 24
number of them are free, but <u>Parks Digest</u> is $27.89 a year. 36

| 1 | 2 | 3 | 4 | 5 | 6 | 7 | 8 | 9 | 10 | 11 | 12

LANGUAGE ARTS

B. PROOFREADING

B. Compare this table with the body of Table 13 on the next page. Key a list of the errors, correcting them as you key.

Date	Resort	State	Price (Mil)
1989	Steamboat	Colorado	$110
1989	Stratton	Vermont	85
1990	Heavenly Valley	Colorado	80
1898	Brackenridge	California	65
1990	Snowshoe	West Virginia	20

FORM 19
(continued)

7. Enter the guide words and the lines as follows:
   a. Press home and tab; then key *To:*.
   b. Press home, tab, F8, Esc; then key *30,* press the space bar, and press F8.
   c. Press home and tab; then key *Invoice No.:*.
   d. Press home, tab, F8, Esc; then key *7,* press the space bar, and press F8.
   e. Press Enter twice. Press home and tab; then press home and tab again.
   f. Press F8 and Esc; then key *30,* press the space bar, and press F8.
   g. Press home and tab; then key *Date:*.
   h. Press home, tab, F8, Esc; then key *14,* press the space bar, and press F8.
   i. Press Enter twice. Then press home and tab, home and tab.
   j. Press F8 and Esc; then key *30,* press the space bar, and press F8.
   k. Repeat Steps i and j, and press Enter once after the last line.
8. In Table Edit, decrease the width of Columns A, C, and D by 5 spaces each. Increase the width of Column B by 15 spaces.
9. Change the top and bottom lines of cells A2–D2 to double.
10. In the document screen, enter the column headings in bold, and center them. Enter *Subtotal* in cell B13, *Plus 5% tax* in cell B14, and *TOTAL AMOUNT DUE* in cell B15.
11. In Table Edit, enter the formula A3*C3 in cell D3. Then copy the formula down the column 9 times. Enter the formula *D3+D4+D5+D6+D7+D8+D9+D10+D11+D12* in cell D13. Enter *D13*.05* in cell D14. Enter *D13+D14* in cell D15.
12. Delete the inside lines from Columns A, B, C, and D, excluding Row 2.
13. Justify each column as follows: A, center; B, left; C, right; D, right [*block each column,* 2, 1 (Cell), *correct number*]. Selecting Cell prevents the copy in the address block and the column headings from shifting.
14. Exit Table Edit, and save the invoice.

FORM 20
INVOICE

Retrieve Form 19, and save it under a different name. Then use Insert (typeover) to complete the invoice with the following data. When all the data has been entered in the Table Edit screen, select Calculate to perform the necessary calculations. Return to the document screen, and delete the zeros appearing in the empty rows.

Do not key the dollar signs on the invoice.

WordPerfect 6 users: See Student Guide, p. 92.

(Current Date) / Invoice No. 1384 / Belmont Electronics / 3509 Hillsdale / Wichita, KS 67230

3 ProCom 486SX computers @ $2,600.75 each
1 Model LPU laser printer @ $1,475.99
10 Cases laser printer paper @ $27.50 per case
5 LPU toner cartridges @ $80.50 each

Subtotal / Plus 5% tax / TOTAL AMOUNT DUE

FORMATTING

R. WORDPERFECT: LINE HEIGHT

Line height: Sh-F8, 1, 4, 2, *set position,* Enter, F7

WordPerfect 6 users: See Student Guide, p. 93.

Line height is the amount of space from the base of one line to the base of the next line. WordPerfect automatically adjusts the line height for the largest font used.

If you do not want the line height adjusted, set a fixed line height (Sh-F8, 1, 4, 2, *0.167″—the line height for normal font,* F7).

SKILLBUILDING

C. DIAGNOSTIC PRACTICE: ALPHABET

Turn to the Diagnostic Practice: Alphabet routine at the back of the book. Take the Pretest and record your performance. Then practice the drill lines for those reaches on which you made errors. Finally, repeat the Pretest and compare your performance.

D. Take two 1-minute timed writings. The last two digits of each number provide a cumulative word count to help you determine your wam speed.

D. NUMBER PRACTICE

1801 3802 3403 2904 3805 4606 1107 0208 3909 4810 8711 9112
3813 3914 3015 3416 1217 9918 0719 6820 0621 5622 2123 2024
3425 3026 2227 9828 5729 5930 3631 4032 2433 2934 0135 2636
7137 3438 6439 8340 2941 4942 1243 3444 0945 8746 6947 0348

E. Spacing: double. Take two 3-minute timed writings. Compute your speed and count errors.

Goal: 36 wam/3′/4e

E. 3-MINUTE TIMED WRITING

Everyone is aware that his or her actions must never 12
exceed the law. However, it is sometimes true that being 23
legally right does not justify our actions. All of us have 35
our own code of ethics, or rules of conduct that go beyond 47
legal rules and tell us how to act when the law is silent. 59

Ethical people should first ask themselves if what 70
they say and what they write are true and then ask if these 82
are in the best interests of their organization. They 93
should always try to achieve their own goals while acting 105
in an ethical manner. 109

| 1 | 2 | 3 | 4 | 5 | 6 | 7 | 8 | 9 | 10 | 11 | 12

DOCUMENT PROCESSING

TABLE 13
4-COLUMN TABLE

RECENT SKI RESORT PURCHASES
(1988–90)

Date	Resort	Location	Price (Mil.)
1989	Steamboat	Colorado	$110
1989	Stratton	Vermont	85
1990	Heavenly Valley	California	80
1988	Breckenridge	Colorado	65
1990	Snowshoe	West Virginia	20

FORMATTING

Q. WORDPERFECT: MATH (TABLES)

WP MATH (TABLE)

Enter formula: Alt-F7, 5, 2, *enter formula*

Calculate: Alt-F7, 5, 1

WordPerfect 6 users: See Student Guide, p. 90.

The Math option in Table Edit enables you to enter formulas to add (+), subtract (−), multiply (*), and divide (/). For example, to add 2 rows of a 3-row column, position the cursor in the cell where you want the total to appear (in Form 19, cell A3). Then select Math (5) and Formula (2). Enter the formula: A1+A2. If numbers have not yet been keyed in the table, the cell will display 0.00.

To calculate the total, position the cursor anywhere within the table, and select Calculate (Alt-F7, 5, 1).

DOCUMENT PROCESSING

FORM 19
INVOICE

Table Review
Create: Alt-F7, 2, 1

Delete lines: Alt-F7, *block cells, rows, or columns,* 3, 5, 1

Create double rule: Alt-F7, *block cells, rows, or columns,* 3, 4 or 3, 3

Join columns/rows: Alt-F7, 7, Y, F7

Adjust column width: Alt-F7, Ctrl-right or left arrow

Tab within columns: Home, Tab

WordPerfect 6 users: See Student Guide, p. 91.

Create the invoice form for the Krandal Computer Company, following these steps:

1. Center and key *INVOICE* in Very Large, all-capital letters on Ln = 1″. Return to normal font, and press Enter twice.
2. Center and key the company name and address in Large, bold type with single spacing. Return to normal font, and press Enter twice.
3. Create a table with 4 columns and 15 rows. Center the table horizontally.
4. In Table Edit, join the cells in Row 1 (*highlight the cells,* 7, Y).
5. In the document screen, position the cursor in cell A1, and press Enter twice.
6. Clear all tabs, and set five relative tabs: 0.3″, 0.7″, 3.8″, 4.4″, 5.1″.

(Continued on next page)

INVOICE

Krandal Computer Company
2378 Park Place
Wichita, KS 67204

To: ______________________ Invoice No.: ________
______________________ Date: ____________
____
____

Quantity	**Description**	**Price**	**Amount**
			0.00
			0.00
			0.00
			0.00
			0.00
			0.00
			0.00
			0.00
			0.00
			0.00
	Subtotal		0.00
	Plus 5% tax		0.00
	TOTAL AMOUNT DUE		0.00

REPORT 10

Spacing: Double

INVESTING IN THE SKI RESORT INDUSTRY

By I. William Berry

A review of industry and demographic data shows that Valdese Associates should not explore further the possible purchase of a ski resort either in the Northeast or in the Northwest.

Industry Trends

Neither past performance nor the outlook for the future provides any support for investing in a ski resort.

Past Performance. Most of the $7 billion U.S. ski resort industry lost money last year. Analysts attribute the poor economic showing to a combination of bad weather, a weak economy, uncontrolled costs, and overbuilding.

Future Outlook. Strict environmental controls are making it difficult for resorts to make the capital improvements that are needed to attract more business. In addition, the weak housing market and tax-law changes have weakened condominium sales, which formerly provided a major share of resort profits.

Demographic Data

By its nature, skiing tends to attract 25- to 35-year-olds in the middle- to upper-income brackets. But as the U.S. population ages and as a weak economy continues, the interest in skiing will probably dwindle, making the purchase of a ski resort a risky investment for Valdese Associates.

LETTER 15
BLOCK STYLE

May 5, 19— / Mr. Hiro Matsushita / Director of Planning / Valdese Associates / 30 South Wacker Drive / Chicago, IL 60606-1233 / Dear Mr. Matsushita:

As you requested, I have studied the feasibility of Valdese Associates' investing in the U.S. ski resort industry. I reviewed industry and demographic data and spoke with several resort operators.

The enclosed report summarizes my initial reactions and may be used for your Investment Committee meeting in July. A more detailed report will be prepared in time for your annual planning meeting in August. I've also enclosed a table showing the recent selling prices of ski resorts. Incidentally, all resorts were purchased by Japanese concerns.

Please call me if you wish additional information for your July committee meeting or if you wish me to explore additional segments of the market for the August report.

Sincerely, / Malcolm J. Davis / Management Consultant / *(Your Initials)* / Enclosures

FORMATTING

P. CREATING FORMS

Before using desktop publishing to create forms, you should first do a thumbnail sketch of how you want the form to look (see the illustration in the side margin). As you sketch the form, identify margins, spacing, font sizes and styles, placement of graphics, and so on. Then, using your thumbnail sketch, design your form in WordPerfect.

DOCUMENT PROCESSING

FORM 18*
TELEPHONE MESSAGE FORM

*(Forms 1–17 appear in Lessons 61–120.)

Horizontal lines: Alt-F9, 5, 1
Vertical lines: Alt-F9, 5, 2
Create figure box: Alt-F9, 1, 1
Add graphic to figure box: Alt-F9, 1, 1, 1, *filename,* F7
Edit figure box: Alt-F9, 1, 2, *figure number,* Enter, 9
Create text box: Alt-F9, 3, 1
Edit text box: Alt-F9, 3, 2, *text box number,* Enter, 9

WordPerfect 6 users: See Student Guide, p. 88.

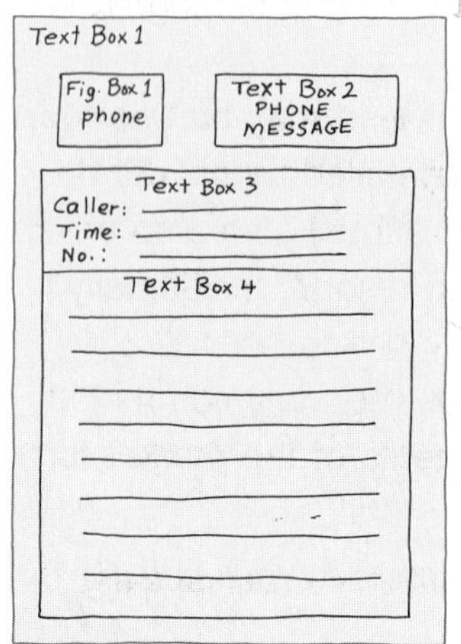

The thumbnail sketch of the telephone message form in the side margin shows that the form consists of one figure box and four text boxes. Create the form, following these steps:

1. Set the options for a figure box to no borders and 0% gray shading; then create Figure Box 1 with these settings:
   Filename: TELPHONE.WPG
   Anchor Type: Page
   Vertical Position: 1.5″
   Horizontal Position: 3″
   Size: 1″ wide × 1″ high
   Wrap Text: Yes
2. Set the options for a text box to double borders and 0% gray shading; then create Text Box 1 with these settings:
   Anchor Type: Page
   Vertical Position: 1″
   Horizontal Position: Margin, Center
   Size: 3.6″ wide × 5″ high
   Wrap Text: Yes
3. Set the options for a text box to no borders and 0% gray shading; then create Text Box 2 with these settings:
   Anchor Type: Page
   Vertical Position: 1.5″
   Horizontal Position: 4″
   Size: 1.75″ wide × 1″ high
   Wrap Text: Yes
4. With the cursor at Ln = 0″ in Text Box 2, center and key the heading *PHONE MESSAGE,* double-spaced and in Large font.
5. Set the options for a text box to double borders and 0% gray shading; then create Text Box 3 with these settings:
   Anchor Type: Page
   Vertical Position: 2.5″
   Horizontal Position: 2.75″
   Size: 3″ wide × 1″ high
   Wrap Text: Yes
6. In Text Box 3, set the line spacing to 1.3, and use normal font. With the cursor at Ln = 0″, key *Caller:, Time:,* and *No.:,* with single spacing. After the first callout, press the Escape key, enter *18* for the repeat value, key an underline, and press Enter. Then repeat the process for the remaining lines, and be sure to align them at the left.
7. Set the options for a text box to no borders and 0% gray shading; then create Text Box 4 with these settings:
   Anchor Type: Page
   Vertical Position: 3.5″
   Horizontal Position: 2.75″
   Size: 3″ wide × 2.25″ high
   Wrap Text: Yes
8. In Text Box 4, on Ln = 0″, press the Escape key, enter *26* for the repeat value, and key an underline. Press Enter; then repeat the process to create the 12 single-spaced lines in the text box.

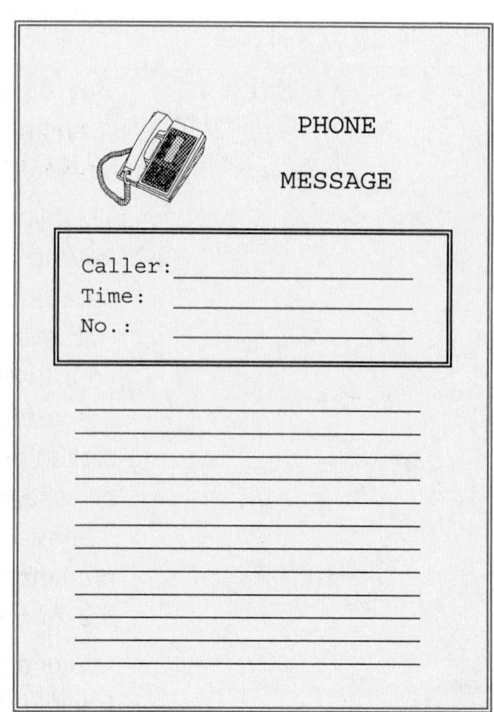

Progress Test on Part 2

TEST 2-A
3-MINUTE TIMED WRITING

Spacing: Double

```
     When doing a tax return for a small business, the use     12
of Schedule C will be required.  In the first stage, the       24
gross income is found.  Once gross income is determined, a     35
careful check of all the deductions and expenses is made.      46
Analyzing all of these dollar amounts is very important        57
because it can reduce the net profit that will be carried      69
forward so that a person's taxable income is found.  Using     81
a tax table or a tax rate schedule, a tax person can find      93
the amount of tax that is owed.  To complete Schedule C       103
will require hours.                                           108
| 1 | 2 | 3 | 4 | 5 | 6 | 7 | 8 | 9 | 10 | 11 | 12
```

TEST 2-B
LETTER 16
BLOCK STYLE

(Current Date) / Mr. Ralph Sheldrake, Director / Administrative Office Services / Seneca Pharmaceutical, Inc. / 62 Fontana Avenue / Nashville, TN 37204 / Dear Mr. Sheldrake:

Your inquiry about the training program that we have available for data-entry clerks has come to my attention. I believe that we have just the training package that you are looking for.

I am enclosing a copy of this instructional package to review on a ten-day trial basis without charge. When you have had an opportunity to review it, I am confident that you will be impressed with its capability to train your data-entry clerks.

In two weeks I will contact you to arrange a time when I can meet with you to answer any questions you may have about the program. At that time we can determine whether you would be interested in using this program on a full-time basis.

Sincerely yours, / Donald C. Williams / Account Executive / *(Your Initials)* / Enclosure

N. Take three 30-second timed writings on each line as you concentrate on infrequently used letters.

N. ALPHABET REVIEW: INFREQUENT LETTER PRACTICE

J James objected to joining Joe and John on a jaunt to Japan. 12
K Ken knew Ike liked cake and asked Kay to bake it this week. 12
X Alex Cox, a Texan, expects to visit Max in Dixie next Xmas. 12
Z Zo was amazed and dazzled by the size of the puzzle prizes. 12

| 1 | 2 | 3 | 4 | 5 | 6 | 7 | 8 | 9 | 10 | 11 | 12

O. Spacing: Double
Take two 5-minute timed writings. Compute your speed and count errors.

Goal: 55 wam/5′/5e

O. 5-MINUTE TIMED WRITING

Insurance. What is it, and why does it work? The 11
business of insurance is based on the central concept of 23
sharing of loss. The idea has the beauty of simplicity 34
combined with practicality. If risks, defined as chances 45
of loss, can be split among many members of a particular 57
group, they need not jeopardize any single member of that 68
group. Thus misfortunes that could be punishing to one 80
can be made bearable for all. 86

The idea and practice of sharing risk originated in 97
antiquity. Many years ago, Chinese merchants devised an 108
ingenious way of protecting themselves against the chance 120
of a financially ruinous accident in the dangerous river 131
rapids along their trade routes. They simply divided their 143
cargoes among several boats. If the rapids claimed one of 155
the boats, no merchant lost all his goods. Each stood to 167
lose only a small portion. 172

Although the ancient Chinese may not have thought of 184
their scheme as insurance, the principle they employed is 195
strikingly similar to the property and casualty insurance 207
of today. Over the years, insurers have expanded their 218
horizons to provide coverage against most known perils. 230
Consumers may now buy policies ranging from fire to the 241
harsh forces of storms, cyclones, and earthquakes; from 252
the actions of white-collar thieves to the tragic results 264
of one person's negligence, in terms of harm to another. 275

| 1 | 2 | 3 | 4 | 5 | 6 | 7 | 8 | 9 | 10 | 11 | 12

TEST 2-C
TABLE 14

Spacing: Double

Center horizontally and vertically.

GLOBE COMPUTER SUPPLIES, INC.

Sales of Computer Furniture

Item	Number	Percent
Workstation	370	26.2
Riser	334	23.7
Printer Stand	273	19.3
Storage Hutch	147	10.5
Mobile Micro Cart	132	9.3
PC Tilt & Swivel	88	6.2
Shelf Riser	68	4.8
TOTAL	1,412	100.0

TEST 2-D
REPORT 11

Spacing: Double

JOB SPECIFICATIONS

By Judith Durish

Personel [n] departments have the responsibility of working with department supervisors to determine the specifications or requirements for a given ~~job~~ position. Two common criteria often found in job specifications are education and experience.

Education Requirements

Some education beyond the secondary level is becoming more and more common when job openings are ~~announced~~ advertised. This postsecondary education can be at a private business school, a two-year community college, or a four-year college.

Experience Requirements

There are two aspects of experience that may be required. One deals with time spent in the work force; ~~and~~ the other deals with specific skills used on the job.

Time in Work Force. There might be a requirement that an individual have a minimum number of years in a certain position to be considered for the advertised job.

Specific Skills on Job. It is possible that the job being advertised requires an ~~person~~ individual who has some specific skills. For example, the applicant must know "WordPerfect."

J. Take three 12-second timed writings on each line. The scale gives wam for a 12-second timed writing.

J. 12-SECOND SPRINTS

My social security number (106-72-3854) was issued in 1967.
Read pages 495–527 before 8:30 a.m. Friday for English 106.
The 193 men and 287 women voted 264 to 216 for the $50 tax.
We purchased a new Model 45 for $3,760 on October 28, 1994.
Michael won the huge lottery with 8, 9, 17, 25, 36, and 40.

| | | | 5 | | | |10| | | |15| | | |20| | | |25| | | |30| | | |35| | | |40| | | |45| | | |50| | | |55| | | |60

K. Change every singular noun to a plural noun.

K. TECHNIQUE PRACTICE: CONCENTRATION

If the man, woman, and child want to vacate the old apartment, the manager must issue the permit to make the transfer legal. The tenant must approve the plan before the vacancy or listing can be printed in the newspaper.

L. Take three 30-second timed writings on each line. Try not to slow down for the capital letters.

L. TECHNIQUE PRACTICE: SHIFT KEY

Sue, Pat, Ann, and Gail left for Rome on November 16, 1994.
The St. Louis Cardinals and New York Mets played on Monday.
Tom Herr took Flight 481 for San Francisco and Los Angeles.
Karen Cook's new address is 51 Baron Street in Provo, Utah.
President Harry Truman was born in Missouri on May 8, 1884.

| 1 | 2 | 3 | 4 | 5 | 6 | 7 | 8 | 9 | 10 | 11 | 12

M. Take a 1-minute timed writing on the first paragraph to establish your base speed. Then take four 1-minute timed writings on the remaining paragraphs. As soon as you equal or exceed your base speed on one paragraph, advance to the next one.

M. SUSTAINED PRACTICE: CAPITALIZATION

History buffs love delving into the pages of old books 12
to try to re-create images of what the world was once like. 24
Some folks prefer becoming experts in one particular region 36
or country, while others concentrate on one period in time. 48

Many students of history, scholarly and amateur alike, 12
have been drawn to a significant region in Central America. 24
The forests that currently stretch across many borders were 36
once inhabited by a unique band of people called the Mayas. 48

They emerged in the land of the Yucatan peninsula more 12
than three millennia ago and created a culture that thrived 24
while Europe withered in the Dark Ages. Classic Mayan life 36
had already faded when the Spanish invaded centuries later. 48

Today a bold idea is taking form in Mexico, Guatemala, 12
Honduras, Belize, and El Salvador--all homes of the ancient 24
Mayas. Plans are to develop a monorail through the forests 36
connecting the Mayan sites. It will be named La Ruta Maya. 48

| 1 | 2 | 3 | 4 | 5 | 6 | 7 | 8 | 9 | 10 | 11 | 12

PART

3

SKILLBUILDING

Correspondence, Reports, and Employment Documents

OBJECTIVES

KEYBOARDING

To key 40 words a minute on a 5-minute timed writing with no more than 5 errors.

LANGUAGE ARTS

To improve language arts skills, including correct grammar and spelling and the correct use of punctuation marks, capitalization, and numbers.

To proofread documents and correct errors.

To develop keyboard composing skill.

WORD PROCESSING

To use the following WordPerfect commands: Search and Replace, Page Numbering, Widow/Orphan Protection, Footnotes, Endnotes, Dot Leaders, and Font Size.

DOCUMENT PROCESSING

To format memorandums and modified-block style letters.

To format one- and two-page unbound and bound reports with enumerations, footnotes, endnotes, bibliographies, and supplementary pages.

To prepare employment documents, including a resume, a letter of application, and a follow-up letter; and take an employment test.

© Andy Sacks/Tony Stone Worldwide

SKILLBUILDING

D. PACED PRACTICE

Turn to the Paced Practice routine at the back of the book. Take three 2-minute timed writings, starting at the point where you left off the last time.

PRETEST. Take a 1-minute timed writing; compute your speed and count errors.

E. PRETEST: DISCRIMINATION PRACTICE

Losing income can make one very uneasy. Debts quickly 12
mount. A merry attitude gets flung aside, and the weeks in 24
which there is no income make one behave differently. This 36
is a time to look at all options and consider viable moves. 48

| 1 | 2 | 3 | 4 | 5 | 6 | 7 | 8 | 9 | 10 | 11 | 12

PRACTICE.
Speed Emphasis: If you made no errors on the Pretest, key each line twice.
Accuracy Emphasis: If you made 1 or more errors on the Pretest, key each group of lines (as though it were a paragraph) twice.

F. PRACTICE: LEFT HAND

vbv bevy vibe above brave bevel beaver viable adverb behave
wew were week twine jewel where glowed twelve review brewer
ded dead bead added tweed edits graded doomed impede decide
fgf figs golf defog gaffe flung finger gifted flight forgot

G. PRACTICE: RIGHT HAND

klk milk like bulky klutz locks kettle linked buckle tackle
uyu your buys youth unify bushy uneasy yogurt runway hourly
oio boil oily ivory optic comic income orient losing choice
jhj jump head juror heavy eject hasten jovial reject wishes

POSTTEST. Repeat the Pretest (E) and compare performance.

H. POSTTEST: DISCRIMINATION PRACTICE

I. Take a 1-minute timed writing on the first paragraph to establish your base speed. Then take four 1-minute timed writings on the remaining paragraphs. As soon as you equal or exceed your base speed on one paragraph, advance to the next one.

I. SUSTAINED PRACTICE: NUMBERS

It is conventional wisdom today that the ever-changing 12
work force has greatly affected the need of working parents 24
to find quality, affordable child care in accessible areas. 36
Without support many parents just don't know where to turn. 48

A main source of aid is the Dependent Care Tax Credit. 12
For the 1.2 million dual-income families who earn less than 24
$15,000 per year, the tax credit helps them to find and pay 36
for child care. Almost half of all those qualified use it. 48

More than 70 percent of women aged 25 to 34 are in the 12
work force, which has made 12.8 million dual-career couples 24
with 8.8 million children under 6 years of age. Meanwhile, 36
7 million kids under age 14 are home alone part of the day. 48

Other statistics show that between 1970 and 1980, over 12
14 million women entered the labor force. Between 1990 and 24
2000, another 9 million will enter it. The number of homes 36
run by women has increased dramatically in the recent past. 48

| 1 | 2 | 3 | 4 | 5 | 6 | 7 | 8 | 9 | 10 | 11 | 12

Memorandums

Margins: 1 inch • Tab: 0.5 inch • Spacing: Single • Drills: 2 times • Format Guide: 19

Goals:
To improve speed and accuracy; to format interoffice memorandums.

A. WARMUP

1 A 14-page report was faxed to 26 new offices in all 13 12
2 zones in this region. Total costs for my project were very 24
3 high, $98,750; and there likely will be numerous questions. 36

| 1 | 2 | 3 | 4 | 5 | 6 | 7 | 8 | 9 | 10 | 11 | 12

SKILLBUILDING

PRETEST.
Take a 1-minute timed writing; compute your speed and count errors.

B. PRETEST: CLOSE REACHES

4 Did anybody try to stymie the enemy when he loaded his 12
5 weapon? Sad to say, all fifty of them had no choice but to 24
6 attempt to avoid more bloodshed by not making a loud noise. 36

| 1 | 2 | 3 | 4 | 5 | 6 | 7 | 8 | 9 | 10 | 11 | 12

PRACTICE.
Speed Emphasis: If you made 2 or fewer errors on the Pretest, key each line twice.
Accuracy Emphasis: If you made 3 or more errors, key each group of lines (as though it were a paragraph) twice.

C. PRACTICE: ADJACENT KEYS

7 tr traded tragic sentry trace tries stray extra metro retry
8 po pocket poorly teapot point poise pound spoke vapor tempo
9 sa salads sanded mimosa sadly safer usage essay visas psalm
10 oi boiled noises choice oiled doing coins avoid broil spoil

D. PRACTICE: CONSECUTIVE FINGERS

11 my myself myrtle myopia myths myrrh enemy foamy roomy slimy
12 ft drafts soften thrift after often fifty lifts craft graft
13 ny anyone canyon colony nylon nymph vinyl agony corny funny
14 lo loaded blouse pueblo loans locks along color hello cello

POSTTEST.
Repeat the Pretest (B) and compare performance.

E. POSTTEST: CLOSE REACHES

FORMATTING

F. INTEROFFICE MEMORANDUMS

An interoffice memorandum is usually sent from one person to another in the same organization. Plain paper, letterhead stationery, or special memo forms may be used. Follow these steps to format a memo on plain paper or letterhead stationery:

1. Margins: 1-inch side; 2-inch top.
2. Heading lines: bold; double spaced.
3. Tab: 1 inch left tab to align heading information.
4. Double-space the heading lines; triple-space to key the body.
5. Double-space and key your reference initials.

UNIT THIRTY • DESKTOP PUBLISHING: FORMS

146-150 LESSONS

Margins: 1 inch • Spacing: Single • Drills: 2 times • Format Guide: 131–133

Goals for Unit 30

Begin each day with approximately 15 minutes of skillbuilding, selecting activities from pages 362–365. In the remaining class time, complete as many production jobs from pages 366–372 as you can.

1. To improve accuracy and speed on alphabet and number keys.
2. To key 55 wam for 5 minutes with no more than 5 errors.
3. To improve proofreading skills.
4. To learn about Table Math, fixed line height, and landscape printing in WordPerfect.
5. To create and complete invoices, calendars, expense reports, and auto usage forms using special features of desktop publishing and WordPerfect.

A. WARMUP

1 After analyzing our inventory, Bev placed an order for 12
2 8 items @ $156, 9 items @ $47, and 20 items @ $93. She was 24
3 quite sure the order could be expected in just three weeks. 36

| 1 | 2 | 3 | 4 | 5 | 6 | 7 | 8 | 9 | 10 | 11 | 12

LANGUAGE ARTS

Study the rules at the right. Then key lines 4–7, making necessary changes.

B. NUMBERS

Rule: Use *st, d,* or *th* only if the day precedes the month.

The income tax forms must be sent by the 15th of April.

Rule: When two numbers appear together and both are in figures or words, separate them with a comma.

On page 237, 12 short activities must be completed.

4 The November 11th holiday is called Veterans Day.
5 The projected completion date is the 3rd of April.
6 In 1992 33 clients filed suit against the equipment company.
7 On Account 254H3, $279.39 was credited.

C. Compare this paragraph with the second paragraph of the 5-minute timed writing on page 365. Key a list of the words that contain errors, correcting the errors as you key.

C. PROOFREADING

8 The idea and practise of sharing risk originated in
9 antiquity. Many years ago, Chinese merchants deviced an
10 ingenious way or protecting themself against the chance
11 of a financeally ruinous accident in the dangerous river
12 rapids along the trade routes. They simply divided their
13 cargos among several boats. If the rapids klaimed one of
14 the boats, no merchant lost all the goods. Each stood to
15 loose only a small portion.

DOCUMENT PROCESSING

MEMO 1

Tab: 1 inch

Key bold headings: *MEMO TO:, FROM:, DATE:,* and *SUBJECT:*

Most memos are keyed with blocked paragraphs (no indentions) and 1 blank line between paragraphs.

The use of *MEMO TO:* eliminates the need to key the word *MEMORANDUM* at the top of the document. After keying the colon at the end of each bold heading, tab once to reach the point where the heading entries begin.

Key your initials for the reference initials.

↓2 inches | Tab

MEMO TO: Curtis Marlowe, Home Designs↓2

FROM: Doug Nestell, Sales Director↓2

DATE: October 18, 19--↓2

SUBJECT: Timber Creek Site↓3

Some observations seem appropriate now that the laying of wiring and conduits for Phase I of the Timber Creek site is being finalized. It is my understanding that a high percentage of Timber Creek residents likely will be first-time home buyers.↓2

Cost will be an important criterion; but on the basis of our previous experience with this type of development, other factors should be considered. Our model homes should reflect today's informal life-style. The use of a great room rather than both a family room and a living room is one way to reduce costs. Also, since both the husband and wife in most homes will work outside the home, there should be two-car garages. We have also found that many people like the option of leaving certain areas unfinished; these can be finished later as the family grows and as finances permit.↓2

I shall be happy to meet with you to discuss these concerns.↓2

bjh

MEMO 2

Tab: 1 inch

MEMO TO: Marian Dickenson, Sales Associate

FROM: Doug Nestell, Sales Director

DATE: October 18, 19—

SUBJECT: Timber Creek Model Homes

The first model homes at the Timber Creek site will be ready for showing by January 1. On the basis of your sales performance during the past year, I would like to have you assume total marketing responsibility for the project.

This may well come as a complete surprise to you. For that reason, please delay your decision until November 1. You likely will want to think through the nature of this assignment and discuss implications with your family.

I know that you can do a fine job with this project; I hope your answer will be "Yes!"

(Your Initials)

FORMATTING

U. CREATING PAIRED STYLES

WordPerfect 6 users: See Student Guide, p. 87.

Follow these steps to create the paired styles for Report 84 which follows.

1. Create a paired style with the name *Number*. Leave the description blank.
2. Key "5" to access the Enter options; then key "2" to turn the style off by pressing Enter.
3. Key "4" to open the codes window.
4. Using Reveal Codes, be sure the cursor is over the comment code [Comment], which should be highlighted.
5. Change to bold and Large font.
6. Press the right arrow key once to move to the right of the comment code and press F4 to turn on Indent.
7. Press F7 two times to return to the styles menu.
8. Follow Steps 2–5 to create another paired style with the name *Example*.
9. In the codes window, press F4 to turn on Indent.
10. Change to italic and to font size = Small.
11. Press F7 three times to return to the document screen and continue on to Report 84. The styles will be saved when you save the report.

DOCUMENT PROCESSING

REPORT 84
REPORT FORMATTED WITH STYLES

WordPerfect 6 users: See Student Guide, p. 88.

Follow these steps to format Report 84:

1. Center the report title 2 inches from the top in Very Large, bold type.
2. Press the right arrow key two times to move past the very large and bold codes.
3. Press Enter three times to leave 2 blank lines after the title.
4. Turn on the first style (Alt-F8, *highlight NUMBER,* 1).
5. Key the number 1 and the period. Then press Enter to turn off the style.
6. Key the rule sentence. Then press Enter two times to leave 1 blank line after the rule.
7. Turn on the second style (Alt-F8, *highlight EXAMPLE,* 1).
8. Key the example sentence; then press Enter to turn off the style.
9. Press Enter two times to leave 1 blank line after the example; then continue with the remaining text in the same manner.

Use the default tab settings of 0.5″ for indenting the numbered items.

GRAMMAR

1. When establishing agreement between subject and verb, disregard intervening phrases and clauses.

The doctor, not the interns, is working there.

2. Verbs in the subjunctive mood (those that talk of conditions which are improbable, doubtful, or contrary to fact) require the plural form.

I wish I were on that harbor cruise.

3. Use a singular pronoun with a singular antecedent (the word for which the pronoun stands) and a plural noun with a plural antecedent.

Neither Mr. Brown nor Robert finished his work.

4. Use nominative pronouns (*I, he, she, we, they,* and so on) as subjects of a sentence or clause.

The programmer and he are reviewing that.

5. Use objective pronouns (*me, him, her, us, them,* and so on) as objects in a sentence or clause.

The folders are for Susan and not him.

Lesson 42 Memorandums

Margins: 1 inch • Tab: 0.5 inch • Spacing: Single • Drills: 2 times • Format Guide: 19–21

Goals:
To key 38 wam/3'/3e; to format interoffice memorandums.

A. WARMUP

1   All 32 graduates were given the 555-7469 number. They 12
2 were excited and amazed at how quickly they could get 1,108 24
3 research questions proofed. They just couldn't believe it! 36

| 1 | 2 | 3 | 4 | 5 | 6 | 7 | 8 | 9 | 10 | 11 | 12

LANGUAGE ARTS

B. COMMAS

B. Study the rules at the right. Then key lines 4–7, making necessary changes.

Rule: Use a comma to separate two independent clauses in a compound sentence when they are joined by *and, but, or,* or *nor.*

The bus was late, but he was able to get there on time.

Rule: Use commas to separate three or more items in a series when the last item is preceded by *and, or,* or *nor.*

The invoice, contract, and cashier's check were enclosed.

4 Joan works in Plainview but Joyce works in Gwinn.
5 Two men came to the house and they installed the furnace.
6 Promotions were received by Matt Pamela and Sissy.
7 The grapes plums and peaches were sent from California.

SKILLBUILDING

C. PACED PRACTICE

Turn to the Paced Practice routine at the back of the book. Take three 2-minute timed writings, starting at the speed at which you left off the last time.

D. 3-MINUTE TIMED WRITING

D. Spacing: Double
Take two 3-minute timed writings. Compute your speed and count errors.

Goal: 38 wam/3'/3e

8   The profit motive is the one main force that drives 11
9 the economy of this country. Strong arguments are voiced 23
10 which support the belief that all of the profits should be 35
11 used either to expand business growth or to pay those who 46
12 own the stock. 49
13   In the past few decades, most business firms seem to 61
14 be judged more and more by the extent to which profit 72
15 dollars are used to satisfy citizens' needs. An example 83
16 would be the providing of quality day-care centers for 94
17 parents who work. Also, there are more and more concerns 106
18 about the environment and consumer needs. 114

| 1 | 2 | 3 | 4 | 5 | 6 | 7 | 8 | 9 | 10 | 11 | 12

REPORT 83
Continued

8. Do not press Enter after keying the last column. Instead, insert the style **Horiz Rule* and continue with the next product.

9. After all products have been entered, turn off columns, and press Enter twice. Create a full-width horizontal line 0.25" wide with 25% shading.

Use the appropriate Compose commands to format the fractions 1/4 and 1/2.

Using the Style command means that you do not have to turn columns off, insert a horizontal line, and then turn columns back on each time you have to insert a rule in the document.

23

Product	Price	Features
Add-a-Closet	$35.00	This well-priced closet provides additional dust-free garment storage anywhere in your home. The quilted vinyl bag features a see-through window at the top and three zippers for quick access. 36" x 19" x 64" high.
Drawer Liners	$12.50	Our exclusive ivy-patterned paper is a pretty and practical way to line drawers, chests, and boxes. Six 24" x 18" sheets per package.
Newspaper Recycling Rack	$16.00	This efficient rack makes newspaper recycling almost effortless. Just slip a grocery bag into the angled rack, and slide newspapers into the bag (plastic clips hold it open neatly). Sturdy tubular plastic; assembles in minutes. 14" x 15¼" x 23" high.
Portable Closet	$142.00	As functional as it is stylish, this portable closet from Italy provides enclosed hanging storage wherever it's needed. The heavy-weight jute shell is moisture-proof and zips closed for use with mothballs. Easy to assemble. 30½" x 20" x 67" high.
Willow Hassocks	$45.00	Lidded, natural willow hassocks are great for storing blankets, needlework, craft supplies, or toys. They also make comfortable footstools. Woven in China of full willow. 16½" diameter.

FORMATTING

WP

SEARCH
F2, *search string,* F2, F2
REPLACE
Alt-F2, *Y/N, search string,* F2, *replacement string,* F2

When keying a search string, be sure to use the exact capitalization of the text you are searching for.

WordPerfect 6 users: See Student Guide, page 21.

E. WORDPERFECT: SEARCH AND REPLACE

Use Search to locate text or codes in a document. Position the cursor where you want the search to begin (usually the start of the document), press F2, and enter what you want to search for (the "search string"). Press F2 to begin the search. The cursor will move to the first occurrence of the search string. To continue searching for the same search string, press F2 twice.

Use Replace to switch text or codes with other text or codes (for example, to replace BTC with Bolton Tire Company). Position the cursor where you want to begin, and press Alt-F2. Answer "yes" to confirm each replacement. Enter what you want to search for, and press F2. Enter what you want as a replacement, and press F2. The cursor will move to the first occurrence of the search string. Press "Y" to replace or "N" to skip to the next occurrence. If you say "no" to confirmation, WordPerfect automatically replaces all occurrences of the string.

F. ATTACHMENT NOTATION

Attachment (rather than *Enclosure*) is keyed below the reference initials when material is physically attached (stapled or clipped) to a memorandum.

Example:

(Your Initials)
Attachment

DOCUMENT PROCESSING

MEMO 3

Tab: 1 inch

MEMO TO: Randy A. Garner, President

FROM: Doug Nestell, Sales Director

DATE: October 20, 19--

SUBJECT: Marketing of Timber Creek site

The Timber Creek project continues to be a high-priority venture for the company. Curtis Marlowe and his staff assure me that the the models under construction have been designed to attract first-time homes buyers, with respect to both features and cost.

¶ You will be pleased to learn that Marian Dickenson has agreed to assume total marketing responsibility for the project. She has informed me that a tentative plan for media exposure will be ready for our review with in ten days. She will likely have some quite imaginative strategies in her plan.

¶ I am confident that the quality reputation of Graner Homes, Inc., will be further enhanced by the Timber Creek project. A schedule of progress reports for the next year is attached.

jlk
Attachment

Use your own reference initials.

FORMATTING

S. WORDPERFECT: STYLE

WP

STYLE
Create: Alt-F8, 3, *make selections,* F7, F7, F7.
Insert: Alt-F8, *highlight,* 1
Edit: Alt-F8, *highlight,* 4

WordPerfect 6 users: See Student Guide, p. 83.

Style enables you to insert formatting codes and text into a document without rekeying the data each time. For example, you can create a style for chapter titles that will print them with a horizontal line above, centered in Extra-Large font, and bold. Then, at the beginning of a new chapter, you simply insert that style and the text will be automatically formatted.

A style is saved with the document (it also can be saved as a separate file) and can be edited or deleted. However, whenever you edit a style, any existing text will be reformatted to conform to the new style. To create a style, press Alt-F8, and key "3." Give the style a descriptive name (up to 12 characters). Select the type of style—paired or open. An open style is turned on and stays on; all text after the open style code will conform to that style. A paired style is turned on and off; any text between the on and off codes will conform to that style.

If desired, enter a description to further identify the style. Then, key "4" (Codes) and enter the commands and text (if any) for the style.

To insert the style into a document, position the cursor where you want the style to begin, and select the style (Alt-F8, *highlight style,* 1).

T. CREATING AN OPEN STYLE

If the Columns command is not turned off, the horizontal line will extend only across the column instead of from margin to margin.

WordPerfect 6 users: See Student Guide, p. 86.

Follow these steps to create a style for Report 83 which follows. This style will turn columns off, insert a horizontal line, and turn columns on again.

1. Create an open style with the name **Horiz Rule* (Alt-F8, 3, 1, *name,* Enter, 2, 2) (the asterisk ensures that the style will be at the top of the Style list). Leave the description blank.
2. Key "4" to open the Codes window. Then, define 3 parallel columns with these margins: (1) 1″ and 3″, (2) 3.25″ and 4″, (3) 4.25″ and 7.5.″
3. Press Enter and insert a horizontal line using the default settings. Press Enter twice and turn columns on.
4. Press F7 three times to return to the Document screen and continue on to Report 83. The style will be saved when you save the report.

DOCUMENT PROCESSING

REPORT 83
CATALOG PAGE WITH PARALLEL COLUMNS

The key to DTP competence is following each step carefully.

WordPerfect 6 users: See Student Guide, p. 87.

Follow these steps to format Report 83:

1. Switch to full justification.
2. Insert a horizontal rule at the top of the document with these features: Horizontal Position = left, Length = 5.75″, Width = 0.25″, Gray Shading = 25%.
3. On the same line (Ln = 1″), key the page number "23" in Extra-Large font, flush right. Return to Normal font and press Enter three times.
4. Repeat Step 2 from "Creating a Style" to define the columns. Then, turn columns on.
5. In Large font, center each column heading; use Ctrl-Enter (hard-page break) at the end of each heading to move from column to column.
6. Do not press Enter after keying the last column heading. Return to Normal font and insert the style **Horiz Rule* (Alt-F8, *highlight style,* 1). Use View Document to ensure that your style is correct. If it isn't, edit the style as necessary (Alt-F8, *highlight style,* 4).
7. Key the first column flush left, insert a hard-page break, and center and key the amount in the second column. Insert a hard-page break, and key the third column letting word wrap end each line.

(Continued on next page)

MEMO 4

Tab: 1 inch

The use of nicknames and the omission of middle initials and courtesy titles reflect the informal nature of memos as compared with letters.

MEMO TO: Gayle Allenstein
FROM: Hank Swanson, Personnel Director
DATE: October 20, 19--
SUBJECT: Promotion to Department Head

You will be pleased to learn that on November 1, you will be promoted to the position of Head of the Housewares Department. This is a reflection of the confidence we have in you on the basis of your performance at Layton's Department Store over the past 18 months.

The Housewares Department plays a key role in achieving the objectives of our anchor store in downtown Lowell. There is a need for someone with broad experience in the retail field who can provide leadership in this department.

Gayle, I am confident that as Head of the Housewares Department, you will fit in well as a member of the Layton management team. Congratulations!

Remember to key your own reference initials.

MEMO 5

Retrieve Memo 4. There are some new changes in the November 1 personnel assignments. Gayle Allenstein is now being assigned to head the Home Appliance Department rather than the Housewares Department. Use the Search and Replace commands to make the necessary revisions in Memo 4 to Gayle.

Modified-Block Style Letters

Margins: 1 inch • Tab: 0.5 inch • Spacing: Single • Drills: 2 times • Format Guide: 21

Goals:
To improve speed and accuracy; to format modified-block style letters.

A. WARMUP

```
     Jack Jacobson said he acquired G & H Imports from Troy   12
Frazier in November of 1993.  The exact price was $685,240.   24
Mr. Jacobson now owns seven (7) retail outlets in the mall.   36
| 1 | 2 | 3 | 4 | 5 | 6 | 7 | 8 | 9 | 10 | 11 | 12
```

REPORT 81
Continued

ellite terminal versus serving them from the Kansas City hub?

- What business will be lost, if any, should delivery be available only from Kansas City?
- What are the opinions of Roadway's staff and major customers about the consolidation?

Procedures

Personal interviews were conducted with the Roadway Carriers staff in Overland Park on May 6 and 7. Connie Hook, terminal manager, and Jeff Parker, sales representative, were interviewed, primarily from the operations point of view. (A copy of the interview form is included in Appendix A.)

Interviews were conducted with managers from three of Roadway's top accounts in Overland Park (included in Appendix B):

Roadway personnel and customers were interviewed.

- Robert A. Foltz, automotive traffic manager at Borg-Warner
- Sharon O'Gilliam, distribution manager at Eli Walters Inc.
- Brian J. Moskowitz, transportation director at Overland Park Paint and Tile Supplies

Secondary data was gathered from transcripts from the ICC and journal articles, as well as from Roadway's corporate financial records since 1979.

The interview data was combined with the secondary data to provide a basis for determining the feasibility of this proposed consolidation.

REPORT 82
MAGAZINE ARTICLE

Retrieve and reformat Report 73 (page 315) to match the format used for Report 81. Key the title in the title block, using Extra-Large font. Double-space, and key the subtitle in Large font. Use the title for a header and the subtitle and page number as a footer. Advance to Ln = 4.63″ to begin the text. Select an appropriate statement from the section "Steps in Problem Solving" to insert into a graphics box, and place the box at an appropriate point in the text. Change the numbered list to a bulleted list. Delete the Bibliography.

LANGUAGE ARTS

B. PROOFREADING

B. Compare this paragraph with the second paragraph of Letter 18 on page 94. Key a list of the errors, correcting the errors as you key.

The Suncourt was designed specially for the small family. The modest monthly association fees will free you from such chores as lawn mowing and exterior maintainance of the property. This extra liesure time will enable the two of you to enjoy the swimming pool, tennis courts and other health club facilities funded by the association fees.

SKILLBUILDING

C. SUSTAINED PRACTICE: PUNCTUATION

C. Take a 1-minute timed writing on the first paragraph to establish your base speed. Then take several 1-minute timed writings on the remaining paragraphs. As soon as you equal or exceed your base speed on one paragraph, advance to the next one.

Many young people rent their own apartments after they 12
complete their education and secure their first jobs. Some 24
acquire a feeling of contentment that lasts for many years. 36

After living in rented apartments for a few years, the 12
people wish for greater independence. The thought of one's 24
becoming a first-time homeowner begins to suddenly develop. 36

The possibilities are numerous; four familiar types of 12
homes are co-operative apartments, condominiums, one-family 24
houses, and townhomes that vary greatly in style and price. 36

First-time owners' choices are based on these factors: 12
space (square footage), "sweat equity" required, negotiated 24
cost, and appearance and quality of the whole neighborhood. 36

| 1 | 2 | 3 | 4 | 5 | 6 | 7 | 8 | 9 | 10 | 11 | 12

FORMATTING

D. BUSINESS LETTERS IN MODIFIED-BLOCK STYLE

The modified-block style is one of the most commonly used formats for business letters.

1. Use 1-inch side margins.
2. Set a tab at the center of the page. Delete preset tabs, then set a relative tab at 3.25 inches (center).
3. Key the date 2 inches from the top of the page at the tab setting.
4. Key the inside address 1 inch below the date at the left margin.
5. Double-space before and after the salutation.
6. Single-space the body of the letter, but double-space between paragraphs. Paragraphs may be indented, but the preferred style is blocked.
7. Double-space after the body and key the complimentary closing at the center tab (3.25 inches).
8. Space down 4 lines and key the writer's identification at the center.
9. Double-space and key your reference initials at the left margin.

Corporate Travel Consultants
18601 Lenox Square
Atlanta, GA 30326

↓2 inches

March 18, 19-- ↓1 inch

Dr. Charles Edwards
University of Hawaii
Honolulu, HI 96844 ↓2

Dear Dr. Edwards: ↓2

I have referred your letter of March 9, in which you asked us about the Braves' home baseball games in July, to the box office of the club. I am sure you will be receiving the schedule and list of ticket rates right away. ↓2

You might want to zero in on the big double-header that is set for July 28. The braves will be meeting the Padres, and that ought to be one of the bright spots of the season. The good news is that tickets are still available. ↓2

Enclosed is a fine booklet about other Atlanta events that may be of interest to you. If there is any other information you need or any way I can help to make your visit to Atlanta more enjoyable, please give me a call. ↓2

Sincerely yours, ↓4

Mrs. Carol Heinz
Sports Consultant ↓2

tps
Enclosures

MODIFIED-BLOCK STYLE. The date, complimentary closing, signature, and writer's identification begin at the center of the page.

REPORT 81
Continued

Press Enter before creating each figure box. Make each box 2 inches wide and 1.3 inches high, and be sure the vertical position is 0. To add the text, in the Definition screen, press 9 for Edit. Switch to Center Justification and Large font. Key the text (which is a "call-out caption"), leaving 1 blank line before the text and pressing Enter after each line.

Use View Document or Print Preview to see how the page will look when printed.

Let WordPerfect determine your page break. It may be slightly different from the one shown here. Ensure that paragraphs are divided correctly (Widow/Orphan control).

WordPerfect 5.1:
Bullets: Ctrl-V, **

WordPerfect 6:
Bullets: Ctrl-W, 4,0

DEFINING THE PROBLEM

Extent of the Problem

Thirty-three of the top fifty carriers as of 1979 were no longer in business by the end of 1990 (Baker, 1991, p. 47). To attract business lost by failed carriers, surviving carriers have dramatically increased their discounts. For example, Roadway Carriers has increased its inbound and outbound discounts from 15 percent in 1987 to 45 percent today (Foltz, 1991).

Accompanying the revenue declines are increases in employee wages and benefits, fuel costs, and new-equipment costs. All this has been happening while the country's economy is in a recession.

Because costs are rising while revenue is dropping, it is necessary to find ways to operate more economically. One way that a carrier can cope with rising costs is to consolidate its smaller satellite operations with its larger hub operations.

Costs are
rising while
revenues are
dropping.

Problem Statement

To study the feasibility of consolidating, the following problem is addressed in this report: What is the feasibility of Roadway Carriers consolidating its Overland Park satellite operation with its larger Kansas City hub operation?

In order to answer this question, the following subproblems must be addressed:

- What are the comparable costs of serving Roadway's 250 Overland Park customers from the Kansas City sat-

10

(Continued on next page)

DOCUMENT PROCESSING

LETTER 17
MODIFIED-BLOCK STYLE

Tab: 3.25 inches

↓ 2 inches *(Current Date)* ↓ 1 inch

enter six

Mr. and Mrs. Charles Kolb-Norman
2308 Hannegan Road
Bellingham, Wa 98225 6

Dear Mr. and Mrs. Kolb- Norman:

Delores Matlon, who hosted the open house at our Ridgeway model last Saturday, has referred your unanswered questions to me. We are pleased that you are interested in a Garner home.

The usual payment down is 20 per cent of the total selling price, but some lending agencies require a smaller amount in certain situations. Garner Homes is not itself involved in the financing of its homes, but we work closely with the financial institutoins shown on the enclosed list.

¶ Yes, the lot that you prefer can accommodate a walk out basement. Delores will be in touch with you soon. We can have your new ridgeway ready for occupancy within 90 days.

Sincerely,

Douglas A. Nestell
Sales Director

(Your Initials)
Enclosure

LETTER 18
MODIFIED-BLOCK STYLE

Tab: 3.25 inches

Stacey Covell and her daughter are buying a home. Use the current date as you format a letter to Ms. Covell / 4304 Keller Lane / Mount Vernon, WA 98273-4156 / Dear Ms. Covell:

We at Garner Stacey Homes feel that your selection of a Suncourt townhome is just the right choice for you. Marian Dickenson informs me that she particularly enjoyed working with you over the past few months.

The Suncourt was designed especially for the small family. The modest monthly association fee will free you from such chores as lawn mowing and exterior maintenance of the property. This extra leisure time will enable the two of you to enjoy the swimming pool, tennis courts, and other health club facilities also funded by the association fees.

All townhomes and one-family units at the Timber Creek site are unconditionally guaranteed for the first year of occupancy. If you have any questions or concerns, please let us know. Thank you, Ms. Covell, for selecting a Suncourt townhome.

Sincerely, / Douglas A. Nestell / Sales Director / *(Your Initials)*

REPORT 81
Continued

10. Insert a hard-page break at the end of page 9 to ensure that the side heading (now on page 10 of the report) is not separated from the text that follows it. A hard-page break is not needed at the end of report page 10.
11. Format the side headings in Very Large size (not bold), leaving 2 blank lines before and 1 blank line after.
12. Insert a graphics figure box after the second paragraph on page 10 and another after the first paragraph of the "Procedures" section on page 11.

Do not begin the second page of the report until your printout looks similar to this one. Depending on your hardware, your page may have slight variations from the one shown here.

WordPerfect 5.1:
Dash: Ctrl-V, --

WordPerfect 6:
Dash: Ctrl-W, 4,34

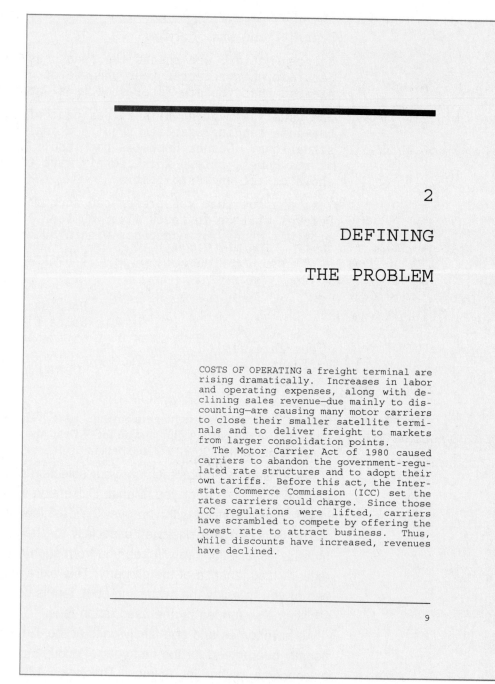

2

DEFINING

THE PROBLEM

COSTS OF OPERATING a freight terminal are rising dramatically. Increases in labor and operating expenses, along with declining sales revenue—due mainly to discounting—are causing many motor carriers to close their smaller satellite terminals and to deliver freight to markets from larger consolidation points.

The Motor Carrier Act of 1980 caused carriers to abandon the government-regulated rate structures and to adopt their own tariffs. Before this act, the Interstate Commerce Commission (ICC) set the rates carriers could charge. Since those ICC regulations were lifted, carriers have scrambled to compete by offering the lowest rate to attract business. Thus, while discounts have increased, revenues have declined.

9

(Continued on next page)

LETTER 19
MODIFIED-BLOCK STYLE

Tab: 3.25 inches
Date: Current

Mr. and Mrs. Matthew A. Longstreet are newly retired and have just purchased a Parkview model townhome at Garner's Gillette site in Bellingham. The real estate agent involved was Maria Quintero (not Marian Dickenson). Revise Letter 18, using Search and Replace. The Longstreets live at 3705 41st Street / Bellingham, WA 98226.

Modified Block Style Letters

Margins: 1 inch • Tab: 0.5 inch • Spacing: Single • Drills: 2 times • Format Guide: 21–23

Goals:
To key 38 wam/3′/3e; to format modified-block style letters.

A. WARMUP

"Do you know the glass factory has produced as many as 12
762 dozen large jars in one day?" Mavis asked. At 35 cents 24
per jar, I can acquire my boss's needs for exactly $981.40. 36

| 1 | 2 | 3 | 4 | 5 | 6 | 7 | 8 | 9 | 10 | 11 | 12

SKILLBUILDING

B. DIAGNOSTIC PRACTICE: ALPHABET

Turn to the Diagnostic Practice: Alphabet routine at the back of this book. Take the Pretest and record your performance. Then practice the drill lines for those reaches on which you made errors. Finally, repeat the Pretest and compare your performance.

C. Spacing: Double
Take two 3-minute timed writings. Compute your speed and count errors.

Goal: 38 wam/3′/3e

C. 3-MINUTE TIMED WRITING

There surely is some truth to the notion that those 11
with high-level jobs are exposed to more stress factors 23
than those who have fairly routine jobs. And yet many top 34
executives seem to work and live in a tranquil state, while 46
others with quite routine jobs live in a heightened state 58
of anxiety. 60

Why is this so? While there is no one easy answer, 72
there seem to be two major reasons. The first is that 83
some people manage stress by being highly organized in both 95
their personal and work lives. A second factor is that 106
these people have a daily exercise routine. 114

| 1 | 2 | 3 | 4 | 5 | 6 | 7 | 8 | 9 | 10 | 11 | 12

FORMATTING

ALTERNATING HEADERS AND FOOTERS
Sh-F8, 2, 3 *(header) or* 4 *(footer), select header/ footer number and placement option*
Insert page number in header/footer: Ctrl-B
Suppress header/footer: Sh-F8, 2, 8, *select*
Edit: Sh-F8, 2, 3 *(header) or* 4 *(footer), select number,* 5

WordPerfect 6 users: See Student Guide, p. 80.

P. WORDPERFECT: ALTERNATING HEADERS AND FOOTERS

Alternating headers and footers can be used so that one format appears on even-numbered pages and a different one appears on odd-numbered pages.

1. Position the cursor at the beginning of the document (or the page) where you want the header or footer to begin.
2. Create the header or footer: Sh-F8, 2, 3 *(header) or* 4 *(footer).*
3. Select A for the first header or footer or B for the second header or footer.
4. Then select the page on which the header or footer should appear.
5. In the header/footer screen, enter text as you normally would, including such features as underlining and bold. To include automatic page numbering position the cursor in the header or footer where you want the page number to appear and press Ctrl-B.
6. Press F7 once to create another header or footer or to suppress the header or footer on a page. Press F7 twice to return to your document.

COMPOSE
Bullet (•): Ctrl-V, **
Dash (—): Ctrl-V, --
1/2 (½): Ctrl-V, /2
1/4 (¼): Ctrl-V, /4

WordPerfect 6 users: See Student Guide, pp. 81 and 82.

Q. WORDPERFECT: COMPOSE

Compose enables you to display and print special characters not found on the keyboard. Although there are many such characters (depending on the capabilities of your printer), the commands for printing four common characters not found on the keyboard are shown at the left.

R. DESKTOP PUBLISHING FORMATS

Follow these formatting instructions for Reports 81 and 82 (prepared in this unit).

1. Use composed characters for dashes (instead of two hyphens) and bullets.
2. Key the first three words of the first line of the body of the report in all-capital letters.
3. Do not indent the first paragraph that begins a new section of the report. Indent other paragraphs .25 inch.

DOCUMENT PROCESSING

REPORT 81
RESEARCH REPORT

WordPerfect 6 users: See Student Guide, p. 82.

Follow these steps to create Report 81 (Section 2, page 1, is shown on page 356).

1. Set left and right margins of 1.5 inches and change to full justification.
2. Set absolute left tabs at 3, 3.25, and 3.5 inches.
3. Set the new page number to "9."
4. Create alternating headers. For odd-numbered pages, key the heading *DEFINING THE PROBLEM* flush right, then press Enter. Create a hòrizontal line (use default settings) and press Enter. For even-numbered pages, key the heading at the left margin, then press Enter. Create a horizontal line (use default settings) and press Enter.
5. Suppress the header on the first page of Section 2 (page 9).
6. Create alternating footers. For both footers, create a horizontal line (use default settings) and press Enter two times. For odd-numbered pages, insert the page number (Ctrl-B) flush right. For even-numbered pages, insert the page number at the left margin. Return to your document.
7. Press Enter three times (Ln = 1.5″) and create a horizontal line, changing the width to 0.1 inch. Press Enter once.
8. Advance to line 2.77 inches, change to Extra-Large font, and key the chapter number *2* flush right. Press Enter twice, then key *DEFINING THE PROBLEM* (as shown on page 356) with a blank line between keyed lines.
9. Return to Normal font, press Enter, and advance to line 5.77 inches. Press F4 (Left Indent), and begin keying the report (as shown on page 356).

(Continued on next page)

DOCUMENT PROCESSING

LETTER 20
PERSONAL-BUSINESS LETTER IN MODIFIED-BLOCK STYLE

Tab: 3.25 inches
Date: 2 inches

Use November 2, 19—, as the date as you format this personal-business letter to be sent to the Sales Manager at Meister's Nursery and Landscaping / 3410 Oneta Avenue / Youngstown, OH 44509-2175. The letter is from Sheldon Y. Friede / 4782 Saranac Avenue / Youngstown, OH 44505-6207.

Dear Sales Manager:

On April 15 my wife and I purchased eight trees from you: four silver maples at your branch in Warren and four Japanese red maples at your branch in Niles.

After about three months one silver maple and one red maple had died. I telephoned both the Warren and Niles branches several times, but no one returned my messages.

As these trees were expensive, I fully expect that you will replace them next spring. I shall look forward to hearing from you.

Sincerely yours,

Miss Marsha
633 WPM

LETTER 21
MODIFIED-BLOCK STYLE

Tab: 3.25 inches

Use today's date as you format this letter to be sent to Mr. Wayne B. Saatzer / 3427 Stromquist Avenue / Lowell, MA 01852-6905 / Dear Mr. Saatzer:

Yesterday we received your letter in which you inquired about employment in our Security Division. Your timing was good, as we do have a position open at the present time.

In order to be considered an official applicant for the position of security officer, you must appear in person at our Personnel Department located on the fourth floor of our downtown Layton store. An Application for Employment form must be completed by you at that time.

When you become an official applicant for a position at Layton's Department Store, you will be kept informed about the status of your application. The interview process for finalists will be completed within two weeks, and our decisions will be made one week later. You will hear from us soon.

Yours truly, / Holly Jean Lainsbury / Personnel Department / *(Your Initials)*

LETTER 22
MODIFIED-BLOCK STYLE

Tab: 3.25 inches
Date: Current

Ms. Lorna J. Jordan has inquired about employment as a buyer in the Purchasing Department at Layton's Department Store. Ms. Jordan lives at 637 Melrose Avenue, Apt. 209 / Lowell, MA 01854. Layton's does have one buyer's position open at this time; retrieve and revise Letter 21 as needed.

N. Take three 30-second timed writings on each line as you concentrate on infrequently used letters.

N. INFREQUENT LETTER PRACTICE

Q 64 Quail are quite quiet and quick, but Quentin got his quota.
X 65 Maxie expects sixty extra boxes of deluxe texts next month.
Y 66 Every entry in Addy's diary displayed loyalty to your city.
Z 67 Zeke was amazed at the size of the dozen zebras in the zoo.

| 1 | 2 | 3 | 4 | 5 | 6 | 7 | 8 | 9 | 10 | 11 | 12

O. Spacing: Double
Take two 5-minute timed writings. Compute your speed and count errors.

Goal: 54 wam/5′/5e

O. 5-MINUTE TIMED WRITING

Corporations in our country have seen great changes 11
in the last decade as a result of downsizing, mergers, and 23
acquisitions, and the need to stay competitive in a global 35
market. The eighties witnessed a dramatic decline in the 47
total number of employees among the largest companies in 58
the nation. Turmoil in the labor market has prompted many 70
firms to rethink their staffing models and make the move 81
toward a more flexible work environment. 90

There are all sorts of ways to make a work setting 101
more flexible. Job sharing is a popular example. In job 112
sharing two employees split one full-time job with each 124
working a portion of the hours. Flextime is another work 135
schedule that grants a wide range of starting and quitting 147
times based on employees' personal needs. A third way, 158
telecommuting, is an arrangement whereby employees work 169
out of their homes and are linked to their office via the 181
phone or a computer. 185

Compromises in scheduling will continue to grow as 196
the job market tightens and more and more employees face 208
commitments outside of work, such as child and elder care 219
responsibilities. In addition, some firms feel it is in 231
their best interest to be responsive to the needs of their 242
employees. More than almost any other benefit, flexible 254
work hours give people the power they need to adjust and 265
balance home with work. 270

| 1 | 2 | 3 | 4 | 5 | 6 | 7 | 8 | 9 | 10 | 11 | 12

Lesson 45: Letters and Memorandums With Copies

Margins: 1 inch • Tab: 0.5 inch • Spacing: Single • Drills: 2 times • Format Guide: 23

Goals:
To improve speed and accuracy; to format interoffice memorandums and modified-block style letters; to format copy notations.

A. WARMUP

```
1      The Baxter/Kaczmarek Company distributes 10 dishwasher  12
2 detergent brands; and our jovial washers can't quite decide  24
3 which of three selling for $2.47, $3.59, and $3.68 is best.  36
  | 1 | 2 | 3 | 4 | 5 | 6 | 7 | 8 | 9 | 10 | 11 | 12
```

LANGUAGE ARTS

B. COMPOSING

B. Answer each question with a complete sentence.

4 What is your closest friend's best quality and why is this important to you?
5 How much would you spend on dinner in a nice restaurant and what would you order?
6 What is your career goal and how do you hope to achieve it?
7 Why is it important to have a balanced diet?
8 What one trait is most valued in an employee and why is it important?
9 If you could live anywhere in the world, where would you reside and why?

C. SPELLING

C. These words are among the 500 most frequently misspelled words in business correspondence.

```
10 address courses accounting return successful request review
11 maximum security either council project already using while
12 reference amount therefore supervisor university commitment
13 recommendation effective authorized adequate correspondence
14 forward district increased regarding included lease follows
```

SKILLBUILDING

D. 12-SECOND SPRINTS

D. Take three 12-second timed writings on each line. The scale shows your wam speed for a 12-second timed writing.

```
V 15 Vivian was very vexed when Dave waved a flag at five doves.
X 16 Tex and Max were vexed at lax tax codes enforcement by Rex.
Y 17 Cowboys yodeled as they swayed back and forth by the dairy.
     | | | | 5 | | | | 10 | | | | 15 | | | | 20 | | | | 25 | | | | 30 | | | | 35 | | | | 40 | | | | 45 | | | | 50 | | | | 55 | | | | 60
```

E. PROGRESSIVE PRACTICE: ALPHABET

Turn to the Progressive Practice: Alphabet routine at the back of the book. Take six 30-second timed writings, starting at the point where you left off the last time.

I. Key each sentence on a separate line.

I. TECHNIQUE PRACTICE: ENTER KEY

Decorate the room. Attend the seminar. Go to the theater.
Watch the inauguration. Go to the rally. See the recital.
Run in the marathon. Bake the bread. Vacuum the bedrooms.
Visit the nursing home. Sell the ticket. Drive the truck.

J. Take three 12-second timed writings on each line. The scale gives wam for a 12-second timed writing.

J. 12-SECOND SPRINTS

Because he was very lazy, Jack paid for six games and quit.
Rex says Jack played a very quiet game of bridge with Inez.
Jerry loves pizzas and got quite a few when Alex came back.
Mary, Jenny, and I will quietly pack five dozen huge boxes.

| | | | 5 | | | |10| | | |15| | | |20| | | |25| | | |30| | | |35| | | |40| | | |45| | | |50| | | |55| | | |60

K. As you key this paragraph once, untangle the transpositions. This means that you must read ahead for understanding.

K. TECHNIQUE PRACTICE: CONCENTRATION

Employee benefits, also known as benefits fringe, must be carefully evaluated when select you a job. The benefits received from a job be can equal to one-third of salary the received. Thus the of importance benefits be must obvious.

L. PROGRESSIVE PRACTICE: ALPHABET

Turn to the Progressive Practice: Alphabet routine at the back of the book. Take five 30-second timed writings, starting at the point where you left off the last time.

M. Take a 1-minute timed writing on the first paragraph to establish your base speed. Then take four 1-minute timed writings on the remaining paragraphs. As soon as you equal or exceed your base speed on one paragraph, advance to the next one.

M. SUSTAINED PRACTICE: SYLLABIC INTENSITY

People continue to rent autos for personal use and for their work, and the car rental business just keeps growing. When you rent a car, look carefully at the insurance costs. You should also know whether you must pay a mileage charge.

It is likely that a good deal of insurance coverage is a part of the standard rental cost. But you might be urged to procure extra medical, property, and collision coverage. If you accept, be ready to see an increase in your charges.

Perhaps this is not necessary, as you may already have the kind of protection you desire in a policy that you have at the present. By reviewing your own automobile insurance policy, you could save yourself a significant sum of money.

Paying mileage charges could evolve into a significant bill. This will be especially evident if the trips planned involve destinations that are many miles apart. Complete a total review of traveling plans prior to making a decision.

| 1 | 2 | 3 | 4 | 5 | 6 | 7 | 8 | 9 | 10 | 11 | 12

FORMATTING

F. COPY NOTATIONS

It is good business practice to make file copies of all documents you prepare. You may want to print additional originals or make photocopies. You may also need copies to send to people other than the addressee of the original document.

A copy notation is keyed on a document to indicate that someone else is receiving a copy of that document.

1. The copy notation is keyed on the line below the reference initials or below the attachment or enclosure notation.
2. At the left margin, key a lowercase *c* followed by a colon and two spaces and the name of the person receiving the copy.
3. If more than one person is receiving a copy, list the names, single spaced, one beneath the other.

```
                              Sincerely yours,


                              Douglas A. Nestell
                              Sales Director

jlp
c:  Paula Marini
```

DOCUMENT PROCESSING

MEMO 6

The word RE is sometimes used in place of the word SUBJECT in a memo or a letter.

The three enumerated entries should be treated as separate paragraphs.

Attachments 2 is the appropriate entry when two items are attached.

MEMO TO: Randy Shequen / Manager, Warren Branch / **FROM:** Margie Hooverman, Co-owner / **DATE:** November 6, 19— / **RE:** Communication Breakdown

Because of a letter (copy attached) I received from Mr. Sheldon Y. Friede, the following actions have been taken: 1. I have sent a letter of apology to Mr. Friede; a copy is also attached. 2. The replacement project has been scheduled on our master calendar for next May. Glenda Bizzano and you will provide the replacement trees from your branch outlets. 3. A meeting has been scheduled in my office with you, Glenda, and George Lambrecht for the purpose of reviewing our present policies so that communication breakdowns like this do not happen in the future.

Randy, let's view this as an opportunity for both you and Glenda to improve communication procedures at your branches.

Your Initials / Attachments 2 / c: Mr. George Lambrecht, Co-owner

MEMO 7

Revise a copy of Memo 6 to send to Glenda Bizzano / Manager, Niles Branch. Use Search and Replace (*Randy* to *Glenda*) to make the necessary changes.

SKILLBUILDING

PRETEST. Take a 1-minute timed writing; compute your speed and count errors.

PRACTICE.
Speed Emphasis: If you made no errors on the Pretest, key each line twice.
Accuracy Emphasis: If you made 1 or more errors on the Pretest, key each group of lines (as though it were a paragraph) twice.

POSTTEST. Repeat the Pretest (D) and compare performance.

D. PRETEST: VERTICAL REACHES

Janice and her escort were late for a dance at the re- 12
sort. The drummers in the band had just started to play as 24
they came in. It seems Janice injured the back of her knee 36
on the bank of the river during a cruise late that morning. 48

| 1 | 2 | 3 | 4 | 5 | 6 | 7 | 8 | 9 | 10 | 11 | 12

E. PRACTICE: UP REACHES

at late flatly rebate atomic rather repeat attest atom what
dr draw drowsy sundry driver adrift drying tundra drum drug
ju jump junior justly jumble adjust injure jurist jury junk
es ages thesis access esteem resort smiles escape desk nest

F. PRACTICE: DOWN REACHES

ca scat scales cattle casual scarce recall fiscal cash call
nk rank blanks anklet unkind donkey tinker chunky wink bank
ba tuba ballot cabana bakery abates global basket balk band
sc disc script ascend scheme escort fiasco scolds scar scab

G. POSTTEST: VERTICAL REACHES

H. Take a 1-minute timed writing on the first paragraph to establish your base speed. Then take four 1-minute timed writings on the remaining paragraphs. As soon as you equal or exceed your base speed on one paragraph, advance to the next one.

H. SUSTAINED PRACTICE: ROUGH DRAFT

Are you eating wisely? If you're like most Americans, 12
you have never been hungrier for information about food and 24
health. As medical research transforms yesterday's beliefs 36
into today's fallacies, many folks are changing their ways. 48

For instance, many currant discussions have focussed on 12
the value of fiber in our deits, but did you know there are 24
two types of fiber? Oatmeal is high in fiber while 36
wheat bran is known for it's high amount of insoluble fiber. 48
What are there diferences? Insoluble fiber adds bulk 12
to the content of the intestines, which might ward off colon 24
cancer. Soluble fiber adds bulk to the stomachs contents, 36
making diets feel stuffed and help reduce cholestrol. 48

Americans typicaly eat half the amount daily of fiber 12
recomended by the national cancer institute. A serving of 24
some sereals can supply up to one third of the daily quote. 36
Other first rate sources are certain fruits and vegetables. 48

| 1 | 2 | 3 | 4 | 5 | 6 | 7 | 8 | 9 | 10 | 11 | 12

LETTER 23
MODIFIED-BLOCK STYLE

Tabs: 0.4 and 3.25 inches

November 8, 19--

Mr. Sheldon Y. Friede
4782 Saranac Avenue
Youngstown, OH 44505-6207

Dear Mr. Friede:

This is in response to your recent letter:

Each numbered item in a letter or a memo is treated as a separate paragraph, arranged with the number at the left margin and turnover lines indented 4 spaces.

Use Indent (F4) for turnover lines.

1. Your tow trees will be replaced without cost next spring. The new trees will match the others in both size and color. A copy of our warranty policy enclosed is for your review.

2. The survival rate for trees can no be perfect; however, we we are indeed sorry that you have had to have this temporary setback.

3. The communication break down with our two office branches should not have occurred. We will take steps to ensure that this will not happen in the future. You can be confident that the appearance of your yard will be restored as soon as conditions are right next spring.

Yours truly,

Margie Hooverman, co-owner

(Your Initials)

Enclosure

c: Mr. George Lambrecht, co-owner
Mr. Randy Shequen, Warren Branch
Ms. Glenda Bizzano, Niles Branch

UNIT TWENTY-NINE • DESKTOP PUBLISHING: REPORTS

141–145 LESSONS

Margins: 1 inch • Spacing: Single • Drills: 2 times • Format Guide: 129–131

Goals for Unit 29

Begin each day with approximately 15 minutes of skillbuilding, selecting activities from pages 347–350. In the remaining class time, complete as many production jobs from pages 351–357 as you can.

1. To improve accuracy and speed on alphabet and number keys.
2. To key 54 wam for 5 minutes with no more than 5 errors.
3. To improve proficiency in composing at the keyboard.
4. To develop proficiency in using WordPerfect Graphics, Alternating Headers and Footers, Compose (characters), Columns, and Style.
5. To format and key research reports and catalog pages.

A. WARMUP

```
1      Three law firms (Quayle & Juster, Gixen & Razacco, and   12
2 Villani & Benson) in Cook County handled the most cases for   24
3 last year.  They processed 852, 967, and 1,430 total cases.   36
  | 1 | 2 | 3 | 4 | 5 | 6 | 7 | 8 | 9 | 10 | 11 | 12
```

LANGUAGE ARTS

B. COMMAS

Study the rules at the right. Then key lines 4–7, making necessary changes.

Rule: Use commas to set off a transitional expression (such as *therefore*) or an independent comment (such as *of course*) when they interrupt the flow of the sentence.

David told him, however, that they will graduate.

Rule: Use a comma to set off an expression in apposition (that is, a word, phrase, or clause that identifies or explains the other terms).

The new nurse, Peter Sulentic, was assigned to that wing.

```
4 In addition the other three will be interviewed on Monday.
5 The custodian Marvin Budde will help mount the banners.
6 Jan Leonard, a local CPA, will discuss the new tax laws.
7 We will not of course be able to maintain that price.
```

C. COMPOSING

Prepare a memo in response to Mr. Wilson's memo (Memo 30, p. 300). Indicate that you believe the summer rates he suggested are appropriate and that he should go ahead with the description for the brochure. Suggest, however, that he add the word "Directory" after "MOBIL Travel" in the description. Supply the current date and an appropriate subject for the memo.

Two-Page Reports

Margins: 1 inch • Tab: 0.5 inch • Spacing: Single • Drills: 2 times • Format Guide: 23–25

Goals:
To study the use of semicolons; to key 39 wam/3'/3e; to use proofreaders' marks; to format a two-page unbound report.

A. WARMUP

```
1      A crazy dog ran in Lanes 1, 2, and 3; and then it took   12
2 a quick jump over the extra lanes labeled 4, 5, and 6.  The   24
3 "feat" was accomplished on 07/08/90 near seats 201 and 203.   36
  | 1 | 2 | 3 | 4 | 5 | 6 | 7 | 8 | 9 | 10 | 11 | 12
```

LANGUAGE ARTS

B. SEMICOLONS

B. Study the rules at the right. Then key lines 4–7, making necessary changes.

Rule: Use a semicolon to separate two independent clauses that are not joined by *and, but, or,* or *nor.*

Cindy will be here before next Saturday; Julie will not.

Rule: If either of the independent clauses in a compound sentence contains a comma, separate the clauses with a semicolon rather than a comma.

If you wish, the job is yours; but there will not be a wage increase.

```
4 Brian applied for a promotion, Scott did not.
5 Kim held the pieces; and Michael attached the hinges.
6 Lee will bring a fax machine, I will return it Tuesday.
7 As usual, Sean is the captain; but Jan is the substitute.
```

C. PROOFREADERS' MARKS

The most frequently used proofreaders' marks were introduced on page 66, Lesson 32. Additional proofreaders' marks are presented below. Study all the marks carefully before keying Report 12, page 102.

Proofreaders' Mark	Draft	Final Copy
SS Single-space	SS [first line / second line	first line second line
ds Double-space	ds [first line / second line	first line second line
V or ∧ Insert punctuation	if he's not ∧	if he's not,
# Insert space	all#ready to	all ready to
new/~~old~~ Change word	and ~~if~~ when you	and when you
. . . Don't delete	a ~~true~~ story (dotted)	a true story
Delete and close up	co-operation	cooperation
/ Use lowercase letter	our /President	our president
○ Spell out	the only (1)	the only one
] Move right	Please send	Please send (moved right)
[Move left	[May I	May I

PART 8 SKILLBUILDING
Desktop Publishing

OBJECTIVES

KEYBOARDING

To key 57 wam on a 5-minute timed writing with no more than 5 errors.

LANGUAGE ARTS

To improve language arts skills, including the correct use of punctuation marks, capitalization, numbers, abbreviations, grammar, and spelling.

WORD PROCESSING

To use previously learned WordPerfect commands to format various document processing assignments.

DOCUMENT PROCESSING

To use desktop publishing to create various business forms, reports, announcements, fliers, transparencies, business cards, advertisements, brochures, and newsletters.

Stock Boston/Brian Smith

D. Spacing: Double
Take two 3-minute timed writings. Compute your speed and count errors.

Goal: 39 wam/3′/3e

D. 3-MINUTE TIMED WRITING

```
     Software has changed to a great extent the way we take   12
care of business in the office.  There was a time not that    24
long ago when pens and pencils were used to record all of     35
our daily business transactions.  Today all such work is      47
quickly done by a spreadsheet on our computers.  For many     58
years, we also used those same pens and pencils to organize   70
our thoughts on tablets.  Next came the typewriter to speed   82
up the process, and today we use word processing to create    94
output tenfold.  Software packages will continue to help     106
increase the work we produce on the job each and every day.  117
| 1 | 2 | 3 | 4 | 5 | 6 | 7 | 8 | 9 | 10 | 11 | 12
```

FORMATTING

E. TWO-PAGE REPORTS

The second and any additional pages of a report are formatted as follows:

1. Side margins: 1 inch
2. Top margin: 1 inch
3. Page number: keyed at the right margin, 1 inch from the top of the page.
4. Body: begins a double space below the page number and is double spaced.
5. Bottom margin: 1 inch

WordPerfect has a default bottom margin of 1 inch and will insert a soft page break (indicated by a line of hyphens) when you reach the bottom margin. If it is necessary to change a page break, position the cursor where you want the page to break and insert a hard page break (Ctrl-Enter).

WP

PAGE NUMBERING
Sh-F8, 2, 6, 4, 3, F7

SUPPRESS PAGE NUMBERING
Sh-F8, 2, 8, 4, Y, F7

NEW PAGE NUMBER
Sh-F8, 2, 6, 1, *no.*, F7, F7

WordPerfect 6 users: See Student Guide, page 23.

F. WORDPERFECT: PAGE NUMBERING

To have WordPerfect number each page of your document in the upper right corner of the page, position the cursor at the top of the first page and enter the appropriate commands (Sh-F8, 2, 6, 4, 3, F7).

Usually page 1 is not numbered. To suppress (turn off) page numbering on page 1, position the cursor at the top of the first page, press Sh-F8, then enter 2, 8, 4, and Y. Press F7 to return to your document.

To begin numbering pages with a page number other than 1 (for example, the first page of section 2 of a report might begin with page number 10), use New Page Number. Position the cursor at the top of the first page to be numbered, press Sh-F8, then enter 2, 6, 1, and the page number you want to start numbering with (in this case, 10). Then press F7 twice to return to your document.

WP

WIDOW/ORPHAN PROTECTION
Sh-F8, 1, 9, Y, F7

WordPerfect 6 users: See Student Guide, page 24.

G. WORDPERFECT: WIDOW/ORPHAN PROTECTION

The last line of a paragraph by itself at the top of a new page is called a *widow*; the first line of a paragraph by itself at the bottom of a page is called an *orphan*. To ensure that at least two lines of a paragraph are carried to the top of a new page or are left at the bottom of a page, position the cursor at the top of your document and turn on Widow/Orphan Protection (Sh-F8, 1, 9, Y, F7).

TEST 7-D
REPORT 80
BOUND REPORT,
PAGE 36

Spacing: Double

36

that the operation be closed if in their judgment the hazards could result in sevre injury or death to employees.

Automotive

Company-Owned Vehicles. The company holds bodily injury and properaty insurance damage to cover the companys legal responsibility and libaility for operation of motor cars. The company and it's authorized employees are covered for cliams of negligence that could result in the damage too property of others, or bodily injury to 3rd parties within the limits of the michigan no-Fault Act.

The firm does carry collision insurance to cover damage to firm-owned cars.

Damage to vehicles company owned, rented or leased by a division is the responsbility of th division.

Privately Owned Vehicles. The firm does carry property dmaage or liability insurance for the protection of all private owners of autos.

Those using privately owned vehicles on company's business should have insureance in amount that will cover there legal responsibility.

Professional

Employes. All workers working with in the scope of their duties are coverde by the companys professional liability self insured funds.

REPORT 12
TWO-PAGE REPORT

Spacing: Double

Turn on Widow/Orphan Protection.

Enter the Page Numbering command at the top of page 1, then suppress the page 1 number.

JUDGING A COMPUTER SYSTEM
By Marilyn Clark

Judgeing the effectiveness of a computer system has taken on a new dimension in the past few years if for no particular reason other than the wide range of computer systems from which the user can select. It is important that we investigate the criteria that be considered in making this decision.

Criterion 1: Speed

This is probably the most critical criterion considered when one purchases a computer system. The value of a computer is directly related to its speed, and a computers speed is often measured in megahertz(MHz). A MHz is equivalent to one million cycles per second, and many of today's micro-computers run 30 to 40 MHz.

Criterion 2: Flexibility This second criterion is now especially important because of the rapid turn over of hardware and software in the computer industry. The flexibility of a computer system is important for two general reasons:

To accommodate a variety of programs. Hundreds and possibly thousands of software packages are available today to meet the needs of computer users. The computer you purchase must be able to accomodate this variety of soft ware and be flexible enough to change with the increasing sophistication of software packages. **To Permit Expandability.** Because of the substantial investment you make in a computer, you do not want to commit your resources to a computer that cannot be expanded to handle (1) newer, more powerful operating systems; (2) "memory-hungry" software packages; (3) network interfaces; and (4) additional users.

Criterion 3: Convenience

A 3d consideration is convenience. Is it easy to learn how to operate your computer? Does the manufacturer stand by it's waranty, and is it difficult to obtain repairs. How convenient is it to buy parts for your computer (such as memory boards and drives) if you want to expand your system? these questions need to be answered and the answers should be weighed before you purchase a computer system new.

TEST 7-B
LETTER 112
BLOCK STYLE WITH STANDARD PUNCTUATION

Tina Harrison, Employee Relations, wishes to send a letter by fax to Mr. Lawrence G. Que at Wolverine Products, 581 Spring Street, Ann Arbor, MI 48103. Send a copy of the letter to Roy Logan. Supply an appropriate salutation and closing lines.

As you requested in your telephone call last week, we are enclosing a copy of our insurance coverage for company-owned and privately owned vehicles. The basic provisions are as follows:

> We do not offer collision insurance to cover damage to company-owned vehicles. Also, we do not carry property damage or personal liability insurance for the protection of employees who use their own vehicles on company business.

We have found over the years that it is more expensive to have insurance coverage for collision than it is to replace the few cars that need to be replaced. The responsibility for damage to company vehicles owned, rented, or leased by a division is placed upon the division itself. Employees using privately owned vehicles should have insurance in an amount that will cover their legal responsibility.

I hope this information will be helpful to you.

TEST 7-C
TABLE 67
BOXED TABLE WITH BRACED HEADING

A TWO-YEAR COMPARISON
OF NEW-CAR SALES

County	Total Sales		Percent of Increase/Decrease
	1990	1992	
Beriren	2,143	2,752	28.4
Cass	765	968	-8.8
Midland	2,840	3,275	15.3
Ingham	1,769	2,311	7.4
Ottawa	301	480	59.5
Van Buren	1,072	946	-44.4

REPORT 13
TWO-PAGE REPORT

Spacing: Double

Retrieve Report 12 and make the following changes:

1. Change the title to ***JUDGING COMPUTER EFFECTIVENESS.***
2. Use your name in the byline.
3. Change the side headings to the following:
   Computer Operating Speed
   System Flexibility
   Overall Convenience
4. Transpose the two paragraphs that begin with paragraph headings (Paragraphs 4 and 5).
5. Delete the final enumerated item under the ***Expandability*** heading.
6. Replace the final question in the ***Convenience*** section with the following: *How far would you have to travel to secure replacement parts (if needed), or how many days would you have to wait if you ordered them from the dealer?*

Bound Reports

Margins: 1 inch • Tab: 0.5 inch • Spacing: Single • Drills: 2 times • Format Guide: 25–27

Goals:
To improve speed and accuracy; to format a two-page bound report.

A. WARMUP

```
     Buzz & Jackie moved to Texas on 8/15/94 and were quite   12
glad to learn that their computers (Carton 2-A) and printer   24
(Carton 7-F) arrived by truck yesterday (8/30/94) at 6 p.m.   36
 | 1 | 2 | 3 | 4 | 5 | 6 | 7 | 8 | 9 | 10 | 11 | 12
```

LANGUAGE ARTS

B. SPELLING

B. These words are among the 500 most frequently misspelled words in business correspondence.

```
assistance compliance initial limited corporation technical
operating sufficient operation incorporated writing current
advise together prepared recommend appreciated cannot based
benefit disability analysis probably projects before annual
issue attention location association participation proposed
```

SKILLBUILDING

C. PRETEST: ALTERNATE- AND ONE-HAND WORDS

PRETEST.
Take a 1-minute timed writing; compute your speed and count errors.

```
     I will defer the amendment that will attract a minimum   12
of a million visitors eastward to the island since it might   24
create a problem.  Did their auditors turn down my request?   36
 | 1 | 2 | 3 | 4 | 5 | 6 | 7 | 8 | 9 | 10 | 11 | 12
```

Progress Test on Part 7

TEST 7-A
5-MINUTE TIMED WRITING

Spacing: Double

The office employee who gets the most work done in the 12
modern office is the one who has the ability to plan for 23
work. Planning is a major portion of today's office work. 35
Plans must include the major details for completing the 47
next task. Such details include whether or not the task is 59
to be completed on a typewriter or microcomputer, the types 71
of supplies and references needed, and the format preferred 83
by the originator. There can be no details left to chance. 94

The employee must decide whether or not the formatting 106
of the task can be completed with a software program and if 118
one is available. If a program is available, who will do 130
the keying and who will be responsible for completing the 142
task? If the task consists of addressing an envelope or 153
completing a business form, on what equipment may it best 165
be completed? These are but a few common questions which 176
must be answered when planning for the production of office 188
work. Planning, which can best be refined when on the job, 200
is a much needed skill in the office. 208

The arrangement of the workstation is one other very 219
important aspect of planning for work in an office. The 231
real expert has at hand whatever materials will be used to 242
complete a task. These materials may include a reference 254
manual, a good dictionary, and other critical materials. 265

| 1 | 2 | 3 | 4 | 5 | 6 | 7 | 8 | 9 | 10 | 11 | 12

PRACTICE.

Speed Emphasis: If you made 2 or fewer errors on the Pretest, key each line twice.

Accuracy Emphasis: If you made 3 or more errors, key each group of lines (as though it were a paragraph) twice.

D. PRACTICE: ALTERNATE HANDS

```
12 visible signs amendment visual height turndown suspend maps
13 element amend endowment signal handle ornament auditor half
14 figment usual authentic emblem island clemency dormant snap
15 problem chair shamrocks profit thrown blandish penalty form
```

E. PRACTICE: ONE HAND

```
16 trade poplin greater pumpkin eastward plumply barrage holly
17 exact kimono created minikin cassette opinion seaweed union
18 defer unhook reserve minimum attracts million scatter plump
19 serve uphill exceeds killjoy carefree homonym terrace onion
```

POSTTEST.
Repeat the Pretest (C) and compare performance.

F. POSTTEST: ALTERNATE- AND ONE-HAND WORDS

G. PACED PRACTICE

Turn to the Paced Practice routine at the back of the book. Take four 2-minute timed writings, starting at the speed at which you left off the last time.

FORMATTING

H. BOUND REPORTS

A left bound report requires a wider left margin for binding. To format a bound report, reset the left margin to 1.5 inches. Leave the right margin at 1 inch.

DOCUMENT PROCESSING

REPORT 14
TWO-PAGE BOUND REPORT

Left Margin: 1.5 inches
Right Margin: 1 inch
Spacing: Double

Key the title, side headings, and paragraph headings in bold.

Turn on Widow/Orphan Protection and Page Numbering.

MANAGING YOUR TIME

The Key to Success in an Office

Using your time more efficiently in an office will help you get more work done in less time. Wasted time cannot be recovered; therefore, the suggestions given in this report will help you better manage your time.

Plan Your Work Each Day

Take a few minutes at the beginning of each workday to plan your day's activities. Decide which tasks you need to finish first and which tasks can be completed at a later time.

Obtaining Necessary Materials. Gather all necessary supplies and materials that you will need to accomplish the tasks you have decided must be completed first. Have all your paper, pens and pencils, folders, and correspondence at your desk and within easy reach if you need to use them.

Completing Individual Tasks. Regardless of the work in which you are involved, it is usually better to finish one task before beginning another. However, if your supervisor assigns you a priority task that must be accomplished immediately, the original task may have to be completed at a later

(Continued on next page.)

LETTER 111

Get this in the mail by July 19. As usual, please check for additional errors!

Mr. Leland G. Paulin
Krevitz and Paulin, Attorneys-at-Law
52 Laurentian St.
Sault Sainte Marie, Ontario
CANADA P6B4G

Subject: Schneidermann Arbitration Case

Dear Mr. Paulin:

been
I have informed that your firm is now representing Lanmoore Engineering Designs, Ltd. with respect to our joint arbitration hearing. As you likely are now aware, the case will be heard before the London Court of International Arbitration in in London, England on November 15. Rockford International has had a good relationship with Lanmoore that dates back to our first years of partnership. This is the first time that our marketting efforts have resulted in an arbitration setting. As we have been selling subassembly components to Schneidermann Engineering in Germany for several years, we are surprised that this situation has developed.

video
Jim Watters of our legal department has informed me that the two of you have scheduled a conference with members of your staffs in early August. I shall look forward to recieving a summary of these discussions.

Sincerely yours

Carter B. Phillips
Vise President for Marketing

c : Jim Waters

time. If this happens, be sure to identify the point of your progress on your original task so that you can resume your work with little hesitation.

Before you begin any task, be sure to read directions and have a thorough understanding of what must be done. If you need to ask someone a question, be sure you have reviewed all of your materials for a possible answer before interrupting that person. If there are several questions you need to ask, write them down so that you ask them in the proper sequence.

Spend Your Time Wisely

Although you may want to work from beginning to end to finish a task, it is sometimes better to take a short break or two when the task is of considerable length. All of us need to take a few minutes to relax both mentally and physically. We will finish our task in less time by doing so.

REPORT 15
TWO-PAGE BOUND REPORT

Left Margin: 1.5 inches
Spacing: Double

Retrieve Report 14 and make the following changes:

1. Add your name for a byline.
2. Transpose the two paragraphs that begin with paragraph headings.
3. Add the following sentence to the final paragraph: *Use good judgment in deciding when and for how long you should take a break.*

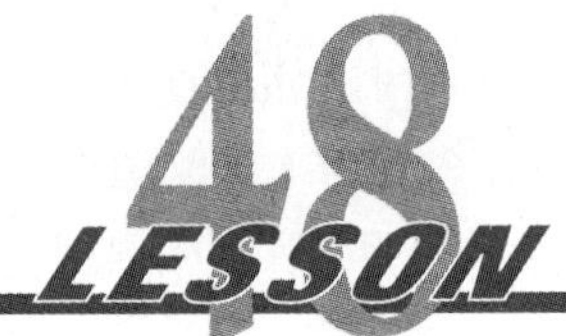

Lesson 48 Footnotes

Margins: 1 inch • Tab: 0.5 inch • Spacing: Single • Drills: 2 times • Format Guide: 27

Goals:
To key 39 wam/3'/3e; to format a report with footnotes.

A. WARMUP

```
1      Rex and Inez won, and their score was 98-76; but Jamal  12
2 (from Qatar) scored the most points of the week (45), and I  24
3 believe his score beat Guy's former records (32, 31, & 30).  36
  | 1 | 2 | 3 | 4 | 5 | 6 | 7 | 8 | 9 | 10 | 11 | 12
```

LANGUAGE ARTS

B. COMPOSING

B. Answer each question with a complete sentence.

4 What are your least favorite chores?
5 If you were to give a speech, what topic would you choose and why?
6 What skills are the most important to you?
7 What kinds of exercise would you prefer to maintain your health?
8 If you were an actor or actress, what role would you prefer to play?
9 What is your favorite pastime?
10 Describe what the weather was like last weekend.
11 What does your best friend think is your strongest asset?

MEMO 37
TWO-PAGE DICTATED
MEMO REPORT

This is Carter Phillips. Please transcribe this dictation of a memo report right away. I would like you to look up some information in reference works to fill in various parts of the report.

This report is being sent to Sheryl Alvarez, Director of South American Operations. Please remember to enter an appropriate subject line. Here is the body of the memo:

The enclosed materials will provide useful background information as you prepare for our next meeting to review our South American operations.

Deliberate decisions were made during the 1980s by Rockford International not to market our products to domestic companies in Brazil. This was true even though the market potential is significant in a country with a population of . . . .

(Would you please look up the population of Brazil and insert it here.)

Our position began to change when Brazil developed a comprehensive environmental program for the Amazon region in 1989. The subsequent move toward an increasingly diversified economic climate has altered our views. We are now ready to move forward.

(Let's put a side heading here labeled "Present Concerns," and then go back and put one after the first paragraph labeled "Background.")

Brazil's government land policies combined with a high inflation rate have led to a severe economic recession. The people suffer from a severe maldistribution of income, and the country's foreign debt is among the largest in the world.

The literacy rate for the population of Brazil is . . . *(please look this up for me)* compared with . . . *(please look this up also)* in the United States.

(Let's put another side heading here labeled "Reasons for Optimism.")

Brazil is fortunate to have extensive mineral reserves. Of particular importance are iron, coal, tin, and oil. But the country also has rich fields of diamonds, gold, nickel, and gemstones.

The present form of government is a . . . . *(Please check to see what the exact wording should be.)*

Efforts are being made to more equitably distribute income throughout the country. The present numbers of such items as television sets, radios, and telephones would seem to indicate that there is a tremendous potential in the consumer market.

Sheryl, I look forward to seeing you on August 23 in Sao Paulo.

SKILLBUILDING

C. TECHNIQUE PRACTICE: CONCENTRATION

C. Take three 30-second timed writings on each line. Try to maintain the same speed on all three lines.

```
It is not a good idea to key the long words at a fast pace.
They might attempt to make the trip before the first month.
Reluctant administrators scheduled supervisory conferences.
| 1 | 2 | 3 | 4 | 5 | 6 | 7 | 8 | 9 | 10 | 11 | 12
```

D. 3-MINUTE TIMED WRITING

D. Spacing: Double
Take two 3-minute timed writings. Compute your speed and count errors.

Goal: 39 wam/3′/3e

```
     Ergonomics is the study of matching the worker to his      12
or her environment.  The key to making this principle work      24
is to organize the work space and equipment for the very        35
best match.  One of the prime elements in making ergonomics     47
work is the design of hardware, mainly the computer system,     59
for the office worker.  The screen should have extra knobs      71
for brightness and contrast, and it also should provide a       82
color that is very easy to look at.  The screen should tilt     94
so that it gives off little glare.  The keyboard should        106
tilt at a slight angle when it rests flat on the desk.         116
| 1 | 2 | 3 | 4 | 5 | 6 | 7 | 8 | 9 | 10 | 11 | 12
```

FORMATTING

E. REPORTS WITH FOOTNOTES

Footnote references indicate the sources of facts or ideas in a report. A superscript (raised) number is keyed after the fact or idea in the body of the report. The footnote reference is keyed at the bottom of the same page, separated from the text by a single space and a 2-inch underline. Footnotes are keyed a double space below the underline, single-spaced, and the first line is indented 0.5 inch. The footnote includes the superscript number and the reference. Double-space between footnotes.

When the last page of a multipage report contains a footnote, the divider line and footnotes are keyed at the bottom of the page—not below the last line of text.

Those workers who initially resisted the technology declare it is easy to learn and has enabled them to compete with any business that has previously published such documents as reports, newsletters, and company brochures."[1] The cost of laying out a page has now been cut considerably with this revolutionary technology.[2] It is no wonder, then, that companies worldwide are overly enthusiastic about hiring trained personnel with these skills.[3] ↓1

________________ ↓2

[1] Louise Plachta and Leonard E. Flannery, *The Desktop Publishing Revolution*, 2d ed., Computer Publications, Inc. Los Angeles, 1991, pp. 558-559. ↓2

[2] Terry Denton, "Newspaper Cut Costs, Increases Quality," *The Monthly Press*, October 1992, p. 160. ↓2

[3] Mary Ann Kennedy, "Office Skill Trends," *Personnel Digest*, August 1992, p. 43.

WP

FOOTNOTES
Create: Ctrl-F7, 1, 1
Edit: Ctrl-F7, 1, 2

WordPerfect 6 users: See Student Guide, page 25.

F. WORDPERFECT: FOOTNOTES

Use the Footnote command to create and automatically format and position footnotes within your document. To create a footnote, position the cursor where the footnote number is to appear in the text, and enter the appropriate commands (Ctrl-F7, 1, 1). Press F7 (do *not* press Enter) when you finish. Footnotes will be correctly positioned on the page. If you delete or add footnotes, the remaining notes will be renumbered. To view footnotes in place before printing, use View Document (Sh-F7, 6).

REPORT 79
MINUTES OF A MEETING WITH PARALLEL COLUMNS

No rush with these minutes. Next week will be fine.

Rockford International

Minutes of Executive Committee Meeting

July ~~17~~ 4, 19--

Introduction	Barbara J. Rosemont, President of Rockford International, reported that ~~early~~ preliminary sales figures for the second quarter of the calendar year show a 17% increase over projected figures. She indicated that she plans to send a communication to all employees expressing her personal appreciation for their performance.
Kangas-Rockford	Josh Bransen reported that Bob Wilson will go to Finland on September 4 to finalize arrangements for the Kangas-Rockford endeavor. *Can you supply a better word?*
Annual Meeting	Joe Rosemont reviewed ~~arrangements~~ *plans* for the annual meeting, scheduled for December 3. Earlier rumors of demonstrations by anti-military groups appear to be unfounded.
Contract for Rockford-China	Jim Watters reported on progress with the Rockford-China project, ~~indicating that it appears that there will be~~ no roadblocks ~~set up~~ by the government of the people's Republic of China *are expected*.
North Atlantic Oil Fields	Bobbi Kjome provided *the following* information relating to the proposed purchase of either Jovaag Enterprises in Norway or Emerson Electronics, Ltd, in England.

Be sure to verify my spelling. Thanks!

	Square Footage	Number of Employees	Year Built
Jovaag	42,000	178	1983
Emerson	35,000	164	1977

SS

Foreign Visitor Program	Valerie Thomas reported on the dramatic growth of our visitor foreign program. The results are directly tied to increases in foreign sales, licensing, training, and consulting.
CONCLUDING REMARKS	*Carter Phillips thanked everyone for their work and then adjourned the meeting.*

REPORT 16
ONE-PAGE UNBOUND REPORT WITH FOOTNOTES

Spacing: Double

SHOPPING FOR A HOME

(Part I)

Buying a home is a proces that many of us will go through in our life time. If we are like many prospective buyers, we will experience this decision three or four major times in our working years. A home is typically the largest purchase we will make, and it deserves therefore our careful attention.

Considered by many as the important criteria in shopping for a home is its site.[1] The site should be on land that is well drained and free from from flooding that can cause extensive damage. Check the area city zoning plan to determine if you have chosen a site that is free from flooding and highwater levels that can cause extensive damage.

You should also check to see if the ground is stable. Ground that shifts can cause cracks in foundations and walls.

You should also consider the quality of construction when shopping for a home. Slight cracks and sign of settling are not a major concern. Kramer and Reynolds state that "larger cracks may indicate unstable ground and poor construction techniques and this is a very serious concern".[2] If you are looking for a home with a basement, check for any water leaks along the basement walls or along the ground level of the exterior walls.

Use the Footnote command to format the footnotes (Ctrl-F7, 1, 1).

---

[1] "Building a Home for Tomorrow," *homes & gardens*, Apr. 27, 1992, pp. 17-24.

[2] David L. Kramer and Leslie T. Reynolds, *Strategies for Building a Home Better*, Bandana Books, St. Louis, MO, 1992, p. 214.

Key titles of books and magazines in italics (if available). Otherwise, underline them.

LETTERS 107–110 Please send this letter to the following four people who will be taking tours and attending workshops at our Jacksonville plant in October.

Mr. Daniel M. Yoo
Sampoong, Apt. 20
203 Seoul
KOREA
Mr. Yoo
Korean
Japan, the Netherlands, and Turkey

Mrs. Kirsten Vande Berg
Box 487
Odyk Utr
NETHERLANDS
Mrs. Vande Berg
suitable
Korea, Japan, and Turkey

Ms. Kim Ichikawa
6/23/26
Kamiaokinishiki
JAPAN
Ms. Ichikawa
Japanese
Korea, the Netherlands, and Turkey

Mr. Cem Atamturk
Bagdad Cad
No. 181
TURKEY
Mr. Atamturk
Turkish
Korea, Japan, and the Netherlands

____
____
____
____

Please get these letters ready for me to sign on July 23.

Dear ______________:

~~Provisions~~ Arrangements have been completed for ~~the~~ your visit to our Rockford Electronics Plant in Jacksonville, FL. The following information is provided so that you can finalize your plans:

1. The tours and ~~workshops~~ seminars have been scheduled for the week of October 22.
2. All sessions will be conducted in English. If ~~needed~~ necessary, you ~~you~~ may arrange for a __________ translator to attend the sessions with you. If you desire, however, we will do our best to make these arrangements.
3. The other foreign visitors are from ____________________. Hotel arrangements have been made for the four of you at the Plaza Hotel near the Rockford plant.

Please let us know when your plane will arrive at Jacksonville Municipal Airport so that we can have some one meet you and take you to the hotel. If you have questions about your visit, please let me know.

Sincerely yours,

Carter B. Phillips
Vice President for Marketing

REPORT 17
TWO-PAGE UNBOUND REPORT WITH FOOTNOTES

Retrieve Report 16 and make the following changes:

1. Change the page reference in footnote 1 to *p. 19.*

2. Add the following paragraphs and references to the end of page 2 of the report:

Spacing: Double

Remember to suppress the page number on the first page.

The walls, ceiling, and floors (if you have a basement) need to be checked for proper insulation. "Both the depth and 'R' factor need to be checked for proper levels."[3] In addition, cross braces should have been used between the beams supporting a floor.

Finally, a thorough check should be made of the heating, cooling, and electrical systems in the home. "These features are often overlooked by prospective home owners; nevertheless, they are as critical as any others to be examined."[4]

---

[3]"Home Construction in the 90's," *Family Living,* October 9, 1992, p. 75.

[4]Randall Evans and Marie Alexander, *Home Facilities Planning,* Bradshaw Publishing, Salt Lake City, Utah, 1992, p. 164.

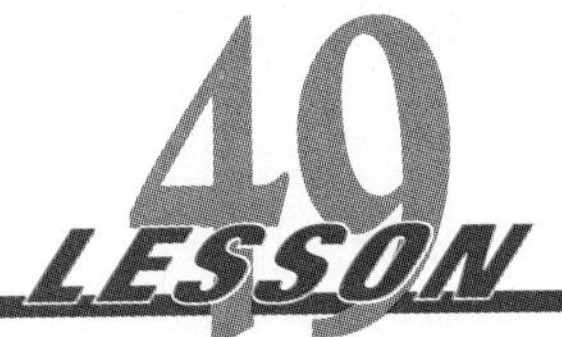

Endnotes

Margins: 1 inch • Tab: 0.5 inch • Spacing: Single • Drills: 2 times • Format Guide: 27–29

Goals:
To increase speed and accuracy; to key a report with endnotes.

A. WARMUP

```
1      Jack paid for six games and quit; as he walked to Room  12
2 389, he realized that he had scored 76 points more than Bev  24
3 (on Game #5) and 40 points more than Jeffrey (on Game #12).  36
  | 1 | 2 | 3 | 4 | 5 | 6 | 7 | 8 | 9 | 10 | 11 | 12
```

SKILLBUILDING

B. 12-SECOND SPRINTS

B. Take three 12-second timed writings on each line. The scale shows your wam speed for a 12-second timed writing.

```
4 You must try to key as fast as you can on these four lines.
5 The screens were very clear, and the print was easy to see.
6 We will not be able to print the copy until later on today.
7 The disk will not store any of the data if it is not clean.
  | | | |5| | | |10| | | |15| | | |20| | | |25| | | |30| | | |35| | | |40| | | |45| | | |50| | | |55| | | |60
```

MEMO 35 Please date and send this on the 19th.

MEMO TO: Della Stenerud, Director
Rockford Scandinavian Office
FROM: CBP
DATE: July 19, 19--
SUBJECT: Considered Purchase of Jovaag Enterprises

I have studied your report on the considered purchase of Jovaag Enterprises in Porsgrunn, Norway. As we move into the North Atlantic oil market, the production of control systems in the area likely will result in significantly reduced manufacturing costs.

There is one other manufacturing site near the North Atlantic oil fields that is also being considered. In order to expedite a decision on the selection, a team of three people headed by Bobbi Kjome will be visiting Norway in about two weeks.

Della, would you please have information relating to the questions on the enclosure ready for the team members' review when they arrive.

Enclosure

MEMO 36 The manufacturing site referred to in the second paragraph of the Jovaag Enterprises memo is Emerson Electronics, Ltd., located in Manchester, England. Please revise the Jovaag memo, and address it to Margaret Milford, director of the Rockford British office. Steve Keane has been appointed to serve as head of the team for the visit to England.

C. Take a 1-minute timed writing on the first paragraph to establish your base speed. Then take several 1-minute timed writings on the remaining paragraphs. As soon as you equal or exceed your base speed on one paragraph, advance to the next one.

C. SUSTAINED PRACTICE: ROUGH DRAFT

```
     An entrepreneur can be defined as an innovative person   12
who assumes the risks of starting a business to develop new   24
products or ideas.  Such people have high levels of energy.   36
     What is it we know about entrepreneurs that make them    12
different from average small business owner?  Many times,    24
a new idea, a few dollars, and drive are what they require.   36
     Also, the entrepreneur normally starts as sole owner     12
but soon changes to a corp. so that much more capital can     24
be found for expanding the business as quickly as possible.   36
It should be noted that entrepreneurs are not always the      12
same as inventors.  entrepreneurs invent may a product but    24
they also have the needed skills to market it with success.   36
 | 1 | 2 | 3 | 4 | 5 | 6 | 7 | 8 | 9 | 10 | 11 | 12
```

FORMATTING

D. ENDNOTES

Like footnotes, endnotes indicate sources of facts or ideas in a report. However, endnotes are placed on a separate page at the end of the report. To format the endnotes page follow these steps:

1. Center and key the title **NOTES** in all-capital letters 2 inches from the top of the page, in bold, and followed by a triple space.
2. Indent the first line of the reference 0.5 inch. Key the reference number (not a superscript), a period, and 2 spaces. Key the note single spaced with a double space between notes.

WP

ENDNOTES
Create: Ctrl-F7, 2, 1
Edit: Ctrl-F7, 2, 2

WordPerfect 6 users: See Student Guide, page 26.

E. WORDPERFECT: ENDNOTES

Use the Endnote command to create endnotes. Position the cursor where the endnote number is to appear in the text and enter the appropriate commands (Ctrl-F7, 2, 1). To indent the first line of an endnote, press the left arrow key once and the tab key once. Then press the right arrow key once, space twice, and key the endnote. Press F7 (not Enter) when you finish keying the endnote.

To begin the endnotes on a separate page, insert a hard page break (Ctrl-Enter) at the end of your document. Key the heading 2 inches from the top of the page and press Enter once if your line spacing is set for double or twice if line spacing is set for single. Use View Document to see the endnotes.

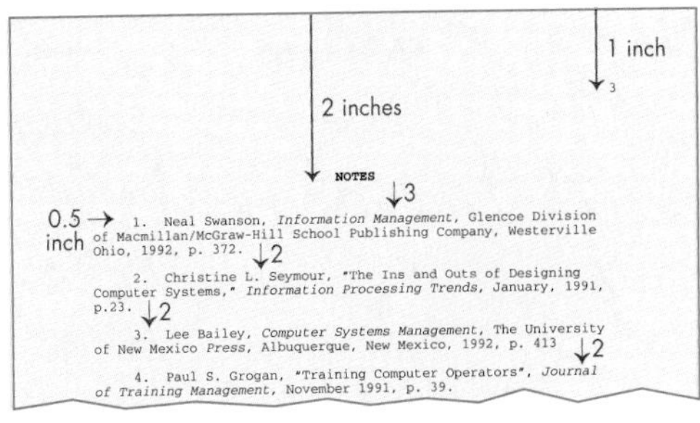

Note: WordPerfect will number the Endnotes page at the top right like all other pages. If you prefer to have the Endnotes page numbered at the bottom center, use the Page Numbering command to make the change (Sh-F8, 2, 6, 4, 6, F7).

TABLE 64

QUOTATION FOR PROPOSED INITIAL ORDER

Leave 4 spaces between columns.

Kangas-Rockford

Effective ~~on~~ August 1, 19--

Because this table extends to the default 1-inch margins, do not double-indent the footnote. Set a tab at 1.5 inches to indent the first line.

Number	Item	~~Item~~ Price*	Total
1,000	XLB Transformer	$ 19.60	
1,000	103 Wiring board	4.20	
1,000	4B Resistor network	3.12	
4,000	MPN Transistor	.07	
2,000	4CD Capacitor, Ceramic	~~.65~~ 56	
4,000	6D Resistor	.12	
~~1~~ 2,000	2CD Diode	.89	
1	Temperature Test Station	184,000.00	
1	Diagnostic Test Fixture	3,600.00	
1	Test Strength Fixture	12,047.00	
1	Swaging Press	3,200.00	
1	Oscilloscope	7,355.00	
TOTAL			

Increase item prices 10% (round to nearest cent); then enter the totals.

ds

*All prices are in U. S. dollars and are subject to change on 60 days' written notice. All prices are f.o.b. Jacksonville, Florida, USA, and do not include any ~~added~~ applicable taxes.

TABLE 65

Kangas-Rockford may wish to delay ordering the testing equipment until January 1. Please prepare a separate table for these items (the last five entries). The prices should reflect a 15 percent increase rather than 10 percent. These prices are effective January 1, 19--. Change the title to Quotation for Testing Equipment Order.

TABLE 66

We'll also have to prepare an August 1 quotation for just the other items (first seven entries). Please use the prices that were increased 10 percent.

DOCUMENT PROCESSING

REPORT 18
TWO-PAGE REPORT WITH ENDNOTES

Spacing: Double

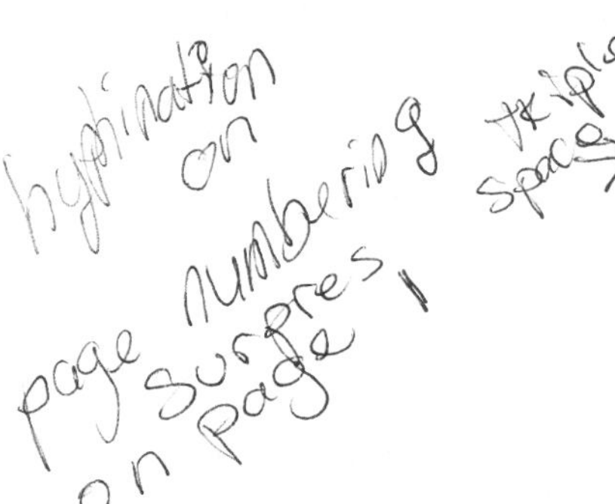

DESIGNING A COMPUTER SYSTEM

Designing a computer system involves a variety of different operations such as word processing, data processing, communications, printing, and other office-related functions. Because of computers, these areas can be integrated into a very powerful computer system.

Designing the System

One of the first steps is to determine what information is going to be computerized and what personnel will need these resources.[1] This decision should involve all departments in the planning stage of system design. If necessary, you may have to invite input from those departments which are going to be closely involved in computer use after the system has been designed.

There may also be a need to acquire the systems design experience of outside experts—people whose careers consist primarily of planning and developing computer systems for management.[2]

Selecting Hardware and Software

Bailey believes that "the selection of software precedes any hardware choices. Too many people, however, select the hardware first and then try to match their software with the computer."[3] After the software has been selected, a decision must be made as to whether hardware should be purchased or leased. Although many firms decide to purchase their own hardware, others have taken the route of time-sharing or remote processing whereby the costs of processing data can be shared with other users.

Training Operators

Many firms neglect this important phase of designing a computer system. It is not enough to offer a one-week training course in an applications package and then expect proficiency from a worker. Training must occur over time to help those who will be using computers every day on the job.

Begin the Notes on a separate page.

Endnotes are arranged in numeric order, following the order of reference numbers in the report (not in alphabetic order as in a bibliography). The first line is indented 5 spaces; turnover lines start at the left margin.

NOTES

1. Neal Swanson, *Information Management,* Glencoe Division, Macmillan/McGraw-Hill School Publishing Company, Westerville, Ohio, 1992, p. 372.

2. Christine L. Seymour, "The Ins and Outs of Designing Your Computer System," *Information Processing Trends,* January 1991, p. 23.

3. Lee Bailey, *Computer Systems Management,* The University of New Mexico Press, Albuquerque, New Mexico, 1992, p. 413.

LETTER 106
FORM LETTER FOR DUPLICATION

Please date this letter July 28. As usual, correct any errors I may have made. Leave the inside address blank. Key the salutation 3 inches from the top.

ds To Share Holders of Rockford International:
It is with a great deal of pleasure that we send you this ~~second~~ report on our entry in to the Scandinavian market.

Our early discussions with firms in Norway are progressing about on schedule. Our big news is that we will soon likely enter into a relationship with Kangas Automation, Inc. in Finland. They will purchase selected Rockford components to be resold with their equipment under the tradename Kangas-Rockford. They are confident that the western ~~soviet~~ states will become large users of their products. We look forward to seeing most of you at our annual meeting. If you are not planing to attend, the enclosed proxy must be returned to our office by September 1 19--.

in the former Soviet Union

Sincerely Yours,

CarterB. Phillips
Vice President for Marketing

MEMO 34

MEMO TO: Jim Watters
Legal Department
From: CBP
Date:
Subject: Contract for Rockford-China

Please correct any errors.

There are still several unresolved issues relating to our establishment of a wholly foreign-owned enterprise in the Peoples Republic of China (PRC).

1. ~~Our first concern is that~~ Rockford-China must be able to accept orders from ~~any~~ customers within the PRC in either local or foreign currency without Government interference.

2. ~~Also,~~ Rockford-China must be able to pay duties in local chinese currency for imported components, sub-assemblies, and complete products in order to utilize locally generated revenues.

We must be able to hire local chinese people through out the PRC.

3. Rockford-China must have the freedom to set sales prices in any currency and to pay dividends without Government interference.

4.

Please incorporate these provisions in the draft agreement, which, it is hoped, will be ready for signing within a month.

Please initial this for me and get it over to the Legal Department right away.

REPORT 19
TWO-PAGE UNBOUND REPORT WITH ENDNOTES

Retrieve Report 18 and add the following paragraph (as well as the accompanying endnote) as the final paragraph and the final endnote in the report.

Spacing: Double

Finally, it should be recognized that training is an ongoing responsibility. As technology, software, hardware, and procedures change, training must occur regularly and on a continuing basis.[4]

4. Paula Blair, *Administrative Management,* Southern Publishing Company, Atlanta, Georgia, 1992, p. 420.

Special Report Pages

Margins: 1 inch • Tab: 0.5 inch • Spacing: Single • Drills: 2 times • Format Guide: 29

Goals:
To key 39 wam/3'/3e; to format a table of contents; to format a title page.

A. WARMUP

Jo made $8.74 (9% profit) on six dozen jewelry pieces, 12
but I quickly found that Al would have to sell $53.20 worth 24
of oranges so May could buy 16 boxes of Mother's Day cards. 36

| 1 | 2 | 3 | 4 | 5 | 6 | 7 | 8 | 9 | 10 | 11 | 12

LANGUAGE ARTS

B. PROOFREADING

B. Compare this paragraph with the first paragraph of Report 18 on page 110. Then key a list of the words that contain errors, correcting the errors as you key.

Desining a computer system involves a vareity of
diferent operations such as word processing, processing
data, comunications, printing, and other office related
functions. because of computers these areas can be made
into a powerful computer.

SKILLBUILDING

C. 3-MINUTE TIMED WRITING

C. Spacing: Double
Take two 3-minute timed writings. Compute your speed and count errors.

Goal: 39 wam/3'/3e

In just a short period of time, computers have changed 12
the way goods and services are now produced. We often think 24
of the computer as a means by which we can work with just 36
numbers or words. There are quite a few other ways in which 48
the computer can also be used. In the production of goods, 60
however, firms are more apt to use robotics. Robotics is 72
the use of computer-driven machines to do the work formerly 84
done by humans. A robot can be used to do such tasks as 95
weld, sew, mark, and select on an assembly line. It is 106
amazing what businesses expect from their computers now. 117

| 1 | 2 | 3 | 4 | 5 | 6 | 7 | 8 | 9 | 10 | 11 | 12

LETTER 105

Please prepare the following letter to be sent to Mr. Uno Kukkonen, President of Kangas Automation, Inc., at 2728 Maki Street in Helsinki, Finland.

Ms. Della Stenerud of our Scandinavian office in Stockholm has been keeping me informed of developments with your firm. It is my understanding that Kangas Automation, Inc., wishes to enter into a relationship with Rockford International to purchase selected electronics components. These would then be resold with certain Kangas equipment under the trade name Kangas-Rockford.

Some provisions are not discussed in the proposed contract. Conditions for payment, remedies for damage, and term length for the agreement must also be addressed. Mr. Robert W. Wilson, our chief financial officer, will be flying to Finland on September 4 to discuss these items with members of your staff.

We at Rockford look forward to this new association.

CBP

PS: Thank you, Mr. Kukkonen, for the invitation to visit your plant in Helsinki. I look forward to doing this when I go there for the formal signing of the agreement.

REPORT 78
AGENDA

For tomorrow's meeting!

ds

ROCKFORD INTERNATIONAL ← Bold
Executive Committee Meeting
Wednesday, July ~~17~~ 14, 19--

Opening Remarks . . . . Barbara J. Rosemont
Kangas Automation, Inc. . . . . . . Josh Bransen
Annual Meeting . . . . Joseph E. Rosemont, Jr.
Contract for Rockford-China . . . . . . Jim Watters
North Atlantic Oil Market . . . . . . Bobbi Kjome
Foreign Visitor Program . . . . . . Valerie Thomas
Concluding Remarks . . . . Carter B. Phillips

Please use your thesaurus to find a different word

FORMATTING

If a report title or subtitle must be divided between 2 lines, try to have the second line shorter than the first, resulting in an inverted pyramid.

WordPerfect 6 users: See Student Guide, page 28.

D. TITLE PAGE

Reports should have a title page, which at the very least, shows the report title, the writer's name and identification, and the date. The title (and subtitle, if any) are keyed on the top part of the page; the writer's name and identification are keyed in the center of the page; and the date is keyed on the lower part of the page.

To format a title page, follow these steps:

1. Access the Format menu (Sh-F8), then turn on Center Page (2, 1, Y) and press Enter to return to the Format menu.
2. Then turn on Center Justification (1, 3, 2) and press F7.
3. Key the report title in all-capital letters and bold. Double-space and key the subtitle with initial capital letters in regular type.
4. Space down 2.5 inches (15 lines) and key the words "Prepared by" followed by a double space.
5. Key the writer's name and identification on separate lines, single spaced.
6. Space down 2.5 inches (15 lines) and key the date.
7. Turn off Center Justification (Sh-F8, 1, 3, 1).

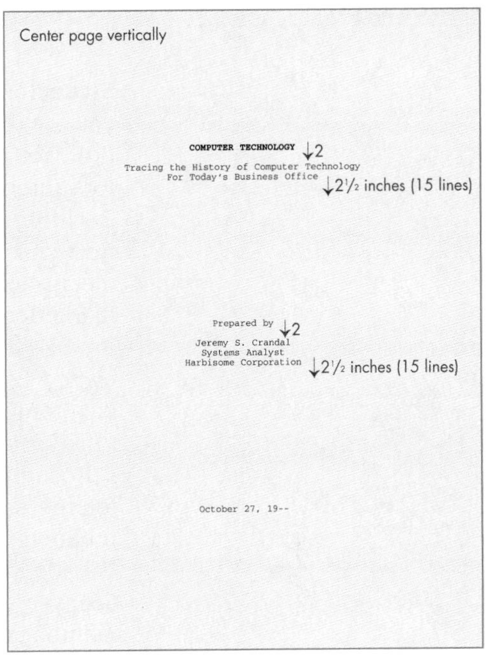

Center page vertically
COMPUTER TECHNOLOGY ↓2
Tracing the History of Computer Technology
For Today's Business Office
↓2½ inches (15 lines)
Prepared by ↓2
Jeremy S. Crandal
Systems Analyst
Harbisome Corporation
↓2½ inches (15 lines)
October 27, 19--

E. TABLE OF CONTENTS

A table of contents (see page 113) is usually supplied with a report. The table of contents identifies the major sections of a report and the page numbers where they can be found.

1. Use the same margins that were used for the report.
2. Align roman numerals at the period.
3. Center and key the title 2 inches from the top of the page in all-capital letters and bold followed by a triple space.
4. Follow an outline format—key the major headings in all-capital letters; triple-space before and double-space after them.
5. Key subheadings with initial capital letters and single spacing.
6. Align page numbers flush right and key them with dot leaders—a series of periods that help guide the reader's eye across the page to the page number on the same line.

WP

DOT LEADERS
Sh-F8, 1, 8, *set tab,* period
OR: Alt-F6, Alt-F6
FLUSH RIGHT
Alt-F6

WordPerfect 6 users: See Student Guide, page 29.

F. WORDPERFECT: DOT LEADERS

To insert dot leaders, access the tab ruler (Sh-F8, 1, 8). Set a right tab at the right margin (6.5 inches). Position the cursor under the tab setting and key a period. When you tab to that position, a line of periods will be inserted.

Another method for inserting dot leaders is to press Flush Right (Alt-F6) twice. Pressing Flush Right once positions the cursor at the right margin; pressing it again inserts the dot leaders.

DOCUMENT PROCESSING

Q. INTEGRATED OFFICE PROJECT
ROCKFORD INTERNATIONAL

Situation: Today is July 16, 19—, and you are the secretary to Mr. Carter B. Phillips, vice president for marketing of Rockford International in Jacksonville, Florida. Rockford International was founded by Rockford Electronics, Inc., in 1983 to handle its exports and to coordinate other marketing functions in foreign countries. As 53 percent of its stock is currently owned by Rockford Electronics, the parent company continues to be a strong force in all management decisions.

Rockford International is responsible for the sales of all Rockford Electronics products outside the United States and Canada. Additionally, the firm acts as the licenser to foreign enterprises for the manufacture of Rockford products as well as the distribution of Rockford products. At times these goods are distributed under a different brand name and may even have a localized logo.

The primary products are transmitters, which are designed to relay electrical impulses of mechanical movements. Many other electronic instruments and components are manufactured by Rockford, however.

Mr. Phillips has a number of jobs ready for you to complete. Read through the materials first so that you can ask for clarification right away.

You are expected to format documents properly, capitalize correctly, and review all jobs for errors that Mr. Phillips may have missed. Use whatever WordPerfect features are needed to complete the jobs. Use the modified-block letter style with standard punctuation for all outgoing correspondence, and include this closing:

```
Sincerely yours,



Carter B. Phillips
Vice President for Marketing
```

Once you have looked over your work assignments and have cleared up any questions, you will need to prioritize the jobs. Determine the priority levels (1, 2, and 3) of the jobs according to these guidelines:

1. Those items which have been identified by Mr. Phillips as having high priority or which, in your judgment, should be in this category.
2. Those items which are timely but, on the basis of their content, do not warrant a high-priority label.
3. Those items which may be delayed until after you have completed the jobs in Levels 1 and 2.

TABLE 63
JOB PRIORITY LIST

Create the table shown below. List the job names and numbers in Column 1 and print the table. In Column 2, show their priority (according to the directions above). Next, complete the jobs in order of priority. Check off each job (in Column 3), as you complete it.

JOB PRIORITY LIST

Job	Priority	Completed
Letter 105		
Report 78		
Letter 106		
Memo 34		

DOCUMENT PROCESSING

REPORT 20
TITLE PAGE

Center each line horizontally. Follow the spacing indicated on page 112.

THE SECRETARY IN TODAY'S AUTOMATED OFFICE

Maintaining Traditional Skills While
Developing High-Tech Competence

Prepared by
Phyllis G. Browe
Systems Analyst
The Western Office Group

December 9, 19--

REPORT 21
TABLE OF CONTENTS

Tabs: Relative; Decimal, 0.3; Left, 0.6; Left, 1.0; and Right, 6.5 inches

Use dot leaders (rows of periods) to lead the eye across the page.

Press tab before keying the roman numerals.

↓ 2 inches **CONTENTS**
↓ 3

I. THE EARLY YEARS OF TECHNOLOGY . . . . 1 ↓ 2

A. Vacuum Tubes 3
B. Transistors 4
C. Integrated Circuits . . . . 4 ↓ 3

II. HARDWARE DEVELOPMENTS . . . . 5 ↓ 2

A. Computer Terminals 6
B. Monitors and Keyboards 8
C. Modems 9
D. Scanners 10
E. Printers . . . . 11 ↓ 3

III. SOFTWARE DEVELOPMENTS . . . . 13 ↓ 3

IV. THE FUTURE OF TECHNOLOGY . . . . 17 ↓ 2

A. Artificial Intelligence 20
B. Parallel Processing 22

N. Take three 12-second timed writings on each line. The scale gives wam for a 12-second timed writing.

N. 12-SECOND SPRINTS

69 Ms. Sue Bell lives at 67 Stagg Road, Apt. 3, Austin, Texas.
70 Did Peter Danforth publish it on Sunday in Berlin, Vermont?
71 The American Management Association will meet in Miami, FL.
72 The Warren County Historical Society will meet on Thursday.

O. DIAGNOSTIC PRACTICE: NUMBERS

Turn to the Diagnostic Practice: Numbers routine at the back of this book. Take the Pretest and record your performance. Then, practice the drill lines for those reaches on which you made errors. Finally, repeat the Pretest and compare your performance.

P. Spacing: Double
Take two 5-minute timed writings. Compute your speed and count errors.

Goal: 53 wam/5′/5e

P. 5-MINUTE TIMED WRITING

73 There is a consistent theme to comments on what skills 12
74 will be necessary in building a healthy career in American 24
75 business in the future: a solid grounding in humanities 35
76 and social sciences. In the computerized, high-tech age 47
77 to come, many people believe that some technical specialty 58
78 will be the only key to success. However, it is crucial 70
79 to realize that computer skills are neither the only, nor 81
80 the chief, tool you will need. 88
81 Business will continue to need people with the ability 100
82 to communicate clearly, both verbally and through written 111
83 correspondence. Those employees who can sift through the 123
84 complexities of business relationships and act not simply 134
85 on commands from above but on the strength of their own 146
86 observations will be quickly promoted. And finally, those 157
87 who are adaptable, who are not upset by change but appear 169
88 ready and able to ride with it, will succeed best. In the 181
89 future, change will be even more constant than it is now: 193
90 no line of work, no job will be immune to it. 202
91 Schools around the country are changing their courses 214
92 to fit this new challenge: to prepare their students for 225
93 fast-moving, high-growth management positions. There will 237
94 continue to be some technical training included, but the 248
95 vote is in: communication skills will rank above all the 260
96 rest for some time to come. 265

Resumes

Margins: 1 inch • Tab: 0.5 inch • Spacing: Single • Drills: 2 times • Format Guide: 31

Goals:
To improve speed and accuracy; to format a resume.

A. WARMUP

1 The mixture (fresh water and lemon) quickly gave Jacob 12
2 Dolze a chance to prove that his 6/25/90 statement was true 24
3 and that the mixture sells for $1.37/ounce and $1.48/ounce. 36

| 1 | 2 | 3 | 4 | 5 | 6 | 7 | 8 | 9 | 10 | 11 | 12

SKILLBUILDING

PRETEST.
Take a 1-minute timed writing; compute your speed and count errors.

B. PRETEST: VERTICAL REACHES

4 He knew about the rival races away from home and today 12
5 ordered Gilbert to skip the seventh race. The race at Cole 24
6 may be one that Gilbert may want to enter at an early date. 36

| 1 | 2 | 3 | 4 | 5 | 6 | 7 | 8 | 9 | 10 | 11 | 12

PRACTICE.
Speed Emphasis: If you made 2 or fewer errors on the Pretest, key each line twice.
Accuracy Emphasis: If you made 3 or more errors, key each group of lines (as though it were a paragraph) twice.

C. PRACTICE: UP REACHES

7 aw aware flaws drawn crawl hawks sawed awful flaw bawl draw
8 se seven reset seams sedan loses eases serve used seed dose
9 ki skids kings kinks skill kitty kites kilts kits kids kick
10 rd board horde wards sword award beard third cord hard lard

D. PRACTICE: DOWN REACHES

11 ac races pacer backs ached acute laced facts each acre lace
12 kn knave knack knife knows knoll knots knelt knew knee knit
13 ab about abide label above abode sable abbey drab able cabs
14 va evade avail value vapor divan rival naval vain vale vane

POSTTEST.
Repeat the Pretest (B) and compare performance.

E. POSTTEST: VERTICAL REACHES

FORMATTING

WP

FONT SIZE
Ctrl-F8, 1, *size*

Some font sizes are printer-dependent. Try each size with your printer to see which fonts are available.

WordPerfect 6 users: See Student Guide, page 29.

F. WORDPERFECT: FONT SIZE

Use Font Size to increase the size of type for headings or to decrease the size of type for supplementary information. You can choose from two sizes that are smaller than normal (fine or small) and three sizes that are larger than normal (large, very large, or extra large). Position the cursor where you want the different-sized text to begin and enter the appropriate commands (Ctrl-F8, 1, *size*). Key the text and press the right arrow key to return to normal text. Or, if the text already exists, block the text and enter the same commands (Ctrl-F8, 1, *size*).

Because most computer screens are unable to display these different font sizes, use View Document (Sh-F7, 6) to see how your document will look when it is printed.

I. This paragraph is made up of very short words, requiring the frequent use of the space bar. Take three 1-minute timed writings. Do not pause before or after striking the space bar.

I. TECHNIQUE PRACTICE: SPACE BAR

He had the car in the shop. He knew that the cost for 12
the work might be high. If the items to be fixed will cost 24
more than $200, he knew that he would skip it. It does not 36
make any sense to put more cash into the auto at this time. 48

| 1 | 2 | 3 | 4 | 5 | 6 | 7 | 8 | 9 | 10 | 11 | 12

J. Take three 1-minute timed writings. Note that the last two digits of each number are a cumulative word count and give your wam.

J. NUMBER PRACTICE

5601 7802 1203 4404 7605 9806 1207 3808 2609 5610 6111 7412
3913 4014 5515 9116 2017 4918 2119 5820 6121 9622 3223 9024
6525 2426 8327 4028 6629 7030 8431 1232 5733 6534 9735 2836
8037 4338 7639 2140 1941 1442 3043 2244 4745 6646 3247 5048

K. Each of these sentences contains two words that are not used properly. Correct those words as you key each sentence twice.

K. TECHNIQUE PRACTICE: CONCENTRATION

During the past weak, he didn't know weather he could sing.
The wait of the patience was recorded on all four charts.
Place the stationary in the envelop to be mailed tomorrow.
He held a conservation with the school principle yesterday.

L. PROGRESSIVE PRACTICE: ALPHABET

Turn to the Progressive Practice: Alphabet routine at the back of the book. Take five 30-second timed writings, starting at the point where you left off the last time.

M. Take a 1-minute timed writing on the first paragraph to establish your base speed. Then take four 1-minute timed writings on the remaining paragraphs. As soon as you equal or exceed your base speed on one paragraph, advance to the next one.

M. SUSTAINED PRACTICE: SYLLABIC INTENSITY

Did you ever walk into a big store to make a purchase, 12
say a pair of slacks, only to find no one is around to help 24
you? Or, perhaps, there are salesclerks in a far corner of 36
the store, but they simply look away as you seek some help? 48

If you have heard this before, you are not alone. For 12
many years the firms which have focused on service, such as 24
department stores, restaurants, and gas stations, have used 36
a service approach which values equipment more than people. 48

Attracting and keeping clients in today's market means 12
using a completely different model. Line managers at sharp 24
businesses are changing the old approach to a new one which 36
puts service workers first and designs systems around them. 48

This emerging model of service emphasizes the value of 12
having a great recruitment, selection, and training process 24
in place. In addition, this approach links compensation to 36
performance, meaning that we consumers obtain good service. 48

| 1 | 2 | 3 | 4 | 5 | 6 | 7 | 8 | 9 | 10 | 11 | 12

G. RESUMES

When you apply for a job, you may be asked to submit a resume. The purpose of a resume is to convey your qualifications for the position you are seeking. In addition to personal information (name, address, telephone number), your resume should also include a summary of your educational background and special training, previous work experience, and any activities or accomplishments that relate to the position for which you are applying. A resume may also include your career goal and references. References should consist of at least three people who can tell a prospective employer what kind of worker you are. Always obtain permission from these people you want to use as references *before* using their names.

Often, your resume creates the first impression you make on a prospective employer; be sure it is free of errors.

A variety of styles is acceptable for formatting a resume (see Illustrations 1 and 2 below). Choose a style (or design one) that is attractive and that enables you to get all the needed information on one or two pages.

List all items in reverse chronological order (most recent first).

If work experience is your strongest asset, list it first.

You may also list the names and addresses of at least three specific references. Be sure to obtain permission before using someone's name as a reference.

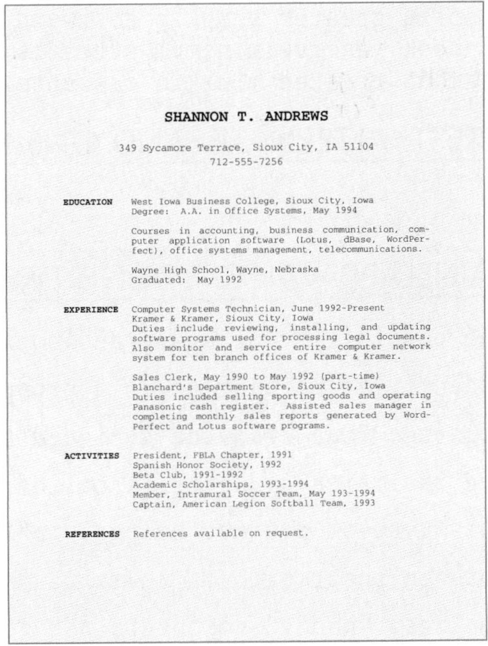

SHANNON T. ANDREWS

349 Sycamore Terrace, Sioux City, IA 51104
712-555-7256

EDUCATION West Iowa Business College, Sioux City, Iowa
Degree: A.A. in Office Systems, May 1994

Courses in accounting, business communication, computer application software (Lotus, dBase, WordPerfect), office systems management, telecommunications.

Wayne High School, Wayne, Nebraska
Graduated: May 1992

EXPERIENCE Computer Systems Technician, June 1992-Present
Kramer & Kramer, Sioux City, Iowa
Duties include reviewing, installing, and updating software programs used for processing legal documents. Also monitor and service entire computer network system for ten branch offices of Kramer & Kramer.

Sales Clerk, May 1990 to May 1992 (part-time)
Blanchard's Department Store, Sioux City, Iowa
Duties included selling sporting goods and operating Panasonic cash register. Assisted sales manager in completing monthly sales reports generated by WordPerfect and Lotus software programs.

ACTIVITIES President, FBLA Chapter, 1991
Spanish Honor Society, 1992
Beta Club, 1991-1992
Academic Scholarships, 1993-1994
Member, Intramural Soccer Team, May 193-1994
Captain, American Legion Softball Team, 1993

REFERENCES References available on request.

Illustration 1

SHANNON T. ANDREWS

927 Dace Avenue, Sioux City, IA 51101
712-555-7256

EDUCATION

West Iowa Business College, Sioux City, Iowa
Degree: A.A. in Office Systems, May 1994

Courses in accounting, business communication, computer application software (Lotus, dBase, WordPerfect), office systems management, telecommunications, desktop publishing, programming (Pascal).

Wayne High School, Wayne, Nebraska
Graduated: May 1992

EXPERIENCE

Programmer, June 1992-Present
Teledyne Inc., Omaha, Nebraska
Duties include writing Pascal programs to monitor quality control within Research and Development.

Sales Clerk, May 1990 to May 1992 (part-time)
Blanchard's Department Store, Sioux City, Iowa
Duties included selling sporting goods and operating Panasonic cash register. Assisted sales manager in completing monthly sales reports generated by WordPerfect and Lotus software programs.

ACTIVITIES

President, FBLA Chapter, 1991
Academic Scholarships, 1993-1994

REFERENCES

References available on request.

Illustration 2

To prepare a resume that is similar to Illustration 1, follow these steps:

1. Use a 2-inch top margin.
2. Center and key the name in extra large size and bold. Turn off bold, change to large size, and double-space.
3. Key the address and telephone number on separate lines, followed by a triple space. Change to normal size.
4. Clear all tabs and set a left tab at 1.25 inches.
5. Key the word *Education* in all caps and bold at the left margin.
6. Press tab and key the name and address of the school and any degrees earned.
7. Double-space, indent (F4), and key the course information. Double-space, indent again, and complete the Education information.
8. Triple-space before beginning each new section.

SKILLBUILDING

PRETEST. Take a 1-minute timed writing; compute your speed and count errors.

PRACTICE.
Speed Emphasis: If you made no errors on the Pretest, key each line twice.
Accuracy Emphasis: If you made 1 or more errors on the Pretest, key each group of lines (as though it were a paragraph) twice.

POSTTEST. Repeat the Pretest (D) and compare performance.

H. Take a 1-minute timed writing on the first paragraph to establish your base speed. Then take four 1-minute timed writings on the remaining paragraphs. As soon as you equal or exceed your base speed on one paragraph, advance to the next one.

D. PRETEST: ALTERNATE- AND ONE-HAND WORDS

In their opinion, the ornamental bicycle from Honolulu 12
may be regarded as an authentic antique. It deserves to be 24
treated well because it will attract many new visitors from 36
Texas and Ohio to most downtown streets in July and August. 48

| 1 | 2 | 3 | 4 | 5 | 6 | 7 | 8 | 9 | 10 | 11 | 12

E. PRACTICE: ALTERNATE-HAND WORDS

maps visual suspend amendment turndown visible height signs
form profit penalty shamrocks blandish problem thrown chair
snap emblem dormant authentic clemency figment island usual
half signal auditor endowment ornament element handle amend

F. PRACTICE: ONE-HAND WORDS

serve uphill exceeds killjoy carefree homonym terrace onion
trade poplin greater pumpkin eastward plumply barrage holly
defer unhook reserve minimum attracts million scatter plump
exact kimono created minikin cassette opinion seaweed union

G. POSTTEST: ALTERNATE- AND ONE-HAND WORDS

H. SUSTAINED PRACTICE: ROUGH DRAFT

The possibility of aging and not being able to live as 12
independently as we want to is a prospect that no one wants 24
to recognize. One resource designed to counter some of the 36
negative realities of aging is called the Handyman Project. 48
This type of ~~project~~ program helps support elders and disabled 12
residents in their efforts to maintain the[ir] homes. As the 24
name implies, "handy" volunt[e]rs per form minor home repairs 36
such as tight[e]ning leaky faucets and fixing broken windows. 48
[¶] Other type[s] of work include: painting, plumbing, yard 12
work, and carpentery. The volunteers are all as divers[i]fied 24
as the word itself. You may find a retire[e] working next too 36
an executive or a student ~~helping~~ assisting a lisensed electrician. 48
Their back grounds may vary, but [w]that they share is the 12
~~hope~~ desire to put their ~~ca~~pabilities to good use. Volunteers ~~take~~ find 24
a high level of personnal satisfaction after ~~doing~~ finishing a job 36
~~but~~ and spending time with an elder who really needs the help. 48

| 1 | 2 | 3 | 4 | 5 | 6 | 7 | 8 | 9 | 10 | 11 | 12

DOCUMENT PROCESSING

REPORT 22
RESUME

Tab: 1.25 inches

Use full justification.

Key the resume below in the same format as Illustration 1 on the preceding page.

↓2 inches

SHANNON T. ANDREWS
↓2

349 Sycamore Terrace, Sioux City, IA 51104
712-555-7256
↓3

EDUCATION West Iowa Business College, Sioux City, Iowa
Degree: A.A. in Office Systems, May 1994 ↓2

Courses in accounting, business communication, computer application software (Lotus, dBase, WordPerfect), office systems management, telecommunications. ↓2

Wayne High School, Wayne, Nebraska
Graduated: May 1992 ↓3

EXPERIENCE Computer Systems Technician, June 1992-Present
Kramer & Kramer, Sioux City, Iowa
Duties include reviewing, installing, and updating software programs used for processing legal documents. Also monitor and service entire computer network system for ten branch offices of Kramer & Kramer. ↓2

Sales Clerk, May 1990 to May 1992 (part-time)
Blanchard's Department Store, Sioux City, Iowa
Duties included selling sporting goods and operating Panasonic cash register. Assisted sales manager in completing monthly sales reports generated by WordPerfect and Lotus software programs. ↓3

ACTIVITIES President, FBLA Chapter, 1991
Spanish Honor Society, 1992
Beta Club, 1991-1992
Academic Scholarships, 1993-1994
Member, Intramural Soccer Team, May 1993-1994
Captain, American Legion Softball Team, 1993 ↓3

REFERENCES References available on request.

REPORT 23
RESUME

Revise Report 22 making the following changes:

1. Change the name, address, and phone number to very large size, and change the address to: *927 Dace Avenue, Sioux City, IA 51101.*
2. Change the side headings to large size and center them. Triple-space before and double-space after the headings.
3. Add desktop publishing and programming (Pascal) to the Education section.
4. Replace the first work experience with: *Programmer, June 1992–Present / Teledyne Inc., Omaha, Nebraska / Duties include writing Pascal programs to monitor quality control within Research and Development.*
5. Delete the Spanish Honor Society, Beta Club, Softball Team, and Soccer Team entries in the Activities section.

UNIT TWENTY-EIGHT • INTEGRATED OFFICE PROJECT: INTERNATIONAL MARKETING

136-140 LESSONS

Margins: 1 inch • Spacing: Single • Drills: 2 times • Format Guide: 121–129

Goals for Unit 28

1. To improve accuracy and speed on alphabet and number keys.
2. To key 53 wam for 5 minutes with no more than 5 errors.
3. To develop proficiency in spelling commonly misspelled words.
4. To format a variety of documents for an international company—letters, memos, tables, agendas, and minutes.
5. To transcribe copy from simulated dictation.

Begin each day with approximately 15 minutes of skillbuilding, selecting activities from pages 334–337. In the remaining class time, complete as many production jobs from pages 338–346 as you can.

A. WARMUP

1 The office required a purchase order of 18 items @ $45 12
2 and 20 items @ $62. Adding a 7% sales tax jumps that price 24
3 to $2,193.50. Be careful to check and validate every size. 36

| 1 | 2 | 3 | 4 | 5 | 6 | 7 | 8 | 9 | 10 | 11 | 12

LANGUAGE ARTS

B. CAPITAL LETTERS

Study the rules at the right. Then key lines 4–7, making necessary changes.

Rule: Capitalize the names of places, such as *streets, buildings, parks, monuments, rivers, oceans,* and *mountains.* Do not capitalize short forms used in place of the full name.

He vows that the water in Lake Superior is crystal clear.

Rule: Capitalize *north, south, east, west,* and derivative words when they designate definite regions or are an integral part of a proper name.

They have already gone to the South for the winter.

4 He lives just two blocks from the Lincoln park zoo.
5 Their new store will be located across from the Square.
6 Two shops are located in the Northern part of Catalina County.
7 One of the subsidiary companies is located back east.

C. SPELLING

C. These words are among the 500 most frequently misspelled words in business correspondence.

8 portion efficient premises customers consultant filed sales
9 extremely document concerning conference authorization role
10 versus brought assessed assigned volume applicable quantity
11 substantially advisory charge continuous shall would versus
12 temporary evaluation complaint retirement reviewed evaluate

Letters of Application

Margins: 1 inch • Tab: 0.5 inch • Spacing: Single • Drills: 2 times • Format Guide: 31

Goals:
To key 39 wam/5'/5e; to format a letter of application.

A. WARMUP

1 Do not jeopardize an equal tax by having Mack vote too 12
2 swiftly on 11/23/92. Last year my precinct (the 46th) tied 24
3 when voting on Resolutions 50 & 78--it was a fierce battle! 36

| 1 | 2 | 3 | 4 | 5 | 6 | 7 | 8 | 9 | 10 | 11 | 12

LANGUAGE ARTS

B. PROOFREADING

B. Compare this paragraph with the fourth paragraph of Report 18, page 110. Then key a list of the words that contain errors, correcting the errors as you key.

4 Bailey believed that "a selection of software precedes
5 the hardware choices. Two many people, however, select the
6 hardware first and then try to match the software with the
7 computer."[3] After the software has been chosen, a decision
8 must be made as to weather hardware should be purchased or
9 leased. Although most firms decide to purchase there own
10 hardware, others have taken the route of time sharing or
11 remote processing whereby the cost of proccessing data will be
12 shared with other people.

SKILLBUILDING

C. TECHNIQUE PRACTICE: TAB KEY

C. Set tabs every 1.5 inches. Use the tab key to go from column to column. Key lines 13–18 once.

13	aisle	above	blank	begin	candy
14	canal	cycle	drain	eagle	fifth
15	given	hoist	ivory	jewel	knack
16	large	money	notch	ounce	patch
17	quick	ready	stand	troop	under
18	video	waist	excel	youth	zebra

D. TECHNIQUE PRACTICE: CONCENTRATION

Change every singular noun to a plural noun.

19 If the man, woman, and child want to vacate the old
20 apartment, the manager must issue the permit to make the
21 transfer legal. The tenant must approve the plan before
22 the vacancy or listing can be printed in the newspaper.

Change every plural noun to a singular noun.

23 The managers asked your assistants to key the letters and
24 reports that the officers had dictated earlier. When the jobs
25 had been completed, the secretaries consulted your assistants.
26 Your assistants discovered the errors and had the jobs redone.

Change all first-person pronouns to the second person and vice versa; for example, change *I* to *you* and change *you* to *I* or *me*.

27 You must give me your recipe for success in your career
28 if I intend to follow you. If I become a broker also, you
29 can help me by giving me some leads and other contacts; you
30 could also have me subcontract a few of your small accounts.

WP

REVIEW
Flush Right: Alt-F6
Horizontal Lines: Alt-F9, 5, 1
Graphics Figure Boxes:
Options: Alt-F9, 1, 4
Create: Alt-F9, 1, 1

WordPerfect 6 users: See Student Guide, p. 79.

T. TITLE PAGE

Create a title page for the report as a separate document named 77T. Use the copy in the illustration.

1. Advance to Ln = 1.5″. Change to Very Large font, and key the title in all-capital letters and bold; center and double-space the lines. Return to normal font (press the right arrow twice; then press Enter).
2. Advance to Ln = 7.5″ and create a horizontal line, width 0.05″. Press Enter twice.
3. Access the Graphics Figure Option menu, and change the gray shading to 10 percent. Create a figure box using the file name *GLOBE2-M.WPG.* For the caption, backspace to delete the figure number; change to Small font and key *International Development Corp.* Set the Horizontal Position to Right; change the Size to 1.5″ wide × 1″ high; change Wrap Text to No.
4. Key the rest of the title page in bold, using normal font. Leave 1 blank line before the writer's name and department and 2 blank lines before the date.
5. Advance to Ln = 9.25″ and create a horizontal line, width 0.05″.

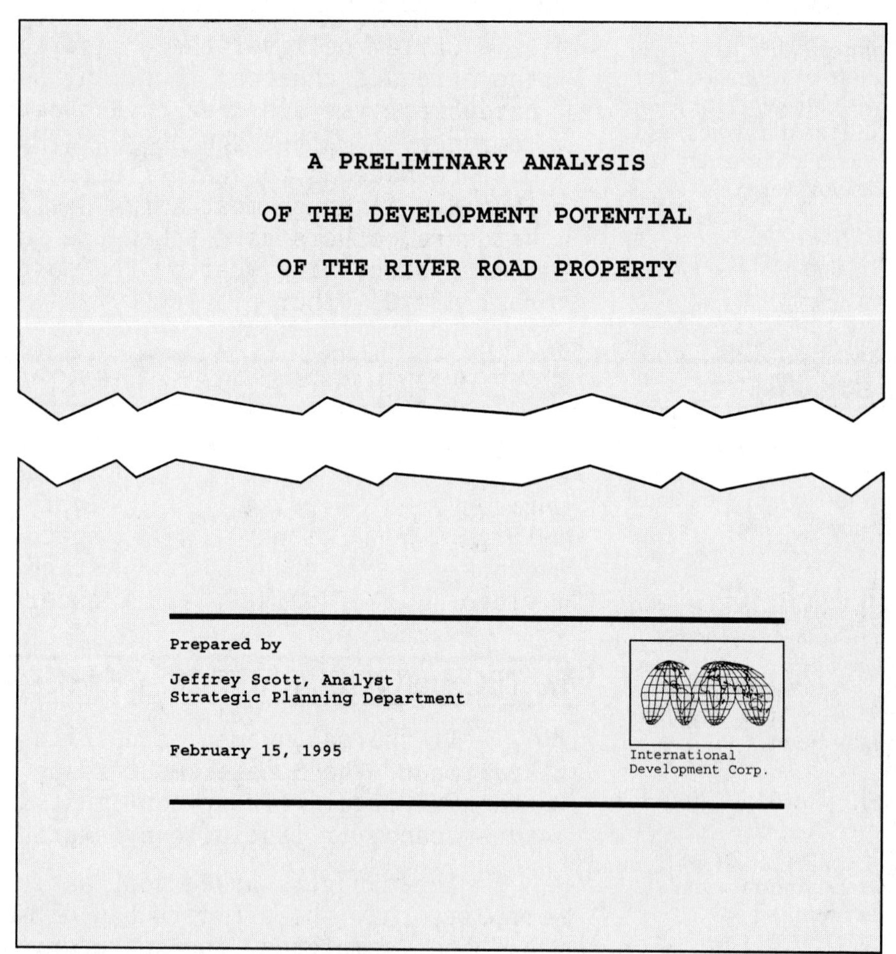

A PRELIMINARY ANALYSIS

OF THE DEVELOPMENT POTENTIAL

OF THE RIVER ROAD PROPERTY

Prepared by

Jeffrey Scott, Analyst
Strategic Planning Department

February 15, 1995

International
Development Corp.

U. COMPLETING THE REPORT

1. Proofread all pages for format and keystroking errors.
2. Assemble the pages in this order: title page, contents, body, appendix, references, and a blank page for a back cover sheet.
3. Staple the report at three places along the left edge.

E. Spacing: Double
Take two 5-minute timed writings. Compute your speed and count errors.

Goal: 39 wam/5′/5e

E. 5-MINUTE TIMED WRITING

```
     Applying for a job is likely to be one of the most      11
critical steps in your career.  This is the one chance you   23
have to impress a prospective employer, and it is very true  35
that first impressions are lasting ones.  Without a doubt,   47
at this time you want to look your very best and put forth   58
the strongest case you can for yourself.                     67
     Be sure that the clothes you choose for your interview  79
are free of lint and wrinkles and that they typify clothes   90
worn by those who now work for the company.  When you talk  102
with the interviewer, you should use language that sends    114
your message clearly, succinctly, and accurately.  When you 126
are asked a question, answer it completely, but don't give  137
excessive answers to any of the questions you are asked.    149
Recognize that you should ask a question or two at the end  161
of the interview.  Often the interviewer might want to know 173
if you have done any background research on the company and 185
would like to ask any questions about its operations.       195
  | 1 | 2 | 3 | 4 | 5 | 6 | 7 | 8 | 9 | 10 | 11 | 12
```

FORMATTING

F. LETTERS OF APPLICATION

A letter of application is sent along with a resume to a prospective employer. Together, the letter and the resume serve to introduce a person to the organization.

The letter of application should be no longer than one page and should include: (1) the job you are applying for and how you learned of the job, (2) the highlights of your enclosed resume, and (3) a request for an interview.

DOCUMENT PROCESSING

LETTER 24
MODIFIED-BLOCK STYLE

Whenever possible, it is best to address the letter to a *person* rather than to a *title* when applying for a job.

March 15, 19— / Ms. Kay Brewer, Personnel Director / Blanchard Computer Systems / 2189 Dace Avenue / Sioux City, IA 51107 / Dear Ms. Brewer:

Please consider me as an applicant for the position of data records operator advertised in the March 13 edition of the *Sioux City Press.*

In May I will graduate with an A.A. degree in Office Systems from West Iowa Business College. As indicated in my resume, which is enclosed, I have completed courses in Lotus, dBase, WordPerfect, and office systems. These courses are ideally suited for the position at Blanchard because these software packages are used in all of your Sioux City offices.

The position with your company is very appealing to me. If you wish to interview me for this position, please call me at 712-555-7256.

Sincerely, / Shannon T. Andrews / 349 Sycamore Terrace / Sioux City, IA 51104 / Enclosure

Begin the references on a new page, leaving a 2-inch top margin.

Use Hanging Indent (F4, Sh-Tab) to format each reference.

↓ 2 inches

REFERENCES

Browne, Mary, and Andrew J. Allison, *Real Estate Management,* American Realty Association, New York, 1993.

Halphin, A. J., "How Much Is Your Property Really Worth?" *Real Estate Quarterly,* June 1989, pp. 47–51.

MacFarline, Douglas M., Personal Interview, November 28, 1994.

Webler, J. Sandra, "How to Manage Your Property Like a Pro," *Investments,* November 1991, pp. 85–91.

Wilson, Ronald R., Personal Interview, December 3, 1994.

S. CONTENTS PAGE

Create a table of contents for the report as a separate document named 77C. Use centered, side, and paragraph headings.

1. Set relative left tabs at 0.3 inch and 0.6 inch and a relative right dot leader tab at 6 inches.

2. Center the title *CONTENTS* in bold and all-capital letters 2 inches from the top of the page; then triple-space.

3. After you key each entry, press Tab to insert dot leaders; then key the page number on which the heading appears. Your page numbers may differ from those shown here.

↓ 2 inches

CONTENTS

LETTER 25
BLOCK STYLE

August 10, 19-- / Personnel Director / Arlington Communications / 2403 Sunset Lane / Arlington, TX 76015-3148 / Dear Personnel Director: / I have always been interested in working for you and was encouraged to apply for a position in your company.

The two part time jobs I held during the summer months at your company convinced me that arlington comunications a leader in the field and a place where I could make a contribution. My strengths have always been in the arts, as you can see on the resume, which reveals a number of courses in English, and speech.

If you would like to interview me this summer or fall, call me at (214) 555-2340. I look forward to hearing from you.

Sincerely yours, / Kenneth R. Talbot / 6892 Center Road / Garland, TX 75041-9285 / Enclosure

Employment Tests

Margins: 1 inch • Tab: 0.5 inch • Spacing: Single • Drills: 2 times • Format Guide: 31

Goals:
To improve speed and accuracy; to key an employment test.

A. WARMUP

1 About 10 to 18 excited jackals squeezed through a gate 12
2 to freedom. Their pelts are worth less than $23 (top-grade 24
3 pelt); on May 7, 1995, we were able to get from $36 to $46. 36

| 1 | 2 | 3 | 4 | 5 | 6 | 7 | 8 | 9 | 10 | 11 | 12

LANGUAGE ARTS

B. SPELLING

B. These words are among the 500 most frequently misspelled words in business correspondence.

4 means entry valve officer industry similar expenses patient
5 quality provisions judgment academic cooperation previously
6 foreign construction especially secretary indicated closing
7 manufacturing assessment continuing monitoring registration
8 accordance products presently policies implemented capacity

SKILLBUILDING

C. 12-SECOND SPRINTS

C. Take three 12-second timed writings on each line. The scale gives your wam speed for a 12-second timed writing.

9 We all had fun in the sun when we spent a day at the beach.
10 Mary will be able to buy a new desk when this one gets old.
11 Take time each day to do those things that are fun for you.
12 This is the first time we have had to stop and look around.

| | | | 5 | | | | 10 | | | | 15 | | | | 20 | | | | 25 | | | | 30 | | | | 35 | | | | 40 | | | | 45 | | | | 50 | | | | 55 | | | | 60

REPORT 77
Continued

Spell-check your report to check for errors. However, remember that you must also proofread carefully for omitted or repeated words, errors that form a new word, and formatting errors.

Summary and Conclusions

At the request of Mr. Arthur J. Simon, the Strategic Planning Department performed a preliminary financial analysis of the feasibility of developing the River Road property. The International Development Corporation purchased this 15-acre, residentially zoned lot in Davenport, Iowa, in 1992 for $40,000.

Data were collected by interviewing real estate professionals and by calculating internal rates of return for four possible development alternatives: young family, growing family, empty nest, and custom home. It was found that building homes for the growing family (for example, 1,500-square-foot, three- or four-bedroom houses) would be the most profitable development plan, yielding an internal rate of return of nearly 20 percent.

The Strategic Planning Department recommends that this preliminary research be followed by an in-depth risk analysis, evaluating such factors as the supply of and demand for new homes, population composition and growth, and income levels in the Davenport metropolitan area.

Begin the appendix on a new page, leaving a 2-inch top margin.

The header and footer should appear on all pages of the report, except the title page and table of contents.

WordPerfect 6 users: Do not key the dollar sign.

Strategic Planning Department *Page 7*

APPENDIX

TABLE A. SUMMARY OF CASH FLOW AND INTERNAL RATE OF RETURN

(All Dollar Figures in 000)

Item	Young Family	Growing Family	Empty Nest	Custom Home
Cash Outflows				
Year 1	$ 148.6	$ 155.3	$ 162.0	$ 158.6
Year 2	369.0	436.4	874.7	456.8
Year 3	929.7	1,118.6	1,298.0	1,292.6
Year 4	561.7	683.2	1,122.2	717.4
Year 5	785.9	956.0	972.7	717.4
Year 6	1.0	1.0	1.0	1.0
TOTAL	$2,795.9	$3,350.5	$4,430.6	$3,343.8
Cash Inflows				
Year 1	$ 0.0	$ 0.0	$ 0.0	$ 0.0
Year 2	0.0	0.0	0.0	0.0
Year 3	332.5	475.0	897.7	456.0
Year 4	997.5	1,425.0	1,596.0	1,520.0
Year 5	665.0	950.0	1,496.2	912.0
Year 6	931.0	1,330.0	1,296.7	912.0
TOTAL	$2,926.0	$4,180.0	$5,286.6	$3,800.0
Rate of Return	4.5%	19.8%	16.2%	12.0%

River Road Property Development Report

D. PROGRESSIVE PRACTICE: NUMBERS

Turn to the Progressive Practice: Numbers routine at the back of the book. Take six 30-second timed writings, starting at the point where you left off the last time.

E. PROOFREADING SKILLS

An interview may also consist of taking an employment test to determine the background knowledge and level of skill you possess in certain areas. Proofreading and language arts are two skills that are considered essential for office employees.

The remaining exercises in this lesson are designed to test your ability to find and correct mistakes in spelling, punctuation, and grammar. Proofread each of the exercises carefully before you key it in final form with all errors corrected. Format the letter in block style. Provide any missing information that is required to complete each of the jobs.

DOCUMENT PROCESSING

EMPLOYMENT TEST A

APPLICATION LETTER 26

November 14, 19-- / Mr. Margin T. Hegman / 182 Bonanza Avenue / Anchorage, AK 99502 / Dear Mr. Hegman:

We are delighted that you will be with us for our business conference on Febuary 15th. Your presentation on "CD-ROM, the future of multi-media presentations," is timely and will be well recieved by our audience. You can expect from 100 to 150 participants in your session that will be held from 1:00 p.m. to 2: 45 p.m. in Conference Room 2.

Also enclosed with this letter is a parking permit that will allow you to park at the hotel Alexander. Just place the permit in your wind shield, and the parking lot attendant will let you enter without charge. The permit is good for all 3 days of the Conference should you choose to attend some of our other conferences while you are in San Francisco.

Please complete and return to me the speaker equipment form with this letter that is enclosed. We have most any equipment you need for your presentation; but in the event you have some unique request, we want all your equipment needs will be met.

Please be sure to call me at 415-555-3874 if there are any questions you have concerning the conference. We look forward to seeing you in March. / Sincerely, / Jane R. Kelley / conference chair / Enc.

REPORT 77
Continued

Cost information was tested for reasonableness by comparison with the costs for comparable projects. For example, the costs for Country Club Estates (custom homes) averaged $56 per square foot, according to Mr. MacFarline (1994). He further stated that the Beau Pre (luxury condominium) development incurred costs in the $50 to $60 range; in Orchard Glen (less expensive condominiums), costs ranged from $40 to $50 per square foot, including land. On the basis of this information, the costs used for these alternatives appear reasonable.

The structural cost per home for each alternative was then multiplied by the number of homes to be built each year, as shown in Table 2.

Use WordPerfect's View Document or Print Preview command to check format.

TABLE 2. NUMBER OF HOMES TO BE BUILT YEARLY

Time	Young Family	Growing Family	Empty Nest	Custom Home
Year 1	0	0	0	0
Year 2	5	5	9	3
Year 3	15	15	16	10
Year 4	10	10	15	6
Year 5	14	14	13	6
TOTAL	44	44	53	25

Selling Prices. The following selling prices of each alternative are based on those found in comparable developments, as determined by local real estate ads and by interviews of real estate professionals:

Use the same formats for this table and the tabular display that were used for the previous ones.

Young Family...... $70,000
Growing Family....$100,000
Empty Nest $105,000
Custom Home $160,000

Using a real estate agency for the sale of an entire development such as this was recommended by Mr. MacFarline. Sales commissions are calculated at 5 percent of selling price. This commission is reflected as a deduction from the selling price at the time of sale. The net selling price per home is multiplied by the number of homes expected to be sold per year. The results of the cost and selling price estimates and the internal rate of return are shown in Table A, in the appendix.

On the basis of this analysis, growing-family-style homes would be the most profitable alternative, with an internal rate of return of 19.8 percent, followed in order by empty nest (16.2 percent), custom home (12.0 percent), and young family (4.5 percent).

(Continued on next page)

EMPLOYMENT TEST B
REPORT 24

The following page from a company report contains several errors in punctuation, spelling, and grammar that must be identified and corrected.

Double-space the report, use standard margins for an unbound report, number the page as *Page 3* and correct the errors.

Income Stock Fund. The Income Stock Funds' objective is curent income with the prospect of increasing dividend income, and the potential for capital appreciation.

The first six month's of the fiscal year produced a total return of 25.4% including a dividend income distribution, of $.38 per share. Electric utilties petroleum and drugs is the largest holdings in the portfolio. Net assets of the fund has grown to $225.7 million from $104.5 million on September 1.

Income fund. The Income Fund's investment objective are maxamum current income without undue risk to principle. Consitant with this objective, the fund held 68.3% in mortgage securities 12,8% in corporite bonds, and 19.9% in high yield electric utility comon stocks.

The fund also has a portion invested in high yeild common stocks which have yeilds almost as high as bonds, and offer the potential for increasing dividends overtime. These comon stocks react quickly to changes in interest rate levels, and genrally have the highest price volatilety in the fund's portfolio.

Money Market Fund. The money Market Fund's investment objective is maximum curent yield without undue risk to principle. There are no deviation from this policy in order to achieve aditional yield. During the past six months the yield advantage increased from 25 basis points to 29 basis points. Net assits of the fund have grown to $1,375.5 milion from $927.5 milion on September 30.

EMPLOYMENT TEST C
TABLE 15

Prepare the following table with double spacing. Arrange the items in the "Expense" column alphabetically. Supply missing information where necessary. Check totals for accuracy.

STATEMENT OF EXPENSES
June 30, 19--

Expense	Income Stock	Income Fund	Money Market
Management Fees	$923,928	$232,687	
Postage	43,369	19,921	130,472
Legal Fees	1,968	1,968	1,968
Audit Fees	13,715	13,715	13,715
Registration Fees	35,427	11,823	66,121
Miscellaneous	10,871		29,513
TOTAL EXPENSES	1,290,278	288,743	2,780,431

REPORT 77
Continued

The cost to develop the land, including roads, utilities, sewers, and removal of trees where needed, is estimated to be $203,000 (Wilson, 1994). A $50,000 reserve for contingencies was added to this amount, for a subtotal of $253,000. To this total was added the cost of landscaping which ranges from $10,000 to $50,000, depending on the alternative.

For cash-flow calculations, the total cost of land development is divided over three years, as illustrated in Table 1.

Format the table as shown, with the title in bold and column headings in bold and shaded. Leave 3 blank lines before and after a table with a title.

WordPerfect 6 users: Do not key the dollar sign.

TABLE 1. LAND DEVELOPMENT COSTS PER YEAR

Time	**Young Family**	**Growing Family**	**Empty Nest**	**Custom Home**
Year 1	$ 87,666	$ 94,333	$101,000	$ 97,666
Year 2	87,667	94,333	101,000	97,667
Year 3	87,667	94,334	101,000	97,667
TOTAL	$263,000	$283,000	$303,000	$293,000

Other land-related costs include the original purchase price of $40,000 and legal and architectural fees of $20,000. Some of these costs have already been incurred; the remaining costs are reflected at the beginning of the project. Property taxes of $1,000 are also recorded for each year. Though this expense will increase as land-development improvements are made, the decrease in total property due to the sale of homes will offset the change in value.

Structural Costs. The first stage of land development is planned to take one year, with construction of homes beginning in the project's second year. Construction costs in general for the Davenport area range from $45 to $60 per square foot (Wilson, 1994). For this study, $45 per square foot was used for the two low-end alternatives. For custom homes, $60 per square foot was used, and $50 per square foot was selected for condominiums, since common walls and plumbing will reduce their cost.

These values are multiplied by the square footage of each home for a total cost per home as follows:

Center this tabular display, setting a left tab and a right dot-leader tab as needed. Leave 1 blank line before and after the display. Leave 6 spaces between columns.

Young Family...... $56,070
Growing Family.... $68,220
Empty Nest $74,750
Custom Home $119,400

(Continued on next page)

Follow-Up Letters

Margins: 1 inch • Tab: 0.5 inch • Spacing: Single • Drills: 2 times • Format Guide: 33

Goals:
To key 39 wam/5'/5e; to format a follow-up letter.

A. WARMUP

```
1      Jack Fox placed 15 big quartz vases in the top drawer,   12
2 and on 4/26/93 he paid $58.70 for a new vase (at a 10% dis-   24
3 count).  When must he buy another vase for the 8/3/93 show?   36
  | 1 | 2 | 3 | 4 | 5 | 6 | 7 | 8 | 9 | 10 | 11 | 12
```

LANGUAGE ARTS

B. CAPITAL LETTERS

B. Study the rules at the right. Then key lines 4–7, making necessary changes.

Rule: Capitalize the names of specific course titles. However, do not capitalize the names of subjects or areas of study (except for any proper nouns or adjectives in such names).

Both students enrolled in College Algebra 105, even though they are majoring in history.

Rule: Capitalize a noun followed by a number or letter that indicates sequence. Do not capitalize the nouns *line, note, page, paragraph,* and *size.*

They will leave for Ottawa at 7:25 p.m. on Flight 68.

```
4 She was advised to enroll in a College Algebra course.
5 Many students were interested in a French Literature course.
6 The logical place for table 7 is at the top of page 16.
7 The $125.07 amount for invoice 94-683 is due on Monday.
```

SKILLBUILDING

C. SUSTAINED PRACTICE: ROUGH DRAFT

C. Take a 1-minute timed writing on the first paragraph to establish your base speed. Then take several 1-minute timed writings on the remaining paragraphs. As soon as you equal or exceed your base speed on one paragraph, advance to the next one.

```
 8      Early word processing software was heralded as a major   12
 9 breakthrough in technology.  Up to that time, any revisions   24
10 required total rekeying of the copy to free it from errors.   36
                       enabled                   to
11      Word processing helped office workers save all their    12
12 work they had keyed for use at a later time.  All documents   24
13 could now be stored on a disk and called up sometime later.   36
              marvelous feature
14 The next characteristic of most software word processing      12
                                      #
15 came with the advent of spellcheckers that would check for    24
       l
16 speling errors we might have made in the work we prepared.    36
             recent                         #
17      More current developments in wordprocessing included an  12
       i                                               ly
18 abilty to work with graphics and text simultaneous.  The      24
                                              capabilities
19 software now has some very nice desktop publishing features.  36
   | 1 | 2 | 3 | 4 | 5 | 6 | 7 | 8 | 9 | 10 | 11 | 12
```

REPORT 77
Continued

3. Empty Nest: The empty nester is seeking a smaller home because the children have grown and moved away. The parents now have high disposable incomes, and a condominium may meet their needs.

   The single-story, three-bedroom condominium proposed for this submarket has many luxurious amenities but is limited to 1,495 square feet. The sunroom provides glass and exposure to the outdoors, considered important by purchasers in this submarket.

4. Custom Home: The custom-home buyer is seeking a home in the Davenport area with a selling price above $120,000. This buyer has a disposable income of more than $65,000 and desires a home with such status appointments as skylights and spa-style bathrooms. Buyers in this submarket often contract directly with a builder to construct a home to their own personal specifications rather than purchasing a home in a development.

   The floor plan selected for this submarket contains 1,990 square feet and has four bedrooms and three baths, as well as vaulted ceilings, a spa-style master bath, and a private deck off the master suite.

Financial Analysis

The financial analysis was prepared by applying cost data to the floor plans selected. Several intermediate calculations supplied data for a cash-flow analysis, which in turn provided the basis for an internal-rate-of-return calculation for each alternative.

Land Development Costs. On the basis of a visual inspection of the geographic conditions of the property, conservative estimates of buildable land were developed. Roads were then planned to provide for lots that are at least 150 feet deep.

Costs per foot associated with roads, utilities, and sewers were obtained by extrapolation from a 1991 quotation received for a different real estate project. (This level of estimation was considered adequate for the purpose of this preliminary study.)

(Continued on next page)

D. Spacing: Double
Take two 5-minute timed writings. Compute your speed and count errors.

Goal: 39 wam/5′/5e

D. 5-MINUTE TIMED WRITING

Dozens of suggestions have been given for what to do 12
at an interview. Here are just a few guidelines to help 23
you during this important phase of your career. 33
It is critical that you are not late for an interview; 45
in fact, try to give yourself a little extra time for car 56
trouble or traffic delays. Be sure to introduce yourself 68
when you arrive at the interview and tell that person why 79
you are there. When you are asked in for the interview, 91
extend your hand if the interviewer offers to shake hands. 103
During the interview, maintain good eye contact; pay close 115
attention to what is being said, and be a good listener. 126
When you are asked a question, speak loudly and clearly. 138
Be conscious of the rate you are speaking and the volume of 150
your voice. Point out your strengths, not your weaknesses. 162
Finally, at the end of the interview you should express an 174
interest in the job and in the company. Before you leave, 186
find out when a hiring decision will be made. 195

| 1 | 2 | 3 | 4 | 5 | 6 | 7 | 8 | 9 | 10 | 11 | 12

FORMATTING

E. FOLLOW-UP LETTERS

As soon as possible after your interview (preferably the next day), you should send a follow-up letter to the person who conducted your interview.

In the letter, thank the person for the interview, highlight your particular strengths, and restate your interest in working for that organization.

DOCUMENT PROCESSING

LETTER 27
BLOCK STYLE

April 7, 19-- / Ms. Kay Brewer / Blanchard Computer Systems /
2189 Dace Avenue / Sioux City, IA 51107 / Dear Ms. Brewer:

you
Thanks for the opportunity of interviewing with Blanchard
computer Systems yesterday. The interview gave me a very posi-
positive
tive feeling about the company and the description you shared
me with convinced me that blanchard is in deed at the top of the
of the companies I have visited computer
list. It appears to me that strengths in software application
and office systems
soft ware would blend in well with your company profile.

I look forward to hearing you from soon regarding you decision on this position.

Sincerely, / Shannon T. Andrews / 349 Sycamore Terrace /
Sioux City, IA 51104

Single space

sign it

My name

Review Step 3 of the directions on page 325 for heading formats.

Findings

The findings are organized by the development alternatives for the 15-acre parcel of land and by according to the financial analysis.

Development Alternatives

Following

Based upon a review of current real estate literature, four development alternatives were selected for this study: young family, growing family, empty nest, and custom home. The size of the house selected for each submarket was determined by averaging the square footage of recent sales of similar homes in the Davenport area.

1. Young Family: The young family is making it's first purchase of a new home. They are moving from rental or otherwise limited accommodations into their first new home. This submarket represents households from a rental or used-home arrangement. In the Davenport market, they are characterized as having disposable income of $34000 or less.

no u/s

no ¶

On the basis of current mortgage rates in the Davenport area, a buyer in this submarket cannot afford more than $70,000 for a home. ¶ Since family size is still small (less than four), a 1,246-square-foot home was selected for planning purposes.

no ¶

The floor plan has no first-floor laundry or private master bath, though there is a full bath on each level. Inexpensive construction materials would be used wherever possible.

2. Growing Family: The growing family is seeking a larger house. This submarket is identified as having more disposable income because the breadwinners have become are more established in their careers. They requires more space, particularly in sleeping quarters. ¶ The floor plan proposed for this submarket has 1,516 square feet of living area, including a first-floor laundry room and four bedrooms, both important selling points for a growing family.

home

the growing family

(Continued on next page)

LETTER 28
MODIFIED-BLOCK STYLE

September 12, 19-- / Ms. Carole Rothchild / Personnel Director / Arlington Communications / 2403 Sunset Lane / Arlington, TX 76015-3148 / Dear Ms. Rothchild:

It was a real pleasure meeting with you yesterday and learning of the wonderful career opportunities at Arlington Communications. I enjoyed meeting all the people, especially those working in the Publications Division.

I believe my experience and job skills match nicely with those you are seeking for a desktop publishing individual, and this position is exactly what I have been looking for.

Please let me hear from you when you have made your decision on this position. I am very much interested in joining the professional staff at Arlington Communications.

Sincerely yours, / ~~Kenneth R. Talbot~~ / 6829 Centerville Road / Garland, TX 75041-9285

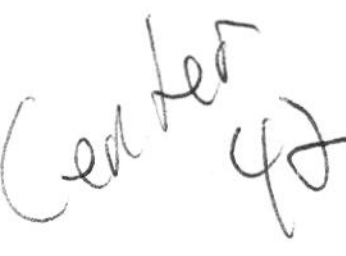

Integrated Employment Project

Margins: 1 inch • Tab: 0.5 inch • Spacing: Single • Drills: 2 times • Format Guide: 33

Goals:
To improve speed and accuracy; to reinforce employment skills.

A. WARMUP

```
1      Thomas Barrows of Phoenix, Arizona (602-555-8175), ran   12
2 just as quickly as he could as he competed in the Jergens &   24
3 Vance 15-kilometer race on Friday--1st prize was $493 cash!   36
  | 1 | 2 | 3 | 4 | 5 | 6 | 7 | 8 | 9 | 10 | 11 | 12
```

LANGUAGE ARTS

B. COMPOSING

B. Answer each question with a sentence or two.

4 Why do you need to prepare yourself for an interview?
5 Why is it important to get good grades in school?
6 What section do you prefer to read in the newspaper and why?
7 How can good communication skills help you achieve your goals?
8 What are the three most important environmental issues today?
9 What advantages do you see in studying a foreign language?
10 Why are ethics important in business?
11 How can you improve your confidence in speaking before a group?

Let WordPerfect end your pages. Your line and page breaks may differ from those shown here.

Use Block Protect to make sure that all displays (tables, tabular displays, and long quotations) do not split between two pages.

Procedures

the basis of

Mr. Ron Wilson, a local builder, and Mr. Douglas MacFarline, a local realtor, were interviewed to obtain cost and design information for the home layouts selected for each submarket. Financial data fegarding cost, selling price, and number of units were collected, and the alternatives were rated ~~based~~ on their ~~attractiveness~~. feasibility

discuss

Several books and monographs on real estate ~~address~~ the feasibility study process. For example, Browne & Allison (1993, pp. 119-176) explain the mathmatics of different methods of évaluation and document the advantages and disadvantages of each method.

DS This simplified internal-rate-of-return calculation illustrated by Halphin (1989, p. 49) ~~was~~ is used in this analysis. According to Webler:

Net-present-value & internal-rate-of-return comparisons are the two most frequently utilized methods of calculating yield on residential real estate properties, partly because of their empirical accuracy and partly because of their ease of calculation. Although somewhat more difficult to determine, the internal rate of return is also somewhat more precise. (1991, p. 85)

To obtain information about existing neighborhoods which are comparable to the 4 alternatives under consideration, Mr. MacFarline was interviewed and the City of Davenport Street Index for 1994 was consulted.

a detailed Thus, data from interviews with local real estate experts, along with ~~the~~ financial analysis, ~~of the costs and projected profits~~, provided the basis for determining the development potential for the River Road property.

(Continued on next page)

SKILLBUILDING

C. PACED PRACTICE

Turn to the Paced Practice routine at the back of the book. Take four 2-minute timed writings, starting at the speed at which you left off the last time.

D. DIAGNOSTIC PRACTICE: NUMBERS

Turn to the Diagnostic Practice: Numbers routine at the back of this book. Take the Pretest and record your performance. Then practice the drill lines for those reaches on which you made errors. Finally, repeat the Pretest and compare your performance.

DOCUMENT PROCESSING

In this unit you learned how to prepare a resume, an application letter, and a follow-up letter—all of which are frequently used by job applicants.

You will now use all of these skills in preparing the documents necessary to apply for the job described in the newspaper ad appearing below.

REPORT 25
RESUME

Prepare a resume for yourself as though you are applying for the job appearing in the ad in the next column. Use actual data in the resume. Assume that you have just graduated from a postsecondary program. Include school-related activities, courses you will have completed, and any part-time or full-time work experience you may have acquired. Make the resume as realistic as possible, and provide as much information as you can about your background.

LETTER 29
APPLICATION LETTER

Prepare an application letter to apply for the position described in the ad at the right. Date your letter March 10. Emphasize the skills you have acquired during your years in school and while working in any part-time or full-time positions. Use Letters 24 and 25 (pages 118 and 119) as guides for your letter.

LETTER 30
FOLLOW-UP LETTER

Assume that your interview was held on March 25 and that you would very much like to work for Tri-State Publishing. It is now the day after your interview. Prepare a follow-up letter expressing your positive thoughts about working for Tri-State. Use Letters 27 and 28 (pages 123 and 124) as guides for your letter.

COMPUTER APPLICATIONS SPECIALIST

Tri-State Publishing, a New York City based publisher specializing in trade and industrial titles, has an immediate opening for a Computer Applications Specialist whose primary responsibilities include word processing and desktop publishing.

This is an entry-level position within the Public Relations Department in our Philadelphia office. Applicant must have had training in WordPerfect and desktop publishing (preferably PageMaker or Ventura). Knowledge of computer operating systems is also helpful.

Excellent company benefits available that include a comprehensive medical and dental program, disability insurance, and a company credit union.

If interested, send a letter of application and resume to:

Mr. David E. Frantelli
Personnel Department
Tri-State Publishing
9350 Andover Road
Philadelphia, PA 19114

Tri-State is an Equal Opportunity Employer

FORMATTING

R. WORDPERFECT: GO TO

WP GO TO

Ctrl-Home, *page no.*, Enter

WordPerfect 6 users: See Student Guide, p. 78.

Use Go To to move quickly to a certain location within a document. For example, to move to a specific page of a long report, press Ctrl-Home, enter the page number you want to go to, then press Enter. To return to your previous location, press Ctrl-Home twice.

DOCUMENT PROCESSING

REPORT 77
LEFT-BOUND, SINGLE-SPACED, MULTIPAGE REPORT

Side margins: 1.5 inches, 1 inch

Business reports are often single-spaced to save file space, save paper, and lower copying costs.

WordPerfect 6 users: See Student Guide, p. 78.

Format this business report as follows:

1. Use a 2-inch top margin for the first page, the appendix, and the References page and a 1-inch top margin for all other pages. On all pages use a 1.5-inch left margin and 1-inch right and bottom margins.
2. Center the report title in all-capital letters and bold. Center the other heading lines in normal type.
3. Format report headings as follows:

Format	*Centered*	*Side*	*Paragraph*
Bold	yes	yes	yes
Justification	center	left	tab
Spacing before	double	double	double
Spacing after	double	double	2 spaces

4. Single-space the body of the report, and use full justification.
5. Be sure Widow/Orphan Protection and Hyphenation are turned on.
6. Create a header for every page (see the illustration on the next page). While in the header screen, key *Strategic Planning Department* in small font and italics, press Flush Right, key *Page,* space, and then press Ctrl-B and Enter. Create a horizontal line and accept all the default settings; then press Enter again and Exit. Suppress the header for page 1.
7. Create a footer for every page. While in the footer screen, create a horizontal line and accept the default settings. Press Enter; then center in small font and italics *River Road Property Development Report.* Press Exit twice to return to the document.

A PRELIMINARY ANALYSIS OF THE DEVELOPMENT POTENTIAL OF THE RIVER ROAD PROPERTY

Jeffrey Scott, Analyst
Strategic Planning Department
February 15, 1995

In early 1992 a 15-acre parcel of residential property located on River Road between Route 72 and the Davenport Country Club in Davenport, Iowa, was offered for sale. ~~Based~~ On the basis of the demand for housing and the desirability of the location, the International Development Corporation purchased this property as an investment in May 1992.

In an October 8, 1994, memo, Mr. Arthur J. Simon, vice president ~~of~~ for development, requested that the Strategic Planning Department conduct a preliminary analysis of the property to assess its development potential. At his request, a risk analysis was not performed.

The report continues on the next page.

(Continued on next page)

UNIT TWELVE • SKILL REFINEMENT

Skillbuilding and Correspondence Review

Margins: 1 inch • Tab: 0.5 inch • Spacing: Single • Drills: 2 times • Format Guide: 35

Goals:
To key 40 wam/5′/5e; to review correspondence formats.

A. WARMUP

```
1      Val bought two tickets for the concert at $19.75.  The  12
2 next day the price was $24.30.  He was amazed at that quick  24
3 jump in price of 23.0%.  His three tickets cost him $63.80.  36
  | 1 | 2 | 3 | 4 | 5 | 6 | 7 | 8 | 9 | 10 | 11 | 12
```

LANGUAGE ARTS

B. GRAMMAR

B. Study the rules at the right. Then key lines 4–7, making necessary changes.

Rule: A verb must agree with its subject in number and person.

Your purchase order for 12 printers was received on May 4.

Rule: The following words are always singular and take singular verbs: *each, neither, either, much,* and pronouns ending in *-body, -thing,* and *-one.*

Neither of them is responsible for the depreciation error.

```
4 The deliveries by the farmer was according to schedule.
5 The manager, along with four trainers, are going tomorrow.
6 Everybody in the adjoining offices were happy for her.
7 Either of them are qualified for the receptionist job.
```

SKILLBUILDING

C. 12-SECOND SPRINTS

C. Take three 12-second timed writings on each line. The scale gives your wam speed for a 12-second timed writing.

```
J  8 Judge Jones justly joined Judge Jettig on a major judgment.
Q  9 Quentin quietly and quickly quoted that eloquent quotation.
X 10 Alex took extra time to execute the exercise on a tax exam.
Z 11 Buzz was amazed at the size of the dozen zebras at the zoo.
     | | | |5| | | |10| | | |15| | | |20| | | |25| | | |30| | | |35| | | |40| | | |45| | | |50| | | |55| | | |60
```

D. NUMBER PRACTICE

D. Take two 1-minute timed writings. The last two digits of each number provide a cumulative word count to help you determine your wam speed.

```
12 3601 4802 5903 1104 2705 8306 9407 5508 6609 2310 9511 7612
13 4913 3814 6615 3916 4017 1918 2119 7320 9821 4822 6323 8424
14 6525 7226 1427 9028 3329 4930 5431 2832 3933 7834 9135 2036
15 7837 8938 5539 4240 1841 6742 3643 2844 1045 2846 3747 8848
```

E. DIAGNOSTIC PRACTICE: ALPHABET

Turn to the Diagnostic Practice: Alphabet routine at the back of this book. Take the Pretest and record your performance. Then practice the drill lines for those reaches on which you made errors. Finally, repeat the Pretest and compare your performance.

O. Clear all tabs. Then set four new tabs every 1 inch. Key lines 74–77, using the tab key to go across from column to column.

O. TECHNIQUE PRACTICE: TAB KEY

651	433	982	261	186
143	819	627	934	418
352	769	970	585	291
418	829	635	472	759

P. DIAGNOSTIC PRACTICE: ALPHABET

Turn to the Diagnostic Practice: Alphabet routine at the back of this book. Take the Pretest and record your performance. Then, practice the drill lines for those reaches on which you made errors. Finally, repeat the Pretest and compare your performance.

Q. Spacing: Double
Take two 5-minute timed writings. Compute your speed and count errors.

Goal: 52 wam/5′/5e

Q. 5-MINUTE TIMED WRITING

```
     What is happening in the communications field?  This       12
question is being asked by scientists and business persons      23
alike.  Fiber optics, satellite dishes, multiple television     35
stations, electronic mail, talking computers, and mobile        47
phones are springing up all over.  All of these changes         58
force us to rethink what we mean by information.  It is         69
not just data but also knowledge; that knowledge part of        81
almost everything important to our future is increasing         92
at a startling pace.                                            96
     Our ability to assemble, analyze, and communicate data    108
out of which knowledge can be constructed is expanding at a    120
rate faster, in some cases, than we can digest.  More than     132
one person has gone back to school just to catch up with       143
the wealth of new materials.  Computers will continue to       154
have a central role in the era of explosive growth just        166
ahead.  The next few years will show great gains in our        177
communications capacity, especially regarding computers and    189
broadcast technology.                                          193
     This growth will create new businesses and bolster        204
many existing ones, while at the same time making others       216
obsolete.  For those that are a success, the potential for     228
development is amazing.  It will help make new jobs for        239
tomorrow's graduates, improve the living standards we now      250
enjoy, and probably complicate our way of life.                260
```

| 1 | 2 | 3 | 4 | 5 | 6 | 7 | 8 | 9 | 10 | 11 | 12

F. Spacing: Double
Take two 5-minute timed writings. Compute your speed and count errors.

Goal: 40 wam/5'/5e

F. 5-MINUTE TIMED WRITING

Is your life a little crazy? Do you find yourself 11
always feeling nervous or anxious? At the end of the day 23
are your shoulder muscles tight and sore? If the answer 34
to these questions is yes, then perhaps you are suffering 46
from an ailment that affects thousands each day: stress. 57

The complex lives we lead often play havoc with our 69
good intentions to just relax and take things slowly. At 80
times we feel quite stressed out and unable to function 92
as we would like. Demands from work, family, and friends 103
might pull us in many directions. 110

There are easily a dozen ways to manage stress. From 122
a physical standpoint, it is essential to learn to relax 133
your body. When nervous, most people take fast, shallow 145
breaths causing their heart rate to increase. Try taking 156
slow, deep breaths instead and you will soon sense your 168
breathing pattern return to its normal state. 177

In our hectic lives, it is too easy to let stress get 189
the best of you. Remember, all you have to do is relax. 200

| 1 | 2 | 3 | 4 | 5 | 6 | 7 | 8 | 9 | 10 | 11 | 12

DOCUMENT PROCESSING

LETTER 31
BLOCK STYLE

(Current Date) / Ms. Wilma Newman, Director / Fremont Cooperative Nursery School / 121 Lincoln Highway / Fremont, NE 68025 / Dear Ms. Newman:

Thank you for your recent inquiry about having an article published in our magazine *Only for Children.* We are very pleased with the reception that this publication has received throughout Nebraska and some of the surrounding states. Consider the following points:

1. Our editor for that publication, Valerie Ritter, has final responsibility for accepting materials for publication. Send your article directly to her for consideration.

2. The magazine is published bimonthly; if your article is accepted for publication, you will receive a $100 payment.

Again, thank you for your interest in having an article published in one of our publications. I'm sure that Ms. Ritter will look forward to hearing from you.

Sincerely yours, / (Ms.) Maridel B. Ash / Editorial Director / *(Your Initials)*

J. Insert the necessary vowels as you key each sentence once.

J. TECHNIQUE PRACTICE: CONCENTRATION

B-th -f th- b-g f-rms -n t-wn -ls- k-pt th--r w-rk-rs b-sy.
Th- tw- g-rls t--k th- d-y -ff t- s-- th- n-w sh-w -n t-wn.
-f th- w-rk -s h-ndl-d r-ght, th- gr--ps m-y m-k- - pr-f-t.
Th- m-n m-y t-k- th- l-nd by th- l-k- -nd s-ll -t f-r l-ss.

K. Take three 1-minute timed writings. Note that the last two digits of each number are a cumulative word count and give wam.

K. NUMBER PRACTICE

2301 7402 6503 9804 1705 3106 4407 8208 9509 1610 2911 4412
9813 7214 8515 1616 2317 7518 8119 4220 3921 8422 1923 8824
6625 9526 1127 9328 1429 6530 1931 4332 6333 8834 6535 1236
3737 1538 2239 4940 9141 9342 4443 1244 9845 2646 8347 1248

L. Take three 12-second timed writings on each line. The scale gives wam for a 12-second timed writing.

L. 12-SECOND SPRINTS

Check #349 was for $1,240.35; check #404 was for $1,756.20.
Check these purchase orders: (1) #9, (2) #87, and (3) #98.
On 9/23 she (Pat) paid $180, which is 42% less than I paid.
The discount of 25% on the $1,500 freezer amounted to $375.

| | | | 5 | | | | 10 | | | | 15 | | | | 20 | | | | 25 | | | | 30 | | | | 35 | | | | 40 | | | | 45 | | | | 50 | | | | 55 | | | | 60

M. Key each sentence on a separate line.

M. TECHNIQUE PRACTICE: ENTER KEY

See that movie. Listen to those albums. Visit the museum.
Look at the photos. See the monuments. Watch the sitcoms.
Attend the seminar. Sign the petition. Review the script.
Take a walk. Join the class. Be on time. Go to the bank.

N. Take a 1-minute timed writing on the first paragraph to establish your base speed. Then take four 1-minute timed writings on the remaining paragraphs. As soon as you equal or exceed your base speed on one paragraph, advance to the next one.

N. SUSTAINED PRACTICE: ALTERNATE-HAND WORDS

The eight people in that group decided that their work 12
would only get done if they selected one person to be chair 24
of their group. They also decided to handle all their work 36
in a formal manner. They began to debate the major issues. 48

When the eight of them began formal discussion on some 12
of the major issues, the need for a chair was very evident. 24
The chair would be sure to handle the usual work with ease. 36
In addition, the chair would set the mission for the group. 48

One issue that needed to be settled right up front was 12
the question of how to handle proxy votes. It seemed for a 24
short time that a fight over this issue would result. With 36
the chair taking charge, the group reached a good solution. 48

The group worked diligently in attempting to solve the 12
issues that were being discussed. All of the concerns that 24
were brought to the group were reviewed in depth, and those 36
that required greater discussion were placed on the agenda. 48

| 1 | 2 | 3 | 4 | 5 | 6 | 7 | 8 | 9 | 10 | 11 | 12

LETTER 32
BLOCK STYLE

(Today's date) / Ms. Victoria F. Eng / 85 Holly Drive / Chadron, NE 69337 / Dear Ms. Eng:

Thank you very much for your inquiry about Allwood Publications. It is a pleasure to respond.

We have six magazines. Their names, the names of their editors, and their cost per year are on the enclosed table. All are subscription magazines—that is, they are not sold at newsstands.

If you would like any other details, please let me know. In the meantime, I will share a copy of your letter with Stephanie Pasquini, Sales Coordinator.

Sincerely yours, / Louis C. Hass / Editorial Assistant / (Your Initials) / Enclosure / c: Stephanie Pasquini

Skillbuilding and Correspondence Review

Margins: 1 inch • Tab: 0.5 inch • Spacing: Single • Drills: 2 times • Format Guide: 35

Goals:
To improve speed and accuracy; to review correspondence formats.

A. WARMUP

Invoice #13765 for $8,924 was for extra work needed to 12
install the computer network. The size of the computer lab 24
totals 720 square feet. It is just right for many classes. 36

| 1 | 2 | 3 | 4 | 5 | 6 | 7 | 8 | 9 | 10 | 11 | 12

LANGUAGE ARTS

B. SPELLING

B. These words are among the 500 most frequently misspelled words in business correspondence.

executive distribution specific carried extension requested
recommended access alternative programs budget could issued
indicated family until objectives calendar could these your
fiscal past possibility administrative students accommodate
transportation employee's categories summary offered estate

SKILLBUILDING

C. PRETEST: DISCRIMINATION PRACTICE

PRETEST.
Take a 1-minute timed writing; compute your speed and count errors.

Polly alerted an astute older gentleman to wear proper 12
colored suits to the opera. If one is of medium build, the 24
suits will look better and one can project his best manner. 36

| 1 | 2 | 3 | 4 | 5 | 6 | 7 | 8 | 9 | 10 | 11 | 12

SKILLBUILDING

D. PACED PRACTICE

Turn to the Paced Practice routine at the back of the book. Take three 2-minute timed writings, starting at the point where you left off the last time.

PRETEST. Take a 1-minute timed writing; compute your speed and count errors.

E. PRETEST: CLOSE REACHES

```
     Casey hoped that we were not wasting good grub.  After   12
the sun went down, he swiftly put the oleo and plums in the   24
cart.  Bart opened a copy of an old book, Grant had a swim,   36
and Curtis unearthed a sword in a hole in that grassy dune.   48
| 1 | 2 | 3 | 4 | 5 | 6 | 7 | 8 | 9 | 10 | 11 | 12
```

PRACTICE.

Speed Emphasis: If you made no errors on the Pretest, key each line twice.

Accuracy Emphasis: If you made 1 or more errors on the Pretest, key each group of lines (as though it were a paragraph) twice.

F. PRACTICE: ADJACENT KEYS

```
as mask last past easy vase beast waste toast reason castle
op hope flop open mops rope opera droop scope copier trophy
we west owed went weld weep weigh weary wedge wealth plowed
rt hurt port cart dirt fort court party start hearty parted
```

G. PRACTICE: CONSECUTIVE-FINGER REACHES

```
sw swat swim swan swig swap swift sweet sword switch swirly
un tune spun unit dune punt under prune sunny hunter uneasy
gr grow grim grab grub grew great graze gripe grease grassy
ol role oleo pool sold hole troll folly polka stolen oldest
```

POSTTEST. Repeat the Pretest (E) and compare performance.

H. POSTTEST: CLOSE REACHES

I. Take a 1-minute timed writing on the first paragraph to establish your base speed. Then take four 1-minute timed writings on the remaining paragraphs. As soon as you equal or exceed your base speed on one paragraph, advance to the next one.

I. SUSTAINED PRACTICE: NUMBERS

```
     The workers of the new millennium will surely be quite   12
unlike workers today or the work force in the past.  At one   24
time almost all Americans were farmers until the industrial   36
revolution moved the work site to the factories and cities.   48

     With the passage of numerous years, in the late 1940s,   12
the baby boom hit, and the workers became men leaving their   24
families in the suburbs each morning and commuting to their   36
offices, labs, and assembly lines between 9 a.m. and 5 p.m.   48

     It is now the 1990s, and ever growing numbers of women   12
and minorities will account for more than 90 percent of new   24
entrants into the work force.  By 2000 the labor force will   36
grow by 21 million; perhaps 15 percent will be white males.   48

     What will all these employees be doing?  Manufacturing   12
positions may decline by more than 800,000 jobs by the year   24
2000, while the forecast is that engineering and managerial   36
jobs will see a growth of 165,000 and 85,000, respectively.   48
| 1 | 2 | 3 | 4 | 5 | 6 | 7 | 8 | 9 | 10 | 11 | 12
```

PRACTICE.
Speed Emphasis: If you made 2 or fewer errors on the Pretest, key each line twice.
Accuracy Emphasis: If you made 3 or more errors, key each group of lines (as though it were a paragraph) twice.

D. PRACTICE: LEFT HAND

```
12 rtr trip trot sport train alert courts assert tragic truest
13 asa mass salt usage cased cease astute dashed masked castle
14 sds used said winds bands seeds godson woodsy shreds wields
15 rer rear rest overt rerun older before entire surest better
```

E. PRACTICE: RIGHT HAND

```
16 mnm menu numb hymns unmet manly mental namely manner number
17 pop post coop opera pools opens polite proper police oppose
18 olo tool loon solos color lower locker oldest lowest frolic
19 iui unit quit fruit suits built medium guided helium podium
```

POSTTEST.
Repeat the Pretest (C) and compare performance.

F. POSTTEST: DISCRIMINATION PRACTICE

DOCUMENT PROCESSING

This memorandum dated today is from Maridel Ash, Editorial Director, to Valerie Ritter, Editor of *Only for Children.* The subject is Potential Article.

MEMO 8

I recently received a letter from Wilma Newman, of the Fremont Cooperative Nursery School. She expressed an interest in having an article published in Only For Children. I have asked her to communicate directly with you regarding this possibility. Attached, you will find a copy of her letter to me and my response to her.

If you have any questions about my response to her, please get in touch with me. I hope she contacts you, since we are always looking for appropriate articles.

By the way, please plan to attend an important meeting of all editors on Thursday, October 10, at 10 a.m. in H-110. We will review publication schedules for next year.

MP attachment

MEMO 9

This memorandum dated today is from Maridel Ash to Raymond Cozza in Sales/Marketing about Achievement Awards in Sales/Marketing.

I was delighted to receive the information regarding sales/marketing revenue generated for the month of March by individuals reporting to you. To see Nancy Ostrowski as the top employee, with over $30,000 of revenue for the month, was a special delight. I know how much you have worked with Nancy in getting her to this point. Congratulations on helping her achieve this milestone.

We will be sponsoring a recognition luncheon for the employees who have achieved the best sales figures for March. Please invite Nancy, Joseph Simon, Kimberley Harris, David Klein, and Kathleen Lake to join us for this luncheon on April 14 at 12 noon at the Brookside Inn on Country Park Road.

131-135 LESSONS

Margins: 1 inch • Spacing: Single • Drills: 2 times • Format Guide: 117–121

Goals for Unit 27

Begin each day with approximately 15 minutes of skillbuilding, selecting activities from pages 321–324. In the remaining class time, complete as many production jobs from pages 325–333 as you can.

1. To improve accuracy and speed on alphabet and number keys.
2. To key 52 wam for 5 minutes with no more than 5 errors.
3. To improve proofreading skills.
4. To review bound reports, tables in reports, long quotations, and enumerated items.
5. To review numerous WordPerfect features—Headers, Footers, Table, Widow/Orphan Protection, Block Protect, Graphics Figure Boxes, and Indent.
6. To format a multipage, left-bound business report.
7. To prepare supplementary pages of a business report—title page, table of contents, appendix, and References page.

A. WARMUP

Part #139 from Klaus & Backey was quoted at $756. The 12
same item from Justern & Zurich was found for $624. It was 24
found that Part #89 had an extra charge of $90 for service. 36

| 1 | 2 | 3 | 4 | 5 | 6 | 7 | 8 | 9 | 10 | 11 | 12

LANGUAGE ARTS

B. GRAMMAR

Study the rules at the right. Then key lines 4–7, making necessary changes.

Rule: Use nominative pronouns (*I, he, she, we, they,* and so on) as subjects of a sentence or clause.

Was it she who established the volunteer program?

Rule: Use objective pronouns (*me, him, her, us, them,* and so on) as objects in a sentence or clause.

The Akroyd Lumber assignment was completed by her and me.

Most of the equations were correctly solved by Tara and I.
It was him who captivated them at Friday's concert.
The technician and her were able to meet the deadline.
The revised quotations are to be sent to either he or she.

C. PROOFREADING

C. Compare this paragraph with the last paragraph of the 5-minute timed writing on page 324. Key a list of the words that contain errors, correcting the errors as you key.

This growth will create new busineses and bolster many exiting ones, while at the same time make others obsolete. For these that are a sucess, the potential for development is amazing. It will help new jobs for tommorow's graduates, improve the living standards we enjoy, and probably complicate our way of life.

LETTER 33
MODIFIED BLOCK STYLE
PERSONAL-BUSINESS

(Current Date)

Ms. Valerie Ritter, Editor
Only for Children
Allwood Publishing Company
115 Grand Street
Omaha, NW 61803-0073

Dear ~~Editor:~~ Ms. Ritter:

I received a letter from Ms. ~~Maridel~~ Ash, Editorial Director for Allwood Publishing, telling me to contact you if I was interested in having an article published. in Only for Children

For the past 6 years, I have been ~~supervising~~ directing the Fremont Cooperative Nursey School. I have 12 staff members helping me with an average of about 100 ~~students~~ children in each quarter. About 3 years ago, we began a unique program of community involvement with the children in our program. Everyone in the town has been extremely supportive of the program.

Enclosed is an article that ~~explains~~ describes this program. I believe it would be of interest to the readers of ~~the~~ your magazine. Please let me know if you can use it in a future issue of the magazine.

Sincerely yours,

Wilma Newman, Director
Fremont Cooperative Nursery
121 Lincoln Highway
Fremont, NE 68025

Reminder: Place the return address after the signature in a personal-business letter.

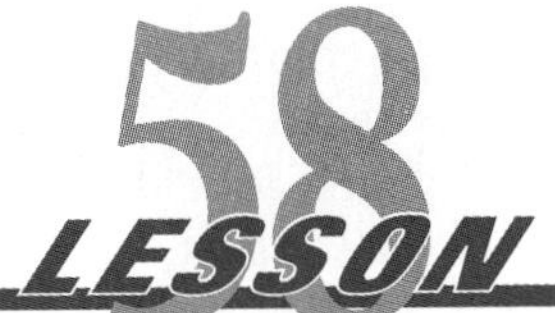

Skillbuilding and Report Review

Margins: 1 inch • Tab: 0.5 inch • Spacing: Single • Drills: 2 times • Format Guide: 35–37

Goals:
To key 40 wam/5'/5e; to review report formats.

A. WARMUP

1 Tickets #180-219 were issued to Granth & Bextley. The 12
2 cost for those 40 tickets came to $376. The 15 tickets for 24
3 Jomass & Olizetti for $141 were delivered to Quince Murphy. 36

| 1 | 2 | 3 | 4 | 5 | 6 | 7 | 8 | 9 | 10 | 11 | 12

TABLE 61
5-COLUMN BOXED TABLE WITH BRACED HEADINGS

Key the appropriate years in the subtitle (last year and this year).

WordPerfect 6 users: Do not key the dollar sign.

ALBERT DALTON, INC.

A Comparison of 19-- and 19-- Sales

Eastern Region		Total Sales and Percent Increase		
State	Manager	This Year	Last Year	% Increase
Connecticut	H. Brown	$ 1,234,678	$ 1,109,345	11.30
Delaware	L. Case	238,190	218,000	9.26
Maine	S. Zinn	471,324	410,134	14.92
Maryland	G. Kee	2,894,563	2,594,563	11.56
Massachusetts	K. Lewis	3,391,010	3,215,785	5.45
New Hampshire	R. Robin	196,325	150,632	30.33
New Jersey	J. Smith	1,364,978	1,277,645	6.84
New York	U. Gee	4,683,911	4,372,843	7.11
Pennsylvania	I. Frank	2,796,552	2,561,210	9.19
Vermont	E. Gomez	361,421	347,310	4.06
Virginia	H. Lucas	1,887,332	1,704,231	10.74
TOTALS		$19,520,284	$17,961,698	8.68

TABLE 62
4-COLUMN OPEN TABLE

Review the format for an open table in the Reference Section, page R-12.

Retrieve Table 61 and reformat it as an open table using the Table feature. Then, make the following changes:

1. Add an asterisk after the last word in the subtitle to indicate a footnote reference.
2. Delete the braced headings *Eastern Region* and *Total Sales and Percent Increase.*
3. Delete the last column containing the percent of increase.
4. Add the following footnote below the table: **This year's sales increased 8.68 percent over last year's sales.*

LANGUAGE ARTS

B. PROOFREADING

B. Compare this paragraph with the last paragraph of the timed writing that follows. Key a list of errors, correcting the errors as you key.

Poeple in other counties do have sharply varied ways of doing things. Each american businessperson who studies these customs quickly learns their value when she or he visits faraway nations on busness.

SKILLBUILDING

C. PACED PRACTICE

Turn to the Paced Practice routine at the back of the book. Take four 2-minute timed writings, starting at the speed at which you left off the last time.

D. 5-MINUTE TIMED WRITING

D. Spacing: Double
Take two 5-minute timed writings. Compute your speed and count errors.

Goal: 40 wam/5'/5e

This globe of ours is full of many exotic places where 12
travelers can visit. However, one should realize that even 24
though it is fun to go to these places, these spots are not 36
just for tourists. Business is becoming a global endeavor. 48
Each savvy businessperson knows that to be a success in 59
today's market, one must know about the world. 68

Asia is a region where cultural norms are very unlike 80
those in the United States. Doing business in Asia means 92
more than just hopping on a plane, meeting a few clients, 103
and closing the deal. For example, in Japan, clean socks 115
with no holes in the toes are crucial, since shoes come off 127
each time you visit someone's home or dine on straw mats 138
in a restaurant. And in China, a highly valued trait is 150
that of always being sure to be on time. 158

People in other countries do have sharply varied ways 170
of doing things. Each American businessperson who studies 181
these customs quickly learns their value when he or she 193
visits faraway nations on business. 200

DOCUMENT PROCESSING

REPORT 26
TWO-PAGE UNBOUND REPORT WITH FOOTNOTES

Spacing: Double

WOMEN AND CHILD CARE

By *(Your Name)*

A number of factors have had a tremendous impact on the role of women in the labor market and in our society. This report will first discuss some of the factors that have impacted the role of women in society and then will explore some of the issues dealing with child care.

(Continued on next page.)

REPORT 76
MINUTES OF A MEETING

Tabs: 1.5 inches; 3.25 inches
Top margin: 2 inches

Key the side headings in all-capital letters and bold. Triple-space before each heading.

Use Indent (F4) for the paragraph copy.

Begin the closing lines at the center.

Ergonomics Committee

Minutes of the Meeting

August 10, 19--

ATTENDANCE The Ergonomics Committee, met on August 10, 19--, in the Conference Room. The Members present were Michael Davenport, Susan Lowe, Huang Zhi-Heng, Alexandra Collins, and Frances Hartland. Alexandra Collins, Chairperson, called the meeting to order. at 9:30 a.m

Alphabetize the members' names

OLD BUSINESS The members of the committee looked at reviewed they proposal for a new lighting system for all floors. They agreed to continue to work with John Lipson, of General Lighting, Inc., on selecting the lighting system. Micheal Davenport will secure further data on the effectiveness of either indirect or semi-indirect lighting for the computer work areas.

proper

NEW BUSINESS The Committee reviewed a request from the accounting department for the purchase of new floor coverings. The Department requested that provisionals be monitored made to prevent the electrostatic charges that carpeting creates from interfering with any sensitive equipment. The committee asked Hueng Zhi-Heng to investigate where such carpeting could be purchased in the metropolitan area.

Business

A request from the Sales Department for seven six new computer desks was sent back to the Department for more data justification.

ADJOURNMENT The meeting was adjourned at 11:30 a.m. The next meeting has been scheduled for September 15 in the Conference Room.

Respectfully Submitted,

Susan Lowe, Secretary

Changing Role of Women

During the past 30 years, a major revolution has been taking place regarding the role of women in our society. A major factor has been the continuing increase in the number of women in the labor force.[1] This increased participation in the labor force on the part of women is due to several factors. First, women have been getting more and more education for careers. Second, more and more women are in the position of being a single parent. The need for income is critical. Even in those situations where there are two parents, the increased cost of living and continuing inflation have made it necessary for the family to have a second income.

Opportunities for women in the labor force have grown tremendously in the past several years. While the number of women attaining top-management positions is still relatively small, the number of women in middle-management and supervisory positions has shown continued growth. According to recent statistics, close to six million women were employed as executives, administrators, and managers in the different employment categories.[2]

Child-Care Issues

Of course, as women increase their participation in the labor force, many questions are raised regarding the child care available to them. This issue has been debated by Congress and is of concern to many business organizations. Recent statistics show that in the past 15 years, the number of 3- to 5-year-olds enrolled in nursery schools has increased by more than 150 percent.[3] At the same time, more and more business organizations have begun their own child-care facilities to meet the needs of their employees. The number of church-related nursery schools has also increased. Many states are now regulating child care by establishing standards to be met by typical nursery schools.

---

[1]Ruth A. Lupo, "Women in the Labor Force," *U.S. Labor Bulletin,* December 1992, p. 78.

[2]Thomas G. Laskert, *Becoming Managers/Supervisors,* American Management Association, New York, 1991, p. 241.

[3]Margaret Hajducky, "Child Care Issues," *Working Women,* October 1992, p. 37.

REPORT 27
TWO-PAGE UNBOUND REPORT WITH ENDNOTES

Retrieve Report 26 and reformat it as follows: delete the two side headings; omit the third paragraph; change the footnotes to endnotes.

REPORT 75
NEWS RELEASE

Spacing: Double
Top margin: 2 inches

From the left margin, key NEWS RELEASE in large font, all-capital letters and bold, and key the remaining heading information flush right.

NEWS RELEASE

From Byron Kirkland
International Office Supplies
4508 Broadway
New York, NY 10040

Release February 14, 19--

50TH ANNUAL OFFICE SUPPLIES SHOW

New York City, Feb. 10--The 50th Annual Office Supplies Show will be held at the Javitts Convention Center for one week beginning March 7. Over 500 manufacturers and suppliers will be presenting their latest office equipment and supplies.

Ms. Sally Churchill, President of the International Office Supplier's Association, states that this year's show will be an extravaganza because the association is celebrating it's 50th anniversary and the latest lines of office equipment and supplies will at last under one roof for everyone.

Members of the association will have hands-on demonstrations on various desktop and notebook computers. Apex Computer Company will be introducing its latest personal computer, the X-15. All firms marketing computer soft ware and supplies will have booths adjacent to the computer demonstration areas.

Some of the outstanding sessions to be held throughout the week will be concerned with the computer and the workforce, ergonomics and the computer workforce, and skills needed by employees. Mr. Jason Babcock, President of Wilson Computers, Inc., will deliver the opening address, and Ms. Dorothy Selinger, President of Moskovis Computers, will present the annual award's address.

Skillbuilding and Table Review

Margins: 1 inch • Tab: 0.5 inch • Spacing: Single • Drills: 2 times • Format Guide: 37–39

Goals:
To improve speed and accuracy; to review table formats.

A. WARMUP

1 Three of our employees (Zeeker, Quigley, & Justex) are 12
2 to be paid for the overtime. Their social security numbers 24
3 are as follows: 154-28-0277, 147-28-5881, and 156-34-5998. 36

| 1 | 2 | 3 | 4 | 5 | 6 | 7 | 8 | 9 | 10 | 11 | 12

LANGUAGE ARTS

B. Answer each question with a sentence or two.

B. COMPOSING

4 Why do people procrastinate?
5 How do you judge the value of a friendship?
6 Why is punctuality important?
7 What qualifications should a teacher possess?
8 How do you make a decision?
9 How can you improve your listening skills?
10 Why do magic tricks fascinate most people?

SKILLBUILDING

C. Set four tabs every 1 inch. Key lines 11–14, pressing the tab to move from column to column.

C. TECHNIQUE PRACTICE: TAB KEY

11	Aurora	Urbana	Geneva	Moline	Illinois
12	Laurel	Towson	Avenel	Elkton	Maryland
13	Elmira	Oswego	Albany	Selden	New York
14	Vienna	McLean	Dublin	Reston	Virginia

PRETEST.
Take a 1-minute timed writing; compute your speed and count errors.

D. PRETEST: HORIZONTAL REACHES

15 The legal facts gave our lawyers a sense that we could 12
16 be ready to wrap up this case quickly. When a written copy 24
17 of our testimony is given us, we shall be extremely joyous. 36

| 1 | 2 | 3 | 4 | 5 | 6 | 7 | 8 | 9 | 10 | 11 | 12

PRACTICE.
Speed Emphasis: If you made 2 or fewer errors on the Pretest, key each line twice.
Accuracy Emphasis: If you made 3 or more errors, key each group of lines (as though it were a paragraph) twice.

E. PRACTICE: IN REACHES

18 wr wrap wren wreak wrist wrote writer unwrap writhe wreaths
19 ou pout ours ounce cough fouls output detour ousted coupons
20 ad adds dead adult ready blade advice fading admits adheres
21 py pyre copy pygmy pylon happy pyrene choppy pyrite pyramid

F. PRACTICE: OUT REACHES

22 yo yoga your youth yodel yowls yogurt joyous yonder younger
23 fa fact farm faith sofas fakes faulty unfair famous defames
24 up upon soup upset group upper upturn supply uplift upsurge
25 ga gate gave cigar gains legal gazing legacy gawked garbage

POSTTEST.
Repeat the Pretest (D) and compare performance.

G. POSTTEST: HORIZONTAL REACHES

TABLE 60
BALANCE SHEET WITH LEADERS

Center the table vertically.

Leave 2 spaces between money columns.

To keep your place when keying a financial statement, put a ruler or card under the line being keyed, and keep moving it as you go down the page.

Refer to Table 32 (page 199) for setting a dot leader tab stop 2 spaces before the first amount column.

Create a double underline (Ctrl-F8, 2, 3) for the totals.

Leave 2 blank lines above each section heading.

Spread-center each section heading by leaving 1 space between letters and 3 spaces between words.

WordPerfect 6 users: See Student Guide, p. 78.

E-Z OFFICE SUPPLIES, INC.
BALANCE SHEET
April 30, 19—

A S S E T S		
Current Assets:		
Cash	$ 8,500.35	
Accounts Receivable	450.00	
Merchandise Inventory	17,363.15	
Office Supplies	1,000.00	
Prepaid Insurance	900.00	
Total Current Assets		$ 28,213.50
Fixed Assets:		
Office Equipment	$17,340.00	
Building	76,000.00	
Land	21,000.00	
Total Fixed Assets		114,340.00
Total Assets		$142,553.50
L I A B I L I T I E S		
Current Liabilities:		
Accounts Payable	$ 9,421.32	
Notes Payable	40,000.00	
State Income Tax Payable	574.00	
Federal Income Tax Payable	2,938.00	
Federal Unemployment Tax Payable	300.00	
State Unemployment Tax Payable	540.00	
FICA Taxes Payable	586.00	
Total Current Liabilities		$ 54,359.32
Long-Term Liabilities:		
Mortgage Payable		25,000.00
Total Liabilities		$ 79,359.32
O W N E R ' S E Q U I T Y		
Larry Osborn, Capital		63,194.18
Total Liabilities and Owner's Equity		$142,553.50

TABLE 16

ALLWOOD PUBLISHING COMPANY
Marketing Leaders for March

Employee	Revenue
Nancy Ostrowski	$32,400
Joseph Simon	29,900
Kimberley Harris	28,600
David Klein	27,800
Kathleen Lake	26,400

TABLE 17

ALLWOOD PUBLISHING COMPANY

Departmental Employees

Put in alphabetic order

Department	Supervisor	Number of Employees
Personnel	Agnes Rossi	10
Accounting	Chinnapa Jayachandran	14
Editorial	~~Grace Whitford~~ Maridel Ash	21
Sales/Marketing	Raymond Cozza	~~17~~ 16
Tech^ni^cal/Design	John Imperato	15

TABLE 18

ALLWOOD PUBLISHING COMPANY

Magazines Published

Title	Editor	Current Orders	Price per Year
News of the World	Jesse Young	15,239	$22.50
Only for Children	Valerie Ritter	17,355	13.95
Recent Happenings	Wayne Lee Frost	11,463	15.80
Sports Events	Joseph Giannini	23,148	21.95
Women's Issues	Edith Hoxie	10,642	12.50
World of Cars	Thomas Preston	14,650	18.95

TABLE 59
4-COLUMN RULED TABLE
WITH FOOTNOTE

Spacing: Double

extend rule to table width

CITY

VOLUME OF SALES BY POPULATION ☆

CITY	Popualation	Stores Unites	Volume of Sales
Chicago	2,977,250	12	$10,345,451
Cleveland	521,700	8 (6)	9,461,3007 (43)
Detroit	1,035,920	10	4,670,820
Columbus	569,570	6 (4)	9,861,278
Indianapolis	707,130 (2)	6 (3)	4,236,576
milwaukee	599,380	4	6,987,340 (5,789)
Minneapolis	344,760	3	3,560,896
Pittsburgh	375,230	44	6,450,899

extend to margins

extend to table width

☆ "Population of U. S. Cities (1988)," *The World Almanac and Book of Facts*, Pharos Books, New York, 1991, p. 557.

REPORT 74
ITINERARY

Tabs: Relative, 1.5″; right dot leader, 6.5″
Top margin: 2 inches

Insert dot leaders between the first line of the second column and the third column.

MS. MELBA LAZARUS / Itinerary for Dayton Store Visit / September 15, 19—

8:15–9:00 / BREAKFAST / Knapp's Restaurant / Breakfast with Ms. Alexis Smith, store manager.
9:15–11:30 / TOUR STORE / Mulbury Avenue Store / Ms. Alexis Smith and Mr. David Layton, assistant manager, will conduct a tour of all departments. Individual department heads will present their staff.
12:00–1:30 / LUNCH / Radisson Hotel / Attend the Economic Club of Dayton's weekly luncheon with Ms. Smith.
1:45–3:00 / COMPUTER OPERATIONS / Executive Offices / Mr. Charles Blackman, department head, will discuss the store's computer system and its link with the companywide system.
3:30–4:30 / INTERVIEW / Executive Offices / Ms. Louise Fass, anchorwoman for WTPK, will conduct an interview relating to the store's success in Dayton and the exceedingly high growth of the company.
5:00–6:30 / RECEPTION / Cafeteria / Attend a reception in your honor by all employees of the Dayton store.

Skillbuilding and Employment Documents Review

Margins: 1 inch • Tab: 0.5 inch • Spacing: Single • Drills: 2 times • Format Guide: 39

Goals:
To key 40 wam/5'/5e; to review formats for employment documents.

A. WARMUP

```
     Get 10 items @ $87, 15 items @ $92, and 9 items @ $96.  12
The entire bill is $3,114.  After checking the invoice with  24
extra care, ship the order to P. J. Quincy in Greenlee, AZ.  36
| 1 | 2 | 3 | 4 | 5 | 6 | 7 | 8 | 9 | 10 | 11 | 12
```

SKILLBUILDING

B. DIAGNOSTIC PRACTICE: NUMBERS

Turn to the Diagnostic Practice: Numbers routine at the back of this book. Take the Pretest and record your performance. Then practice the drill lines for those reaches on which you made errors. Finally, repeat the Pretest and compare your performance.

C. Spacing: Double
Take two 5-minute timed writings. Compute your speed and count errors.

Goal: 40 wam/5'/5e

C. 5-MINUTE TIMED WRITING

```
     Time is elastic; it can be stretched to include the        11
activities you enjoy doing as well as the tasks you are         23
obliged to do.  How do people with crazy schedules find the     35
time for all they do?  The secret is quite simple:  they        46
don't find the time for their interests; they make it.          57
     For example, did you ever notice how much time you         68
spend waiting in the supermarket checkout line or at the        80
doctor's office?  Even though it is only ten minutes here       91
or five minutes there, when you add it all up, it can be       103
substantial.  You could use the extra minutes to read a new    115
book or magazine.                                              118
     Successful time managers also know that it is critical    130
to break a task down into small pieces.  Say you wanted to     142
learn French.  Few people could set aside the time required    154
to devote to the project.  But what if you tried to learn      165
just ten new words each day?  It might take you longer, but    177
in the end you would surely master a new language.  Making     189
dreams come true is what time management is all about.         200
| 1 | 2 | 3 | 4 | 5 | 6 | 7 | 8 | 9 | 10 | 11 | 12
```

REPORT 73
TWO-PAGE UNBOUND REPORT WITH AUTHOR/ YEAR CITATIONS

Spacing: Double

Refer to page R-9 of the Reference Section for formatting a report with author/year citations.

Read the rough-draft copy before formatting the report. Make any notes necessary to format the report.

The Bibliography is page 3.

Use WordPerfect's Page Numbering feature to number pages. Suppress the page number for page 1.

Clear all tabs, then set relative tabs at 0, 0.5, and 0.9 for the enumeration and the bibliography.

To format the hanging indent in the bibliography, press F4 (Indent) then Sh-Tab.

DECISION MAKING < ds
Introduction < ts

An employee, regardless of his or her position, who ~~has the ability to~~ can make decisions ~~based upon~~ using problem-solving abilities is of paramount importance in the office today. Wade and Smith (1993) indicate that decision making is a matter of course in an office.

There are minor and major decisions made ~~by~~ each working day. Such decisions ~~are~~ involve which ~~evaluator~~ elevator to take to the office and which computer system would best meet the needs of the firm.

Purpose

The purpose of this ~~paper~~ report is to ~~show~~ reveal to office ~~workers~~ employees the steps in problem solving.

Scope

This report will be limited to ~~four~~ five common steps in problem solving.

Steps in Problem Solving

Conover, Gordon, and Ramsetter (1994) suggest~~ed~~ that the problem-solving sequence involes five steps:

1. Defining the Chqallenge. Theproblem must be clearly defined.
2. Search(ing) for alternatives. All alternative(s) should be identified.
3. Weighfing alternatives. Each alterantive must be carefully weighed and considered as a solution.
4. Making the selection. Which alternative is best?
5. Evaluating the outcomes. Was the problem solved?

Acquiring Problem-SØlving Skills

Whose reponsibility is it to assist individuals in developing problem-solving skills? Lamson (1993) indicates that our education(al) system is inefficient because it is too general. If our schools are nost assisting in the acquisin(tio) of these skills, then where will employees acquire them?

Conclusion

Problem-solving skills are a necessity in today's business world; therefore businesses must take steps to assist in the acquisition of these skills.

begin new page here →

BIBLIOGRAPHY

Conover, Hobart H., Sanford D. Gordon, and Vera Ramsetter, *Business Dynamics*, ~~Second Edition~~ 2d ed., Glencoe Publishing Company, Missions Hills, Calif~~ornia~~, 1994, p. 97.

Lamson, Charles, "Education Today," *Business Training*, Vol. 28, No. ~~2~~ 3, March, 1994.

Wade, John, and Larry Smith, *Office Systems*, 3rd ~~Edition~~ ed., Johnson Press, Boston, 1993, p. 230.

LETTER 34
APPLICATION LETTER

Key this letter in block format.

(Current Date) / Ms. Anna B. Krajewski / Personnel Department / Compu-Serve Systems / 1531 Roosevelt Avenue / Peoria, IL 61603 / Dear Ms. Krajewski:

I saw your advertisement in Friday's edition of the *Peoria Express,* and I am interested in being considered for the position of assistant network administrator. Enclosed is a copy of my resume, which gives details of my education and work experience.

During the past two years, my work at Bentley & Simon has required me to use the computer on a regular basis. In addition, my course work at Iron Hills gave me skills that I could easily transfer to the position you advertised.

I will be happy to come for an interview at your convenience. Please call me any day after 5 p.m. at 309-555-8407.

Sincerely yours, / Joseph B. Hawkins / *Pick up address from below.* / Enclosure

REPORT 28
RESUME

Key the name in extra-large size and bold. Key the address in large size.

JOSEPH B. HAWKINS

151 Greenwich Street, Peoria, IL 61603

309-555-8407

OBJECTIVE To obtain a position with computer operations responsibilities in an automated office.

EDUCATION Iron Hills Junior College, Peoria, Illinois
A.A. in Automated Office Technology, May 1992

Hoover High School, Peoria, Illinois
Academic Curriculum; Graduated: June 1990

EXPERIENCE Bentley & Simon, Peoria, Illinois
Position: Data Entry Clerk
June 1990-Present
Responsibilities: Entering legal time spent into computer accounts of clients; generating monthly computer statements to clients.

Caselli Florist Shop, Peoria, Illinois
Position: Clerk
June 1988–June 1990
Responsibilities: Assisted in taking orders at front desk. Handled telephone orders.

ACTIVITIES Iron Hills: Student Government Delegate; Intramural Basketball; Office Automation Club

Hoover H.S.: Varsity Basketball and Baseball; Class Treasurer; Key Club

REFERENCES Furnished on request

REPORT 72
THREE-PAGE BOUND REPORT

Spacing: Double

Left margin: 1.5 inches

Refer to the Reference Section for formatting a bound report.

Revise Report 71, making the necessary changes on the first two pages. The formatting changes will make this a three-page report.

Key the quotation listed at the bottom of the rough-draft portion of page 2 as the first sentence of the report.

Retrieve Report 71 and make these changes starting on page 2. Switch to a bound report format.

Since the partnership between the selling of equipment and the offering of training is increasing,[3] it is imperative that look for assistance from our manufacturers to help we train our employees.

Pertinent Questions. What costs, if any, will we be asked to absorb? Will the training occur at our ~~office~~ firm or will our ~~workers~~ employees be asked to travel elsewhere, and at whose expense? How many employees can be accommodated in any ~~one~~ particular training session? ~~May~~ Should we consider, as other firms ~~are,~~ have the use of self-directed teams in training?

Self-Directed Teams. ~~A~~ Self-directed teams ~~is a~~ are small groups of employees, with each group responsible for an entire work process or segment. This concept could prove ~~very~~ valuable for us, as an ~~whole~~ entire unit would be learning the new equipment ~~rather than one or two employees~~ at the same ~~a~~ time. If we ~~undertook~~ use the self-directed team approach, we might be able to save money as well as reduce employee time away from the job.

Key the following quotation as the first sentence of the report, and insert the new endnote.

A recent survey by Packer Research in Atlanta indicates that 41 percent of all U. S. organizations with 100 or more employees in the U.S. provide some form of computer-based training.

[3]Albert D. Springer, "Corporate Training Today," <u>Industrial Training</u>, Vol. 6, No. 8, August 1993, p. 56.

TABLE 58
4-COLUMN BOXED TABLE WITH BRACED HEADING

Use WordPerfect's Table feature to create this table.

Center the table horizontally and vertically. Center the column headings over the columns.

Read through the entire copy before keying the table. Check the total for each column.

WordPerfect 6 users: Do not key the dollar sign.

ADVERTISING EXPENDITURES

January through July 199-

Month	Media Type		
	Magazine	Newspaper	Radio
January	$ 2,~~3~~4 45	$ ~~9~~8 50	$ 760
February	3,456	1,560	~~5~~4 00
March	~~2~~1,985	1,390	1,500
April	4,687	2,431	966
~~MAY~~ May	1,778	2,34~~9~~8	1,~~7~~6 85
June	1,~~5~~6 40	3,776	1,050
TOTAL	$15,991	$12,355	$6,501

Progress Test on Part 3

TEST 3-A
5-MINUTE TIMED WRITING

Spacing: Double

Most people file their income tax forms around the 11
middle of April. They have a choice as to whether they use 23
the standard deduction or itemize their deductions. The 35
wise taxpayer will use the method that is in his or her 46
best interest. When it is time to complete your income tax 58
forms, it may be quite beneficial if Schedule A is used 69
to compute your deductions. The amount saved by using this 81
form can be quite large. There are several sections on the 93
form. The first one deals with health expenses, which 104
might be deductible depending on the income you earned. 116
Some taxes and certain types of interest may also be used. 128
There are other sections that cover gifts, theft and other 139
types of losses, moving expenses, job expenses, and other 151
types of expenses. The major job of completing this 162
schedule is in keeping all the needed records through the 173
course of the year, but the benefits may be quite large. 185
One may be very well rewarded for the extra amount of time 197
that this may take. 200

| 1 | 2 | 3 | 4 | 5 | 6 | 7 | 8 | 9 | 10 | 11 | 12

TEST 3-B
LETTER 35
MODIFIED-BLOCK STYLE

Use the current date.

The correct salutation is *Dear Mr. Beilow:*

Treat each item in the enumeration as a separate paragraph.

Please send the following letter to Mr. Robert D. Beilow, Director of Athletics, Mountainview Community College, 157 Valley Road, Winslow, AZ 86047.

As you are aware, the eight conferences of the quad states have now agreed to sponsor a basketball tournament to determine a champion from the quad states of Arizona, Colorado, New Mexico, and Utah.

1. The tournament will be held on the campus of Farmington Community College in Farmington, New Mexico, on March 19–21.

2. Each school must make its own travel arrangements. Lodging and meals will be available at Farmington. (Details are enclosed.)

3. On the basis of advertising and ticket revenues, each school participating in the tournament will receive some compensation.

Please call me if you have any questions about this invitation.

Sincerely, / Carline J. Wuoka / Administrator / *(Your Initials)* / Enclosure

TABLE 56*
4-COLUMN OPEN TABLE

Spacing: Double

Center the table horizontally and vertically.

*Tables 1–55 appear in Lessons 1–120.

CAR SALES
Week of July 20, 19--

Year	Make	Model	Representative
1993	Buick	Park Avenue	Lewis Leslie
1992	Cadillac	Brougham	Mable Smith
1993	Chrysler	Imperial	John Guin
1991	Ford	Taurus	Jim Knox
1993	Lincoln	Town Car	Mary Lee

FORMATTING

P. TABLES WITH FOOTNOTES

WordPerfect 6 users: See Student Guide, p. 77.

To format tables with footnotes, follow these steps.

1. Key an asterisk (or some other symbol) at the appropriate point within the table to indicate there is a footnote.
2. *Open Table:* Single-space after the last line of the table. (If the table was created using the Table feature, position the cursor on the first blank line after the table.)
   Ruled Table: Double-space after the final rule of the table.
   Boxed Table: Position the cursor on the second blank line after the table.
3. Set 2 left tabs. Set the first tab to align with the left edge of the table and set the second tab 5 spaces to the right of the first. (If you created an open table, at the first tab, key a 1-inch underline to separate the footnote from the body of the table; then double-space.)
4. Press Sh-F4 (double-indent) to have turnover lines wrap correctly and press Tab to indent the first line of the footnote. Double-space between footnotes.

DOCUMENT PROCESSING

TABLE 57
3-COLUMN BOXED
TABLE WITH FOOTNOTE

Key the table using WordPerfect's Table feature.

Center the table horizontally and vertically. Center the column headings over the columns.

WordPerfect 6 users: Do not key the dollar sign.

DETROIT METRO AIRFARES*

Detroit to:	Full Coach	Lowest Discount
Atlanta	$364	$109
Boston	388	109
Chicago	123	29
Dallas	449	134
Los Angeles	614	184
New York/Newark	315	89

*"Business Monday," Detroit Free Press, November 28, 1994, p. 12F.

TEST 3-C
REPORT 29
UNBOUND REPORT
WITH FOOTNOTES

Spacing: Double

BASKETBALL TOURNAMENT

By Charlotte Luna

On March 19, 19--, an exciting new competition will be inaugurated when the eight conference winners in the basketball programs in the community colleges of the quad states of (AZ), (CO), (NM), and (UT) meet in farmington, (NM).

NEW AGREEMENT

According to the agreement reached by the athletic directors from community colleges in the quad states, the eight league conferences in the (4) states will send their conference champion winner to a basketball tournament during the third week end of March to determine the quad states champion.[1]

Financial Benefits

The revenues ~~raised~~ generated from advertising and ticket sales will be ~~returned~~ distributed to the participa~~nts~~ting schools after the appropriate expenses have been deducted. The share of revenues earned will be based on the ~~record~~ achievement of the teams at the tournament.[2] Thus the tournament champion will collect the biggest share of revenues.

---

[1] ~~Thomas Foley~~ Pat Muranka, "Basketball Tournament Becomes a Reality", *Quad States Community College Newsletter*, July 1992, p. 12.

[2] Ibid.

TEST 3-D
MEMO 10

Use the current date and send this memo to Marvin Palomaki, Athletic Director from Debra Marchant, Tournament Manager, concerning the Quad States Tournament.

The participating colleges in the quad states tournament have been sent the packet of information and forms. As this is my first experience in coordinating the activities for an event like this, I am very appreciative of everything that you have done to help me.

Housing arrangements have been made at the Manson Inn, and all meals will be provided at the Farmington Community College dining hall. The contracts for the officials (including referees) have all been received. All media personnel are being kept informed of the developments.

Please look over the attached list; have I overlooked anything?

(Your Initials) / Attachment

DOCUMENT PROCESSING

REPORT 71
TWO-PAGE UNBOUND REPORT WITH SIDE HEADINGS AND ENDNOTES

Spacing: Double

Refer to the Reference Section for formatting a two-page report with side headings and endnotes.

Format a header for each page entitled *Rough Draft (Current date)* and a footer *Checked by:*.

Use WordPerfect's Page Numbering feature to number pages in the top right corner. Suppress the page number on page 1.

Double-space after the title, single-space the writer's name and title, and triple-space after the writer's title.

Double-space before and after side headings. Key side and paragraph headings in bold.

Use WordPerfect's Endnotes feature to format the endnotes on a separate page.

BETTER TRAINING ON EQUIPMENT
Tena Harrington
Corporate Training Director

How can we do a better job of training our employees on new equipment so that less time is spent attempting to decipher the owner's manual? One way is to use the services of equipment manufacturers. Koontz[1] believes that comprehensive training from equipment manufacturers should be a matter of course for companies such as ours. If Koontz is correct, what steps should we now take to ensure that we, too, avail ourselves of this training?

Steps to Better Training

Koontz[2] indicates that as a purchaser and user of equipment, we can take three steps that will lead us to getting the most equipment-specific training. They are as follows:

1. Setting clear goals for what the training is to accomplish.
2. Assessing the skills of current employees who will be taught new skills or updated on current skills.
3. Making training needs known to the equipment manufacturers.

We have, for a number of years, implemented the first two steps, but we have not usually undertaken the third step.

There are questions that need to be answered by our units before we implement the third step.

Questions Concerning Training by Equipment Manufacturers

Since the partnership between the selling of equipment and the offering of training is increasing,[3] it is imperative that we train our employees.

Pertinent Questions. What costs, if any, will we be asked to absorb? Will the training occur at our office or will our workers be asked to travel, and at whose expense? How many employees can be in any one training session? May we consider, as other firms are, the use of self-directed teams?

Self-Directed Teams. A self-directed team is a small group of employees responsible for an entire work process or segment. This concept could prove very valuable for us, as a whole unit would be learning the new equipment rather than one or two employees at a time. If we undertook the self-directed team approach, we might be able to save money as well as employee time away from the job.

NOTES

1. Anthony Koontz, "Three Steps to Better Equipment Training," *Training in the Workplace,* Vol. 2, No. 5, July 1994, p. 21.
2. Ibid.
3. Addison Fales, "All in the Family," *Technical Training,* Vol. 7, No. 2, August 1994, p. 25.

PART

4

SKILLBUILDING

Correspondence, Reports, and Tables

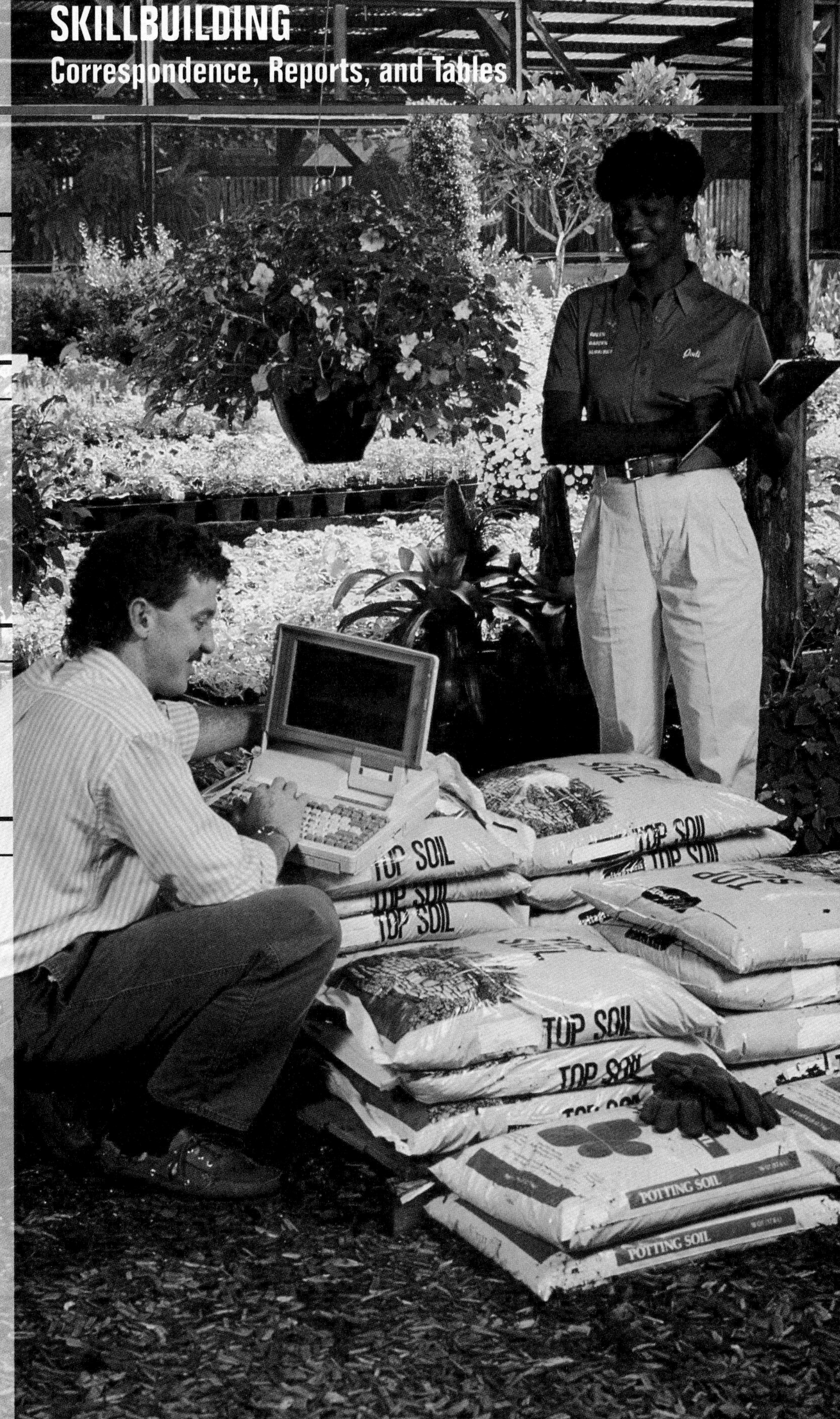

OBJECTIVES

KEYBOARDING

To key 43 words a minute on a 5-minute timed writing with no more than 5 errors.

LANGUAGE ARTS

To improve language arts skills.

To proofread and correct errors.

To develop keyboard composing skill.

WORD PROCESSING

To review WordPerfect commands and learn to use: Initial Codes, Block Protect, Repeat Value, and Double Underline.

DOCUMENT PROCESSING

To review the formatting of correspondence, reports, and tables. To format business letters with tables, indented paragraphs, subject lines, and copy notations.

To format bound and unbound reports with side headings, enumerations, endnotes, footnotes; book manuscripts; a news release; and a magazine article.

To format tables, ruled tables, and financial statements.

Ruttle Graphics, Inc./Maria Paraskevas

M. Take three 30-second timed writings on each line. Remember to use the caps lock key when keying in all-capital letters.

M. TECHNIQUE PRACTICE: CAPS LOCK KEY

He observed the YIELD and CAUTION signs on the way to work.
Was there a sign FOR RENT or FOR SALE in front of his home?
Did the WANT AD section of the BOSTON NEWS help him at all?
ENTRANCE and EXIT signs were to be placed at various doors.

| 1 | 2 | 3 | 4 | 5 | 6 | 7 | 8 | 9 | 10 | 11 | 12

N. PROGRESSIVE PRACTICE: NUMBERS

Turn to the Progressive Practice: Numbers routine at the back of the book. Take five 30-second timed writings, starting at the point where you left off the last time.

O. Spacing: Double
Take two 5-minute timed writings. Compute your speed and count errors.

Goal: 51 wam/5'/5e

O. 5-MINUTE TIMED WRITING

Have you ever tried to accomplish a task only to find 12
that you just couldn't concentrate? Many factors in your 23
work environment directly affect your body and your ability 35
to focus on your tasks. When you are working, it is best 47
if distractions are minimal. When you are able to focus 58
your attention and fully concentrate on your job duties, 70
you are operating at maximum efficiency. 78

Experts agree that the largest amount of information 90
you receive from your environment is gathered through your 101
eyes. Therefore, proper lighting is high on the priority 113
list of a good work environment. Inadequate lighting makes 125
it difficult for the eyes to focus, and it takes more time 137
for the appropriate information to be deciphered by the 148
brain. This extra effort can cause fatigue and eyestrain. 160
As the day goes on, it becomes more difficult and tiresome 172
to perform. 174

Room lighting should also not be so bright that you 186
must squint to see. The cumulative effects of continually 197
shifting your body, neck, and head to avoid bright lights 209
or reflections can cause enough stress or strain to produce 221
or aggravate other symptoms such as neck pain, back pain, 233
muscle tension, and fatigue. Manage your tasks with zest 244
each day by investing in a lighting system that works. 255

| 1 | 2 | 3 | 4 | 5 | 6 | 7 | 8 | 9 | 10 | 11 | 12

UNIT THIRTEEN • WORDPERFECT AND CORRESPONDENCE REVIEW

61-65 LESSONS

Margins: 1 inch • Spacing: Single • Drills: 2 times • Format Guide: 39–41

Goals for Unit 13

1. To improve accuracy and speed on alphabet, number, and symbol keys.
2. To key 40 wam for 5 minutes with no more than 5 errors.
3. To develop proficiency in spelling commonly misspelled words.
4. To format and key various forms of correspondence—business letters, personal-business letters, and memorandums.

Begin each day with approximately 15 minutes of skillbuilding, selecting activities from pages 140–143. In the remaining class time, complete as many production jobs from pages 144–151 as you can.

A. WARMUP

```
1      Pam inquired about Flight #670 to Zurich for April 21.  12
2 She found that the cost was $853 for a two-way ticket.  She  24
3 discovered that Flight #97 would be an extra $50 on June 4.  36
  | 1 | 2 | 3 | 4 | 5 | 6 | 7 | 8 | 9 | 10 | 11 | 12
```

LANGUAGE ARTS

B. ABBREVIATIONS

B. Study the rules at the right. Then key lines 4–7, making necessary changes.

Rule: Abbreviations made up of single initials in all caps usually require no periods and no internal spaces. **Exceptions:** geographic names and academic degrees

The FIFO inventory valuation method is being used.

Rule: Abbreviations made up of single initials in small letters require a period after each initial but no space after each internal period. **Exceptions:** rpm, mpg, mph

The shipment of tires was to be made f.o.b. destination.

```
4 The N.F.C. and A.F.C. champions met in the Super Bowl.
5 Kamran was proud to receive his BS degree in the U.S.A.
6 The eom statement has an error in the amount of $79.42.
7 An m.p.g. average is affected by speed, roads, and weather.
```

C. SPELLING

C. These words are among the 500 most frequently misspelled words in business correspondence.

```
8 operations health individual considered expenditures vendor
9 beginning internal pursuant president union written develop
10 hours enclosing situation function including standard shown
11 engineering payable suggested participants providing orders
12 toward nays total without paragraph meetings different vice
```

I. Take three 30-second timed writings on each line. Try not to slow down for the capital letters.

I. TECHNIQUE PRACTICE: SHIFT KEY

Alan, John, and David went to London on Tuesday, August 24.
The Atlanta Falcons were playing the New York Giants today.
Karl took Flight 53 for Dallas and Fort Worth on August 31.
Tim Bell's new address is 18 Reston Road in Preston, Idaho.

| 1 | 2 | 3 | 4 | 5 | 6 | 7 | 8 | 9 | 10 | 11 | 12

J. Insert the necessary capitalization as you key these sentences twice.

J. TECHNIQUE PRACTICE: CONCENTRATION

Lee and john went to cape cod, massachusetts, on october 8.
President lyndon b. johnson was born near stonewall, texas.
The cities of ogden, salt lake city, and provo are in utah.
One campus of the university of wisconsin is in eau claire.
Many visitors go to zion national park in springdale, utah.

K. Take three 12-second timed writings on each line. The scale gives wam for a 12-second timed writing.

K. 12-SECOND SPRINTS

The firm sent 12,534 statements in 1989 and 13,760 in 1990.
Invoice 346 for $1,825.50 was sent to 197 Hamburg Turnpike.
Our plane leaves from Gate 19 or 20 at either 7:53 or 8:46.
Merle was paid $609 on November 13 and $584 on November 27.

| | | | 5 | | | | 10 | | | | 15 | | | | 20 | | | | 25 | | | | 30 | | | | 35 | | | | 40 | | | | 45 | | | | 50 | | | | 55 | | | | 60

L. Take a 1-minute timed writing on the first paragraph to establish your base speed. Then take four 1-minute timed writings on the remaining paragraphs. As soon as you equal or exceed your base speed on one paragraph, advance to the next one.

L. SUSTAINED PRACTICE: CAPITALIZATION

For many people, the rite of passage after the college 12
years is a vacation: hiking across this country, traveling 24
overseas, or spending a few weeks relaxing by the mountains 36
or shore. These scenes certainly paint a relaxing picture. 48

However, there is one feature of traveling that is not 12
so enjoyable: tipping. Once you start on your first trip, 24
you must learn whom to tip, how much, and when. When trips 36
are taken in the United States, tipping should be expected. 48

Outside the United States, a similar tip is given, but 12
check the bill, especially when paying by American Express, 24
Visa, or MasterCard. In Germany, restaurants routinely add 36
the service charge to the bill, and you may not realize it. 48

Feeling broke? Try visiting Iceland, Sweden, Denmark, 12
Norway, or Finland, where tipping is not fostered. Tipping 24
in New Zealand or Australia is done only by foreigners, and 36
in Japan it is confined to traditional inns called Ryokans. 48

| 1 | 2 | 3 | 4 | 5 | 6 | 7 | 8 | 9 | 10 | 11 | 12

SKILLBUILDING

D. 12-SECOND SPRINTS

D. Take three 12-second timed writings on each line. The scale gives your wam speed for a 12-second timed writing.

13 Rick made the dog sleighs for the six girls and their pals.
14 They paid a helpful neighbor to sit with their eight girls.
15 Pam did not cut the oak but let the men cut the fir for us.
16 The six forms she got from my firm may do for that problem.

| | | | 5 | | | | 10 | | | | 15 | | | | 20 | | | | 25 | | | | 30 | | | | 35 | | | | 40 | | | | 45 | | | | 50 | | | | 55 | | | | 60

E. PRETEST: ALPHABET REVIEW

E. PRETEST. Take a 1-minute timed writing; compute your speed and count errors.

17 The skill of listening is just as important as are the 12
18 skills of speaking and writing. Quite often we hear an em- 24
19 ployer say that workers are not paying attention to what is 36
20 being said. Listening is expected of everybody and prized. 48

| 1 | 2 | 3 | 4 | 5 | 6 | 7 | 8 | 9 | 10 | 11 | 12

F. PRACTICE: ALPHABET KEYS

F. PRACTICE.
1. Key lines 21–46 (A–Z) once.
2. Check the Pretest (E) for those keys on which you made errors, and key the corresponding lines 2 more times.

21 A Alan also last easy vain bacon canoe attest ballad author
22 B Beth baby able best bibb derby limbo budget burger bronze
23 C Chip coco cold care fact crazy civic carpet octave scopes
24 D Dave date adds drop dent adore diner redeem hidden worded

25 E Ella ease else eyed epic treat check esteem elated talked
26 F Faye fold fair cuff fort beefs draft friend grafts finder
27 G Glen good gold ages page vigor begun grates legion jargon
28 H Hope hash high huge such north laugh thrust though chided

29 I Iris into inch tile fill music pinch picnic impart deceit
30 J John junk just join jowl bijou banjo jabber junior hijack
31 K Kate cork kind seek hawk kitty knack kinder shrink awaken
32 L Lane look alas late lime elate skill locale collar bleach

33 M Mary mate maid main amen moody smile memory motion muffin
34 N Nate note neon wind fend longs mints noodle nation inland
35 O Opal oleo tool code fold opens order mascot report casino
36 P Paul pork pine spot tips props soupy dipped purple upbeat

37 Q Quip quiz quad quit quay quaff equal square piqued squirm
38 R Rose rage roar rare rate resin orbit arrear droves drench
39 S Sara suit sale easy skis sable ashes attest tassel assort
40 T Tony toot unto tile test stair trash fitted ratify stayed

41 U Ural undo unit used upon truth union assume scours adjust
42 V Vera vail veto vest wave value vivid evenly avowed lavish
43 W Wilt were avow crow gnaw swept waits awards winked wigwag
44 X Xeno exit jinx oxen axle sixty taxed coaxed exiled exceed

45 Y Yale yawl yard eyed stay dimly yeast choppy yearly yellow
46 Z Zeke zest zero zone cozy pizza tizzy dozing zapped sneeze

G. POSTTEST. Repeat the Pretest (E) and compare performance.

G. POSTTEST: ALPHABET REVIEW

SKILLBUILDING

PRETEST. Take a 1-minute timed writing; compute your speed and count errors.

PRACTICE.

Speed Emphasis: If you made no errors on the Pretest, key each line twice.

Accuracy Emphasis: If you made 1 or more errors on the Pretest, key each group of lines (as though it were a paragraph) twice.

POSTTEST. Repeat the Pretest (D) and compare performance.

H. Take a 1-minute timed writing on the first paragraph to establish your base speed. Then take four 1-minute timed writings on the remaining paragraphs. As soon as you equal or exceed your base speed on one paragraph, advance to the next one.

D. PRETEST: COMMON LETTER COMBINATIONS

Della Kily will return to Detroit because she believes 12
her income will increase. She will share an apartment with 24
Joanne to save on rent. Their rental was lowered, however, 36
because of the intense complaints of the outraged dwellers. 48

| 1 | 2 | 3 | 4 | 5 | 6 | 7 | 8 | 9 | 10 | 11 | 12

E. PRACTICE: WORD BEGINNINGS

re redo retake reform remake revamp return rewrite reactive
in into income indent insole intact intone invalid indebted
be beam belong become before bemuse betray betroth befuddle
de deny decide defend design detain devise depress deformed

F. PRACTICE: WORD ENDINGS

ly duly likely calmly gamely hardly kindly clearly directly
ed aged handed farmed melted played traded reached shielded
nt dent relent patent invent recant cement figment poignant
al dial mental cereal bridal fungal normal literal informal

G. POSTTEST: COMMON LETTER COMBINATIONS

H. SUSTAINED PRACTICE: ROUGH DRAFT

The pattern of employment in our country is undergoing 12
some major changes. Companies are slowly paring down their 24
permanent staffs to just a core group of managers and other 36
high-powered people and are using temporaries for the rest. 48

This trend is creating an acordian effect in the work 12
force: the ability to expand and contract as the time and 24
the balance sheets dictate. Have this bit of flexibility 36
~~would~~ will be a key ingredient in the competative fights to come. 48
All of these changes ~~would~~ will make it tough for ~~all~~ the unions 12
to stay a float. They do not have a satisfactery manner for 24
organizing such employes. Unions ~~can~~ could try to change in to 36
social agenceis providing help for members out side of work. 48

Such services as elder or child care, counseling, debt 12
managment, and even health care maybe of great asistance 24
as employers find it more and more dificult to offer these 36
benfits. Unions may find their niche by filling this gap. 48

| 1 | 2 | 3 | 4 | 5 | 6 | 7 | 8 | 9 | 10 | 11 | 12

H. PRETEST.
Take a 1-minute timed writing; compute your speed and count errors.

H. PRETEST: NUMBER AND SYMBOL REVIEW

```
47      Hall & Smith's catalog listed #489 (personal computer)  12
48 and #267 (disk) at a 15% discount.  One-fourth (1/4) of all  24
49 of their items were on sale at 9:30 a.m.  Ms. "Tillie" Yang  36
50 said the $7.50 tray sold well.  However, the $9.65 did too.  48
   | 1 | 2 | 3 | 4 | 5 | 6 | 7 | 8 | 9 | 10 | 11 | 12
```

I. PRACTICE.
1. Key lines 51–60 once.
2. Check the Pretest (H) for those keys on which you made errors, and key the corresponding lines 2 more times.

I. PRACTICE: NUMBERS

```
51 00 ;p0 000 0 pod, 00 pie, 00 par, 00 pale, 00 push, 00 past
52 11 aq1 111 1 ask, 11 add, 11 art, 11 quit, 11 zero, 11 zest
53 22 sw2 222 2 sew, 22 six, 22 was, 22 wise, 22 axes, 22 exam
54 33 de3 333 3 den, 33 dew, 33 end, 33 edge, 33 cede, 33 code
55 44 fr4 444 4 for, 44 far, 44 red, 44 rave, 44 very, 44 five

56 55 fr5 555 5 tar, 55 tag, 55 get, 55 gear, 55 boat, 55 verb
57 66 jy6 666 6 joy, 66 jog, 66 yet, 66 year, 66 nary, 66 navy
58 77 ju7 777 7 jug, 77 jib, 77 urn, 77 unto, 77 must, 77 mush
59 88 ki8 888 8 kit, 88 key, 88 icy, 88 inky, 88 kilt, 88 kite
60 99 lo9 999 9 lot, 99 log, 99 old, 99 oils, 99 loot, 99 oleo
```

J. PRACTICE.
1. Key lines 61–66 once.
2. Check the Pretest (H) for those keys on which you made errors, and key the corresponding lines 2 more times.

J. PRACTICE: SYMBOLS

```
61 % ft5% 18% 25% - ;--;- Smith-Brown's interest rate was 18%.
62 " ;'"' ;"' "A" / ;//;/ "Ed" and/or "Bo" got it for 1/5 off.
63 $ fr4$ $18 $35 : ;::;: Ken sold shares for $45 at 9:30 a.m.
64 ( lo9( 1(1 (1( ) ;p0); () Ike (the favorite) moved quickly.
65 & ju7& j&j &j& ; ;;;;; Mo & Joe's sold it; but Al's didn't.
66 # de3# #82 #20 ' ;'';' Jay's #67 and #33 were like Marie's.
```

K. POSTTEST.
Repeat the Pretest (H) and compare performance.

K. POSTTEST: NUMBER AND SYMBOL REVIEW

L. Take a 1-minute timed writing on the first paragraph to establish your base speed. Then take four 1-minute timed writings on the remaining paragraphs. As soon as you equal or exceed your base speed on one paragraph, advance to the next one.

L. SUSTAINED PRACTICE: SYLLABIC INTENSITY

```
67      The thought of owning a business can make a person get  12
68 very excited.  To be your own boss and to call the shots is  24
69 a worthy aim.  Think of your answers to some big questions.  36

70      What are your knowledge and background of this product  12
71 or service that you will provide?  Are you prepared to make  24
72 a detailed, credible business plan for the first two years?  36

73      How is your product or service different from those in  12
74 your marketing area?  Why would a client come to you rather  24
75 than support one of the other vendors located in your area?  36

76      Are your resources and credit adequate to help provide  12
77 the financial support necessary for the early stages?  Have  24
78 you got a clear understanding of all the financial aspects?  36
   | 1 | 2 | 3 | 4 | 5 | 6 | 7 | 8 | 9 | 10 | 11 | 12
```

LESSONS 126-130

Margins: 1 inch • Spacing: Single • Drills: 2 times • Format Guide: 111–117

Goals for Unit 26

Begin each day with approximately 15 minutes of skillbuilding, selecting activities from pages 308–311. In the remaining class time, complete as many production jobs from pages 312–320 as you can.

1. To improve accuracy and speed on alphabet and number keys.
2. To key 51 wam for 5 minutes with no more than 5 errors.
3. To improve proficiency in composing at the keyboard.
4. To format reports with a variety of features—side headings, endnotes, author/year citations, and long quotations.
5. To format itineraries, financial statements, news releases, and minutes of a meeting.
6. To format tables with a variety of features—open, boxed, braced, long and short column heads, and footnotes.

A. WARMUP

1 Sales by three travel agencies (Quill & Jebson, Keef & 12
2 Zane, and Bate & Virgil) exceeded all prior amounts. Total 24
3 sales recorded were $1,924,565; $1,240,830; and $1,970,000. 36

| 1 | 2 | 3 | 4 | 5 | 6 | 7 | 8 | 9 | 10 | 11 | 12

LANGUAGE ARTS

B. NUMBERS

Study the rules at the right. Then key lines 4–7, making necessary changes.

Rule: Use figures for house numbers.

She said their new address will be 532 Lakeview Drive.

Rule: Do not use a decimal with even amounts of money.

The new salary for the advertising position is $32,000.

4 The package was delivered to him at Eighteen Walnut Lane.
5 They bought the house at 348 West Garfield Avenue.
6 He received a $50 bill from his parents for his birthday.
7 A mortgage loan was obtained in the amount of $126,000.00.

C. COMPOSING

Prepare a letter in response to Ms. Wilkinson (Letter 91, p. 299) indicating that you would like to make a change in your September 18 order for a Style E numbering machine. After looking at the catalog page, you have decided to purchase a Style C, three-movement numbering machine, Catalog No. R1-NM-3. Indicate that a new purchase order is enclosed that specifies this change. Close your letter by thanking Ms. Wilkinson for bringing the error to your attention. Ms. Wilkinson's address at Lakeland Office Products is 248 Crescent Drive, Baltimore, MD 21218-0345. Provide a suitable salutation and closing.

M. Key each sentence on a separate line.

M. TECHNIQUE PRACTICE: ENTER KEY

```
Move the desk.  Hook up the computer.  Hang the photograph.
File the invoices.  Lower the chairs.  Sharpen the pencils.
Adjust the new vertical blinds.  Update the client records.
Empty the baskets.  Polish the credenza.  Remove the files.
```

N. DIAGNOSTIC PRACTICE: ALPHABET

Turn to the Diagnostic Practice: Alphabet routine at the back of this book. Take the Pretest and record your performance. Then practice the drill lines for those reaches on which you made errors. Finally, repeat the Pretest and compare your performance.

LINE SPACING
Sh-F8, 1, 6, *no.*, F7

WP

WordPerfect 6 users: Units 13 and 14 review word processing commands from Lessons 1–60. The notation **WP6,** p. xx, indicates the Student Guide page where WordPerfect 6 instructions can be found.

O. WORDPERFECT: LINE SPACING

Line spacing sets the amount of space between keyed lines. To change the line spacing at any point on the page, position the cursor at the start of the line where you wish the new spacing to begin and enter the appropriate commands. Key a "1" for single spacing (the default setting), "2" for double spacing, and so on. All text after the line-spacing code will reflect the new spacing. Line spacing can be changed as often as you wish within a document.

P. Spacing: Double.
Take two 5-minute timed writings. Compute your speed and count errors.

Goal: 40 wam/5′/5e

P. 5-MINUTE TIMED WRITING

```
     A place for everything and everything in its place.      12
This old adage makes sense for today's businessperson who     23
is concerned with both neatness and efficiency on the job.    35
Whether you do your work at a desk in an office or in a       47
spare room in your home, these three guidelines may help      58
you be more organized:  adequacy, closeness, and grouping.    70
     Adequacy means sufficient for a specific requirement.    82
Quite simply, when your desk no longer holds your work, you   94
must add to your space or reduce the amount of work on your  106
desk.  The next tip, closeness, means keeping those things   118
you use most often nearby.  For example, current projects    129
should be on wall shelves or in top drawers where they can   141
most easily be reached.                                      146
     And finally, it is helpful to group the things you      157
need according to their use.  Books, records, forms, and     168
other supplies for each project should all be kept in just   180
one place.  Use these tips to organize your space, and you   192
will present a sharp, professional image.                    200
| 1 | 2 | 3 | 4 | 5 | 6 | 7 | 8 | 9 | 10 | 11 | 12
```

LETTER 104
TWO-PAGE LETTER IN BLOCK STYLE

Key the day before the month instead of after, with no separating comma, when using a military-style date.

Key the name of the country in all capital letters on a separate line in a foreign address.

A blind copy *(bc:)* notation is used when the addressee is not intended to know that one or more other persons are being sent a copy of the letter. Key the *bc* notation on the file copy at the left margin on the second line after the last item in the letter.

When preparing a letter with a blind copy, print one copy of the letter; then add the blind copy notation and print another.

```
Sincerely yours,


Jerry Lawlor
Manager

rp
c:   Alex Smith

bc:   Mary Brown
```

1 October 19— / Mr. T. Patrick Van Kampen / Jakarta International School / P.O. Box 79 / JKS / Jakarta 12430 / INDONESIA / Dear Mr. Van Kampen:

It was a pleasure to hear and meet you last week at the annual meeting of the International Society of Businessmen and Businesswomen.

You certainly challenged our members with your speech "Where Do We Get Skilled Employees?" I think that most of us in the United States were of the opinion that we were the only industrialized country where a large number of new employees lacked adequate basic skills.

At the end of your speech, you indicated that you would like to know about some of the activities that various firms were undertaking to alleviate the problem. Listed below are some of the steps we have been taking.

1. All new employees, regardless of position, are tested in the areas of mathematics, grammar, spelling, and writing. If an individual is poor in any one of the areas, he or she is urged to take a refresher course or complete a recognized course in the particular area. We do hire employees, even though their skill(s) may be less than we would like, on a temporary basis until they complete the necessary course work or improve their test scores within a set time frame.

2. Individuals who have been employed with us over a number of years are monitored (observed) in their use of the basic skills. If they show a weakness in everyday use of a skill or skills, they are required to attend the appropriate skill course during working hours. This incentive has paid dividends for us, as it has reduced the number of terminations and the cost of hiring new employees and has raised the morale of all employees.

3. Employees who are terminated because of new technology or changes in our manufacturing processes are given the opportunity to improve their basic skills as well as acquire new job skills at our local community college at no cost to them.

These are but three of the activities we undertake to ensure that our employees continue to maintain or improve their basic skills.

It is interesting to note the changes that are occurring in our schools today. They, too, are aware that something must be implemented to ensure that all learners achieve the basic skill levels. All of the states have enacted legislation requiring additional course work in the basic skills as well as an insurance that when the learner has completed high school, he or she will have acquired the basic skills.

I would be interested in learning what other individuals are telling you about their company's activities with regard to basic skills improvement.

Again, thank you for your excellent presentation.

Sincerely yours, / David Prina, Personnel / urs / c: G. Blackman / bc: R. Ray

Q. WORDPERFECT: HYPHENATION

 **WP6:** p. 4.

HYPHENATION—AUTOMATIC
Sh-F8, 1, 1, F7
HYPHENATION PROMPT
Position the cursor at division point,
Ctrl-Hyphen

Use Hyphenation to maintain a more even right margin. WordPerfect will automatically divide most words correctly. If it needs help, a screen prompt will ask you to position the hyphen (use the arrow keys) at a correct division point; then press Esc. If the word should not be hyphenated, press F1.

To manually divide a word not in WordPerfect's hyphenation dictionary, press Ctrl-Hyphen at the division point.

R. WORDPERFECT: PAGE BREAK

 **WP6:** p. 8.

PAGE BREAK
Ctrl-Enter

When you reach the end of a page, WordPerfect inserts a soft page break (shown by a line of dashes). Soft page breaks will shift as copy is added or deleted.

A hard page break (shown by a line of equal signs) can be inserted wherever you want a new page to begin (for example, to start a centering activity on a new page).

To insert a hard page break, position the cursor where you want the new page to start, and press Ctrl-Enter. Hard page breaks will not shift as copy is deleted.

To delete a hard page break, position the cursor at the left margin immediately below the line of equal signs, and press Backspace.

S. WORDPERFECT: REVEAL CODES

 **WP6:** p. 1.

REVEAL CODES
Alt-F3 or F11

Sometimes when you issue a command, WordPerfect inserts a hidden code into the document. For example, pressing Enter at the end of a line inserts a hard-return code [HRt]. To see these hidden codes, use Reveal Codes: Alt-F3 or F11. The screen splits in half, with the top half showing the text as you keyed it and the bottom half showing the same text with the codes. To delete a hidden code, position the cursor to the right of the code and press Backspace.

To return to the normal screen, press Alt-F3 or F11 again.

T. WORDPERFECT PRACTICE

1. Turn Hyphenation off and key the paragraph below, letting word wrap end your lines for you. (Your lines will probably end at the same point as those shown.)
2. Insert a hard page break.
3. Turn Hyphenation on and key the paragraph a second time. If prompted, insert a hyphen at an appropriate word-division point.
4. Turn on Reveal Codes and locate the codes WordPerfect inserted at the paragraph indention, at the end of each line, in each hyphenated word, and at the hard page break.
5. Print both pages.

```
     The main attractions for the children in a municipal
recreation league are the supervised sports activities.  The
neighborhood youngsters sign up for either basketball camp or
swimming relays.  Last year our recreation league was run by Al
Biggerstaff.  He was assisted in basketball by Anne Smith and in
swimming by Marc Jaderstrom.  Nearly a hundred children
participated.
```

LETTER 102 (Continued)

We, too, are aware of the limited parking. Presently we are negotiating with the owners of the vacant lot across the street, and we believe that by next fall we will have additional parking.

In the meantime, we are providing a rapid-shuttle bus service from a lot south of the theater. Enclosed is a pass to use the shuttle service.

Sincerely yours / Lewis Hamlin, Manager / *(Your Initials)* / Enclosure

LETTER 103
BLOCK STYLE WITH STANDARD PUNCTUATION ON MONARCH STATIONERY

Retrieve Letter 102 and make the following changes:

1. Send the letter to Mr. Brad Paddock, 203 Brackett Street, Portland, ME 04102.
2. Delete the last sentence of the second paragraph and add: *We are very sorry for the damage to your right-rear light when you were parking in limited space in our lot last week. Please send me a copy of the charges for repairing your light, and we will reimburse you. We hope to have additional parking space next fall.*
3. Change the last paragraph to read: *In the meantime, enclosed is a pass for our rapid-shuttle service. Present the pass to the driver of any theater bus at the public parking lot two blocks south of the theater. There is ample parking space there, and the buses leave every 5 minutes.*
4. Add the postscript: *PS: Also enclosed are two complimentary tickets to our next Paul Simon concert.*

MEMO 33

MEMO TO: Loren Roe
FROM: Judy Berry
DATE: July 1, 19--
RE: Summer Picnic

The annual summer picnic is scheduled at Porter Park on July 11. Enclosed is a list of the activities that we plan to offer.

Do you believe the list is comprehensive enough to satisfy most employees? Should softball and swimming be added? I know that Porter Park has a number of softball fields that we could reserve. The swimming pool at the park is small, but it could handle 25 of our group in addition to the regulars at the park.

I need to get the list of activities to the employees by Monday. Please let me have your responses by Friday.

urs
Enclosure

 **WP6:** p. 12.

SPELLER
Ctrl-F2, 3

U. WORDPERFECT: SPELLER

Proofreading and correcting errors are an essential part of document processing. The WordPerfect Speller enables you to check documents quickly for any misspelled words.

To spell-check your document, press Ctrl-F2, then enter "3." The Speller compares the words in your document with words in its dictionary. When a word is not found, it is highlighted and a list of replacement words is displayed. To choose a listed word, enter its letter.

If a highlighted word is correct, skip the word by entering "1" or "2." If the word is incorrect but no list is provided, enter "4" to edit the word. When the spell-check is complete, press any key.

Although the Speller will find misspelled words, it will not find omitted words or wrong words (such as "sing" for "sign" and "wiring" for "writing"). Therefore, you must still proofread every document carefully.

WP **WP6:** p. 11.

VIEW DOCUMENT
Sh-F7, 6

V. WORDPERFECT: VIEW DOCUMENT

Using View Document, you can see what a document looks like and make any format changes before it is printed. To view a document, press Sh-F7, then enter "6." Select option 3 to see the full page. Press F7 to return to your document.

W. WORDPERFECT PRACTICE

1. Change line spacing to double, and key the following passage.
2. Use the Speller to identify and correct errors. Then proofread manually for errors not caught by the Speller.
3. Use View Document to see how your document will look when printed.
4. Print the document.
5. Turn on Reveal Codes, and delete the code for double spacing.
6. Reprint the document.

The chef at the Hyatt Regency was asked to serve her special Roquefort dressing, a favorite of Mr. Fittipaldi, a former winner of the Indy 500.

After the luncheon, which ends at 1:30 p.m., we will use the blue Aerostar van to take everyone to Cypress Street Park, where Mr. Fittipaldi will tape the 30-second public-service announcement on AIDS.

The AIDS announcement will air throughout the months of February and March on Stations KLMC-TV and WABC-TV.

FORMATTING

PAPER SIZE

Create New Form: Sh-F8, 2, 7, 2

Name Paper Type: 9, *name,* F7

Change Paper Size: 1, o, *width,* Enter, *height,* Enter

Specify Location: 5, 1 *(Continuous)* or 3 *(Manual Feed),* F7

Select Form: Sh-F8, 2, 7, *highlight form,* 1, F7

WordPerfect 6 users: See Student Guide, p. 76.

Q. WORDPERFECT: PAPER SIZE/TYPE

To format documents on paper (forms) other than 8.5 × 11 inches (the default size), use Paper Size/Type. To create a form for Baronial stationery, follow these steps:

1. At the top of a page, press Sh-F8. Then key 2 (Page), 7 (Paper Size), 2 (Add), 9 (Other).
2. Key the form name, Baronial, and press Enter.
3. Define the paper size. Key 1 and *o* (the letter). Enter the width (5.5″) and press Enter. Enter the height (8.5″) and press Enter.
4. Key 5 (location) and select either 1 for continuous-form paper or 3 for manual-feed paper; then press F7.
5. Key 1 and press F7 to select Baronial stationery, or press F7 twice to return to an 8.5″ × 11″ document.

Repeat steps 1–5 to create a form for Monarch stationery (7.25″ wide by 10.5″ high).

From then on, to format a document on Baronial or Monarch stationery, simply select the form (Sh-F8, 2, 7, *highlight form,* 1, F7).

R. FORMATTING ON BARONIAL OR MONARCH STATIONERY

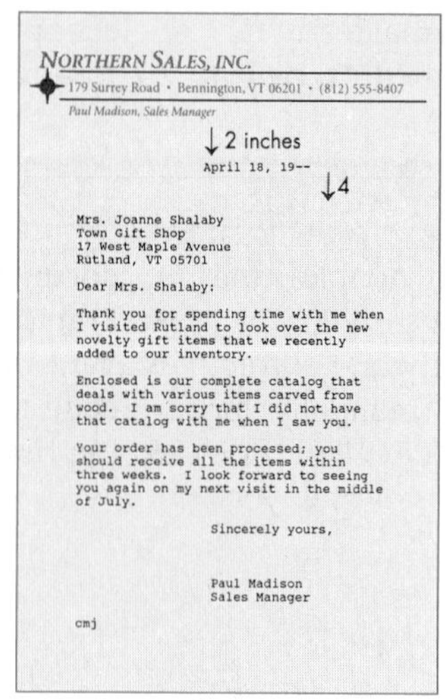

NORTHERN SALES, INC.
179 Surrey Road • Bennington, VT 06201 • (812) 555-8407
Paul Madison, Sales Manager

↓ 2 inches

April 18, 19--

↓ 4

Mrs. Joanne Shalaby
Town Gift Shop
17 West Maple Avenue
Rutland, VT 05701

Dear Mrs. Shalaby:

Thank you for spending time with me when I visited Rutland to look over the new novelty gift items that we recently added to our inventory.

Enclosed is our complete catalog that deals with various items carved from wood. I am sorry that I did not have that catalog with me when I saw you.

Your order has been processed; you should receive all the items within three weeks. I look forward to seeing you again on my next visit in the middle of July.

Sincerely yours,

Paul Madison
Sales Manager

cmj

Baronial stationery (5.5″ × 8.5″) accommodates up to 125 words. Use 0.75-inch side margins. Begin the date 2 inches from the top and the inside address 4 lines below the date.

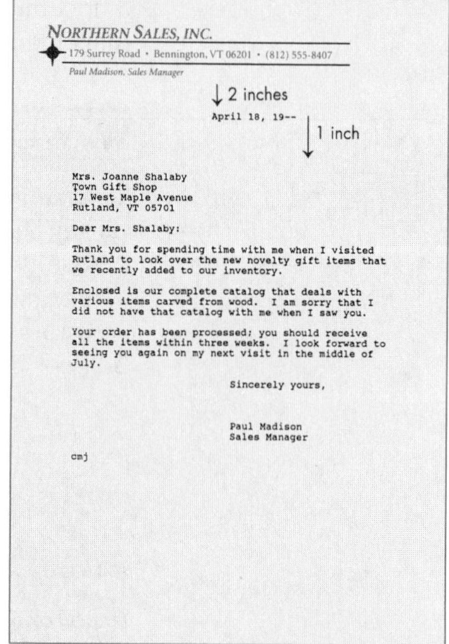

NORTHERN SALES, INC.
179 Surrey Road • Bennington, VT 06201 • (812) 555-8407
Paul Madison, Sales Manager

↓ 2 inches

April 18, 19--

↓ 1 inch

Mrs. Joanne Shalaby
Town Gift Shop
17 West Maple Avenue
Rutland, VT 05701

Dear Mrs. Shalaby:

Thank you for spending time with me when I visited Rutland to look over the new novelty gift items that we recently added to our inventory.

Enclosed is our complete catalog that deals with various items carved from wood. I am sorry that I did not have that catalog with me when I saw you.

Your order has been processed; you should receive all the items within three weeks. I look forward to seeing you again on my next visit in the middle of July.

Sincerely yours,

Paul Madison
Sales Manager

cmj

Monarch stationery (7.25″ × 10.5″) accommodates up to 250 words. Use 1-inch side margins. Begin the date 2 inches from the top and the inside address 1 inch below the date.

DOCUMENT PROCESSING

LETTER 102
BLOCK STYLE WITH OPEN PUNCTUATION ON BARONIAL STATIONERY

(Current Date) / Ms. Anne Olmsted / 562 Congress Street / Portland, ME 04101 / Dear Ms. Olmsted

Thank you for your recent note concerning parking at our theater when there are special events.

(Continued on next page.)

DOCUMENT PROCESSING

LETTER 36*
BLOCK STYLE

Addison & Moore
2701 WILSHIRE BOULEVARD • LOS ANGELES, CA 90057-1076 • 213-555-2200

↓ 2 inches

April 3, 19-- ↓ 1 inch

Ms. Janice Jackson, President
Weston & Weston, Inc.
3667 Highland Avenue
Jersey City, NJ 07304-1034 ↓ 2

Dear Ms. Jackson:

Thank you for your letter of March 28 in which you asked me to address your local Rotary Club. I am happy to accept your invitation to speak on human relations in business.

Human relations development is a very current topic in the business world today. Businesses, more than ever, want to hire employees who can work to better serve customers and the firm. As you know, I have just completed a two-year study of human relations in business. It is interesting to note that the study indicates that more than 95 percent of all businessmen and businesswomen still believe that any employee with this ability is a major asset to the firm.

Enclosed is a copy of my article "Human Relations--Today and Tomorrow." If you feel this article would be of interest to the members of your club, I would be happy to have copies available.

I plan to arrive at the Holiday Inn Center by 11:30 a.m. as you have requested. It will be a pleasure to see you again.

Sincerely yours, ↓ 4

James F. Rainey
Human Relations Consultant ↓ 2

~~urs~~
Enclosure

*Letters 1–35 appear in Lessons 1–60.

Block style: All lines begin at the left margin.

Always respect a woman's preference in selecting *Miss, Mrs.,* or *Ms.* If her preference is unknown, use the title *Ms.*

Standard punctuation consists of a colon after the salutation and a comma after the complimentary closing.

To indicate that an item is enclosed with a letter, key the word *Enclosure* a single space below the reference initials of a business letter.

LETTER 101
MODIFIED-BLOCK STYLE WITH INDENTED PARAGRAPHS, STANDARD PUNCTUATION

Leave 3 blank lines before and after a table with a title in a letter.

October 1
~~September 29~~, 19--

Seneca
Mr. Donald Landes
416 ~~Senoca~~ Street
Settle, WA 98111

Dear Mr. Landis:

Thank you for your letter of September 23 in whihc you inquired about interest rates on a 30 year ~~payment~~ mortgage for a home.

As you ~~asked,~~ requested we ~~did a~~ review ~~of~~ what local banks are asking as interst on a 30-year mortgage. Listed below ~~are the rates.~~

INTEREST RATES ON 30-YEAR MORTGAGES

Banks	Adjustable ~~30-Year~~	Fixed ~~30-Year~~
Banc Two	5 7/8%	8 5/8%
Fịrst National	5 3/8%	8 6/8%
Opympia Savings	5 7/8%	8 6/7%
Washington National	5 5/8%	8 3/8%

There are differences; however you should take into consideration any costs as they vrry by ~~businesses.~~

Sincerely yours,

~~Fidlety Financial Services~~

Sharn Zablotney
Financial Analyst

urs
c: Kurt Jergins

LETTER 37
BLOCK STYLE

Names of published works may be underlined or italicized.

June 3, 19— / Hampton Associates, Inc. / 830 Market Street / San Francisco, CA 94102-1925 / Ladies and Gentlemen:

I recently read an article in *Business Week* concerning how computer buyers can make standards happen. It was a very interesting article.

It indicates that if customers demand standard products when they purchase computers, participate in standard-setting groups, and band together with other customers, they will do better in the long run.

Have you had customer groups assist you or provide you with information on the adoption of more computer standards, such as in the areas of industrywide interfaces, a mix and match of computer gear and programs, and building the best system for each application utilized?

I would appreciate any data that you might furnish for me with relationship to customers and your firm working together to set past or future standards.

Sincerely yours, / Alice Karns / Vice President / *(Your Initials)*

LETTER 38
PERSONAL-BUSINESS LETTER IN BLOCK STYLE

Personal-business letter in block style: All lines begin at the left margin. The return address is keyed under the writer's name. Reference initials are not used.

October 1, 19— / Dr. James L. Rowe / 2345 South Main Street / Bowling Green, OH 43402 / Dear Jim:

Thank you for your letter of September 25 in which you inquired about my trip to New York City.

I plan to leave on October 15 for a two-week business/vacation trip to the city. While at Columbia University, I will be conducting a workshop on the utilization of voice-activated equipment.

My work at Columbia will be completed on October 22, after which I plan to attend a number of plays, visit the Metropolitan Museum of Art, and take one of the sightseeing tours of the city.

If you would care to join me on October 22, please let me know. I would be most happy to make reservations at the hotel for you and to purchase theater tickets. Why don't you consider joining me in the "Big Apple."

Sincerely, / Bryan Goldberg / 320 South Summit Street / Toledo, OH 43604

LETTER 39
PERSONAL-BUSINESS LETTER IN BLOCK STYLE

March 11, 19— / Mr. Sam Lukens / 1367 Lockland Road / Atlanta, GA 30316 / Dear Sam:

Did you receive my letter of March 1? I wrote you concerning my article on word processing.

As you know, I have had some problems in writing the article as a result of my changing software. I was so thoroughly knowledgeable about Apex that when I changed to Mars, I became somewhat confused. I need your help with the descriptions for some of the function keys.

Perhaps you have received my letter, and your answer is in the mail. If not, please call me at 602-555-6241.

Sincerely, / Lillian Smith / 1816 Vernon Avenue / Scottsdale, AZ 85257

MEMO 32

Along with your reference initials, key a file name under which the memo would be stored (for example: ODONNELL.urs).

MEMO TO: Jill O'Donnell, Customer Service

FROM: Glenn Omura, Accounting

DATE: October 1, 19—

RE: Lapsed Maintenance Agreements on Appliances

Notify the following four individuals that their maintenance contracts have lapsed. The termination date of the current contract, amount due for uninterrupted service, and years of service are listed after each individual's name and address.

Mr. Charles E. Parks, 1437 Bannock Avenue, Denver, CO 80202, October 15, 19—, $125, four years.

Mrs. Alice Colson, 200 East 14th Avenue, Denver, CO 80203, October 17, 19—, $95, ten years.

Ms. Brenda Parker, 1730 South Colorado Boulevard, Denver, CO 80222, October 17, 19—, $145, five years.

Miss Kathy Paradise, 480 South Marion Parkway, Denver, CO 80209, October 20, 19—, $98, one year.

Please indicate to these customers that if they renew their contracts now, there will be no interruption in the service we provide. I think that you should indicate how much we value them as customers. This may be just a small courtesy, but I do believe it will enhance public relations for us.

(FILE NAME.Your Initials)

LETTERS 97–100

FORM LETTER IN BLOCK STYLE WITH STANDARD PUNCTUATION

WordPerfect 6 users: See Student Guide, p. 76.

WP MERGE

Create a mailing list (secondary file) using the addresses and data in Memo 32. Use the following fields: (1) Name; (2) Street Address; (3) City, State, and ZIP; (4) Title and Last Name; (5) Date; (6) Amount; and (7) Year(s).

Key the form letter as a primary file. Then, merge the mailing list with the letter.

(Current Date) / *(Field 1)* / *(Field 2)* / *(Field 3)* / Dear *(Field 4):*

The maintenance contract on your Wilcox appliance(s) expired on *(Field 5).* If you are to receive uninterrupted maintenance service and/or repair service, you must sign and return the enclosed contract and *(Field 6)* by November 1.

I am sure that you will want to continue the maintenance service and/or repair service that we have offered you over the past *(Field 7).* Wilcox Appliances, as you know, provides the quickest and most reliable appliance maintenance and repair service in the Denver area.

Enclosed are a contract to continue your maintenance and/or repair service and an addressed envelope in which to return the contract and check. You are one of our most valued customers, and we hope that we will have the opportunity to serve you in the future.

Sincerely yours, / WILCOX APPLIANCES / Jill O'Donnell / Customer Service / *(FILE NAME.Your Initials)* / Enclosures 2

X. WORDPERFECT: TAB SET

 **WP6:** p. 3.

TAB SET
Sh-F8, 1, 8, *tab position,* F7, F7

Clear all tabs: Ctrl-End

Set multiple tabs: *tab position for first tab, comma, amount of space between tabs*

Set tabs in spaces rather than inches: *tab position,* U

Switch to absolute tabs: T, 1

WordPerfect has default tabs set every 0.5 inch (5 spaces). Pressing the tab key moves the cursor 0.5 inch to the right.

To change the tab settings, enter the appropriate commands to access the tab ruler (Sh-F8, 1, 8). To clear the default tabs, position the cursor at the beginning of the line and press Ctrl-End; to clear an individual tab, position the cursor under the tab and press Delete.

To set a left tab (indicated by the letter "L"), enter the position number (e.g., "0.5"). You must enter 0 and a decimal point before any number less than 1. To set a tab in terms of spaces rather than inches, enter "U" (for units) after the number (e.g., "3u" for a tab 3 spaces from the left margin).

To set tabs at regular intervals, enter the position number for the first tab, a comma, and the amount of space between the tabs (e.g., "0, 1.5" for tabs 1.5 inches apart beginning at the left margin).

To set a right tab (for aligning text or numbers at the right), enter the position number, press Enter, then key "R." To set a decimal or "dec" tab (for aligning numbers at the decimal point), enter the position number, press Enter, then key "D."

Relative tabs (tab settings measured from the left margin) is the default setting. To switch to absolute tabs (tab settings measured from the edge of the page), access the tab ruler, enter "T" (Type) then "1" (Absolute).

Y. WORDPERFECT: INDENT

 **WP6:** p. 18.

INDENT
Left indent: F4
Double indent: Sh-F4
Hanging indent: F4, Sh-Tab

Left Indent (F4) is used to indent all lines from the left margin to the next tab setting without having to press Tab for each line. To end Indent, press Enter.

Double Indent (Sh-F4) is used to indent all lines from both the left and right margins the same number of spaces as the next tab setting.

Hanging Indent (F4, Sh-Tab) is used to leave the first line of a paragraph flush with the left margin and to indent all remaining lines to the next tab setting.

Z. WORDPERFECT: FULL JUSTIFICATION

 **WP6:** p. 17.

JUSTIFICATION—FULL
Sh-F8, 1, 3, 4, F7

Full Justification is used to align text at both the left and right margins. The spaces between letters and words are expanded or compressed as necessary to align the text.

To turn on Full Justification, position the cursor where you want Full Justification to begin and enter the appropriate commands (Sh-F8, 1, 3, 4, F7). Full Justification can be turned on or off at any point in a document.

AA. WORDPERFECT PRACTICE

AA. Read the information at the right. Then format the enumerated items as shown.

```
1.  Clear all tabs, and set a left relative tab at 0.4 inch.

2.  Switch to full justification.

3.  Key the passage.  After keying the number and the period,
    press Left Indent (instead of Tab) to align the lines of
    each enumerated item.  Single-space the lines of each
    enumerated item, but double-space between items.

4.  Use the Speller to help proofread the document.  After
    correcting all errors, print the document.
```

Note: Don't forget that in addition to using the Speller, you must always proofread a document manually because the Speller does not check for omitted words or typographical errors that form a new word.

LETTER 96
PERSONAL-BUSINESS LETTER, BLOCK STYLE WITH STANDARD PUNCTUATION

(Current Date)

Ms. Beth Rutter
J. W. Knapps, Inc.
105 West Main Street
South Bend, IN 46601-1360

Dear Ms. Rutter:

Last week I purchased a green pullover sweater at your mall store. The sweater was on sale for $48.50.

The sweater is unraveling in the back. I have worn the sweater only once, underneath a jacket. How do I replace the sweater?

I have the sales slip and all of the tags from the sweater. May I go to your downtown store, or do I have to go to the mall? I am within walking distance of the downtown store.

Please let me know this week so I can replace the sweater. My telephone number is 555-7279.

Sincerely,

John Burns
331 West Wayne Street
South Bend, IN 46601

MEMO 31

Use WordPerfect's Move command to move text in and delete text from the document.

Retrieve Memo 30 and make the following changes:

1. Move the first paragraph and the display paragraph to the end of the memo.
2. Delete all occurrences of the word *hotel* from the table.
3. Replace the last row of the table with: *Cottage, 2 Bedrooms, $290.*
4. In the last sentence of the summer rates paragraph, delete *of one of our competitors* and insert *from Sea and Golf Resorts.*
5. Add a new last paragraph: *May I have your response in two days.*

LETTER 40
MODIFIED-BLOCK STYLE

Modified-block style: The date line, complimentary closing, and writer's identification begin at center. Paragraphs are blocked.

See page R-13 in the Reference Section for proofreaders' marks.

Human Relations Consultants, Inc.
150 STATE STREET, TRENTON, NJ 08608-200348
PHONE 609-555-3339

↓2 inches

May ~~April~~ 3, 19-- ↓1 inch

Mr. Michael Mc Ginty
Starr & Morgan Company
One DuPont Circle
Washington, DC 20036-2133

Dear Mr. McGinty:

It was a pleasure to see you again at our sales conference last week. Your winning ~~our~~ the "Golden Apple" Award for the most sales for the ~~month~~ year was well deserved.

We comend you for obtaining the Westerminster Account. None of our companys sales representatives have ever been able to ~~do~~ accomplish this feate. Just the idean of a new account at over 500,000 is mind-boggling to say the least. How did you do it? Did you:

1. Spend considerable time with the President, Mr. Arch Davis or the Director of Purchasing, Ms. Betsy Matin?

2. CØnduct a series of hands-on workshops for the employees and managers?

3. Develop a special marketing campaign for Westmister it self or use a regular campaign model?

~~Can you~~ Please let me know what your strategies were for this sale. I am sure that our representatives ~~should~~ would profit from your excellent work.

Sincerely yours, ↓4

Robert Miley
President ↓2

urs
c: R. Olson , Director of Sales

Numbered items are treated as separate paragraphs, with the number at the left margin and turnover lines indented 0.4 inch. Use the Indent command (F4) to align turnover lines.

A copy notation (c:) is keyed below the reference initials (or below an enclosure notation if used).

FORMATTING

P. DEEP-LETTERHEAD AND LEFT-WEIGHTED STATIONERY

DEEP LETTERHEAD. When the letterhead is deeper than 2 inches, key the date 0.5 inch below the letterhead.

DISPLAY PARAGRAPHS. Use WordPerfect's double-indent command to indent 0.5 inch from each margin. Double-space before and after.

COMPANY NAME IN CLOSING LINES. Key in all capital letters a double space below the complimentary closing. Leave 3 blank lines between the company name and the writer's name.

LEFT-WEIGHTED STATIONERY. Reset the left margin 0.5 inch to the right of the widest item in the left column of the letterhead.

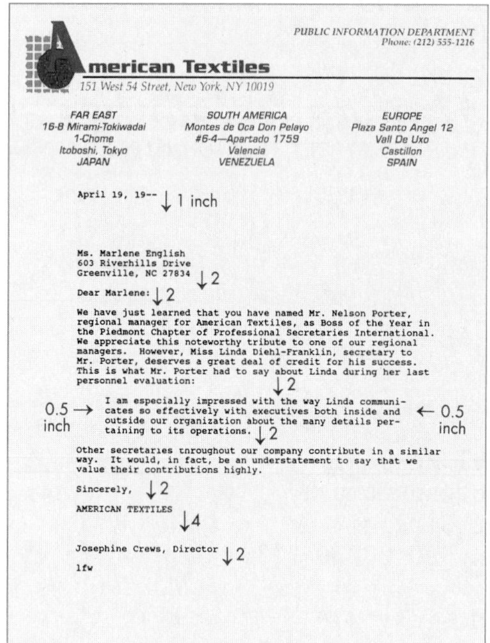

PUBLIC INFORMATION DEPARTMENT
Phone: (212) 555-1216

American Textiles
151 West 54 Street, New York, NY 10019

FAR EAST	SOUTH AMERICA	EUROPE
16-8 Mirami-Tokiwadai	Montes de Oca Don Pelayo	Plaza Santo Angel 12
1-Chome	#6-4—Apartado 1759	Vall De Uxo
Itoboshi, Tokyo	Valencia	Castillon
JAPAN	VENEZUELA	SPAIN

April 19, 19-- ↓ 1 inch

Ms. Marlene English
603 Riverhills Drive
Greenville, NC 27834 ↓ 2

Dear Marlene: ↓ 2

We have just learned that you have named Mr. Nelson Porter, regional manager for American Textiles, as Boss of the Year in the Piedmont Chapter of Professional Secretaries International. We appreciate this noteworthy tribute to one of our regional managers. However, Miss Linda Diehl-Franklin, secretary to Mr. Porter, deserves a great deal of credit for his success. This is what Mr. Porter had to say about Linda during her last personnel evaluation: ↓ 2

0.5 inch → I am especially impressed with the way Linda communicates so effectively with executives both inside and outside our organization about the many details pertaining to its operations. ↓ 2 ← 0.5 inch

Other secretaries throughout our company contribute in a similar way. It would, in fact, be an understatement to say that we value their contributions highly.

Sincerely, ↓ 2

AMERICAN TEXTILES ↓ 4

Josephine Crews, Director ↓ 2

lfw

DEEP-LETTERHEAD STATIONERY. Block-style letter with standard punctuation.

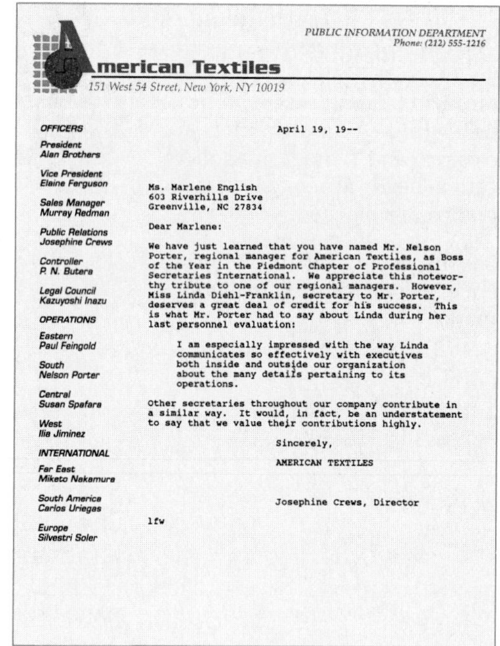

PUBLIC INFORMATION DEPARTMENT
Phone: (212) 555-1216

American Textiles
151 West 54 Street, New York, NY 10019

OFFICERS
President
Alan Brothers
Vice President
Elaine Ferguson
Sales Manager
Murray Redman
Public Relations
Josephine Crews
Controller
P. N. Butera
Legal Council
Kazuyoshi Inazu

OPERATIONS
Eastern
Paul Feingold
South
Nelson Porter
Central
Susan Spafara
West
Ilia Jiminez

INTERNATIONAL
Far East
Miketo Nakamura
South America
Carlos Uriegas
Europe
Silvestri Soler

April 19, 19--

Ms. Marlene English
603 Riverhills Drive
Greenville, NC 27834

Dear Marlene:

We have just learned that you have named Mr. Nelson Porter, regional manager for American Textiles, as Boss of the Year in the Piedmont Chapter of Professional Secretaries International. We appreciate this noteworthy tribute to one of our regional managers. However, Miss Linda Diehl-Franklin, secretary to Mr. Porter, deserves a great deal of credit for his success. This is what Mr. Porter had to say about Linda during her last personnel evaluation:

I am especially impressed with the way Linda communicates so effectively with executives both inside and outside our organization about the many details pertaining to its operations.

Other secretaries throughout our company contribute in a similar way. It would, in fact, be an understatement to say that we value their contributions highly.

Sincerely,

AMERICAN TEXTILES

Josephine Crews, Director

lfw

LEFT-WEIGHTED STATIONERY. Modified-block style letter with open punctuation.

DOCUMENT PROCESSING

LETTER 94
BLOCK STYLE ON DEEP-LETTERHEAD STATIONERY

(Letterhead requires 2.5 inches.)

Italicize or underline titles of published works.

Treat this quotation as a display paragraph.

May 10, 19— / Mrs. Jean Harris / 8216 East Vernon / Scottsdale, AZ 85257 / Dear Mrs. Harris:

Thank you for your recent letter in which you extol the service of our restaurant. The letter was so well written and the statements about our staff were so complimentary that we wondered if we could print a portion of your letter in one of our advertisements. May we use the following in the *Phoenix Magazine*?

> Your service is one of the best I have experienced in the Valley. The staff has to be the best of any restaurant in the United States because of its tender, loving care for every detail.

We in the hospitality industry know that it is only by providing an outstanding environment and outstanding service and food that we can succeed.

You are always welcome at The Oasis. Please let me know the next time you are to be with us, and I personally will greet you.

Sincerely, / THE OASIS RESTAURANT / Adrian Joyaux / President / *(Your Initials)*

LETTER 95
MODIFIED-BLOCK STYLE ON LEFT-WEIGHTED STATIONERY

Revise Letter 94 for left-weighted stationery (printed copy is 1.5 inches wide) in modified-block style with open punctuation. Use *Dear Jean* as the salutation, add *and The National Restaurant Journal* after *Phoenix Magazine*, and delete the company name in the closing lines.

FORMATTING

 **WP6:** p. 5.

BLOCK
Alt-F4 or F12, *highlight text*

BB. WORDPERFECT: BLOCK

Block is used to highlight a section of text, such as a word, phrase, sentence, or paragraph. You can then perform other commands, such as underlining or deleting the block of text.

To define a block, position the cursor under the first character you wish to block and press Alt-F4 or F12. WordPerfect will display "Block On" at the bottom of your screen. Next, move the cursor to the right of the last character you wish to block. The block of text is now highlighted, and you can issue another command, such as pressing F8 to underline.

 **WP6:** p. 11.

BOLD
F6

CC. WORDPERFECT: BOLD

Bold text prints darker than normal text. Use bold to highlight or display text. To bold text, press F6, key the text, then press F6 again (or the right arrow key) to turn off bold. To bold existing text, position the cursor under the first character to appear in bold, block the remaining text to appear in bold, then press F6.

 **WP6:** p. 15.

DATE INSERT
Date Text: Sh-F5, 1
Date Code: Sh-F5, 2

DD. WORDPERFECT: DATE INSERT

If the date on your computer is correct, use Date Insert to insert the date as text into your document. Position the cursor where you want the date to appear and press Sh-F5. Then enter "1" to select Date Text.

If you want to insert the date into your document and also have it change to the most current date each time you retrieve the document, press Sh-F5, then enter "2" to select Date Code.

DOCUMENT PROCESSING

MEMO 11*

*Memos 1–10 appear in Lessons 1–60.

Tab: 1 inch

↓ 2 inches

MEMO TO: Shirley Atwood, Purchasing Manager

FROM: Clinton Jones, Accounting Manager

DATE: *(Current)*

SUBJECT: Purchase of Marx Software↓3

Remember to bold the guide words, double-spacing between each line. Triple-space after the subject line to begin the body, and block the paragraphs.

Please order the Marx Software for use in the Accounting Department. We have tested it and its configuration appears to meet the needs of our staff.

Mable Youngblood and Marvin Knots will attend the three-day orientation program established by the Marx Company. Mable and Marvin were selected because they will be the principal managers of the unit in which the software is to be installed.

It is my understanding that James Clayton, the local representative of Marx, has discussed the price and terms of the sale with you. Is this so?

urs
c: Jason Black, President

MEMO 30*

Read through the entire copy of Memo 30 before beginning to key.

*Memos 1–29 appear in Lessons 1–120.

Review the proofreaders' marks on page R-13 in the Reference Section.

Use WordPerfect's double-indent command to format the second paragraph.

Use WordPerfect's Table feature to format the three-column table. Leave 3 blank lines before and after a table with a title in a letter or memo.

In memorandums, the words *In Re:* and *Re:* may be used in place of the guide word *Subject:*.

Adjust the width of each column so that text in each cell remains on one line.

MEMO TO: Larry Bean, Sales Manager

FROM: Nelson L. Wilson, Vice President

DATE: *(Current Date)*

RE: Brochure Copy

I think that we should use the following ~~attached~~ description on the first page of our boorchure. It really summs up what we have to offer.

> Worldwide Resort if's located just ten ~~nine~~ miles north of beautiful Ocen City, Maryland. With a growing list of accolads, it may soon be the dictionary next to the word best. The MOBIL Travel Guide honors the resot with a five-star ~~four~~ rating. found in

What do you think of these rates for the summer season? Please let me know if you think they should be higher. Attached is a brochure of one of our competitors, listing their summer rates.

NIGHTLY ROOM RATES

April 16, 19--, through October 14, 19--

Resort / Hotel	Suite / Room	Rate
Tower / Hotel	1 Bedroom	$150
Shores	Studio	$190
Seaside	2-Bedroom Suite	$250
Golfside (Upper)	2-Bedroom Suite	$200
Golfside (Lower)	2-Bedroom Suite	$175
Hotel	1 Bedroom	$125

urs
Attachment

MEMO 12

MEMO TO: All Departments

FROM: Allison Baker, Vice President

DATE: Octoebr 14, 19--

SUBJECT: New Vice President

I am happy to ~~tell you~~ announce that Mr. Keith MacPhee was appointed as our new vice president for Finance starting ~~February 20~~ March 1.

Keith, as you know, has had a very successful caeers with us during the past 15 years? He was originall employes as an accountant in the Accounting department where he was instrument in establishing our system wide programs in Accounting.

I am sure that ~~each and all of you~~ everyone will want congratulate ~~him~~ Keith on his ~~program~~ promotion.

urs
c: Personnel

MEMO 13

MEMO TO: Annette O'Brien, Human Resources

FROM: Juan Garcia, Vice President

DATE: (Current)

SUBJECT: Performance Appraisals

I have felt for a long time that we must revise our policies for appraising workers both for retention and for promotion. I must say now that I agree with you that the supervisors need training in this aspect of supervision. Most of them were promoted because they could perform the jobs they supervise and not because of any insight into the principles of supervision.

Will you please outline a course in employee evaluation to present to Mr. Houston for approval. I would prefer either a one-day workshop or two half-day workshops. Please let me have an initial draft by next Friday.

Thanks for your help.

DOCUMENT PROCESSING

LETTER 91*
BLOCK STYLE, STANDARD PUNCTUATION

*Letters 1–90 appear in Lessons 1–120.

September 25, 19— / Mr. Hector Aviles / Purchasing Agent / Logan & Smith, Inc. / 825 Lake Drive / Baltimore, MD 21217-3815 / Dear Mr. Aviles:

Thank you for your recent order for office supplies. We have a question about an item listed on Purchase Order 3478, dated September 18, 19—.

The purchase order listed one numbering machine, Style E, 6 wheels, but Catalog No. R1-NMSP is for a striking pad. Did you want to order a numbering machine or a striking pad? Enclosed is a copy of the page from our Fall 19— catalog on which the items are listed.

Our Style E, 6-wheel numbering machine offers you a choice of four movements: consecutive, duplicate, triplicate, and repeat; however, you may request special additional movements.

Please let us know which item you wish to purchase so that we can make our shipment to you on time.

Sincerely yours, / LAKELAND OFFICE PRODUCTS / Mary Beth Wilkinson / urs / Enclosure / PS: Just call me to let me know the correct item.

LETTER 92
PERSONAL-BUSINESS LETTER MODIFIED-BLOCK STYLE WITH INDENTED PARAGRAPHS, STANDARD PUNCTUATION

(Current Date) / Ms. Louise Santiago / Dart Container Corporation / 1633 South Caron Street / Tulsa, OK 74119-2419 / Dear Ms. Santiago:

My resume is enclosed. Please consider me a candidate for the accounting position that you listed in today's *Tulsa State Journal.*

Since graduating from college, I have been employed for three years as a CPA at Jones, Smith, and Brown Associates. My position includes the auditing of accounts for many local clients.

Currently, I am seeking a salary of $41,000. However, I am willing to negotiate this amount.

I am eager to meet you and to have the opportunity for an interview for the accounting position. You may call me at 352-6578 during working hours or at 352-7821 after 5 p.m.

Sincerely yours, / Bruce Coleman / 1425 South Carson / Tulsa, OK 74105 / Enclosure

LETTER 93
MODIFIED-BLOCK STYLE, OPEN PUNCTUATION

(Current Date) / Mr. Wilbur L. Brown / Story Oldsmobile / 3850 Memorial Drive / Decatur, GA 30032 / Dear Mr. Brown / Subject: United Fund Drive

Are you willing to be the chairperson of the local United Fund Drive?

As we have in the past, we are again looking to leaders such as you to provide the leadership for this important task. Your name was submitted to us as one who is well known throughout the area. Please consider this position as one of the most eminent roles you have been asked to assume.

We hope your answer will be "Yes." Please call me at 675-3200 during working hours or at 689-3454 after 5 p.m. with your answer.

Sincerely yours / Leland Garner / urs / c: United Fund Drive Committee

Margins: 1 inch • Spacing: Single • Drills: 2 times • Format Guide: 43–45

Goals for Unit 14

Begin each day with approximately 15 minutes of skill-building, selecting activities from pages 152–155. In the remaining class time, complete as many production jobs from pages 156–163 as you can.

1. To improve accuracy and speed on alphabet and number keys.
2. To key 41 wam for 5 minutes with no more than 5 errors.
3. To improve proficiency in composing at the keyboard.
4. To gain proficiency in formatting tables.
5. To format and key unbound and bound reports.
6. To format and key endnotes and footnotes.

A. WARMUP

```
1      Customers with bad debts (Zak & Juster, Power & Baxen,  12
2  and Quinn & Haven) had the following amounts due:  $185.90,  24
3  $247.38, and $1,356.  We asked our attorney to take action.  36
   | 1 | 2 | 3 | 4 | 5 | 6 | 7 | 8 | 9 | 10 | 11 | 12
```

LANGUAGE ARTS

B. ABBREVIATIONS

B. Study the rules at the right. Then key lines 4–7, making necessary changes.

Rule: Spell out compass points used as ordinary nouns and adjectives or when included in street names. **Exception:** Abbreviate compass points without periods when they are used *following* a street name.

That lot is two blocks east of North Winnebago Drive.

Rule: Abbreviate units of measure when they occur frequently, as in technical or scientific work, on forms, and in tables. Do not use periods.

The 4- by 6- by 10-ft sizes are the most popular.

```
4 The shipping address is 4500 E. Country Club Road.
5 Ship the order to 3208 36th Street, Northeast, in Biloxi.
6 New quotations are $3.47 a gal and 95 cents a qt.
7 The 9 3/4-in by 2-ft 6-in tablet contains 292.5 sq in.
```

C. COMPOSING

C. Answer each question with a short paragraph.

8 What section do you prefer to read in the newspaper and why?
9 How can good communication skills help you achieve your goals?
10 What are the three most important environmental issues today?
11 What advantages do you see in studying a foreign language?
12 Why are ethics important in business?
13 How can you improve your confidence in speaking before a group?

Why are employers so interested in elder care? Rising 12
interest is the result of the coalescence of several recent 24
trends--most notably, the aging of our people. In the past 36
few decades, life expectancy has risen to very high levels. 48

Another trend is the increased participation of women, 12
the primary caregivers, in the paid work force. This trend 24
is forcing employers to recognize that work and family life 36
are inextricably intertwined and they need to be proactive. 48

| 1 | 2 | 3 | 4 | 5 | 6 | 7 | 8 | 9 | 10 | 11 | 12

N. PACED PRACTICE

Turn to the Paced Practice routine at the back of the book. Take three 2-minute timed writings, starting at the point where you left off the last time.

O. Spacing: Double. Take two 5-minute timed writings. Compute your speed and count errors.

Goal: 50 wam/5′/5e

O. 5-MINUTE TIMED WRITING

It is easy to see why many of us are distracted by 11
noise on the job. Keyboards tapping, telephones ringing, 23
office machines running, air-conditioning vents blowing, 34
and loud voices all may interfere with our concentration. 46
We realize the reason we were hired: to perform certain 57
tasks that help our company function in a more productive 69
manner. Distractions can reduce our ability to perform 80
effectively, but what can we do to quiet things down? 91

The first step is to examine our work environment in 103
order to identify the trouble spots. Equipment noise can 114
sometimes be reduced with proper maintenance or by calling 126
the equipment dealer or manufacturer to see what can be 137
done about loud, irritating, or distracting sounds. The 149
telephone ring can be controlled by adjusting the volume 160
control, usually located on the side or the bottom of the 172
phone. Just be sure not to turn the volume down so low 183
that you miss calls when you are away from your desk. 194

Other distracting noises and voices can be reduced 205
with specially padded room dividers. Although this may 216
become expensive, the consequences of not fixing a noisy 227
office can be worse. Dealing with a hearing loss can be 239
stressful and have a negative impact on job performance. 250

| 1 | 2 | 3 | 4 | 5 | 6 | 7 | 8 | 9 | 10 | 11 | 12

SKILLBUILDING

PRETEST. Take a 1-minute timed writing; compute your speed and count errors.

PRACTICE. *Speed Emphasis:* If you made no more than 1 error on the Pretest, key each line twice.
Accuracy Emphasis: If you made 2 or more errors, key each group of lines (as though it were a paragraph) twice.

POSTTEST. Repeat the Pretest (D) and compare performance.

D. PRETEST: COMMON LETTER COMBINATIONS

The insurance agents began to input the weekly renewal 12
data into the computer. They quickly decided which amounts 24
had to be increased by adding yearly totals to the formula. 36

| 1 | 2 | 3 | 4 | 5 | 6 | 7 | 8 | 9 | 10 | 11 | 12

E. PRACTICE: WORD BEGINNINGS

re- react ready refer relax remit renew repel really reveal
in- incur index infer input inset inert inept inches insert
be- befit began being below beach beams bears beauty beside
de- deals debit debug decay deeds delay denim decent delude

F. PRACTICE: WORD ENDINGS

-ly apply daily early hilly lowly madly truly simply weekly
-ed acted added based cited dated hired sized opened showed
-nt agent count event front giant meant plant amount fluent
-al canal decal equal fatal ideal local usual actual visual

G. POSTTEST: COMMON LETTER COMBINATIONS

H. Take a 1-minute timed writing on the first paragraph to establish your base speed. Then take four 1-minute timed writings on the remaining paragraphs. As soon as you equal or exceed your base speed on one paragraph, advance to the next one.

H. SUSTAINED PRACTICE: ROUGH DRAFT

The interest in our global economy is growing by leaps 12
and bounds. Many of our politicians and leaders realize it 24
is essential that we keep abreast of all that is happening. 36
Economists are very busy studying this growing development. 48
For example, the rapid movement to a com m on market for 12
the twelve european countries must be watched closely. The 24
import and export markets from this union will be critical. 36
The consumer market from this union will surpass our own. 48
When reveiwing all the change s taking place in Eastern 12
Europe, there is also the realization that a ~~national~~ global economy 24
is pending. Again, this can change many things in the ~~U.S.A.~~ United States. 36
The interest in free market trade in this area is exciting. 48
One of the major reason s behind all these developements 12
is the ~~fast~~ rapid growth of technology. It is now very easy for 24
busineses s to share in formation and data across many miles. 36
Conducting busness with distant clients has become common. 48

| 1 | 2 | 3 | 4 | 5 | 6 | 7 | 8 | 9 | 10 | 11 | 12

H. Key each sentence on a separate line.

H. TECHNIQUE PRACTICE: ENTER KEY

47 Debit the account. Balance the checkbook. Add the assets.
48 Take the discount. Send the statement. Compute the ratio.
49 Review the accounts receivable. Calculate the inventories.
50 Prepare the statement. Send the catalog. Call the client.

PRETEST. Take a 1-minute timed writing; compute your speed and count errors.

I. PRETEST: NUMBER AND SYMBOL KEYBOARD REVIEW

51 The company paid $400 (25% of the total) for those #73 12
52 tiles. Gant & Nease and/or Dixon & Stahl won't sell 16,819 24
53 leftover "duds." A Dorfe-Morre share is $27 (58% more than 36
54 one year ago). The firm's owner/manager sold 39 #46 lamps. 48

| 1 | 2 | 3 | 4 | 5 | 6 | 7 | 8 | 9 | 10 | 11 | 12

PRACTICE.
Speed Emphasis: If you made no errors on the Pretest, key each line twice.
Accuracy Emphasis: If you made 1 or more errors on the Pretest, key each group of lines (as though it were a paragraph) twice.

J. PRACTICE: NUMBERS

55 0 ;p0 000 0 pins 00 pets 00 pals 00 parts 00 pails 00 plans
56 1 aq1 111 1 aunt 11 ants 11 apes 11 quips 11 zeros 11 zones
57 2 sw2 222 2 sets 22 sips 22 suns 22 suits 22 walls 22 watts
58 3 de3 333 3 dots 33 dams 33 eggs 33 elves 33 carts 33 colts
59 4 fr4 444 4 fads 44 figs 44 rims 44 roads 44 vases 44 volts

60 5 fr5 555 5 fins 55 fans 55 rats 55 rules 55 vines 55 vests
61 6 jy6 666 6 jabs 66 jugs 66 yaks 66 yards 66 masts 66 nests
62 7 ju7 777 7 jars 77 jets 77 ukes 77 units 77 males 77 notes
63 8 ki8 888 8 kegs 88 kits 88 imps 88 ideas 88 kilts 88 knots
64 9 lo9 999 9 lads 99 lids 99 oars 99 ovens 99 lumps 99 lists

K. PRACTICE: SYMBOLS

65 % f5% 28% 37% 49% 10% 65% 73% 91% 38% 47% 23% 119% and 150%
66 $ f4$ $27 $89 $71 $70 $206 $382 $5,623 $6,912 and $2,582.39
67 # d3# #45 #70 #46 #50 #54 #160 and 14# 74# 80# 51# and 475#
68 & j7& 39 & 34 & 481 & 104 & Harris & Parks, Garcia & Miller
69 () 19(;0) (fruit) (3%) (soldiers) (638) ($579) and (women)

POSTTEST. Repeat the Pretest (I) and compare performance.

L. POSTTEST: NUMBER AND SYMBOL KEYBOARD REVIEW

M. Take a 1-minute timed writing on the first paragraph to establish your base speed. Then take four 1-minute timed writings on the remaining paragraphs. As soon as you equal or exceed your base speed on one paragraph, advance to the next one.

M. SUSTAINED PRACTICE: SYLLABIC INTENSITY

70 Taking care of older people is not a new trend. It is 12
71 an issue that has long been dealt with by spouses and adult 24
72 children. What has changed, though, is that there are many 36
73 companies that help their employees with elder care issues. 48

74 Help may come in many ways, ranging from financial aid 12
75 in the form of special accounts to programs held at the job 24
76 site. Some places are even providing direct help to elders 36
77 by building or sponsoring day care or in-home respite care. 48

| 1 | 2 | 3 | 4 | 5 | 6 | 7 | 8 | 9 | 10 | 11 | 12

(Continued on next page)

I. Tab: Center.
The opening lines of a letter require the quick operation of the Enter key. Key these opening lines 3 times as quickly as possible.

I. TECHNIQUE PRACTICE: LETTER OPENING

↓ 2 inches
→TAB *(Current Date)*↓ 1 inch

Mr. Roger Allgor
Personnel Manager
Farview Travel Services
51 East Longview Boulevard
Wichita, KS 67202↓2

Dear Mr. Allgor:

J. Tab: Center.
The closing lines of a letter require the quick operation of the Enter and tab keys. Key these closing lines 3 times as quickly as possible.

J. TECHNIQUE PRACTICE: LETTER CLOSING

→TAB Sincerely yours,↓4

→TAB Melanie B. Kaplan
→TAB Director of Sales↓2

urs
Enclosure

K. Take two 1-minute timed writings on each line. Try not to slow down for the capital letters.

K. TECHNIQUE PRACTICE: SHIFT KEY

41 Sue and Alan took Marsha to the Washington Monument in May. 12
42 On Al's trip to Nova Scotia, he stopped in Portland, Maine. 12
43 Cedar Rapids and Des Moines are the largest cities in Iowa. 12
44 Marie moved to 16 North Hollywood Boulevard in Los Angeles. 12

| 1 | 2 | 3 | 4 | 5 | 6 | 7 | 8 | 9 | 10 | 11 | 12

L. Key this paragraph once, concentrating on each letter keyed. Then take three 1-minute timed writings, trying to increase your speed each time.

L. TECHNIQUE PRACTICE: CONCENTRATION

45 El uso de la bicicleta es muy popular en Barranquilla. 12
46 Cuando el tiempo es bueno a toda la gente joven le gusta ir 24
47 a pasear en bicicletas. Me gusta ir a montar en bicicleta. 36

| 1 | 2 | 3 | 4 | 5 | 6 | 7 | 8 | 9 | 10 | 11 | 12

M. Take a 1-minute timed writing on the first paragraph to establish your base speed. Then take four 1-minute timed writings on the remaining paragraphs. As soon as you equal or exceed your base speed on one paragraph, advance to the next one.

M. SUSTAINED PRACTICE: CAPITALIZATION

48 Many people like to plan summer trips by auto in order 12
49 that they will see many sites. We all like discussing many 24
50 things we have seen or special places that we have visited. 36

51 If you know anyone who has driven to Florida, you will 12
52 most likely hear about the time spent at Walt Disney World. 24
53 This is one of the top tourist attractions in this country. 36

54 Anyone who has spent some time in Virginia would share 12
55 some comments about a trip to Virginia Beach, Williamsburg, 24
56 or Busch Gardens. Memories of Richmond may also be shared. 36

57 A trip to Boston will be fondly remembered. Following 12
58 the Freedom Trail is exciting. Seeing the Old North Church 24
59 and the Bunker Hill Monument can make history come to life. 36

| 1 | 2 | 3 | 4 | 5 | 6 | 7 | 8 | 9 | 10 | 11 | 12

SKILLBUILDING

D. 12-SECOND SPRINTS

D. Take three 12-second timed writings on each line. The scale gives wam for a 12-second timed writing.

13 Because he was very lazy, Jack paid for six games and quit.
14 David quickly put the frozen jars away in small gray boxes.
15 Two sax players in the jazz band gave a quick demo for Tom.
16 Max quickly amazed Joan Bishop with five magic card tricks.

| | | | 5 | | | | 10 | | | | 15 | | | | 20 | | | | 25 | | | | 30 | | | | 35 | | | | 40 | | | | 45 | | | | 50 | | | | 55 | | | | 60

E. PRETEST: ALPHABET KEYBOARD REVIEW

PRETEST. Take a 1-minute timed writing; compute your speed and count errors.

17 As quickly as Liz raked the leaves, the wind blew them 12
18 back on the lawn. She fantasized about a giant vacuum that 24
19 just quietly plucks up extra junk and fills bags and boxes. 36
20 She was hoping to clean the whole yard by the late morning. 48

| 1 | 2 | 3 | 4 | 5 | 6 | 7 | 8 | 9 | 10 | 11 | 12

F. PRACTICE: ALPHABET KEYS

PRACTICE.

Speed Emphasis: If you made no errors on the Pretest, key each line twice.

Accuracy Emphasis: If you made 1 or more errors on the Pretest, key each group of lines (as though it were a paragraph) twice.

21 A Amy Alex anew save cake alack badge afraid fearful Alaska
22 B Bea Bill bird abet base brake about aboard cobbler Brazil
23 C Cal Carl city acid crow click acute accrue lacking Canada
24 D Dot Dale dice edge daze drape adorn padded bedtime Denver

25 E Eve Emma be eve ease greed enrage excerpt eclipse England
26 F Fae Ford if fry fame hefty fluffy fearful fanfare Florida
27 G Guy Greg go gag gang rigid groggy lodging garbage Georgia
28 H Hal Hank oh hot hush bunch hither hatchet haughty Houston

29 I Ike Ivan ire lie into inset niacin lithium implied Ithaca
30 J Joe Jodi jam jab jury joker jacket perjury enjoyed Jasper
31 K Kim Kurt keg ark kilt knock kicked bracket package Kansas
32 L Lee Lois lay ale lack allot lively gallery fulfill London

33 M May Marty mine mimic hammer emblem member summary Montana
34 N Ned Nancy noun ninth banner animal notion enliven Norfolk
35 O Ola Oscar onto spoon potion noodle option opinion Oakland
36 P Pam Paula pulp primp appeal proper pauper peppery Prussia

37 Q Quent quip aqua quote equip quill conquer tranquil Quincy
38 R Ralph rest tray arrow razor rural rustler occurred Rwanda
39 S Sandy sues sash asset spots issue success scissors Sweden
40 T Trent tint that tempt start otter emotion attitude Toledo

41 U Ursula ugly pouch nurse uncut trust unique bureau Uruguay
42 V Violet vast cover serve valve avert lively voting Venezia
43 W Warren ward owner threw await swarm coward window Wyoming
44 X Xerxes axle oxide maxim excel vixen flaxen excite Xanthus

45 Y Yancy yak dye yelp yoga pray yummy trying skyway Yokosuka
46 Z Ziska zip zoo zero daze lazy ozone buzzer snazzy Zanzibar

G. POSTTEST: ALPHABET KEYBOARD REVIEW

POSTTEST. Repeat the Pretest (E) and compare performance.

N. Take two 1-minute timed writings on each line as you concentrate on infrequently used letters.

N. ALPHABET REVIEW: INFREQUENT-LETTER PRACTICE

Y You and your young friend may buy a yellow yacht in a year. 12
Z I was amazed at the size of a dozen lazy zebras at the zoo. 12
Q She quickly qualified for equal quarterly quotas of quills. 12
X Lex expects those extra deluxe taxis in exactly six months. 12

| 1 | 2 | 3 | 4 | 5 | 6 | 7 | 8 | 9 | 10 | 11 | 12

O. Take three 12-second timed writings on each line. The scale gives your wam speed for a 12-second timed writing.

O. 12-SECOND SPRINTS

A queen received prized onyx and ruby jewels from the king.
V. Peh felt lazy and quit working on the jumbled tax forms.
Sixty equals only five dozen, but we promised Jackie eight.
Bill Gavin was quite amazed about the extra copy for jokes.

| | | | 5 | | | |10 | | | |15 | | | |20 | | | |25 | | | |30 | | | |35 | | | |40 | | | |45 | | | |50 | | | |55 | | | |60

P. Spacing: Double.
Take two 5-minute timed writings. Compute your speed and count errors.

Goal: 41 wam/5′/5e

P. 5-MINUTE TIMED WRITING

Human resource experts all over the country face tough 12
challenges in today's market. They are trying to match the 24
best people to the vacancies to be filled. How can job 35
seekers increase their chances of landing the job that they 47
want? One of the key traits an interviewer looks for is 59
enthusiasm. What do you think are some of the ways that a 70
person can show an upbeat attitude? 78

One way is to take a close look at your resume and 89
cover letter. When writing to a firm, it is helpful to 100
use strong action verbs. Tell how well organized you are 112
or what you have accomplished. This can make you appear 123
dynamic and might help to bring your resume to the top of 135
the stack. 137

A second idea is to take the time to practice your 148
communication skills. An applicant who quietly mumbles 159
his or her name when meeting someone new is not making a 171
good first impression. A firm handshake, good eye contact, 183
and a melodic pitch to the voice will all help give off the 195
aura of a happy, vibrant person who can do the job. 205

| 1 | 2 | 3 | 4 | 5 | 6 | 7 | 8 | 9 | 10 | 11 | 12

UNIT TWENTY-FIVE • CORRESPONDENCE REVIEW

LESSONS 121-125

Margins: 1 inch • Spacing: Single • Drills: 2 times • Format Guide: 105–111

Goals for Unit 25

1. To improve accuracy and speed on alphabet and number keys.
2. To key 50 wam for 5 minutes with no more than 5 errors.
3. To develop proficiency in spelling commonly misspelled words.
4. To format letters with a variety of features—postscripts, subject lines, copy notations, indented paragraphs, blind copy notations, military date, foreign address, and deep letterheads.
5. To use Merge and Paper Size/Type in WordPerfect to format letters and memos.
6. To format memorandums with a variety of features—three-column tables, attachments, extensive revisions, and merged information.

Begin each day with approximately 15 minutes of skillbuilding, selecting activities from pages 295–298. In the remaining class time, complete as many production jobs from pages 299–307 as you can.

A. WARMUP

```
1      Buz was quite pleased with his travel plans.  The trip  12
2 to Mexico City was on Flight #634 on May 21.  The return is  24
3 set for June 5 on Flight #178.  The plane ticket cost $790.  36
  | 1 | 2 | 3 | 4 | 5 | 6 | 7 | 8 | 9 | 10 | 11 | 12
```

LANGUAGE ARTS

B. COMMAS

Study the rules at the right. Then key lines 4–7, making necessary changes.

Rule: When a dependent clause *precedes* the independent clause, separate the clauses with a comma.

If the quota is reached, a sizable bonus will be paid.

Rule: Use commas to set off a nonessential expression (that is, a word, phrase, or clause that may be omitted without changing the basic meaning of the sentence).

Our new goals, you must admit, are quite reasonable.

```
4 As you know, if it rains the art show will be held indoors.
5 When the shipment arrives Susan will prepare the display.
6 Our group wants Cory, the current senator, to be a candidate.
7 Michelle who was recently promoted puts in very long days.
```

C. SPELLING

C. These words are among the 500 most frequently misspelled words in business correspondence.

```
8 committees indicates edition meeting major attached clients
9 capital sewer consumer amounts clients specified loan point
10 generally survey juvenile suggestions laboratory throughout
11 achieve average consider competitive guarantee institutions
12 compensation excess utilization congratulations significant
```

FORMATTING

WP **WP6:** p. 7.

CENTER—HORIZONTAL
Sh-F6

JUSTIFICATION—CENTER
Sh-F8, 1, 3, 2, F7

Q. WORDPERFECT: HORIZONTAL CENTERING

Horizontally centered text has equal spaces to the left and right of it.

To center a single line of text, position the cursor at the left margin, press Sh-F6, key the line, then press Enter. To center several lines of text, position the cursor at the left margin, turn on Center Justification (Sh-F8, 1, 3, 2, F7), and key the lines. Remember to turn off Center Justification (Sh-F8, 1, 3, 1, F7) when you finish.

To center an existing line of text, position the cursor at the beginning of the line, press Sh-F6, then press the down arrow key. To center several lines of existing text, block the text to be centered, press Sh-F6, then answer "yes" to the screen prompt *[Just: Center]?*.

WP6: p. 9.

CENTER PAGE
Sh-F8, 2, 1, Y, F7

R. WORDPERFECT: VERTICAL CENTERING

The concept of vertical centering is similar to horizontal centering. Text that is vertically centered has equal space above and below it. Documents should appear to be framed on all sides of the page with equal side margins and equal top and bottom margins.

To center text vertically (between the top and bottom margins) on a page, position the cursor at the top left of the page; then enter the appropriate commands (Sh-F8, 2, 1, Y, F7). Although text will not appear centered on the screen, it will be vertically centered when you print.

WP6: p. 6.

UNDERLINING
F8

S. WORDPERFECT: UNDERLINING

To underline text as you key it, turn on Underlining by pressing F8. Then, key the text and press F8 again (or the right arrow key) to turn off Underlining. To underline existing text, block the text to be underlined, then press F8.

DOCUMENT PROCESSING

TABLE 19*

*Tables 1–18 appear in Lessons 1–60.

Spacing: Double

Center the table horizontally and vertically.

Review:

1. The key line consists of the longest item in each column plus 6 spaces between the columns.
2. Column headings for this table are blocked at the left.
3. For additional review of tabulation, see page R-12 in the Reference Section.

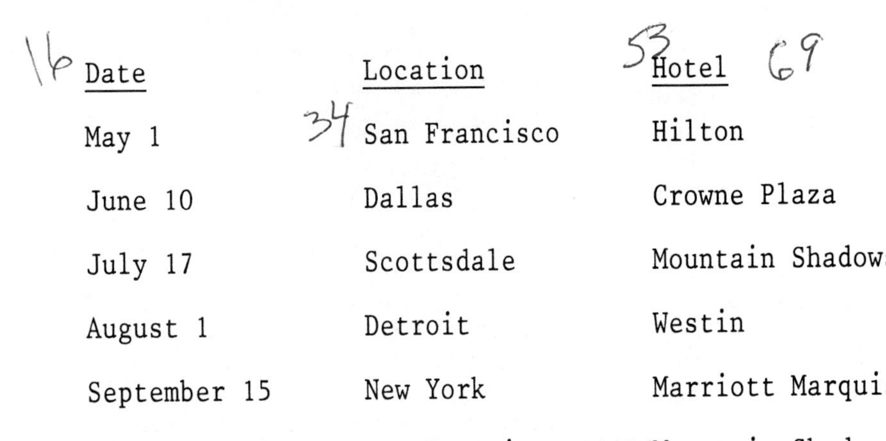

SOFTWARE DEMONSTRATION LOCATIONS ↓2

Demonstrations Start at 10:30 a.m. ↓3

Date	Location	Hotel
May 1	San Francisco	Hilton
June 10	Dallas	Crowne Plaza
July 17	Scottsdale	Mountain Shadows
August 1	Detroit	Westin
September 15	New York	Marriott Marquis

Key Line: September 15123456San Francisco123456Mountain Shadows

PART 7

SKILLBUILDING

Correspondence, Report, and Table Review
Integrated Office Project: International Marketing

OBJECTIVES

KEYBOARDING

To key 53 wam on a 5-minute timed writing with no more than 5 errors.

LANGUAGE ARTS

To improve language arts skills, including the correct use of punctuation marks, capitalization, numbers, abbreviations, grammar, and spelling.

WORD PROCESSING

To use previously learned WordPerfect commands to format various document processing assignments.

DOCUMENT PROCESSING

To review the formatting of business and personal correspondence, reports, and tables.

To format a multipage business report.

To apply high-level formatting skills while completing an integrated office project in international marketing.

Stock Boston/Joe Sohm

TABLE 20

Spacing: Double

Center the table vertically and horizontally.

Set a right tab for number columns and their column headings and a left tab for word columns and their column headings.

AIR MILEAGE

Selected Cities

Origination	Destination	Miles	Airline
Los Angeles	Las Vegas	234	Northwest
Chicago	New York	733	United
Detroit	Cincinnati	229	Delta
Cleveland	Houston	1,091	Continental
Dallas	San Francisco	1,465	American

TABLE 21

Spacing: Double

Center the table vertically and horizontally.

Set a left tab for Column 1 and right tabs for Columns 2 and 3.

Review:

1. The underline is the full column width.
2. "TOTAL" is keyed at the first tab.
3. The $ sign in the bottom line must align with the $ sign above it.

THIRD

~~FOUR~~-QUARTER SALSE] Center

Ending September 31, 19-- (0)

MONTH		Sales Quota	Actual Sales
July		$ 335,400 (5)	$ 350,610 (1)
August	Leave 6 Spaces	370,760 (5)	246,230 (3)
Stepember		386,824 (7)	425,110
TOTAL		$1,094,154 (07)	$1,121951

TABLE 22

Spacing: Double

Center the table vertically and horizontally.

Set right tabs for Columns 2, 3, and 4.

LONGACRE PUBLISHING COMPANY

Staff, Texts Sold, and Sales Volume, 19--

Division	Staff	Texts	Sales Volume
Adult	54	20	$ 1,250,300
Elementary	110	75	5,369,765
Secondary	106	62	4,125,377
College	101	73	5,671,356
TOTAL	371	230	$16,416,798

TEST 6-D
REPORT 70

TWO-PAGE UNBOUND REPORT WITH ENDNOTES

Spacing: Double

End page 1 at an appropriate point.

CRITERIA TO USE IN DETERMINING OFFICE SALARIES

By Kathy McCormack

As the need for office workers increased over the past two decades, the need to determine appropriate office salaries was evident. There are three criteria that companies consider when establishing the salaries for their office workers. Each of the three criteria will now be discussed.

Company Philosophy Toward Office Salaries

Companies, influenced by the quality of workers they hope to attract and retain, may adopt a policy of paying office salaries that are the same as, more than, or less than the average salaries paid by surrounding firms. Some managers consider the theories of behaviorists like Maslow and Herzberg in setting office salaries.[1] Of course, a basic factor to consider in setting salaries for office workers is that the salaries cannot exceed the ability of the firm to pay and still earn a profit.

Expectations of Office Employees

Like other employees at every level in an organization, office workers bring to their jobs their own expectations. Salary is one such area. These employees consider the supply of and demand for office workers. They evaluate the amount of education and training that is necessary for them to perform their jobs satisfactorily.

Office Salaries Paid by Other Companies

The local going rates for office salaries are extremely strong determinants and guides in establishing office salaries. Information from salary surveys that have been conducted on a local, regional, or national level can be useful. For example, the AMS publishes the results of a salary survey once a year.[2] It is important that a business firm have someone in the personnel department who is given major responsibility for keeping abreast of changing salary rates for office workers.

NOTES

1. John F. DeVries, *Office Administration,* Crane Publishing Company, Chicago, 1988, p. 87.

2. Patricia B. Wilcox, "Office Salaries," *Management World,* September/October 1988, p. 34.

TABLE 23

Spacing: Single

A $700 LOAN COMPOUNDED ANNUALLY
FOR SEVEN YEARS AT 7 PERCENT

Yr	Interest	Value
1	$00.00	$ 700.00
2	49.00	749.00
3	52.43	801.43
4	56.10	857.53
5	60.03	917.56
6	64.23	981.79
7	68.72	1,050.51
8	78.68	1,129.19

FORMATTING

T. WORDPERFECT: DOT LEADERS AND FLUSH RIGHT

WP **WP6:** p. 29.

DOT LEADERS
Set tab, period
OR: Alt-F6, Alt-F6
FLUSH RIGHT
Alt-F6

Dot leaders (rows of periods) help guide the reader's eye from one column to the next. To insert a dot leader, access the tab ruler (Sh-F8, 1, 8). Next, enter the tab setting and then a period. For example, to insert a dot leader at the right margin for a table of contents, at the tab menu you would key "6.5, R, *period*." When you tab to that point, a row of dots will appear between the previous text and the tab setting.

Another method for inserting dot leaders is to press Flush Right (Alt-F6) twice. Pressing Flush Right once positions the cursor at the right margin; pressing it again inserts the dot leaders.

DOCUMENT PROCESSING

TABLE 24

Spacing: Single

Use default margins.

PURCHASING MANAGERS ASSOCIATION

Executive Board

President . . . . Mark Mabrita
Dell Corporation

Vice President . . . . Chris Weston
Collingswood & Sanders

Recording Secretary . . . . Inge Klopping
Central Wholesale Pharmaceuticals, Inc.

Corresponding Secretary . . . . Paul Lunt
Westhampton Office Supplies

Treasurer . . . . Ethel Jones-Tyler
Dunn Metallic Industries

Historian . . . . Dorothy J. Windsor
Dell Corporation

Newsletter Editor . . . . William H. Hart
L & M Transfer Company

TEST 6-C
LETTER 90
MODIFIED-BLOCK STYLE
WITH INDENTED
PARAGRAPHS

Current Date / Mr. Donald Hart, President / Welco Aluminum / 178 Washington Street / Henderson, NC 27536 / Dear Mr. Hart:

Thank you for your recent inquiry concerning the benefits package that we provide for business firms like yours. We have just recently begun working with some organizations in the Henderson area. I am glad to hear that you received a favorable reference about us from Thomas Glass in Oxford.

The enclosed brochure will give you a broad overview of the benefits that we could provide for your employees. You can get more information in one of the following ways:

1. Call us at 1-800-555-1840 to ask one of our representatives to visit you at your site.

2. Attend an open house that we are holding at the Stonehedge Inn in Raleigh on Friday, May 15, from 1 to 4 p.m.

3. If you will be attending a trade show or conference in the near future, let us know where and when it will be held. We will have one of our agents meet you there.

Thank you again for your interest in the benefits package that Liberty can provide for you. I will look forward to meeting you at some future time.

Sincerely yours, / Martha Browning / Industrial Account Agent / urs / Enclosure

REPORT 30*
UNBOUND REPORT

*Reports 1–29 appear in Lessons 1–60.

Spacing: Double

The heading of a report is keyed in uppercase and bold. The byline is keyed a double space below the heading in normal type and followed by a triple space. The body is double-spaced.

Side headings and paragraph headings are keyed in upper- and lowercase and bold. Double-space before and after side headings.

See pages R-6 and R-7 in the Reference Section for formatting an unbound report.

↓ 2 inches

EMPLOYEE TRAINING PROGRAMS ↓ 2

By *(Your Name)* ↓ 3

change to spacing

There are various training techniques used in business and industry to update employees' skills and/or to ~~assist them in~~ help employees acquir~~ing~~e new skills. Some of the various techniques used in training will be discussed in this report.

3 before

On-the-Job Training and Lectures

change back to 2

On-the-job training and lectures are the ~~three~~ two most frequently used methods of training.

Do not triple

On-the-job Training. On-the-job training permits individuals to train at the workplace, thus saving time and money. This method lets the trainer use the workstation in place of a classroom.

Lectures. Lectures are often used because they are low-cost methods of instruction. Lectures usually are one-way communication techniques with little interaction on the part of the learner. They are often ineffective when used to introduc~~ing~~e employees to new techniques and orient~~ation~~ them to new programs of work.

Conference

In this ~~the conference~~ method ~~of instruction,~~ small groups of employees are taught by a conference director. This method of instruction results in considerable give-and-take between the director and participants.

Progress Test on Part 6

TEST 6-A
5-MINUTE TIMED WRITING

Spacing: Double

Business firms are deeply involved with a lot of 11
different groups in our society. These groups include the 23
workers of the firm, the stockholders, the consumers or the 35
public at large, all the firms that compete with one 45
another, the tax collectors for the city and state and 56
federal governments, and quite a few others, ranging from 68
health bureaus to welfare offices. It's hard to fully 79
realize just how many persons and agencies are affected by 91
each success and failure on the business scene. 100

Those who work for a firm are involved in its welfare 112
for two reasons. First, the effects which they exert will 124
be factors in determining how much success the business 135
does or does not enjoy; and second, if a firm does badly, 147
not only the employees' incomes but also their chances of 158
advancement may be jeopardized. Thus a company has a right 170
to employee loyalty; employees have the right to expect a 182
fair wage, good working conditions, and a future. 192

Each business firm matters to the whole community. It 204
provides jobs for citizens, revenue for the stores and for 216
all kinds of supply vendors, more market value for property 228
and housing, and its fair share of taxes. It is absolutely 240
essential that business succeed in every community. 250

| 1 | 2 | 3 | 4 | 5 | 6 | 7 | 8 | 9 | 10 | 11 | 12

TEST 6-B
FORM 17
MEMO FORM

MEMORANDUM

North States Power Company

TO:

FROM: Louise E. Bates, CEO

DATE: April 17, 19--

SUBJECT:

U. WORDPERFECT: LEFT AND RIGHT MARGINS

 **WP6:** p. 14.

MARGINS—LEFT AND RIGHT
Sh-F8, 1, 7, *new margins,* F7, F7

WordPerfect's default side margins are 1 inch. To change margins, position the cursor where you want the new margins to begin, and enter the appropriate commands. Margins can be changed as often as desired within a document.

V. WORDPERFECT: TOP AND BOTTOM MARGINS

 **WP6:** p. 16.

MARGINS—TOP AND BOTTOM
Sh-F8, 2, 5, *position,* F7, F7

WordPerfect has default top and bottom margins of 1 inch. To leave a larger top margin for just one page, press Enter to space down the correct number of lines.

To change top or bottom margins on every page, position the cursor at the top left margin of the page and enter the appropriate commands.

W. WORDPERFECT: PAGE NUMBERING

 **WP6:** p. 23.

PAGE NUMBERING
Sh-F8, 2, 6, 4, 3, F7

SUPPRESS PAGE NUMBERING
Sh-F8, 2, 8, 4, Y, F7

NEW PAGE NUMBER
Sh-F8, 2, 6, 1, *no.,* F7, F7

To have WordPerfect number each page of a document in the upper right corner of the page, position the cursor at the top of the first page and enter the appropriate commands (Sh-F8, 2, 6, 4, 3, F7). Note that WordPerfect can also insert the page numbers in a variety of other positions.

Usually page 1 is not numbered. To suppress (turn off) page numbering on page 1, position the cursor at the top of page 1, press Sh-F8, then enter "2," "8," "4," and "Y." Press F7 to return to your document.

To begin numbering with a page number other than 1 (for example, the first page in section 2 of a report might be page 10), use New Page Number. Position the cursor at the top of that page, press Sh-F8, then enter "2," "6," "1," and the page number you want to start with (in this case, 10). Then press F7 twice to return to your document.

X. WORDPERFECT: WIDOW/ORPHAN PROTECTION

 **WP6:** p. 24.

WIDOW/ORPHAN PROTECTION
Sh-F8, 1, 9, Y, F7

The last line of a paragraph that appears alone at the top of a page is called a *widow;* the first line of a paragraph that appears alone at the bottom of a page is called an *orphan.* To ensure that at least two lines of a paragraph are at the top or bottom of a page, position the cursor at the start of a document and turn on Widow/Orphan Protection (Sh-F8, 1, 9, Y, F7).

Y. WORDPERFECT: FOOTNOTES

 **WP6:** p. 25.

FOOTNOTES
Create: Ctrl-F7, 1, 1
Edit: Ctrl-F7, 1, 2

Use the Footnote command to create and automatically format and position footnotes within your document. To create a footnote, position the cursor where the footnote number is to appear in the text, and enter the appropriate commands. Press F7 (do *not* press Enter) when you finish. If you delete or add footnotes, the remaining notes will be renumbered. To view the document with the footnotes in place before printing, use View Document.

Z. WORDPERFECT: ITALICS

 **WP6:** p. 20.

ITALICS
Ctrl-F8, 2, 4

To italicize text, enter the appropriate commands and key the text; then repeat the commands (or press the right arrow key) to turn off italics. To italicize existing text, first block the text; then enter the italics commands. Be sure your printer is capable of printing italics before selecting this command.

REPORT 69
FLIER

WordPerfect 6 users: See Student Guide, p. 74.

Follow these steps to format Report 69.

1. Create a figure box with these settings:
   Filename: BALLOONS.WPG
   Caption: Up Up and Away to Greater Savings (delete the figure number)
   Anchor: Paragraph
   Vertical Position: 0″
   Horizontal Position: Margin, Right
   Size: 3.30″ wide × 2.35″ high
   Wrap Text: Yes
2. Advance to Ln = 1.17″; then center and key in all-capital letters and bold: SPECIAL ONE-WEEK. Turn off bold.
3. Center and key these two lines:
   "No Hassle—No Risk"
   End of Summer Sale
4. Press Enter two times and center and key three asterisks (***).
5. Press Enter four times; center and key the company name and address:
   ALLIANCE OFFICE PRODUCTS
   901 N. Harrison
   E. Lansing, MI 48823
6. Press Enter three times and center and key 3 asterisks (***).
7. Press Enter five times; then key in all-capital letters and bold the heading:
   Microcomputer Supplies--
8. Press Enter two times and key the following lines, double-spaced at the first tab position:
   Furniture
   Hardware
   Software
9. Press Enter three times and key in all-capital letters and bold:
   Furniture--
10. Press Enter two times and at the tab stop key:
    Conference and Folding Chairs
11. Press Enter once and create a figure box with these settings:
    Filename: TELPHONE.WPG
    Caption: Call Us for All of Your Office Needs (delete the figure number)
    Anchor: Page
    Vertical Position: 6.33″
    Horizontal Position: Margin, Right
    Size: 3.25″ wide × 2.35″ high
    Wrap Text: Yes
12. Press Enter once and key the next three lines with double-spacing at the tab stop:
    Office Furniture
    Office Seating
    Shelving
13. Press Enter three times and key in all-capital letters and bold:
    Office Equipment--
14. Press Enter two times and key the next four lines, double-spaced:
    File Cabinets
    Office Supplies
    Report Binders
    Shelf Files
15. Press Enter to reach Ln = 9.67″ and center and key:
    Your Honest Office Products Supplier

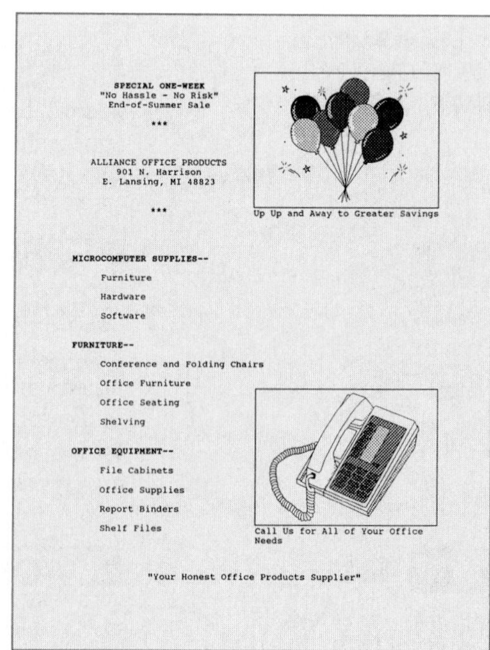

SPECIAL ONE-WEEK
"No Hassle - No Risk"
End-of-Summer Sale

***

ALLIANCE OFFICE PRODUCTS
901 N. Harrison
E. Lansing, MI 48823

***

Up Up and Away to Greater Savings

MICROCOMPUTER SUPPLIES--

Furniture

Hardware

Software

FURNITURE--

Conference and Folding Chairs

Office Furniture

Office Seating

Shelving

OFFICE EQUIPMENT--

File Cabinets

Office Supplies

Report Binders

Shelf Files

Call Us for All of Your Office Needs

"Your Honest Office Products Supplier"

DOCUMENT PROCESSING

REPORT 31
TWO-PAGE UNBOUND REPORT WITH FOOTNOTES

Spacing: Double

Use the appropriate WordPerfect commands to number page 2 in the upper right corner of the page.

Use the WordPerfect Footnote command (Ctrl-F7, 1, 1, *text,* F7) to create, format, and position the footnotes within the document.

The titles of publications may be either underlined (F8, *text,* F8) or formatted in italics (Ctrl-F8, 2, 4, *text,* Ctrl-F8, 3).

LEADERSHIP SKILLS NEEDED IN BUSINESS

By ~~Sally Rodriguez~~ Marsha

Leadership skills are needed now more than ever in business and industry if our nation is to maintain a leading role in the business world of tomorrow. With the advent of a common European community without boundaries, the Japanese influence throughout the world, and the development of a common North American business community, we must have leaders with vision and the appropriate skills for meeting the challenges of the new century.

Each of the skills that a successful leader needs will be discussed in the succeeding pages of this report.

Leadership

Leadership has been defined in a variety of ways. One of many is "the behavior of an individual when he (or she) is directing the activities of a group toward a shared goal."[1]

A successful leader is one who is committed to ideas—ideas for future products and services, for improving the firm's market position, and for the well-being of his or her employees. A leader possesses a value system that is ethically and morally sound. In addition, a leader has a set of beliefs that is a basis for his or her decisions affecting the firm, employees, and society.

Skills That a Leader Needs

A good leader must have the prerequisite skills if he or she is to be effective in business. Quible[2] lists such skills as characteristics. They are "getting others to cooperate, delegating responsibilities, understanding subordinates, and using fairness." However, Quible discusses human relations, teaching, coaching, and communications as special skills a leader should possess. These skills are often acquired on the job with the assistance of other leaders within the firm.

---

[1]Judith R. Gordon, *A Diagnostic Approach to Organizational Behavior,* 2d ed., Allyn and Bacon, Inc., Boston, 1987, p. 393.

[2]Zane K. Quible, *Administrative Office Management: An Introduction,* 4th ed., Prentice-Hall, Englewood Cliffs, N.J., 1988, pp. 212–216.

MEMO 29
(Continued)

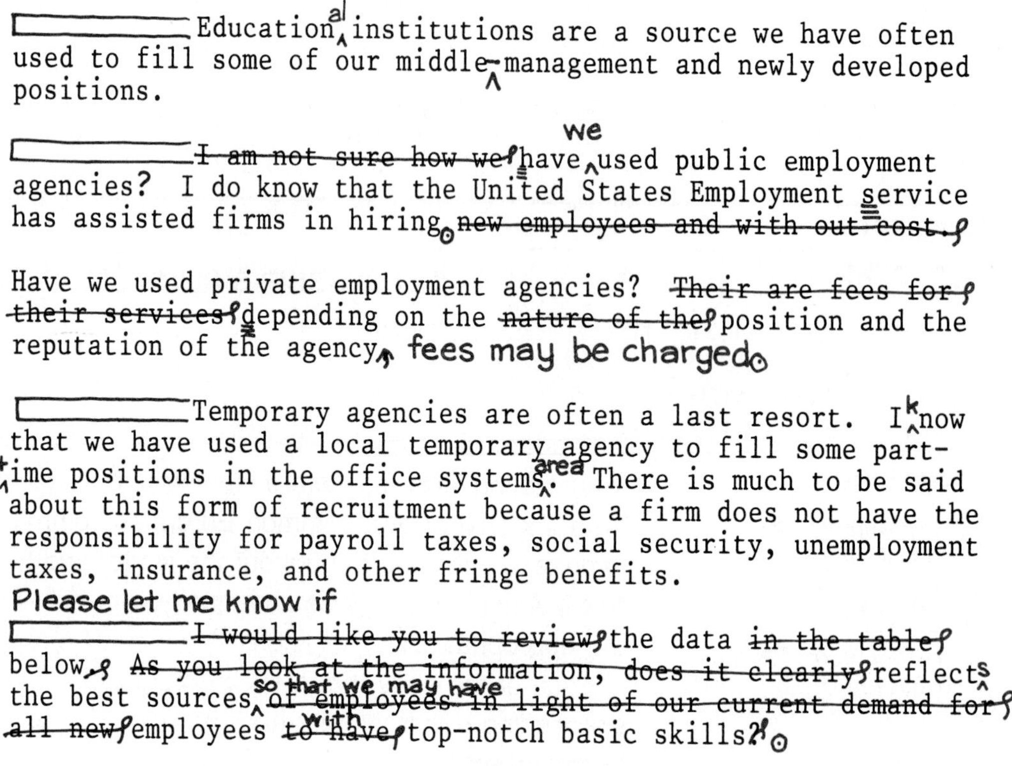

Education[al] institutions are a source we have often used to fill some of our middle-management and newly developed positions.

~~I am not sure how we~~ have [we] used public employment agencies? I do know that the United States Employment service has assisted firms in hiring ~~new employees and with out cost.~~

Have we used private employment agencies? ~~Their are fees for their services~~ depending on the ~~nature of the~~ position and the reputation of the agency, fees may be charged.

Temporary agencies are often a last resort. I [k]now that we have used a local temporary agency to fill some part-time positions in the office systems [area]. There is much to be said about this form of recruitment because a firm does not have the responsibility for payroll taxes, social security, unemployment taxes, insurance, and other fringe benefits.

Please let me know if ~~I would like you to review~~ the data ~~in the table~~ below. ~~As you look at the information, does it clearly~~ reflect[s] the best sources so that we may have ~~of employees in light of our current demand for all new~~ employees ~~to have~~ with top-notch basic skills?

Use the Table feature of WordPerfect to format the table.

SOURCES AND NUMBER OF EMPLOYEES HIRED, 1992-1994

Sources	1992	1993	1994
Advertising	12	11	8
Data Banks	--	--	--
Educational Institutions	3	4	6
Employee Referral	4	5	3
Private Agencies	--	--	--
Promoting from Within	10	12	9
Public Agencies	--	--	--
Temporary Agencies	16	20	21
Unsolicited Applications	8	9	6
TOTAL	53	61	53

FORMATTING

AA. WORDPERFECT: SEARCH AND REPLACE

 **WP6:** p. 21.

SEARCH
F2, *search string,* F2, F2
REPLACE
Alt-F2, *Y/N, search string,*
F2, *replacement string,* F2

Use Search to locate text or codes in a document. Position the cursor where you want the search to begin (usually the start of the document), press F2, and enter what you want to search for (the "search string"). Press F2 to begin the search. The cursor will move to the first occurrence of the search string. To continue searching, press F2 twice.

Use Replace to switch text or codes with other text or codes (for example, replace Smythe with Smith). Position the cursor where you want to begin, and press Alt-F2. Press "Y" to confirm each replacement. Enter what you want to search for, and press F2. Enter its replacement, and press F2. The cursor will move to the first occurrence of the search string. Press "Y" to replace or "N" to skip to the next occurrence. If you said "no" to confirmation, WordPerfect will automatically replace all occurrences of the string.

BB. WORDPERFECT: MOVE (MOVE, COPY, DELETE)

 **WP6:** p. 18.

MOVE (MOVE, COPY, DELETE)
Move: Ctrl-F4, *option,* 1, *position cursor,* Enter
Copy: Ctrl-F4, *option,* 2, *position cursor,* Enter
Delete: Ctrl-F4, *option,* 3

Use Move to highlight text and then move, copy, or delete it. Position the cursor anyplace within the text and press Ctrl-F4. Select 1 (sentence), 2 (paragraph), or 3 (page). Then select 1 (move), 2 (copy), or 3 (delete). If you choose to move or copy, position the cursor where you want the text to be placed and press Enter. If you choose 3 (delete), the text will be automatically deleted.

To move a partial section of text, block the text, then press Ctrl-F4. Select 1 (block), then select either move, copy, or delete. To move or copy, position the cursor where you want the copy to be placed and press Enter.

CC. WORDPERFECT: ENDNOTES

 **WP6:** p. 26.

ENDNOTES
Create: Ctrl-F7, 2, 1
Edit: Ctrl-F7, 2, 2

Endnotes are created much like footnotes. WordPerfect numbers and formats them correctly at the end of your document. To create an endnote, position the cursor where the endnote number is to appear in the text and enter the appropriate commands. To indent the first line of an endnote, press the left arrow key once and the tab key once. Then press the right arrow key once, space twice, and key the endnote. Press F7 (do *not* press Enter) when you finish.

To begin the endnotes on a separate page, insert a hard page break (Ctrl-Enter) at the end of your document. Key the heading for the notes page in bold. If line spacing is set for double, press Enter once; if set for single, press Enter twice.

DOCUMENT PROCESSING

REPORT 32
UNBOUND REPORT
WITH ENDNOTES

When using Search and Replace, change capitalization as needed.

Retrieve Report 30 and make the following changes.

1. Use Search and Replace to replace all occurrences of *Training* with *Training/Development.*
2. Use Move to move the last paragraph including the *Conference* side heading to immediately below the introductory paragraph.
3. Replace the last sentence in the introductory paragraph with *The most popular techniques used will be discussed in this report.*
4. Insert endnote number 1 at the end of the second paragraph and endnote number 2 at the end of the third paragraph (see page 163 for the endnote text). Format the endnotes on a separate page with the heading ***NOTES*** centered on Ln = 2″.

MEMO 29
TWO-PAGE
MEMORANDUM REPORT
WITH TABLE

Format the heading for page 2 of the memo the same as you would for a two-page letter. (See Unit 18, page 208 or page R-5 in the Reference Section.)

MEMO
TO: Lucy White

FROM: Martin Beck, Personnel

DATE: (current)

SUBJECT: Sources of Recruitment

In attending various personnel management meetings, talking ~~association~~ with other ~~personnel~~ managers, and reading~~s~~ various journal articles, I have become aware of how important it is ~~for the future of our firm~~ to have the best-qualified employees in light ~~lieu~~ of the current economy and our desire to be the premier firm ~~leader~~ in our product field. Therefore, I think that we must ~~should~~ review our sources of recruiting.

In the past, we have used internal and external sources for recrutment. Listed below are my thoughts ~~ideas~~ about each of these sources.

Internal

Our employees have for the most part referred excellent individuals to us. The only major problem we have had with employee referral is that once in a while an individual may not succeed, and the individual employee is often embarassed.

Promoting our own employees is a source ~~place~~ that we have utilized. As you know ~~are aware~~, this source ~~we have been able to~~ saves time and money ~~with this source~~ because we have not had the expense of recruiting or lengthy training. Additionally, it ~~Promoting employees from within does~~ boosts morale and loyalty to the firm. A draw back often occurs from our not being able to bring fresh ideas to the firm.

transpose

Some firms are now using data banks. These data banks are computer files on the qualifications of current employees. One can quickly scan a file to see if an employee is qualified for a vacant or new ~~job~~ position.

External

One source we have used in the past is unsolicted applications. This source has provided us with employees who have had outstanding qualifications. If we have not installed a data bank on this source, I think we ~~should~~ must.

We have been very successful in recruiting employees though our advertizing in the local papers, on radio and television, and in trade magazines. This method does result in our obtaining a large number of responses; however, the pool is larger.

(continued on next page)

NOTES

1. Sandra Lattimer, "Spilling the Beans," Academic Journal, June 1994, p. 4.

2. "Stop Talking and Listen," Education Life, October 1995, p. 38.

FORMATTING

DD. WORDPERFECT: FONT SIZE

WP6: p. 29.

FONT SIZE
Ctrl-F8, 1, *size*

Use Font Size to increase the size of type for headings or to decrease the size of type for supplementary information. You can choose from two sizes that are smaller than normal (*small* or *fine*) and three sizes that are larger than normal (*large, very large,* or *extra large*). Position the cursor where you want the different-sized text to begin, enter the appropriate commands, and key the text; press the right arrow to return to normal text. Or, block existing text and enter the appropriate commands.

Because most computer screens cannot display these different font sizes, use View Document (Sh-F7, 6) to see how your document will look when printed.

DOCUMENT PROCESSING

REPORT 33
ANNOUNCEMENT

Spacing: Double

Turn on Center Page and Justification—Center. Key the title in bold, using Extra Large, and key the rest of the announcement using Large. Leave 2 blank lines after the title; then switch to double spacing for the body of the announcement. Press Enter twice before and after "NEW WORK SCHEDULES EXPLAINED." Format the line in bold and italics.

NOTICE

Emergency meeting of Local 437
Office Workers International
Monday, March 13, at 4 p.m.
Canteen Area, Building 5

NEW WORK SCHEDULES EXPLAINED

Come meet your district representatives.
Get your questions answered.

TABLE 55
BOXED TABLE WITH BRACED COLUMN HEADINGS

Before formatting Table 55, review Unit 20 on the Table features of WordPerfect.

Center the column headings.

WordPerfect 6 users: Do not key the dollar sign in the Amount columns.

BARKER-FOWLER ELECTRICAL REPAIR
COMPARISON OF ACTUAL AND PROJECTED OPERATIONS

For the Month Ended October 31, 19--

Category	Actual		Projected	
	Amount	% of Sales	Amount	% of Sales
Sales	$22,845	100.0	$22,900	100.0
Cost of Goods	3,200	14.0	4,800	21.0
Profit	19,645	86.0	18,100	79.0
Expenses	15,438	67.6	15,000	65.5
Net Income	4,207	18.4	3,100	13.5

LETTER 89
PERSONAL-BUSINESS LETTER

Format the letterhead using large font and bold for the name. Use Flush Right to key the telephone number. Format the horizontal line, using the default settings.

Key the letter, leaving the appropriate spacing before (use Advance) and after the date line.

If the return address is provided at the top of the letterhead, it does not need to be repeated in the closing lines.

Set this up as an open table.

Margaret L. Conklin
202 Locust Street
Weston, OH 43569 Telephone: 419-555-4452

September 22, 19--

Mr. Clark Roberts, Sales
The Highsmith Co., Inc.
W5527 Highway 106
P.O. Box 800
Fort Atkinson, WI 53538-0800

Dear Mr. Roberts:

I recently received your fall catalog and would like to order the following:

2	Brown Plastic Files, D41-28288
10	Green 3-Ring Binders, D41-52263
30	One-Step Binder Index Systems, D41-52451
3	Suspension Frames, D41-59838

I am interested in your Sirco Computer Console. Do you have a console in a walnut finish rather than oak? If so, would you please send me a brochure and the price of the console.

Sincerely yours,

If the return address is provided at the top of the letterhead, it does not need to be repeated in the closing lines.

Margaret L. Conklin

LESSONS 71-75

Margins: 1 inch • Spacing: Single • Drills: 2 times • Format Guide: 47–51

Goals for Unit 15

Begin each day with approximately 15 minutes of skillbuilding, selecting activities from pages 164–167. In the remaining class time, complete as many production jobs from pages 168–175 as you can.

1. To improve accuracy and speed on alphabet and number keys.
2. To key 42 wam for 5 minutes with no more than 5 errors.
3. To improve proofreading skills.
4. To gain proficiency in using macros for memos in WordPerfect.
5. To format tables within correspondence.
6. To format correspondence in modified-block style with indented paragraphs.
7. To format subject lines in various types of correspondence.
8. To format and key correspondence from various sources, especially handwritten and rough-draft copy.

A. WARMUP

```
1      Invoice #1874 for $1,862 was for Brad Quigley; Invoice   12
2 #1967 for $864 was for Alexis Jenik; Invoice #2042 for $350   24
3 was for Dominick Zaccaro.  These amounts were all past due.   36
  | 1 | 2 | 3 | 4 | 5 | 6 | 7 | 8 | 9 | 10 | 11 | 12
```

LANGUAGE ARTS

B. SEMICOLON/HYPHEN

B. Study the rules at the right. Then key lines 4–7, making necessary changes.

Rule: Use a semicolon to separate items in a series if any of the items already contain commas.

The cities selected are Boise, ID; Memphis, TN; and Buffalo, NY.

Rule: Hyphenate a compound adjective (two or more words that function as a unit to describe a noun) that comes *before* a noun. **Exception:** If the first word is an adverb ending in *ly,* do not hyphenate.

Mr. Montgomery has made some cost-effective decisions.

```
4 The meetings will be held on Monday, April 5, Monday, April
  12, and Monday, April 19.
5 Other cities considered were Provo, Utah, St. Cloud,
  Minnesota, and Greensboro, North Carolina.
6 A decision was made to purchase three high speed printers.
7 The group was challenged to develop a long range plan.
```

C. PROOFREADING

C. Compare this paragraph with the first paragraph of the 5-minute timed writing on page 167. Key a list of the words that contain errors, correcting the errors as you key.

```
8       Foriegn companies and the folks who manager them are
9  buying slices of American busness and expanding them from
10 coast to coast.  The result is more U.S. workers
11 that will have to live what it is like to have a boss from
12 another part of the country.
```

LETTER 88
(Continued)

Insert an appropriate Page 2 heading.

Leave 3 blank lines before and after a table with a title.

We plan to use various instructional strategies; for example, case studies, small-group descussions and role playying. The best training takes palce when the learenr is directly involved in the process.

Listed below are the session topics, the director(s), special events, and dates for the training program.

APPRAISING AND EVALUATING EMPLOYEES center and bold

Topics	Directors	Special Events	Dates
Appraising Performance	l'Huillier		May 6
Analyzing Jobs	Kopaca	Consultant	May 13
Evaluating Jobs	l'Huillier	Film	May 20
Administering Salaries	Kopaca		May 27
Measuring Output	L'Huillier	Field trip	June 3
Improving Productivity	L'Huillier and Kopaca		June 10

I will be glad to discuss the fees cost of this programs with you. As you know, we have always provided an good excellent program at a minimal cost. Please write or call me at your earliest convenience so that we may develop your program as soon as possible.

Sincerely yours

Wendy Humphries
training director

urs

Key the postscript as the last item in the letter, preceded by 1 blank line.

PS: I will be out of twon next week.

SKILLBUILDING

PRETEST. Take a 1-minute timed writing; compute your speed and count errors.

PRACTICE. *Speed Emphasis:* If you made no more than 1 error on the Pretest, key each line twice.

Accuracy Emphasis: If you made 2 or more errors on the Pretest, key each group of lines (as though it were a paragraph) twice.

POSTTEST. Repeat the Pretest (D) and compare performance.

D. PRETEST: CLOSE REACHES

Old Uncle Evert lived northeast of the swamp, opposite 12
a dirty old shop. Last week we asked him to agree to allow 24
Aunt Gretel to purchase a jeweled sword for her next birth- 36
day. He fooled us all by getting her a new topaz necklace. 48

| 1 | 2 | 3 | 4 | 5 | 6 | 7 | 8 | 9 | 10 | 11 | 12

E. PRACTICE: ADJACENT KEYS

as asked asset based basis class least visas ease fast mass
op opera roped topaz adopt scope troop shops open hope drop
we weary wedge weigh towed jewel fewer dwell wear weed week
rt birth dirty earth heart north alert worth dart port tort

F. PRACTICE: CONSECUTIVE FINGERS

sw swamp swift swoop sweet swear swank swirl swap sway swim
un uncle under undue unfit bunch begun funny unit aunt junk
gr grade grace angry agree group gross gripe grow gram grab
ol older olive solid extol spool fools stole bolt cold cool

G. POSTTEST: CLOSE REACHES

H. Take two 1-minute timed writings on each line as you concentrate on infrequently used letters.

H. ALPHABET REVIEW: INFREQUENT-LETTER PRACTICE

J Jill Jenkins adjusted her jogging jacket and jumped across. 12
K Kaye Kane packed stacks of bricks in the back of the truck. 12
Q Quentin Quamm was quite quiet but quickly requested equity. 12
X Rex Truex got excited as he expertly fixed those six taxis. 12

| 1 | 2 | 3 | 4 | 5 | 6 | 7 | 8 | 9 | 10 | 11 | 12

I. Take a 1-minute timed writing on the first paragraph to establish your base speed. Then take four 1-minute timed writings on the remaining paragraphs. As soon as you equal or exceed your base speed on one paragraph, advance to the next one.

I. SUSTAINED PRACTICE: NUMBERS

A committee was appointed in order to begin making the 12
plans for our annual meeting. It was made up of 12 members 24
from the Hills Region, 10 from Valley, and 8 from Stanhope. 36

The members in charge of exhibits are hoping to invite 12
34 exhibitors to utilize 50 booths in Convention Hall at 87 24
Midway. Last year we had 26 exhibitors at this conference. 36

The members in charge of the luncheon are hoping for a 12
total of 350 persons for lunch at $17.50 each. Last year a 24
ticket cost $16.40 for all those who attended the luncheon. 36

Attendance at last year's meeting was 1,230. The goal 12
for this year is to have 1,410 people. This will enable us 24
to project an increase of 180 people, a 14.63 percent rise. 36

| 1 | 2 | 3 | 4 | 5 | 6 | 7 | 8 | 9 | 10 | 11 | 12

LETTER 88
TWO-PAGE, MODIFIED-BLOCK STYLE LETTER WITH OPEN PUNCTUATION

Spacing: Single

Refer to the Reference Section (page R-5) for formatting a two-page letter.

Read the letter before keying. Refer to the Reference Section (page R-13) for a review of proofreaders' marks.

Change the style to modified block with open punctuation. Do not indent paragraphs.

(Current Date)

Mr. Larry Dwyer
Personnel Department
Erickson and Lee Company
3735 Booth Street
Kansas City, KS 66103-1304

Dear Mr. Dwyer

It has been a pleasure to aid you and your company with the various educational programs you have implemented over the past few years. i hope that we can continue this relationship.

We are announcing a new personnel program for next year. This programs will include two-week sessions on the following personnel areas: appraising performance, analyzing jobs, evaluating work, administering wages, measuring output, and improving productivity. I am sure that you company will want to give this program for your supervisors.

The program will be under the direction of Dr. Alice l'Huillier, professor, Personnel Managemment, Tufts University. Dr. L'Huillier, as you now, is one of the leading authroities in personnel management today. He has conducted many training programs for all of the major firms in the United States and is the writer of many articles and text in the areas of personnel managemetn and management.

Each of the five sessions will be conducted in your firm's corporate headquarters. The program is tailor-made so that sessions can be offered in any sequence you wish; however, we think the order in which we schedule them maybe the best for most firms. Each session will last one and half hours and will be conducted by Dr. L'Huillier and/or her assistant Mr. Timothy Kopaca.

Instructional materials will be provided each student and are covered by the fee charged for the program. As it has in the past, I am sure your firm will provide times for your employees to attend the sessions. We expect each participant to be an integral part of these training sessions.

(continued on next page)

J. NUMBER PRACTICE

J. Take two 1-minute timed writings. The last two digits of each number provide a cumulative word count to help you determine your wam speed.

3301 5502 6603 8804 2205 4406 9907 7708 1109 2110 3111 4112
5613 6714 2015 3816 9117 9018 3719 5220 1921 7922 5923 2024
8225 6026 4127 8728 4229 7930 2131 6432 5833 2834 3035 9736
1437 3638 1239 8240 5441 9142 3443 7844 6845 4046 9547 8248

K. 12-SECOND SPRINTS

K. Take three 12-second timed writings on each line. The scale gives your wam speed for a 12-second timed writing.

I need seats 10, 29, 38, 47, and 56 for today's first game.
Flight 29 leaves at 10:47, while Flight 38 leaves at 10:56.
We had 2,945 employees in 1988 and 1,036 employees in 1978.
He mailed out 10, 29, 38, 47, and 56 packages in five days.

| | | | 5 | | | |10| | | |15| | | |20| | | |25| | | |30| | | |35| | | |40| | | |45| | | |50| | | |55| | | |60

L. TECHNIQUE PRACTICE: ENTER KEY

L. Key each sentence once on a separate line.

Call the client. Answer the letter. Prepare the mailings.
Fax the response. Ship the package. Forward the estimate.
Copy the document. Collate the handout. Add the receipts.
Deposit the cash. Reconcile the checks. Post the account.

M. TECHNIQUE PRACTICE: CONCENTRATION

M. Change every plural noun to a singular noun.

The managers asked the secretaries to key the letters and reports that the officers had dictated earlier. When the jobs had been completed, the secretaries consulted your assistants. Your assistants discovered the errors and had the jobs redone.

N. SUSTAINED PRACTICE: ALTERNATE-HAND WORDS

N. Take a 1-minute timed writing on the first paragraph to establish your base speed. Then take four 1-minute timed writings on the remaining paragraphs. As soon as you equal or exceed your base speed on one paragraph, advance to the next one.

The chairman of that civic club also has to make a new 12
amendment to change the shape of the map for downtown. The 24
rich visitor owns eight of the giant lots that are visible. 36
The town did not permit the antique-shop owner to relocate. 48

The problem with the audit is that the city will blame 12
our firm. Some may not wait for us to make a profit on the 24
deal. If that is the case, we shall refuse to participate. 36
A panel is hard at work to correct the major discrepancies. 48

I once lived in the downtown section of Knoxville. My 12
best neighbor there was a guy named Michael Bono. The only 24
problem with him was that he tended to act like an elitist. 36
He spent lots of time in his home with some of his friends. 48

Phil and Edward had wasted a million pumpkins by scat- 12
tering the vegetables along the street in Sweetwater, Ohio. 24
Everyone was quite aggravated by the great waste of effort. 36
This was especially true of his closest friends and family. 48

| 1 | 2 | 3 | 4 | 5 | 6 | 7 | 8 | 9 | 10 | 11 | 12

REPORT 68
TWO-PAGE UNBOUND REPORT WITH HEADERS, FOOTERS, AND ENDNOTES

Spacing: Double

Format a header for each page entitled *ROUGH DRAFT (Current Date)* and the footer *CHECKED BY:*.

Use WordPerfect's Endnotes feature to format the endnotes on a separate sheet.

Review the Reference Section (R-8) before formatting the page of endnotes.

ARE WE ON TRACK FOR THE '90s?

By Malcolm Lund

The personal computer will affect our company in many ways over the next decade. It will impact on how we process information, produce our goods and services, hire employees, network throughout our organization, and purchase computers and related equipment. Just think what has happened in only one decade. Schlender states it well: "The PC rendered the typewriter nearly extinct, turned secretaries into word processing experts, pulled small businesses into the information age, and inspired man-machine love affairs every bit as passionate as automobiles have."[1]

What are the predictions for firms such as ours for the future?

Predictions

Many predictions are being made about the computer industry for the remainder of the '90s. Some of these predictions are discussed below:

Pioneers' Predictions. Two early pioneers of the personal computer industry—Steven P. Jobs, Apple Computer cofounder, and William G. Gates III, Microsoft cofounder—in a face-to-face interview predicted the following:

1. Razzle-dazzle technology will emerge faster than ever.
2. Data networks will come of age.
3. Users could confront a bewildering array of choices.
4. Japan's electronics companies will become more of a force.
5. Computers will finally change the nature of organizations and office work.[2]

Predictions by Others. Writers for *Business Week* indicated that the bulk of the computer market will be standards-based desktop computers.[3]

Recommendations

If these predictions occur, then we should establish a committee to determine what changes we should make with regard to our firm's organization, the continued use of PCs, and our networking throughout the company.

NOTES

1. Brenton R. Schlender, "The Future of the PC," *Fortune,* August 26, 1991, p. 40.
2. Ibid., pp. 40–41.
3. John W. Verity, with Gary McWilliams, Joseph Weber, and Alice Cuneo, "The Computer Slump Becomes a Sea of Change," *Business Week,* August 19, 1991, p. 106.

O. DIAGNOSTIC PRACTICE: ALPHABET

Turn to the Diagnostic Practice: Alphabet routine at the back of this book. Take the Pretest and record your performance. Then practice the drill lines for those reaches on which you made errors. Finally, repeat the Pretest and compare your performance.

P. Clear all tabs. Then set four new tabs every 1 inch. Key lines 73–76, using the tab key to go from column to column.

P. TECHNIQUE PRACTICE: TAB KEY

73	171	292	383	464	595
74	626	737	828	909	210
75	387	910	621	745	973
76	517	620	864	389	402

Q. PACED PRACTICE

Turn to the Paced Practice routine at the back of the book. Take three 2-minute timed writings, starting at the speed at which you left off the last time.

R. Spacing: Double
Take two 5-minute timed writings. Compute your speed and count errors.

Goal: 42 wam/5'/5e

R. 5-MINUTE TIMED WRITING

77 Foreign companies and the folks who manage them are 11
78 buying slices of American business and expanding them from 23
79 coast to coast. The result is more and more U.S. workers 35
80 who will have to learn what it is like to have a boss from 47
81 another part of the world. 52
82 Once an American agrees to work for a foreign company, 64
83 he or she is faced with the job of adjusting to its unique 76
84 style. Take the task of making decisions. American bosses 88
85 tend to move quickly on things. They are not afraid of 99
86 acting on their own or making a mistake. Foreign bosses, 111
87 on the other hand, take a long time to analyze the facts 122
88 and tend to make more decisions in a group. 131
89 There may also be different ideas about how long the 142
90 workday should last. For the Japanese, long hours are the 154
91 norm; it is rare for them to leave their jobs before ten 166
92 at night. Americans who are used to heading home early 177
93 may be viewed as lazy. A final tip for those anxious to 188
94 succeed with a foreign boss: buckle down and learn the 199
95 language spoken in the home office and use it often. 210

| 1 | 2 | 3 | 4 | 5 | 6 | 7 | 8 | 9 | 10 | 11 | 12

LETTERS 80, 81, 82, 83, 84, 85, 86, 87
FORM LETTERS IN BLOCK STYLE WITH STANDARD PUNCTUATION

MERGE

First create a mailing list (secondary file) using the addresses in Memo 28. Then key the form letter as a primary file. After you finish keying the file, merge the mailing list from Memo 28 and the form letter.

Use a file name with your reference initials that identifies the letter.

(Current Date) / (FULL NAME) / (COMPANY NAME) / (STREET ADDRESS) / (CITY), (STATE) (ZIP) / Dear (NAME): / Subject: Renewal Notice for *Software News*

Your firm's subscription to *Software News* will expire in approximately eight weeks. If (COMPANY NAME) is to keep abreast of current and future software developments, you will want to extend your subscription to the magazine.

Over the past 12 months we have published a variety of articles on new software and its uses in firms such as (COMPANY NAME), on the future development of and research on desktop computers as they relate to employee usage and satisfaction, and on how users in firms are accepting and implementing the new software packages.

Whatever you do, don't delay. Act now to be sure that *Software News* keeps arriving without interruption at your firm. Just complete the enclosed renewal form, and return it in the enclosed addressed envelope.

Sincerely yours, / SOFTWARE NEWS / Arnold Smythe / Circulation Manager / (FILE NAME) / Enclosures 2

TABLE 54
RULED TABLE

Spacing: Double

STARR-HARRISON, INC.

Year-to-Date Sales of Selected Mason Products

Model	First Quarter	Second Quarter	Third Quarter	Total for Year
11-1075	$42,084	$48,650	$43,791	$134,525
11-1079	1,379	1,465	1,821	4,665
12-1003	15,367	15,894	16,253	47,514
12-1025	4,549	5,412	5,880	15,841
13-1650	10,002	8,876	11,453	30,331
13-1655	8,392	9,416	9,832	27,640
13-1771	10,456	9,781	9,890	30,127
TOTAL	$92,229	$99,494	$98,920	$290,643

FORMATTING

S. WORDPERFECT: MACROS

WP

MACROS
Create:
Ctrl-F10, Alt-*letter name,* Enter, *description,* Enter, *keystrokes,* Ctrl-F10

Execute:
Alt-*letter*

Edit:
Ctrl-F10, Alt-*letter name,* 2, *edit,* F7

WordPerfect 6 users: See Student Guide, p. 31.

A *macro* is a special file that you can create to store often-used keystrokes and commands. For example, you can create a macro that will automatically insert the guide words on a memo form and one that will automatically insert the closing lines of a letter.

To create a simple macro, press Ctrl-F10 and define (or name) the macro. The easiest way to name a macro is to hold down the Alt key and enter a single letter (for example, "Alt-M" for memo), then press Enter. Next, give your macro a short description (such as "Memo Heading") and press Enter. At this point, enter the keystrokes you want recorded, including any commands, tab settings, and the like. Correct any errors as you go along, and when you finish, press Ctrl-F10.

To execute a macro, position the cursor where you want the macro to begin and press Alt and the letter name of the macro. The keystrokes you recorded will be entered into your document. If your macro does not work as you intended, use the appropriate commands to edit the macro and correct the errors (Ctrl-F10, Alt-*letter name,* 2, *edit,* F7).

DOCUMENT PROCESSING

MEMO 14

WordPerfect 6 users: See Student Guide, p. 32.

Create a macro to automatically insert the guide words in a memo heading:

1. Position the cursor at the left margin.
2. Press Ctrl-F10 and define (name) the macro (hold down the Alt key and key the letter "M").
3. Describe the macro as "Memo Heading" and press Enter. Then press Enter until you reach Ln = 2″.
4. Turn on Caps Lock and Bold and key **MEMO TO:**, then turn off Caps Lock and Bold and press Tab.
5. Press Enter two times.
6. Repeat steps 4 and 5 to key **FROM:**.
7. Repeat steps 4 and 5 to key **DATE:**.
8. Repeat steps 4 and 5 to key **SUBJECT:**; then press the Up Arrow key six times.
9. Press Ctrl-F10 to save the macro.
10. Delete the copy (including all codes and commands) from the screen; then execute the macro by pressing Alt-M. Your cursor should be at the tab position for "Memo To:."

Use the Macro "Alt-M" to format the heading entries. This memo from Sam Steele, Executive Director, is for Edo Dorati, Cabaret Pops Conductor. Use the current date and Irving Berlin Concert as the subject.

Before beginning to format Memo 14, review the proofreaders' marks on page R-13 in the Reference Section.

Italicized words may be either formatted in italics or underlined.

Key your own initials for the reference initials.

#

Our Patron Advisory Program Committee recommends in its ~~theire~~ attached letter that the Irving Berlin concert begin with some pre-World War I hits, followed by songs from the '20s and '30s. Favorites from this era are hit songs from *Music Box Revue, Puttin' on the Ritz,* and *Follow the Fleet.* After the intermission, the committee suggests songs from the '40s and '50s, hits from *Annie get your Gun, Call Me Madam,* and *Easter Parade.*

A planning meeting has been scheduled for you, Dolly Carpenter (the Rehearsals Coordinator), and me on March 9 at 10 a. m. at Orchestra Hall. I shall look foreward to seeing you then.

ds

dal

Attachment

c: Dolly Carpenter

DOCUMENT PROCESSING

MEMO 28

Key the memorandum, making the necessary corrections.

Use Indent instead of Tab for keying a two-line subject line.

Be sure the first line of each address in Column 2 aligns with those in Column 1.

Use a reference-initial format that identifies the file name under which the memorandum would be stored on a disk—for example: CARLSON.URS.

The name of a publishing company can be the same as the name of the publication; for example, *Toledo Daily News.* Underline or italicize the name when it refers to the publication but not when it refers to the company, as in an inside address.

MEMO

TO: Alice Carlson

FROM: Arnold Smythe

DATE: (Current Date)

SUBJECT: Mailing List for Selected Firms Whos e Subscriptions to Software News Expires in Eight Weeks

Listed below ~~are~~ is a selected list of ~~companys~~ firms whose subscription to Software News expires in eight weeks. ~~I~~ We want to be sure that they renew their subscriptions because of their influence on adoptions and their prestige.

Please ~~S~~send the ~~attached~~ enclosed form letter with the appropriate names and addresses, to the designated idndividuals as soon as ~~you can~~ possible.

Mr. Alex Whitmore
Allison & Sons
1801 Inveꜱtment Plaza
Cleveland, OH 43213-2305

Mrs. Susan Meiske-Rose
Arts and Crafts, Inc.
121 East Seventh Street
St. Paul, MN 55101-1332

Mr. Mark Riordion
Vice President
Riordion Software, Inc.
23030 Peachtree Road, NW
Atlanta, GA 31709-2317

Ms. Zenalda Diaz
A-One Markets
423 Commercial Square
Cincinnati, OH 45202-1006

Ms. Elsie Stonehouse
Diamond Foods, Inc.
Commonwealth Building
719 Griswold
Detroit, MI 48226-1785

Ms. Mary V. Moore
First National Bank
11 North Pennsylvania
Indianapolis, IN 46204-1321

Ms. Sandy Ramos
Toledo Daily News
606 Madison Street
Toledo, OH 43604-2376

Mr. Albert Chan
Montrose Associates
705 Hamilton
Peru, IN 46970

(FILE NAME)
Enclosure

MEMO 15

MEMO TO: Frank Janowicz / Ticket Manager / **FROM:** Sam Steele / Executive Director / **DATE:** March 1, 19— / **SUBJECT:** Ticket Sales Campaign

We tentatively have scheduled 114 concerts for Orchestra Hall for the calendar year beginning September 1, 19—. The attached list shows the new season ticket prices for the main floor, mezzanine, balcony, and gallery.

These prices are grouped in 11 different concert categories which reflect the varied classical tastes of our patrons. These groupings also consider preferences for day of the week, time of day, and season of the year.

Please see me at 3 p.m. on March 10 so that we can review our ticket sales campaign. Last year's season ticket holders have had ample time to renew their subscriptions; we must now concentrate on attracting new season subscribers. I shall look forward to reviewing your plans on the 10th. *(Your Initials)* / Attachment

Continue to execute the macro for the bold heading entries when formatting memos.

A reminder: The paragraphs in memorandums are always blocked.

MEMO 16

MEMO TO: Dolly Carpenter, Rehearsals Coordinator
FROM: Sam Steele, Executive Director
DATE: March 1, 19--
SUBJECT: Summer Cabaret Pops Concert

We are pleased that you will be our rehearsals coordinator for this summer's Cabaret Pops concerts. The five biweekly concerts will run from June 13 through August 8.

As the concert schedule is much lighter during the summer months, I am quite confident that you will be able to use the Orchestra Hall stage for all rehearsals. This is the preference of Edo Dorati, who will be the conductor for this year's Cabaret Pops concerts.

I look forward to seeing you on June 1.

Remember your reference initials.

FORMATTING

T. TABLES IN OTHER DOCUMENTS

To format a table that is part of a letter, memorandum, or report:

1. Leave 1 blank line above and below a table without a title (regardless of whether the table has column headings) and 3 blank lines above and below a table with a title.
2. Single-space the body of the table.
3. Keep the table within the margins of the document. If necessary, the normal 6 spaces between columns may be reduced to a minimum of 2 spaces.
4. Never split a table between two pages. If it will not fit at the bottom of the page on which it is first mentioned, place it at the top of the next page.

O. Key this paragraph twice as you concentrate on some of the commonly used symbols.

O. NUMBER AND SYMBOL PRACTICE

```
What high prices!  The tag shows 50# @ $2.49 and 10# @ 78¢.
But the new ad* for Frost & Coyne shows prices that are 36%
lower.  Let's build an inventory (an up-to-date one) now by
buying at these "summer discount prices."  Don't you agree?
```

P. DIAGNOSTIC PRACTICE: ALPHABET

Turn to the Diagnostic Practice: Alphabet routine at the back of this book. Take the Pretest and record your performance. Then practice the drill lines for those reaches on which you made errors. Finally, repeat the Pretest and compare your performance.

Q. Spacing: Double
Take two 5-minute timed writings. Compute your speed and count errors.

Goals: 50 wam/5′/5e

Q. 5-MINUTE TIMED WRITING

```
     Major businesses across the land have found a unique      12
means to assist nonprofit organizations by using a new type    24
of marketing designed to do well by doing good.  Advocates     35
call it a great idea because each player wins:  the company    47
promotes its product, while the charity gains funding.         58
     Unsure what this new pitch is all about?  Chances are     70
good that you see some examples of this means of corporate     82
sponsorship each time you shop in a grocery store or read a    94
magazine circular.  It occurs whenever you, the consumer,     105
purchase something and the company that makes the product     117
agrees to donate a portion of the proceeds to the nonprofit   129
agency of its choice.  So if you buy a box of soap flakes,    141
you may be helping the Special Olympics.  And if you pay      152
for that box by credit card, you may be helping to fight      164
cancer or Alzheimer's disease.                                170
     The trend for giving gifts with strings attached is      181
likely to stretch into the next few decades as budgets get    193
smaller and tighter.  For companies, the link to a cause      205
can help make a product stand out.  And for charities that    216
are facing reduced government dollars and fewer corporate     228
contributions, having their names linked to a product can     239
make the difference between their continuing or folding.      250
| 1 | 2 | 3 | 4 | 5 | 6 | 7 | 8 | 9 | 10 | 11 | 12
```

DOCUMENT PROCESSING

LETTER 41
BLOCK STYLE

WordPerfect 6 users: See Student Guide, p. 33.

Create a macro to automatically insert the closing lines for Letter 41 (block style) below. Follow these steps:

1. Press Ctrl-F10 and define (name) the macro Alt-C (press and hold down the Alt key while you key "C"), then press Enter.
2. Give the macro a short description such as "Closing" and press Enter.
3. Key "Sincerely yours," and press Enter four times.
4. Key "Samantha A. Steele, Executive Director" and press Enter once.
5. Key "Philadelphia Orchestral Association" and press Enter twice.
6. Correct any errors, then press Ctrl-F10 to save the macro and F7 to exit the document.

Use March 2, 19—, as the date for this letter to Ms. Maureen Testa / 372 Central Park West, Apt. 812 / New York, NY 10025-4690. Use an appropriate salutation. Execute the macro "Alt-C" to insert the complimentary closing.

We are ~~pleased~~ delighted that you will be with us for (4) Cabaret Pops concerts this year. Your appearance in Next in Order on Broadway, which earned you a Tony Award nomination, has won you thousands of new fans in the Philadelphia area. They are looking forward to seeing you at Orchestra hall.

ss [As your agent and I discussed on # the telephone, the four concerts have been scheduled on the following dates (for 8 p.m.):

Cole Porter Revisited	June 13
Big Bands of the Forties	June 27
A Century of Irving Berlin	July 11
Blues, Blues, Blues	July 25

Center the table between the margins, with 6 spaces between columns.

Our Cabaret Pops Series continues to be a poplar summer offering. While most of our patrons are serious classical music devotees, they also enjoy the ~~lighter~~ diversion offered by our posp concerts.

Sincerely yours,

Samantha A. Steele, Executive Director
Philadelphia Orchestral Association

your initials.P23

A word processing file reference number is often used in combination with the reference initials. The P23 indicates that this letter is stored on disk P as document 23.

LETTER 42
BLOCK STYLE

Be sure to change the file reference number to *P24*.

Revise Letter 41 from Ms. Steele as follows: This letter is to be sent to Mr. Rodney Graae / 42 Harris Court / Trenton, NJ 08648. Mr. Graae received a Tony Award nomination for his appearance in *Time for Dreams* on Broadway. Also, he will be appearing in five concerts; in addition to the four listed, he will also be one of the vocalists for the *Beatles Favorites From the '60s* concert on August 8.

J. Take three 1-minute timed writings. The last two digits of each number provide a cumulative word count to help you determine your wam speed.

J. NUMBER PRACTICE

43 6601 5902 1103 3904 4005 5606 9007 3408 3609 8810 5611 2112
44 3213 4714 5615 8916 7017 1318 4419 2820 5921 6022 9223 4424
45 7325 5026 2227 9428 1929 3930 4431 2132 8933 6234 3835 2036
46 8937 2738 5839 6040 3241 5742 1843 2444 9345 9146 8847 4848

K. Take three 12-second timed writings on each line. The scale gives wam for a 12-second timed writing.

K. 12-SECOND SPRINTS

47 Flight #97 to Tulsa cost $543; Flight #34 to Reno was $561.
48 One-sixth or 1/6 equals 16.7%; 80% is equal to four-fifths.
49 Trace these policies: (1) #2428, (2) #1894, and (3) #1627.
50 On 10/28 he (Bart) paid $97, which is 36% less than I paid.

| | | | 5 | | | | 10 | | | | 15 | | | | 20 | | | | 25 | | | | 30 | | | | 35 | | | | 40 | | | | 45 | | | | 50 | | | | 55 | | | | 60

L. Clear all tabs. Then set four new tabs every 1 inch. Key lines 51–54, using the tab key to go across from column to column.

L. TECHNIQUE PRACTICE: TAB KEY

51	prize	pizza	amaze	sizes	zebra
52	mixed	extra	sixth	boxes	fixed
53	quick	quiet	quite	quart	quilt
54	judge	jumps	jokes	enjoy	banjo

M. Key this Italian paragraph once, concentrating on each letter keyed. Then take three 1-minute timed writings, trying to increase your speed each time.

M. TECHNIQUE PRACTICE: CONCENTRATION

55 Ti ringrazio per la foto che mi hai mandato, anche per 12
56 tutti auguri che hai mandato. Noi siamo tutti bene e spero 24
57 che la tua famiglias anche si trovano tutti en bene salute. 36

| 1 | 2 | 3 | 4 | 5 | 6 | 7 | 8 | 9 | 10 | 11 | 12

N. Take a 1-minute timed writing on the first paragraph to establish your base speed. Then take four 1-minute timed writings on the remaining paragraphs. As soon as you equal or exceed your base speed on one paragraph, advance to the next one.

N. SUSTAINED PRACTICE: ALTERNATE-HAND WORDS

58 The city planners appointed a panel of eight people to 12
59 handle the work. The chair of the panel will keep a formal 24
60 record of meetings. The chair will also sign any form that 36
61 panel members may wish to send to any visitor to a meeting. 48

62 When the chair called the first meeting for that panel 12
63 to order, all five members were available. The chair asked 24
64 each member to sign a form for reimbursement of expenses to 36
65 all panel meetings. The work for the panel was determined. 48

66 After that initial meeting, the chair was planning for 12
67 another meeting during the following week. Since all panel 24
68 members were available, the chair set an agenda. The chair 36
69 plans to give out assignments for all of the panel members. 48

70 The planners were anxious to have the group submit its 12
71 plans by the end of the first quarter of the year. This is 24
72 in keeping with the objective of having each section within 36
73 the governing board prepared for the final budget hearings. 48

| 1 | 2 | 3 | 4 | 5 | 6 | 7 | 8 | 9 | 10 | 11 | 12

LETTER 43
BLOCK STYLE

(Current Date) / Master Gyms, Inc. / 4201 Castine Court / Raleigh, NC 27613-5981 / Ladies and Gentlemen:

We have 494 apartments here at Fountain Ridge. As the Recreation Coordinator for the complex, I have concerns not only about the leisure-time activities of our residents but also about the health and physical fitness of the more than 1,100 people who call Fountain Ridge home.

Our recreation facilities are excellent. In addition to our two outdoor tennis courts and swimming pool, we also have the following indoor facilities: two racquetball courts, swimming pool, whirlpool bath, sauna, steam room, and two billiard tables. However, we have no workout equipment.

During the next few months we will be equipping a new gymnasium. The dimensions of the gym are shown on the enclosed sketch. There will be exercise bicycles, treadmills, and rowing machines. In addition, we would like to install a muscle-toning machine that includes features such as the following: leg press, chest press, shoulder press, arm pull, leg pull, arm lift, leg lift, and sit-up board.

Do you have a sales representative serving this area who could meet with me within a week or ten days? As an alternative, perhaps you have some brochures, including prices, that could be sent to me.

Sincerely yours, / Rosa Bailey-Judd / Recreation Coordinator / *(Your Initials)* / Enclosure

LETTER 44
BLOCK STYLE

Use today's date and send this letter to Mr. Kent R. Raudenbush / Choice Athletic Equipment Co. / 5800 Moreland Avenue / Athens, GA 30601-4279. Use an appropriate salutation and complimentary closing. This letter is also from Rosa Bailey-Judd / Recreation Coordinator. Use your own reference initials, key an enclosure notation, and send a copy to Mr. Larry Hackworth, Manager.

Thank you for being so kind when I visited your showroom last week. Having Joe present to actually demonstrate the use of each muscle-toning device was very helpful. I really feel that I am now aware of the special features of your equipment.

Please send me a quotation that includes the cost of your equipment, delivery and installation charges, and taxes. A specification sheet is enclosed.

Please provide this information quickly, as we hope to make a selection within ten days.

D. PACED PRACTICE

Turn to the Paced Practice routine at the back of the book. Take three 2-minute timed writings, starting at the speed at which you left off the last time.

PRETEST.
Take a 1-minute timed writing; compute your speed and count errors.

E. PRETEST: VERTICAL REACHES

```
     The third skier knelt on the knoll and secured a loose  12
ski as the race was about to begin.  Each of the rival team  24
members awaited the starting signal way above the crowd.  A  36
variety of trophies and awards would go to all the winners.  48
| 1 | 2 | 3 | 4 | 5 | 6 | 7 | 8 | 9 | 10 | 11 | 12
```

PRACTICE.
Speed Emphasis: If you made no more than 1 error on the Pretest, key each line twice.
Accuracy Emphasis: If you made 2 or more errors on the Pretest, key each group of lines (as though it were a paragraph) twice.

F. PRACTICE: UP REACHES

```
aw away award crawl straw drawn sawed drawl await flaw lawn
se self sense raise these prose abuse users serve send seem
ki kind kites skill skier skims skips skits kilts king skid
rd lard third beard horde gourd board guard sword cord curd
```

G. PRACTICE: DOWN REACHES

```
ac ache track paced brace races facts crack acute back aces
kn knob knife kneel knows knack knelt known knoll knot knew
ab drab about label table above abide gable abbey able abet
va vain vague value valve evade naval rival avail vats vase
```

POSTTEST.
Repeat the Pretest (E) and compare performance.

H. POSTTEST: VERTICAL REACHES

I. Take a 1-minute timed writing on the first paragraph to establish your base speed. Then take four 1-minute timed writings on the remaining paragraphs. As soon as you equal or exceed your base speed on one paragraph, advance to the next one.

I. SUSTAINED PRACTICE: NUMBERS

```
     The membership director for a national association was  12
compiling a report on membership statistics for each region  24
in the association.  This would be presented to the leaders  36
of the organization at an upcoming meeting of the officers.  48

     Membership was organized into five regions.  The total  12
number of members for the past year was 12,562.  This was a  24
decline of 2,420 from the previous year.  This decrease has  36
created a great deal of discussion on the part of officers.  48

     The southern region had a membership of 3,640 for this  12
past year.  It had 3,120 members in the previous year; this  24
meant it had an increase of 16.7 percent.  Its goal for the  36
new year was 4,100 members.  This goal would be attainable.  48

     The other four regions had membership totals of 3,172,  12
2,289, 1,950, and 1,511.  In one of the regions, a decrease  24
of 244 members took place; in another, there was a decrease  36
of 226 members.  The other two regions had small decreases.  48
| 1 | 2 | 3 | 4 | 5 | 6 | 7 | 8 | 9 | 10 | 11 | 12
```

FORMATTING — U. MODIFIED-BLOCK STYLE WITH INDENTED PARAGRAPHS

Paragraphs in the body of a modified-block style letter may be indented (usually 0.5 inch) or blocked at the left margin. However, paragraphs in a block-style letter are never indented.

Mr. Daniel Vlasuk
8 Hillside Avenue
Peabody, MA 01869

Dear Mr. Vlasuk:

It is likely that the new warehouse will be built at the intersection of Maple Ridge Avenue and 44th Street. This area has been surveyed and construction plans have been drawn up.

We are now in the process of obtaining the necessary building permits from the city. As soon as the city approves the plans and issues these permits, construction will begin. We expect that to be some time in March.

DOCUMENT PROCESSING

LETTER 45
MODIFIED-BLOCK STYLE WITH INDENTED PARAGRAPHS

When correspondents are on a first-name basis, the first name is appropriately used in the salutation.

(Current Date)

Leave 5 blank lines here

Mr. Timothy E. Kerfeld
1260 Glenmar St., APT. 4
Wilburton, Ok 74578
ds
Dear Tim:

e engagement sent
As we agreed, your fiance's ring is being shipped today by National Express overnight. It will be delivered to you in person tomorrow morning.

\# self
You were wise to include both Jodi andyour in the selection of the diamond. Though the dollar amount represents a significant investment, the sentimental aspect should also be considered. Jodi will treasure the ring because the two of you were involved in the selection all the more.

ed educated
I was impress with the way in which both of you had taught yourselves about the various criteria for diamond selection. Many people seem to believe think that size alone (represented by carat weight) determines the value of a diamond. Your knowledge that cut, color, and clarity are also important factors enabled you to make a wise choice. ¶ Thank you for choosing Dorsheim's for this important purchase. We look forward to helping you and Jodi with your fine jewelry and gift selections in the future.

Sincerely,
3 blank lines here
Beth E. Dryden, GG.
c

(Your Initials)

Unless there are legal reasons for a complete signature, the sender usually will sign with only the first name in the closing if the first name is used in the salutation.

LETTER 46
MODIFIED-BLOCK STYLE WITH INDENTED PARAGRAPHS

A revision of Letter 45 is to be sent from Ms. Dryden to Mr. Clifford A. Reuter / 1830 Rolling Meadow Road / Enid, OK 73701. Use *Dear Mr. Reuter:* as the salutation, and change *fiancee's engagement ring* to *wife's diamond ring* in the first paragraph. Also, use the search and replace commands to change *Jodi* to *Mrs. Reuter* throughout the letter.

LESSONS 116-120

Margins: 1 inch • Spacing: Single • Drills: 2 times • Format Guide: 95–103

Goals for Unit 24

1. To improve accuracy and speed on alphabet and number keys.
2. To key 50 wam for 5 minutes with no more than 5 errors.
3. To improve proofreading skills.
4. To format various letters—personal-business, business, two-page—and memorandums from typeset and rough-draft input.
5. To format tables in a variety of styles.
6. To format reports with a variety of features—side headings, paragraph headings, endnotes, and long quotes.
7. To use various features of WordPerfect in completing documents.

Begin each day with approximately 15 minutes of skillbuilding, selecting activities from pages 278–281. In the remaining class time, complete as many production jobs from pages 282–290 as you can.

A. WARMUP

1 Flight #1120 to Phoenix on August 19 was quoted at the 12
2 rate of $464. Flight #357 to Las Vegas on July 7 was given 24
3 as $385. Becky Zinn confirmed the rates with Bill Walmach. 36

| 1 | 2 | 3 | 4 | 5 | 6 | 7 | 8 | 9 | 10 | 11 | 12

LANGUAGE ARTS

B. NUMBERS

B. Study the rules at the right. Then key lines 4–7, making necessary changes.

Rule: When two numbers come together in a sentence and one is part of a compound adjective, spell the first number unless the second number would make a much shorter word.

They have begun constructing three 16-story condominiums.

Rule: In high-level executive writing, hyphenate all compound numbers between 21 and 99 (or *21st* and *99th*), whether they stand alone or are part of a number over 100.

He has already received twenty-two congratulatory letters.

4 The real estate agent showed them 3 4-bedroom houses.
5 The package contained one hundred fifty 10-dollar bills.
6 A dividend will be paid for thirty-four years in a row.
7 My company plans to have a big 25th anniversary party.

C. PROOFREADING

C. Compare this paragraph with the last paragraph of the 5-minute timed writing on page 281. Key a list of the words that contain errors, correcting the errors as you key.

8 The trend for give gifts with strings attached is
9 liekly to stretch in to the next few decades as bugets get
10 smaller and tighter. For companys, the link to a cause
11 can help make a product standout. And for chairties that
12 are facing reduced goverment dollars and fewer corporate
13 contributions, having their names linked to a produce can
14 make the difference between continuing or folding.

MEMO 17

Remember to use the macro command for the memo heading.

If necessary, refer to the Reference Section to review proper format for memos (page R-4) and tables (page R-12).

Center the table between the margins, with 6 spaces between columns.

MEMO TO: Larry Hackworth, Manager
FROM: Rosa Bailey-Judd, Recreation Coordinator
DATE: Current
SUBJECT: Fitness Room

The new Fitness Room will be ready for use in about one month. Your leadership in bringing this about is sincerely appreciated. After extensive investigation (much reading and several interviews), I likely will be requesting approval soon to purchase the following equipment:

Number	Type
4	exercise bicycles
2	treadmills
2	rowing machines
1	muscle-toning machine

Three other types of equipment were seriously considered, but those listed above enable users to reach objectives without excessive cost and duplication.

Thanks again for your full support and cooperation with this project.

MEMO 18

Retrieve Memo 17 and make the following revisions: Send this memo to Pete Chamberlin / Maintenance Supervisor. Delete the second sentence in the first paragraph, and change the last paragraph to read as follows: *I am aware that Larry has discussed normal custodial needs with you. In addition, there will be a need for someone to keep the equipment in good operating condition; I shall talk with you about this soon.*

FORMATTING

V. SUBJECT LINES

A subject line indicates what a letter is about. It is keyed below the salutation at the left margin, preceded and followed by 1 blank line. (The term *Re* or *In re* may be used in place of *Subject.*)

Mrs. Melanie Stewart
511 Whitley Drive
Gahanna, OH 43230

Dear Mrs. Stewart:

Subject: Kindergarten Preregistration

Kindergarten preregistration for the coming school year is being held on Wednesday, May 15 from 9 a.m. to 1 p.m.

On that day, you are welcome to tour the facility. Staff members will be available to answer questions and to tell you about the various programs that are available.

LETTER 79
TWO-PAGE LETTER IN BLOCK STYLE WITH OPEN PUNCTUATION, DISPLAY PARAGRAPH, AND BOXED TABLE

Please key this letter for Tom Panian.

April 27, 19--

Ms. Charlene Jo Helbert ← 2307 Reeves Avenue
Ogden Ut 84401

Thank you for your letter in which you inquired about the air traffic control program here at the Chandler Air Traffic Control School. Your first question was an inquiry as to what an air traffic controller does. I am confident that these statements from our new bulletin will provide a good answer for you:

> Air traffic controllers are responsible for the safe, methodical, and expeditious movement of air traffic. They are men and women with special skills who can handle complex and precise tasks and yet remain alert in pressure situations.

You allso inquired about job opportunities. ~~Qualified~~ graduates from CATCS continue to be in high demand. Almost all of our graduates obtain~~ed~~ positions with the Federal Aviation Administration (FAA), which is in the Dept. of Transportation. Most of them work at en route centers, where air traffic is controlled along established air ways in the geographic area served by each center. Others work at FAA airport traffic control towers. The table below details the placement of our December 19-- graduates:

Center the information in the columns.

Sex	FAA INSTALLATIONS	
	En Route Center	Airport Tower
Male	8	6
Female	9	3

Our Instructors are particularly well qualified. All have at least five years of experience in air traffic control positions. Our instructional facilities are excellent, equipped with the latest in instructional media and technology.

Our advanced students spend ~~some~~ much of thier time in a simulated lab setting. The instructional media are programed so that the learner encounters very real air traffic control situations.

A packet of materials, including an application form, is ~~being sent to you today.~~ enclosed. If you have ~~any~~ other questions, please ~~do~~ let me know.

Yours truly

CHANDLER AIR TRAFFIC CONTROL SCHOOL

← 3 blank lines

Thomas V. Panian
Admissions Director

DOCUMENT PROCESSING

LETTER 47
MODIFIED-BLOCK STYLE WITH INDENTED PARAGRAPHS

Subject lines are keyed at the left margin after the salutation, preceded and followed by 1 blank line.

Center a table between the margins, with 6 spaces between columns.

(Current Date) / Mrs. Katie Holister / 11426 Prairie View Road / Kearney, NE 68847 / Dear Mrs. Holister: / Subject: Site for New Elementary School

As you are aware, your 160-acre farm, located in the northeast quarter of Section 25 in Tyro township, is a part of Independent School District 17. Each of our three elementary schools occupies two acres and is adjoined by an 8-acre park. The schools and their adjoining parks are:

Evelyn Moen Elementary School	Maple Grove Park
Percy Miller Elementary School	T. J. Blomgren Park
Spring Creek Elementary School	Spring Creek Park

We are now in the early planning stages for a fourth elementary school. As your farm is centrally located, the District 17 Board has directed me to initiate discussions with you for the purchase of 8 acres of land.

Please call me at your convenience to arrange a meeting with you and/or your attorney and me. I look forward to our discussions.

Yours truly, / Irvin J. Hagg / Superintendent of Schools / *(Your Initials)* / c: District 17 Board

LETTER 48

Retrieve Letter 47 so that several errors can be corrected. Mrs. Hollister's name is spelled incorrectly, and her farm is located in Section 26. The names of the two parks for the Moen and Miller schools should be reversed. Also, the discussions will be about the purchase of 10 acres of land, not 8.

LETTER 49
PERSONAL-BUSINESS LETTER IN BLOCK STYLE

March 21, 19--

Dr. Arif Gureshi
8726 E. Ridge Drive
Morehead, KY 40351

Dear dr. Gureshi:

Your book The Middle East In The Year 2000 has been getting excellent reviews. The citizens of Morehead are highly pleased that a respected member of one of our local colleges is receiving much national attention. Our book discussion group here in Morehead, composed of members of AAUW (American Association of University Women) has selected your book for discussion at our May meeting. We would like you to be a participant; your attendance at that meeting would be a real highlight.

I shall call you next week; our members are hoping that will be able to attend and that a date can be mutually arranged.
Sincerely,

Theresa A. Gorski
2901 Garfield Court
Morehead, KY 40351

MEMO 26

MEMO TO: Jane Pfeiffer
FROM: Warren D. Ebert, Director
DATE: April 26, 19__
SUBJECT: Case Study for Orientation Course

I know that you are always on the lookout for ideas for the Orientation to Air Traffic Control course. The enclosed case might be of interest.

The case involves the accident that occurred on January 18, 1990, when Eastern Airlines Flight 111, a Boeing 727, struck a Beech 100 at the Atlanta Hartsfield International Airport.

Let's get together to discuss the ways in which this case might relate to course objectives.

MEMO 27

Please revise the Pfeiffer memo, and send it to Lee Montoyo for his Basic Radar course. The case involves the accident that occurred on December 3, 1990, when a Northwest Airlines Boeing 727 collided with a Northwest Airlines Douglas DC-9 at the Detroit Metropolitan Airport.

TABLE 53
BOXED TABLE WITH BRACED COLUMN HEADING

WordPerfect 6 users: Do not key the dollar sign.

COMPENSATION EXPENDITURES

Group	First Quarter, 19__			
	January	February	March	Totals
Administration	$ 42,833	$ 42,833	$ 51,834	$137,500
Instructional	106,250	106,250	106,250	318,750
Staff	14,779	16,542	18,179	49,500
TOTALS	$163,862	$165,625	$176,263	$505,750

LETTER 50
PERSONAL-BUSINESS LETTER IN BLOCK STYLE

Retrieve Letter 49 and revise it as follows: Date the letter June 14, 19—, and address it to Ms. Margot Ault / 13894 Combs Ferry Road / Lexington, KY 40509. The title of Ms. Ault's new book is *Wilderness Passages.* Change the second sentence in the first paragraph to read as follows: *The citizens of Morehead are highly pleased that one of our former residents is receiving national attention.* (The discussion of Ms. Ault's book is scheduled for the September meeting.)

LETTER 51
PERSONAL-BUSINESS LETTER IN MODIFIED-BLOCK STYLE WITH INDENTED PARAGRAPHS

March 28, 19— / Ms. Theresa A. Gorski / 2901 Garfield Court / Morehead, KY 40351-2687 / Dear Ms. Gorski:

I am looking forward to being a guest at your AAUW book group meeting on May 17.

Since I spoke to you on the phone earlier this week, there has been a new development. My editor, Mr. Dwight Friesen, will be in Morehead that day to conduct a seminar at Culver College. As he will be staying overnight, I would like to bring him along. He is truly one of our country's experts on the cultures of Middle Eastern countries.

As you know, my wife Tana is a member of the local AAUW chapter. She, Dwight, and I will look forward to being at the Federated Women's Club building at 7:30 p.m. on May 17.

Sincerely, / ~~Arif Gureshi~~ Ms. Mc / 8726 East Ridge Drive / Morehead, KY 40351-7268 / c: Mr. Dwight Friesen

LETTER 52
PERSONAL-BUSINESS LETTER IN MODIFIED-BLOCK STYLE WITH INDENTED PARAGRAPHS

Remember to italicize the book title.

Date the letter October 2, 19—. This letter is also going to Ms. Gorski. It is from Margot Ault / 13894 Combs Ferry Road / Lexington, KY 40509.

Dear Theresa:

Thank you for inviting me to attend your book group's discussion of my new novel, Wilderness Passages. This was my first opportunity to discuss the book with a group this large, all of whom had already read it.

I am returning the honorarium check for $100. Please apply the amount to your college scholarship fund.

It was wonderful to see so many of my old friends again. Thank you for this special evening.

Sincerely,

Enclosure

LETTERS 75, 76, 77, 78
MERGE LETTERS IN
BLOCK STYLE

Please send this letter to the following four people, who have applied for our two vacant faculty positions.

Roy A. Rossback	Carol E. Tarmann
2414 Bush Lake Road	4467 14th Avenue East
Gwinn, MI 49841	Denver, CO 80220
team lab instructor	basic radar instructor
eight	five
Air Force control tower	airport control tower
Judith Ann Smith	Tyrone J. Williams
804 Humphrey Avenue	5416 Imperial Highway West
Farmington, MN 55024	Los Angeles, CA 90045
team lab instructor	team lab instructor
fourteen	nine
en route center	en route center

April 25 , 19--

____
____
____

Dear ________ :

We are pleased to have received your application for a positoin as a __________ at the Chandler Air Traffic Control school. Even though you provided a copy of your resume would you please also complete the enclosed Application Form and return it to our office in the envelope that is also enclosed.
ds The __________ years of experience you have haad at an ________ are appropriate for this position. We shall look forward to receiving your completed application form. ¶ Our plan is to ~~choose~~ select candidates for interviews after June 1. We shall inform you of ~~of~~ the status of your application at that time.

W. Ebert
Enclosures 2

76-80 LESSONS

Margins: 1 inch • Spacing: Single • Drills: 2 times • Format Guide: 51–57

Goals for Unit 16

Begin each day with approximately 15 minutes of skillbuilding, selecting activities from pages 176–179. In the remaining class time, complete as many production jobs from pages 180–187 as you can.

1. To improve accuracy and speed on alphabet and number keys.
2. To key 43 wam for 5 minutes with no more than 5 errors.
3. To develop proficiency in spelling commonly misspelled words.
4. To improve proficiency in formatting footnotes in a report.
5. To gain proficiency in using Block Protect and Initial Codes in WordPerfect.
6. To gain proficiency in formatting a display in a report.
7. To format a news release, magazine articles, and book manuscripts.
8. To format and key various types of reports with different features.

A. WARMUP

1 Request 18 items @ $74 and another 21 items @ $53. If 12
2 you add the 6% sales tax, the total purchase will amount to 24
3 $2,591.70. Just analyze the invoice before making payment. 36

| 1 | 2 | 3 | 4 | 5 | 6 | 7 | 8 | 9 | 10 | 11 | 12

LANGUAGE ARTS

B. UNDERLINE/PERIOD

B. Study the rules at the right. Then key lines 4–7, making necessary changes.

Rule: Underline titles of complete published works, and use quotation marks around titles that represent only a part of a complete published work.

One of the required books was entitled <u>Family Finance</u>.

Rule: Use a period to end a sentence that is a polite request, suggestion, or command if you expect the reader to respond by *acting* rather than by giving a yes-or-no answer.

Will you please send your check for $142.38 before May 1.

4 I read the article entitled A Right Price for Your House.
5 The article was in Friday's issue of the <u>Washington Post</u>.
6 May I have a copy of the proposal before the meeting?
7 Will you please inform me if I can be of any further help.

C. SPELLING

C. These words are among the 500 most frequently misspelled words in business correspondence.

8 practice continue regular entitled course resolution assist
9 weeks preparation purposes referred communication potential
10 environmental specifications original contractor associated
11 principal systems client excellent estimated administration
12 responsibility mentioned utilized materials criteria campus

REPORT 67
MAGAZINE ARTICLE

Tab: 0.3 inch

THE EARLY DAYS OF RADAR 8

sophisticated equipment is now being used at all large air traffic control centers throughout the world.

ds THE 1920s
The work of some two German scientists, Heinrich Hertz and Christian Hulsmeyer, led to the development of what we now call Radar. Their work attracted the attention of Guglielmo Marconi, who made a recommendation recommended to the Institute of Radio Engineers in 1922 that their experiments should be investigated for any practical applications. The resulting system was used successfuly for the first time at the Carnegie Institute in Washington in 1925 by Gregory Breit and Merle A Tune.

ds The 1930s (bold)
In late 1930 Dr. A Hoyt Taylor of the U. S. Naval Research Laboratory began investigating the use of radar to detect the presence of other ships and aircraft. These experiments were conducted in full cooperation with scientists in England. By 1931 it was possible to detect both ships and planes under favorable conditions. ¶ Dr. Taylor indicated that the next step was to develop some instruments that would automatically collect, record, and analyze data to show the exact position, angle, and speed of approaching ships and planes.

Both the army and the navy continued the further development of radar devices through the 1930s. The first demonstration of radar equipment to Army officials took place in 1938 when a device designed for control of anti-aircraft guns and search lights was used. The SCR-268 was the first radar set actually used by the Army.

The Signal Corps Laboratory developed a radar instrument in 1939 for detecting airplanes at much greater distances. After a a succesful demonstration for the Secretary of War, it was adopted for military use.

> The United States and Great Britain endeavored together on the improvement of radar . . . .

ds The 1940s (bold)
The U. S. and Great Britain endeavored together on the improvement of radar into the 1940s. The two countries agreed in late 1940 to share information on their technological advancements.

CATCS ALUMNI REVIEW Summer 19--

LETTER 74
BLOCK STYLE

Retrieve the Glatzer letter, and make the necessary revisions so that a similar letter can be sent to Mrs. Carmen Marquez-Shroyer, who is president of the California Chapter of the Air Traffic Control Organization. Her address is shown in the directory of advisory board members, which you recently prepared. Revise the second paragraph by requesting that she conduct a two-hour seminar during the first half of July on the benefits of ATCO membership, both to the profession and to the individuals who join.

SKILLBUILDING

PRETEST.
Take a 1-minute timed writing; compute your speed and count errors.

PRACTICE.
Speed Emphasis: If you made no more than 1 error on the Pretest, key each line twice.
Accuracy Emphasis: If you made 2 or more errors on the Pretest, key each group of lines (as though it were a paragraph) twice.

POSTTEST.
Repeat the Pretest (D) and compare performance.

D. PRETEST: ALTERNATE- AND ONE-HAND WORDS

The usual visitors to the rocky island are from either 12
the city of Lakeland or Honolulu. They like to visit hilly 24
areas and taste the giant fruit. The eight signs that girl 36
made gave us an extra boost and some added revenue as well. 48

| 1 | 2 | 3 | 4 | 5 | 6 | 7 | 8 | 9 | 10 | 11 | 12

E. PRACTICE: ALTERNATE-HAND WORDS

also angle field bushel ancient emblem panel sight fish big
both blame fight formal element handle proxy signs girl and
city chair giant island visitor profit right their laid cut
down eight laugh theory chaotic visual shape usual work she

F. PRACTICE: ONE-HAND WORDS

acts hilly award uphill average poplin refer jolly adds him
area jumpy based homily baggage you'll serve union beat ink
case onion brave limply greater kimono taste plump draw oil
gave pupil extra unhook wastage unholy wages imply star you

G. POSTTEST: ALTERNATE- AND ONE-HAND WORDS

H. Take three 12-second timed writings on each line. The scale gives your wam speed for a 12-second timed writing.

H. 12-SECOND SPRINTS

Check #187 was for $2,056.50 and Check #98 was for $190.20.
Carlson & Son won't buy #4; H & N won't buy #5; but I will.
"One-tenth or 1/10 equals 10%; one-half or 1/2 equals 50%."
Pay these expenses: (1) travel, (2) food, and (3) lodging.

| | | | 5 | | | |10| | | |15| | | |20| | | |25| | | |30| | | |35| | | |40| | | |45| | | |50| | | |55| | | |60

I. Take a 1-minute timed writing on the first paragraph to establish your base speed. Then take four 1-minute timed writings on the remaining paragraphs. As soon as you equal or exceed your base speed on one paragraph, advance to the next one.

I. SUSTAINED PRACTICE: SYLLABIC INTENSITY

As we have learned more and more about the benefits of 12
exercise, large numbers of people have gotten involved in a 24
broad range of sports. They want their workouts to be fun. 36

There are those who become puzzled after they discover 12
that they perform much better when they are practicing than 24
when competing. They can't keep their minds on their game. 36

Some of these discouraged athletes have sought counsel 12
from sports psychologists. They tell these special experts 24
that they handicap themselves because of these self-doubts. 36

Just as when working with professional athletes, there 12
is a basic challenge for the sports psychologist: What can 24
I do to rebuild confidence and refine concentration skills? 36

| 1 | 2 | 3 | 4 | 5 | 6 | 7 | 8 | 9 | 10 | 11 | 12

LETTER 73
BLOCK STYLE

Mr. Orlyn R. Glatzer
1706 Belasco Avenue
Sacramento, CA 95815

Subject: June Seminar at CATCS

The Chandler Air Traffic Control School is only three years old, but our program continues to be going very well. Among our varied efforts to bring enrichment to our program, we are continuing with our monthly seminar series.

We would like you to conduct a one-hour seminar again for our students on a date convenient for you during the first half of June. We would prefer that your topic be a current relevant issue in the state of California.

I shall call you on Thursday to finalize plans.

W. Ebert

By FAX

REPORT 66
ITINERARY

WARREN D. EBERT
Nevada Itinerary
May 18-19, 19--

Monday, May 18

San Jose / Las Vegas . . . . Southwest 64
Leave 7:10 a.m.; arrive 8:50 a.m.
Seat 7E; nonstop; breakfast
Las Vegas / Reno . . . . Nevada-Utah 1824
Leave 4:20 p.m.; arrive 6:35 p.m.
Seat 5A; 1 stop

Tuesday, May 19

Reno / San Jose . . . . CalCoastal 372
Leave 2:00 p.m.; arrive 2:50 p.m.
Seat 4C; nonstop

J. This paragraph is made up of very short words, requiring frequent use of the space bar. Key the paragraph twice. Do not pause before or after striking the space bar.

J. TECHNIQUE PRACTICE: SPACE BAR

```
     If I can see you at one or two, I can get to my job by   12
six and not be late.  I will try to take a cab or walk to a   24
bus stop for a ride.  My boss wants me to be on time for my   36
shift.  If I work for six hours, I will have my time in for   48
the week.  I will then see if I can join all of you at one.   60
```

| 1 | 2 | 3 | 4 | 5 | 6 | 7 | 8 | 9 | 10 | 11 | 12

K. Take two 1-minute timed writings. The last two digits of each number provide a cumulative word count to help you determine your wam speed.

K. NUMBER PRACTICE

```
3801 4702 1803 9304 6305 8006 2807 3308 5909 6110 9011 1212
4813 1914 7915 5316 8117 2418 7619 3720 9421 5922 7023 2324
8825 4126 6827 3128 9629 7530 5331 2632 1733 8834 6235 4036
2737 8538 5539 1140 3941 4642 9943 6744 7345 8146 3947 5248
```

L. DIAGNOSTIC PRACTICE: NUMBERS

Turn to the Diagnostic Practice: Numbers routine at the back of this book. Take the Pretest and record your performance. Then practice the drill lines for those reaches on which you made errors. Finally, repeat the Pretest and compare your performance.

M. Take a 1-minute timed writing on the first paragraph to establish your base speed. Then take four 1-minute timed writings on the remaining paragraphs. As soon as you equal or exceed your base speed on one paragraph, advance to the next one.

M. SUSTAINED PRACTICE: ROUGH DRAFT

```
     When you begin a new job, a few things can help ensure   12
success.  The first deals with getting along with others in   24
the workplace.  Maintaining a good rapport with supervisors   36
and coworkers should always be a prime goal of new workers.   48
     Listen[ing] carefully to instructions and endeavoring to   12
~~finish~~ [complete] assigned tasks accurately are quite important.  It   24
is ~~necessary~~ [essential] that a new worker understand what must be done   36
and then finish ~~the~~ [that] task in an efficient, accurate manner.   48
     Another useful tip is being a ~~cooperative~~ [dependable] worker.  When   12
a [new] worker maintains a ~~fine~~ [good] attendance pattern, it['s] just   24
like [a] good credit [rating].  Do not be late for work, and be   36
very certain that [your] absences from work are [at a minimum.]   48
     It's ~~essential~~ [vital] for ~~you~~ [one] to become part of [the] team quickly.   12
Learn to cooperate with [other] workers in ~~your~~ [the] office, and ask   24
question[s] when ~~i~~[u]nsure of some thing.  In order for a unit~~e~~[d] or   36
department to suc[c]eed, [everyone should be working together.]   48
```

| 1 | 2 | 3 | 4 | 5 | 6 | 7 | 8 | 9 | 10 | 11 | 12

REPORT 65
MINUTES OF MEETING

bold — CHANDLER AIR TRAFFIC CONTROL SCHOOL

ds Minutes of Faculty Meeting
April 15, 19--

2 blank lines

bold

ds REVIEW OF MINUTES
The minute(s) of the CATSC faculty meeting (held) on April 1 were reviewed and approved. There was one correction; the faculty and staff family picnic will be held at Hodges Park on Sunday, May 22 (not on Saturday, May 21), at 3 p. m.

ds TEXT AND REFERENCES — bold
Brad Danielson and Fran Hybbert reported that they are reviewing five text books and about a dozen published documents ~~that~~ (which) could be considered for adoption for the Advanced Radar course.

ds COURSE OBJECTIVES FOR ADVANCED RADAR COURSE — bold
There was agreement that all basic radar ~~program~~ (course) objectives relating to interpreting and performing radar procedures should be achieved by all enrollees in the advanced radar course at the 85% level. ¶ In addition to other topics previously identified, there was agreement that the following topics should be added: instrument approaches, traffic advisories, merging target procedures, aircraft safety alerts and aircraft emergency procedures.

ds ADJOURNMENT — bold
The ~~faculty~~ meeting was adjourned at 9:35 a.m.; the next ~~faculty~~ meeting will be held in two weeks.

Respectfully Submitted,
your name ___
Administrative Assistant

MEMO 25

MEMO TO: All Faculty

FROM: Warren D. Ebert, Director

DATE: April 42, 19--

SUBJECT: (Faculty) Meeting on April 29

A meeting for ~~all~~ instructional faculty has been scheduled for 8 a.m. on April 29, 19-- to continue a review of the following as ~~as~~ they relate to the new course entitled advanced radar, which will begin in January.

1. ~~Program~~ (Course) Description: A ~~program~~ (course) description that reflects course objectives will be developed.

2.[3] Test and References: Brad Danielson and Fran Hybert will submit their recommendations at the meeting.

3.[2] Course Objectives: The committee will distribute a ~~revised~~ list on Apr. 26; please review this list before the meeting.

N. Insert the necessary capital letters as you key these sentences twice.

N. TECHNIQUE PRACTICE: CONCENTRATION

66 Pat met mr. and mrs. hajducky when they flew to sacramento.
67 American flight 110 to nova scotia made a stop in hartford.
68 Lynn and john left for paradise island on saturday, july 6.
69 see the new york mets game at shea stadium with bob carlin.

O. Clear all tabs. Then set new tabs every 1 inch. Key lines 70–73, using the tab key to go across from column to column.

O. TECHNIQUE PRACTICE: TAB KEY

70	coins	await	eagle	berry	dairy
71	horse	fruit	jelly	gable	igloo
72	major	unite	offer	ledge	night
73	roast	phase	toast	valve	strap

P. PACED PRACTICE

Turn to the Paced Practice routine at the back of the book. Take four 2-minute timed writings, starting at the speed at which you left off the last time.

Q. Spacing: Double
Take two 5-minute timed writings. Compute your speed and count errors.

Goal: 43 wam/5′/5e

Q. 5-MINUTE TIMED WRITING

74 The paradox of time is that people rarely think they 12
75 have enough when in fact all of us have the same amount. 23
76 Time goes by faster and faster; days blur; seasons tumble 35
77 after seasons. It seems as if the faster we go, the faster 47
78 time goes. Most people compensate for this by trying to do 59
79 things quickly, by cramming more into the same space. 69
80 We walk faster, talk faster. In our cars, otherwise 81
81 calm people become Type A personalities, impatient at the 93
82 slightest delay. This furious pace can be seen by visiting 105
83 any big city. Pedestrians hurry down the street checking 116
84 their watches. Shoppers zip in and out of stores clutching 128
85 their bags. It almost seems as if one must rush about when 140
86 visiting a big city just to keep up. 148
87 Our perception of how fast time passes also depends on 160
88 what we are doing: it is one thing while we are on a trip, 172
89 another if our fingers are caught in a car door. In our 183
90 busy lives, it often appears impossible to try to find a 194
91 quiet moment for ourselves, but we must learn to give time 206
92 to time, to plan for a day and for a decade. 215

| 1 | 2 | 3 | 4 | 5 | 6 | 7 | 8 | 9 | 10 | 11 | 12

LETTER 72
BLOCK STYLE

Ms. Brenda J. Boettcher
Office for Compliance Review
State of California
3902 Bacchini Avenue
Sacramento, CA 95828

Dear Ms. Boettcher:

A table summarizing the ethnic composition of our January 19-- entering class is enclosed.

You will note that exactly half of our students are female. Also, 12 of the 28 students are in the nonwhite categories.

Please let me know if further information is needed.

W. Ebert

PS: Our detailed report, which analyzes the ethnic composition for all applicants for the July 19-- class, will be forwarded by August 1.

TABLE 52
RULED

ETHNIC COMPOSITION
January 19 -- Entering Class

Category	Male	Female
American Indian or Alaskan Native	2	0
Asian or Pacific Islander	1	2
Black	2	1
Hispanic	2	2
White	7	9

FORMATTING

R. REPORTS WITH A DISPLAY

WordPerfect 6 users: See Student Guide, p. 33.

A paragraph that is quoted or considered essential to a report may be "highlighted" or displayed by using single spacing and a 0.5-inch indent from both the left and right margins to make it stand out from the rest of the report. Use the Double-Indent command (Sh-F4) to double-indent the paragraph to be displayed.

DOCUMENT PROCESSING

REPORT 34
TWO-PAGE UNBOUND REPORT

Spacing: Double

Because this is a two-page report, the page numbering command must be entered on page 1 (top right) of this report, then suppressed for that page (Sh-F8, 2, 6, 4, 3, Enter, 8, 4, Y, F7).

Single-space and indent from both margins the displayed paragraph.

WordPerfect 6 users: Suppress page numbering—Sh-F8, Page, Supress, Page Numbering, OK, OK, Close.

Do widow/orphan

TRAVEL POLICY
Effective July 1, 19--

As of July 1, 19--, the travel policy guidelines will be changed to adhere to Rockmart's limited-expenditures position that was mandated at the board meeting on June 1, 19--. This travel policy will apply to all employees of Rockmart and will cover both in-state and out-of-state travel.

The new travel policy, as stipulated by the board on June 1, is as follows:

Shift F4

All Rockmart employee travel will be restricted to an amount not greater than $500 per month for in-state travel and $1,000 per month for out-of-state travel. This dollar amount will apply to transportation, lodging, and meals.

Travel budgets for each division vary during the months of the year. Because of this variation, division managers may request that their travel monies be "banked" so that the months of extensive travel can be accommodated by this policy.

Therefore, divisions are requested to submit quarterly travel reports to the Albuquerque office no later than 14 days prior to the quarter during which travel is anticipated. Travel Form A94-022 is to be used for all requests submitted after July.

Form A94-022 requires that all transportation costs, lodging expenses, and meals be filed with

[continued on next page]

DOCUMENT PROCESSING

IN-BASKET EXERCISE

CHANDLER AIR TRAFFIC CONTROL SCHOOL

Situation: Today is April 23, 19—. You are working as an administrative assistant for Mr. Warren D. Ebert, director of the Chandler Air Traffic Control School, located in San Jose, California. Mr. Ebert is on a business trip to Washington, D.C., and has left the following jobs in your in-basket for you to complete during his absence. You should save everything on a data disk.

Use WordPerfect's table, column, header, and footer functions as needed for the preparation of tables, the directory, and the magazine article, making adjustments as needed.

Mr. Ebert prefers his letters in block style with standard punctuation and this closing:

Sincerely yours,

Warren D. Ebert
Director

REPORT 64
DIRECTORY

Use Newspaper columns. Turn off columns before keying the date.

Please prepare a two-column directory of CATCS advisory board members. Use ADVISORY BOARD MEMBERS as the title, and alphabetize by last name.

Hernandez, Enrique J.
Pilot Coastal
California^Airlines
2489 Redondo Street
San Francisco, CA 94124
415-555-3673

Pham, Hoan Khai
Air Traffic Controller
South California Center
2608 43d Street ~~West~~
Los Angeles, CA 90008
ds 213-555-1768
Malzachar, M.#C.
Manager
San Diego Midway Airport
1457 Vista De La Orilla
San Diego, CA 92117
619-555-2038

Margaret M. O'Connor,
Instructional Dean
Arizona Aviation Center
10026 Black Canyon Drive (N.)
Phoenix, AZ 85051
602-555-4379 ↓2

April 23, 19--

Marquez-Shroyer, Carmen
Air traffic controller
Central California Center
4306 Laurite (Ave.) East
Fresno, CA 93725
ds 209-555-8175
Jackson, Kathryn M.
Pilot
Nevada - Utah Commuter Airline
803 Natasha Way
ss Reno, NV 89512

702-555-4693

Johnson , Thomas A.
Vice President for Operations
California Coastal Airlines
22 Oakmont Circle
Cupertino, CA 95014
ds 408-555-3276
Seidler, Naomi V.
Assistant Secretary
U.S. Dept. of Transportation
6025 Lee Highway
Arlington, VA 22205
703-555-8149

REPORT 34
(Continued)

the division--and subsequently with regional headquarters--no later than 10 days after completion of the travel. These expenses will be itemized individually for each trip. Related expenses (duplicating, telephone, and similar expenses) are to be included on page 2 of Form A94-022.

This policy supersedes Policy A90-324, dated March 1990, and will be in effect until further notice.

REPORT 35
TWO-PAGE UNBOUND REPORT

Spacing: Double

widow & orphan hyphenation

Note: The footnotes for both report pages are shown on the next page.

PAPER SELECTION

Choosing the Right Paper for your office

Selecting the right paper to use in your office isa decision that today requires considerable thought. A decade or so ago the decision required little ~~work~~ effort because options were very limited. In the '60s and '70s we looked for just a few basic ingredients in our paper: paper size, content rag, and weight. Although colored paper was evident 20 ~~and~~ or 30 years ago, it's use in the business office was just limited to a few applications.

Today paper comes in thousands of colors, finishes, prices, textures, and weights. You can combine these choices with papre that is smooth, glossy, speckled, re cycled, or first run.[1] In todays market, it is also very common to consider paper that is compatible with laser printers, since that is where the printing industry appears to be going. ¶ Because of the remarkable technological advances that have been made in the printing industry, in the 1990s, we now have a greater choice in the texture of. For example, the paper we use ~~to~~ we can now send out our office correspondense on letterhead paper that has intricately cut paterns or designs ~~cut right into~~ on the surface.[2]

These advances are inded remarkeable when you consider that of all the elements a designer works with (i.e. ~~paper~~, layout and design, color, type, and images), paper is probably dealt with the most conservatively.

When you are selecting the paper appropriate for your office, ~~there are~~ a number of questions ~~that~~ need tobe asked. Only after you have obtained satisfactory answers to these questions should you make ~~a~~ your decision on paperchoice. The questions are as follows: Does the paper--

[continued on next page]

N. Clear all tabs. Then set four new tabs every 1 inch. Key lines 64–67, using the tab key to go across from column to column.

N. TECHNIQUE PRACTICE: TAB KEY

165	343	298	126	618
304	981	762	493	804
235	976	890	558	129
841	982	563	204	975

O. Take three 12-second timed writings on each line. The scale gives wam for a 12-second timed writing.

O. 12-SECOND SPRINTS

Mr. James J. Baylorth lives at 15 Kent Street, Parma, Ohio.
Dr. Marcia Bates and Dr. Robert Gorem will be in Las Vegas.
The National Association of Realtors could meet in El Paso.
Morris County includes Budd Lake, Dover, and Morris Plains.

| | | | |5| | | |10| | | |15| | | |20| | | |25| | | |30| | | |35| | | |40| | | |45| | | |50| | | |55| | | |60

P. Spacing: Double
Take two 5-minute timed writings. Compute your speed and count errors.

Goal: 50 wam/5'/5e

P. 5-MINUTE TIMED WRITING

Do you like the idea of helping run a food bank for 11
the homeless? How about tutoring grammar school children 23
in math? Or teaching adults to read? In the coming years, 35
you may not have to work for a nonprofit organization in 46
order to be able to help out in this way. Your job may 58
give you some time to volunteer in your community. 68
More and more employers are recognizing their role 79
in keeping charities running. Many companies do this by 90
asking their employees to help out both on and off company 102
time. What kind of return on investment does this type of 114
help bring to the company? Unlike direct cash donations, 126
the gift of people power brings little in the way of tax 137
relief. However, there are many who call this a win-win 148
situation for all three groups: employers, employees, and 160
nonprofits alike. 164
With mergers giving companies a bad name and a growing 176
shortage of employees, many are discovering that volunteer 188
programs are an effective way to quell an upset public. 199
There are over a thousand companies that send some workers 211
into the community each year. For employees, such efforts 223
offer the chance to brush up on old skills or learn new 234
ones. For companies, this gives a chance to provide some 245
service for less cost. 250

| 1 | 2 | 3 | 4 | 5 | 6 | 7 | 8 | 9 | 10 | 11 | 12

REPORT 35
(Continued)

1. Come in the shade, texture, and weight you want?
2. Meet laser printer requirements?
3. Fit your budget?
4. Suit the audience intended?
5. Convey your intended message?[3]

If you have positive response to each of these question you are on your way to selecting the paper that is appropriate for you.

---

[1]Elizabeth Adler, "Paper," *Publish*, Sept. 1991, p. 76.

[2]Carmen Reynolds, "Today's paper standards," *Communications Technology*, March 1993, p. 42.

[3]Adler, p. 83.

FORMATTING

S. NEWS RELEASES

To format a news release:

1. Use 1-inch side margins and a 2-inch top margin.
2. Double-space the body, and indent paragraphs 0.5 inch.
3. Key "NEWS RELEASE" in large font, all capital letters, and bold, at the left margin.
4. Begin the identifying information at the top margin, flush right.
5. Center the title of the news release in all-capital letters with bold print.
6. Key a date line—city, state, abbreviated date, and a dash—before the first sentence.

DOCUMENT PROCESSING

REPORT 36
NEWS RELEASE

Spacing: Double

↓2 inches

NEWS RELEASE

From Jeanette Bullard
Nevada Systems Association
2483 Carter Drive
Reno, NV 89509

Release April 17, 19-- ↓2

↓3

NSA SPONSORS SYSTEMS MEETING ↓3

Reno, NV, Apr. 15--The Nevada System Association hosted the annual National Systems Association convention in Reno from Apr. 13 through Apr. 15. More than 800 computer systems personel attended the meeting, which attracted representatives from as far away as Puerto Rico and Toronto.

Next year's meeting will be held April 10-13 in Columbus, Ohio. The them will be "Communication technology inthe decade."

At this meeting, computer manufacturers revel some of their latest advances in laser printing technology. Color printers purchased for business use can compete with previously found quality only in high volume operations such as printing.

I. This paragraph is made up of very short words, requiring frequent use of the space bar. Take three 1-minute timed writings. Do not pause before or after striking the space bar.

I. TECHNIQUE PRACTICE: SPACE BAR

```
36      In just a few days, we will be taking a long trip to a  12
37 small town in the woods.  This will give us some time to be  24
38 quiet and take a good, long rest.  There is no way to reach  36
39 us in that town, and we shall not plan to call at any time.  48
    | 1 | 2 | 3 | 4 | 5 | 6 | 7 | 8 | 9 | 10 | 11 | 12
```

J. Key lines 40–43 twice each as you concentrate on number reaches. Notice that each number uses the same reaches as the preceding word.

J. NUMBER PRACTICE

```
40 we 23 it 85 ore 943 the 563 top 590 yet 635 out 975 two 529
41 et 35 or 94 tie 583 you 697 yet 635 pup 070 rip 480 tip 580
42 up 70 to 59 rot 495 pie 083 owe 923 wit 285 pet 035 wet 235
43 re 43 ie 83 toy 596 pot 095 owl 929 pit 085 yet 635 put 075
```

K. Each of these sentences contains two words that are not used properly. Correct those words as you key each sentence twice.

K. TECHNIQUE PRACTICE: CONCENTRATION

```
44 The assistance were board with the jobs they were assigned.
45 The advise from the personal department will help the man.
46 Please seize righting about the failures of our new workers.
47 An access amount of desert was being offered after dinner.
```

L. PROGRESSIVE PRACTICE: ALPHABET

Turn to the Progressive Practice: Alphabet routine at the back of the book. Take six 30-second timed writings, starting at the point where you left off the last time.

M. Take a 1-minute timed writing on the first paragraph to establish your base speed. Then take four 1-minute timed writings on the remaining paragraphs. As soon as you equal or exceed your base speed on one paragraph, advance to the next one.

M. SUSTAINED PRACTICE: SYLLABIC INTENSITY

```
48      Do you want a safe, fast, and easy way to improve your  12
49 health?  Try walking; it may be the best thing you could do  24
50 for yourself.  Although people have been walking for years,  36
51 it is but in recent times that it has been seen as a sport.  48

52      The new approach towards walking began about ten years  12
53 ago when one shoe company produced the first shoe made just  24
54 for walking.  Currently, there are many companies that make  36
55 hundreds of models all geared to make walking safe and fun.  48

56      Podiatrists believe that walking improves skeletal and  12
57 muscular development by exercising and toning all the bones  24
58 and muscles in the body.  Walking with excellent posture is  36
59 a good way to strengthen the back, stomach, and upper legs.  48

60      Whether you call it aerobic walking, power walking, or  12
61 exercise walking, it has fast become a favorite workout and  24
62 participation sport in America.  There are easily a million  36
63 Americans maximizing their health by striding for exercise.  48
    | 1 | 2 | 3 | 4 | 5 | 6 | 7 | 8 | 9 | 10 | 11 | 12
```

REPORT 37
NEWS RELEASE

Margins: 1 inch
Spacing: Double

Retrieve Report 36 and make the following changes;

1. Add the following as the third paragraph: *CD-ROM technology was also highlighted during the sessions and the product demonstrations. CD-ROMs will become the norm for storing information.*
2. Add the following side headings to the news release:
   Laser Technology as the heading for the paragraph on laser printing.
   CD-ROM Technology as the heading for the paragraph on CD-ROMs.

FORMATTING

T. MAGAZINE ARTICLES

Magazine Article Page Heading

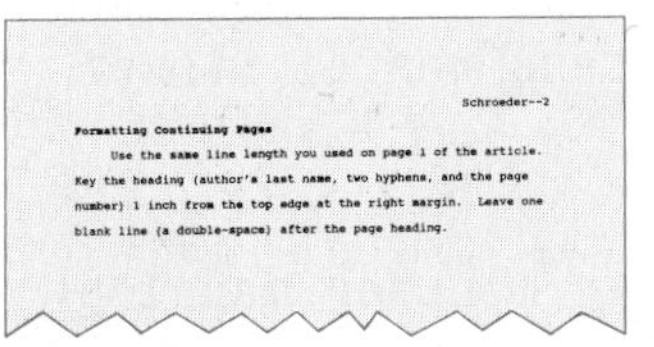

Schroeder--2

Formatting Continuing Pages

Use the same line length you used on page 1 of the article. Key the heading (author's last name, two hyphens, and the page number) 1 inch from the top edge at the right margin. Leave one blank line (a double-space) after the page heading.

WordPerfect 6 users: See Student Guide, p. 34.

Read the instructions for preparing a magazine article in the report that follows before you begin the report. To include the author's name with the page number in the continuing pages of the report (Illustration 1), follow these steps. Turn on Page Numbering (Sh-F8, 2, 6, 4, 3). Select Option 2 from the Page Numbering menu. Key the author's name and two hyphens, then press Enter to insert the WordPerfect page number symbol (^B). Press Enter again to return to the Page Numbering menu. Suppress the page number on page 1 and return to your document (8, 4, Y, F7).

DOCUMENT PROCESSING

REPORT 38
MAGAZINE ARTICLE

Margins: 1.75 inches
Spacing: Double
Tab: 0.5 inch, 0.9 inch

Headers, footers, and page numbers do not appear on-screen. Use View Document (or Print Preview) to check placement of the page number for this report.

↓ 2 inches

FORMATTING A MAGAZINE ARTICLE ↓ 2

By Jeremy N. Shroeder ↓ 3

To format a magazine article, which is classified as a report, you follow many of the formatting rules for preparing reports. However, a few differences need to be pointed out. The information in this article identifies the formatting rules that are common to many magazines.

One measure of the success of an article is the writer's ability to prepare a document that is pleasing to the eye of the editor. These guidelines will help you prepare a quality document for a magazine.

Formatting Rules

To prepare a quality manuscript, you must make your article look professional. Here are a few suggestions:

1. Use a 5-inch line for the article.
2. Except on page 1, key the author's name and the page number at the top right on all pages of the article.
3. Follow the style required by the magazine to which you are sending your article.
4. If enumerations are used, indent the first line 0.5 inch. Turnover lines indent 0.9 inch. Double-space the enumerations.

Formatting Continuing Pages

Use the same line length you used on page 1 of the article. Key the heading (author's last name, two hyphens, and the page number) 1 inch from the top edge at the right margin. Leave one blank line (a double space) after the page heading.

SKILLBUILDING

PRETEST. Take a 1-minute timed writing; compute your speed and count errors.

D. PRETEST: DISCRIMINATION PRACTICE

Lois said the rear of the long train was right next to 12
the column of poplar trees. A robber had entered a red car 24
and stolen a case of grapefruit juice and ten cases of soda 36
pop. The officer quickly arrested him; the train moved on. 48

| 1 | 2 | 3 | 4 | 5 | 6 | 7 | 8 | 9 | 10 | 11 | 12

PRACTICE. *Speed Emphasis:* If you made no more than 1 error on the Pretest, key each line twice.

Accuracy Emphasis: If you made 2 or more errors on the Pretest, key each group of lines (as though it were a paragraph) twice.

E. PRACTICE: LEFT HAND

rtr art part trip sort trot start train skirt depart strobe
asa ash mass sand cash salt grass salad trash splash salmon
sds sad used suds said pods based drips curds stride guards
rer red rear fear rest pier tread lower press rental flower

F. PRACTICE: RIGHT HAND

mnm menu mine numb meant named melon column mention mansion
pop post poor coop point troop poise police popular operate
olo tool yolk loon spoil lodge color stroll lottery rolling
iui unit suit quit quiet unite juice sluice biscuit uniform

POSTTEST. Repeat the Pretest (D) and compare performance.

G. POSTTEST: DISCRIMINATION PRACTICE

H. Take a 1-minute timed writing on the first paragraph to establish your base speed. Then take four 1-minute timed writings on the remaining paragraphs. As soon as you equal or exceed your base speed on one paragraph, advance to the next one.

H. SUSTAINED PRACTICE: ROUGH DRAFT

In one way or another, the great majority of women who 12
were born in the Baby Boom generation, and their daughters, 24
will probably be deeply involved in the work force from now 36
on. These women will greatly change the future job market. 48

Woman will account for two thirds of the net growth in 12
the work force in the years to come, even through their rate 24
of entry in to the job market may slow. By the next century 36
it will most liely level to a bit below the male job rate. 48

The portion of adult women at work will rise faster 12
then thier total numbers, reaching three our of five in the 24
near future. Women's number will grow in managerial rank 36
and in many entrpreneurial business which will open. 48

Additionally, the disparty not found between male and 12
female earning will narow. This will be do to increased 24
legal presure and, more signifcantly, the growing business 36
experience and educational background that women will have. 48

| 1 | 2 | 3 | 4 | 5 | 6 | 7 | 8 | 9 | 10 | 11 | 12

REPORT 39
MAGAZINE ARTICLE

Margins: 1.75 inches
Spacing: Double

Remember to include the author's name with the page number.

DISCOUNT SERVICES FOR USPA MEMBERS

By Brenda K. Allen

As an employee of USPA, you are eligible for a wide range of discount services available to all employees and their dependents. These consumer savings provide you with tremendous buying power for a wide variety of items and services, from automobiles to jewelry to travel plans. Here are some examples of the quality merchandise and services that are available from USPA.

Auto Pricing and Purchase

You can order the most sophisticated auto information guide on the market. It will give you information on suggested retail prices, vehicle specifications, safety equipment, and factory option packages.

When you are ready to make your purchase, a team of company experts will work with you to ensure that you are getting the best possible price through a network of nationwide dealers.

Extended Services

A wide range of services will appeal to you, especially when you are ready to travel by auto.

Emergency Road Service. You can enjoy the security of emergency road service through the USPA Road and Travel Plan. This comprehensive plan also includes discounts on hotels and motels.

Car Rental Discounts. Special rates from four of the largest auto rental agencies make this service extremely popular with our employees.

Travel Service. As a USPA traveler, you can take advantage of our exclusive discounts and bonuses on cruises and tours. Our travel plan provides daily and weekend trips to over 100 destinations. Take advantage now of this wonderful opportunity to let USPA serve all your travel needs.

LESSONS 111-115

Margins: 1 inch • Spacing: Single • Drills: 2 times • Format Guide: 87–95

Goals for Unit 23

1. To improve accuracy and speed on alphabet and number keys.
2. To key 50 wam for 5 minutes with no more than 5 errors.
3. To improve proficiency in composing at the keyboard.
4. To gain an understanding of and an orientation to an in-basket exercise.
5. To format a variety of reports—directory, minutes of meeting, itinerary, and magazine article.
6. To format letters and memorandums with various features.
7. To format boxed tables with braced column headings.

Begin each day with approximately 15 minutes of skillbuilding, selecting activities from pages 266–269. In the remaining class time, complete as many production jobs from pages 270–277 as you can.

A. WARMUP

```
1      A requisition has been completed to purchase 8 items @   12
2 $71 and 30 items @ $59.  Just add a 6% sales tax for a cost   24
3 of $2,478.28.  Analyze, check, and verify the gross weight.   36
  | 1 | 2 | 3 | 4 | 5 | 6 | 7 | 8 | 9 | 10 | 11 | 12
```

LANGUAGE ARTS

B. Study the rules at the right. Then key lines 4–7, making necessary changes.

B. NUMBERS

Rule: Spell out fractions that stand alone, and use figures for mixed numbers.

The gauge shows that the tank is over one-third full.
Expenses are nearly 2 1/2 times higher than last year.

Rule: To form the plurals of figures, add *s*.

That particular stock is now priced in the high 30s.

```
4 They now control about 2/3 of the market in that region.
5 The recipe called for two and one-half cups of flour.
6 That form of technology was introduced in the 1970's.
7 The temperatures were in the 90s every day of the month.
```

C. COMPOSING

Compose the body of a letter to respond to Letter 57, Unit 18, page 208. Use the following suggestions for each paragraph:

Paragraph 1. Tell Mr. Fabereisen that you are pleased with his thorough inspection of the Larch Street building and that his information was clear and to the point.

Paragraph 2. Tell Mr. Fabereisen that you are still interested in purchasing the building but would like to have a soils engineer review the available compaction reports. Ask if he can provide you with a list of people he would recommend to do this for you.

Paragraph 3. Thank Mr. Fabereisen for his prompt response in this matter.

FORMATTING

WP

INITIAL CODES
Sh-F8, 3, 2, *enter codes,* F7, F7

WordPerfect 6 users: See Student Guide, p. 34.

U. WORDPERFECT: INITIAL CODES

To change WordPerfect's default settings in a single document, enter format changes in Initial Codes instead of in your document. For example, the default margins for footnotes or endnotes are 1 inch. In order for footnotes or endnotes in a bound report to be formatted with the same margins as the report, you must set the left margin (1.5") in Initial Codes. Position the cursor at the top of your document and press Sh-F8, 3, 2. Then set the left margin (Sh-F8, 1, 7, 1.5"). Press Enter four times to return to Initial Codes, then press F7 twice.

WordPerfect 6 users: See Student Guide, p. 36.

V. BOOK MANUSCRIPTS

Follow these steps when formatting the individual pages for a book manuscript:

1. Key the manuscript in standard "bound report" format.

2. Position the page number in the top right corner of every page (Sh-F8, 2, 6, 4, 3, F7).

DOCUMENT PROCESSING

REPORT 40
BOOK MANUSCRIPT

Left margin: 1.5 inches
Spacing: Double

Set all formatting commands in Initial Codes.

Note: The portion of book manuscript at the right begins with *page 142.* Set the Page Numbering command to begin with page 142.

WordPerfect 6 users: See Student Guide, p. 36.

142

Storing information in an office can take many forms. Information must be stored so that it can be found quickly when it is needed. Most information today is stored either on paper, on magnetic disks, or on laser disks.

Paper Storage

Most of the written or printed information that was created in the past two decades is still being stored on paper. In fact, some authorities estimate that we currently have over a trillion pages of information stored on paper.[1] Current predictions are that we will continue to store information on paper, and storage systems must be updated often to meet this demand.

Magnetic Storage

Magnetic storage is in common use today, and its most popular forms are the floppy disk, the hard disk, and CD-ROM. Some floppy disks can hold as much as 400 pages of information, and about six floppy disks can store about one file drawer of paper. A hard disk can store many more pages than a floppy disk. Today's hard disks can store over 100,000 pages, or about 40 file drawers of paper documents.

Laser Storage

Optical disk storage (CD-ROM) can hold yet more information than either the floppy disk or the hard disk. An optical disk is written and read by lasers. One laser optical disk is capable of storing over 6.8 gigabytes of information.[2] As prices continue to come down, optical disks could eventually replace magnetic storage.

---

[1]Sharon Lund O'Neil, *Office Information Systems,* 3d ed., Glencoe Division, Macmillan/McGraw-Hill School Publishing Company, Westerville, Ohio, 1990, p. 197.

[2]Ibid., p. 201.

TABLE 51
ADVERTISEMENT

WordPerfect 6 users: See Student Guide, p. 73.

Follow these steps to format Table 51, illustrated below:

1. Change left and right margins to 0.5″.
2. Create a figure box with no border for TROPHY.WPG with Anchor = Page; Vertical Position = 1.1″; Horizontal Position = Margin, Center; Size = 1″ × 1″; Wrap Text = No.
3. Center "TROPHY" in Extra Large font and bold. Press Enter twice. Set absolute tabs at 2.1″ (left) and 6.3″ (right). Tab once to key "COMPUTER" and once more to key "SUPPLIES." Return to normal font.
4. Press Enter four times, and center "Serving the Boston Area . . ." in Very Large italic font. Return to normal font.
5. Press Enter three times, and center "HOLIDAY SPECIALS" in Extra Large font, Small Caps. Return to normal font.
6. Press Enter two times and create a 5-column, 9-row table.
7. Enter the data for the table, placing a blank line before and after each horizontal entry.
8. Extend the columns so that all lines are single-spaced.
9. Center and add shading to the column headings.
10. Use left justify for the first two columns and right justify for the last three columns.
11. Change the horizontal line between the Epson and Panasonic brands to thick.

TROPHY

COMPUTER  **SUPPLIES**

"Serving the Boston Area Since 1975"

HOLIDAY SPECIALS

Printer	Stock No.	Quantity 1	Quantity 6	Quantity 12
Epson LQ 850	RB850-B	$9.95	$8.95	$7.95
Epson LQ 1050	RB1050-B	$10.25	$9.25	$8.25
Epson FX 1050	RB1050X-B	$8.75	$7.75	$6.75
Epson LQ 2550	RB2550-B	$12.95	$11.95	$9.95
Panasonic KX-P1080	RB1080-B	$7.80	$6.80	$5.80
Panasonic KX-P1124	RB1124-B	$8.25	$7.25	$6.25
Panasonic KX-P1524	RB1524-B	$9.85	$8.85	$7.85
Panasonic KX-P1624	RB1624-B	$10.25	$9.25	$7.95

REPORT 41
BOOK MANUSCRIPT

Left margin: 1.5 inches
Spacing: Double

Retrieve Report 40 and make the following changes:

1. Delete the last sentence in the paragraph entitled **Paper Storage.** Add the following to the end of that paragraph:

   Today, most paper documents are stored by one of four methods. Each of these methods is described in the following enumeration.

   1. Vertical filing is the most common method for paper storage. In this method, all paper is stored in drawers, and each drawer is stacked on top of another.
   2. In lateral filing, papers are arranged to face the sides of the cabinet.
   3. In open-shelf filing, everything is stacked vertically so that you can see everything that is stored on the shelf.
   4. In rotary filing, a document can be accessed by turning or rotating the "cabinet" until it is in front of you.

2. Add the following paragraph headings to the section entitled **Magnetic Storage:**

   Floppy Disks as the heading before the sentence that starts with "Some floppy disks. . . ."
   Hard Disks as the heading before the sentence that starts with "A hard disk. . . ."

FORMATTING

W. WORDPERFECT: BLOCK PROTECT

WP BLOCK PROTECT
Block text (F12 or Alt-F4, *highlight text*), Sh-F8, Y

WordPerfect 6 users: See Student Guide, p. 37.

Block Protect keeps a block of text (for example, a table) from being split between two pages. If all of the block will not fit on one page, the entire block will be moved to the next page. To keep a block of text together, move to the start of the block, press F12 or Alt-F4, highlight the text to be blocked, then press Sh-F8, and enter "y."

DOCUMENT PROCESSING

REPORT 42
BOOK MANUSCRIPT

Left margin: 1.5 inches
Spacing: Double

Set all formatting commands in Initial Codes.

Note: Set Page Numbering to begin with *page 62.*

62

Every year that goes by reveals that computers are becoming increasingly more popular in the nation's business offices. These computers are used by managers, supervisors, office personnel, and others who manipulate data on a day-to-day basis. Using computers has become a way of life for all of these people, and their daily routines have changed dramatically because of computers.

Among those people who use computers as tools to help them perform office activities at a faster pace and with more accuracy, most reveal that they use a computer for one of five basic functions: word processing, spreadsheet, database, communications, and programming. Also mentioned as very popular uses of computers are graphics and desktop publishing.

In a recent survey on how people use computers in an office, the greatest percentage of respondents (29 percent) indicated that word processing is the package they use most often. Following closely in second place was spreadsheet software, with 23 percent of the respondents indicating an interest in this package. The third most frequent response was database, with 19 percent of all respondents indicating this choice. These results and other findings are revealed in Table 5, page 63.

[continued on next page]

FORMATTING

S. WORDPERFECT: TABLE REVIEW

WP TABLE REVIEW
Create table: Alt-F7, 2, 1

Switch between screens: *position cursor inside table,* Alt-F7

Center table horizontally: 6, 3, 3, F7

Adjust column width: Ctrl–Right or Left Arrow

Center a row: 2, 1, 3, 2

Apply shading: 3, 8, 1

Delete top line: 3, 3, 1

Right-justify a column: 2, 1, 3, 3

Insert row/column: Ins

WordPerfect 6 users: See Student Guide, p. 72.

WordPerfect's powerful Table command, in combination with other DTP features, can be used to format many documents. Follow these steps to format Table 49:

1. Change left and right margins to 1.5″, clear all tabs, and set an absolute right tab at 7″.
2. Change the option for figure boxes to border style = none on each side.
3. Create a figure box (Filename = STAR-5.WPG) at the top left margin, with a width of 0.75″ (set Width/Auto Height).
4. Key the company name in Extra Large font size and bold and the address in regular-size type; then press Enter five times (Ln = 2.11″).
5. Key "Price List" in Extra Large font size, tab, and then key the date in regular-size type. Press Enter twice.
6. Create a table with 5 columns and 6 rows.
7. Switch to the document screen (Alt-F7), and key the data in the table in regular-size type. (You will format the table later.)
8. Block the column headings, and switch to the small font size.
9. Return to the table edit screen and format the table as follows (use the Block command to format more than one cell at a time):
   a. Center the table horizontally.
   b. Widen Column A so that each title fits on one line. Shorten Columns B and E so that the headings appear as shown in the illustration.
   c. Center and apply gray shading to the column headings.
   d. Remove the top lines from the interior rows of the table.
   e. Right-justify the number columns.

DOCUMENT PROCESSING

TABLE 49
PRICE LIST

WordPerfect 6 users: See Student Guide, p. 73.

STAR PUBLICATIONS
333 West Lane, Westfield, MA 01085

Price List July 1, 19--

Magazine	No. of Issues	Cover Price	Regular Price	Sale Price
Alamo Sports Weekly	52	101.40	51.48	25.74
Lone Star Cooking	27	106.65	49.95	24.99
Outdoor Living	12	30.00	24.00	12.00
Southwest Industry	13	38.35	35.95	18.99
Texas History	6	15.00	12.00	9.97

TABLE 50
PRICE LIST

Retrieve Table 49, change the date to September 1, 19—, and add the following magazines (in alphabetic order). Adjust Column A to fit the titles on single lines.

Southern Hospitality / 10 / 25.00 / 18.00 / 9.97
Mexican Affairs / 12 / 39.00 / 28.00 / 24.50
Texas Entrepreneur / 54 / 155.40 / 69.66 / 34.98
Plains Speaking / 12 / 28.00 / 22.00 / 10.50

REPORT 42
(Continued)

Block protect the table.

Leave 3 blank lines (2 double spaces) before and after a table that contains a title within a report.

Table 5

BUSINESS COMPUTER USAGE

(Most Popular Software Packages)

Type of Package	Percent
Word Processing	29
Spreadsheet	23
Database	19
Communications	9
Programming	7
Graphics	6
Desktop Publishing	5
Other	2
TOTAL	100

It is likely that in the future computers will be used even more heavily in the business office than they are today. The greatest usage will likely come from people who conduct the majority of their business on a computer or use peripheral equipment (such as a modem or fax machine) to communicate their ideas to others across the nation and around the globe.

REPORT 43
BOOK MANUSCRIPT

Left margin: 1.5 inches
Spacing: Double

Retrieve Report 42 and make the following changes:

1. Add a footnote to the final sentence of Report 42. The source is as follows: Brandon T. Oliver, "Computer Usage in Business," *Business Technology News,* March 1992, pp. 17–18.
2. Add the following paragraphs as a continuation of Report 42:

At the turn of the century, we will be working with computers that are smarter, faster, smaller, and more powerful. All of this will be made possible because of the advent of more advanced chip technology. As Robichaud states in his information processing text:

Block protect the indented paragraph to keep all of its lines together.

> Computer chips being developed today have four times the storage capacity of any memory chip used in computers today. The memory cells in these chips are so small that 48,000 of them fit in an area the size of the period at the end of this sentence.[2]

It is a fact that tomorrow's computers will be used extensively in all areas of business. The information revolution is certainly here to stay.

---

[2]Beryl Robichaud et al., *Introduction to Information Processing,* 4th ed., Glencoe Division, Macmillan/McGraw-Hill School Publishing Company, Westerville, Ohio, 1989, p. 349.

REPORT 62
2-COLUMN ABSTRACT

Your job may look different from what is shown here.

↓ 1 inch

The Feasibility of Consolidating Roadway's Overland Park Terminal With the Kansas City Operation

Abstract

THE COSTS OF OPERATING a freight terminal are rising quite dramatically. The increase in labor and operating expenses, along with declining sales revenue, are causing many motor carriers to close their smaller satellite terminals and to deliver freight to markets from larger consolidation points.

BACKGROUND

The purpose of this study was to judge the possibility of consolidating the Roadway Overland Park satellite operation with its larger Kansas City hub operation. Specifically, the investigation included determining the comparable costs of consolidation, whether any business would be lost, and the opinions of Roadway's staff and major customers about the proposed consolidation.

Interviews with some of Roadway's staff and major customers, journal articles, and corporate records provided the data for solving the problem.

FINDINGS

An analysis of the data indicates that consolidating the two separate operations would probably result in a first-year net cost savings of approximately $45,000, with subsequent-year savings of $35,000 to $40,000 annually.

A gross estimated first-year cost saving of $60,000 will be realized by eliminating two positions. Further, $15,000 can be realized by renting the Overland Park building and property for other purposes.

Offsetting this $75,000 gross gain is an estimated increase of $12,000 in additional transportation cost as well as an estimated $18,000 loss of business due to closing the Overland Park terminal.

RECOMMENDATION

We recommend that Roadway close their Overland Park satellite but refrain from selling the property for six months until the effect of the closure can be determined.

We further recommend that the satellite's transportation marketing director be provided released time to develop a plan for working with our major Overland Park customers to ease the transition to Kansas City.

Progress Test on Part 4

TEST 4-A
5-MINUTE TIMED WRITING

Spacing: Double

If you are to be a success in the world of work, you 12
must possess the ability to get along with others. Men and 24
women of all ages, experience, and education have found 35
this ability a key requirement for success in jobs in which 47
people work side by side. Those who lack the know-how they 59
need for getting along with others will not win advancement 71
nearly as quickly as do those who may have less knowledge 82
and skill but more ability in getting along with others. 94
You have to ask yourself what the knack of getting along 105
with others is and what you hope to do to achieve it. 116

Getting along with others is somewhat hard to define, 128
but it is expressing yourself in a manner that shows you 139
recognize and respect how others feel. No one can be sweet 151
all the time, but no one ever has to be rough or mean. No 163
one should insult or bully others or ignore their feelings 175
and expect those people to become friends or to provide 186
help up the ladder of success. The maxim about treating 197
others the way you wish them to treat you is a good formula 210
that you can use for business. 215

| 1 | 2 | 3 | 4 | 5 | 6 | 7 | 8 | 9 | 10 | 11 | 12

TEST 4-B
LETTER 53
MODIFIED-BLOCK LETTER WITH INDENTED PARAGRAPHS

(*Current Date*) / Mr. Joseph Alholm, Jr. / Regional Manager / Sunshine Household Products, Inc. / 158 Prince Street / Boston, MA 02113 / Dear Joe: / Subject: Sales in New England Region

Although Sunshine Household was removed from the umbrella of Capital Products last year, I have been getting sales figures for each of the districts.

Enclosed is the sales data concerning the New England region. This information is absolutely essential to you as you make long-range plans and strategies. While I no longer have responsibility for Sunshine products, I am pleased to note the New England Region met its sales quota.

I am also pleased that the Portland office is having such a banner year. It would be good if some of the excitement from that office would touch the Boston crew; you might want to see what the problem is in Boston.

Sincerely yours, / Jack Canton / Vice President of Marketing / (*Your Initials*) / Enclosure

FORMATTING

R. WORDPERFECT: COLUMNS

WP COLUMNS

Define and turn on columns: Alt-F7, 1, 3, *make selections,* F7, 1

Turn off columns: Alt-F7, 1, 2

Force a column break: Ctrl-Enter

Move between columns while editing: Ctrl-Home, ← or →

WordPerfect 6 users: See Student Guide, p. 69.

WordPerfect enables you to format two kinds of columns: newspaper and parallel. Newspaper columns are read from top to bottom (like the columns in this textbook).

Parallel columns are read from left to right. For example, in a catalog the product name might appear in Column 1 and a multiline description might appear in Column 2. With parallel columns the first line of each column always aligns.

You can define from 2 to 24 columns on a page and can turn columns on or off as needed. To delete columns, enter Reveal Codes and delete the Column On code.

As you key text in newspaper columns, the lines will automatically wrap within a column until you reach the bottom of the page. Text is then moved to the top of the next column. To force a column to break before the end of a page, insert a Hard-Page Break (Ctrl-Enter) at the point where you want to end the column.

When you finish keying a parallel column, insert a Hard Page Break (Ctrl-Enter) in order to move the cursor to the next column. If the text in a column extends past the end of a page, the text will wrap to the next page, remaining in the same column.

DOCUMENT PROCESSING

REPORT 61
2-COLUMN REPORT

WordPerfect 6 users: See Student Guide, p. 70.

Key Section R above as two equal newspaper columns. Key the title 2 inches from the top of the page in all-capital letters and bold, then triple space. Define the columns using the default settings: type (newspaper), number of columns (2), distance between columns (0.5″), and margins (1″). Use single spacing, full justification, and a 0.3-inch paragraph indention (do not indent the first paragraph). Insert a Hard Page Break to align the columns at the bottom. Your printout should look similar to the illustration at the right.

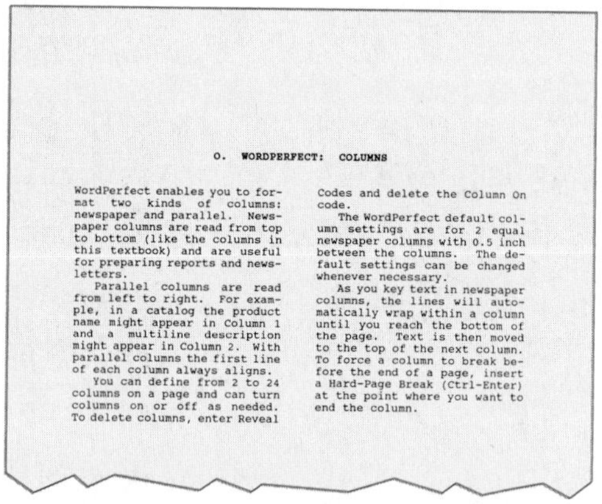

O. WORDPERFECT: COLUMNS

WordPerfect enables you to format two kinds of columns: newspaper and parallel. Newspaper columns are read from top to bottom (like the columns in this textbook) and are useful for preparing reports and newsletters.

Parallel columns are read from left to right. For example, in a catalog the product name might appear in Column 1 and a multiline description might appear in Column 2. With parallel columns the first line of each column always aligns.

You can define from 2 to 24 columns on a page and can turn columns on or off as needed. To delete columns, enter Reveal Codes and delete the Column On code.

The WordPerfect default column settings are for 2 equal newspaper columns with 0.5 inch between the columns. The default settings can be changed whenever necessary.

As you key text in newspaper columns, the lines will automatically wrap within a column until you reach the bottom of the page. Text is then moved to the top of the next column. To force a column to break before the end of a page, insert a Hard-Page Break (Ctrl-Enter) at the point where you want to end the column.

REPORT 62
2-COLUMN ABSTRACT

WordPerfect 6 users: See Student Guide, p. 71.

Follow these steps to format Report 62 shown on page 263.

1. Insert a graphic horizontal line 0.1″ wide at the top of the page.
2. Create a footer that contains a horizontal line using the default settings.
3. Set a relative left tab at 0.3 inch.
4. Press Enter five times (Ln-1.77″). Center the title in Very Large font; the subtitle in Large font. Double-space before and triple-space after the subtitle.
5. Switch to full justification.
6. Define the columns using the default settings, then turn on columns.
7. Key the body of the newsletter, letting word wrap end lines and move to a new column.
8. Format the side headings in all-capital letters and bold with one blank line above and below.

REPORT 63
3-COLUMN ABSTRACT

WordPerfect 6 users: See Student Guide, p. 71.

Retrieve Report 62 and make the following changes:

1. Change the side margins to 0.75 inch.
2. Delete the column-define and column-on codes (use Reveal Codes).
3. Switch to left justification.
4. Define and turn on three equal newspaper columns with 0.25 inch between columns. (Scroll through the document using the down arrow key to reformat it to three columns.)
5. Print the document and determine where you need to insert a Hard Page Break (Ctrl-Enter) to make the columns end as evenly as possible. If necessary, add the date in parentheses (September 19—) as the last line of Column 3 so that the columns will end more evenly.
6. Print a final copy of the abstract.

TEST 4-C
TABLE 25

Spacing: Single

Center the table horizontally and vertically.

SUNSHINE HOUSEHOLD PRODUCTS, INC.

Third-Quarter Sales for New England Region

District	Sales	Quota	Percent of Quota
Boston	$1,380,000	$1,500,000	92.0
Concord	975,800	950,000	102.7
Hartford	1,115,000	1,000,000	111.5
Portland	860,000	800,000	107.5
Providence	1,150,000	1,200,000	95.8
TOTAL	$5,480,800	$5,450,000	100.6

TEST 4-D
REPORT 44
BOUND REPORT PAGE 26

Spacing: Double

Depreciation Expenses

With the new legislation ~~concerning~~ regarding tax reform, there has now been a change in calculating our depreciation expenses on any assets put in service after January 1, 1987. This new system, which is called the "Modified Accelerated Cost Recovery System",) must be understood in order to comply with Internal Revenue Service ~~code~~ directives.

To compute the MACRS deduction, multiply the unadjusted basis of the asset by a percentage taken from the MACRS tables. These tables are available in our corporate tax department. First, determine the number of years it will take to fully depreciate or recover the cost or other ~~amount~~ basis of the asset. Then, referring to the table, follow the column with the correct number of years to determine the rate for depreciation in ~~every~~ each year of the life of the asset. This system enables us to recover a greater portion of the cost of our assets in the beginning years of their being in service, compared with taking a straight-line depreciation, ~~gives~~ which spreads the cost evenly through out the life of the asset.

Section 179 Expense Deduction. It is possible to deduct up to ~~$5,000~~ $10,000 of certain property in the year of acquisition instead of recovering that amount under MACRS. This deduction will only be taken with the approval of our Director of Accounting.

REPORT 60
FLIER

WordPerfect 6 users: See Student Guide, p. 67.

Follow these steps to create the voting ballot shown here.

1. At the top of the page, center and key in Extra Large font and bold the title:
   PRESIDENTIAL VOTING BALLOT
2. Change to Normal font and press Enter.
3. Advance to Ln = 6.5″ and set absolute tabs at 4 inches and 4.5 inches.
4. Tab to the first tab stop and create a figure box with these settings:
   Anchor: Character
   Vertical Position: Baseline
   Size: 0.25″ wide × 0.25″ high
   Wrap Text: No
5. Exit the figure box and press Tab. Next, key in Large font the first candidate's name:
   D. Arnold
6. Press Enter two times and Tab once. Then create a second figure box with the settings listed in Step 3.
7. Tab again and key in Large font the second candidate's name:
   T. Hayes
8. Repeat Steps 4 through 6 for the remaining names, but do not press Enter after keying the last name.
   S. Blakely
   M. Fang
9. Set the options for a figure box to "no borders."
10. Create another figure box with these options:
    Filename: PRESNT-1.WPG
    Anchor: Page
    Vertical Position: 2″
    Horizontal Position: Margin, Center
    Size: 5.5″ wide × 4″ high
    Wrap Text: No
11. Set the options for a text box to "no border, no shading."
12. Create a text box with these options:
    Anchor: Page
    Vertical Position: 2.2″
    Horizontal Position: 3.7″
    Size: 2.5″ wide × 3.65″ high
    Wrap Text: No
13. Key the remaining text:
    Exercise your voting rights! Check mark the box below next to your choice for president of our league.

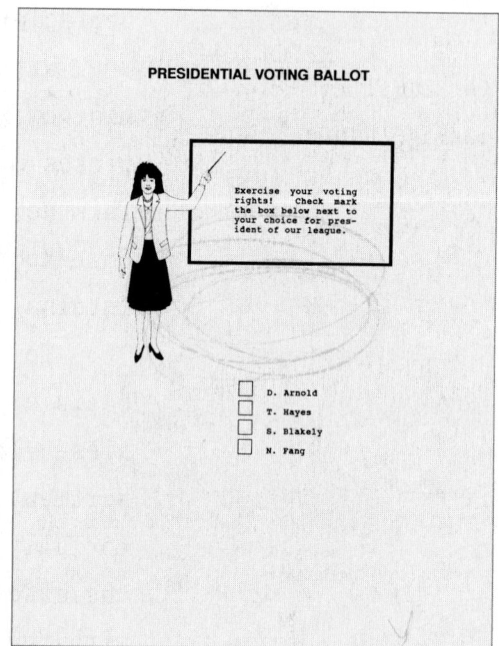

PART 5

SKILLBUILDING

Specialized Correspondence, Reports, and Tables

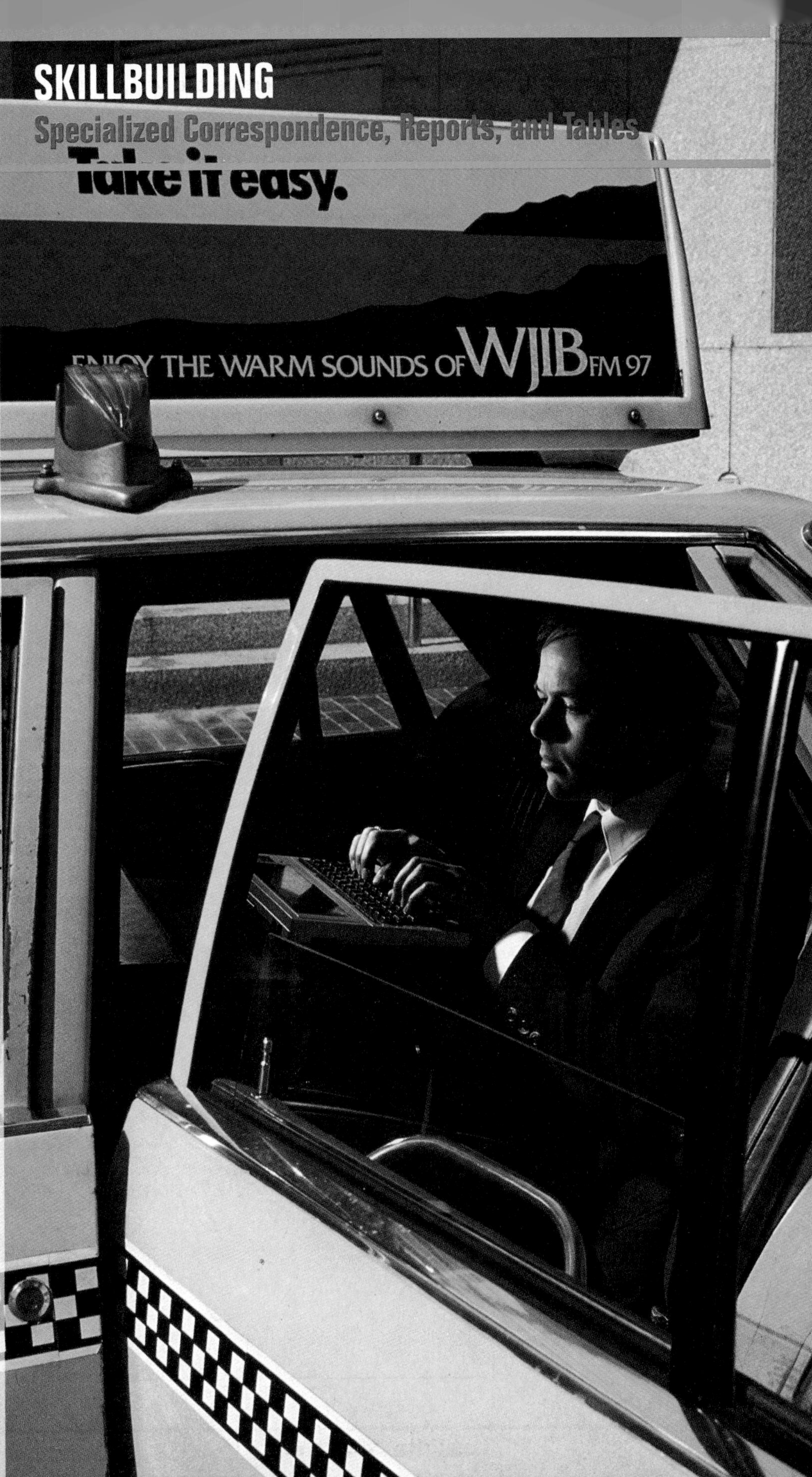

OBJECTIVES

KEYBOARDING

To key 47 words a minute on a 5-minute timed writing with no more than 5 errors.

LANGUAGE ARTS

To improve language arts skills.

To proofread and correct errors.

WORD PROCESSING

To learn to use these WordPerfect commands: Repeat Value, Double Underline, Merge, Switch, Window, Headers, Footers, Thesaurus, Text In/Out, and Tables.

DOCUMENT PROCESSING

To format three- and four-column ruled tables with long and short column headings.

To format correspondence with displays and enumerations for various styles of stationery and window envelopes and to create form letters.

To format specialized reports such as minutes of meetings, itineraries, procedures manuals, legal documents and to format author/date citations.

To format specialized tables using different font sizes.

Leo de Wys, Inc./Ed Braverman

REPORT 59
(continued)

Press the right arrow key twice and Enter once.

5. Advance to Ln = 6″, switch to center justification, and key in Large font the next line: 7 days/6 nights in oceanfront accommodations. Press Enter and key: Plus round-trip plane fare from Los Angeles. Press the right arrow key once and Enter three times.
6. Change to Extra Large font and key the next line: $1,575 complete. Then press the right arrow key once and Enter twice.
7. Key in Large font and italics the last two lines:
   Call KRT TRAVEL SERVICES for details
   555-3024

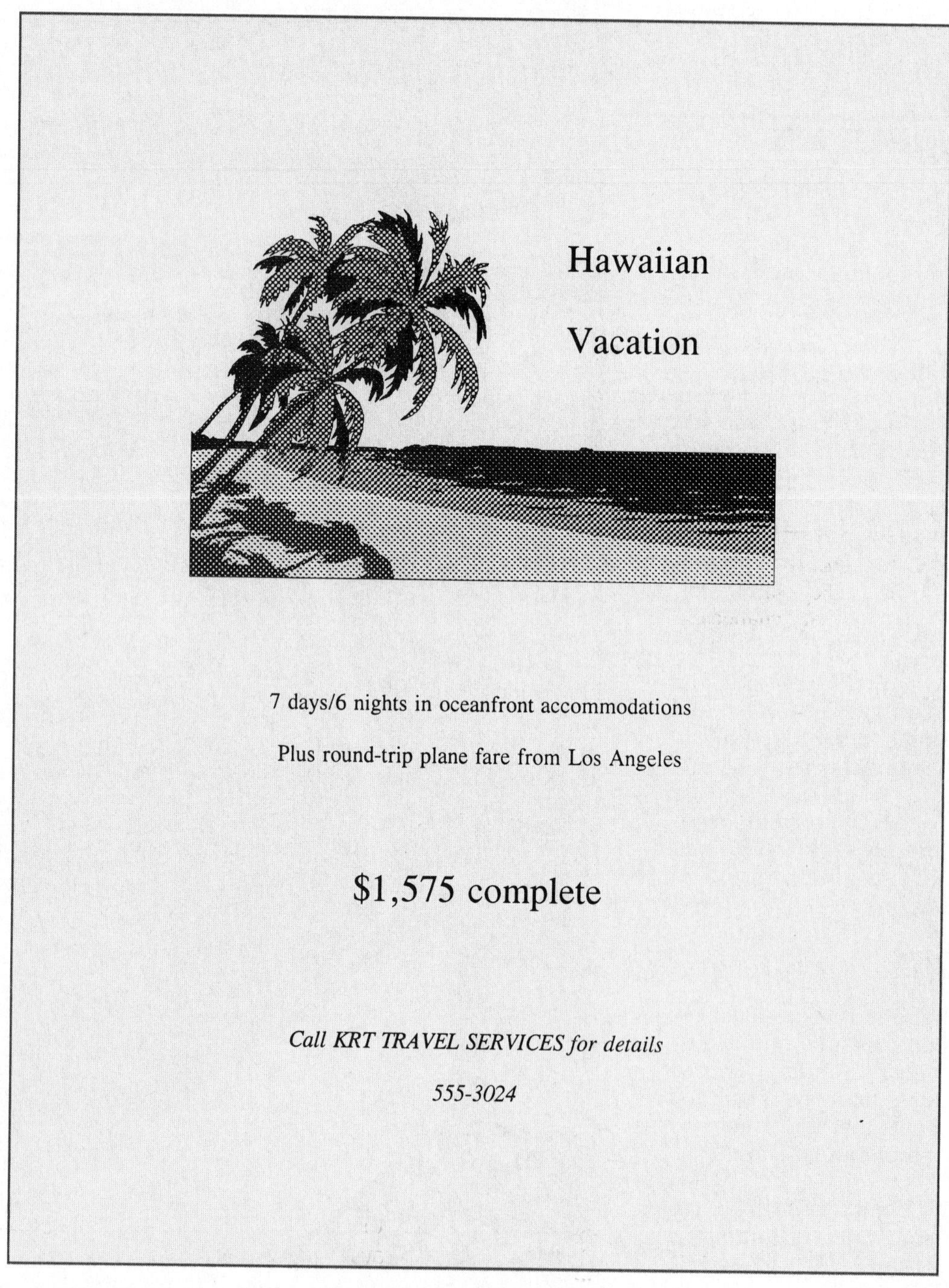
Hawaiian
Vacation
7 days/6 nights in oceanfront accommodations
Plus round-trip plane fare from Los Angeles
$1,575 complete
Call KRT TRAVEL SERVICES for details
555-3024

UNIT SEVENTEEN • TABLES AND FINANCIAL STATEMENTS

81-85 LESSONS

Margins: 1 inch • Spacing: Single • Drills: 2 times • Format Guide: 57–63

Goals for Unit 17

Begin each day with approximately 15 minutes of skillbuilding, selecting activities from pages 191–194. In the remaining class time, complete as many production jobs from pages 195–202 as you can.

1. To improve accuracy and speed on alphabet and number keys.
2. To key 44 wam for 5 minutes with no more than 5 errors.
3. To improve proficiency in composing at the keyboard.
4. To format short and long column heads in tables.
5. To gain proficiency in using Repeat Value and Double Underline.
6. To format and key ruled tables and financial statements.
7. To format and key correspondence with tables.

A. WARMUP

```
1      Joe quickly boarded Flight #578 to Phoenix on July 20.  12
2 He spent $9.75 on snacks and magazines.  On his return trip  24
3 on Flight #641, he spent $43.50 to have two gifts for home.  36
  | 1 | 2 | 3 | 4 | 5 | 6 | 7 | 8 | 9 | 10 | 11 | 12
```

LANGUAGE ARTS

B. COMMAS

B. Study the rules at the right. Then key lines 4–7, making necessary changes.

Rule: When a dependent clause *precedes* the independent clause, separate the clauses with a comma.

If the quota is reached, a sizable bonus will be paid.

Rule: Use commas to set off a nonessential expression (that is, a word, phrase, or clause that may be omitted without changing the basic meaning of the sentence).

Our new goals, you must admit, are quite reasonable.

```
4 As you know, if it rains the art show will be held indoors.
5 When the shipment arrives Susan will prepare the display.
6 Our group wants Cory, the current senator, to be a candidate.
7 Michelle who was recently promoted puts in very long days.
```

C. COMPOSING

Compose the body of a memo to respond to Memo 11, Unit 13, p. 150, using the following suggestions for each paragraph:

Paragraph 1. Confirm that you have discussed the price and terms of the Marx software with James Clayton and that the site license for the accounting software will cost around $550.

Paragraph 2. Indicate that Bonnie Chandler will be attending the three-day orientation in place of Mable Youngblood because of a previous meeting Mable had scheduled during that week.

Paragraph 3. Close with a positive paragraph that shows how very much interested you are in receiving the software.

REPORT 58
SALE ANNOUNCEMENT

WordPerfect 6 users: See Student Guide, p. 65.

Follow these steps to format the sales announcement shown here.

1. Change the border options for a figure box to "none."
2. Create three figure boxes with these options:
   a. Filename: PC-1.WPG
      Anchor: Page
      Vertical Position: Top
      Horizontal Position: Margin, Left
      Size: 3″ wide × 2.6″ high
   b. Filename: FLOPPY-2.WPG
      Anchor: Page
      Vertical Position: 4″
      Horizontal Position: Margin, Right
      Size: 3″ wide × 2.6″ high
   c. Filename: PRINTR-3.WPG
      Anchor: Page
      Vertical Position: 7″
      Horizontal Position: Margin, Left
      Size: 3″ wide × 2.6″ high
3. Create three text boxes, each with the same anchor type, vertical position, and size as the corresponding figure box in Step 2. Change the shading option to 0% before you create the boxes.
4. Change the horizontal position for Text Boxes 1 and 3 to Margin, Right.
5. Key the text in each box using center justification, bold, and Very Large font.
   Text Box 1: Spread each line by leaving 1 blank space between letters. Leave 1 blank line before the first line and 2 blank lines between each keyed line.
   C A R M E L
   C O M P U T E R
   C E N T E R
   Text Box 2: Leave 1 blank line before the first line and 2 blank lines between each keyed line.
   Computers
   Software
   Laser Printers
   Text Box 3: Leave 1 blank line before the first line and 2 blank lines after it. Leave 2 blank lines before the last line. Single-space the two middle lines.
   Anniversary Sale
   8 a.m.–10 p.m.
   Saturday, July 3
   Keystone Mall

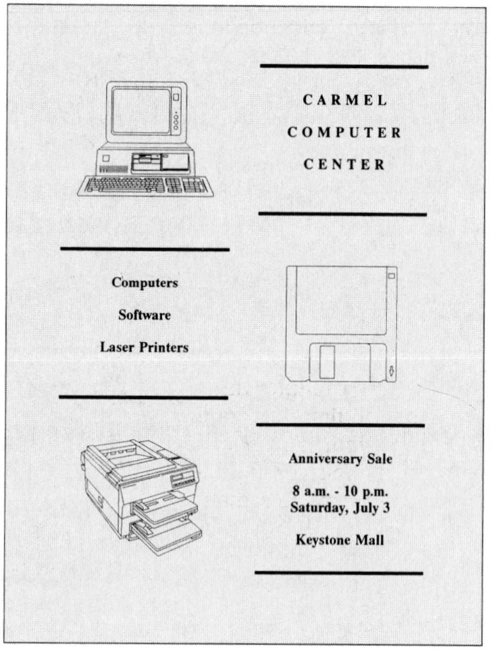

REPORT 59
FLIER

WordPerfect 6 users: See Student Guide, p. 67.

Follow these steps to format Report 59 (shown on the next page):

1. Change the border option for a figure box to "none."
2. Create a figure box with the following options:
   Filename: BKGRND-1.WPG
   Anchor: Page
   Vertical Position: Top
   Horizontal Position: Margin, Full
   Size: 6.5″ wide × 4″ high
   Wrap Text: No
3. Advance to Ln = 2″ and switch to double spacing. Set an absolute tab at 5 inches.
4. Tab to Pos = 5″ and key in Extra-Large font and bold:
   Hawaiian Vacation

SKILLBUILDING

PRETEST.
Take a 1-minute timed writing; compute your speed and count errors.

D. PRETEST: VERTICAL REACHES

```
     Just what does Dr. Carlson think is the basic cause of   12
Justin's scalp problem?  A patch of hair at the back of his   24
neck can be treated with a new drug.  I dread that it might   36
leave quite a bad scar, but Dr. Carlson thinks it will not.   48
| 1 | 2 | 3 | 4 | 5 | 6 | 7 | 8 | 9 | 10 | 11 | 12
```

PRACTICE.
Speed Emphasis: If you made no more than 1 error on the Pretest, key each line twice.
Accuracy Emphasis: If you made 2 or more errors on the Pretest, key each group of lines (as though it were a paragraph) twice.

E. PRACTICE: UP REACHES

```
at atlas atone attic batch gates sweat wheat atom bath what
dr draft drank dryer drain drama dread dream drag drew drug
ju judge juice jumpy junks juror julep jumbo judo jump just
es essay nests tests bless dress acres makes uses best rest
```

F. PRACTICE: DOWN REACHES

```
ca cable caddy cargo scare decay yucca pecan cage calm case
nk ankle blank crank blink think trunk brink bank junk sink
ba bacon badge basin tubal urban scuba basic baby back base
sc scale scalp scene scent scold scoop scope scan scar disc
```

POSTTEST.
Repeat the Pretest (D) and compare performance.

G. POSTTEST: VERTICAL REACHES

H. Take a 1-minute timed writing on the first paragraph to establish your base speed. Then take four 1-minute timed writings on the remaining paragraphs. As soon as you equal or exceed your base speed on one paragraph, advance to the next one.

H. SUSTAINED PRACTICE: ROUGH DRAFT

```
     It has been said that the most important tool required   12
for successful business leadership in the future will be an   24
ability to work with people.  A leader must be able to push   36
workers to be creative and to put forth their best efforts.   48
A leader must akknowledge the fact that people are the        12
most important resource in any enter prise.  Workers must be  24
made to feel part of our team.  It is essential for leaders   36
to encourage employees to contribute suggestions and ideas.   48
     Leaders need to maximize out put with limited resources  12
and carefully monitor the alocation of resource.  That is     24
specially critacal when the economy is sluggish.  The leader  36
is judged by reveiwing the loss and profit statement.         48
     Sucessful leaders at ever level know that no one has     12
all the ansers.  However, they also under stand that having   24
employees who work will together and who share comon goals   36
and objectives might increase the productivity of any unit.   48
| 1 | 2 | 3 | 4 | 5 | 6 | 7 | 8 | 9 | 10 | 11 | 12
```

FORMATTING

Q. WORDPERFECT: GRAPHICS TEXT BOXES

WP

GRAPHICS TEXT BOXES
Create: Alt-F9, 3, 1
Edit: Alt-F9, 3, 2, *figure no.*, Enter
Change options: *position cursor*, Alt-F9, 3, 4

WordPerfect 6 users: See Student Guide, p. 64.

Like figure boxes, text boxes can contain pictures, text, or both. The major difference between the two is that text boxes have horizontal rules and shading, although these default settings can be changed. To enter text, key "9" (Edit) while in the text-box definition menu. You can use such options as different font sizes, centering, and bold in the text box.

DOCUMENT PROCESSING

REPORT 57
MEETING ANNOUNCEMENT

Note: Options for graphics boxes must be set before the boxes are created.

WordPerfect 6 users: See Student Guide, p. 65.

Create the meeting announcement illustrated in the next column following these steps:

1. At the top of the page, set the option for borders to "none" for a figure box (Alt-F9, 1, 4, 1, 1, 1, 1, 1, F7).
2. Create and define the figure box (Alt-F9, 1, 1).
   Filename: SCALE.WPG
   Anchor: Page
   Vertical Position: Top
   Horizontal Position: Margin, Center
   Size: 5″ wide × 5″ high
3. Exit the figure box.
4. Set the option for shading to "0" for a text box (Alt-F9, 3, 4, 9, 0, F7, F7).
5. Create and define a text box (Alt-F9, 3, 1).
   Anchor: Page
   Vertical Position: 6″
   Horizontal Position: Margin, Center
   Size: 6″ wide × 3″ high
6. Select Edit (press 9 in the Definition Menu) to add the text to the text box.
7. Center and key in Large font the following line:
   Do not miss the court case of the century!
8. Press Enter three times. Then, center and key in Very Large font, all-capital letters, and bold, the topic:
   TECHNOLOGY VS. EMPLOYEE SAFETY
9. Press Enter three times. Then, center and key in Large font with double spacing the remaining lines:
   Presented by the IBM Computer User's Group
   Monday, April 7, 7 p.m.
   Blair Junior High Auditorium

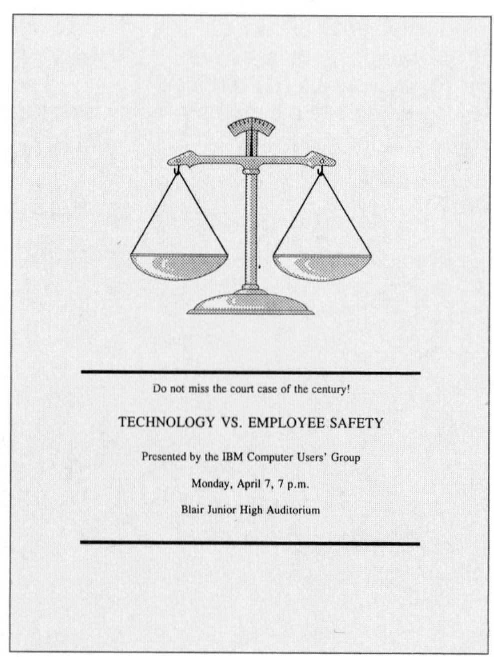
Do not miss the court case of the century!
TECHNOLOGY VS. EMPLOYEE SAFETY
Presented by the IBM Computer Users' Group
Monday, April 7, 7 p.m.
Blair Junior High Auditorium

I. PROGRESSIVE PRACTICE: ALPHABET

Turn to the Progressive Practice: Alphabet routine at the back of the book. Take six 30-second timed writings, starting at the point where you left off the last time.

J. Take three 12-second timed writings on each line. The scale gives wam for a 12-second timed writing.

J. 12-SECOND SPRINTS

```
Vince knew that Maxine just passed her formal biology quiz.
Felix might hit your jackpot even with the bad quiz answer.
Jack Bowman was very excited when my quilt got first prize.
Kyle mixed seven quarts of frozen grape juice with sherbet.
 | | | | 5 | | | |10| | | |15| | | |20| | | |25| | | |30| | | |35| | | |40| | | |45| | | |50| | | |55| | | |60
```

K. Tab: Center. The opening lines of a letter require the quick operation of the Enter key. Key these opening lines 3 times as quickly as possible.

K. TECHNIQUE PRACTICE: LETTER OPENING

```
                        (Current Date)↓1 inch



Ms. Victoria R. Cull
Human Resources Administrator
Crane Financial Services
87 Lincoln Boulevard
Topeka, KS 66603-3161

Dear Ms. Cull:
```

L. Take a 1-minute timed writing on the first paragraph to establish your base speed. Then take four 1-minute timed writings on the remaining paragraphs. As soon as you equal or exceed your base speed on one paragraph, advance to the next one.

L. SUSTAINED PRACTICE: SYLLABIC INTENSITY

```
     Many routine factory jobs and tasks are often not done   12
by people.  Machines now perform some work that was done by   24
members of the labor force.  What happens to these persons?   36
More and more firms are taking steps to solve this problem.   48

     Perhaps you think that this brings about a shortage of   12
jobs for those who are laid off.  This does not necessarily   24
happen because jobs are increasing in many new areas.  Many   36
new jobs which call for different skills have been created.   48

     In order to take advantage of these new emerging jobs,   12
young people must continue their education after completing   24
high school.  People with specialized skills can always see   36
opportunities for using new skills in a different location.   48

     History has continually repeated itself with regard to   12
this phenomenon.  Just review what happened with the intro-   24
duction of the automobile to workers who were involved with   36
horses.  New inventions can invariably require new workers.   48
 |  1  |  2  |  3  |  4  |  5  |  6  |  7  |  8  |  9  |  10  |  11  |  12
```

N. Take two 1-minute timed writings on each line as you concentrate on infrequently used letters.

N. ALPHABET REVIEW: INFREQUENT-LETTER PRACTICE

J Jolly jugglers joined the judge, jury, and jealous jailers. 12
Q I quickly acquired an eloquent quartet for the quiet queen. 12
X Dexter expects extra excise taxes in excess of six percent. 12
Z A dozen puzzled zebras were seized by a dozen dizzy guards. 12

1 2 3 4 5 6 7 8 9 10 11 12

O. DIAGNOSTIC PRACTICE: NUMBERS

Turn to the Diagnostic Practice: Numbers routine at the back of this book. Take the Pretest and record your performance. Then practice the drill lines for those reaches on which you made errors. Finally, repeat the Pretest and compare your performance.

P. Spacing: Double. Take two 5-minute timed writings. Compute your speed and count errors.

Goal: 49 wam/5′/5e

P. 5-MINUTE TIMED WRITING

Frequent business travelers know quite well what the 12
annoying side effects of long-distance plane trips include. 24
That tired, dizzy feeling may stay with a traveler for up 35
to two or three days after a trip. Jet lag, as it is often 47
called, is really the physical disorientation of all bodily 59
and mental functions that occurs when a flight crosses a 71
number of time zones. 75

Our bodies operate by some internal time clock, which 87
tells us when to eat, sleep, and awake. When you change 98
time zones, a watch may be set to that new time, but your 110
body is still operating in the old one. How can you avoid 122
the stress that comes with jet lag? Stay away from such 133
common temptations as late-night movies, free alcoholic 144
drinks, and loads of food served at unusual hours. The 156
main causes of that tired feeling are lack of sleep and, 167
unexpectedly, dehydration. 172

In a pressurized aircraft, it is essential that the 184
humidity be kept at a very low level. Every breath gives 195
up more water, making your skin and mouth feel dry. If you 207
replace this loss of fluid with alcohol, you are worsening 219
the dehydration process. Your best bet for a stress-free 231
trip is to drink all the bottled water you can and take 242
a few power naps. 245

1 2 3 4 5 6 7 8 9 10 11 12

M. Take three 1-minute timed writings on each line. Try not to slow down for the capital letters.

M. TECHNIQUE PRACTICE: SHIFT KEY

Ray, Bob, and John went to Harrisburg on Tuesday, April 20. 12
The Pittsburgh Pirates were playing the Chicago Cubs today. 12
Sue took Flight 261 for Miami and Fort Lauderdale on May 6. 12
Tom Crane's new address is 15 Lincoln Road in Boise, Idaho. 12

N. Change every plural noun to a singular noun.

N. TECHNIQUE PRACTICE: CONCENTRATION

The employees read the letters from the annoyed customers and gave the letters to the managers in charge of the sections to handle. The managers will respond to the questions raised by the customers. Hopefully, the answers will be acceptable.

O. PACED PRACTICE

Turn to the Paced Practice routine at the back of the book. Take three 2-minute timed writings, starting at the speed at which you left off the last time.

P. Spacing: Double. Take two 5-minute timed writings. Compute your speed and count errors.

Goal: 44 wam/5'/5e

P. 5-MINUTE TIMED WRITING

A recent study, directed by a psychology professor, 11
created a method to measure and evaluate the pace of life. 23
Researchers observed how fast pedestrians walked on the 35
downtown streets, how long it took postal clerks to fill 46
out requests, and the number of people wearing watches. 57
Of the six countries studied, only Japan beat the United 69
States regarding the fast pace of public life. 78

Here at home, Boston was shown to be the fastest city, 90
followed by New York and then Salt Lake City. The question 102
that these facts raise is, why? Why are some cities more 114
hectic than others? No one has the entire answer, but one 125
theory suggests that fast cities attract people who enjoy 137
living life in the fast lane and repel people who despise 149
the fast pace. 152

Where you live may affect your health. Smoking, a 163
major risk factor for heart disease, shows the very same 174
regional pattern. Smoking is often linked to stress, and 186
living in a time-pressured environment may cause people to 198
smoke. So the very next time you are about to rush out the 210
door, slow down and don't follow a crazy schedule. 220

J. Key each sentence on a separate line.

J. TECHNIQUE PRACTICE: ENTER KEY

41 Who should go? Can you attend? Why not? Will Ann attend?
42 Someone should go. They asked us. It shouldn't take long.
43 Ask Lynn to go. She may like it. I could go. He will go.
44 When can you go? Can I ride with you? Will you stay long?
45 Thanks for the offer. I'll pay the toll. Let's eat lunch.

K. Insert the necessary capitalization as you key these sentences twice.

K. TECHNIQUE PRACTICE: CONCENTRATION

46 Erik hall is attending notre dame university in south bend.
47 The statue of liberty and the hudson river are in new york.
48 The cities of dallas, austin, and san antonio are in texas.
49 The alexander graham bell museum is located in cape breton.
50 The boston red sox play their games at home in fenway park.

L. Take three 12-second timed writings on each line. The scale gives wam for a 12-second timed writing.

L. 12-SECOND SPRINTS

51 They were 65 or 70 miles south of Freeway #429 at 8:31 a.m.
52 I shipped 20 crates each of items #485 and #697 on July 31.
53 Our city's population grew from 39,612 to 40,587 in a year.
54 She will be on Route 67 for 1,308 of the 2,495 total miles.
55 The 45 teachers and 761 students arrived at 8:30 on May 29.

| | | | 5 | | | |10 | | | |15 | | | |20 | | | |25 | | | |30 | | | |35 | | | |40 | | | |45 | | | |50 | | | |55 | | | |60

M. Take a 1-minute timed writing on the first paragraph to establish your base speed. Then take four 1-minute timed writings on the remaining paragraphs. As soon as you equal or exceed your base speed on one paragraph, advance to the next one.

M. SUSTAINED PRACTICE: SYLLABIC INTENSITY

56 If you would like to be a success as a spouse, parent, 12
57 friend, or worker, you should think about the words you use 24
58 on a daily basis. These words can enable you to go through 36
59 life being pleased with things that must be done every day. 48

60 Through the use of certain words and by regulating the 12
61 tone of voice, one can help to build the self-esteem of any 24
62 person spoken to. This may encourage these others to react 36
63 in a positive way to any type of order that will be issued. 48

64 For example, you might improve your relationships with 12
65 others by trying to show a sympathetic understanding. This 24
66 can be done by giving others a feeling of worthiness. Make 36
67 an effort to find something to admire and praise in others. 48

68 In summary, there are words which achieve miracles. A 12
69 person who masters the art of praising discovers that it is 24
70 possible to have receivers react in a very favorable way to 36
71 the giver. Strive to provide reassurance and appreciation. 48

| 1 | 2 | 3 | 4 | 5 | 6 | 7 | 8 | 9 | 10 | 11 | 12

FORMATTING

Q. TABLES WITH COLUMN HEADINGS

Underlined column headings are used to identify the information in the columns. Blocked column headings are used most often because they are quick and easy to format. When formatting tables, set a left tab to align word columns and their headings at the left and set a right tab to align number columns and their headings at the right.

If a column heading is the longest item in a column, use the column heading to determine the key line.

DOCUMENT PROCESSING

TABLE 26
FOUR-COLUMN TABLE WITH COLUMN HEADINGS

Spacing: Double

The $ sign is not repeated after the first entry in a column of figures.

SALES BONUSES

September 30, 19--

Representative	Region	Manager	Bonus
Bassetto, Sally	Central	Lukens	$11,525
Chan, Xin-Ben	Southern	Wilson	975
Curtis, Bruce	Western	Whittemore	12,500
Daniels, May	Eastern	Zhang	1,675
Ferns, George	Central	Lukens	2,750
Legoff, May	Northern	Everson	875
Rosaen, Nellie	Southern	Wilson	1,375
Silverman, Rod	Eastern	Zhang	12,655

TABLE 27
THREE-COLUMN TABLE WITH COLUMN HEADINGS

Spacing: Double

AUTOMOBILE DEALERS

Company Name	Address	Manager
Beacon Sales, Inc.	5014 Grand River	John F. Lipson
Brooks Imported Cars	1285 Lansing Road	Elsie Stone
Buege Buick, Inc.	3625 Pennsylvania	Alex Larson
Capitol Cadillac	5901 Pennsylvania	Joseph Lewis
Dodge Sales	6131 Saginaw	Jose Ortego
Larson Sales	345 East Mount Hope	May Lewis
Story Oldsmobile	3133 Michigan	Louis Fox
Toyota Sales	134 Grand River	Paul Atkins
White's Ford, Inc.	535 South Cedar	Peter Davis
Wilson Imports	4212 North Larch	Alex Jones

SKILLBUILDING

D. PACED PRACTICE

Turn to the Paced Practice routine at the back of the book. Take three 2-minute timed writings, starting at the speed at which you left off the last time.

PRETEST. Take a 1-minute timed writing; compute your speed and count errors.

E. PRETEST: ALTERNATE- AND ONE-HAND WORDS

```
     Banks must not be carefree with their minimum reserves  12
or they might encounter a problem with the auditor.  Such a  24
case might find a penalty being assessed.  The opinion that  36
most eager bankers have is to exceed the required reserves.  48
| 1 | 2 | 3 | 4 | 5 | 6 | 7 | 8 | 9 | 10 | 11 | 12
```

PRACTICE.

Speed Emphasis: If you made no more than 1 error on the Pretest, key each line twice.

Accuracy Emphasis: If you made 2 or more errors on the Pretest, key each group of lines (as though it were a paragraph) twice.

F. PRACTICE: ALTERNATE-HAND WORDS

```
also amend maps island blame city problem panel formal down
snap rigid lens social visit with penalty right height half
chap burnt such enrich shape dish auditor spend eighty lamb
girl usual tick thrown laugh then suspend slept mantle kept
```

G. PRACTICE: ONE-HAND WORDS

```
fad only craft pupil regret uphill drafter homonym carefree
bed join water nylon target pompon savages minimum exceeded
was hook great knoll teased kimono scatter pumpkin attracts
age milk eager union bazaar limply reserve opinion cassette
```

POSTTEST. Repeat the Pretest (E) and compare performance.

H. POSTTEST: ALTERNATE- AND ONE-HAND WORDS

I. Take a 1-minute timed writing on the first paragraph to establish your base speed. Then take four 1-minute timed writings on the remaining paragraphs. As soon as you equal or exceed your base speed on one paragraph, advance to the next one.

I. SUSTAINED PRACTICE: NUMBERS AND SYMBOLS

```
     The number of people who are completing their shopping  12
through the use of a catalog has increased significantly in  24
the past few years.  The following examples will serve as a  36
sample of the types of activities being processed this way.  48

     Fox & Day included 20 new items in the newest catalog.  12
Item #19 was being imported from Finland and was priced for  24
$99.  This item was handmade by a group of individuals in a  36
distant village in the southwestern region of that country.  48

     A catalog for sports enthusiasts distributed by Gall &  12
Spenillo included items for about 25 different sports.  The  24
items ranged from a low of $18 to a high of $199.  A few of  36
the items (#140 and #221) were imported from other nations.  48

     The catalog from Shafer & Wilson listed new electronic  12
equipment at big savings.  For example, Item #89 was listed  24
at $99, a discount of 60%.  Some items (#41, #97, and #121)  36
were discounted 50%.  There were 433 items in this catalog.  48
| 1 | 2 | 3 | 4 | 5 | 6 | 7 | 8 | 9 | 10 | 11 | 12
```

TABLE 28
THREE-COLUMN TABLE WITH COLUMN HEADINGS

Spacing: Single

Set a right tab for a heading over a column that contains decimals.

Do not key the % sign in a column when the word *Percent* or a % sign is used in the column heading.

Columns that contain both text and numbers (as in Column 1) are aligned at the left.

SALES VOLUME FOR SELECTED CATEGORIES

March 30, 19—

Model	Sales Volume	Percent of Sales
AC-101	$ 14,360	2.19
AD-222	132,158	20.18
BA-110	66,400	10.14
BE-215	215,340	32.87
CB-200	16,980	2.59
CQ-415	89,470	13.66
DF-316	109,365	16.70
DJ-400	10,945	1.67
TOTAL	$655,018	100.00

TABLE 29
THREE-COLUMN TABLE WITH COLUMN HEADINGS

Spacing: Double

VINSON INC. CORPORATE OFFICES

~~June 30~~ July 1, 19--

Name	Company Title	Office
James L. Re~~a~~ed	Chairman of the Board	2106
~~Lousie~~ Lucy Sauce	President	2109
Anthony Koo	Sen~~r~~ior Vice President	2104
~~Betty L.~~ Elizabeth Green	Senior Vice President	2102
William A. Smith	V ice President	~~11~~2207
Jason ~~H~~T. Fox	Vice President	~~11~~2209
Mary L. Lox	Co~~n~~mptroller	2113
Lawrence Bass	Secretary	2101

TABLE 30
THREE-COLUMN TABLE WITH COLUMN HEADINGS

Spacing: Double

MAGAZINE SUBSCRIPTION RENEWALS

APRIL 15, 19--

DEPARTMENT	MAGAZINE	EMPLOYEE
ACCOUNTING	ISSUES IN ACCOUNTING	LEE BROWN
CORPORATE	FORTUNE	JILL LOGAN
MARKETING	JOURNAL OF MARKETING	ALEY MAY
SALES	BUSINESS WEEK	SUSAN MARCH

UNIT TWENTY-TWO • DESKTOP PUBLISHING

LESSONS 106-110

Margins: 1 inch • Spacing: Single • Drills: 2 times • Format Guide: 85–87

Goals for Unit 22

1. To improve accuracy and speed on alphabet and number keys.
2. To key 49 wam for 5 minutes with no more than 5 errors.
3. To develop proficiency in spelling commonly misspelled words.
4. To develop proficiency in using WordPerfect Graphics and Text Boxes, Columns, and Table.
5. To format and key speech handouts, announcements, fliers, and multicolumn abstracts.

Begin each day with approximately 15 minutes of skillbuilding, selecting activities from pages 254–257. In the remaining class time, complete as many production jobs from pages 258–265 as you can.

A. WARMUP

```
1      Three accounting firms (Braxx & Jackson, Zack & Villa,  12
2 and Powl & Yale) placed requests with the collection agency  24
3 to collect the following amounts:  $612.50, $489, and $370.  36
  | 1 | 2 | 3 | 4 | 5 | 6 | 7 | 8 | 9 | 10 | 11 | 12
```

LANGUAGE ARTS

B. CAPITAL LETTERS

B. Study the rules at the right. Then key lines 4–7, making necessary changes.

Rule: Capitalize all official titles of honor and respect when they precede personal names.

One of the new Golden Wildcats members is Dr. Chi Pang Yu.

Rule: Capitalize words such as *mother, father, aunt,* and *uncle* when they stand alone or they are followed by a personal name.

The letter from Aunt Mary was extremely encouraging.

```
4 Mr. Tim Swendsen and Ms. Sara Terrell were both elected.
5 The student debate was coordinated by professor Coleman.
6 The ladies and mother plan to form a string quartet.
7 Many of the regulations had been written by uncle Roger.
```

C. SPELLING

C. These words are among the 500 most frequently misspelled words in business correspondence.

```
8 labor station quarter conditions modifications applications
9 companies questionnaire certainly except pertinent previous
10 agreement brochure ability claimants responsible curriculum
11 liability phase consumer treasurer's coordinator counseling
12 orientation institution enrollment reasonable signed growth
```

FORMATTING

R. RULED TABLES

A ruled table has horizontal rules (lines) that divide the parts of the table. To format a ruled table:

1. Center the table vertically and horizontally.
2. Center and key the title followed by a double space. Center and key the subtitle followed by a single space.
3. Determine the tab settings—absolute left tabs for word columns and right or decimal tabs for number columns.
4. Key a horizontal rule, extending it to the edges of the table. Determine the length of the rule by subtracting the beginning position of the first column from the ending position of the last column. Multiply the answer by 10. For example, in Table 31, subtract 1.25" (the beginning of Column 1) from 7.25" (the end of Column 3) to get 6.0". You will need a 6-inch (or 60-character) line.
5. Double-space and key the column headings. Do not underline column headings in a ruled table.
6. Single-space and key the horizontal rule below the column heads.
7. Double-space and key the table body.
8. Single-space after the last line of the body and key the horizontal rule.
9. Double-space and key the total information; then single-space and key the horizontal rule.

WP

REPEAT VALUE
Esc, *number, character*

WordPerfect 6 users: See Student Guide, p. 28.

S. WORDPERFECT: REPEAT VALUE

Use Repeat Value to repeat a single character a specific number of times. For example, to enter the 6-inch (60-character) divider line in Table 31, tab to the beginning of Column 1, press Escape, enter the number 60 (do not press Enter), then key a single underline. A 6-inch line will be inserted into your document.

DOCUMENT PROCESSING

TABLE 31
THREE-COLUMN RULED TABLE

Align the $ signs at the top and bottom of the column.

CANDIDATES FOR PROMOTION ↓2

January 1, 19-- ↓1

Candidate's Name	New Position Title	Salary
D'Hadilla, Tariocha	Engineer I	$ 47,000
Kolberg, Amy	Accountant II	43,200
Solomon, David	Laboratory Technician	29,100
Tracy, James	Auditor	45,000
Wolter, Karl	Sales Representative	38,000
TOTAL		$202,300

U. WORDPERFECT: LABELS

WP LABELS

Create 3-across labels: Sh-F8, 2, 7, 2, 4, 8, Y, F7, F7, 1, F7

Use existing label form: Sh-F8, 2, 7, *highlight "Labels,"* 1, F7

WordPerfect 6 users: See Student Guide, p. 63.

Mailing labels are often used to simplify the task of addressing envelopes in a word processing environment. WordPerfect has default settings for label sheets with 3 columns of labels across the page and 10 rows of labels down the page. The default settings can be changed by selecting Create from the Paper/Size menu and entering the new settings in the Labels format menu.

If you cannot select labels, you must create them first. Once you have created or selected labels, key the name and address for the first label, pressing Enter after each line. To move to the next label, insert a hard page break (Ctrl-Enter). Use View Document (Sh-F7, 6) to see how the labels will print.

Test your label settings by printing the addresses on a blank page first. Then, adjust the position of the label sheet in the printer as necessary.

DOCUMENT PROCESSING

FORM 16
MAILING LABELS

The addresses are shown in alphabetic order from left to right, formatted in the all-capital letters, no-punctuation style preferred for bulk mailings.

PURCHASING DEPT ABBOTT LABORATORIES ABBOTT PARK RTS 43 & 137 CHICAGO IL 60064-2134	PURCHASING DEPT ACUSON 1220 CHARLESTON RD MTN VIEW CA 94043-2113	PURCHASING DEPT ADOBE SYSTEMS 1585 CHARLESTON RD MTN VIEW CA 94039-2314
PURCHASING DEPT ADVANCED MICRO 901 THOMPSON PL SUNNYVALE CA 94088-9873	PURCHASING DEPT AETNA LIFE 151 FARMINGTON AVE HARTFORD CT 06156-3134	PURCHASING DEPT AFFILIATED PUBLISHING 135 MORRISSEY BLVD BOSTON MA 02107-3274
PURCHASING DEPT AIR PRODUCTS 7201 HAMILTON BLVD ALLENTOWN PA 18195-2154	PURCHASING DEPT ALASKA AIR GROUP 19300 PACIFIC HIGHWAY S SEATTLE WA 98188-2064	PURCHASING DEPT ALBANY INTERNATIONAL ONE SAGE RD MENANDS NY 12204-5184
PURCHASING DEPT ALBERTO-CULVER 2525 ARMITAGE AVE MELROSE PK IL 60160-3124	PURCHASING DEPT ALBERTSON'S 250 PARKCENTER BLVD BOISE ID 83726-2083	PURCHASING DEPT ALCO STANDARD 825 DUPORTAIL RD WAYNE PA 19087-2152
PURCHASING DEPT ALCOA 1501 ALCOA BLDG PITTSBURGH PA 15219-4125	PURCHASING DEPT ALEXANDER & ALEXANDER 1211 AVE OF THE AMERICAS NEW YORK NY 10036-2128	PURCHASING DEPT ALEXANDER & BALDWIN 822 BISHOP ST PO BOX 38724 HONOLULU HI 96813-8085
PURCHASING DEPT ALLEGHENY AIRLINES 55 EAST 52 ST NEW YORK NY 10055-2127	PURCHASING DEPT ALLEGHENY LUDLUM 1000 SIX PPG PL PITTSBURGH PA 15222-4123	PURCHASING DEPT ALLEGHENY POWER 320 PARK AVE NEW YORK NY 10022-2127
PURCHASING DEPT ALLIED-SIGNAL COLUMBIA & PARK AVE MORRISTOWN NJ 07962-2014	PURCHASING DEPT AMAX GOLD 1707 COLE BLVD GOLDEN CO 80401-3032	PURCHASING DEPT AMDAHL 1250 EAST ARQUES AVE SUNNYVALE CA 94088-4087
PURCHASING DEPT AMERADA HESS 1185 AVE OF THE AMERICAS NEW YORK NY 10036-2129	PURCHASING DEPT AMERICAN BRANDS 1700 EAST PUTNAM GREENWICH CT 06870-2036	PURCHASING DEPT AMERICAN CYANAMID ONE CYANAMID PLAZA WAYNE NJ 07470
PURCHASING DEPT AMERICAN ELECTRIC ONE RIVERSIDE PLAZA COLUMBUS OH 43215-6145	PURCHASING DEPT AMERICAN EXPRESS TOWER C WORLD FINANCIAL CENTER NEW YORK NY 10285-2126	PURCHASING DEPT AMERICAN FAMILY 1932 WYNNTON RD COLUMBUS GA 31999-4043
PURCHASING DEPT AMERICAN GENERAL 2929 ALLEN PKWY HOUSTON TX 77019-7135	PURCHASING DEPT AMERICAN GREETINGS 10500 AMERICAN RD CLEVELAND OH 44144-2162	PURCHASING DEPT AMERICAN HOME 685 THIRD AVE NEW YORK NY 10017-2128

LETTER 54
BLOCK-STYLE LETTER WITH THREE-COLUMN TABLE

Leave 1 blank line before and after a table with column headings but no title.

August 1, 19— / Mr. Alex Horton / Vice President for Sales / Bower & Lyons, Inc. / 5623 McCormick Boulevard / Chicago, IL 60659-2317 / Dear Mr. Horton:

Thank you for your letter of July 24 in which you inquired about our company's distributing your new fax machines in Florida.

Listed below are the cities, the number of units in each city and its surrounding area, and our fax representative in that city.

City	Units	Representative
Bradenton	10	Rufus Spencer
Fort Lauderdale	120	Alan Omoto
Miami	115	Virginia L. O'Rourke
Tampa	104	Lewis Garcia

I will be glad to meet with you to discuss the contractual arrangements for our distributing and selling your fax equipment. Please call me at your convenience to establish a date for our meeting.

Sincerely yours, / Louise Atkinson / Vice President / *Your Initials* / c: Jack Martin

LETTER 55
MODIFIED-BLOCK STYLE LETTER WITH FOUR-COLUMN TABLE

Do not indent the paragraphs.

Leave 3 blank lines before and after a table with a title.

March 15, 19— / Mr. Robert Karns, Editor / Office Systems Publications, Inc. / 31 St. James Street / Boston, MA 02116-0326 / Dear Mr. Karns:

I have just compiled the information you requested about our office employees last week. Listed below is the data on our employees' ages and gender for your article.

THE J. THOMPSON COMPANY

Employee Age Distribution and Gender

Age	Male	Female	Total
20–39	31	159	190
40–59	52	64	116
60–65	30	38	68
TOTAL	113	261	374

I hope this information will assist you with your writing.

Sincerely yours, / Jason Smith / Research Director / *Your Initials*

FORM 15
LETTER

Retrieve Form 13, and save it under another file name. Then move the cursor to the end of the file (Ln = 3″), and key this letter, beginning with the inside address.

WESTSIDE TROPHY COMPANY

Trophies, Plaques, and Certificates for All Occasions

July 2, 19--

Customer Relations Manager
Occidental Wholesale Company
11050 York Rd.
Hunt Valley, MD 21030

Dear Customer Relations Manager
~~Ladies and Gentlemen~~:

Last week we placed an order for 100 5" x 7" blank plaques at a net price of $3.95 per plaque. We received your ~~official~~ acknowledgment copy of our order yesterday. We were quite surprised, therefore, to find in the ~~most recent~~ biannual issue of *Award News* your announcement of a discount of 10 per cent on this item.

We have been a customer of your company for many years and have always shown great loyalty to your firm. Will you please issue us a revised acknowledgment of our order that reflects the 10 per cent discount.

Also, would you please have your sales~~man~~ representative call on us to demonstrate for us your new line of laser certificate software. We will soon ~~have a~~ need ~~for~~ approximately 25 copies of such software.

That is why we feel that you should have told us about this discount, which was obviously planned before we placed our order.

Sincerely,

George E. Boyce
Purchasing Department

urs

625 SOUTH BROADWAY, SAN DIEGO, CA 92101 619-555-8000

FORMATTING

T. FINANCIAL STATEMENTS WITH LEADERS

Financial statements are formatted almost like other tables. The exceptions are:

1. Leave 2 spaces between money columns.
2. Set right tabs for money columns.
3. Set a dot leader tab 2 spaces before the dollar sign in the first money column.
4. Indent individual items under major categories 3 spaces.
5. Key a double underline the width of the longest item in the column to indicate a table (financial) total.

UNDERLINE—DOUBLE
Ctrl-F8, 2, 3

WordPerfect 6 users: See Student Guide, p. 38.

U. WORDPERFECT: DOUBLE UNDERLINE

To create a double underline (for example, to indicate a table total), enter the appropriate commands (Ctrl-F8, 2, 3) and then key the text to be underlined; turn off double underline by pressing the right arrow key once.

To double-underline existing text, first block the text to be underlined; then enter the appropriate commands.

DOCUMENT PROCESSING

TABLE 32
INCOME STATEMENT WITH LEADERS

Use the WordPerfect Center Page command to center the financial statement vertically.

Leave 2 spaces between money columns.

Set absolute left tabs at 1.2, 1.5, 1.8, and 2.2; a dot leader tab at 4.0; and right tabs at 4.9, 6.1, and 7.3.

Press the space bar to extend the underline to cover the longest item, including the $ sign. For example, in extending the underline to cover the Sales minus Sales Return column, press the space bar 4 times before keying 825.20.

BARKER-FOWLER ELECTRICAL REPAIR ↓2

INCOME STATEMENT ↓2

For the Month Ended October 31, 19-- ↓3

REVENUE FROM SALES			
3→ Sales		$23,670.25	
Less: Sales Returns	$700.10		
Sales Discounts . . .	125.10	825.20	
Net Sales			$22,845.05
COST OF GOODS SOLD			3,200.00
GROSS PROFIT ON SALES			$19,645.05
OPERATING EXPENSES			
Advertising		$ 1,376.40	
Delivery Service		431.20	
Insurance		150.50	
Payroll Taxes		1,075.00	
Rent		975.00	
Rental (Machine)		100.00	
Salary		10,400.00	
Supplies		375.60	
Utilities		478.31	
Miscellaneous		76.32	
3→ Total Expenses			15,438.33
NET INCOME BEFORE TAXES			$ 4,206.72

DOCUMENT PROCESSING

FORM 12
LETTER

WordPerfect 6 users: See Student Guide, p. 61.

Create a blank letterhead stationery form as shown below:

1. Change the top margin to 0.5″.
2. Create a graphics figure box with these options (press F7 when finished):
   Filename: BICYCLE.WPG
   Horizontal Position: Left
   Size: Set Width/Auto Height = 1″
3. Change to right justification, and key the company name "Charlotte Cycle Center" in extra-large size and bold. Then turn off bold, return to normal-sized text, and press Enter once.
4. Key the two remaining lines of the letterhead, inserting enough space between the phone and fax numbers to make the two lines even.
5. Press Enter once, and switch to left justification.
6. Insert a horizontal line, using the default options.
7. Press Enter repeatedly until Ln = 2″ (or as close as possible to 2″) in the status line, and enter the updated current date code.
8. Press Enter six times (Ln = 3″), and save the blank letterhead form.

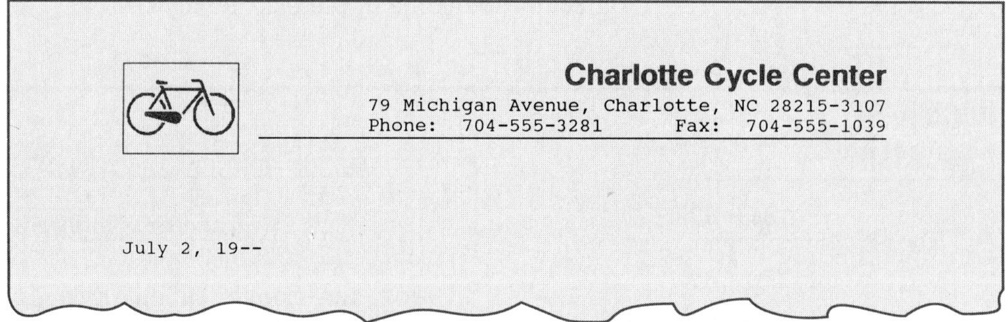
Charlotte Cycle Center
79 Michigan Avenue, Charlotte, NC 28215-3107
Phone: 704-555-3281 Fax: 704-555-1039

July 2, 19--

FORM 13
LETTER

WordPerfect 6 users: See Student Guide, p. 62.

Create a blank letterhead stationery form for Westside Trophy Company (see page 252):

1. Change the top margin to 0.5″ and the bottom margin to 0.0″.
2. Change the option for graphics figure boxes to border style = none on each side.
3. Create a graphics figure box with these options:
   Filename: TROPHY.WPG
   Horizontal Position: Right
   Size: Set Width/Auto Height = 1″.
4. Switch to center justification, and key the company name "WESTSIDE TROPHY COMPANY" in all-capital letters, extra-large size, and bold.
5. Turn off bold, return to normal-sized text, and press Enter twice.
6. Key the second line in normal-sized font and italics: *Trophies, Plaques, and Certificates for All Occasions.*
7. Press Enter three times, turn off italics, and switch to left justification.
8. Insert a horizontal line, changing the vertical position from baseline to 10.2″.
9. Advance the cursor to Ln = 10.3″, and center the company address and phone number in all-capital letters, italics, and small size, leaving 5 spaces between the address and phone number: *625 SOUTH BROADWAY, SAN DIEGO, CA 92101 619-555-8000.* Turn off italics, return to normal-sized text, and press Enter.
10. Advance the cursor to Ln = 2″, and enter the updated current date code.
11. Press Enter six times (to Ln = 3″), and save the blank letterhead form.

FORM 14
LETTER

Using one of the 30 graphics images that comes with WordPerfect or another one that is available to you, create a letterhead design of your own—for you personally, for your institution, for an organization of which you are a member, or for the company where you work.

TABLE 33
BALANCE SHEET WITH LEADERS

Center the table vertically.

Leave 2 spaces between money columns.

To keep your place when keying a financial statement, put a ruler or card under the line being keyed, and keep moving it as you go down the page.

BARKER-FOWLER ELECTRICAL REPAIR↓2

BALANCE SHEET↓2

October 31, 19--↓3

ASSETS↓2

Current Assets:		
Cash	$ 9,475.03	
Change Fund	75.00	
Accounts Receivable	12,581.35	
Merchandise Inventory	8,523.00	
Prepaid Insurance	250.00	
Total Current Assets		$30,904.38
Equipment:		
Repair Equipment	$12,350.00	
Office Equipment	6,230.50	
Total Equipment		18,580.50↓2
Total Assets		$49,484.88↓3

LIABILITIES↓2

Current Liabilities:		
Accounts Payable	$ 435.74	
Sales Taxes Payable	315.00	
Federal Income Taxes Payable	425.00	
FICA Taxes Payable	440.00	
State Income Taxes Payable	212.00	
Federal Unemployment Taxes Payable .	125.00	
State Unemployment Taxes Payable . .	90.00	
State Small Business Taxes Payable .	230.00	
Total Current Liabilities		$ 2,272.74
Long-Term Liabilities:		
Three-Year Bank Note Payable		15,500.00
Total Liabilities		$17,772.74↓3

OWNERS' EQUITY↓2

Fred L. Barker, Capital	$15,856.07	
Lance J. Fowler, Capital	15,856.07	31,712.14
Total Liabilities and Owner's Equity		$49,484.88

FORM 9
MEMORANDUM

WordPerfect 6 users: See Student Guide, p. 60.

Create a blank memorandum form as shown below.

1. On Ln = 1″, key the heading "Memorandum" in all-capital letters and bold, with font size = Ext Large. Press the right arrow key two times to return to normal-sized text, and then press Enter once.
2. Insert a horizontal line 0.05″ wide, and press Enter once.
3. Press Flush Right (Alt-F6) and key the company name, with font size = Small. Return to normal-sized text and press Enter.
4. Advance to Ln = 2″.
5. Format the remaining heading lines as shown below.
6. Save the form.

MEMORANDUM

Graceland Industrial Products

DATE:

TO:

FROM: James L. Cooper, Public Safety

SUBJECT:

FORM 10
MEMORANDUM

Retrieve Form 8, immediately save it under another file name, and key a memorandum from Shelly Rappaport to All Headquarters Personnel on the subject of Identification Cards. Be sure to save the completed memo. Use today's date.

Please stop by this office on July 10 or 11 between the hours of 1 and 3:30 p.m. to pick up your new ID card. Please sign the card as soon as it is issued, and carry it with you at all times. You will be required to relinquish your old ID card before a new one is issued to you.

Beginning July 17, your new card will be required for admission to the company cafeteria and for cashing checks at the cashier's office. Your new card must also be shown when you enter or leave the building before and after office hours and on weekends.

If your card becomes lost or stolen, please notify this office (Extension 5014) immediately. / *(Your Initials)*

FORM 11
MEMORANDUM

Using your own design, create a memorandum form for your instructor at your institution.

FORMATTING

T. WORDPERFECT: GRAPHICS FIGURE BOXES

WP

GRAPHICS FIGURE BOXES

Copy picture into figure box: Alt-F9, 1, 1, 1, *filename,* F7

Edit figure box: Alt-F9, 1, 2, *figure no.,* Enter

Change figure box options: *position cursor,* Alt-F9, 1, 4

WordPerfect 6 users: See Student Guide, p. 60.

WordPerfect's Graphics feature enables you to include images or pictures in your document. WordPerfect comes with 30 graphics (pictures) available. There are other graphics available that can also be used with WordPerfect.

There are five different types of graphics boxes, including figure or text boxes, although any graphics box can display pictures or text or both. Graphics options enable you to adjust the size and position of the text and pictures, the borders around them, and the amount of shading, if any, to be used.

To add a WordPerfect graphic to your document, position the cursor where you want the figure to appear and enter the appropriate commands (Alt-F9, 1, 1, 1). Enter the file name of the graphic or press F5 to list files. Graphics have the extension WPG. Only an outline of the box will be displayed. Use View Document (Sh-F7, 6) to see how your document will look when it is printed. If there is any text on the same line as the graphic, it will wrap around the box.

To change the graphics box or figure (for example, the border around the figure), position the cursor before the graphics box you want to change, access the Options menu (Alt-F9, 1, 4), and make your selections or edit the graphic (Alt-F9, 1, 2).

TABLE 34
FOUR-COLUMN RULED TABLE

Spacing: Double

STEINBAUGH ASSOCIATES
NEW HIRES
June 15, 19--

Employee	SS Number	Division	Rank
Dansby, Julie	237-50-6713	Payroll	G-3
Helma, Thomas	312-78-9267	Finance	G-5
Isaac, Lewis	423-89-2313	Payroll	G-3
Richards, Donald	231-81-4876	Receiving	G-5
Ripley, Keith	237-67-3481	Office	G-5
Seijo, Rose	145-78-6612	Purchasing	G-8
Solomon, Albert	673-33-8923	Sales	G-9
Vasquez, Mary	567-24-7812	Mail	G-3

MEMO 19
MEMORANDUM WITH FOUR-COLUMN RULED TABLE

Leave 3 blank lines before and after a table with a title.

MEMO TO: Kurt Smith, Advertising Designer

FROM: Louise Grooms, Purchasing

DATE: ~~June~~ July 25, 19--

SUBJECT: New Copy for Two-Drawer Filing Cabinets

I have just ~~written~~ completed the copy for our ~~three~~ two-dawer (r) filing cabinets for the 199~~4~~5 catalog. I am sure the following ~~copy~~ table will meet all ~~of the~~ your specifications. ~~established by you.~~

~~THREE~~ TWO-DRAWER FILING CABINETS--~~4~~29" HIGH

Color	Size	Style	Price
Black	Letter	E4-512-P	$163.00
Tropic Sand	Letter	E4-512-K	163.50
Putty	~~Legal~~ Letter	E4-512-L	163.00
Light Gray	Letter	E4-512-Q	1~~7~~56.00
Tropic Sand	Legal	E4-512C-7	195.00
Black	Legal	E4-512C-8	195.50
Putty	Legal	E4-512-9	195.00
Light Gr~~e~~ay	~~Letter~~ Legal	E4-512C-X	187.00

If you have questions about this table as an insert, plea~~e~~se let me know.

initials

GRAPHICS LINES
Horizontal: Alt-F9, 5, 1
Vertical: Alt-F9, 5, 2

WordPerfect 6 users: See Student Guide, p. 57.

R. WORDPERFECT: GRAPHICS LINES

Use Graphics Lines to insert horizontal or vertical rules (lines) into a document. Position the cursor where you want the line and issue the appropriate commands (Alt-F9, 5, and 1 or 2). The default settings are for a line 0.013 inch wide extending the full width of the text page. The default settings can be changed whenever the Graphics: Horizontal Lines menu is displayed.

Graphics Lines will not be displayed on your screen. Use View Document (Sh-F7, 6) to see what the document will look like when it is printed.

ADVANCE
Vertical position: Sh-F8, 4, 1, 3, *measurement from top edge,* F7, F7
Horizontal position: Sh-F8, 4, 1, 6, *measurement from left edge,* F7, F7

WordPerfect 6 users: See Student Guide, p. 58.

S. WORDPERFECT: ADVANCE

Use Advance to position text at an exact vertical and/or horizontal position on a page (for example, to fill in a blank on a printed form).

To move to a new horizontal position, issue the Advance command (Sh-F8, 4, 1); then enter "6" for position and enter the position. The horizontal position is measured from the left edge of the page.

To move to a new vertical position, issue the Advance command (Sh-F8, 4, 1, 3); then enter the vertical position. The vertical position is measured from the top edge of the page.

DOCUMENT PROCESSING

FORM 8
MEMORANDUM

WordPerfect 6 users: See Student Guide, p. 59.

Follow these steps to create the blank memorandum form shown below:

1. Clear all tabs, then set a relative left tab at 1 inch.
2. With the cursor at the left margin on Ln 1″ (see the status line), center the heading "Memorandum" in all-capital letters, extra large, and bold, leaving one blank space between letters. Press the right arrow key twice to return to normal type.
3. Begin the date line on Ln 2″. Key the guide word "Date:" in all-capital letters and bold. Turn off bold, tab to Pos 2″, then press Enter twice.
4. For the remaining heading lines, key the guide word in bold and all-capital letters, turn off bold, and tab to Pos 2″ before pressing Enter twice.
5. After keying "Subject:" in all-capital letters, press tab, press Enter twice, and insert a horizontal line the full width of the text page. Change the line width to 0.05 inch (Alt-F9, 5, 1, 4, 0.05″, F7).
6. Press Enter three times, then save the memo form.

M E M O R A N D U M

DATE:

TO:

FROM:

SUBJECT:

LETTER 56
BLOCK-STYLE LETTER WITH THREE-COLUMN TABLE

July 26, 19— / Ms. Geraldine Hanover / Radcliff & Osborn, Inc. / 1400 Commerce Street / Dallas, TX 75221-2675 / Dear Ms. Hanover:

It was a pleasure to meet you and hear you address the American Management Association's annual meeting in Chicago last week.

Your address—"What Educational Requirement Should Our Workers Possess?"—was outstanding. In checking with our department heads, I found the following:

EDUCATIONAL REQUIREMENTS FOR THE '90s

Arthur Sanders and Son

Position	College Major	Minimal Level
Accountant	Accounting	Community College
Manager	Personnel	University
Secretary	Office Systems	Community College
Systems Designer	Engineering	University

The department heads stated a preference for a four-year degree, but indicated that many of the positions could be filled by a highly trained individual from a community college.

Sincerely yours, / Josephine Larson / Director of Personnel / *(Your Initials)*

TABLE 35
FOUR-COLUMN RULED TABLE

Spacing: Double

Center a table number a double space above the title, and key it in uppercase and lowercase.

Unlike the $ sign, the % sign is used with every number if the word *Percent* does not appear in the column heading.

Table 5

SALARY INCREASES BY LEVEL

Level	Old Salary	New Salary	Increase
T-1	$16,500	$17,500	6.06%
T-2	17,000	18,250	7.35%
T-3	18,500	20,225	9.32%
T-4	19,575	21,000	7.28%
T-5	24,000	26,500	10.42%
T-6	25,700	27,700	7.78%
T-7	28,000	30,000	7.14%
T-8	30,000	32,500	8.33%

FORM 6
MEMORANDUM

A memorandum template is usually created so that the cursor will stop 1 or 2 spaces beyond the guide words to enable you to enter the TO, FROM, DATE, and SUBJECT information at the top of the memo. The formats for memos may vary, depending on where the guide words are located at the top of the page. Use the illustration below to prepare Form 6.

MEMORANDUM

TO: Adrian Cosgrove **DATE:** September 14, 19--

FROM: Cynthia Newsome

SUBJECT: Clip Art Offer

Attached is a new clip art catalog from Magic-Clips, a new distributor of clip art images in the Fort Lauderdale area. As you can see, several volumes are available; and you can choose from business, borders, professional, transportation, and communication topics.

Please circulate the catalog to all your computer graphics and design people to get their reaction to the clip art samples in the catalog. Let me hear from you by September 30 if you would like to order any of the clip art volumes.

(Your Initials)
Attachment

FORM 7
MEMORANDUM

To: Cynthia Newsome / From: Adrian Cosgrove / Date: September 25, 19— / Subject: Clip Art Offer

Our computer graphics and design people have reviewed the Magic-Clips catalog and are impressed by the quality of images the volumes contain. It is apparent that the images were first hand-drawn and then converted to graphics images. The quality is superb.

We would like to order Volumes 1 and 2 in this set and will prepare a purchase order after receiving your authorization. / *(Your Initials)*

FORMATTING

Q. CREATING FORMS

WP

REVIEW
Date Code: Sh-F5, 2
View Document: Sh-F7, 6
Font Size: Ctrl-F8, 1

WordPerfect 6 users: See Student Guide, p. 56.

With its graphics features, WordPerfect can be used to create basic forms that are frequently used, such as letterheads and memorandums.

To create forms, you will be using many different WordPerfect features. To keep track of the WordPerfect codes you will be inserting into your documents, use Reveal Codes. To reduce the size of the Reveal Codes window and, therefore, display more of your document, combine Reveal Codes and Window commands. Press Alt-F3 or F11, then Ctrl-F3. Next, enter "1" and "19."

86-90 LESSONS

Margins: 1 inch • Spacing: Single • Drills: 2 times • Format Guide: 63–69

Goals for Unit 18

Begin each day with approximately 15 minutes of skillbuilding, selecting activities from pages 203–206. In the remaining class time, complete as many production jobs from pages 207–215 as you can.

1. To improve accuracy and speed on alphabet and number keys.
2. To key 45 wam for 5 minutes with no more than 5 errors.
3. To improve proofreading skills.
4. To gain proficiency in using Merge, Switch, Window, and Headers in WordPerfect.
5. To format and key correspondence from various types of input, including handwritten, rough-draft, and unarranged text.
6. To format and key correspondence making various changes for two-page letters, multiple addresses and writers, special letterheads, and window envelopes.
7. To format and key memorandums with different features.

A. WARMUP

Three law firms (Quentin & Brint, Zenith & Jevsen, and 12
Paxen & Krey) submitted statements to collect the following 24
amounts for the legal actions: $872.50, $940.30, and $610. 36

| 1 | 2 | 3 | 4 | 5 | 6 | 7 | 8 | 9 | 10 | 11 | 12

LANGUAGE ARTS

B. COMMAS

B. Study the rules at the right. Then key lines 4–7, making necessary changes.

Rule: Do not use commas to set off an expression that is *essential* to the completeness of a sentence.

Those workers who have seniority will have preference.

Rule: Use commas to set off the year when it follows the month and day.

They will meet on July 24, 1994, in Government Center.

The form was received after you left last evening.
All students, who are commuters, are invited to attend.
The December 31 1995 deadline will not be changed.
The book being published in April 1994 is on schedule.

C. PROOFREADING

C. Compare this paragraph with the last paragraph of the 5-minute timed writing on page 206. Key a list of the words that contain errors, correcting the errors as you key.

More and more companies are trying to provide ethacal guide lines for their employees by clearly stating the type of behavior they expect. If a company wishes to be veiwed as honest, unbiased, and morale, then it must encourage is employees to be responsable for their actions and not to engage in unethical or immorale behaviors.

FORM 3
INVOICE

On December 14, Berkeley Associates prepares Invoice 72236, also to Adams Construction Company, for the following items:

1 16″ band saw, Model G1540, @ 550.00 = 550.00
2 Carbide-tipped router bits, Item 230, @ 14.25 = 28.50
1 12″ wood lathe, Model G1535, @ 450.00 = 450.00
14 Saw gauges, Model SP139, @ 19.95 = 279.30
5 Tabletop drill presses, Model G1390, with 1/2-hp motor and 11″ × 11″ square table, @ 179.95 = 899.75
Subtotal = 2,207.55; Plus Tax = 88.30; TOTAL AMOUNT DUE = 2,295.85

FORM 4
PURCHASE ORDER

A purchase order is prepared by a company to order the goods or services it needs from another firm.

Prepare a purchase order, using the information in the illustration below. Note that the information in the QTY., UNIT PRICE, and AMOUNT columns are right aligned.

Purchase Order No.: 2384

11896 Mackey Street
Shawnee Mission, KS 66210
Phone: 913-555-4832

TO: Hamby's Pool Supplies
184 North River Blvd.
Wichita, KS 67203

DATE: September 11, 19--

QTY.	CAT. NO.	DESCRIPTION	UNIT PRICE	AMOUNT
2	860C67	Patio chaise with 4-position backrest, 27" x 74" x 39"	179.99	359.98
8	860C75	High-back chairs, 24" x 28" x 36"	73.99	591.92
2	860C33	Woven, vinyl-coated, polyester umbrella. Tubular aluminum frame, crank-lift handle, 3-position tilt	99.99	199.98
2	860C25	Patio end table, 16" x 16" x 14"	24.99	49.98
		Subtotal		1,201.86
		Shipping and handling (10%)		120.19
		TOTAL AMOUNT DUE		1,322.05

FORM 5
PURCHASE ORDER

On September 12, Metro Pool Co. prepares Purchase Order 2385 and orders the following items from Swimfest Discount Center, 209 Paramount Parkway, Batavia, IL 60510:

24 18-gauge, heavy-duty water tubes, Cat. No. W16230, @ 4.99 = 119.76
5 16′ × 32′ pool covers with premium polyethylene coating, Cat. No. W92034, @ 117.77 = 588.85
2 Swimming pool pumps, 1 1/2-hp, Cat. No. W12113, @ 295.85 = 591.70
10 Boxes of super algicide (4 per box), Cat. No. W20238, @ 44.75 = 447.50
Subtotal = 1,747.81; Shipping and handling (10%) = 174.78; TOTAL AMOUNT DUE = 1,922.59

SKILLBUILDING

D. PACED PRACTICE

Turn to the Paced Practice routine at the back of the book. Take four 2-minute timed writings, starting at the speed at which you left off the last time.

PRETEST.
Take a 1-minute timed writing; compute your speed and count errors.

E. PRETEST: DISCRIMINATION PRACTICE

Did the new clerk join your golf team? John indicated 12
to me that Beverly invited her prior to last Wednesday. He 24
believes she must give you a verbal commitment at once. We 36
should convince her to join because she is a gifted golfer. 48

| 1 | 2 | 3 | 4 | 5 | 6 | 7 | 8 | 9 | 10 | 11 | 12

PRACTICE.
Speed Emphasis: If you made no more than 1 error on the Pretest, key each line twice.
Accuracy Emphasis: If you made 2 or more errors on the Pretest, key each group of lines (as though it were a paragraph) twice.

F. PRACTICE: LEFT HAND

vbv bevy verb bevel vibes breve viable braves verbal beaver
wew went week weans weigh weave wedges thawed weaker beware
ded dent need deals moved ceded heeded debate edging define
fgf guff gift flags foggy gaffe forget gifted guffaw fights

G. PRACTICE: RIGHT HAND

klk kale look kilts lakes knoll likely kettle kernel lacked
uyu buys your gummy dusty young unduly tryout uneasy jaunty
oio oils roil toils onion point oriole soiled ration joined
jhj jell heed eject wheat joked halved jalopy heckle jigsaw

POSTTEST.
Repeat the Pretest (E) and compare performance.

H. POSTTEST: DISCRIMINATION PRACTICE

I. Take a 1-minute timed writing on the first paragraph to establish your base speed. Then take four 1-minute timed writings on the remaining paragraphs. As soon as you equal or exceed your base speed on one paragraph, advance to the next one.

I. SUSTAINED PRACTICE: NUMBERS AND SYMBOLS

Retailers need to carefully consider the markup on any 12
items that are sold. They also have to be especially aware 24
of their inventory status on various products. Controlling 36
these factors can help ensure the success of the operation. 48

For example, purchasing items that cost $50 each and a 12
markup of 20% would give the retailer a markup of $10 for a 24
selling price of $60. On the other hand, if the markup was 36
30%, the selling price for an individual item would be $65. 48

The inventory on these items (#3410, #4223, and #5920) 12
has been depleted very rapidly. The supplier (Kell & Drew) 24
for these items is located in Cambridge. Place a new order 36
with them. In addition, order a supply of #6120 and #6430. 48

The new items (#6120 and #6430) must be priced at $20, 12
which would be a markup of 40%. Increase the markup to 50% 24
on those items (#3410, #4223, and #5920) being replenished. 36
Kell & Drew will be pleased with this new order for $1,600. 48

| 1 | 2 | 3 | 4 | 5 | 6 | 7 | 8 | 9 | 10 | 11 | 12

FORMATTING

A template is used as a page design in which all elements on the page (such as margins and tabs) can be saved and used as needed to prepare a finished page.

P. TEMPLATES

A template is an image of a "printed" form (such as a purchase order) that is displayed on screen. The template contains data fields that correspond to the blank areas that need to be filled in on a printed form. For example, to complete the invoice shown below, you would have to fill in the invoice number, the date, and the name and address of the buyer; the quantity, the description, and the dollar amount of items; plus any other additional information required on the form.

Templates are designed with preset tab stops at each data field, enabling you to quickly move to each field with a single keystroke—usually Tab or Enter. Use the arrow keys to move within a field.

Some forms software enables you to create your own form, fill it in, then print the completed form. Other forms software is available that enables you to key the data for the fields so that it aligns correctly with the data fields on a printed form inserted into your printer.

DOCUMENT PROCESSING

A seller prepares an invoice (or *bill*) for the buyer, showing an itemized list of the charges for the goods purchased.

INVOICE 72234

DATE May 17, 19--

TO Aims Community College
10234 Hot Springs Drive
Greeley, CO 80634

Berkeley Associates
9582 Pacific Avenue
Atlantic City, NJ 08402
Phone: 609-555-2028
Fax: 609-555-2020

QUANTITY	DESCRIPTION	UNIT PRICE	AMOUNT
6	Model 610 CFM dust collector, 1 1/2 hp, 110/220 volts	199.95	1,199.70
10	Polycrylic finish (1 gal.)	50.25	502.50
1	8" x 65" heavy-duty jointer, Model G1015	625.75	625.75
12	Router pads, Part No. C3238	7.95	95.40
2	Brad nailers, Model G1864	78.99	157.98
	Subtotal		2,581.33
	Sales Tax (5%)		129.07
	Shipping		75.00
	TOTAL AMOUNT DUE		2,785.40

FORM 1
INVOICE

Key Invoice 72234 (in the illustration above) on a template. Proofread carefully, then print the completed invoice.

FORM 2
INVOICE

On October 10, Berkeley Associates prepares Invoice 72235 for Ms. Donna Voice, Purchasing Department, Adams Construction Company, 568 Baxter Blvd., Portland, ME 04103-2783:

3 Portable planers (Model CT-60L) @ 339.99 = 1,019.97

1 10″ contractor-style table saw (Model RSW-10) @ 425.05 = 425.05

2 Drum sanders with 38″ dual drum and 2-hp motor @ 1,275.75 = 2,551.50

12 Adjustable steel bar clamps, 2 1/2″ × 36″ @ 9.50 = 114.00

4 Variable-speed scroll saws with 1.3-amp, 110-volt motor; cut depth, 2″; throat, 15″ deep; tilt to 45 degrees @ 169.95 = 679.80

Subtotal = 4,790.32; Plus Tax = 191.61; TOTAL AMOUNT DUE = 4,981.93

J. Key each sentence on a separate line.

J. TECHNIQUE PRACTICE: ENTER KEY

Cut the lawn. Wash the glasses. Vacuum the kitchen floor.
Paint the bedroom. Dust the furniture. Put up the shades.
Clean out the attic. Repair the window. Spade the garden.
Trim the bushes. Sweep the sidewalk. Replace the battery.
Clean out the cellar. Put up the wallpaper. Wash the car.

K. Insert the necessary capital letters as you key these sentences twice.

K. TECHNIQUE PRACTICE: CONCENTRATION

Diane and jim took the new jersey turnpike to philadelphia.
The chicago bears will play the buffalo bills on october 9.
When visiting san francisco, you can see fisherman's wharf.
Vicki and frank will take megan for a vacation to cape cod.
Take time to explore the piazza san marco in venice, italy.

L. Take three 12-second timed writings on each line. The scale gives wam for a 12-second timed writing.

L. 12-SECOND SPRINTS

Please send me 35 cases of part number 907864 by August 12.
The 1:30 game drew a crowd of 78,569 on Sunday, October 24.
I counted 29 or 30 cars in the lot at 4856 North 17 Avenue.
Models 74, 86, and 93 were out of stock for 15 to 20 weeks.
Order #459367 will likely be received within 18 or 20 days.

| | | | 5 | | | |10| | | |15| | | |20| | | |25| | | |30| | | |35| | | |40| | | |45| | | |50| | | |55| | | |60

M. Take a 1-minute timed writing on the first paragraph to establish your base speed. Then take four 1-minute timed writings on the remaining paragraphs. As soon as you equal or exceed your base speed on one paragraph, advance to the next one.

M. SUSTAINED PRACTICE: CAPITALIZATION

The senior class from the area high school have worked 12
on raising funds for the class trip for the past two years. 24
The class members will be holding a meeting within the next 36
two weeks to make the final selection of their destination. 48

The meeting was scheduled for one day next week. Four 12
class members will give an overview of the choices for this 24
trip. It seems that New York and Boston will be the cities 36
that will receive the most support from many class members. 48

Many of the members of the class are in favor of going 12
to New York City because they are anxious to see the Statue 24
of Liberty and the Empire State Building. In addition, the 36
members of the class are hoping to see the midtown section. 48

The members of the class wanting to go see Boston have 12
a number of sites in mind. They are anxious to see the Old 24
North Church and the Bunker Hill Monument. Some want to go 36
visit Fenway Park, the home of the baseball Boston Red Sox. 48

| 1 | 2 | 3 | 4 | 5 | 6 | 7 | 8 | 9 | 10 | 11 | 12

M. Take three 30-second timed writings on each line. Try not to slow down for the capital letters.

M. TECHNIQUE PRACTICE: SHIFT KEY

Pat left for Boise, Idaho, in May to see Ms. Ann A. French. 12
Diane, Lynn, Dave, Vicki, and Frank left for Bangor, Maine. 12
Megan was to go to Cape Cod, Boston, Fall River, and Dover. 12
Peter and Gina left for Niagara Falls on Saturday, June 22. 12

| 1 | 2 | 3 | 4 | 5 | 6 | 7 | 8 | 9 | 10 | 11 | 12

N. Change every singular noun to a plural noun.

N. TECHNIQUE PRACTICE: CONCENTRATION

The employee read the letter from the annoyed customer and gave the letter to the manager in charge of the section to handle. The manager will respond to the question raised by the customer. Hopefully, the answer will be acceptable.

O. Spacing: Double
Take two 5-minute timed writings. Compute your speed and count errors.

Goal: 48 wam/5′/5e

O. 5-MINUTE TIMED WRITING

Can you relax when you are under pressure? If not, 11
you may want to discover the benefits of taking a power 23
nap. Most people are able to relax when they take a two- 34
week vacation. Other people find that the weekends leave 46
them feeling refreshed. And some people can even unwind 57
every evening after work. But the power nap is designed 68
to relax your body and brain completely anytime, anywhere, 80
in a few quick minutes. 85

The advantage of taking a snooze is not to fall sound 97
asleep in the middle of each day but simply to slow your 108
pulse and breathing rate and reverse many of the natural 120
stress responses in your body. For example, if you enjoy 131
the ocean, slowly count to ten and picture yourself on a 143
beautiful, deserted beach lying in warm sand and listening 154
to waves crashing on the shore. Then count back down to 166
zero and awake rejuvenated and ready to tackle anything. 177

This type of self-hypnosis may be difficult for some 189
folks to learn, but with practice the power nap may become 201
a terrific technique for recharging your batteries in only 212
a few minutes each day. Spare yourself the burnout that 224
comes from constant use of the same mind and body circuits; 236
take a nap instead. 240

| 1 | 2 | 3 | 4 | 5 | 6 | 7 | 8 | 9 | 10 | 11 | 12

N. Take two 1-minute timed writings on each line as you concentrate on infrequently used letters.

N. ALPHABET REVIEW: INFREQUENT-LETTER PRACTICE

J Jovial Joe joked with Josh while they jogged in torn jeans. 12
K Kevin Packard knew that Rick and Kelly liked baked chicken. 12
Q Quincy quietly quoted the quip about the quartet's quarrel. 12
X Max fixed those taxi exits for the six excited taxi owners. 12

| 1 | 2 | 3 | 4 | 5 | 6 | 7 | 8 | 9 | 10 | 11 | 12

O. DIAGNOSTIC PRACTICE: NUMBERS

Turn to the Diagnostic Practice: Numbers routine at the back of this book. Take the Pretest and record your performance. Then practice the drill lines for those reaches on which you made errors. Finally, repeat the Pretest and compare your performance.

P. Spacing: Double. Take two 5-minute timed writings. Compute your speed and count errors.

Goal: 45 wam/5'/5e

P. 5-MINUTE TIMED WRITING

It seems as if there are many people around today who 12
have put themselves into a stressful situation because they 24
have made a decision they feel is morally wrong. Whether 35
it is adjusting sales numbers, borrowing office supplies, 47
or stretching an expense account, they know deep down that 59
they have made unethical choices. 66

Many people contend that there is now a large gray 77
area between right and wrong, and they use it as an excuse 89
not to worry about being ethical. Business students must 100
question that logic. Much of the grayness can be taken out 112
of ethical dilemmas if one takes the time to sort things 124
through. It is easy to charge ahead without thinking and 135
then rationalize your behavior after the fact. But the 146
truth is that there is no right way to do a wrong thing. 158

More and more companies are trying to provide ethical 170
guidelines for their employees by clearly stating the type 181
of behavior they expect. If a company wishes to be viewed 193
as honest, unbiased, and moral, then it must encourage its 205
employees to be responsible for their actions and not to 216
engage in unethical or immoral behaviors. 225

| 1 | 2 | 3 | 4 | 5 | 6 | 7 | 8 | 9 | 10 | 11 | 12

I. PROGRESSIVE PRACTICE: ALPHABET

Turn to the Progressive Practice: Alphabet routine at the back of the book. Take six 30-second timed writings, starting at the point where you left off the last time.

J. Take three 12-second timed writings on each line. The scale gives wam for a 12-second timed writing.

J. 12-SECOND SPRINTS

Jack required an extra big size of shade for his new lamps.
The juniors who excelled did not find the quiz very taxing.
Chocolate-flavored pie is amazingly unique and costs extra.
Six of the women quietly gave the prizes back to the judge.

| | | | 5 | | | |10| | | |15| | | |20| | | |25| | | |30| | | |35| | | |40| | | |45| | | |50| | | |55| | | |60

K. Tab: Center.
The opening lines of a letter require the quick operation of the Enter key. Key these opening lines 3 times as quickly as possible.

K. TECHNIQUE PRACTICE: LETTER OPENING

2 inches ↓ *(Current Date)*
1 inch ↓

Mr. Armando Sabatini
Vice President of Administration
Bentley Technology, Inc.
189 Henderson Street
Norristown, PA 19402-1520

Dear Mr. Sabatini:

L. Take a 1-minute timed writing on the first paragraph to establish your base speed. Then take four 1-minute timed writings on the remaining paragraphs. As soon as you equal or exceed your base speed on one paragraph, advance to the next one.

L. SUSTAINED PRACTICE: CAPITALIZATION

Taking a cruise has become a very popular way to spend 12
a vacation these days. The growth in the numbers of people 24
who have made arrangements to set sail on a cruise ship for 36
a week or more has been phenomenal in these past few years. 48

One of the most popular companies for providing such a 12
vacation is the Norwegian Cruise Line. There are currently 24
seven ships that are sailing on a regular basis out of four 36
different ports. All of these ships take an exotic voyage. 48

As an example, the Norway departs Miami every Saturday 12
afternoon. It alternates its destination every other week. 24
It always stops at St. John and St. Thomas, but it plans to 36
make a stop at some other islands in the alternating weeks. 48

Another ship in this firm always departs from San Juan 12
and follows the same route each week. It departs on Sunday 24
and stops at Barbados, Martinique, St. Thomas, Antigua, and 36
St. Maarten before it returns to its home port of San Juan. 48

| 1 | 2 | 3 | 4 | 5 | 6 | 7 | 8 | 9 | 10 | 11 | 12

FORMATTING

Q. SPECIAL LETTERHEADS

DEEP LETTERHEAD. For a letterhead deeper than 2 inches, key the date 0.5 inch below the letterhead.

DISPLAY PARAGRAPHS. Indent 0.5 inch from each margin. Double-space before and after.

COMPANY NAME IN CLOSING LINES. Key in all-capital letters a double space below the complimentary closing. Leave 3 blank lines between the company name and the writer's name.

LEFT-WEIGHTED STATIONERY. Move the left margin 0.5 inch to the right of the widest item in the left column of the letterhead.

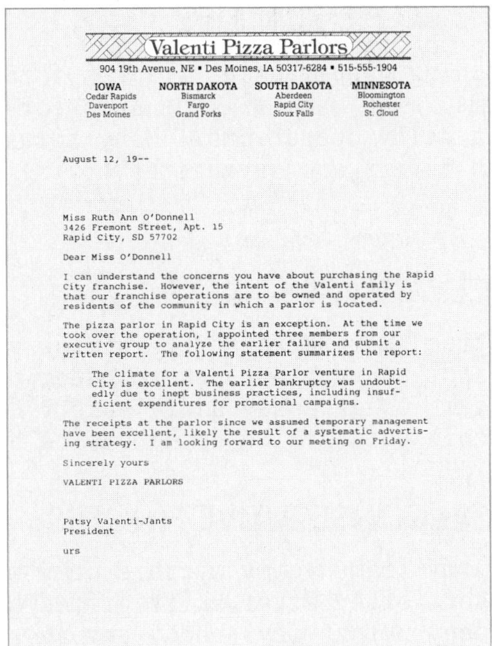

Valenti Pizza Parlors

904 19th Avenue, NE • Des Moines, IA 50317-6284 • 515-555-1904

IOWA	NORTH DAKOTA	SOUTH DAKOTA	MINNESOTA
Cedar Rapids	Bismarck	Aberdeen	Bloomington
Davenport	Fargo	Rapid City	Rochester
Des Moines	Grand Forks	Sioux Falls	St. Cloud

August 12, 19--

Miss Ruth Ann O'Donnell
3426 Fremont Street, Apt. 15
Rapid City, SD 57702

Dear Miss O'Donnell

I can understand the concerns you have about purchasing the Rapid City franchise. However, the intent of the Valenti family is that our franchise operations are to be owned and operated by residents of the community in which a parlor is located.

The pizza parlor in Rapid City is an exception. At the time we took over the operation, I appointed three members from our executive group to analyze the earlier failure and submit a written report. The following statement summarizes the report:

> The climate for a Valenti Pizza Parlor venture in Rapid City is excellent. The earlier bankruptcy was undoubtedly due to inept business practices, including insufficient expenditures for promotional campaigns.

The receipts at the parlor since we assumed temporary management have been excellent, likely the result of a systematic advertising strategy. I am looking forward to our meeting on Friday.

Sincerely yours

VALENTI PIZZA PARLORS

Patsy Valenti-Jants
President

urs

DEEP-LETTERHEAD STATIONERY. Letter shown in block style with open punctuation.

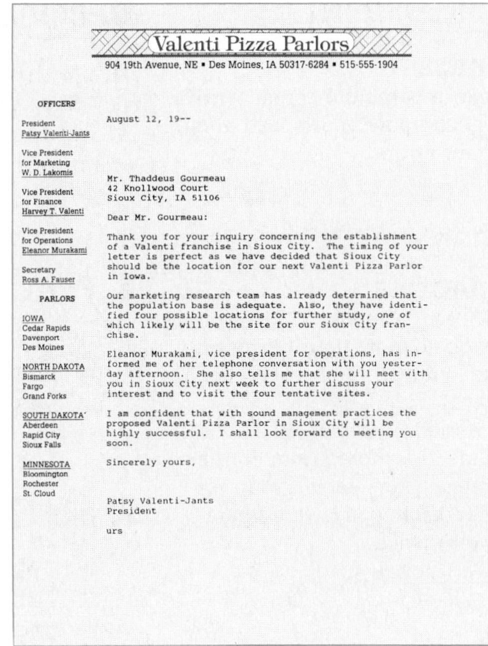

Valenti Pizza Parlors

904 19th Avenue, NE • Des Moines, IA 50317-6284 • 515-555-1904

OFFICERS

President
Patsy Valenti-Jants

Vice President for Marketing
W. D. Lakomis

Vice President for Finance
Harvey T. Valenti

Vice President for Operations
Eleanor Murakami

Secretary
Ross A. Fauser

PARLORS

IOWA
Cedar Rapids
Davenport
Des Moines

NORTH DAKOTA
Bismarck
Fargo
Grand Forks

SOUTH DAKOTA
Aberdeen
Rapid City
Sioux Falls

MINNESOTA
Bloomington
Rochester
St. Cloud

August 12, 19--

Mr. Thaddeus Gourmeau
42 Knollwood Court
Sioux City, IA 51106

Dear Mr. Gourmeau:

Thank you for your inquiry concerning the establishment of a Valenti franchise in Sioux City. The timing of your letter is perfect as we have decided that Sioux City should be the location for our next Valenti Pizza Parlor in Iowa.

Our marketing research team has already determined that the population base is adequate. Also, they have identified four possible locations for further study, one of which likely will be the site for our Sioux City franchise.

Eleanor Murakami, vice president for operations, has informed me of her telephone conversation with you yesterday afternoon. She also tells me that she will meet with you in Sioux City next week to further discuss your interest and to visit the four tentative sites.

I am confident that with sound management practices the proposed Valenti Pizza Parlor in Sioux City will be highly successful. I shall look forward to meeting you soon.

Sincerely yours,

Patsy Valenti-Jants
President

urs

LEFT-WEIGHTED STATIONERY. Letter shown in block style with standard punctuation.

DOCUMENT PROCESSING

LETTER 57
BLOCK STYLE

Format this letter for 2.5-inch deep-letterhead stationery, and insert the company name in the closing lines as illustrated above.

Treat this quotation as a display paragraph. Use Double Indent (Sh-F4) to indent 0.5 inch from both margins.

(Current Date) / Mr. Adolph R. Thompson / 734 28th Avenue South / Grand Forks, ND 58201 / Dear Mr. Thompson:

Your letter in which you inquired about the opening of a second Valenti Pizza Parlor in Grand Forks arrived yesterday. My parents opened the doors of their first parlor almost 20 years ago. When they expanded to a franchise operation in 1985, they adopted the following as one of their guidelines:

> Population size shall be the primary consideration in determining the number of parlors to be authorized in a particular city.

The specific application of this guideline has been to award only one Valenti Pizza Parlor franchise in a city with a population of less than 100,000. As you likely are aware, the population of Grand Forks is somewhat less than this.

I would like to keep your inquiry on file. If this policy should change at some future date, I shall let you know.

Sincerely yours, / VALENTI PIZZA PARLORS / Patsy Valenti-Jants / President / *(Your Initials)*

LETTER 58

Reformat Letter 57 for left-weighted (1.75 inches) stationery as illustrated above.

Retrieve Letter 57 and revise it as follows: Send the letter to Mr. and Mrs. Francis E. Lessar / 426 Second Street, SE / Rochester, MN 55904. Remember to change the salutation. Change *Grand Forks* to *Rochester* in both the first and third paragraphs. Also, delete the company name in the closing lines.

SKILLBUILDING

PRETEST.
Take a 1-minute timed writing; compute your speed and count errors.

D. PRETEST: CLOSE REACHES

Avoiding gloomy sales figures is a point of concern in 12
many firms. The same will be said for the need to trim any 24
losses in daily operations. Many firms look at simple ways 36
to obtain thrift and savings by trying to motivate workers. 48

| 1 | 2 | 3 | 4 | 5 | 6 | 7 | 8 | 9 | 10 | 11 | 12

PRACTICE.
Speed Emphasis. If you made no more than 1 error on the Pretest, key each line twice.
Accuracy Emphasis: If you made 2 or more errors on the Pretest, key each group of lines (as though it were a paragraph) twice.

E. PRACTICE: ADJACENT KEYS

tr trim tree trait strap truce stripe pantry tremor truants
po post spot pours vapor poker powder oppose weapon pockets
sa sash same usage essay sadly safety dosage sample sailing
oi oily coin point voice doing choice boiled egoist loiters

F. PRACTICE: CONSECUTIVE FINGERS

my myth army foamy yummy myrrh stormy mystic gloomy mystery
ft left soft often after shift gifted crafts thrift uplifts
ny onyx deny nylon vinyl phony anyway skinny felony canyons
lo loss solo loser flood color locate floral ballot loaders

POSTTEST.
Repeat the Pretest (D) and compare performance.

G. POSTTEST: CLOSE REACHES

H. Take a 1-minute timed writing on the first paragraph to establish your base speed. Then take four 1-minute timed writings on the remaining paragraphs. As soon as you equal or exceed your base speed on one paragraph, advance to the next one.

H. SUSTAINED PRACTICE: ROUGH DRAFT

The thought of a tax audit is bound to make one just a 12
bit nervous. At the present time, the IRS audits about one 24
of every 100 returns. The amount of income earned is a big 36
factor in determining whether or not an audit will be done. 48

In some cases, tax returns might be audited owing to a 12
mathematical formula on some portion of the tax return. In 24
other cases, there might be some questions about deductions 36
taken. Whatever the reason, an audit should not be feared. 48

Keeping good records and saving them is a major factor 12
if one is called for an audit. Three years can pass from a 24
filing of a tax return until the IRS may call for an audit. 36
During that time, it is essential that all records be kept. 48

If one is called for an audit, the meeting that will be 12
held might prove to be stressful. A review of the rights of 24
one being audited should be conducted. Also, it is critical 36
that a thorough review of the completed return be conducted. 48

| 1 | 2 | 3 | 4 | 5 | 6 | 7 | 8 | 9 | 10 | 11 | 12

FORMATTING

R. TWO-PAGE LETTERS

To format a two-page business letter:

1. Print the first page on letterhead stationery and the second page on plain paper that matches the letterhead.
2. Use a standard format for page 1 and leave at least a 1-inch bottom margin.
3. Key the page 2 heading (addressee's name, page number, and date) 1 inch from the top, blocked at the left margin and followed by a double space.

↓ 1 inch
Mr. Michael J. O'Keefe
Page 2
August 14, 19-- ↓ 2
since May 1, 19--. As you have lived at your present address for eight months of the year, you are required to pay state income taxes on two-thirds of your reported federal taxable income.

WP

HEADERS
Header:
Sh-F8, 2, 3, 1, 2, *text*, Enter, F7
Suppress:
8, 5, Y, F7

WordPerfect 6 users: See Student Guide, p. 39.

S. WORDPERFECT: HEADERS

Use a header to insert information at the top of the second and successive pages of a document. To create a header, move to the beginning of the document and enter the appropriate commands (Sh-F8, 2, 3, 1, 2). Key the information for the header. WordPerfect automatically inserts a blank line after the header. Then, press F7 and suppress the header on page 1 (8, 5, Y). Press F7 to return to your document.

DOCUMENT PROCESSING

LETTER 59

TWO-PAGE LETTER IN MODIFIED-BLOCK STYLE WITH STANDARD PUNCTUATION

Create a header for the second-page heading, then suppress the header on page 1.

Treat this comment as a display paragraph.

August 16, 19— / Mr. Myron D. Maciewski / MDM Furniture and Carpet, Inc. / 4200 Havre Avenue / Great Falls, MT 59405-3287 / Dear Mr. Maciewski:

At your request I inspected the commercial building located at 407 Larch Street on August 15, 19—.

This is a one-story, wood-frame structure with a full basement. It is approximately four years old and has been used as a warehouse facility.

In addition, I reviewed the Franz Intertec report. (The report is enclosed for the record.) Of particular concern are their comments that relate to the fill material on which the building stands:

> Two soil borings were taken on the west side of the building. They revealed that the fill material is in a soft, loose condition.

They go on to say that the fill material is compressible under the weight of the building and the weight of the fill itself. This is a nice way of saying that the structure is going to settle.

The basement floor slab has a number of cracks, some patched, of varying size. I noticed a pattern that seemed to imply a settlement of the west wall area. Further investigation showed that the structure slopes from 1 1/2 to 2 inches toward the west wall. Further settling may require the use of a new procedure called compaction grouting to raise the west wall.

On the basis of a review of the Franz report and my inspection of the facility, I would make two recommendations should you wish to further consider the purchase of the building. First, have the compaction reports that are available in the City Buildings office reviewed by a soils engineer. Second, obtain an estimate from a contractor for compaction grouting.

If I can be of further help, please let me know.

Yours truly, / FABEREISEN & ASSOCIATES, INC. / Francis J. Fabereisen, P.E. / Consulting Engineer / *(Your Initials)* / Enclosure

UNIT TWENTY-ONE • COMPLETING AND CREATING FORMS

LESSONS 101-105

Margins: 1 inch • Spacing: Single • Drills: 2 times • Format Guide: 79–85

Goals for Unit 21

1. To improve accuracy and speed on alphabet and number keys.
2. To key 48 wam for 5 minutes with no more than 5 errors.
3. To improve proofreading skills.
4. To gain proficiency in using Graphics Lines, Graphics Text/Figure Boxes, and Labels in WordPerfect.
5. To gain proficiency in completing electronic forms.
6. To format and key purchase orders and invoices.
7. To format and key mailing labels.
8. To create memorandum forms and letterheads.

Begin each day with approximately 15 minutes of skillbuilding, selecting activities from pages 242–245. In the remaining class time, complete as many production jobs from pages 246–253 as you can.

A. WARMUP

Zeke was anxious to plan his vacation. He had several 12
options. Ten days to Italy was $2,340; ten days to Jamaica 24
was $1,965; or he could go to Quebec for a total of $1,087. 36

| 1 | 2 | 3 | 4 | 5 | 6 | 7 | 8 | 9 | 10 | 11 | 12

LANGUAGE ARTS

B. CAPITAL LETTERS

B. Study the rules at the right. Then key lines 4–7, making necessary changes.

Rule: Capitalize common organizational terms such as *advertising department* and *finance committee* when they are the actual names of units within the writer's own organization and are modified by the word *the*.

Send the new collection plan to the Accounting Department.

Rule: Capitalize adjectives derived from proper nouns. **Exceptions:** congressional, senatorial, constitutional

Almost all of the European countries endorse the plan.

Our purchasing department has advertised for sealed bids.
One result was the formation of a Security Department.
The airport was located 60 miles from the Canadian border.
Each witness testified before the Congressional committee.

C. PROOFREADING

C. Compare this paragraph with the last paragraph of the 5-minute timed writing on page 245. Key a list of the words that contain errors, correcting the errors as you key.

This type of self-hypnosis may be dificult for some folks to learn, but with practise the power map may become a terific technique for recharging your bateries in only a few minets each day. Spare your self the burnout that comes from constant use of the same mind and body circuits; take a nap insted.

MEMO 20

Remember to leave a blank line between the heading entries when formatting memorandums. Also, there are 2 blank lines before the body in a memo.

Remember to use your reference initials when formatting memos.

```
MEMO TO:  Harvey Valenti, Vice-President for Finance
FROM:     Patsy Valenti-Jants, President
DATE:     (Current)
SUBJECT:  Policy for franchise allocation

Eight letters have been received the past three or fuor months
from people who would like to consider opening a second Valenti
Pizza Parlor in cities with a population under 100,000.

                                  present
I have concludded that our policy of awarding only one fran-
chise in a city with a population under 100,000 should be re-
viewed.  Your office can provide useful financial information to
aid me in making the correct decision. ¶ Please provide me with
            net
sales and gross profit figures for all Valenti parlors in the
                                           the
four-state area, along with population numbers for cities in
which they are located, I am asking Bill Lakomis to obtain the
franchise policies of our top 5 or 6 pizza chain competitors.
```

MEMO 21

Retrieve Memo 20 and revise it as follows: This memo is to go to Bill Lakomis, Vice President for Marketing. Delete the second sentence in the second paragraph; and revise the third paragraph, requesting that Bill Lakomis obtain the franchise policies, then tell him that Harvey Valenti is being asked to obtain the sales and net profit figures, along with the population figures.

FORMATTING

T. WINDOW ENVELOPES

No. 10 window envelopes are often used to eliminate the need for addressing envelopes. Letters are prepared so that the inside address shows through the window.

To format a letter for a window envelope, key the date 2 inches from the top of the page followed by a triple space (leaving 2 blank lines). Next, key the inside address followed by a triple space.

To fold a letter for a window envelope so that the inside address appears through the window:

1. Place the letter *face down,* and fold the bottom third of the letter up toward the top.
2. Fold the top third down so that the address shows.
3. Insert the letter into the envelope with the address facing the window and check to be sure it is visible.

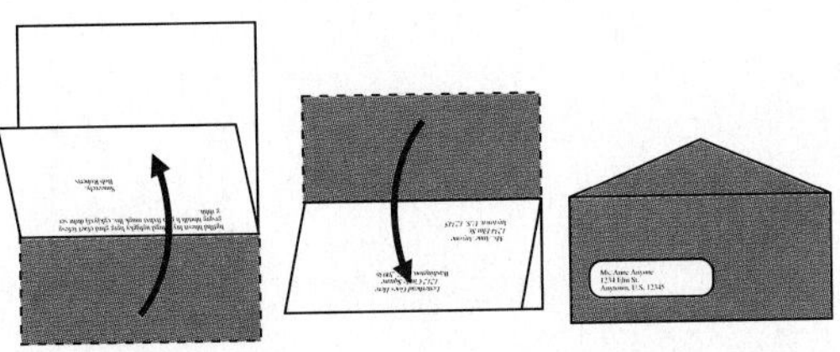

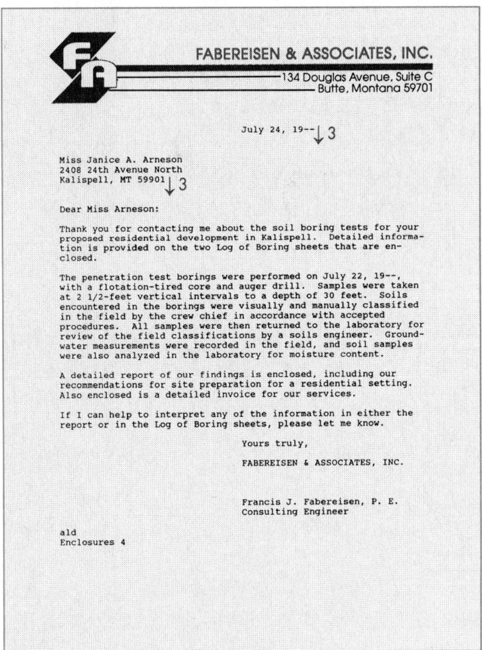

FABEREISEN & ASSOCIATES, INC.
134 Douglas Avenue, Suite C
Butte, Montana 59701

July 24, 19-- ↓3

Miss Janice A. Arneson
2408 24th Avenue North
Kalispell, MT 59901 ↓3

Dear Miss Arneson:

Thank you for contacting me about the soil boring tests for your proposed residential development in Kalispell. Detailed information is provided on the two Log of Boring sheets that are enclosed.

The penetration test borings were performed on July 22, 19--, with a flotation-tired core and auger drill. Samples were taken at 2 1/2-feet vertical intervals to a depth of 30 feet. Soils encountered in the borings were visually and manually classified in the field by the crew chief in accordance with accepted procedures. All samples were then returned to the laboratory for review of the field classifications by a soils engineer. Groundwater measurements were recorded in the field, and soil samples were also analyzed in the laboratory for moisture content.

A detailed report of our findings is enclosed, including our recommendations for site preparation for a residential setting. Also enclosed is a detailed invoice for our services.

If I can help to interpret any of the information in either the report or in the Log of Boring sheets, please let me know.

Yours truly,

FABEREISEN & ASSOCIATES, INC.

Francis J. Fabereisen, P. E.
Consulting Engineer

ald
Enclosures 4

MODIFIED-BLOCK STYLE LETTER FOR WINDOW ENVELOPE

PART

6

SKILLBUILDING

Completing and Creating Forms, Desktop Publishing, and In-basket Exercise

OBJECTIVES

KEYBOARDING

To key 50 words a minute on a 5-minute timed writing with no more than 5 errors.

LANGUAGE ARTS

To improve language arts skills, including the correct use of punctuation marks, capitalization, numbers, and spelling.

To develop composing skill.

To proofread and correct errors.

WORD PROCESSING

To use these WordPerfect features: Lines (horizontal and vertical), Graphics Lines and Text/Figure Boxes, Labels, Columns (newspaper and parallel), and Tables.

DOCUMENT PROCESSING

To fill in forms that are shown on the screen.

To create memorandum forms, letterhead stationery, and mailing labels.

To design announcements, forms, newsletters, and reports.

To apply formatting skills in a simulated office environment.

Highlander Photographics/
Mark MacLeod

DOCUMENT PROCESSING

LETTER 60
MODIFIED-BLOCK STYLE FOR WINDOW ENVELOPE

After formatting Letter 60, fold it for insertion into a window envelope.

Send this letter to Mr. James L. Alvarez / 417 Graham Street / Missoula, MT 59802-6341. Date the letter August 19, 19—.

Dear Mr. Alvarez:

Our firm will be conducting a one-day seminar on Friday, September 23, 19--, in Missoula on a topic that is relatively new. The topic is compaction grouting.

Detailed information for the seminar will be sent to you in about ten days, but you may want to reserve the date on your calendar now. As we expect that many members of the Missoula Builders Association will want to attend, the seminar fee will be only $100.

I, along with other members of our seminar team, shall look forward to seeing you in Missoula on September 23.

Yours truly,

Francis J. Fabereisen, P.E.
Consulting Engineer

If a postscript is added to a letter, it is keyed as the last item in the letter, preceded by 1 blank line. If the paragraphs in the letter are indented, the first line of the postscript should be indented as well.

PS: A social hour and dinner will follow the seminar.

LETTER 61
MODIFIED-BLOCK STYLE FOR REGULAR ENVELOPE

Retrieve Letter 60 and revise it as follows: The letter, dated August 21, 19—, is to be sent to Ms. Gayle A. Dungay / Dungay Construction / 3802 Canyon Drive / Billings, MT 59102. The letter is about a half-day seminar on Thursday, September 22, 19—, on soils testing (not a new topic). The seminar fee will be $50. Use Search and Replace commands to replace *Missoula* with *Billings.*

FORMATTING

U. FOREIGN ADDRESSES

Key the name of a foreign country in all capital letters on a separate line at the end of the address.

February 17, 19--

Ms. Monique LaCroix
747 Lacasse Street
Bordeaux, Gironde
FRANCE

Dear Ms. LaCroix:

TEST 5-C
LETTER 71
BLOCK STYLE WITH
OPEN PUNCTUATION

Supply the closing lines and any necessary notations.

On March 15, 19—, Mr. Raymond Miramontes, Vice President for Sales, Midstate Enterprises, sends a letter to Ancona Marble, Via II Strada, No. 40, Cesano Di Senigallia, Ancona, ITALY. The subject is "May Visit." Mr. Miramontes uses the company name, his name, and his title in the closing lines. Send a copy of the letter to Mr. Paul Sirocco, CEO.

Ladies and Gentlemen

This is to inform you that I will be taking a business trip to Europe during the last two weeks of May in order to purchase items for our decreasing inventory.

I would like to visit Ancona during either May 24–25 or May 28–29. Please let me know which of those dates is better for you, and I will plan on visiting with you at that time.

Please send me your most recent catalog so that I can anticipate any new items that you have available for exporting.

PS: Your last shipment of marble products caused a great deal of enthusiasm with our customers.

TEST 5-D
REPORT 56
REPORT WITH AUTHOR/
YEAR CITATIONS

Spacing: Double

RESPONSIBILITIES OF AN OFFICE SUPERVISOR

By Jean Auriemma

As more and more workers are employed in office environments, it is beneficial to review some of the responsibilities of an office supervisor.

Upward Responsibilities

It is essential that an office supervisor be aware of the expectations of top management. Keeping superiors informed of what is being done in the department and passing along ideas for improvement are musts. At the same time, the office supervisor should interpret employees' needs to management and vice versa (Cohen, 1991, p. 87).

Horizontal Responsibilities

The supervisor must keep a good communications link with other supervisors. There should be cooperation in coordinating the work of the department with that of other supervisors for the good of the firm (Taubald, 1992, p. 15).

Downward Responsibilities

Motivating workers to become more productive is a major goal for an office supervisor. Selecting, orienting, training, and evaluating employees are additional critical tasks (Berkowitz, 1990, p. 16). Scheduling the work for the department and developing harmony, cooperation, and teamwork among the workers are essential.

DOCUMENT PROCESSING

LETTER 62
BLOCK STYLE WITH OPEN PUNCTUATION

No punctuation marks are used after the salutation and the complimentary closing when the open punctuation style is used.

September 4, 19--

Mr. Seane R. Tilden
English China, Lmtd.
852 Sudbury Street N.
Sault ste. Marie, Ontario
CANADA R3B 2Z6
← Dear Mr. Tilden

As the NorthAmerican distributor of several English China patterns you are very well known in the United States. I would like to have my store become an authorized retail outlet for your company. Please provide answers to these questions:

1. Is it true that only ~~pieces~~ samples are stocked in your retail outlets and that all purchases are made by customers on an order basis? This is very appealing to me because of the virtual elimination of inventory costs?
2. What types of information and/or documentation should I send to your office for review?
3. What is the date that I would become an ~~authorized~~ outlet? earliest likely

I look forward to recieving answers to these questions so that I can become a distributor as soon as possible for your china.

Sincerely yours

D.M. Hallam, Owner

(Your Initials)
By Overnight Mail

Key a delivery notation on the line below the enclosure notation (if used) or on the line below the reference initials. A delivery notation comes before a copy notation.

urs
Enclosure
By Fax
c: Mr. M. R. Crews

LETTER 63
BLOCK STYLE WITH RULED TABLE

Refer to the Reference Section (page R-12) for the proper format for a ruled table. Leave 1 blank line before and after the table.

October 24, 19— / Mrs. Huong Quan / 12782 Highway 37 / Greeley, CO 80631-4591 / Dear Mrs. Quan:

Yes, individual pieces of Royal Sheldon and Belmore china may be replaced. Here is the information for the items about which you inquired:

Item	Pattern	Price
Dinner plate	Royal Sheldon	$80
Salad plate	Royal Sheldon	38
Cup	Belmore	42
Saucer	Belmore	32

As these pieces must be special-ordered, there likely will be a delay of about three or four weeks after the order is processed. Fifty percent of the purchase price will be due at the time the order is placed, and the balance will be due when the shipment arrives.

Thank you for contacting Hallam's about your china needs. I am enclosing brochures for both Royal Sheldon and Belmore that include prices.

Sincerely yours, / D. M. Hallam, Owner / *(Your Initials)* / Enclosures 2

Progress Test on Part 5

TEST 5-A
5-MINUTE TIMED WRITING

Spacing: Double

Any person who [1]returns to visit his or her [2]birth site 12
is almost sure [3]to be amazed by changes [4]that have occurred. 24
Some [5]of the oldest buildings [6]will have been replaced by [7]new 36
and modern structures.[8] Other buildings will [9]have been made 48
over in [10]line with some theme for [11]that part of the city. If 60
[12]you look for old stores [13]or other businesses that [14]you 70
recall, it is likely [15]to be vexing, for they [16]aren't there 82
anymore. The [17]fact that no one recognizes[18] you is equally 93
frustrating.[19] You may feel like [20]an outsider, because you 104
[21]truly are one. You get a [22]sense of being a part of [23]history. 116
After you [24]linger for a while in your [25]old neighborhood, 128
you [26]may get back in your car [27]and drive around to look [28]over 140
the town. This likely[29] will be just as shocking.[30] Where 151
there were deluxe[31] houses, apartment towers[32] now exist. Park 163
meadows [33]are shopping malls, and [34]the old swimming hole is [35]in 175
the middle of a tract [36]of look-alike homes. Slowly [37]it will 187
dawn on you [38]that you don't really [39]like that place anymore. 199
[40]Of course, any visitor [41]coming to where you live [42]now is 211
just as likely to [43]have pangs of regret when [44]he or she views 223
all those[45] changes which have [46]happened in that old hometown.[47] 235

| 1 | 2 | 3 | 4 | 5 | 6 | 7 | 8 | 9 | 10 | 11 | 12

TEST 5-B
TABLE 48
BOXED TABLE

EMPIRE MANUFACTURING, INC.

Salesperson	Budgeted Sales	Actual Sales
Mary Ann Stanek	$148,000	$146,750
Lester Boyd	131,000	133,250
James Green	114,000	108,000
Stanley Barusiwicz	103,000	107,500
Linda Lanzi	98,000	99,300

FORMATTING

V. MULTIPLE ADDRESSES AND WRITERS

If a letter is addressed to two people at different addresses, key each name and address one under the other, with 1 blank line between them. If a letter is addressed to two people at the same address, list each name on a separate line of the same inside address.

If a letter is to be signed by two people, key each name and title one under the other, with 3 blank lines between them.

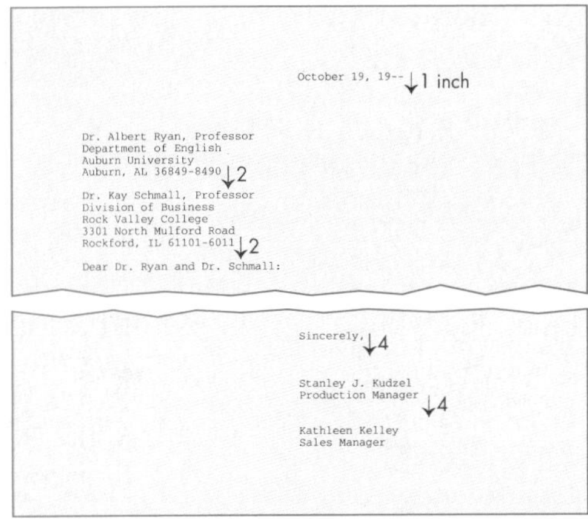

DOCUMENT PROCESSING

LETTER 64
MODIFIED-BLOCK STYLE WITH INDENTED PARAGRAPHS

The format for the date (day, month, year, with no commas) is used by all U.S. military organizations as well as by business organizations, especially for international correspondence.

Paragraph indentions may be used with modified-block style letters but never with block-style letters.

Use Double Indent to display the paragraph, then tab to indent the first line.

Remember your reference initials and the enclosure notation.

12 November 19--

Mr. Douglas R. Powers
City Manager
Municipal Building
406 Wall Street
Midland, TX 79701-3528

Ms. Joanne Starke
Director of Human Resources
City of Midland #
404 Wall Street, Annexb
Midland, TX 79701-3528

Dear Mr. Powers and Mrs. Strake: (blank line)

Yes, the city of Midland can still join the many munici-palities in Texas that have made long-term-care insurance available to their employees, retirees, and spouses at a reasonable cost. ¶ The federal government recently published these statistics:

(blank line) Nearly 60% of those over age 65 will need some type of long-term care, and almost 43% are expected to spend some time in a nursing home.

ds To reconsider adopting of long-term-care coverage would be wise. We would be happy to meet with you further to describe the benefits and exclusions contained in the enclosed materials.

Yours Truly,

Howard J. Larscheide
Executive Director

B. T. Mays
MEIG Chief Administrator

LETTER 70
MODIFIED-BLOCK STYLE
LETTER WITH BOXED
TABLE

March 13, 19--

Mr. Fritz Dietsche, Director
Bureau of Employment
Pascalstrasse 51
5300 Bonn 1
Germany

Dear Mr. Dietsche:

nationality of the

We are happy to provide the information your office requested regarding the work force at our facility in Berlin (Ohmstrasse 4-6, 1000 Berlin 13). On December 31 of this past year, we had 435 full-time employees in the following groups:

Horizontally center the table on the page. Leave 1 blank line before and after the table.

	German		American	
Classification	No.	%	No.	%
Managerial	5	1.43	10	11.90
Clerical	51	14.53	47	55.95
Production	274	78.06	13	15.48
Miscellaneous	21	5.98	14	16.67
TOTAL	351	100.00	84	100.00

Please telephone Mr. Rudi Georg, plant manager, at (30) 41.060 if you have questions or if you desire additional information. Since its opening, our Berlin plant has become a n very integral part of our international production network, and we look forward to expanding our operation within the next few years.

Sincerely,

David C. Perkins, Director
International Operations

urs

MEMO 22

Remember to execute the macro you created to format the heading lines of this memo.

MEMO TO: Nicole Rohlin / Reservations Manager / **FROM:** Ardella Eagle, Manager / **DATE:** January 9, 19— / **SUBJECT:** Season Rates

As you will remember, May 14 will be the last day for our special off-season rates. The new season rates have been established and will go into effect on May 15 and continue through October 31.

The daily rates for two–four persons will be as follows: luxury condominium, $120; beachfront cottage, $99; poolside apartment, $86; and apartment, $76. For more than four persons there will be an additional charge of $15 per person.

The weekly rates for two–four persons will be $765 for a luxury condominium, $653 for a beachfront cottage, $555 for a poolside apartment, and $492 for an apartment. For more than four persons there will be an additional charge of $80 per person.

The photos for the new brochures that you showed me last week are excellent. Now that you have these new rates, we can have the brochures printed in time for our March campaign.

(Your Initials) / c: Accounts Receivable

MEMO 23

Save this memo for use later with Letter 69.

Just as you finish Memo 22, Ms. Eagle hands you a note with changes. Retrieve the memo and make the necessary revisions: The new rates will go into effect on June 1. Also, the luxury condo daily rate will be $130, and the weekly rate will be $820. The beachfront cottage daily rate will be $108, and the weekly rate will be $693. Also, the promotional campaign has been moved up to February.

FORMATTING

W. WORDPERFECT: MERGE

WP

MERGE
Create secondary file:
Field 1 data, F9; *Field 2 data,* F9; *Field 3 data,* F9; Sh-F9, 2.
Create primary file:
Position cursor at point where field is to be inserted, Sh-F9, 1, *Field no.,* Enter
Merge:
Ctrl-F9, 1, *primary file name,* Enter, *secondary file name,* Enter

WordPerfect 6 users: See Student Guide, p. 41.

Merge enables you to create original form letters by combining a secondary file (the mailing list) with a primary file (the form letter). Each person on the mailing list will receive a personalized letter.

Information in the secondary file is organized like data on an index file card. Each item on the card is a *field,* and each card is a *record.* For example, a card for one company would be a record, and the company name, address, and telephone number would be fields. The type of information in each field must be the same for every record.

To create a secondary file, begin a new document and key the field data. At the end of each field, press F9 (do not press Enter). Pressing F9 inserts an end-field code ({END FIELD}) and moves the cursor to the next line where you can key another field. The number of the field will be displayed in the lower left of the screen.

When you have entered all the fields for one record, press F9 to end the last field, then press Sh-F9, 2 to end the record. Continue with this procedure until all records have been created, then save the file.

Next, create the primary file as a separate document. At the point you want the information from a field inserted, press Sh-F9, 1. Key the appropriate field number and press Enter to add the field code to your document. Continue keying the document, inserting fields as needed. When you complete the primary file, save it as a separate document.

To merge the two files, create a third document. Press Ctrl-F9, 1, key the name of the primary file, press Enter, key the name of the secondary file, and press Enter again. Your files will be merged and displayed. You can then print, edit, or save them individually or as a group.

FORMATTING

T. WORDPERFECT: TABLE (continued)

WordPerfect 6 users: See Student Guide, p. 54.

Table 47 that follows requires the use of additional options available when you create a table using WordPerfect's Table.

Two-Line Column Heading. To create a two-line column heading, press Enter (not Tab) at the end of the first line. To align a one-line column heading with a two-line column heading, press Enter before keying the heading.

Delete a Single Line. To delete a single line, position the cursor in the cell where you want to delete the line. From the table-edit screen, issue the Lines command. For Table 47, position the cursor in Cell A2 and enter 3, 3, 1.

Join. A braced column heading is a heading that applies to more than one column (for example, "Job Applications" in the table below).

To create the braced heading, position the cursor in one of the cells you want to join. From the table-edit screen block the cells to be joined and issue the Join command. For Table 47, position the cursor in Cell B1, then enter 7, Y.

Center Column Headings. To center a column heading, highlight the heading and issue the Format command. For Table 47, position the cursor in Cell B1 and enter 2, 1, 3, 2.

Gray Shading. Shading can be used to emphasize certain cells in a table (for example, column headings) or to enhance readability (for example, highlighting every other row).

Block the cells you wish to shade and issue the Lines command. For Table 47, highlight Cells A1, A2, B1-3, then enter 3, 8, 1. Repeat this procedure to shade Cells A15–C15.

DOCUMENT PROCESSING

TABLE 47
BOXED TABLE WITH BRACED HEADING AND SHADING

Prepare Table 47 in the format shown. The table contains 15 rows and 3 columns.

WordPerfect 6 users: See Student Guide, p. 54.

MONTHLY HIRING REPORT

South American Division

Month	**Job Applications**	
	Number Received	**Number Accepted**
January	489	106
February	376	83
March	392	79
April	406	92
May	534	107
June	482	75
July	382	69
August	295	53
September	372	68
October	350	71
November	372	75
December	423	102
TOTAL	4,873	980

DOCUMENT PROCESSING

LETTERS 65, 66, 67, 68
MAIL MERGE OF SECONDARY AND PRIMARY FILES

Format the following secondary and primary files, using the commands shown on page 213. Save the two files separately. Then open a new file, and merge the two files by using the merge commands also shown on page 213.

SECONDARY FILE

First Record

First Field:	Mr. Paul R. Schoutz
Second Field:	1462 Burgan Street
Third Field:	Waco, TX 76704
Fourth Field:	Mr. Schoutz
Fifth Field:	W37392-88
Sixth Field:	Waco
Seventh Field:	July

Second Record

First Field:	Ms. Edith Drevecky
Second Field:	1022 Hearne Drive
Third Field:	Paris, TX 77502
Fourth Field:	Ms. Drevecky
Fifth Field:	P50691-93
Sixth Field:	Paris
Seventh Field:	September

Third Record

First Field:	Mrs. Anne M. Sten
Second Field:	8902 Spur 348
Third Field:	Irving, TX 75039
Fourth Field:	Mrs. Sten
Fifth Field:	I40167-90
Sixth Field:	Irving
Seventh Field:	May

Fourth Record

First Field:	Mr. Roy V. Himler
Second Field:	55 Becket Court
Third Field:	Garland, TX 75040
Fourth Field:	Mr. Himler
Fifth Field:	G48261-91
Sixth Field:	Garland
Seventh Field:	January

PRIMARY FILE

MODIFIED BLOCK STYLE LETTER

(Current Date)

(First Field)
(Second Field)
(Third Field)

Dear *(Fourth Field)*:

Your application for enrollment in our MEIG long-term health care program has now been completed. Your membership number is *(Fifth Field)*; use this number whenever you contact us.

As a retired member from the city of *(Sixth Field)*, you will pay the entire cost on an annual basis. The premium payments will be due on the first day of *(Seventh Field)* each year.

Welcome to our program. You and your spouse can feel confident that you have substantially reduced any concerns that you might have had about future long-term health care needs.

Sincerely yours,

B. T. Mays
Chief Administrator

(FILE NAME)

Along with your reference initials, key a file name under which the letter would be stored; for example:
MEIG.urs

TABLE 45
BOXED TABLE USING
TABLE COMMAND

Margins: 0.5 inch

Make appropriate decisions about column width, format, and the like.

Each column must be wide enough to fit the longest item on a single line.

WordPerfect 6 users: Do not key the dollar sign in the Amount column.

COASTAL ENERGY COMPANY
Accounts Payable Report
September 30, 19--

Name	**Street Address**	**City**	**ST**	**ZIP**	**Amount**
Dominion Steel	11 Nichols Blvd.	Elk Grove	IL	60007	$ 322.50
Oak Federal	832 River St.	Dayton	OH	45405	84.50
DNI Finance	One Indian Pkwy.	Troy	NY	12180	804.10
United Jersey	382 East St.	Canton	OH	44707	56.40
Pope & Stone	401 Pershing	Economy	IN	47311	75.10
Standard Jar	P.O. Box 3725	Voorhees	NJ	08043	536.80
Lorimar Fibers	620 West Main	Houston	TX	77019	1,286.50
Newel, Inc.	10 Light St.	Baltimore	MD	21202	435.78
US Healthcare	11208 Elm Ave.	Boise	ID	83706	732.40
TOTAL					$4,334.08

TABLE 46
OPEN TABLE USING
TABLE COMMAND

WordPerfect 6 users: See Student Guide, p. 54.

Retrieve Table 45 and make these changes:

1. Reformat the table as an open table by removing all the rules.
2. In the table-edit screen, position the cursor anywhere in the Oak Federal row, and use the Delete command (see the menu at the bottom of the screen) to delete this account.
3. Position the cursor anywhere within the first row (Dominion Steel), and use the Insert command to insert another row for the following account: Safeco, 80 Park Plaza, Purchase, NY 10577, 239.45. Return to the document screen (F7), position the cursor in the first column, and add the account.
4. Recalculate the total.

FORMATTING

X. WORDPERFECT: SWITCH/WINDOW

WP

SWITCH
Sh-F3
WINDOW
Open: Ctrl-F3, 1, 11, Enter
Close: Ctrl-F3, 1, 0, Enter

WordPerfect 6 users: See Student Guide, p. 43.

When working with secondary and primary files, it is often easier to see both documents at the same time. To retrieve a second document while you are already working on another, use Switch (Sh-F3). Pressing Sh-F3 will move you to a blank screen. You then can use Retrieve (Sh-F10, *document name*) to retrieve the document or List Files (F5, *select document,* 1) to retrieve a document from the directory. Once you retrieve the second document, you can switch between the two documents and work on either of them by pressing Sh-F3.

To split the screen in half so that both documents appear on screen at the same time, use Window. Press Ctrl-F3 (Screen), 1 (Window), 11 (Lines), Enter. Use Sh-F3 to switch between the two documents. To close Window, press Ctrl-F3, 1, 0, Enter.

DOCUMENT PROCESSING

LETTER 69
MODIFIED-BLOCK STYLE

Subject:, In re:, or *Re:* usually precedes the actual subject but may be omitted in a subject line.

WordPerfect 6 users: See Student Guide, p. 44.

First, retrieve Memo 23 which you saved on page 213. Then use the Sh-F3 Switch command to open a new document, Letter 69. When you get to the point in the letter where you need information from Memo 23, use the Ctrl-F3 Window command to split the screen in half. Then use Sh-F3 to switch between the two documents.

The opening lines for Letter 69 are as follows: January 24, 19— / Mr. and Mrs. Roy Krizan / 925 Sagewood Avenue / Casper, WY 82601 / Dear Mr. and Mrs. Krizan: / Re: New Season Rates for 19—

The season rates at Breezy Point Resort will be in effect from June 1 through October 31. Our new brochures have not arrived from the printer, but I will send you one when they arrive.

The weekly rates for two-four people will be $____ for a luxury condominium, $____ for a beachfront cottage, $____ for a poolside apartment, and $____ for an apartment.

The daily rates for two-four people will be $____ for a luxury condominium, $____ for a beachfront cottage, $____ for a poolside apartment, and $____ for an apartment.

Each unit can accommodate as many as six people. Additional charges for more than four people are $____ a day and $____ a week per person.

Our reservations number is 314-555-1826. We shall look forward to your call.

Sincerely,

Nicole Rohlin
Reservations Manager

Remember your reference initials.

TABLE 43
OPEN TABLE USING TABLE COMMAND

Retrieve Table 42 and format it as an open table (see Step 11).

WordPerfect 6 users: See Student Guide, p. 53. Do not key the dollar sign in Column 3.

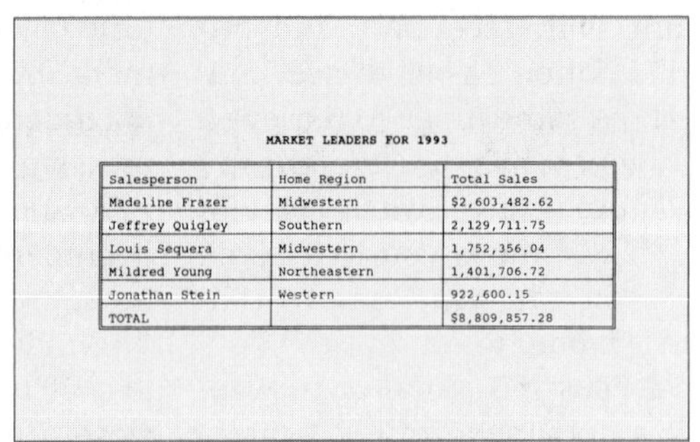

MARKET LEADERS FOR 1993

Salesperson	Home Region	Total Sales
Madeline Frazer	Midwestern	$2,603,482.62
Jeffrey Quigley	Southern	2,129,711.75
Louis Sequera	Midwestern	1,752,356.04
Mildred Young	Northeastern	1,401,706.72
Jonathan Stein	Western	922,600.15
TOTAL		$8,809,857.28

Illustration 3: Unformatted Table

5. **Calculate the total.** Position the cursor in Cell C7 (see the status line) and press Alt-F7 to return to the table-edit screen. Enter 5, 4.

6. **Print the table.** Press F7 to return to the document screen and print the table. Your table should now look like Illustration 3.

7. **Format the number columns.** Since Column C contains numbers, set it for right justification. Press Alt-F7 to return to the table-edit screen. Position the cursor anywhere in Column C and enter 2, 2, 3, 3.

8. **Adjust column widths.** Table creates all columns the same width. To adjust the width of a column, position the cursor within the column and press Ctrl-Right Arrow to make it one character wider and Ctrl-Left Arrow to make it one character narrower. Reduce the width of Columns B and C by three characters.

9. **Center the table horizontally.** In the table-edit screen, enter 6, 3, 3, F7.

10. **Format the column headings.** Block the column headings (F4 or F12), and bold them (2, 1, 2, 2, 1). Add a double line below the column headings by blocking the headings again and entering 3, 4, 3. Press Alt-F7 to return to the document screen, then print your table. It should look like Illustration 1.

11. **Reformat the table as an open table.** Return to the table-edit screen (Alt-F7). To remove all the lines, block the entire table, and enter 3, 7, 1. Unbold the column headings by blocking them and entering 2, 1, 2, 3. Block the headings again and underline them (Alt-F4 or F12, 2, 1, 2, 2, 2). In the document screen, underline the last figure before the Total line in Column C, adding spaces before the first digit to make the underline the same width as the Total figure.

    Print this open table, which should look like Illustration 4.

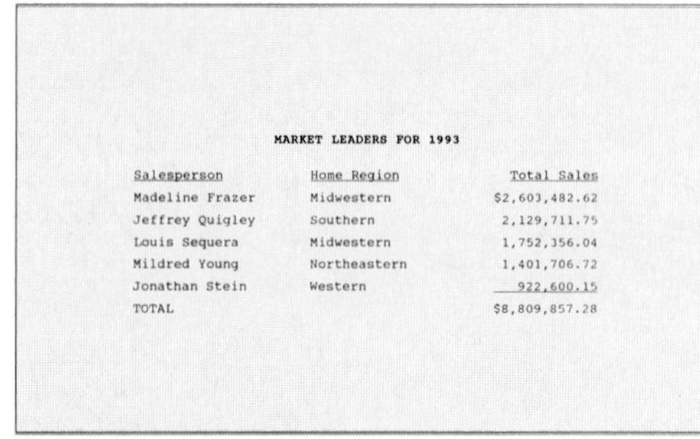

MARKET LEADERS FOR 1993

Salesperson	Home Region	Total Sales
Madeline Frazer	Midwestern	$2,603,482.62
Jeffrey Quigley	Southern	2,129,711.75
Louis Sequera	Midwestern	1,752,356.04
Mildred Young	Northeastern	1,401,706.72
Jonathan Stein	Western	922,600.15
TOTAL		$8,809,857.28

Illustration 4: Open Table

TABLE 44
BOXED TABLE USING TABLE COMMAND

Format Table 44 as shown, using WordPerfect's Table command. Adjust column widths by eye judgment.

WordPerfect 6 users: Do not key the dollar sign in Column 3.

TOP FIVE FRANCHISES

Franchise	**Business**	**Investment**	**No.**
McDonald's	Fast food	$22,500	8,101
Century 21	Real estate	25,000	7,133
KFC	Fast food	20,000	5,707
Dairy Queen	Ice cream	30,000	5,181
Burger King	Fast food	40,000	5,083

91-95 LESSONS

Margins: 1 inch • Spacing: Single • Drills: 2 times • Format Guide: 69–73

Goals for Unit 19

Begin each day with approximately 15 minutes of skillbuilding, selecting activities from pages 216–219. In the remaining class time, complete as many production jobs from pages 220–226 as you can.

1. To improve accuracy and speed on alphabet and number keys.
2. To key 46 wam for 5 minutes with no more than 5 errors.
3. To develop proficiency in spelling commonly misspelled words.
4. To gain proficiency in using Footers and Thesaurus in WordPerfect.
5. To format and key various types of legal documents.
6. To format and key an itinerary.
7. To format and key the minutes of a meeting.
8. To format and key a procedures manual.
9. To format and key reports with side headings and author/year citations.

A. WARMUP

```
1      Our accounts receivable clerk found Invoice #139 for a   12
2 total of $1,894.20 from Max Joy was past due.  In addition,   24
3 Invoice #642 for $975 from Gunther Zak was not quite right.   36
  | 1 | 2 | 3 | 4 | 5 | 6 | 7 | 8 | 9 | 10 | 11 | 12
```

LANGUAGE ARTS

B. APOSTROPHES

B. Study the rules at the right. Then key lines 4–7, making necessary changes.

Rule: To make a singular noun possessive, place the apostrophe before the *s*.

The company's assets had nearly doubled in two years.

Rule: To make a possessive from a singular noun that ends in an *s* sound, be guided by the way the word is pronounced. If a new syllable is formed by making the noun possessive, add an apostrophe and an *s*.

The jurors were all shaken by the witness's testimony.

```
4 Miss Hayward's new car had been stored in the warehouse.
5 A business firms' parking lot must meet zoning standards.
6 Minneapolis' downtown area has been transformed.
7 We helped select the new furniture for our boss' office.
```

C. SPELLING

C. These words are among the 500 most frequently misspelled words in business correspondence.

```
8 coverage schedules substantial ordinance scheduling counsel
9 termination instructions acquisition claimant allowed value
10 techniques capabilities requirement discussion emphasis out
11 participate various concern months provide notify establish
12 entered subsequent particularly communications studies some
```

MEMO 24
MEMO WITH IMPORTED TABLE

On February 1, 19—, Robert Novotny, budget analyst, sends a memo to Edwin Pearce, controller, on the subject "Projected Operating Expenses."

As you requested, I have revised our statement of projected operating expenses to reflect the changes decided upon at our budget meeting last week. The new figures are as follows:

Text In/Out (import): Ctrl-F5, 1, 3, *file name*

Import the DOS text file containing Table 41 at this point. Leave 3 blank lines before and after the table. Format the table title in bold, and underline the column headings and the figure immediately above the Total line.

These are the figures you should use in your annual budget plan to be submitted to the Board of Directors.

FORMATTING

S. WORDPERFECT: TABLE

WP

TABLE
Alt-F7, 2, 1, *no. of columns,* Enter, *no. of rows,* Enter.

Switch between table-edit and document screens: *position cursor inside table,* Alt-F7

WordPerfect 6 users: See Student Guide, p. 49.

MARKET LEADERS FOR 1993

Salesperson	Home Region	Total Sales
Madeline Frazer	Midwestern	2,603,482.62
Jeffrey Quigley	Southern	2,129,711.75
Louis Sequera	Midwestern	1,752,356.04
Mildred Young	Northeastern	1,401,706.72
Jonathan Stein	Western	922,600.15
TOTAL		8,809,857.28

Illustration 1: Table created with WordPerfect's Table

DOCUMENT PROCESSING

TABLE 42
BOXED TABLE USING TABLE COMMAND

See Steps 1–10.

Boxed tables contain both horizontal and vertical rules.

Pay attention to the screen prompts at the bottom of the screen as you enter each command.

WordPerfect 6 users: See Student Guide, p. 50.

The Table feature creates boxed tables consisting of rows (ruled horizontally) and columns (ruled vertically). These rows and columns create cells which are labeled alphabetically from left to right and numerically from top to bottom.

Follow these steps to use Table to create the table shown in Illustration 1.

1. **Center the table vertically.** Turn on Center Page (Sh-F8, 2, 1, Y, F7).
2. **Key the table title.** Center the title in all capital letters and bold. Turn off bold and press Enter twice.
3. **Create the table structure.** Press Alt-F7, 2, 1. Enter the number of columns (3, Enter) and the number of rows (7, Enter). The table structure will be displayed.

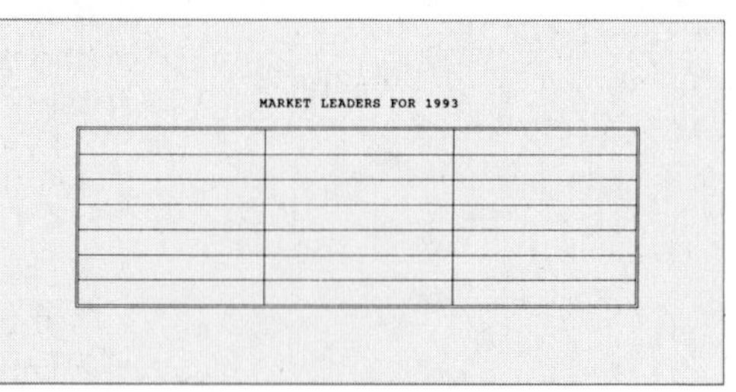

Illustration 2: Table Structure

4. **Enter the table data.** Press F7 to return to the document screen and key the data in the table. Use the arrow keys, Tab, or Sh-Tab to move between columns. At the end of a row, press Tab (not Enter) to move to the start of the next row. Do not key a Total figure for Column C.

D. PACED PRACTICE

Turn to the Paced Practice routine at the back of the book. Take four 2-minute timed writings, starting at the speed at which you left off the last time.

PRETEST.
Take a 1-minute timed writing; compute your speed and count errors.

E. PRETEST: HORIZONTAL REACHES

```
     Art enjoyed his royal blue race car.  He bragged about   12
how he learned to push for those spurts of speed which made   24
him win races.  The car had a lot of get-up-and-go.  He had   36
daily meetings with his mechanics when a race date was set.   48
| 1 | 2 | 3 | 4 | 5 | 6 | 7 | 8 | 9 | 10 | 11 | 12
```

PRACTICE.
Speed Emphasis: If you made no more than 1 error on the Pretest, key each line twice.
Accuracy Emphasis: If you made 2 or more errors on the Pretest, key each group of lines (as though it were a paragraph) twice.

F. PRACTICE: IN REACHES

```
oy ahoy ploy toys loyal coyly royal enjoy decoy Lloyd annoy
ar fare arch mart march farms scars spear barns learn radar
pu pull push puts pulse spurt purge spuds pushy spurs pupil
lu luck blue lure lucid glued lumps value lulls bluff lunge
```

G. PRACTICE: OUT REACHES

```
ge gear gets ages getup raged geese lunge pages cagey forge
da dare date data dance adage dazed sedan daubs cedar daily
hi high hick hill hinge chief hires ethic hiked chili hitch
ra rate rare brag ranch brace ratio bravo rayon prawn races
```

POSTTEST.
Repeat the Pretest (E) and compare performance.

H. POSTTEST: HORIZONTAL REACHES

I. Take a 1-minute timed writing on the first paragraph to establish your base speed. Then take four 1-minute timed writings on the remaining paragraphs. As soon as you equal or exceed your base speed on one paragraph, advance to the next one.

I. SUSTAINED PRACTICE: NUMBERS

```
     The division managers were reviewing the sales figures   12
for the last fiscal year.  They were anxious to review what   24
the sales figures of autos would be for each state.  The 10   36
states in the Southern region had impressive sales figures.   48

     Thomas Hundley was the top salesperson in Alabama.  He   12
sold 70 autos in the past year.  Total revenue generated by   24
the sales was $870,100.  This was a great increase for Tom.   36
He will be recognized at the banquet in Birmingham in June.   48

     Sales in Alabama were the highest for that region.  In   12
reviewing the sales data, there were 4,563 autos sold for a   24
total sales revenue of $56,718,090.  This represented a big   36
increase for the state over sales for just the year before.   48

     The Southern region sold a total of 32,650 cars during   12
the past year.  This gave us a total of $405,957,950 in our   24
revenues for the year.  For the entire region, there was an   36
increase of 1,162 automobiles sold over the preceding year.   48
| 1 | 2 | 3 | 4 | 5 | 6 | 7 | 8 | 9 | 10 | 11 | 12
```

FORMATTING

R. WORDPERFECT: TEXT IN/OUT

TEXT OUT
Ctrl-F5, 1, 1, *file name*
TEXT IN
Ctrl-F5, 1, 3, *file name*

WordPerfect 6 users: See Student Guide, p. 47.

To import (retrieve) or export (save) text in a format usable by other software programs, use Text In/Out to save WordPerfect files as DOS (ASCII) text files which can then be imported into spreadsheets and databases.

To save a WordPerfect file for export as a DOS text file, press Ctrl-F5. Key "1" for DOS text, "1" for save, and then the file name.

Text In/Out can also be used to import DOS text files from spreadsheets and databases into WordPerfect. To import files, press Ctrl-F5. Key "1" for DOS text, "3" to retrieve, and then the file name.

Note: All WordPerfect codes are removed, but the document format is retained by converting tabs to spaces and hard and soft returns to CR/LFs (carriage return/line feeds).

DOCUMENT PROCESSING

TABLE 40
TABLE SAVED AS TEXT FILE FOR EXPORT

Margins: 0.5 inch
Tabs: 1 left and 3 right
Spacing: Single

Prepare Table 40 exactly as shown so that it can be imported as a spreadsheet into another program.

1. Turn on Center Page.
2. Center the key line, leaving 6 spaces between columns. Set the tabs for the columns before keying the heading.
3. Key the three-line table heading with single spacing (do not use bold), and triple-space after the heading.
4. Use the hyphen for the horizontal rules. Except for the triple space before the first rule (after the table heading), single-space above and below these rules.
5. Proofread, then print the table. Save the table as a WordPerfect file, then save the table again under a different name as a DOS text file.

When setting tabs of less than 1 inch, remember to key a zero before the decimal—for example, "0.75."

Do not insert any spaces within the formulas.

```
ALLIED RENT-A-CAR
Sales ($000)
Jun 1-Dec 31, 19--


-----------------------------------------------------------------
Region                Last Yr          This Yr              % Chge
-----------------------------------------------------------------
Northeastern           307.00           156.20         (C8-B8)/B8
Southeastern           381.25           385.21         (C9-B9)/B9
Central                235.79           241.00      (C10-B10)/B10
Western                458.90           530.55      (C11-B11)/B11
Government              87.50            79.75      (C12-B12)/B12
International          279.50           345.75      (C13-B13)/B13
-----------------------------------------------------------------
TOTAL SALES      @SUM(B8..B13)    @SUM(C8..C13)     (C15-B15)/B15
-----------------------------------------------------------------
```

TABLE 41
REVISED TABLE SAVED AS TEXT FILE

Retrieve Table 37 and make these changes:

1. Delete the 1995 and 1996 columns of data, and set new tabs as needed.
2. Change the officers' salaries to $42,500 and the postage to $3,650.
3. Delete these expense categories: payroll taxes and local taxes.
4. Recalculate the total.
5. Delete the 0.5″ margin code.
6. After proofreading and printing Table 41, save it as a DOS text file.

J. Take two 1-minute timed writings. Note that the last two digits of each number provide a cumulative word count to help you determine your wam speed.

J. NUMBER PRACTICE

41 3201 4702 5603 8904 7005 1306 4407 2808 5909 6010 9211 4412
42 8913 2714 5815 6016 3217 5718 1819 2420 9321 4822 9123 8824
43 6625 5926 1127 3928 4029 5630 9031 3432 3633 8834 5635 2136
44 7337 5038 2239 9440 1941 3942 4443 2144 8945 6246 3847 2048

K. Clear all tabs. Then set four new tabs every 1 inch. Key lines 45–48, using the tab key to go across from column to column.

K. TECHNIQUE PRACTICE: TAB KEY

45	straw	safer	dense	purer	trace
46	desks	after	truck	sadly	dance
47	named	roped	along	quite	pound
48	using	enemy	point	loyal	quiet

L. Take three 12-second timed writings on each line. The scale gives wam for a 12-second timed writing.

L. 12-SECOND SPRINTS

49 Invoice #561 was for $850.35; Invoice #421 was for $565.20.
50 *One-fifth or 1/5 equals 20%; two-fifths or 2/5 equals 40%.
51 Check these invoices: (1) #3419, (2) #4623, and (3) #3518.
52 Order #34 from Quinn & Son; Item #78 will be sold by N & B.

| | | | 5 | | | | 10 | | | | 15 | | | | 20 | | | | 25 | | | | 30 | | | | 35 | | | | 40 | | | | 45 | | | | 50 | | | | 55 | | | | 60

M. Insert the necessary vowels as you key these sentences twice.

M. TECHNIQUE PRACTICE: CONCENTRATION

53 Th- --ght m-n w-rk d-wn by th- b-g l-k- f-r th- r-ch w-d-w.
54 H- m-ght m-k- th- --rly tr--n -f h- c-n d- h-s w-rk by s-x.
55 Th- w-m-n -wns h-lf th- l-k- -nd h-lf th- l-nd by th- t-wn.
56 Y-- w-ll w-nt t- d- s-m- f-sh-ng wh-n y-- v-s-t th- -sl-nd.

N. Take a 1-minute timed writing on the first paragraph to establish your base speed. Then take four 1-minute timed writings on the remaining paragraphs. As soon as you equal or exceed your base speed on one paragraph, advance to the next one.

N. SUSTAINED PRACTICE: SYLLABIC INTENSITY

57 The cost of going to school after high school has been 12
58 increasing rapidly during these past few years. There have 24
59 been several studies that have shown how that cost has been 36
60 rising faster than the rate of inflation that we have seen. 48

61 The cost of higher education may depend on the type of 12
62 school that is being considered. For example, the cost for 24
63 a private school is substantially higher than the cost of a 36
64 public one. The reputation of the school is also a factor. 48

65 By analyzing these increases, it will be obvious where 12
66 the rapid growth is taking place. Tuition charges show the 24
67 big jumps, but housing and food are at about the same level 36
68 as inflation. Student activity fees have also skyrocketed. 48

69 Parents with new babies should carefully consider what 12
70 this means. If these increases continue, it is critical to 24
71 consider financial investments. Instead of putting savings 36
72 into regular accounts, different investments may be needed. 48

| 1 | 2 | 3 | 4 | 5 | 6 | 7 | 8 | 9 | 10 | 11 | 12

FORMATTING

Q. TABLES WITH DIFFERENT FONT SIZES

WordPerfect 6 users: See Student Guide, p. 47.

Follow these steps to format Table 39, which contains three different font sizes.

1. Turn on Center Page.
2. Change the font size to Very Large, and center and key the title in bold; then return the font size to Normal and double-space.
3. Center and key the subtitle and date in Normal size; then press Enter once.
4. Change the font size to Fine, center the key line, and record the tab positions from the status line.
5. Position the cursor at the start of the key line (Home, Left Arrow) and delete the key line, including the center and font codes (use Reveal Codes).
6. Set absolute tabs as needed (1 left and 5 right).
7. Change font size to Fine, tab to the first column, and use the underline to draw the first rule, stopping the rule as close as possible to the last right tab position.
8. Key the rest of the table.

Note: When keying in a small-size font, the copy will not appear to be positioned correctly on the screen; however, it will print correctly. Use View Document (Sh-F7, 6) to see how the table will look when it is printed.

DOCUMENT PROCESSING

TABLE 39
TABLE WITH DIFFERENT FONT SIZES

Tabs: 1 left and 5 right

The dollar sign before the first amount in each column aligns with the dollar sign in the Total line.

LEHIGH FINANCIAL SERVICES

Schedule of Accounts Receivable by Age

October 31, 19--

Account Name	Balance	1-30 Days	31-60 Days	61-90 Days	91-120 Days
Chemical Rehab, Inc.	$ 320.00	$ 320.00			
Chesapeake International	68.00		$ 26.00	$ 17.00	$ 25.00
Crown Electric Utility	126.00			126.00	
First Fidelity	800.00	800.00			
Los Altos Products	350.50			257.50	93.00
Monarch Capital	400.00	400.00			
Providence Industries	1,175.32		1,175.32		
Waste Management	905.25	905.25			
TOTAL	$4,145.07	$2,425.25	$1,201.32	$400.50	$118.00

O. Key this paragraph twice as you concentrate on some of the commonly used symbols.

O. SYMBOL PRACTICE

Invoice #3212 to Klekburg & Baines requested the following:
(1) 9 disks @ $2.60 each, (2) 7 tapes @ $2 each, (3) 8 pens
@ $1.10 each, and (4) 18 records @ $6 each; the sum for the
bill is $154.20, with a 7% sales tax adding another $10.79.

P. DIAGNOSTIC PRACTICE: ALPHABET

Turn to the Diagnostic Practice: Alphabet routine at the back of this book. Take the Pretest and record your performance. Then practice the drill lines for those reaches on which you made errors. Finally, repeat the Pretest and compare your performance.

Q. Spacing: Double. Take two 5-minute timed writings. Compute your speed and count errors.

Goal: 46 wam/5′/5e

Q. 5-MINUTE TIMED WRITING

Many Americans are entering the nineties by embracing 12
simpler pleasures and homier values. They are thinking 23
hard about what really matters to them and have decided 34
that having time for family, friends, and relaxation is 45
more important than status symbols and corporate ladders. 57
All over the country folks are trying to find a quieter 68
life with deeper meaning. 74

Part of this zest for down-home values is based on 85
changes in our economy. In the past, families could get 96
by on one salary. The majority of U.S. families now rely 108
on two incomes to keep things running. That extra salary 119
no longer pays for vacations and fancy clothes but instead 131
is used for such things as mortgages, food, and gasoline 143
for the family car. 147

Maybe because people are working so hard for their 158
money, they have become more careful in how they spend it. 170
Renting a movie to watch at home has surpassed the desire 181
to see new releases in the theaters. Gourmet cooking is 193
being replaced by fast, healthy foods which can feed twice 205
the number of people for the same cost. All in all, people 217
are realizing that the value of life may not be in just 228
making money. 230

| 1 | 2 | 3 | 4 | 5 | 6 | 7 | 8 | 9 | 10 | 11 | 12

TABLE 36
RULED TABLE

Center and key the title in bold using extra large size font.

Center the key line and note the position for the start of the two columns as well as the position where the second column ends (to determine the length of the rules).

SOFTWARE WORKSHOP

Time and Place	Topic and Speaker
8 a.m.-9 a.m. Velvet Room	MicroTech Bytes Back Jorge Morales
9 a.m.-10 a.m. Salon I	A Model for Pricing Software Hans M. Allwang
10 a.m.-11 a.m. Salon II	Software Support Options Louise Summer-Ames
11 a.m.-12 noon Grand Ballroom	SDIG Business Meeting Terry Ledesma, President

TABLE 37
OPEN TABLE

Margins: 0.5 inch
Tabs: 1 left and 3 right

Reset margins first.

LEHIGH FINANCIAL SERVICES

Projected Operating Expenses

Expense	1995	1996	1997
Officers' Salaries	$ 6,300	$ 26,400	$ 36,000
Clerical Salaries	26,100	27,200	34,000
Advertising	30,300	49,900	70,400
Depreciation	21,900	28,700	26,600
Office Supplies	12,200	11,500	15,300
Payroll Taxes	10,700	14,600	13,900
Rent	10,400	12,000	12,600
Insurance	6,200	7,600	10,000
Telephone	9,200	8,000	8,900
Professional Services	3,700	7,200	6,000
Printing	4,300	3,600	5,500
Utilities	3,600	3,200	3,300
Hospitalization	2,000	2,800	3,100
Postage	2,000	2,200	3,100
Local Taxes	1,800	2,100	2,800
Travel and Entertainment	4,000	1,800	2,100
Dues and Licenses	2,000	1,200	2,100
TOTAL	$156,700	$210,000	$255,700

TABLE 38
RULED TABLE

Retrieve Table 37 and format it as a ruled table with double spacing.

FORMATTING

R. ITINERARIES

WordPerfect 6 users: See Student Guide, p. 44.

An itinerary is a proposed outline of a trip that provides a traveler with information such as flight and meeting times, travel dates, and room reservations. It may also include notes of special interest to the traveler.

Use dot leaders (Alt-F6, Alt-F6 or Sh-F8, 1, 8, *tab set,* Enter, *R, period,* F7, F7) to place a series of dots between the flush-left entries (such as the cities) and the flush-right entries (such as the flight numbers).

DOCUMENT PROCESSING

REPORT 45
ITINERARY

Tabs: Relative, 0.4 inch; 6.5 inches (right dot leader)
Spacing: as directed
Justification: Full (Sh-F8, 1, 3, 4, F7)

WordPerfect 6 users: See Student Guide, p. 45.

↓2 inches **ATLANTA ITINERARY**

Paula Mc Keenan

July 23-24, 19-- ↓3 (5)

Tuesday, July 23 ↓2

Seattle/Denver . . . . Delta 249
0.4 inch → Leave 2:15 p.m.; arrive 5:33 p.m.
Seat 5C; one stop ↓2

Denver/Atlanta . . . . ~~American~~ Delta 108
Leave 6:30 p.m.; arrive 11:15 p.m.
Seat 8A; nonstop; dinner ↓3

July 24, Wednesday

N.A.B.R. Meeting . . . . Atlanta hilton
General session, ~~8:00-~~9:30 p.m., Alexander Room
Buyers' Forum, 10:15-11:30 a.m., Conference Room A
Regional Meetings, 1:30~~-5:00~~ p.m., Parlors I, II, III, & IV ↓3

Thursday, July 25

Atlanta/Seattle . . . . Delta 250
Leave 9:30 a.m.; arrive 11:28 a.m.
Seat 3a; non stop; snack ↓3

NOTES ↓2

1. A hotel limosine is available at Harts field to take you directly to the Atlanta Hilton, and back to the airport on Thursday.

2. A ~~single-room~~ reservation has been made at the Atlanta Hilton and is guaranteed for late arrival (No. 513-38414-2370).

N. Clear all tabs. Then set four new tabs every 1 inch. Key lines 65–68, using the tab key to go across from column to column.

N. TECHNIQUE PRACTICE: TAB KEY

65	561	343	892	621	816
66	403	189	267	394	408
67	532	679	790	855	921
68	148	289	365	402	579

O. Take three 12-second timed writings on each line. The scale gives wam for a 12-second timed writing.

O. 12-SECOND SPRINTS

69 Tom, Sue, Ann, and Ralph went to see the Statue of Liberty.
70 Radio City Music Hall is located on Avenue of the Americas.
71 Route 80 East goes right into the George Washington Bridge.
72 The New York Stock Exchange is situated in lower Manhattan.

|||||5||||10||||15||||20||||25||||30||||35||||40||||45||||50||||55||||60

P. Spacing: Double
Take two 5-minute timed writings. Compute your speed and count errors.

Goal: 47 wam/5′/5e

P. 5-MINUTE TIMED WRITING

73 Around the world, summer is considered the best time 12
74 for taking a vacation. Hot days, warm nights, and no kids 23
75 in school encourage many people to pack up and go. But 35
76 where you go and for how long varies quite a bit depending 46
77 on where you live. 50
78 In our country, one or two weeks for vacation time is 62
79 quite common. Some people and managers can expect to have 74
80 much more time off. As the trend for Americans to take 85
81 shorter trips several times a year increases, destinations 97
82 are more likely to be close to home. Organized trips are 108
83 popular too, and jaunts to theme parks and all-inclusive 120
84 resorts rank high for families and singles. 129
85 If two weeks off sounds too short, then perhaps you 140
86 should work in Italy, where a month off is typical. The 151
87 Italians quench their thirst for relaxation by visiting 163
88 one of the hundreds of beaches that dot their coastline. 174
89 The Japanese also enjoy vacations by the ocean, with the 186
90 most popular spots being company-owned centers. However, 197
91 if you like long vacations, don't get a job in Japan; the 209
92 average Japanese takes off only eight days a year. It may 221
93 seem short, but even a few days in the sun can make anyone 232
94 feel refreshed. 235

| 1 | 2 | 3 | 4 | 5 | 6 | 7 | 8 | 9 | 10 | 11 | 12

REPORT 46
ITINERARY

Retrieve Report 45 and make the following changes:

1. Change the traveler's name to Justin Ireland; change the travel dates to August 1–3 (Monday–Wednesday).
2. Mr. Ireland will depart from Seattle on American 382 at 9 a.m., nonstop. He will arrive in Atlanta at 5 p.m. The seat is 10A; lunch is served.
3. His return flight on Wednesday is Delta 185, leaving at 10:08 a.m. and arriving in Dallas at 10:39 a.m.; seat 14B.
4. From Dallas to Seattle, Mr. Ireland will fly on Northwest 672, leaving at 12:15 p.m. and arriving in Seattle at 1:32 p.m.; seat 7A. Lunch is served.
5. The confirmation number is 513-38414-2319.

REPORT 47
MINUTES OF A MEETING

Tabs: Relative, 1.5 inches; 3.25 inches

Begin closing lines at the center.

Key the side headings in all capital letters and bold, then press Indent (F4) to begin the paragraphs.

2 inches ↓

PLANNING COMMITTEE
Minutes of the Meeting ↓2
March 15, 19-- ↓2 ↓3

ATTENDANCE The Planning Committee meeting was called to order at 3 p.m. on March 15, 19--, by Michael Nix, chairperson. Members present were Curtis Avery, T. L. Balenger, Shelly Karle, Michael Nix, and Lisa Spense. ↓3

OLD BUSINESS The members of the committee reviewed bids submitted for the purchase of a laser printer. Shelly Karle will contact the two lowest bidders to obtain information on color capabilities. ↓3

NEW BUSINESS The committee reviewed a proposal for a new plant in Redwood City. After much discussion, the committee agreed to contact the county clerk's office and ask for the Redwood City zoning ordinances. ↓2

A request for five microcomputers (with CD-ROM drives) in the Records Office was approved. ↓3

ADJOURNMENT The meeting was adjourned at 4:30 p.m. The next meeting is scheduled for April 16 in the Boardroom. ↓2

Respectfully submitted, ↓4

T. L. Balenger, Secretary

I. This paragraph is made up of very short words, requiring frequent use of the space bar. Take two 1-minute timed writings. Do not pause before or after striking the space bar.

I. TECHNIQUE PRACTICE: SPACE BAR

```
     I will stop by to see you at your office at about one.  12
We can check the order that was sent in by Kay, and then we  24
can plan on lunch at two.  I will take you to that new deli  36
that just opened.  When lunch is over, we can plan to go to  48
see that new pet shop that opened at the mall on Wednesday.  60
| 1 | 2 | 3 | 4 | 5 | 6 | 7 | 8 | 9 | 10 | 11 | 12
```

J. Take two 1-minute timed writings. The last two digits of each number provide a cumulative word count to help you determine your wam speed.

J. NUMBER PRACTICE

```
2301 7402 6503 9804 1705 3106 4407 8208 9509 1610 2911 4412
9813 7214 8515 6116 2317 7518 8119 4220 3921 8422 1923 3824
6625 9526 1127 9328 4029 6530 9031 4232 6333 8834 7535 1236
3737 5038 2239 4940 9141 9342 4443 1244 9845 2646 8347 2048
```

K. Each of these sentences contains two words that are not used properly. Correct those words as you key each sentence twice.

K. TECHNIQUE PRACTICE: CONCENTRATION

```
The principle of the high school was quiet upset on Friday.
Please except the congratulations from the too individuals.
There house was on the rode that went near the new schools.
If the home team could beet them, it would be a great feet.
```

L. PROGRESSIVE PRACTICE: NUMBERS

Turn to the Progressive Practice: Numbers routine at the back of the book Take six 30-second timed writings, starting at the point where you left off the last time.

M. Take a 1-minute timed writing on the first paragraph to establish your base speed. Then take four 1-minute timed writings on the remaining paragraphs. As soon as you equal or exceed your base speed on one paragraph, advance to the next one.

M. SUSTAINED PRACTICE: CAPITALIZATION

```
     An objective held by some people is to visit the fifty  12
states in our land.  While they visit each one, the idea of  24
seeing each capital is appealing.  Can you identify some of  36
the capital cities of our fifty states that are well known?  48

     For example, the capital of Massachusetts has played a  12
major role in our American history.  Boston is very closely  24
associated with the Revolutionary War and is recognized for  36
the role it played in critical events in our early history.  48

     Many of the states in the South have well-known cities  12
that serve as capitals.  In Alabama, the city of Montgomery  24
has played significant roles.  The Confederate States began  36
there in 1861, and Rosa Parks attracted national headlines.  48

     Some state capitals are not as well known.  Would many  12
people be able to identify the capitals of Delaware, Maine,  24
South Dakota, Alaska, and Montana?  The right answers would  36
be as follows:  Dover, Augusta, Pierre, Juneau, and Helena.  48
| 1 | 2 | 3 | 4 | 5 | 6 | 7 | 8 | 9 | 10 | 11 | 12
```

REPORT 48
MINUTES OF A MEETING

Key these minutes in report format. Use single spacing. Key the side headings in bold with a double space before and after.

Minutes of the Meeting
September 8, 19--

N
PERSONEL COMMITTEE

Attendance

of the Personnel Committee ,who chaired the meeting
A special meeting was held in the office of Mr. Carpenter. All members were present except Ron Farley, who was represented by Heather Zukowski. The meeting was called to order at 2 p.m.

Unfinished Business

distributed and
Ms. Samuels reported on the survey of company personnel. ~~A copy of the survey is attached to the minutes.~~ The minutes of the last monthly meeting were read and approved.

New business

n
Mr. Carpenter discussed the need for planing a campaign for letting job applicants know about openings within the company.
position
and Donna Newby
Richard Smiley will draft a promotion piece to be sent to the
Adams
chronicell.

Bismarck
Programs for the H R D Conference to be held in ~~Fargo~~ were distributed to all members. Each committee member ~~were~~ asked to
was
his or her
distribute these copies to all employees in ~~their~~ departments.

~~ADJOURN~~ Adjournment

The meeting for October 9 was adjourned at 3:15 p.m. The next meeting has been scheduled in the Communications Center.

Respectfully submitted,

Blake Lanier, Secretary

FORMATTING

S. PROCEDURES MANUAL

Organizations often prepare procedures manuals to identify the steps or methods to be followed to accomplish a particular task. These manuals are often formatted as unbound reports, but with single spacing. It is important that the pages be clearly labeled. The top of each page may include such items as the company name, a section title, and a page number. The bottom of each page may include the same items or may identify the content on that page (for example, *Policies*).

Employees' Manual Kramer, Inc., Page 5

This procedures manual, therefore, is designed to assist managers who are responsible for developing training programs for all new employees hired in any of the five regional branches of Kramer, Inc. The following paragraphs outline the basic content of a training program.

Introduction

This section should explain the content of the manual and specific ways in which it may be used within the company. It should provide answers to the following questions:

1. Who is the training manual designed for, and what does it contain?
2. Where does the training manual fit within the training program?
3. How should the training manual be used?
   A. As self-paced instructional material?
   B. As classroom material?
   C. As a study guide for students?

Program Philosophy and Goals

The program philosophy and goals section reveals the nature of the training program. These statements provide the context for all courses within Kramer, Inc. This section should focus on two major areas:

1. Program Philosophy
   A. Why does this program exist, and who will benefit from it?

SKILLBUILDING

PRETEST.
Take a 1-minute timed writing; compute your speed and count errors.

PRACTICE.
Speed Emphasis: If you made no more than 1 error on the Pretest, key each line twice.
Accuracy Emphasis: If you made 2 or more errors on the Pretest, key each group of lines (as though it were a paragraph) twice.

POSTTEST.
Repeat the Pretest (D) and compare performance.

D. PRETEST: COMMON LETTER COMBINATIONS

We were careful to pick forty capable persons to serve 12
on the committee. Some complex questions concerning upkeep 24
of the condos were to be part of the discussions. A former 36
member made a motion to table the motion on building plans. 48

| 1 | 2 | 3 | 4 | 5 | 6 | 7 | 8 | 9 | 10 | 11 | 12

E. PRACTICE: WORD BEGINNINGS

for forty forth format former forget forest forearm forbear
con condo conic contra confer convey concur concern condemn
per peril perky period permit person peruse perform persist
com combo comic combat commit common combed compose complex

F. PRACTICE: WORD ENDINGS

ing doing mixing living filing taping sending biking hiding
ble cable nimble fumble dabble bobble capable marble mumble
ion onion nation lotion motion option mention fusion legion
ful awful useful joyful earful lawful helpful sinful armful

G. POSTTEST: COMMON LETTER COMBINATIONS

H. Take a 1-minute timed writing on the first paragraph to establish your base speed. Then take four 1-minute timed writings on the remaining paragraphs. As soon as you equal or exceed your base speed on one paragraph, advance to the next one.

H. SUSTAINED PRACTICE: ROUGH DRAFT

Housing in our society has always been a topic that is 12
hotly debated. For the past several decades, the prices of 24
new and existing homes have climbed higher than the rate of 36
inflation. What are some significant housing developments? 48

Driven by cost res[r]taints, builders ~~would~~ will be encouraged 12
to build smaller homes. To off set smaller and fewer rooms, 24
house builders will offer as much open interior space as is 36
possible. In addition, the lot sizes will also be smaller. 48

¶ Technology ~~would~~ will be a critical factor in all new ~~homes~~ houses 12
in the future. Most homes will be wired for communications 24
and central electronic controls. This will help home owners 36
to keep a ~~style~~ standard of living that's comfort~~i~~able and ~~safe~~ secure. 48

Paying for housing ha~~d~~s always been a concern. ~~A~~ One new 12
method use[d] for financ~~e~~ing new ~~houses~~ homes has been an [d]ajustable- 24
rate mortgage. How ever, there seems to be more interest in 36
get[t]ing a conventional mortgage in today's financial arena. 48

| 1 | 2 | 3 | 4 | 5 | 6 | 7 | 8 | 9 | 10 | 11 | 12

FOOTER
Sh-F8, 2, 4, 1, 2, *text,* F7, F7

WordPerfect 6 users: See Student Guide, p. 45.

T. WORDPERFECT: FOOTERS

Just as you would use a header to insert information at the top of pages, use a footer to insert information at the bottom of pages. To create a footer, move to the beginning of the document and enter the appropriate commands (Sh-F8, 2, 4, 1, 2). Key the text for the footer and press F7 twice. WordPerfect considers the footer as part of the text page. The footer will be printed above the bottom margin.

DOCUMENT PROCESSING

REPORT 49
PROCEDURES MANUAL–PAGE 5

To align the enumerated items, set tabs at 0.9 and 1.3 inch.

Paragraphs are indented 0.5 inch.

Change the page number to 5, then create a header (Sh-F8, 2, 3, 1, 2, *text,* F7, F7) for the information to appear at the top of the page. Create a footer (Sh-F8, 2, 4, 1, 2, *text,* F7, F7) to include *Training Program* at the bottom right of the page.

WordPerfect 6 users: See Student Guide, p. 46.

Employees' Manual — Kramer, Inc., Page 5

This procedures manual, therefore, is designed to assist managers who are responsible for developing training programs for all new employees hired in any of the five regional branches of Kramer, Inc. The following paragraphs outline the basic content of a training program.

Introduction

This section should explain the content of the manual and specific ways in which it may be used within the company. It should provide answers to the following questions:

1. Who is the training manual designed for, and what does it contain?
2. Where does the training manual fit within the training program?
3. How should the training manual be used?
   A. As self-paced instructional material?
   B. As classroom material?
   C. As a study guide for students?

Program Philosophy and Goals

The program philosophy and goals section reveals the nature of the training program. These statements provide the context for all courses within Kramer, Inc. This section should focus on two major areas:

1. Program Philosophy
   A. Why does this program exist, and who will benefit from it?
   B. What company needs are satisfied by this training program?
2. Goal Statements
   A. What tasks, competencies, and goals are satisfied by this program?
   B. What specific skills does this training program develop?

Training Program

FORMATTING

U. AUTHOR/YEAR CITATIONS

When preparing a report, you must document (or cite) any information that is taken from other sources. The author/year method of citation includes the following information in parentheses at the appropriate point within the text: the author's last name, the year of publication (followed by a comma), and the page number; for example (Smith, 1993, p. 52). If the author's name appears within the text, give only the year and page number in parentheses.

If a source has two authors, give both last names joined by *and.* If a source has three or more authors, give the last name of the first author followed by *et al.*

UNIT TWENTY • SPECIALIZED TABLES

96-100 LESSONS

Margins: 1 inch • Spacing: Single • Drills: 2 times • Format Guide: 73–79

Goals for Unit 20

Begin each day with approximately 15 minutes of skillbuilding, selecting activities from pages 227–230. In the remaining class time, complete as many production jobs from pages 231–238 as you can.

1. To improve accuracy and speed on alphabet and number keys.
2. To key 47 wam for 5 minutes with no more than 5 errors.
3. To improve proficiency in composing at the keyboard.
4. To format tables using different font sizes and with two-line column heads.
5. To develop proficiency in using Tables, Text In/Out, and Shading in WordPerfect.
6. To format and key a comparative income statement.
7. To format and key a variety of tables.

A. WARMUP

```
1      Get them a requisition to purchase 18 items @ $105 and   12
2 23 items @ $96.  Just add the 7% sales tax for a total cost   24
3 of $4,384.86.  Be sure to check and verify those two sizes.   36
  | 1 | 2 | 3 | 4 | 5 | 6 | 7 | 8 | 9 | 10 | 11 | 12
```

LANGUAGE ARTS

B. APOSTROPHES

B. Study the rules at the right. Then key lines 4–7, making necessary changes.

Rule: If the addition of an extra syllable to a singular noun would make a word that is difficult to pronounce, add only the apostrophe to make it possessive.

Mrs. Sanders' advice to the strikers was well received.

Rule: To make a plural noun not ending in *s* possessive, place the apostrophe before the *s*.

Place all children's shoes in a display area by the aisle.

```
4 The article featured four of New Orleans's restaurants.
5 Jim Phillips' negotiating skills helped us get a contract.
6 Kathleen and Kris helped in designing the womens' lounge.
7 An announcement of the four alumnis' gifts was published.
```

C. COMPOSING

Compose the body of a letter to respond to Letter 62, Unit 18, p. 211, using the following suggestions for each paragraph:

Paragraph 1. Thank Mr. Hallam for his interest in becoming a distributor for English China, Ltd.

Paragraph 2. Explain that although much of our stock is stored in a warehouse and available only by direct order, our full product line must be displayed by our distributors. Also explain that in order for him to become a distributor, Mr. Hallam must provide us with a five-year business plan and a five-year marketing strategy.

Paragraph 3. Tell Mr. Hallam that once I receive these materials and have looked them over, I will call to arrange a meeting with him to discuss the remaining details.

DOCUMENT PROCESSING

REPORT 50
TWO-PAGE REPORT WITH AUTHOR/YEAR CITATIONS

Spacing: Double

THE FEASIBILITY OF PURCHASING A DTP SYSTEM FOR BLAKE ASSOCIATES

This report will investigate some of the major uses and advantages of desktop publishing to determine if it is feasible to purchase a new DTP system for Blake Associates during the current fiscal year.

Uses of Desktop Publishing

The purchase of a new desktop publishing system would enable Blake Associates to produce its own company newsletter. Currently, our newsletter is drafted in the Communications Department and then sent to Quick Press for layout, design, and typesetting. According to Hirsch (1994), we would also be able to use desktop publishing to produce our annual report.

In addition to the purchase of a desktop publishing system, it would be in the best interests of Blake Associates to obtain a copy of the popular ArtCraft clip art package so that we could use desktop publishing in our advertising campaign. The clip art could also be used to promote our catalog products throughout the year. With desktop publishing, these promotion spots could be created with camera-ready perfection (Slade, 1993, p. 48).

Advantages of Purchasing a DTP System

On the basis of current figures, it is estimated that first-year savings in printing costs for Blake Associates would amount to a minimum of $9,450. Savings in the second year of operation should reach $15,000. According to Collins (1994), printing cost savings in the first five years of operation could approach 80 percent.

REPORT 51
TWO-PAGE REPORT WITH AUTHOR/YEAR CITATIONS

Spacing: Double

Retrieve Report 50 and make the following changes:

1. Replace the last sentence in the advantages paragraph with the following: *We believe that our forms production costs could be reduced from $.20 per form page to $.05 per form page.*
2. Add the following paragraph to the end of the report:

The costs of using an outside vendor for printing our publications will continue to rise. Desktop publishing will enable us to cut those publishing costs dramatically. Telcon Industries had been spending up to $75,000 on printing its newsletter. With desktop publishing, they reduced that outlay to only $35,000 (Byers, 1994).

REPORT 52
REFERENCE LIST

Center and key the title "References" in all-capital letters and bold 2 inches from the top, and use the Hanging Indent command (F4, Sh-Tab) to format the turnover lines.

Byers, Ed, "Newsletter Design," *Personal Publisher,* April 1994, pp. 14–15.

Collins, Wanda, "Taking a Journey With DTP," *DTP Computing,* May 1994, p. 28.

Hirsch, Mitchell, *DTP Manual for Executives,* Computer Press, Denver, 1994.

Slade, Beth, *Desktop Publishing Comes of Age,* Midwestern Book Company, Kansas City, 1993, p. 48.

REPORT 54
POWER OF ATTORNEY

Tabs: 1 inch; center
Spacing: Double

POWER OF ATTORNEY

Be It Known that I, Dale D. Lindsey, have made and appointed and by these presents do make, appoint, and constitute, Teresa R. Lindsey, my true and lawful attorney-in-fact, for me and in my name, place, and stead on my behalf, to do and perform ~~for me~~ anything of any character which I might do or perform for myself if personaly present and acting.

Should my attorney pre decease me or otherwise be unable to perform all the matters and things here in set out to be done and perform, then, and in that event, and thereafter I do hereby constitute and appoint no one my true and lawful attorney-in-fact with full power and authority to do and perform in my name all matters and things herein authorized to be done and preformed by the said attorney-in-fact with all the power and authority here in given.

IN WITNESS WHEREOF, I have executed the fore going Power of Attroney, this twenty-sixth day of June, 19--.

____

Signed and affirmed in the presence of

____________________________ and ____________________________

FORMATTING

THESAURUS
Alt-F1, 1, *letter*

WordPerfect 6 users: See Student Guide, p. 46.

W. WORDPERFECT: THESAURUS

The Thesaurus displays synonyms for words in your text. Position the cursor anywhere in the word you want to look up, and press Alt-F1. To replace the highlighted word with a synonym, enter "1" and the letter of the desired synonym.

DOCUMENT PROCESSING

REPORT 55
POWER OF ATTORNEY

Retrieve Report 54 and make the following changes:

1. In paragraph 1, line 2, use the Thesaurus to replace *appoint* with *designate.*
2. In paragraph 1, line 4, use the Thesaurus to replace *perform* with *execute.*
3. In paragraph 1, line 5, use the Thesaurus to replace *perform* with *accomplish.*
4. In paragraph 2, line 7, use the Thesaurus to replace *power* with *capacity.*

V. LEGAL DOCUMENTS

Two common legal documents are a bill of sale and a power of attorney.

A *bill of sale* is an agreement by which one person agrees to sell a piece of personal property to another. A *power of attorney* gives one person the power to act as an agent, or proxy, for another.

Study the illustrations below; then key Report 53 and Report 54.

Note: Reports 53 through 55 are one-page legal documents and are not numbered. For a two-page legal document, the cumulative page count *(Page 1 of 2, Page 2 of 2)* is centered 1 inch from the bottom. The second page has a 1½-inch top margin.

Note: Key the title in Very Large size and bold.

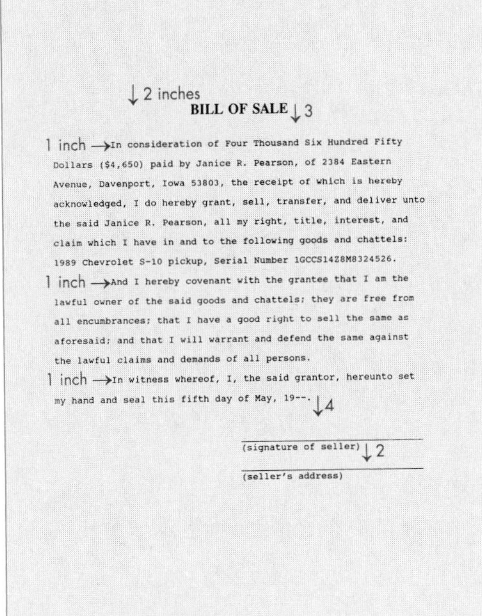

↓2 inches

BILL OF SALE ↓3

1 inch → In consideration of Four Thousand Six Hundred Fifty Dollars ($4,650) paid by Janice R. Pearson, of 2384 Eastern Avenue, Davenport, Iowa 53803, the receipt of which is hereby acknowledged, I do hereby grant, sell, transfer, and deliver unto the said Janice R. Pearson, all my right, title, interest, and claim which I have in and to the following goods and chattels: 1989 Chevrolet S-10 pickup, Serial Number 1GCCS14Z8M8324526.

1 inch → And I hereby covenant with the grantee that I am the lawful owner of the said goods and chattels; they are free from all encumbrances; that I have a good right to sell the same as aforesaid; and that I will warrant and defend the same against the lawful claims and demands of all persons.

1 inch → In witness whereof, I, the said grantor, hereunto set my hand and seal this fifth day of May, 19--. ↓4

(signature of seller) ↓2

(seller's address)

BILL OF SALE

POWER OF ATTORNEY

↓2 inches

POWER OF ATTORNEY ↓3

1 inch → BE IT KNOWN that I, Dale D. Lindsey, have made, constituted, and appointed and by these presents do make, constitute, and appoint, Teresa R. Lindsey, my true and lawful attorney-in-fact, for me and in my name, place, and stead and on my behalf, to do and perform for me anything of any character which I might do or perform for myself if personally present and acting.

1 inch → Should my said attorney-in-fact predecease me or otherwise be unable to perform all the matters and things herein set out to be done and performed, then and in that event and thereafter I do hereby constitute and appoint no one my true and lawful attorney-in-fact with full power and authority to do and perform in my name and stead all matters and things herein authorized to be done and performed by the said attorney-in-fact with all the power and authority herein given.

1 inch → IN WITNESS WHEREOF, I have executed the foregoing Power of Attorney, this twenty-sixth day of June, 19--. ↓4

↓2

SIGNED and affirmed in the presence of ↓2

and

DOCUMENT PROCESSING

REPORT 53
BILL OF SALE

Tabs: 1 inch; center
Spacing: Double

Note: Key the title in Very Large size and bold.

BILL OF SALE ↓3

In consideration of Four Thousand Six Hundred Fifty Dollars ($4,650) paid by Janice R. Pearson, of 2384 Eastern Avenue, Davenport, Iowa 52803, the receipt of which is hereby acknowledged, I do hereby grant, sell, transfer, and deliver unto the said Janice R. Pearson, all my right, title, interest, and claim which I have in and to the following goods and chattels: 1989 Chevrolet S-10 pickup, Serial Number 1GCCS14Z8M8324526.

And I hereby covenant with the grantee that I am the lawful owner of the said goods and chattels; that they are free from all encumbrances; that I have a good right to sell the same as aforesaid; and that I will warrant and defend the same against the lawful claims and demands of all persons.

In witness whereof, I, the said grantor, hereunto set my hand and seal this fifth day of May, 19—. ↓4

Start the signature line at the center.

____
(signature of seller) ↓2

____
(seller's address)

SUPPLEMENTARY TIMED WRITING

Spacing: Double

Employee recruitment has become both more demanding 11
and more urgent in recent years. In order to compete in 23
the global marketplace, many companies are giving their 34
workers duties that require greater levels of trust and 45
power. Finding people able to handle these added tasks is 57
a tall order for recruiters at a time when the typical pool 69
of recruits is shrinking and filled with many folks who are 81
not qualified or interested in taking responsibility for 92
additional jobs. 96

To meet this challenge, smart employers will do two 107
things: expand and refine current recruiting methods and 119
design new ones. Expanding old methods, such as creatively 131
using the help-wanted section in the local paper, seems to 143
be the current plan of action for the majority of firms. 154
While adjusting current systems might be helpful in the 165
short run, they may not be proactive enough to solve future 177
issues unless they are mixed with more unique methods. 188

One way of designing a new recruiting method is to 200
work diligently to obtain a work force that is diverse. 211
For instance, some companies make special arrangements to 223
match the needs of new recruits they are trying to target, 234
such as older folks, students, or the handicapped. Then 246
they market these benefits with certain campaigns designed 258
just for these audiences. A second creative approach is to 270
hire more workers on a temporary basis. Such workers are 281
no longer only support staff or unskilled but now include 293
high-level professionals. 298

All of these changes will require firms to be less 309
biased, better trained, and more holistic in their future 321
thinking on recruiting and hiring goals. They will need to 333
know the facts about what inspires people to join their 344
firms. Smart recruiters will take a long, careful look at 356
hiring strategies, including recruiting materials and their 368
interview process. Since retention can no longer be taken 380
for granted, recruiters will also have to gather data on 391
why workers leave or stay with their company. 400

| 1 | 2 | 3 | 4 | 5 | 6 | 7 | 8 | 9 | 10 | 11 | 12

Diagnostic Practice: Alphabet

The Diagnostic Practice: Alphabet program is designed to diagnose and then correct your keystroking errors. You may use this program at any time after completing Lesson 9.

Directions

1. Key the Pretest/Posttest passage once, proofread it, and identify errors.
2. Note your results—the number of errors you made on each key and your total number of errors. For example, if you keyed *rhe* for *the,* that would count as 1 error on the letter *t.*
3. For any letter on which you made 2 or more errors, select the corresponding drill lines and key them twice. If you made only 1 error, key the drill once.
4. If you made no errors on the Pretest/Posttest passage, turn to the practice on troublesome pairs on page SB-3 and key each line once. This section provides intensive practice on those pairs of keys commonly confused.
5. Finally, rekey the Pretest/Posttest, and compare your performance with your Pretest.

PRETEST/POSTTEST

Jacob and Zeke Koufax quietly enjoyed jazz music on my new jukebox. My six or seven pieces of exquisite equipment helped both create lovely music by Richard Wagner; I picked five very quaint waltzes from Gregg Ward's jazz recordings.

PRACTICE: INDIVIDUAL REACHES

aa Isaac badge carry dared eager faced gains habit dials AA
aa jaunt kayak label mamma Nancy oasis paint Qatar rapid AA
aa safer taken guard vague waves exact yacht Zaire Aaron AA

bb about ebbed ebony rugby fiber elbow amber unbar oboes BB
bb arbor cubic oxbow maybe abate abbot debit libel album BB
bb embed obeys urban tubes Sybil above lobby webby bribe BB

cc acted occur recap icing ulcer emcee uncle ocean force CC
cc scale itchy bucks excel Joyce acute yucca decal micro CC
cc mulch McCoy incur octet birch scrub latch couch cycle CC

dd admit daddy edict Magda ideal older index oddly order DD
dd outdo udder crowd Floyd adapt added Edith Idaho folds DD
dd under modem sword misdo fudge rowdy Lydia adept buddy DD

ee aegis beach cents dense eerie fence germs hence piece EE
ee jewel keyed leads media nerve poems penny reach seize EE
ee teach guest verse Wendy Xerox years zesty aerie begin EE

SUPPLEMENTARY TIMED WRITING

Spacing: Double

There are a few essential items businesspeople today 12
should know about telecommunications in order to be up to 23
date in their field. Although it may seem confusing at 34
first, it is quite simple once you realize that there are 46
just four main components involved in almost all systems. 58
The first part is called transmission and includes all the 69
links along which signals are sent and also the techniques 81
for coding information. The medium may be cable, microwave 93
radio, satellite, fiber optics, or anything else that can 105
carry the signal. 108

The next component is the switches. Switches are the 120
specialized equipment at set points of a communications 131
network. At these points, the signals from transmission 143
links are processed in order to route them to the terminal 155
or computer, translate them from one message format to the 166
next, improve the efficiency of transmission, or handle 178
other aspects of the network control. It is in this area 189
that the technology is moving fastest and is most unstable 201
in terms of products, standards, and vendors. 210

Terminals, devices that access the computer network, 222
are the third area. Most of the time they are personal 233
computers or workstations linked to a distant computer for 245
processing, access to data, or communication of messages 256
to other terminals. They could also be telephones, word 268
processors, some types of workstations, and even a central 279
mainframe computer. 283

The final part is the network. This is a system of 295
switches and transmission links, as well as a listing of 306
the terminal points that can access them and thus contact 318
each other; the U.S. phone system is one such network, with 330
the phone number providing the address. The same phone can 342
link itself into other countries' networks. Even though 353
those systems may use different transmission features and 365
conventions, special switches can translate the protocols. 377
In the same way, a single terminal may access many networks 389
which, in turn, may be interconnected through switches. 400

| 1 | 2 | 3 | 4 | 5 | 6 | 7 | 8 | 9 | 10 | 11 | 12

ff after defer offer jiffy gulfs infer often dwarf cuffs FF
ff awful afoul refer affix edify Wolfe infra aloof scarf FF
ff bluff afoot defer daffy fifty sulfa softy surfs stuff FF

gg again edges egged soggy igloo Elgin angel ogled Marge GG
gg outgo auger pygmy agaze Edgar Egypt buggy light bulge GG
gg singe doggy organ fugle agree hedge began baggy Niger GG

hh ahead abhor chili Nehru ghost Elihu khaki Lhasa unhat HH
hh aloha phony myrrh shale Ethan while yahoo choir jehad HH
hh ghoul Khmer Delhi Ohara photo rhino shake think while HH

ii aired bides cider dices eight fifth vigil highs radii II
ii jiffy kinds lives mired niece oiled piped rigid siren II
ii tired build visit wider exist yield aimed binds cigar II

jj major eject fjord Ouija enjoy Cajun Fijis Benjy bijou JJ
jj banjo jabot jacks jaded jails Japan jaunt jazzy jeans JJ
jj jeeps jeers jelly jerks jibed jiffy jilts joint joker JJ

kk Akron locks vodka peeks mikes sulky links okras larks KK
kk skins Yukon hawks tykes makes socks seeks hiker sulks KK
kk tanks Tokyo jerky pesky nukes gawks maker ducks cheek KK

ll alarm blame clank idled elope flame glows Chloe Iliak LL
ll ankle Lloyd inlet olive plane burly sleet atlas Tulsa LL
ll yowls axles nylon alone blunt claim idler elite flute LL

mm among adman demit pigmy times calms comma unman omits MM
mm armor smell umber axmen lymph gizmo amass admit demon MM
mm dogma imply films mommy omits armed smear bumpy axman MM

nn ankle Abner envoy gnome Johns input knife kilns hymns NN
nn Donna onion apnea Arnes snore undid owned cynic angle NN
nn entry gnash inset knoll nanny onset barns sneer unfit NN

oo aorta bolts coats dolls peony fouls goofs hoped iotas OO
oo jolts kooky loins moral noise poled Roger soaks total OO
oo quote voter would Saxon yo-yo zones bombs colts doles OO

pp apple epoch flips alpha ample input droop puppy sharp PP
pp spunk soups expel typed April Epsom slips helps empty PP
pp unpin optic peppy corps spite upset types apply creep PP

qq Iraqi equal pique roque squad tuque aquae equip toque QQ
qq squab squat squam squaw quail qualm quart queen quell QQ
qq query quest quick quiet quilt quirk quota quote quoth QQ

rr array bring crave drive erode freak grain three irate RR
rr kraft inrun orate Barry tramp urges livre wrote lyric RR
rr Ezars armor broth crown drawl erect freer grade throw RR

SUPPLEMENTARY TIMED WRITING

Spacing: Double

All too often, businesses place too much importance on 12
the rational, logical side of the intellect and neglect the 24
creative, intuitive side. Since creative thought occurs in 36
the mind, it cannot be seen and, therefore, is not easily 48
measured. Perhaps for this reason, there are only a few 59
socially acceptable roles where it is okay to be creative, 71
try out new ideas, or seek different methods for reaching 82
goals. Even when managers claim to want creative ideas 94
from their employees, the fear of taking risks may squelch 105
these efforts. 108

As a result, creative people often find themselves on 120
the outside looking in as new ideas are analyzed over and 132
over again in an effort to minimize or eliminate the risk. 144
It may be next to impossible to start a new product which, 156
in the firm's early days, might have been launched quickly 167
without excessive controls and approvals. As a response to 179
this restraint on imagination, thousands of new businesses 191
are launched every year, many guided by former employees of 203
large companies who found their creativity and innovative 215
ideas stifled. 218

While some creators leave the corporate world to find 230
their own niche by starting a small company, many stay and 241
try to teach their bosses how to better utilize the talents 253
found right in their own department. Although some experts 265
think that creativity comes only from a few special people 277
placed in top jobs, most believe that creativity can, and 289
should, be sought from all employees. If given the right 300
support and time, nearly everyone has the ability to find 312
better systems, strategies, or products. 320

Part of the challenge of inspiring creativity, though, 332
is learning to effectively manage truly creative people, 344
which is not an easy task. They tend to disrupt procedures 356
rather than accept the old ways of working. Their high 367
energy level may result in negative behavior and burnout. 379
Creative folks tend to be driven by a belief that they can 390
overcome obstacles and get around fixed authority. 400

| 1 | 2 | 3 | 4 | 5 | 6 | 7 | 8 | 9 | 10 | 11 | 12

ss ashen bombs specs binds bares leafs bangs sighs issue SS
ss necks mills teams turns solos stops stirs dress diets SS
ss usury Slavs stows abyss asked stabs cords mares beefs SS

tt attic debts pacts width Ethel often eight itchy alter TT
tt until motto optic earth stops petty couth newts extra TT
tt myths Aztec atone doubt facts veldt ether sight Italy TT

uu audio bumps cured dumps deuce fuels gulps huffy opium UU
uu junta kudos lulls mumps nudge outdo purer ruler super UU
uu tulip revue exult yucca azure auger burns curve duels UU

vv avows event ivory elves envoy overt larva mauve savvy VV
vv avant every rivet Elvis anvil coves curvy divvy avert VV
vv evict given valve ovens serve paves evade wives hover VV

ww awash bwana dwarf brews Gwenn schwa kiwis Elwin unwed WW
ww owner Irwin sweet twins byway awake dwell pewee tower WW
ww Erwin swims twirl awful dwelt Dewey owlet swamp twine WW

xx axiom exile fixed Bronx toxin Sioux Exxon pyxie axman XX
xx exert fixes Leonx oxbow beaux calyx maxim exact sixth XX
xx proxy taxes excel mixed boxer axing Texas sixty epoxy XX

yy maybe bylaw cynic dying eying unify gypsy hypos Benjy YY
yy Tokyo hilly rummy Ronny loyal pygmy diary Syria types YY
yy buyer vying Wyatt epoxy crazy kayak Byram cycle bawdy YY

zz Azure Czech adzes bezel dizzy Franz froze Liszt ritzy ZZ
zz abuzz tizzy hazed czars maize Ginza oozes blitz fuzzy ZZ
zz jazzy mazes mezzo sized woozy Hertz fizzy Hazel Gomez ZZ

PRACTICE: TROUBLESOME PAIRS

A/S Sal said he asked Sara Ash for a sample of the raisins.
B/V Beverly believes Bob behaved very bravely in Beaverton.
C/D Clyde and Dick decided they could decode an old decree.

E/W We wondered whether Andrew waited for Walter and Wendy.
F/G Griffin goofed in figuring their gifted golfer's score.
H/J Joseph joshed with Judith when John jogged to Johnetta.

I/O A novice violinist spoiled Orville Olin's piccolo solo.
K/L Kelly, unlike Blake, liked to walk as quickly as Karla.
M/N Many women managed to move among the mounds of masonry.

O/P A pollster polled a population in Phoenix by telephone.
Q/A Quincy acquired one quality quartz ring at the banquet.
R/T Three skaters traded their tartan trench coats to Bart.

U/Y Buy your supply of gifts during your busy July journey.
X/C The exemptions exceed the expert's wildest expectation.
Z/A Eliza gazed as four lazy zebra zigzagged near a gazebo.

SUPPLEMENTARY TIMED WRITING

Spacing: Double

As human beings, our perception of time has grown out 12
of a natural series of rhythms which are linked to daily, 23
monthly, and yearly cycles. No matter how much we live by 35
our wristwatches, our bodies and our lives will always be 47
somewhat influenced by an internal clock. What is of even 59
greater interest, though, are the many uses and perceptions 71
of time based on individuals and their cultures. 81

Rhythm and tempo are ways we relate to time and are 92
discerning features of a culture. In some cultures, folks 104
move very slowly; in others, moving quickly is the norm. 115
Mixing the two types may create feelings of discomfort. 127
People may have trouble relating to each other because they 139
are not in synchrony. To be synchronized is to subtly move 151
in union with another person; it is vital to a strong and 162
lengthy partnership. 167

In general, Americans move at a fast tempo, although 178
there are regional departures. In meetings, they tend to 190
be impatient and want to "get down to business" right away. 202
They have been taught that it is best to come to the point 214
quickly and avoid vagueness. Because American business 225
works in a short time frame, prompt results are often of 236
more interest than the building of long-term relationships. 249

Time is also the basic organizing system for all of 260
life's events. Time is used for setting priorities. For 272
example, lead time varies quite a bit from one culture to 283
the next. When you conduct business with people of other 295
cultures, it is crucial to know just how much lead time is 307
required for each event. For instance, numerous corporate 318
executives have their time scheduled for months in advance. 330
Last-minute requests by phone are viewed as poor planning 342
and could even be perceived as an insult. 350

| 1 | 2 | 3 | 4 | 5 | 6 | 7 | 8 | 9 | 10 | 11 | 12

Diagnostic Practice: Numbers

The Diagnostic Practice: Numbers program is designed to diagnose and then correct your keystroking errors. You may use this program at any time after completing Lesson 14 in the text.

Directions

1. Key the Pretest/Posttest passage once, proofread it, and identify errors.
2. Note your results—the number of errors you made on each key and your total number of errors. For example, if you keyed *24* for *25,* that would count as 1 error on the number *5.*
3. For any number on which you made 2 or more errors, select the corresponding drill lines and key them twice. If you made only 1 error, key the drill once.
4. Make one copy of the drills on page SB-5 that contain all the numbers. (If you made no errors on the Pretest/Posttest passage, key the drills that contain all the numbers, repeat, and then repeat again as you strive to reach new speed levels.)
5. Finally, rekey the Pretest/Posttest, and compare your performance with your Pretest.

PRETEST/POSTTEST

My inventory records dated December 31, 1994, revealed we had 458 pints, 2,069 quarts, and 4,774 gallons of paint. We had 2,053 brushes, 568 scrapers, 12,063 wallpaper rolls, 897 knives, 5,692 mixers, 480 ladders, and 371 step stools.

PRACTICE: INDIVIDUAL REACHES

1 aq aq1 aq1qa 111 ants 101 aunts 131 apples 171 animals a1
They got 11 answers correct for the 11 questions in BE 121.
Those 11 adults loaded the 711 animals between 1 and 2 p.m.
All 111 agreed that 21 of those 31 are worthy of the honor.

2 sw sw2 sw2ws 222 sets 242 steps 226 salads 252 saddles s2
The 272 summer tourists saw the 22 soldiers and 32 sailors.
Your September 2 date was all right for 292 of 322 persons.
The 22 surgeons said 221 of those 225 operations went well.

3 de de3 de3ed 333 dots 303 drops 313 demons 393 dollars d3
Bus 333 departed at 3 p.m. with the 43 dentists and 5 boys.
She left 33 dolls and 73 decoys at 353 West Addison Street.
The 13 doctors helped some of the 33 druggists in Room 336.

4 fr fr4 fr4rf 444 fans 844 farms 444 fishes 644 fiddles f4
My 44 friends bought 84 farms and sold over 144 franchises.
She sold 44 fish and 440 beef dinners for $9.40 per dinner.
The '54 Ford had only 40,434 fairly smooth miles by July 4.

SUPPLEMENTARY TIMED WRITING

Spacing: Double

Pick up any newspaper or turn on any news program on 12
TV, and it seems you will hear yet another story about an 23
oil tanker that has spilled its cargo or a landfill that 35
has reached its limit. As more and more people are paying 46
heed to the environmental concerns, more and more companies 58
are following suit by setting environmental goals. 68

What are the reasons so many firms have a new stance 80
on these issues? First, and foremost, there appear to be 92
more simultaneous threats to our world than in any other 103
moment in time. Our government believes that four out of 115
ten Americans live in places where the air is not healthy 127
to breathe. Other issues include ozone depletion, acid 138
rain, the fouling of thousands of rivers and lakes by raw 149
sewage and toxic wastes, destruction of rain forests, and 161
the greenhouse effect. 166

A second reason for the growing concern over these 177
issues in corporate America is a response to heightened 188
public awareness of the problems. Nine out of ten people 200
say they would be willing to make a special effort to buy 211
products that show concern for protecting the air, land, 223
and water. Membership in environmental groups is soaring. 235
There are now tens of thousands of conservation groups; 246
each town seems to have two or three doing anything from 257
trying to save a trout stream to stopping a shopping mall 269
from being built. 273

In the last two decades, more than a dozen major laws 285
have been passed. As a result, overall pollution levels 296
have dropped. New regulations now focus on management and 308
recordkeeping roles and have fewer quantitative, absolute 319
standards to which firms must adhere. While much has been 331
accomplished, strong maintenance is key to keeping our air, 343
water, and land clean in years ahead. 350

| 1 | 2 | 3 | 4 | 5 | 6 | 7 | 8 | 9 | 10 | 11 | 12

5 fr fr5 fr5rf 555 furs 655 foxes 555 flares 455 fingers f5
They now own 155 restaurants, 45 food stores, and 55 farms.
They ordered 45, 55, 65, and 75 yards of that new material.
Flight 855 flew over Farmington at 5:50 p.m. on December 5.

6 jy jy6 jy6yj 666 jets 266 jeeps 666 jewels 866 jaguars j6
Purchase orders numbered 6667 and 6668 were sent yesterday.
Those 66 jazz players played for 46 juveniles in Room 6966.
The 6 judges reviewed the 66 journals on November 16 or 26.

7 ju ju7 ju7uj 777 jays 377 jokes 777 joists 577 juniors j7
The 17 jets carried 977 jocular passengers above 77 cities.
Those 277 jumping beans went to 77 junior scouts on May 17.
The 7 jockeys rode 77 jumpy horses between March 17 and 27.

8 ki ki8 ki8ik 888 keys 488 kites 888 knives 788 kittens k8
My 8 kennels housed 83 dogs, 28 kids, and 88 other animals.
The 18 kind ladies tied 88 knots in the 880 pieces of rope.
The 8 men saw 88 kelp bass, 38 kingfish, and 98 king crabs.

9 lo lo9 lo9ol 999 lads 599 larks 999 ladies 699 leaders 19
All 999 leaves fell from the 9 large oaks at 389 Largemont.
The 99 linemen put 399 large rolls of tape on for 19 games.
Those 99 lawyers put 899 legal-size sheets in the 19 limos.

0 ;p ;p0 ;p0p; 100 pens 900 pages 200 pandas 800 pencils ;0
There were 1,000 people who lived in the 300 private homes.
The 10 party stores are open from 1:00 p.m. until 9:00 p.m.
They edited 500 pages in 1 book and 1,000 pages in 2 books.

All numbers

a1a s2s d3d f4f f5f j6j j7j k8k 191 ;0; Add 5 and 9 and 16.
Those 67 jumpsuits were shipped to 238 Birch on October 14.
Invoices numbered 294 and 307 are to be paid by November 5.
Flight 674 is scheduled to leave from Gate 18 at 11:35 a.m.

All numbers

a1a s2s d3d f4f f5f j6j j7j k8k 191 ;0; Add 6 and 8 and 29.
That 349-page script called for 18 actors and 20 actresses.
The check for $50 was sent to 705 Garfield Street, not 507.
The 14 researchers asked the 469 Californians 23 questions.

All numbers

a1a s2s d3d f4f f5f j6j j7j k8k 191 ;0; Add 3 and 4 and 70.
They built 1,200 houses on the 345-acre site by the canyon.
Her research showed that gold was at 397 in September 1994.
For $868 extra, they bought 27 new books and 62 used books.

All numbers

a1a s2s d3d f4f f5f j6j j7j k8k 191 ;0; Add 5 and 7 and 68.
A bank auditor arrived on May 26, 1994, and left on May 30.
The 4 owners open the stores from 9:30 a.m. until 6:00 p.m.
After 1,374 miles on the bus, she must then drive 185 more.

SUPPLEMENTARY TIMED WRITING

Spacing: Double

For almost three decades, firms have been trying, with 12
higher and higher levels of success, to harness information 24
technology. The role that top management has played has 35
often not been as useful as it could have been. Managers 47
have helped things happen rather than made them happen. 58
People today must know something about the technology that 70
helps them do their jobs. Telecommunications involves some 82
fairly simple concepts that quickly expand into complex 93
details. The jargon alone is often enough to numb the mind 105
and cause some concern. 110

It makes no sense for managers to try to learn the 121
nuts and bolts of the technology. The field is moving too 133
fast for experts to keep up their knowledge base. What 144
managers need is the same level of basic understanding that 156
a person involved in business has to have about accounting. 168
They should have a sense of the major sections and terms, 180
such as debits and credits. They must be able to interpret 192
a computer plan in the same way that they read a financial 204
statement. That level of knowledge in no way means they 215
are experts, but it enables them to take part in planning 227
and not be scared off because they don't know the topic. 239

When managers deal with technology, they often will be 251
dealing with change because it brings organizational and 263
business issues to the foreground of planning and action. 274
It pushes senior managers to take on a new relationship 286
with what has often been outside their scope. Ten years 297
ago, few executives would have defined an understanding of 309
technology as part of the profile of an effective manager. 321
If they do not do so now, they soon will. Change may be a 333
problem, but it is also a prospect for growth. Technology 344
can pave the way for new growth. 350

| 1 | 2 | 3 | 4 | 5 | 6 | 7 | 8 | 9 | 10 | 11 | 12

Progressive Practice: Alphabet

This skillbuilding routine contains a series of 30-second timed writings that range from 16 wam to 70 wam. The first time you use these timed writings, select a passage that is 2 words a minute higher than your current speed. Take five 30-second timed writings on the passage, trying to complete it within 30 seconds with no errors. When you have achieved your goal, record your results. Then move on to the next passage and repeat the procedure.

16 wam An author is the creator of a document.

18 wam Access means to call up data out of storage.

20 wam A byte represents one character to your computer.

22 wam To store means to insert data in memory for later use.

24 wam Soft copy is text that is displayed on your display screen.

26 wam Memory is the part of a word processor that stores information.

28 wam A menu is a list of choices to guide the operator through a function.

30 wam A sheet feeder is a device that will insert sheets of paper into a printer.

32 wam Boilerplate copy is a reusable passage that is stored until needed in a program.

34 wam Downtime is the length of time that equipment is not usable because of a malfunction.

36 wam To execute means to perform an action specified by an operator or by a computer program.

38 wam Output is the result of a word processing operation. It is in either printed or magnetic form.

40 wam Format refers to the physical features which affect the appearance and arrangement of your document.

42 wam A font is a set of type of one size or style which includes all letters, numbers, and punctuation marks.

SUPPLEMENTARY TIMED WRITING

Spacing: Double

More and more people are retiring at a younger age as 12
new retirement programs are being offered by business firms 24
and by the government. A good number of the people who 35
retire early may even be starting in a new career or a new 47
job. This is happening at a time when the life expectancy 59
for adults has been quickly rising in the past few years. 70

With the increase in life expectancy and the early 82
retirement plans, it can be seen that adults must be sure 93
to plan carefully for their retirement years. If planning 105
is not done, many people who are in good health could find 117
themselves at this point in their lives with plenty of free 129
time and not much to do. As one ages, it is important to 140
look at the activities that one enjoys and to strengthen 152
one's interest in those things. At the same time, it is 163
important to find new interests and hobbies so that the 174
time in retirement will be enjoyed to its fullest. It 185
should be noted that the financial part of retirement must 197
also be planned in a careful way. One should be sure to 209
check all investments. 213

Of course, some retirees enjoy visiting with family 225
and friends. Others plan to travel as much as they can to 236
many parts of the country or of the world. Then one can 248
find some retirees who pursue a hobby with great zeal. 259
Whatever one wants to do, the most critical factor is that 271
planning must be done with care prior to the date one sets 283
for retirement. In this way, one can be sure to have a 294
retirement that brings success. 300

| 1 | 2 | 3 | 4 | 5 | 6 | 7 | 8 | 9 | 10 | 11 | 12

44 wam Ergonomics is the science of adapting working conditions or equipment to meet most physical needs of workers.

46 wam Home position is the starting position of a document; it is typically the upper left corner of the display screen.

48 wam An electronic typewriter is a word processor which has only limited functions; it may or may not have a visual display.

50 wam An optical scanner is a device that can read text and enter it into a word processor without the need to rekeyboard the data.

52 wam Hardware refers to the physical equipment used, such as the central processing unit, display screen, keyboard, printer, or drive.

54 wam A peripheral device is any piece of equipment that extends the capabilities of a computer system but is not necessary for its operation.

56 wam A split screen displays two or more different images at the same time; it can, for example, display two different pages of a legal document.

58 wam A daisy wheel is a printing element that is made of plastic or metal and is used on different printers. Each character is at the end of a spoke.

60 wam A cursor is a special character, often a blinking box or an underscore, which shows where the next keyed character will appear on the display screen.

62 wam The hot zone is the area before the right margin, typically five to ten characters wide, where words may have to be divided or transferred to another line.

64 wam Turnaround time is the length of time needed for a document to be keyboarded, edited, proofread, corrected if required, printed, and returned to the executive.

66 wam A local area network is a system that uses cable or another means to allow high-speed communication among various kinds of electronic equipment within a small area.

68 wam To search and replace means to direct the word processor to locate a character, word, or group of words wherever it occurs in the document and replace it with newer text.

70 wam Indexing is the ability of a word processor to accumulate a list of words that appear in a document, including the page numbers, and then to print it out in alphabetic order.

SUPPLEMENTARY TIMED WRITING

Spacing: Double

The value of team play and of team effort has been a 12
topic of great interest to many different people. There 24
are experts who look at the actions of people in a variety 36
of research studies in order to find out the impact of a 47
unified effort on how much the group is able to achieve. 59
The results are always the same. When a group of people 70
tries to meet a shared goal, it is quite likely that more 82
will be gained. This is true in many environments--office, 93
plant, home, school, or church. It is especially true when 105
one looks at the success of athletic teams. 113

Many business firms have now begun quality circles in 125
their offices and plants. The goal of these circles is to 137
encourage small groups of workers to meet on a periodic 148
basis to find out if any of the procedures or steps that 160
they follow in the jobs they do can be improved. The small 172
groups give each person in the unit a stake in the way the 184
unit functions as a whole. A quality circle recognizes the 195
benefits that can come from a team effort. 205

The concept of team effort is most evident when it 217
comes to athletic events. Each time that a study is made 229
of a championship team in any sport or event, many comments 241
can be made about the team play and the team spirit that 252
were observed. This point is often discussed after a big 264
game by sportswriters and the many fans of a team. A lot 275
of experts, in fact, would back the notion that team effort 286
is more important than the talents of any single player on 298
any one team. 300

| 1 | 2 | 3 | 4 | 5 | 6 | 7 | 8 | 9 | 10 | 11 | 12

72 wam The control key is a special key that never prints but when used with some other key enables you to complete a special function such as checking spelling or changing font sizes.

74 wam A facsimile is an exact copy of a document. It is also the process by which images, such as typed letters, signatures, and graphs, are scanned, transmitted, and then reprinted on paper.

76 wam Compatibility refers to the ability of one machine to share information with another machine or to communicate with the other machine. It can be accomplished by using hardware or software.

78 wam Indexing refers to determining the captions or titles under which a document would most likely be found. The term also encompasses cross-referencing each document under any other possible title.

80 wam Wraparound is the ability of a word processor to move words from one line to another line and from one page to the next page as a result of inserting and deleting text or changing side-margin widths.

82 wam The office is a place in which administrative functions are performed for a company or some other types of businesses. The most common duties include filing, document processing, and scheduling of meetings.

84 wam List processing is an ability of the word processor to keep lists of data that can be upgraded and sorted in alphabetic or numeric order. A list can also be added to any document that is stored in the computer.

86 wam A computer is an electronic device; it accepts data that is input and then processes the data and produces output. The computer performs its work by using one or more stored programs which give the instructions.

88 wam The configuration is the components which make up your word processing system. Most systems include a keyboard that is used for entering data, a central processing unit, at least one disk drive, a screen, and a printer.

90 wam A keypad meter is a device used to monitor the use of the office copier. It can be either a key or a coded card which, when inserted into your copier, unlocks the machine for use and keeps track of the number of copies made.

92 wam An open office is a modern approach to office planning that combines modular furniture with an open layout. The larger offices separate workers by removable partitions instead of permanent walls, which provide greater flexibility.

SUPPLEMENTARY TIMED WRITING

Spacing: Double

Since early settlers first came to this land, our 11
people have always had a strong interest in the actions of 23
our government. When you speak of our national, state, or 35
local government, you can be sure that a lively debate will 47
start. This is most true when election time comes and the 58
candidates speak to the issues. Media reports of debates 70
and of election issues tend to be quite broad and can serve 82
as a gauge of what the voters seem to want. 91

Of course, economic issues are bound to start a major 103
debate on the part of those who pay taxes. Raising taxes 114
or changing the tax laws will often start a debate. One 126
other topic that causes much debate deals with our defense 137
plans. Many candidates have used the issue to form their 149
own base for a national election. If you look at the near 161
past, you can see that issues on defense will always be a 172
major concern. 175

In addition to the economic and defense issues, you 187
will be amazed at how rapidly a lively debate can commence 199
over social issues. For instance, crime, education, and 210
privacy are topics that have been of special concern in 221
recent years. There has also been a good deal of debate 233
over the environment, as well as many questions about our 244
welfare system. A lot of our people have a deep interest 251
in the actions of our judicial bodies and the way in which 268
they respond to the social issues that face our nation. It 280
is easy to see that issues under debate by government are 291
sure to be of concern in years to come. 300

| 1 | 2 | 3 | 4 | 5 | 6 | 7 | 8 | 9 | 10 | 11 | 12

94 wam To scroll means to show a large block of text by rolling it either horizontally or vertically past your display screen. As the text disappears from the top section of the monitor, new text appears at the bottom section of the monitor.

96 wam Justification is a form of printing that inserts additional space between words or characters to force each line to the same length; it can be called right justification, since it forces all the lines to end at the same point at the right.

98 wam A stop code is a command that makes a printer halt while it is printing to permit an operator to insert text, to change the font style, or to change the kind of paper in the printer. To resume printing, the operator must use a special key or command.

100 wam A computerized message system is a class of electronic mail that enables any operator to key a message on any computer terminal and have the message stored for later retrieval by the recipient, who can then display the message on his or her terminal.

102 wam Many different graphics software programs have been brought on the market in recent years. These programs can be quite powerful in helping with a business presentation. If there is a need to share data, using one of these programs can be quite helpful.

104 wam Voice mail has become an essential service that many people in the business world use. This allows anyone who places a call to your phone to leave a message if you cannot answer it at that time. This special feature has helped many people be more productive.

94 wam

Listening is a skill that is an essential component of the communication process. A great many experts have found that lack of good listening skills is a major cause for the breakdown in effective communications. For the first part, there must be understanding. If ideas given by any speaker are not completely understood, it is most likely that there will be a problem. In addition, a listener must attempt to keep an open mind for new ideas to be considered.

A good listener must be active. Three steps should be taking place. Think about what the speaker is saying. The ideas and facts heard should be related to information that the listener knows. Analyze what the speaker is saying and try to read between the lines. It is also essential that a listener have a degree of empathy. This can be achieved by placing oneself in a speaker's place. An attempt should be made to create a strong bonding with the speaker.

96 wam

Speech is a major factor in the communication process. In evaluating the quality of your voice, you should analyze the four factors of pitch, tempo, tone, and volume in order to determine whether or not some improvements must be made. Pitch refers to the sound of a voice. A shrill voice would turn people off. If a voice has a very low pitch, it might be too dull or too hard to hear. The voice which should be the most pleasing is the one having a moderate pitch to it.

The tone of a voice might help reveal the attitude and feelings of the speaker. You should hope to project a tone that is cheerful and pleasant. You should always adapt the tone of the voice to the meaning of the words being spoken. Volume is also a critical factor in evaluating one's voice. A voice should carry to every person in a room. Using good breath control, you can enhance your ability to increase or decrease your voice volume to satisfy any appropriate need.

Progressive Practice: Numbers

This skillbuilding routine contains a series of 30-second timed writings that range from 16 wam to 68 wam. The first time you use these timed writings, select a passage that is 4 to 6 words a minute *lower* than your current alphabetic speed. (The reason for selecting a lower speed goal is that sentences with numbers are more difficult to key.) Take five 30-second timed writings on the passage, trying to complete it within 30 seconds with no errors. When you have achieved your goal, move on to the next passage and repeat the procedure.

16 wam There were now 21 children in Room 211.

18 wam Fewer than 12 of the 121 boxes have arrived.

20 wam Maybe 2 of the 21 applicants met all 12 criteria.

22 wam There were 34 letters addressed to 434 West Cranbrook.

24 wam Jan reported that there were 434 freshmen and 43 transfers.

26 wam The principal assigned 3 of those 4 students to Room 343 at noon.

28 wam Only 1 or 2 of the 34 latest invoices were more than 1 page in length.

30 wam They met 11 of the 12 players who received awards from 3 of the 4 coaches.

32 wam Those 5 vans carried 46 passengers on the first trip and 65 on the next 3 trips.

34 wam We first saw 3 and then 4 beautiful eagles on Route 65 at 5 a.m. on Monday, June 12.

36 wam The 6 companies produced 51 of the 62 records that received awards for 3 of 4 categories.

38 wam The 12 trucks hauled the 87 cows and 65 horses to the farm, which was about 21 miles northeast.

40 wam She moved from 87 Bayview Drive to 657 Cole Street and then 3 blocks south to 412 Gulbranson Avenue.

90 wam

Almost everyone has experienced interviewing for a job during his or her life. For some persons, the interview is a traumatic time. But when a candidate adequately prepares for this interview, it doesn't need to be very frightening. A person should apply only for the jobs for which he or she is professionally prepared. Before an interview one should obtain detailed information about the company with which he or she is seeking employment.

You should always learn the name of the person who will conduct the interview and use the name during the interview. It's also best to take a neat copy of your resume. It goes without saying that suitable business attire is required. As an applicant, you will be judged on personality, appearance, and poise as well as competence. At the end of the interview, it would be wise if you stand, shake hands, and address the interviewer by name.

92 wam

Are you an active listener? Listening is a skill that few people possess. It is one important way to bring about change in people. Listening is not a passive activity, and it is the most effective agent for personality development. Quality listening brings about change in people's attitudes toward themselves and others' values. People who have been listened to become more open to their experiences, less defensive, more fair, or less authoritative.

Listening builds deep positive relationships and tends to constructively moderate the perspective of the listener. Active listening on the job is extremely important whether an employee is in the top levels of management or works at the lower end of the hierarchy. Every worker should try to analyze his or her listening habits to see whether some improvement could be made. Pleasant human interaction will result and yield even more job satisfaction.

42 wam My 7 or 8 buyers ordered 7 dozen in sizes 5 and 6 after the 14 to 32 percent discounts had been granted.

44 wam There were 34 women and 121 men waiting in line at the gate for the 65 to 87 tickets to the Cape Cod concert.

46 wam Steve had listed 5 or 6 items on Purchase Order 241 when he saw that Purchase Requisition 87 contained 3 or 4 more.

48 wam The item numbered 278 will sell for about 90 percent of the value of the 16 items that have a code number shown as 435.

50 wam The manager stated that 98 of the 750 randomly selected new valves had about 264 defects, far in excess of the usual 31 norm.

52 wam Half of the 625 volunteers received about 90 percent of the charity pledges. Approximately 83 of the 147 agencies will get funds.

54 wam Merico hired 94 part-time workers to help the 378 full-time employees during that 62-day period when sales go up by 150 percent or more.

56 wam Kaye only hit 1 for 6 in the first 29 games after an 8-game streak in which she batted 0 for 4. She then hit at a .573 average for 3 games.

58 wam The courier delivered 98 letters during the week to 734 Oak Street and also delivered 52 letters to 610 Pioneer Road as he returned on Route 58.

60 wam Pat said that about 1 of 5 of the 379 swimmers had a chance of being among the top 20. The finest 6 of those 48 divers will receive about 16 awards.

62 wam It rained from 3 to 6 inches, and 18 of the 21 farmers were fearful that 4 to 7 inches more would flood about 950 acres along 3 miles of the new Route 78.

64 wam The 7 sacks weighed 48 pounds, more than the 30 pounds that I had thought. All 24 think the 92-pound bag is at least 6 or 9 or 15 pounds beyond what it weighs.

66 wam They ordered 7 of those 8 options for 54 of the 63 vehicles last month. They now own over 120 dump trucks for use in 9 of the 15 regions in the new 20-county area.

68 wam Andrew was 8 or 9 years old when they moved to 632 Glendale Street from the 1700 block of Horseshoe Lane about 45 miles directly southwest of Boca Raton, Florida 33434.

86 wam

Most of us have had occasion to write business letters from time to time whether to apply for a job, to comment on a product or service, or to place an order. Often it seems to be an easy task to sit and let our thoughts flow freely. In other cases we seem to struggle over the proper wording, trying to say it in just the right way. Writing is a skill that comes with practice and, most of all, with study. One can learn.

There are many writing principles that must be studied to ensure successful letters. Some of these principles are as follows: Use language in your letters that you would be comfortable using face-to-face. Words should be simple and direct. Words should be carefully chosen. Always try to be positive. Emphasize the bright side of a situation when possible. Be kind. Write the way you would like people to always talk.

88 wam

One of the most important areas for a business student to study is report writing. Many people who have worked in business organizations indicated that one of the areas they felt least prepared for was report writing. Most people in college do not know that they'll probably be asked to write reports on the job. Fortunately, most schools are aware of this deficit today and are trying to correct the situation. They are succeeding.

In recent years there has been quite a large increase in the range of report writing courses in the business curricula. Reports might be categorized as horizontal, vertical, and radial. Vertical reports go up and down in the organization and may include status reports or policy statements. Horizontal reports move from person to person or department to department and are informational. Radial reports may be publicized research.

70 wam Claire had read 575 pages in the 760-page book by March 30; David had read only 468 pages. Claire has read 29 of those optional books since October 9, and David has read 18.

72 wam The school district has 985 elementary students, 507 middle school students, and 463 high school students; the total of 1,955 is 54, or 2.84 percent, over last year's grand total.

74 wam Attendance at last year's meeting was 10,230. The goal for this year is to attract 11,150 people. This will enable us to plan for an increase of 920 participants, a 9.89 percent rise.

76 wam John's company has 151 stores, located in 109 cities in the West. The company employs 3,540 males and 2,624 females, a total of 6,164 employees. About 4,750 of the employees are part-time.

78 wam Memberships were as follows: 98 members in the Drama Club, 104 members in Zeta Tau, 82 members in Theta Phi, 75 in the Bowling Club, and 136 in the Ski Club. This meant that 495 joined a group.

80 wam The association had 684 members from the South, 830 members from the North, 992 members from the East, and 751 from the West. The total membership was 3,257; these numbers gave a 9.8 percent increase.

82 wam

Do you enjoy the work you do most of the time? Do you look forward to going to work each day? Even though some people say that their work is unpleasant, the majority of men and women usually find their work generally satisfying. If it isn't, the problem could be that there is a poor fit between the job and the worker. Quality of life at work is a major concern of the management, unions, and labor.

When jobs become boring and routine, workers often become less productive because they do not feel challenged. The concept of job enrichment greatly enhances the types of experiences an employee deals with every day by upgrading the responsibilities of the job. Opportunity for growth is the key to job enrichment. Any organization should select a few jobs that have the best potential for enrichment.

84 wam

More and more women are moving into executive levels in business and industry. Many of these women who pursue careers in management today have moved into their positions after gaining experience as office support personnel. This background gives them a special appreciation for the myriad contributions made by such workers as file clerks, word processors, and other office support staff members working in a firm.

Other women have acquired their managerial roles after earning degrees and gaining experience through jobs in such fields as finance, marketing, accounting, and law. But the measure of success as a manager, no matter what the degrees or past experiences are, is how well one can identify goals and problems and then drive toward the realization of those goals and the resolution of those problems for the company.

Paced Practice

Tab: 0.5 inch

The Paced Practice skillbuilding routine builds speed and accuracy in short, easy steps, using individualized goals and immediate feedback. You may use this program at any time after completing Lesson 9.

This section contains a series of 2-minute timed writings for speeds ranging from 16 wam to 60 wam. The first time you use these timed writings, select a passage that is 2 wam higher than your current keyboarding speed. Use this two-stage practice pattern to achieve each speed goal—first concentrate on speed, and then work on accuracy.

If you are not using the correlated software, have someone call out each 1/4-minute interval as you key. Strive to be at the appropriate point in the passage marked by a small superior number at each 1/4-minute interval.

SPEED GOAL. Take three 2-minute timed writings on the same passage until you can complete it in 2 minutes without regard to errors.

When you have achieved your speed goal, work on accuracy.

ACCURACY GOAL. To key accurately, you need to slow down—just a bit. Therefore, to reach your accuracy goal, drop back 2 wam to the previous passage. Take three 2-minute timed writings on this passage until you can complete it in 2 minutes with no more than 2 errors.

For example, if you achieved a speed goal of 32 wam, you should then work on an accuracy goal of 30 wam. When you have achieved the 30 wam for accuracy, you would then move up 4 wam (for example, to the 34 wam passage) and work for speed again.

12 wam

What is the[1] meaning of work?[2] Why do most[3] people work?[4]
The concept[1] of work and careers[2] is of interest[3] to you.[4]

14 wam

When doing something[1] that is required,[2] you think[3] of it
as working.[4]

16 wam

We often do not[1] consider the amount[2] of time and effort[3]
spent doing a task.[4]

If we did, we would[1] realize that many[2] people work hard[3]
even while playing.[4]

18 wam

For example, people[1] sweat, strain, or even[2] suffer
discomfort[3] when playing a sport.[4]

They do this for fun.[1] If they were required[2] to do it,
they might[3] not be so willing.[4]

78 wam

The ergonomics experts stress the major role furniture plays in the well-being of office workers. Many years ago, we paid little attention to whether our chairs and desks suited our utility and comfort needs. But now we know that various styles, sizes, shapes, and colors have quite an impact on our quality and quantity of work. An informed manager must carefully plan surroundings.

Colors in a workplace may produce important effects on one's moods. Studies show that the cool colors, such as blue and green, are quiet and relaxing. Cool colors should be used in offices that are located in warm areas such as south or west sections of the building. The warm colors, such as red, yellow, and orange, are cheerful and add zip to a job, which may help improve morale.

80 wam

Today we hear a great deal about how important human relations are in management. Job-related human interaction is a comparatively new concern. This can be easily seen if we look at the history of leadership theories as they apply to management practice. When people first started to study leadership, it was expected that certain qualities, such as height, could predict effective leaders.

Next, exceptional leaders were analyzed to see whether they had similar qualities. However, that proposal was not any more successful than the earlier approaches. Now it is generally known that many elements combine to make a person an effective leader. Also, a specific leader's proficiency varies from one situation to another; everyone must develop a style that aids him or her on the job.

20 wam

Spending time on a job is work. For most people, work is something they have to do to survive.

Today, work means more than staying alive. People expect different rewards from their jobs.

22 wam

Work can be interesting, and more and more workers are now saying that their work should be interesting.

Sure, there are many boring jobs, and every job always has some less exciting and more routine features.

24 wam

Today there are many different types of jobs which you may choose from which range from the routine to the exotic.

If you begin your planning early, you can work at different types of jobs and learn from the experience of each.

26 wam

Workers tend to identify with their careers, and their careers in a real sense give them a sense of importance and belonging.

People's jobs also help determine how they spend their spare time, who their friends are, and sometimes even where they live.

28 wam

Work can take place in school, in a factory or office, at home, or outside; it can be done for money or experience or even voluntarily.

It should be quite clear that work can be any activity that involves a type of responsibility. The same thing can be said about a job.

30 wam

A career relates to work that is done for pay. But it means more than a particular job; it is the pattern of work done throughout your lifetime.

A career suggests looking ahead, planning, and setting goals and reaching them. The well-planned career becomes a part of the individual's life.

74 wam

A major part of office activity is deciding what kinds of equipment will best meet company objectives. One should analyze every system, checking for easy and flexible usage. The next step is then defining the requirements of each job in terms of volume of work, space needed, and how each cost fits into the overall budget. Categorize function types, above all.

A complete itemized checklist of every task identifies various functions performed by each employee. This type of data can be obtained through questionnaires, interviews, or observation techniques. Some subjects covered are document creation, employee interaction, scheduling, typing, filing, and telephoning. Technology can then be selected to match job needs.

76 wam

While technology has quite dramatically changed nearly all office procedures in the last decade, the attention to changing human interaction at the workplace because of all of these changes has been largely neglected. Some people have a great deal of enthusiasm for working with different kinds of computers, while others view any computer as a threat, a fearsome complexity.

It is expected that most people's jobs will in time be affected by computers. Therefore, it is imperative to ease employee qualms about learning to operate new equipment. A good point is to nurture a positive attitude toward the computer by convincing employees of two things. First, the office work is made easier. Second, they are much more apt to become more organized.

32 wam Whichever career path is selected, the degree of pride shown in one's work has to be at a high level. Others will judge you by how well you do your work.

Your self-image is affected by what you believe others think of you as well as by what you think of yourself. The quality of your efforts impacts on both.

34 wam If a matter is important to a supervisor or to a firm, it should be important to the employee too. The competent person can be relied on to prioritize and complete.

The higher your job-satisfaction level, the greater is the likelihood that you will be pleased with all aspects of your life. Positive attitudes will bring rewards.

36 wam Whenever people work together, attention must be given to the human relations factor. A quality organization will concern itself with interpersonal skills needed by workers.

Respect, courtesy, and patience are examples of just a few of the words that combine to bring about positive human relationships in the office as well as in other situations.

38 wam The alarm didn't go off. The road was detoured. The baby-sitter is sick. The car wouldn't start. And for some, the list of excuses goes on. Be thankful that this list is not like yours.

You will keep the tardy times to a minimum by planning and anticipating. And you will realize that those who jump the gun by quitting work early at the end of the day have a bad habit.

40 wam Some people take forever to become acquainted with the office routines. Some must have every task explained along with a list of things to be done. Some go ahead and search for new things to do.

Initiative is a trait that managers look for in people who are promoted while on the job. A prized promotion with a nice pay raise can be the reward for demonstrating that a person has new ideas.

68 wam

Enthusiasm is still another work trait that is eagerly sought by most employers. Being enthusiastic means that an employee has lots of positive energy. This is reflected in actions toward the work as well as toward the employer. It has been noted that enthusiasm can be catching. If workers have enthusiasm, they can reach for gold.

It might pay to examine your level of enthusiasm for a given job or project. Analyze whether you help to build up people or whether you aid in giving coworkers a negative or pessimistic attitude. There will always be quite a few job opportunities for workers who are known to possess a wealth of enthusiasm for the work that they do.

70 wam

Understanding is another work habit or trait that is a requirement to be an excellent worker. In this society the likelihood of working with people who have many differences is quite probable. It is essential to have workers who can understand and accept those differences that are evident in other employees who work in each unit or division.

On the job it is imperative that a worker realize that employees will have different aptitudes and abilities. The chances are also great that differences in race, ethnicity, religion, work ethic, cultural background, and attitude can be found. With so many possible differences, it is obvious that a greater degree of understanding is needed.

72 wam

Reviewing the seven previous Paced Practice exercises, it can be concluded that specific work habits or traits can play a major role in determining the success of a worker at a given job or task. Most managers would be quick to agree on the importance of these traits. These habits would most likely be on any performance appraisal forms you might see.

Of course, while these work habits are critical to the success of an individual on the job, there is also the need for specific competencies and abilities for a given job. A new worker must size up the needed blend of these traits in addition to those required competencies. As will be noted, a worker needs many various skills to be a success at work.

42 wam

Newly employed workers are quite often judged by their skills in informal verbal situations. A simple exchange of greetings when being introduced to a client is an example that illustrates one situation.

A new employee might have a very good idea at a small-group meeting. However, unless that idea can be verbalized to the other members in a clear, concise manner, they won't develop a proper appreciation.

44 wam

Many supervisors state that they want their workers to use what they refer to as common sense. Common sense tells a person to answer the phone, to open the mail, and to lock the door at the end of the working day.

It is easy to see that this trait equates with the use of sound judgment. The prize employee should desire to capitalize on each new experience that will help him or her to use better judgment when making decisions.

46 wam

Every person should set as a goal the proper balancing of the principal components in one's life. Few people will disagree with the conviction that the family is the most important of the four main ingredients in a human life.

Experts in the career education field are quick to say that family must be joined with leisure time, vocation, and citizenship in order to encompass one's full "career." The right balance results in satisfaction and success.

48 wam

As we become an information society, there is an ever-increasing awareness of office costs. Such costs are labor intensive, and those who must justify them are increasingly concerned about workers' use of time management principles.

Researchers in the time management area have developed several techniques for examining office tasks and analyzing routines. The realization that "time is money" is only the beginning and must be followed with an educational program.

62 wam Another trait or work habit essential for success on a job is accuracy. Accurate workers are in much demand. The worker who tallies numbers checks them very carefully to be certain there are no errors. When reviewing documents, the accurate worker has excellent proofreading skills to spot all errors.

Since accuracy is required on all jobs, it is critical to possess this trait. An accurate worker is usually quite thorough in all work that is undertaken or completed. If a worker checks all work which is done and analyzes all steps taken, it is likely that a high level of accuracy should be attained.

64 wam Efficiency is another work habit that is much admired. This means that a worker is quick to complete an assignment and to begin work on the next job. Efficient workers think about saving steps and time when working. For example, one should plan to make one trip to the copier versus going for each individual job.

Being efficient means having all the right tools to do the right job. An efficient worker is able to zip along on required jobs, concentrating on doing the job right. Being efficient also means having all needed supplies for the job within reach. This means that a worker can produce more in a little less time.

66 wam Cooperation is another desired work habit. This means that an employee is thinking of all the team members when a decision is made. A person who cooperates is willing to do something for the benefit of the entire group. As a member of a work unit or team, it is absolutely essential that you take extra steps to cooperate.

Cooperation may mean being a good sport if you have to do something you would rather not do. It could also mean a worker helps to correct a major error made by someone else. If a worker has the interests of the organization at heart, it should be a little easier to make a quick decision to cooperate with company endeavors.

50 wam

We all want to work in a pleasant environment where we are surrounded with jovial people who never make a mistake. The realities of the real world tell us, however, that this likely will not happen; the use of corrective action may be required.

For the very reason that this trait is so difficult to cultivate, all of us should strive to improve the manner in which we accept constructive criticism. By recognizing the positive intent of supervisors, each of us can accrue extra benefits.

52 wam

The worker and the firm might be compared in some ways with a child and the family unit. Just as a child at times disagrees with a parent, the worker might question policies of the organization. In both cases, policies must exist for conflict resolution.

One option for a vexed child is to run away from home; an employee may type a letter of resignation. A far better option in both situations is the discussion of differences. The child remains loyal to family, and the employee remains loyal to the company.

54 wam

The person who aspires to a role in management must be equal to the challenge. Individuals who have supervisory responsibilities must make fine judgments as decisions are formed that affect the entire organization. The challenge of managing is trying and lonely.

While other labels are sometimes used to explain basic management functions, the concepts remain the same. The four main functions are involved with planning, organizing, actuating, and controlling of such components as personnel, production, and sales of products.

56 wam

Going to work has always been a major part of being an adult. Of course, many adolescents also have jobs that can keep them extremely busy. The work one does or the job one holds is a critical factor in determining many other things about the way a person is able to live.

Various work habits are as crucial to one's success as the actual job skills and knowledge that one brings to that job. If one is dependable, organized, accurate, efficient, cooperative, enthusiastic, and understanding, one should be recognized quickly by most supervisors.

58 wam

Being dependable is a desirable trait to have. When a worker says that something will be done by a specific time, it is quite assuring to a manager to know that a dependable worker is assigned to it. Workers who are dependable learn to utilize their time to achieve maximum results.

This trait can also be evident with workers who have a good record for attendance. If a firm is to be productive, it is essential to have workers on the job. Of course, the dependable employee not only is on the job, but also is the worker who can be counted on to be there on time.

60 wam

Organization is another trait that can be described as necessary to exhibiting good work habits. To be organized, a worker should have a sense of being able to plan the work that is to be done and then to work that plan. It is quite common to observe that competent workers are well organized.

If an office worker is organized, requests are handled promptly, correspondence is answered quickly, and projects do not accumulate on the desk. In addition, an organized office worker returns all telephone calls without delay and makes a list of activities to be accomplished on a daily basis.